HENRI, DUC DE ROHAN.
From a steel engraving.

Frontispiece.

Portraits

of the

Seventeenth Century

Historic and Literary

By

C. A. Sainte-Beuve

Translated by
Katharine P. Wormeley

With 32 Illustrations

G. P. Putnam's Sons
New York and London
The Knickerbocker Press

Made in the United States of America

Portraits

of the

Seventeenth Century

Historic and Literary

Part I

Translator's Note.

In the following volumes—taken from the *Causeries du Lundi,* the *Portraits de Femmes,* and the *Portraits Littéraires,*—some passages have been omitted ; these relate chiefly to editions that have long since passed away, or to discussions on style that cannot be made clear in English. Also, where two or more essays on the same person have appeared in the different series, they are here put together, omitting repetitions.

Contents of Part I

vii

Contents

Illustrations to Part I

I.

Cardinal de Richelieu.
His Letters and State Papers.

I.

Cardinal de Richelieu.

His Letters and State Papers.

THE fate of Cardinal de Richelieu as a man whose pen or whose dictation produced important works is singular. As such he was long ignored or depreciated. When his "Testament Politique" appeared in 1687, men of judgment recognised the stamp of the master:

"Open his Political Testament," says La Bruyère, "digest that work: it is the picture of his mind; his whole soul is there developed; there we discover the secret of his conduct and of his actions; there we find the source and the fore-shadowing of the many and great events which appeared under his administration; there we see without difficulty that a man who thought with such virility and accuracy must have acted safely and with success, and that he who achieved such great things either never wrote, or must have written as he has done."

In spite of such testimony, well justified on the reading, Voltaire persisted in regarding that same "Testament Politique" as nothing more than a collection of futilities or commonplaces. The learned Foncemagne, who applies himself to refute Voltaire with all sorts of good and demonstrative reasons, has

3

not forgotten that of brilliancy of style and literary talent, things so essential in France! Voltaire continued to triumph apparently, or at least to cast trouble into the minds of even the least ordinary readers. Far from considering this memorable treatise and the maxims of State which it contains as emanations of the austere and serious mind and meditative genius of the cardinal, those who attributed such qualities to him regarded the work as a derogation, and the great Frederick, so fitted to appreciate him, wrote, out of complaisance to Voltaire:

> "The wisest minds may meet eclipse:
> Richelieu made his Testament,
> And Newton his Apocalypse."

As for the other works, political and historical, of Richelieu, their fate was more singular still. In 1730, appeared, under the odd title of "History of the Mother and the Son," meaning Marie de Medicis and Louis XIII, a fragment of history beginning at the death of Henri IV, which was attributed to the historian Mézeray, simply because the manuscript was found after his (Mézeray's) death among his papers. But as in more than one part of the narrative Cardinal de Richelieu spoke in his own name and in his own person, critics took upon themselves to suppose that Mézeray in his youth, out of gratitude for the cardinal's benefits, chose, in this work, to assume his personality and mask himself under Richelieu's name; and they thought to explain by this disguise the various in-

CARDINAL DE RICHELIEU.

congruities of the work. Though the style, at first
sight, is more pompous and flowery than that which
Mézeray usually employed, which at times has a tone
of the *frondeur* and the republican, there was no cause
for wonder, they said, because the author for once had
disguised himself as a courtier and wished to be faithful to the spirit of his part. A few good judges were
not taken in by such poor reasoning; they recognised
the hand of Richelieu himself in more than one passage. Nevertheless, the question was not wholly
cleared up till 1823, when M. Petitot obtained permission to publish the cardinal's own Memoirs which
had long lain buried in the archives of the Ministry of
Foreign Affairs, and now form no less than ten volumes of the Petitot Collection.

All was then made plain: Richelieu's thoughts, of
which mere fragments had hitherto appeared, now
came together, his words assumed their true tone and
all their authority: his style was recognised; for he
had a style, such a man could not fail to have one. It
was seen that in addition to the glory of doing great
things he had conceived the ambition to write of them
in detail and extensively, and to compose, not so much
his Memoirs properly so-called, as a body of history
and of annals: "I own," he said, speaking of this
work of selection and dictation on which, amid so
many other imperative duties, he had spent his vigils,
"I own that although there is more satisfaction in
furnishing the matter for history than in giving history

its form, there is no little pleasure to me in representing that which was done with so much trouble."

While he was tasting the "sweetness of that toil" his illness and the weakness of his constitution, even more than the pressure of affairs, forced him to interrupt his work; it was then that he wrote the "Succinct Narrative" which forms the first chapter, or rather the introduction to the "Political Testament." This narrative is, as he says himself, a "shortened picture," a fine and noble abridged discourse, in which he relates to the king all the great actions of the king, from the time of his (Richelieu's) second entrance to the ministry in 1624 until 1641. In thus attributing everything to his master and affecting to efface himself he does not fear that posterity will be misled and fail to recognise the man who was the principal instrument of great designs so gloriously executed.

Therefore, whoever desires to-day to know and have in hand all the political and historical writings of Richelieu (I am not speaking of his controversial writings as bishop and theologian in his diocese), it is necessary to have: 1st his "Political Testament," preceded by the "Succinct Narrative." 2nd, his Memoirs printed in the Petitot Collection, and later in that of MM. Michaud and Poujoulat; and, 3rd, the collection of his Letters and State-papers, the first volume of which will appear, by the efforts of M. Avenel, in a few weeks, to be followed by four other volumes in quarto.

Richelieu usually wrote little with his own hand; he dictated; but in this sort of transmission he never allowed a secretary to write as he pleased. His secretaries, among whom one named Charpentier held first rank, were no more than copyists and transcribers. Never was any thing written in his name if he were absent. He did not sign what were called " office-letters."

" Richelieu," says M. Avenel, " had, near his person day and night, several private secretaries, but he had no *bureaux* [departments]. The secretaries of State, who were no more than head-clerks, came to take his orders and executed, each in his own office, the work agreed upon, submitted it, when necessary, to the prime-minister, but signed it themselves. Richelieu signed only what was written in his own cabinet."

Many of his letters are dated in the night; he rose when an idea seized him and called a night secretary, who wrote it instantly.

Not only did Richelieu never sign a letter he had neither written nor dictated, but this prime-minister, whose spirit chose to be everywhere present, often dictated letters, instructions and dispatches that he did not sign; these were signed by the secretaries of State or their agents. In a word, Richelieu was apt to do the work of others rather than let any one encroach upon his, or upon his absolute authority. In this immense cabinet labour the part of the secretaries was, as we see, almost nothing and purely material. That of Richelieu was not only chief, but continual and sovereign.

It is a pleasure to approach and study the great man through these new and complete documents which show him to us at his origin and in all the stages of his fortune. Richelieu, born September 5, 1585, the youngest son of an ancient family of Poitou, was at first destined to be a soldier. But one of his brothers who was appointed to the bishopric of Luçon having made himself a Carthusian monk, Richelieu was obliged to take the cassock rather than let the bishopric escape his family. Henri IV named him for it, and negotiated the appointment through his ambassador in Rome. Richelieu was at that time only a few months over twenty years of age; he was forced to make many appeals before he received the pope's sanction, and went in person to Rome, where he was consecrated April 17, 1607. After his return we find him in his diocese, which had long been without a bishop; for Richelieu's brother had never resided there, and, in fact, had never been consecrated, nor had his predecessor resided there. The young bishop, arriving in a region full of Protestants and where there had long been much discord, took his episcopal functions seriously, informed himself as to his rights, and did his duty. The town of Luçon was little more than a village, the poor inhabitants of which were crushed by taxes; he writes to obtain some lessening of the burden. In these first letters of Richelieu we are not made conscious of the heart of a pastor, but there does appear a spirit of order and equity which requires that justice and proportionate burdens shall exist around him. He does not fear, in one place, to compare the load laid upon the common people to that of the beasts of burden, which ought to be proportioned to their strength. "It is the same thing," he adds, "with subsidies in regard to the common people; if not moderate, even though useful to the public they will not fail to be unjust."

In all that I have to say of Richelieu I shall endeavour to speak with truth, without bias, and with no idea of disparagement; the public mind has abandoned, through experience, that idea, which tended to misconceive and undervalue in him one of the most courageous artizans of the grandeur of France. I shall nevertheless avoid the other extreme, which might go to systematic apotheosis; I shall try to restrain admiration in all that concerns him within the limits of good sense and humanity. He will help me himself to do this, if I may venture to say so, for more than one of the sayings with which he judged of other men can, if turned upon himself, show wherein lay too much passion and harshness.

This powerful being, destined to hold France at his feet and make Europe tremble, began by being very poor and in great straits. He writes as follows to a certain Mme. de Bourges in Paris, who usually did his household commissions and had lately bought the decorations of which his church was in need:

"April, 1609.

"Madame, I have received the copes you sent me, which came extremely àpropos ; they are very handsome, and have been received as such by the company to whom I owed them.   .   .   .   I am now in my barony, beloved, so they try to make me think, by every one ; but I can only tell you so now, for all beginnings are fine, as you very well know.   I shall not want for occupation here, I assure you ; all is so ruined that much energy will be required to restore it.   I am extremely ill-lodged ; I have no place where I can make a fire on account of smoke ; you can imagine that I do not long for the depth of winter ; and there is no remedy but patience.   I can assure you that I have the worst bishopric in France, the muddiest, the most disagreeable ; I leave you to think what the bishop is.   There is no place here to take a walk ; neither garden, nor alley, nor anything whatever; so that my house is a prison.

"I leave this topic to tell you that we could not find among my clothes a tunic and a white silk dalmatic that belonged to the white damask trimmings which you had made for me ; and this makes me think they were left behind.   .   .   ."

A number of letters to Mme. de Bourges treat in this way of his household and his domestic affairs, about which he jokes rather pleasantly.   In his journeys to Paris, whither he came sometimes to preach and to breathe Court air, he feels he wants an abiding place, a house of his own, for convenience and decorum, instead of merely hiring furnished rooms.   He consults this same Mme. de Bourges, a good household economist.

"If you will give me good advice," he writes, "you will oblige me very much, for I am very irresolute, principally about a house, fearing the quantity of furniture that may be needed.   On the other hand, being of your humour, that is to say, rather vain-glorious, I should like, as I am more at my ease, to make a better appearance, which I could do more conveniently in a house of my own.   Poor nobility is quite pitiful, but there is no remedy; against fortune keep good heart."

Among these early letters, where, as I need not remark, we are still amid the language of the sixteenth
century, there are some in which Richelieu assumes
the bishop, the consoler, and, occasionally, the director
of souls.   He is adequate and seemly, but little at ease
in these rôles.   The letters of consolation that he addresses to persons who have lost their nearest and
dearest are over-strained, subtle, and suggest even
less the contemporary than the pretentious and rather
antiquated forerunner of Balzac.[1]   To the Comtesse de
Soissons, on the occasion of the death of her husband,
he says, strangely enough and as if to persuade her
that she had gained rather than lost: " If you desire
your welfare it is better to have an advocate in heaven
than a husband on earth."   On one occasion, giving
inward and wholly spiritual counsel to a devout soul
tried by discouragements and difficulties in prayer, he
attempts the language of mystical science in which he
is easily surpassed by the Fénelons and Saint-François
de Sales.   We find him more in character and in the
tone that comes easily to him in the following letter,
written to one of his grand-vicars who has taken, he
thinks, too much liberty:

" 1610.

" Monsieur, I have read the letter you have written me touching the
differences between the Sieur de La Coussaye and yourself.   I cannot
do otherwise than blame them, desiring that those who handle the
affairs of my diocese should live peaceably with one another.   I
write the same to the Sieur de La Coussaye, and I so inform you, in order

[1] Jean-Louis de Balzac, 1594–1654; one of the creators of French
prose.

that you may each arrange to live in peace.   You are both my grand-vicars, and as such you ought to have no other object than to carry things along to my satisfaction, which can be done, provided it be also to the glory of God.   It seems, from your letter, that you were in bad humour when you took your pen; as for me, I like my friends so well that I desire to know only their good humour, and it seems to me that they ought not to show me any other.   If a gnat stings you you ought to kill it, and not try to make those who, by the grace of God, are so far saved from such pricking, feel the sting.   I know, God be thanked, how to govern myself, and I know, moreover, how those who are under me ought to govern themselves.   .   .   .   I think it right that you should warn me of disorders which may exist in my diocese; but it is necessary to do so more coolly; there being no doubt that heat would, in these days, anger those who have hot blood, like me, if they had no means of warding it off.   .   .   ."

The stage is still narrow.   Richelieu in his relations with the outside world is obliged to pay many civilities, practice much suppleness, and bow low before the powers of the day.   But wherever he felt himself master he already applied his method and made the stamp of his character felt.

I perceive this no less in another letter addressed to a certain M. de Préau, in which, after speaking of threatened troubles in the interior of France (1612) and omens of war without, he adds, hopefully: " The wise conduct, affection and fidelity of many good servitors guarantee us from ills within.   As for those without, I shall baptise them with another name if they bring us opportunity to enlarge our borders and cover ourselves with glory at the cost of the enemies of France." There we hear the instinctive cry of that soul of courage and virtue, which, in its ambitions, was patriotic and French above all else, and was destined in future to fuse its personal passions in the grandeur of its public purpose. There is a saying of Montesquieu which seems to show such absolute misconception that I have difficulty in comprehending how it came from so great a mind: " The most mischievous [*méchants*] citizens of France," he says in one of his " Pensées," " were Richelieu and Louvois." We will set aside Louvois, who is not in question here; but Richelieu, a bad citizen of France! To what a point must Montesquieu have been imbued with the old parliamentary spirit, or with the modern philosophic idea, on the day when that saying escaped him! A citizen is precisely what Richelieu was; a patriot, ardent for the public grandeur of the State; as much so, at the very least, as the two Pitts were great patriots and citizens of England.

We see dawning in Richelieu's Letters the first gleams of his favour at Court, without, however, learning much more about it than he tells us in his Memoirs. His first political act, properly so-called, was the harangue he pronounced in presenting the report of his Order at the closure of the States-General, February 23, 1615. He was chosen as orator, and acquitted himself with honour and applause. A tone of high authority and reason makes itself felt through the pomposity of the speech in certain places. He knew the queen, Marie de Medicis personally, and had already insinuated himself into her confidence. It was about this time that he first saw the Maréchal d' Ancre.

"I won his heart," he says, " and he formed an esteem for me the first time we conferred together.   He told some of his familiars that he had a young man in hand who was capable of teaching a lesson to *tutti borboni*.   The esteem lasted always; but his goodwill diminished wholly; first because he found oppositions in me which he did not expect; secondly, because he noticed that the queen's confidence leaned wholly to my side.[1]   .   .   ."

What was the state of the kingdom when Richelieu, then thirty-one years of age, became minister for the first time?   Although this first and rather obscure ministry, separated from the glorious second by an interval of seven years, lasted only five months (Oct. 31, 1616 to April 24, 1617) we already discover, by looking closely into it, the distinctive features of Richelieu's policy, the vigorous application of his principles to the same evils he was later to cure, and the dawning efficacy of the same remedies which were on the point of taking effect when the murder of Maréchal d'Ancre stopped all and threw everything into abeyance.   Richelieu's great career was destined to begin twice before succeeding: " There are times," he says, energetically, " when Fortune begins but cannot complete her work."

France, after the death of Henri IV, had fallen from the most flourishing and prosperous condition and government into a miserable state of things.   The queen-regent, Marie de Medicis, lazy, obstinate, and without fixed views, was still surrounded by the chief

[1] The Italian adventurer, Concini; favourite and prime-minister of the queen-regent, Marie de Medicis, assassinated at the instigation of the Duc de Luynes in 1617.

councillors of Henri IV, Villeroy, Jeannin, the chancellor Sillery, but the hand of the master was henceforth lacking to them.   The princes and nobles were
lifting their heads on all sides and taking arms; the
Protestants seized the occasion to confederate and
form a State within the State and against the State.
The country had been, since 1610, beneath a continual, and in some sort a chronic Fronde, a Fronde
the more dangerous because it was nearer to the
League, and chiefly because the great fomenters of
trouble had preserved intact their elements of power.
In the royal succession, so suddenly brought about by
murder, the crown conquered by Henri IV was held,
as in the later Fronde, by the hand of a woman on
the head of a child.   Richelieu, in his Memoirs, has
admirably pictured the misery of this period anterior
to his coming into office, and what he calls the cowardice and corruption of hearts:

" The times were so miserable," he says, " that the ablest among
the nobles were those who were most industrious in causing quarrels;
and the quarrels were such, and there was so little safety in estab-
lishing anything, that the ministers were more occupied in finding the
necessary means to preserve themselves than the means that were
necessary to govern the State."

Thus these ministers, the queen's councillors, men
trained and perfected in the old policy, now presented
to imminent dangers and the growing exigencies of
princes and nobles, nothing better than compromises,
delays, and, finally, concessions over which they merely
tried to haggle as much as possible.   On the morrow

of the death of Henri IV, the queen might have seen
the weakness of her councillors. It was a question
of publishing a Declaration in the name of the late
king immediately proclaiming her Regent. Villeroy,
the boldest among them, offered to draw up the document and sign it; the chancellor Sillery, "who had a
heart of wax," says Richelieu, would not seal it, giving as a reason that if he did so the Comte de Soissons
would be furious with him and kill him. "He ought,
on such an occasion," cries Richelieu, "to have despised his life for the safety of the State—but God does
not give that grace to every man." He often recurs
to this idea: that the courage which undertakes wise
and just things for the public good is a special gift of
God; and this is not in him a form of words; evidently he believed it. Speaking of the vain and fruitless ending of the States-General in 1614 he adds:

"The whole work of this Assembly had no other effect than to
overburden the provinces with the tax to be paid to their deputies,
and to show to the world that it is not enough to know evils if there
is no will to remedy them; the which will God gives, when it pleases
him to make the kingdom prosper, and the great corruption of the
ages does not hinder."

Richelieu is not a philosopher; his lofty mind, which
is, above all, a sound mind armed with a great character, pays tribute to the ideas and prejudices of his
day. In many places he speaks as if he believed in
omens, horoscopes, and sorcery; he is superstitious;
but also he is sincerely religious; he believes in the
gift of God extended over certain men destined to be

the instruments of public salvation; if the wrongs
committed against public persons seem to him of quite
another order from those committed against private
individuals, the wrongs done by those public persons
themselves seem to him graver and of heavier weight
in view of their responsibility and the far extent of
consequences. It was he who wrote, on the last
page of his Political Testament, "Many could save
themselves as private individuals who damn themselves in fact as public personages."

Let Voltaire laugh if he likes at these maxims and
see therein the trace of a small mind! For all that,
they give the only superior morality which serves as
guarantee in public personages, which saves them
from pure Machiavellianism; we rejoice when we find
the sign of this religious spirit under one form or another, this sacred sentiment of divinity invoked and
recognised by all great heads and founders of States
and leaders of peoples. In some it is but a vain and
hollow formula proclaimed on occasions and ceremo-
nies; but in others in whom this basis of belief is
real the accent never deceives; we feel it readily.

At sight of the ruin of the kingdom and the weakness of councillors during these years of the regency, Richelieu suffered greatly, asking himself if an
avenger would not appear. The queen had no fixed
views, and let herself be led sometimes by one and
sometimes by another of her ministers, according as
she thought herself the better or the worse for the

2

last advice: which is, remarks Richelieu, "the worst
thing in politics, where nothing is so needed to preserve reputation, strengthen friends, and terrify adversaries, as unity of mind and continuance of the
same purposes and means." It was then that he
began to take part himself, in the character of confidant, at first secretly, as an unseen counsellor; but,
after a certain day, we are conscious, in the actions
of the queen, of a persistence and vigour in which
they were hitherto lacking.

She had signed the Peace of Loudun, May 3, 1616,
for which the rebellious princes made her pay dearly;
but what she had done for these pretended reformers
and champions of the public weal had whetted rather
than sated their insatiable appetites. Returning to
Paris with the young king, she found herself compelled to share authority with the Prince de Condé;
the mansion of the latter was besieged by the crowd
of courtiers and became the true Louvre; the other
Louvre being left to solitude. Richelieu, very intimate with Barbin, steward of the queen's household
and a man of good judgment, who had just been
appointed secretary of State, must have acted and
made his influence felt through him at this decisive
moment. The queen, listening to the energetic counsels then given to her, and perceiving the growing
intrigues of the Prince de Condé and his allies, the
Bouillons, Vendômes, and others, who, under pretext of rising against the Maréchal d'Ancre, were

conspiring against herself and her son, decided to have the Prince de Condé arrested in the Louvre. She chose for the execution of this order Thémines, of whom Henri IV had said to her: "He is a man who will recognise nothing but the quality of royalty, and will obey nought else"—a characteristic then becoming rare indeed! Richelieu, who unravels for us all these intrigues and paints them with more than one stroke of Tacitus, adds that Thémines, who arrested the Prince de Condé, if he did well was fully aware of it, for from that day he was never satisfied, no matter what rewards the queen heaped upon him:

"She made him marshal of France, gave him one hundred and some thousand crowns in ready money, made his eldest son captain of her guards, gave to Laugières, his second son, the office of first equerry to Monsieur; and yet, with all that, he still whined and complained: so dearly do men sell the little good that is in them, and so small a value do they put on the benefits they receive from their masters."

Richelieu the historian is full of such strokes of a consummate moralist who has gone, by experience, to the depths of the hearts of men.

As soon as the Prince de Condé was arrested (September 1, 1616), the whole aspect of things changed; the crowd of courtiers who had deserted the Louvre returned to it instantly; each desiring to show himself and testify thus to his fidelity:

"Some did it sincerely," says Richelieu, "some with intentions and desires quite the contrary; but there were none who did not approve of what her Majesty had done; many even declared that they envied the luck of the Sieur de Thémines, who had had the good fortune to be employed on the enterprise: but the fact was, the Court was at this time so corrupt that it would have been hard to find any other man capable of saving the State by his fidelity and courage."

The great seigneurs, accomplices of the Prince de Condé, seeing him taken, escaped and left Paris instantly. Pretence was made of pursuing a few, M. de Vendôme for instance; but the desire they had to escape was much greater than the desire to capture them in those sent to do so. Unfaithfulness and disloyalty were betrayed on all sides. The Prince de Condé was hardly arrested before, in order to ransom himself out of prison, he offered to reveal all and betray the secrets of his party and his cabal: "which did not show as much generosity and courage," remarks Richelieu, "as a man of his condition ought to have."

It was then that the queen saw herself in the way to form a Council of ministers decisively, having already made certain changes: for the new situation a new policy was needed. The old councillors, Villeroy and Jeannin, were set aside, or nearly so; the Keeper of the Seals, Du Vair, self-styled philosopher and a man of renown in letters, had succeeded Sillery as chancellor, in which office he made a poor figure, and was good only at shackling public business. The very day of the arrest of the Prince de Condé, all the old councillors, including Sully, reappeared at the Louvre to make representations to the queen on this *coup d' État,* of which they did not appreciate the necessity and which threw them therefore into consternation.

It was about this moment that Richelieu was called to the Council, where his friends Barbin and Mangot had preceded him. He had been employed for some time in confidential negotiations and was designated to go as ambassador extraordinary to Spain. That mission suited him well; but the proposal of the queen to enter her Council, which was brought to him by Maréchal d'Ancre, carried the day: "Besides the fact that I was not honourably permitted," he says, "to deliberate on this occasion, in which the will of a superior power seemed to me absolute, I admit that there are few young men who could refuse the splendour of an office that promised both favour and employment." On entering the Council he became, from the very first day, its most important personage. He had, as he tells us, the portfolios of War and of Foreign affairs, also precedence over his colleagues as bishop; and all that at thirty-one years of age! He was the soul of this first little ministry, composed of rather obscure men, though firmly united with one another; a vigorous and energetic Cabinet, to which nothing lacked for the accomplishment of great things but time to last, and not to have been born under the shadow of Maréchal d'Ancre's patronage, a banner that made it unpopular.

Sully, jealous and hurt, expressed himself as much scandalised. We find in his Memoirs a letter to the young king in which a good Frenchman (a personage whom Sully does not disavow) speaks indignantly of seeing Maréchal d'Ancre, his wife, and Mangot, "those three creatures with their Luçon [Richelieu] ruling the whole kingdom, presiding at the Councils of State, dispensing the dignities, arms, and moneys of France." The old minister of Henri IV misconceives and rejects the successor who was destined to maintain and enlarge the work of Henri IV. From the depths of his grumbling retreat facing toward the past, Sully will never do justice to Richelieu; but, in these first moments, the error is perhaps permissible; for Maréchal d'Ancre still masked him.

Richelieu, in some very fine historical and moral pages, defining for us the character of this maréchal who was, above all else, vain and presumptuous and who clung to appearing powerful rather than to being so in fact, shows distinctly in what this ministry, supposed to be wholly given over to the favourite, was not his vassal; and we are admirably made to feel that if Luynes had not intervened, if the maréchal had lived, a struggle between Richelieu and him for the sole favour of the queen-mother would quickly have come about. Richelieu making himself more and more useful and necessary, and affecting, as he always did in all circumstances of which he was not the master, to withdraw and keep aloof, the queen would have had to choose between the two.

The great seigneurs in the provinces continued

their intrigues and their appeal to arms. One of them, the Duc de Bouillon, had the boldness to write to the king to make complaints. The king returned an answer in which, for the first time, is seen the finger, the lion's claw of Richelieu. This vigorous act of Louis XIII which "showed more of royal majesty than his past conduct," was nevertheless not received by the body of the people as it should have been, on account of Maréchal d'Ancre. That which would have been recognised as advantageous to the service of the king and the good of the State if the favourite had not been there, was taken in bad part by the people, and envenomed by the malcontents; such was the rock, the wrecking-point of Richelieu's first ministry, and he himself knew it to be so.

Nevertheless he worked to enlighten opinion; he thought of Europe and dispatched three ambassadors extraordinary, one to England, one to Holland, and M. de Schomberg to Germany. We have the Instructions that he gave to Schomberg; they form an historical summary of the situation of France as strong as it is skilful, a justification of the measures of his government, and a first tracing out of the new policy. They begin with these words:

" The chief thing that M. de Schomberg must keep before his mind is that the object of his mission to Germany is to disperse the factions that may be formed there to the prejudice of France, to put forward the name of the King as much as he can, and establish powerfully his authority."

The nobles in the provinces spring to arms for the

fourth time.   The king puts forth a Declaration; and, as words signify nothing if they are not supported by arms, Richelieu raises and organises three armies at once: one that marches into Champagne, a second into Berry and the Nivernais, and a third in the Île-de-France.   Thanks to these prompt and energetic meas-ures, to which they were not hitherto accustomed, the nobles disperse and take refuge in towns and fort-ified places, where they are soon reduced to capitu-late.   Affairs were in this state, and the party of the princes "as low" as possible, when all was changed in the twinkling of an eye by the death of Maréchal d'Ancre, who was killed April 24, 1617, by order of the king at the instigation of the Duc de Luynes. The favourite of the king caused the killing of the favourite of the queen-mother.   The ministry, of which the maréchal was more the apparent than the real head, Richelieu being its already efficacious in-spirer, was overthown by the same blow.

Richelieu relates that he was paying a visit to a rector of the Sorbonne when they brought him the news of the death of the maréchal.   He returned to the Louvre after having conferred a moment with his colleagues: "Continuing my way," he says, "I met divers faces which having smiled upon me two hours earlier no longer recognised me; many also who made me feel no change for the change of fortune."

He was the only member of the ministry whom Luynes seemed at first to spare and to wish to except from dismissal and public vengeance. In his description of the scenes that followed the murder of the maréchal, Richelieu proves himself a great painter of history. He shows us oronically the king, whom Luynes puts upon a billiard-table, that he may be seen more easily by the guilds of the city and by the deputies from the States who came to congratulate him. "It was," says Richelieu, "like a renewal of the ancient custom of Frenchmen who carried their kings at their accession on shields around the camp." He points to Luynes as the most dangerous enemy of the Maréchal d'Ancre because he was less so of his person than of his fortunes: "He bore him the hatred of envy, which is the most malignant and most cruel of all." He makes us see the insolence which, on this death of a favourite, merely changes its object. Richelieu, who will one day be considered cruel and pitiless himself— and who is so at times, though his chief vengeances mingle with State interests — considers, àpropos of the murder of the maréchal, that it was done "through hasty advice, unjust, and of evil example, unworthy of the royal majesty and virtue of the king." He thinks it would have been enough to make him a prisoner and send him back to Italy; and he blames so sanguinary a beginning of the new government.

It is to be remarked that Richelieu, when writing, though inflexible, is never inhuman. When he shows us Marie de Medicis forced to quit the Louvre, accompanied by her servants, all with sadness painted on their faces: "There was scarcely a person," he takes pleasure in noting, "who had so little the sentiment of humanity that the sight of this almost funeral procession did not move to compassion." Speaking of the odious and even barbarous treatment inflicted on the wife of the maréchal, and of her execution after she was condemned as a sorceress to have her head cut off on the scaffold, and her body and head burned to ashes, he uses words of extreme pity:

"On leaving her prison and beholding the great multitude of people crowding to see her pass: 'How many persons,' she said, 'have gathered to watch a poor, afflicted woman go by!' And presently, seeing some one to whom she had done an ill turn with the queen, she asked his pardon; so much did the true and humble shame she felt before God for having injured him take from her all shame before men. And so marvellous an effect did the blessing of God upon her have, that, by a sudden change, all those who were present at that sad spectacle became quite other men, drowning their eyes in tears of pity for this desolate woman. . . ."

I suppress a few touches of bad taste. He ends by remarking that what he says is not the result of partiality; it is the simple truth itself that compels him to speak thus: "For there is no one, however odious, who, ending their days in public with resolution and modesty, will not change hatred to pity, and draw tears from those who, at an earlier moment, have desired to shed their blood."

I like to set these words of Richelieu, so worthy of a great soul, against what was cruel and pitiless in his later conduct, by which he exceeded, on certain occasions, the necessities of even the most austere policy.

During his first ministry we find him, in those few months, doing all he could to break down the revolt of the princes and nobles and to re-establish the royal authority at the point from which it ought never to have fallen. We can perceive, even in that short time, his distinct intention to raise France abroad, and not suffer her to fall away from the rôle and title of "umpire of Christianity" which Henri IV had won to the crown. In his Instructions to M. de Schomberg, ambassador to Germany, and also in the letters written in the king's name to M. de Béthune, ambassador to Italy, Richelieu never ceases to claim that glory, and almost that function which belonged of right to France as being the "heart" of all Christian States. The republic of Venice was quarrelling with the Archduke of Grätz; Louis XIII, by Richelieu's advice, desired that the affair be appealed to him; and as the war in Piedmont was being prolonged in spite of all efforts on the spot to arrest it, Louis XIII also desired that the Duc de Savoie should send an envoy to Paris to negotiate with the Spanish ambassador accredited there, believing that the affair could be better settled near his own person. With this view he dispatched an ambassador to Spain to obtain the agreement of the Catholic King. When Venice, playing a double game, made terms with the Archduke of Grätz through the channel of Spain only, Louis XIII took offence; he complained of being defrauded of one of his noblest rights, that of holding the scales: "It seems," he

writes, "that they [the republic of Venice], falling into
voluntary ingratitude, desire, exempting themselves
from gratitude to me, to deprive me of the glory that is
due me for the accomplishment of so good a work by
transferring it to others." In that we see the finger
of Richelieu and his seal on foreign affairs during his
five-months' rule in the ministry, and in the midst of
civil troubles that seemed to compromise the very existence of the State. He is tenacious of showing to
Europe, from the very first, what he nobly expresses
in his Instructions to Schomberg: "Never vessel will
resist so great a tempest with less of damage than
will be seen in ours."

Richelieu, fallen from his first ministry, accompanies Queen Marie de Medicis in her exile to Blois (May,
1617). Soon, however, his presence in that little
Court gives umbrage to his enemies; calumny impli-
cates him in various intrigues, from which his common
sense sufficed to keep him aloof. He himself asks the
king to send him back to his diocese; he is taken at
his word, and for some time we see him in his priory
of Coussaye playing the bishop, even the recluse,
"reduced to a little hermitage," and apparently resolved to let "time flow gently onward among books
and neighbours." It was during this interval that he
wrote a book of controversy against Protestants,
seeming to be solely occupied with the duties of his
bishopric.

In placing a certain confidence in the letters which

we have of Richelieu we must not forget that we do
not possess them all; that the most important were
in cipher and have not come down to us. Neither
have we his secret letters, those in which he talked
to his intimates from a full heart — *à cœur saoul,* as
he says himself. In all that he reveals to us of his life
at divers periods there is always an undercurrent of
negotiations that escapes us. Suffice it therefore to
discern his general line of conduct.

He was not left tranquil in his retreat very long; he
was still too near the queen; calumny riddled him at
Court, and he himself was the first to instigate a sort
of exile; he requests that he may be ordered to some
other place "where he can live without calumny,
being, as he is, without fault and without just blame."
Thereupon he receives an order to go to Avignon (April,
1618); he remains there nearly a year in retirement.
Meantime the queen, escaping from the castle of Blois
by night (February, 1619), took refuge with the Duc
d'Épernon. Luynes, then ruler, feared that in obeying
the influence of that old seigneur and the mischief-
makers by whom she would be surrounded, she would
become a great danger. It was then that Richelieu's
active friends, Père Joseph, Bouthillier, and others, be-
stirred themselves, and fixed attention upon him as
the most suitable negotiator to recall and soften the
mind of the queen, to whom he had never ceased
to be agreeable. Richelieu reappears in that delicate
rôle, as semi-avowed agent. He leaves Avignon; is

arrested on his way by some too-zealous servants of the king, who think him still in disgrace, but soon make haste to excuse themselves. He reaches Angoulême on the Wednesday of Holy Week (March 27, 1619), and there, where he thought to enter port, he found, he says, "the greater tempest." He is received with an evil eye by all the other councillors who fear his influence towards moderation and his wise counsel. The queen dissimulates; he and she understand each other. He lets us be present at some of the bickerings of the little Court. Soon he becomes the necessary man, and concludes the negotiation that reconciles the mother with the son. That treaty made, he arranges the interview which is to seal the reconciliation, at Cousières near Tours. The favourites, the Luynes, are present with an eye on everything and keeping watch over the emotions of nature between mother and son. Richelieu, nevertheless, attains his end, he fulfils his mission, and from that day the king, to reward the good service, asks the pope on his behalf for the cardinal's hat; which, however, he did not receive until three years later. Thus it was that at the very moment when Richelieu's fortunes seemed irretrievably ruined they were suddenly repaired, and henceforth insensibly rose and broadened without further check.

Nevertheless, the years that immediately followed left him still in a secondary position, in which he had need of all his insinuation, suppleness, and patience.

The Duc de Luynes triumphed at Court, and reigned throughout the kingdom. Richelieu remained attached to the queen-mother in her government of Anjou; he is the superintendent of her household, and, correctly speaking, the minister of this semi-exile; for, in spite of the meeting and the embraces at Cousières, evil passions interposed and worked at sowing fresh discord between mother and son. The Prince de Condé, whom Marie de Medicis had put in prison solely in the king's interests, was released, and that prince of the blood became her active enemy, serving all the evil purposes of Luynes. Richelieu was strongly of opinion that the queen, to thwart these intrigues, ought to go straight to Court, make Nature speak for her in the heart of the king, and boldly drive into nothingness this malignancy. But other counsellors of the queen thought otherwise, supporting their opinion with plausible reasons. Fearing to lose the confidence of his mistress, Richelieu, out of prudence, felt himself obliged to adopt their opinion, "imitating wise pilots who yield before tempests. There being no advice so judicious," he reflects, "that it may not have a bad issue, one is often obliged to follow opinions that we least approve." Even when he reveals to us the many hindrances and disappointments that barred his fortunes, Richelieu's style is never irritable and shows neither anger nor vexation.

The power and the pretensions of Luynes and his

brothers keep on increasing and rouse universal repro-
bation. Greedy of honours and possessions, and without the slightest patriotic ambition, they monopolise
all governments, offices, fortified places, and castles;
they buy up for themselves and cheapen the royal
companies and the pick of all others; the taxes levied
on the people are appropriated to these private sales:
"In a word," says Richelieu, "if the whole of France
were for sale they would buy France from France itself." Richelieu is in the Opposition, as we should
now say; he is too patriotic at this time not to be,
but he is so in a manner of his own.

The nobles and the seigneurs, whom he had formerly combated are now, it seems, rising on his side,
and in the name of the queen-mother; they surround
the latter with intrigues, and under pretence of delivering the kingdom from the favourite, they are thinking only of their private interests. Seeing them arrive
at Angers, Richelieu effaces himself and takes no part
in their deliberations. Between two papers drawn up
in the queen's name, one more moderate, more prudent, and not tending to civil war, the other bitter,
violent, in short a manifesto of hostility, he is of opinion to choose the first, all the more because they have
not force enough to support the second. He fears to
give pretext to these powerful and turbulent allies who
"after ruining the varlets" will next, out of ambition,
attack the masters. He thinks that "there is no peace
so bad that it is not better than civil war." Luynes

advances into Maine with the king's troops; all the seigneurs and captains grouped around the queen-mother at Angers make countless plans that interfere with one another. Every one prays for the queen: she has all hearts, she has even many arms, and yet she is about to be vanquished in the twinkling of an eye. "God permits it, as I think," says Richelieu, "to make it plain that the peace of States is of such great importance in his sight that he often deprives of success enterprises that would trouble it, however just and legitimate they are."

Speaking of the part taken by Richelieu at this critical moment, some men of the period accused him of having betrayed the interests of the queen-mother and the confederates. The Duc de Rohan, that fomenter of civil war, accuses him of having intentionally advised the queen to make "a trembling defence." No; Richelieu gave then, even to the men of war, the best counsel, which was not followed; but the true explanation, in my opinion, is that he was not in heart with the confederates. Richelieu remained the past and the future minister of the monarchy even under dismissal and exile; he is conscious of his coming destiny; he does not belie his future.

Nothing can be more piquant than the portrait he draws of the principal leaders in the affray and rout that goes by the name of the "Pont-de-Cé" (August 7, 1620): it was a panic. The boasters, the cowards, the brave (in small number), each and all have their

3

place. It is an ironical picture such as Philippe de Commynes might have painted, and he ends it by considerations worthy of him, worthy of the man who remained, at all times, royalist:

> " I learned on this occasion that any party composed of various bodies having no other bond than that their excitability gives them . . . has no great subsistence; that whatever is maintained only by precarious authority has no great duration; that those who combat legitimate power are semi-defeated by their imagination; thoughts come to them that not only are they exposed to the loss of their lives in battle but, what is worse, by the arm of the law if captured; they think of the executioner as they face the enemy, rendering the fight very unequal; for there is little courage stiff enough to rise above such considerations with as much resolution as if they were not aware of them."

Such Richelieu is still at heart when he finds himself reluctantly involved in armed revolt and sedition. It is he who, on the morrow of the defeat at Pont-de-Cé, contributes most to healing matters and to bring about a peace which Luynes the victor did not, for once, abuse to his own advantage.

So long as Luynes governed the king, there was no great place possible for Richelieu. About this time the favourite had a passing fancy to form connection with the queen; he seems to have even sought alliance with Richelieu, and the niece of the one married the nephew of the other. But the two men were incompatible, and Richelieu had then no other real security than the goodwill and confidence of the queen-mother. To all the hazardous advice that was given to the latter he urged the opposition of consistent prudence and patience. Seeing the excessive good

fortune and the poor discretion and conduct of the
adversary, he felt with his sound good sense that it
behoved them only to wait and hold fast: "It is not
in France as in other countries," thought he; "in
France the best remedy we can have is patience.
. . ." And he expresses, àpropos of our light-
mindedness, so fruitful of reverses, distressing ideas
that would be too discouraging if he himself, man of
authority and organisation, did not come erelong to
oppose and correct them by his own example. But
for those who seek to find cause against our nation in
his words let me add that, according to him, this
French levity often bears its own remedy within
itself; for, if it sometimes casts us down frightful precipices it does not leave us there, but "pulls us up
so quickly that our enemies, unable to take right
measures on such frequent variations, have no leisure
to profit by our faults."

While Richelieu takes patience and waits, war begins in the south of France against the Protestants
who have organised themselves into churches and
chosen for leader and generalissimo the Duc de Rohan
(1621). Rebellion is manifest; the king goes down
there in person, full of courage; but Luynes ill knows
how to prepare the ground and afford him occasions
for acting. Before Montauban, for instance, Luynes
relies too much on information he obtains from a
traitor. He plans the advance of the king, who is
repulsed: "It is well," says Richelieu, 'not to neglect

small advantages; but it is dangerous to depend upon them, especially for a great prince who ought rather to win than to filch victories." How noble and how well said that is! Richelieu has his system of the way a devoted prime-minister ought to bring forward and put in relief a courageous king; he suffers in seeing that Luynes knows nothing of that art, nor of the jealousy for the honour of his master's arms that he ought to have.

If Luynes had lived, Richelieu's fortunes would have been long delayed, perhaps for ever. When he disappears, carried off by a sudden illness (December 14, 1621), in the midst of this very campaign which he had undertaken without ability to bring it to an end, Richelieu, in describing his death, his character and his person, has flashes of colour and passion such as Saint-Simon, a century later, might have given. Luynes, in the midst of his other defects, had one which, in France, would spoil even the best qualities, he was not personally brave. At the siege of Montauban, Constable of France as he was, he never approached the town within cannon-shot. He amused himself by sealing, filling the office of Keeper of the Seals, while others fought: a good Keeper of the Seals in war-time, people said, and a good constable in times of peace. "At the height of his cowardice," cries Richelieu, "he never ceased to talk as if he were riddled with wounds and covered with the blood of the enemy . . . " "The height of his cowardice" is one of those involuntary expressions which characterise a great and brave historian.

The whole portrait of Luynes is one of extreme beauty; it should be read as a whole; I can note only a few salient points which reflect the character of Richelieu himself. He is bent on showing Luynes as little fitted for the height to which favour had lifted him; a height that merely made him giddy and insolent: " Such minds," he says, " are capable of every fault; especially when men come, as this one did, to favour without having passed through public offices; men who see themselves suddenly above rather than in public affairs, and are masters of the Council without ever having entered it."

" He had," he says again, " a mediocre and timid mind, little faith, no generosity; too feeble to stand firm under the rush of great fortune . . . . He wished to be Prince of Orange, Count of Avignon, Duke of Albert,[1] King of Austrasia,[2] and would not have refused more had he seen his way to it. Flattery carried him to such a point that he thought all the laudations bestowed upon him were true, and that the grandeur he attained was the least of his merits. . . . He was full of fine words and promises that he never kept faithfully; when he gave his most positive word persons felt the most certain that he would not keep it; and when he promised his affection it was then that its object had reason to doubt it: so faithless was he without shame, measuring honour solely by utility."

Richelieu reproaches Luynes for seeking to apply to France the narrow and tyrannical policy that is practicable only in the lesser provinces of Italy, where all

[1] Ancre in the department of the Somme.
[2] Eastern part of the empire of the Merovingian kings:—TR.

the subjects are immediately under a hand they fear:
"It is not the same in France," he says, "a great,
spacious country, parted by many rivers, with provinces very far from the seat of the king." In this
whole picture Richelieu indirectly reveals to us his
private thoughts; in representing to us the odious
favourite it is evident that he is feeling how he himself would differ from him. Richelieu, for example,
does not think himself tyrannical in the same manner
as the predecessor whom he scathes:

> "He, on the contrary," he says, "having the power in hand, scorned
> to gratify any one, believing that it sufficed him to hold their persons by
> force, and that he had no need to attach their hearts. But in that he
> was greatly mistaken; for it is impossible that a Government can exist
> under which none are satisfied and all are treated with violence. Se-
> verity is very dangerous where no one is content; laxity where there is no
> satisfaction is dangerous also; the only means by which it can exist is
> by uniting severity with just satisfaction to those who are governed;
> which will end in the punishment of the bad and the reward of the
> good."

Richelieu's theory is in those words; it is true, as he
tells us elsewhere, that where it is absolutely necessary
to choose, he considers punishment more necessary
than reward, and he puts it in the front rank.

Machiavelli said: "It is not the violence that repairs
but the violence that destroys which should be condemned." It is best, however, that in all that is permanent, all that is founded to last, the idea of violence
should fade away; and Richelieu, in his government,
never attained to this course of regular, almost impas-
sive, action. He was certainly of the race of royal

souls, but he was not born king. It was the resistance and effort he had to make to maintain the royalty
he held as a loan that made him sometimes tyrannical in
action and manner.   Montesquieu said of Louis XIV :
" He had a soul that was greater than his mind."   In
Richelieu the mind was as great as the soul and
seemed to fill it but never to overflow it.

Richelieu does not enter the ministry immediately on
the death of Luynes; the ministers at Court dread him,
knowing that he is full of ideas and of force of judgment; they retard as much as they can the moment
when the king will take particular notice of him, fearing to see him at once at the head of affairs : " I have
had this misfortune," he says, " that those who had
power in the State have always wished me ill, not for
any harm that I had done them, but for the good they
believed was in me."   Do what they would, however, in vain did they oppose fate and sink deeper
daily into wastefulness and blunders; the moment approaches—it has come—and Richelieu henceforth is
inevitable.

We will leave him to reign.   But it is essential, that
I may not fall below my own idea, to say a few more
words about that Political Testament in which he laid
down, in a rather sententious form, the summing up
of his experience and the ideal of his doctrine.

Among the objections that Voltaire raised against
the authenticity of that work, there is one, among
others, that strikes me by its weakness and even its

misconception: " Admit," he says, addressing M. de
Foncemagne, "admit that after all you do not believe
there is a single word from the cardinal in this Testament: in good faith, do you think that Sir Robert
Walpole would ever have thought of writing a political catechism for George I?" But Richelieu is
precisely the contrary of Robert Walpole: he is a
man who believes in God, in the nature of kings, in a
certain moral grandeur in public affairs, in virtue belonging to each Order of the State—lofty rectitude in
the Clergy, generosity and purity of heart in the
Nobles, integrity and gravity in the Parliaments; all
this is what he desires at any cost to maintain or restore. Richelieu likes and prefers honest men· in
what memorable terms does he speak in his Memoirs
of the heroic gravity of Achille de Harlay and of the
prud'homie of President Jeannin!

In the Political Testament there is a remarkable
chapter entitled: "On Letters"; that is to say, on
classical literature and on education. In it Richelieu
explains his ideas about a wise administration and
dispensation of literature, and, considering the date at
which he wrote, it proves his lofty foresight. One
might really think he had the eighteenth century and
something of the nineteenth before his eyes.[1] He
cannot admit that in a State every one, without difference, should be brought up to be learned. "Just as a
body which had eyes in every part of it would be a

[1] The French Academy was founded by Richelieu in 1635:—Tr.

monster," he says, "so would a State be if all its subjects were learned men; we should see little obedience,
while pride and presumption would be common."
And again: " If Letters were degraded to all sorts of
minds, we should see more men capable of forming
doubts than of solving them, and many would be
more fitted to oppose truths than defend them." He
cites in support of his opinion Cardinal Du Perron, that
friend of fine literature, who would have liked to see
less colleges established in France on condition that
they were better, supplied with excellent professors,
engaged with worthy studies only, fit to preserve in
its purity the fire of the temple. The rest of the
young manhood would naturally go, he thought, to
the mechanical arts, to agriculture, commerce, the
army; whereas by applying them all indifferently to
studies " without the capacity of their minds being
first examined, nearly all remain with a mediocre tinge
of Letters and fill France with disputers [*chicaneurs*]."
This opinion of Richelieu, coming after the inundation
of the sixteenth century and before the deluge of the
eighteenth, is Bonald's legislation unadulterated; and,
on whichever side we look at it, expressed at that
time and with that precision, it bears witness to the
profound insight of a statesman.

This rôle of statesman, which, at every social crisis,
is the chief and the most actual, is not the only
rôle; two forces in conflict govern the world. While
Richelieu was expressing these forecasts and fears,

Descartes was preparing free access for all minds not only to Letters but to the Sciences by teaching mathematical doubt.   There is much to meditate upon in those two names.

On superficial reading, the Political Testament may seem to be composed of rather trite and commonplace maxims: but read it carefully, and you will always find the statesman and the experienced moralist.   In all the reforms that he proposes, Richelieu shows himself full of moderation; he takes account of accomplished facts; and even in correcting evils he desires to proceed with gentleness and caution.   He is one of those architects who prefer to remedy the faults of an old building, and bring it by their art to satisfactory symmetry, rather than pull it down on pretence of building another quite perfect and complete.   However ardent may have been Richelieu's nature and his fire of ambition, it remains evident that his mind in its foundation was essentially just and temperate.   In his moral descriptions, and in the examination of conditions that he exacts from men chosen to be political councillors, he certainly had in view this one or that one of those whom he had known; and his observations are so just and strong that merely in transcribing them here it seems as though we could put the right names beneath both virtues and defects:

"The greatest minds," says Richelieu, "may be more dangerous than useful in the management of affairs; if they have not more lead than quicksilver, they are worth nothing to the State."

"Some are fertile in invention and abundant in thoughts, but so variable in their designs that those of evening and those of morning are always different; and such men have so little persistency in their resolutions that they change the good ones as often as the bad ones and are constant to none."

"I can say with truth, knowing it from experience, that the levity of some men is not less dangerous in the administration of public affairs than the malice of others. There is much to fear from minds whose vivacity is accompanied with little judgment, and, even if those who excel in judgment have no great force they may nevertheless be useful to the State."

"Presumption is one of the great vices that men may have in public office; if humility is not required of those who are called upon to lead States, modesty is absolutely necessary."

"Without modesty great minds are so in love with their opinions that they condemn all others, better though they be; the pride of their natural characters joined to their authority soon renders them intolerable."

Such are the counsels, or rather the specifications of experience given by a man who did not pass for modest, but who certainly was still less presumptuous. In reading carefully Richelieu's State maxims, a doubt has possessed me at times: I ask myself whether, in the historical judgment formed upon him, too much of the unpopularity that easily attaches to strong powers in periods of public relaxing, has not been allowed to enter; and whether, from afar, we do not now judge him, even in his glory, too much through the imputations of the enemies who survived him. Richelieu was vindictive; was he as much so as was said of him? He certainly did not think so when he said: "Those who are vindictive by nature, who follow their passions rather than reason, cannot be considered to have the requisite integrity for the management of the State. If a man is subject to revenge, to put him in authority is to put a sword in the hand of a madman."

Such words show that the mind of Richelieu was far from tending to violent extremes. I leave these divers problems, these apparent contradictions between some of his thoughts and his acts, for future historians to agitate; the fame of Richelieu (and fame, he said, is the sole payment of great souls) can only increase with the years and the centuries; he is of those who have most contributed to give consistency and unity to a great nation which, in itself, has too little of them; he is, under that head, one of the most glorious political artisans that ever existed, and the more the generations are battered by revolutions and ripened by experience the more will they approach his memory with circumspection and respect.

II.

The Duc de Rohan.

Henri, Duc de Roban.

The Protestant Leader.

THE sixteenth century, which produced so great a number of good captains and writers of the sword, had, as it were, a last scion in the Duc de Rohan, who, under that double aspect, made himself illustrious during the first third of the following century. He is the last great man the Reformed religion produced in France; and it is the right of the historians of that party to study him with complacency and peculiar admiration. For us, who content ourselves with feeling his force, his merit — merit always thwarted and obscured by certain shadows — he attracts us chiefly as a writer, and it is on that side that I wish to render account of him to myself in presence of my readers, adding nothing to the idea, very lofty already, that we ought to form of him, and exaggerating nothing.

The fact is, we are at the present time in the habit of exaggerating many things. The study of the past, where great talents have lighted beacons that attract

all sorts of minds, is becoming a fashionable enthusiasm and a snare.　It is time for criticism, if it still dares
to be critical, to lay upon this enthusiasm certain restrictions and to remind it of some salutary rules.　In
France, we do things too often by fits and starts; the
fever of the present day is to rehabilitate all that comes
to hand or within the reach of every one.　A few old
papers found, which often, if read carefully (but nothing is more difficult than to read carefully, especially if
the words are not in print), tell us nothing more than
we knew before; a few unpublished documents which,
in every case, ought to combine with notions already
acquired and positive, these are the pretexts for an upsetting; accepted judgments are reversed, reputations
are made anew, we all blow our trumpets for the discoveries we think we have made, and in our eagerness to succeed we readily grant all to our neighbour
so that in return he may grant all to us.　I see many
hod-carriers who pretend to be architects, and copyists
saying to themselves: "I, too, am a painter."—But
this is not the time and place to treat of so grave
and delicate a question.　Happily the Duc de Rohan is
not in need of rehabilitation; he needs only to be
studied, and we have only to study him.

　He came of a proud, strong race, descended from the
ancient dukes and kings of Brittany, allied by descent
and marriage with the principal sovereign families of
Europe.　"I shall content myself," writes one of his
earliest biographers, "by merely saying one rather

fine and rather peculiar thing: to whatever part of
Europe he went he was related to those who reigned
there." We all know the speech of his sister, replying to a gallant declaration from Henri IV, "I am
too poor to be your wife, and too well-born to be your
mistress." [1]

Born at the castle of Blein in Brittany in 1579, Henri
de Rohan, the eldest of his family, was brought up
with great care by his widowed mother, Catherine de
Parthenay, who fixed upon him from childhood her
pride and hopes. He was proficient in all exercises
that made part of the education of a noble and a man of
war; and he likewise applied himself to things of the
mind, especially history, geography, and mathematics,
which he said was the true science of princes. It was
told that he neglected the ancient languages, Latin
and Greek, being more eager after things than words.
However that may be, it would not have injured him
to know Latin, fond as he was of studying ancient
authors and of annotating Cæsar, of whom he was to
make, in his leisure hours, a sort of breviary. He
read also, like Henri IV, Amyot's translation of
Plutarch, and kindled with enthusiasm for the Greek
and Roman heroes; Epaminondas and Scipio being
his models. In short, he received from his excellent
mother a hardy and virile education, which his own

---

[1] It is singular that Sainte-Beuve does not here mention the proud
motto of the Rohans: *Roi ne peux, prince ne veux, Rohan je suis—*
"King I cannot [be], prince I will not [be], Rohan I am."—TR.

4

nature welcomed and the austerity of his religious communion confirmed: his youth was ardent, frugal, and serious.

Henri IV distinguished him among all the young nobles and loved him. As Vicomte de Rohan, he made his first campaign under the king's eye at the siege of Amiens, when sixteen years of age. This was his first school of war. The peace of Vervins (1598), which was to give France years of repose and a national felicity long unknown, made the warlike zeal of the young man useless, and he resolved to travel. His first idea was to push on to the East and see the empire of the Turks: "not from superstition," he says, like most of those who go to visit Jerusalem, but to instruct himself during the active years of his novitiate and to study the diversities of peoples and countries. Circumstances thwarted this first intention, and he fell back on travelling through European Christendom (1600–1601). He has left a narrative of his journey, dedicated to his mother, and written to preserve his own recollections and to please his friends. This *coup-d'œil* of a tourist of twenty years of age through France, Germany, Italy, Holland, and Great Britain, shows plainly the qualities and the solid inclinations of a mind that was preparing itself to play a great part. He notes everywhere, as a future commander and statesman, the site of fortresses, fortifications, commerce, the genius of nations, the form of governments. For a man who was said to have no taste for classical study, he takes such interest in antiquities and quotes so much Latin that we must believe his first biographer exaggerated his repugnance and his ignorance in that respect.

Venice impressed him keenly by its originality of aspect, its arsenal, its fine police, its palaces, even its pictures and its fantastic magnificences.

"In a word," he says, "if I tried to note down all that is worthy of it paper would fail me : content thyself, therefore, my Memory, in remembering that having seen Venice thou hast seen one of the collections of the marvels of the world, from which I depart as enraptured and content at having seen it as I am sad at having stayed so short a time ; for it deserves, not three or four weeks but a century to study it to the level of its merits."

He stays longer in Florence and from there makes a trip to Rome and Naples. Though he stayed but a week in Rome, and seems to have ransacked at full speed her curiosities and ruins, he is not too unjust or too calvinistic in his remarks upon her.

But after Venice he finds nothing more interesting nor more admirable than Amsterdam and the government of the United Provinces; he prefers the latter to that of Venice. He likes Holland, even that which is rather sad about her, even her difficulties, even that long war she had successfully maintained against powerful Spain for her independence as a country. Holland, under the illustrious princes of Nassau, was always the ideal land of Reformed religionists. He ends his journeyings in England and Scotland where, more even than elsewhere he is received with

distinction and hospitality by the sovereigns of the two
countries.   Queen Elizabeth calls him her "Knight";
and James VI, treating him as a cousin, invited him
to be godfather to his son, just born, afterwards the
unfortunate Charles I of England.   In concluding his
narrative, Rohan draws a species of parallel between
the genius of the different peoples and their government.   What he says of the good qualities and defects of the French nation in comparison with the
English shows him to be a judicious and impartial
observer.   As for the nobility and aristocracy of France,
he considers them (without enough reason perhaps)
far more fortunate than those across the Channel:
"As much," he says, "because the latter pay taxes like
the people, as for the rigour of the law, which is so
constantly exercised against them that some hold it as
an honour, and rest the grandeur of their families on the
number of their forbears who have had their heads cut
off; which is very rare among us."   Here speaks the
young man, and before the days of Richelieu.   He
sees only the agreeable advantages he then enjoyed:
"the privileges of the nobility in France, its liberty,
the familiarity with which the king treats it, in place
of the superstitious reverence that the English pay to
their king"—all things well fitted to seduce even so
solid a mind as that of young Rohan.   It was not
until the day of Louis XIV that the fatal levelling of the
nobility was really felt; it was permissible amid the
gracious sallies and smiles of Henri IV to mistake its

actual position.   Nevertheless, one year later, the head
of Biron was to fall.

Henri IV had a true friendship for young Rohan; in
him he saw a pupil, a future lieutenant for his military
projects; doubtless he also discerned a head capable
of upholding and leading the Reformed party in future
years, and of opposing his own better views to the
perpetual intrigues of the Maréchal de Bouillon.   He
desires to confirm him in grandeur and makes him
duke and peer (1602): his first idea was to marry him
to a princess of Sweden, but this project did not take
shape.   Rohan married the daughter of Sully, becoming the son-in-law of the man who was daily gaining
more importance in the State and more credit with its
master.   Rohan himself received the office of colonel-
general of the Swiss Guard.   He served in this capacity in 1610, and was one of the principal leaders in
the army that awaited Henri IV for that great and
mysterious enterprise of which, to all appearance,
the siege of Juliers was to be the signal.   He was
thirty-one years of age, and the noblest and most brilliant career lay open before him; when suddenly the
knife of Ravaillac, taking from France a great king,
took also from all generous hearts their true guide.

"If ever," says Rohan, "I had reason to join my regrets to those
of France, it was at the unhappy death of Henri the Great, so full of
gloom and fatal results for us; yet for him it may, perhaps, be
reckoned, from a worldly point of view, as fortunate. . . . After
his accession to the throne (1589) he employed eight years in bringing the kingdom to obedience; and these years, though toilsome,

were the happiest of his life ; for, in augmenting his reputation he augmented his State : the true happiness of a magnanimous prince does not consist in long possessing a great empire, which may serve to plunge him into pleasures only, but in having from a little State made a great State, and satisfied not his body but his spirit. One often sleeps worse among delights on good mattresses than on gabions, and there is no such rest as that which is acquired through labour."

Rohan thinks (and this judgment is characteristic of him) that those eight laborious and victorious years— victory so contested and bought by such perils and vigils — were happier to Henri IV than the twelve years of peace and felicity, during which he governed his kingdom without further struggle. Rohan is, in his way, a hero, but a thwarted hero, who will always have a burden to bear upon his shoulders; one might almost think from those words of his that he found more pleasure than resignation in bearing it; he loved effort.

He foresees all the evils that will follow the king's death, all the ambitions that already are whetting their appetites.

" In his lifetime he [Henri IV] restrained evil-doers by his authority; by his death all fear in evil-doing is removed, liberty seems given to worthless men. The still recent memory of his name bears with it some respect, but every day that carries us away from it is a sure step into the path of disobedience. Those who witnessed the reign of Charles IX, with the consequent evils that France suffered after it, can easily judge of the danger she is now in. . . . I regret in the loss of our invincible King, that of France. I mourn his person, I deplore the lost opportunities, and I sigh in the depths of my heart over the manner of his death. Experience will teach us in a short time the legitimate cause we have to regret and mourn him. The people already shudder and seem to foresee their misery; the cities are guarded as if they expected a siege; the nobles look for safety to the most important in their own body, but find them all dis-united; there is every occasion for fear and none for security. In short, one must either not be a Frenchman, or regret the loss of the happiness of France. I mourn in him the loss of his courtesy, his familiarity, his good humour, his pleasant conversation. The honour that he did me, the good cheer with which he favoured me, the admittance that he gave me to his most private places, oblige me not only to mourn him but also to no longer like myself where I was accustomed to see him. I mourn for the noblest and most glorious enterprise that was ever spoken of . . . an opportunity I shall never see again; certainly not under so great a captain, nor with the same desire on my part to serve it and learn my pro-fession. . . . Is it not, for me, a subject of great regret to lose the only opportunity that ever came to me to prove to my king — and O God, what a king! — my courage, my affection, my fidelity? Surely when I think of it my heart breaks. A lance-thrust given in his presence would have pleased me more than now to win a battle. I should have more esteemed one word of praise from him in this profession, of which he was the greatest master in his time, than those of all other living captains. . . . I part my life in two, and call the first, that which I have now lived, happy, because it served the great Henri, and that which I have to live unhappy, employing it in regretting, mourning, complaining, and sighing."

Rohan did not pass the rest of his life mourning and sighing, nor even in serving inviolably (as he vows to do at the end of this paper) France, the young king and his mother. But he had good reason to consider his career as cut in two by King Henri's death. Instead of the way lying open before him, that of a great captain of generous and loyal French-men, beneath the great man of whom he would have been the illustrious lieutenant and second, he was henceforth to find himself engaged, by force of cir-cumstances, in a life of faction, of struggle in all

directions, of disputes at every step, wrangles with
his own people and with the envious orators of his
own party, in rebellion before the armies and the
person of the king, and continually in alliance with
foreigners. He was now to train and consume his
faculties as an able statesman and a skilful soldier on
manœuvres in which selfish interests and personal
ambitions made, with the names, perpetually invoked,
of God and conscience, a most equivocal mixture that
even those assiduously given to it found difficulty in
distinguishing apart.

His *Mémoires*, which cover, from his point of view,
the whole history of France from the death of Henri
IV to the end of the third war against the Reformers,
when La Rochelle fell (1610–1629), exhibit the complication of events and the obstructions to the writer.
The first religious civil war seems to have been begun,
in 1621, against Rohan's will, although he became its
instrument and most energetic champion. There happened to him that which so often happens to leaders
of party : it is the parties and the Assemblies that lead
them. The Assembly of Protestants, convoked at
La Rochelle, believing that the guarantees to their
Churches were threatened, even by the conditions of
the Edict of Nantes, and excited by the Vicomte de
Favas, pushed forward to a rupture. Rohan's prudence made him see the peril ; the point of honour
and the instinct of a soldier made him brave it. Most
of the nobles of the Reformed religion, who seemed

at first to take the same course, made terms, little by little, and withdrew. Rohan, with his brother Soubise, was left to bear the brunt of the defence. His governments in Poitou fell into the power of the royal armies. He organised the resistance in the South, and succeeded in throwing succour into Montauban, in spite of the vicinity of the two royal armies. His plan was to act in the true military manner: to dismantle the small places he could not hold, and to fortify the large ones, Nîmes, Montpellier, Uzès: "We had," he says, "a sufficient number of men to make a lively resistance; but the shortsightedness of the people and the private interests of the governors of the towns caused my advice to be rejected, for which they afterwards repented sorely."

Leader of a league, and that a religious league, Rohan had to struggle against all the disadvantages of that position: fanatical forebodings and denunciations from within, popular violence, excesses and crimes to punish, self-willed and headstrong troops, difficult to collect or retain under the flag. He got along as best he could, sometimes for three months, with unpaid troops, holding his own against the armies of the enemy, laying several sieges; but, after all, being forced to desist from what he was on the point of attaining, "as much through the ill-humour of his colonels as because the harvests were beginning, which is a time when the poor of lower Languedoc earn much money."

These are but glimpses, but they give an idea of the
nature of the genius and the firmness required to make
as good a show as Rohan did in such a style of war;
I leave it to others to admire him for it. Great
occasions were lacking, but he ennobled as much as
he could the lesser ones. There is one place in his
narrative where the Duc de Luynes (the favourite in
power, who had married his cousin), asks for a con-
ference with him at a league from Montauban; Rohan
trusts himself to him, and gives us the details of the
interview and of their speeches, — that of Luynes
and his own reply :

"I should be my own enemy," says Rohan to Luynes, "if I did not
desire the good graces of my King and your friendship. I shall never
refuse the gifts and honours of my master, nor your good offices as
an ally. I have fully considered the peril in which I am; but I ask
you to also consider your own. You are universally hated, because
you alone possess that which every man desires to have. The ruin of
those of the Reformed religion is not so near that malcontents will not
have time to form parties. Reflect that you have already harvested
all that promises, mingled with threats, can ever obtain for you, and
that all who now remain to us are fighting for the religion they
believe in. . . ."

He ends by refusing to lend himself to any personal
conclusion that would separate him from the general
interests. For these religious wars, having once begun, even against his will, it is to Rohan's honour
that he never put his hand to private negotiations,
nor sacrificed his party. It is for this, as much as for
his talents as a commander, that he is distinguished
from the other seigneurs who, sooner or later, deserted

their party, and he deserves that the French Protestant cause shall remain for ever identified with his name.

After the death of Luynes, and after many similar parleys, mingled with various bold attacks, Rohan, who sees the people to be weary of war, and that forage for his much-diminished cavalry will last only eight days longer, and who, moreover, has lost all hope of succour from foreign co-religionists, confers with the new connétable, Lesdiguières, to draw up a treaty (October, 1622) which saved and maintained the principal points necessary to the Reformed party, and in which his own interests were not altogether forgotten. After which, he is not only pardoned by the king, but he has a dazzling moment of favour at Court. Richelieu, then approaching power with slow step, had not yet reached it; when he did so, pacifications were conducted differently.

But this peace, obtained by bargaining, was ill-kept. The Duc de Rohan was forced to submit at Montpellier to an affront from the governor, M. de Valençay, and to a species of imprisonment. Besides which, he had to defend himself in his own party against censors who, for the most part, had kept their arms folded during the war, and to "justify his good intentions blamed and his best actions calumniated." We begin now to see the thankless and difficult part he had to play, which was destined to become far more so in his two following wars, with Richelieu in power.

There is a race of brilliant, favoured warriors and fortunate heroes: Rohan is not of it. He is of those to whom adversity serves as a continual school, and even as a strengthener; men who snatch glory bit by bit, in fragments only. He is not of that group of Captains — the Condés, the Luxembourgs, the Villars, the Saxes — of whom we may say that fortune smiled upon them like Venus, like a woman. He is of the race of grave men, thwarted men, morose men; whose very brilliancy is darkened and sombred; who have more merit than opportunity or luck, esteemed though often defeated; and who do the utmost that they can with a dismembered and rebellious cause; he is, in short, of the race of the Colignys, and of William of Orange; less French, perhaps, than foreign in physiognomy. In place of the lightning-flash of the French nature, the Reform has placed upon his brow its thoughtful seal, its frown, proclaiming less the inspired warrior than the reasoning soldier.

We may follow and study closely the narrative that M. de Rohan has written of the religious civil wars under Louis XIII and the noted part that he played in them, but we cannot, even by placing ourselves at the most neutral point of view and avoiding all questions of the Church,—we cannot, I say, take a strong interest in him, or desire at any moment his success and the triumph of his arms. He is definitively against France; he fights against the nation; he conspires against its grandeur, and makes common cause with the foreigner.

I desire, in this rapid outline and while stating the principal facts, to shock no true and noble feeling, to slight no claim of the human conscience; and yet I must maintain the line which is ever the most direct, the only French line, that of the broad and royal road. The question, so sacred to us, of tolerance and respect for all convictions and professions of sincere faith compatible with social order, had in that day not been evolved. A few men who had enough wisdom and firmness of judgment to understand it and to forestall its solutions, spoke to deaf ears; and when they tried, like l'Hôpital, to introduce moderation publicly by edicts, they merely lent immediate arms to passions. In that heated atmosphere, which had not been sufficiently worked over in every direction, which had not yet vented all its storms, and where the numerous currents of indifference had not as yet worked their way, how could there be tolerance? Satisfaction, full and exclusive, dominion, the upper hand, was what they wanted.

Henri IV was the only man who was able to calm this spirit; he did it by his skill, his justice, his force so wisely tempered by dexterity. He died too soon; and when he was gone it was difficult indeed for the ill-appeased fermentations, stirred up afresh by the air without, not to burst once more into flames. The Duc de Rohan felt, from the moment of that death, that his party was released from tutelage; the Reformers lost with Henri IV their guardian, and also the powerful hand that restrained them. Their policy ought to have been to fortify themselves in the places of safety they had preserved, and to recover others that they had lost; in a word, in order to make themselves respected they ought to have made themselves more feared than ever.

"I know," said Rohan to the Assembly of Saumur (1611), "they will oppose us if we ask more than we possessed in the time of the late king; I know that we ought, in order to insure peace during the infancy of this reign, to content ourselves with the same treatment. To that it may be answered that the change of things causes apprehension. . . . How many alarms have we not received since the unhappy day of the parricide of our Henri the Great! The law of States changes with the times; no one can give positive maxims; what is useful to one king is hurtful to another."

The princes of the blood, the Condés, by their conversion to Catholicism had not, Rohan thought, weakened the position of the Reformers; for those princes, if they supported the party, had to be supported by it, and often carried on their own affairs to its injury. What is certain is that, in default of the princes, it was the higher nobles who took their place, who took the initiative and the command of the armed rebels; and the house of Rohan was in the front rank of this active rôle. It gave itself to the common cause with a devotion that cannot be contested; neither the Maréchal de Bouillon, whose career was ending and who had long been only a consulting power, nor the old Lesdiguières, who was thinking of being converted and returning to his former brethren, nor the Trémouilles, the La Forces, the Châtillons, whose resolutions were never long-breathed,—not one of these attempted in the new uprising to dispute the supremacy of the Rohans.

Without here speaking of his mother, a strong woman, of *vieille roche*, the inspirer and soul of all resistance, to whom we shall presently return; without speaking of his wife, — the daughter of Sully, a dainty and charming beauty, the most volatile of wives, but faithful politically and an active and devoted auxiliary,—Rohan had for his second a brother, Benjamin de Rohan, known under the name of Soubise, a sailor, high admiral of the Reformed Church just as Rohan was the generalissimo ashore and in the mountains. During the first war, of 1621, Rohan, not willing to let himself be shut up in his town of Saint-Jean d'Angely, left that place in charge of Soubise, who held out against the army of the king, received with doffed hat the royal summons to surrender, and replied with these words in writing, which have come down to us: "I am the very humble servant of the king, but the execution of his commands is not within my power. [Signed:] Benjamin de Rohan." Forced to surrender after a siege of twenty-four days in virtue of a capitulation which took the form of letters of pardon, Soubise, although in issuing from the town he had asked forgiveness of the king on his knees, went straight into the same war that same year and continued the work

of resistance and rebellion, in which he never slack-
ened. He thought he had in the depths of his con-
conscience (such are the sophistries of the spirit of
faction) that which released him from the engage-
ment he had taken and absolved him in the last
resort. Taking refuge in England, during the truces,
returning with English vessels, which he strove to
take into the port of La Rochelle, leader and pilot
of foreigners to our shores, his whole conduct in
those years casts a sorry light on the most vulner-
able side of the policy of Rohan, that elder brother
with whom he was so fully in accord, so unanimous,
planning in concert with him at all times, and willing
to be disavowed for appearance' sake when the occasion demanded. Soubise, unsubdued and unsub-
duable, in whom the idea of duty towards the sovereign
of France did not exist, determining, in the last extremity, to make a piratical war rather than submit
to his king, represents very well the Frenchman who
forgets himself and who is to a certain point denat-
uralised, or, at least (for I would not say an unjust
thing of a vanquished man), denationalised.

M. de Rohan had more prudence: prudence and
obstinacy are the two distinctive traits of his character. He claims, through it all, to remain a good
Frenchman; he has always the air of taking arms
against his will, in self-defence, and because he could
not in honour do otherwise without failing in his
duty to the Reformed Church. But, arms once taken,

he never lays them down until there are no means left to prolong the struggle; and there are no expedients he does not employ to force his people to imitate him and follow him to the end. His Memoirs, very good to read, are far from being a complete narrative to which we can trust implicitly; he conceals where it suits him to do so. Orator, man of discussion and persuasion as much as he was a warrior, a whole very important side of his talent and of the part he played has disappeared from sight. In his harangue before the town-council of Montauban during the first war, he said: "I beg you to believe that I will never abandon you, no matter what happens. When there are but two persons left to the Religion, I shall be one of the two." He kept that promise throughout the wars and renounced it only when all had failed him. No scruple withheld him from making terms either with the King of England (that was natural) or with foreign co-religionists, with the Duc de Savoie, or even with the King of Spain, whose succour he had long hoped for, expecting a subsidy from him as a last resource. The Spanish doubloons and the *Catholicon,* the subject of so much sarcasm against the League, would have seemed to Rohan purified by passing through his hands.

A double reading is interesting to make here that of the Memoirs of Rohan in comparison with the Memoirs of Richelieu. What a different policy !

5

what a conflicting game ! what opposing views
and sentiments, reflected in their very manner of
speech and expression!   Let us guard against forgetting that those who did not succeed have against
them many equivocal appearances and beginnings,
which might have quite another air had the issue
been otherwise: a ray of sunshine falling at the right
moment changes the landscape.   "But because,"
says Rohan somewhere, "histories are made by the
victorious only, we usually find none esteemed but the
children of fortune." That is true.   Nevertheless, it is
Richelieu who is right in this struggle, who has on his
conscience the great cause he serves, the noble monarchy he continues, the incomparable France he is
perfecting.   Words and language tell it; through images his thoughts gleam; Rohan envelops himself
where Richelieu develops.

It was not until the second civil war that Rohan
came face to face with the supremacy of the haughty
cardinal, in whom, up to that time, he had seen only
one favourite the more:

"To that man's favour," he says, speaking of the Marquis de
La Vieuville, "succeeded that of Cardinal de Richelieu, introduced
by La Vieuville into public affairs; that is how all those favourites
serve one another faithfully. . . . The support that the Cardinal
gets from the queen-mother [Marie de Medicis] has made his favour last
much longer than that of others, and has also made him more insolent."

Rohan seems to have been some time in perceiving
that he had encountered in Richelieu his great and
fatal adversary.

The second war was begun by Soubise, who gave the signal for it (January, 1625) by an audacious act. Feeling that La Rochelle, that bulwark of the Protestant cause, was becoming more and more blockaded by Fort Louis and from the direction of the islands of Ré and Oléron, and that the city would stifle if it did not have free communication with the sea, Soubise went to Blavet (Port Louis), seized a number of large vessels that were being equipped, and, after various adventures, succeeded in bringing away his prizes. Master of the sea, he gave hope and courage to the Rochelle people, who at first had pretended to disavow him. Rohan, though concurring with him on every point, had hitherto not chosen to take up arms, even lending himself to a semblance of negotiation with the Court; he now began to declare himself, "constrained to do so," he says, "to show that it was not his inability, as people imagined, that prevented it, but his desire to pacify all things."

He had already gone through many of the towns, accompanied by a great number of ministers, haranguing, saying prayers, and having a Bible carried before him, faithful to his double rôle of Captain and servant of the Religion. On the 1st of May, 1625, he began his armed enterprises, failed in his attack on Lavaur, but made all the towns on his way declare themselves. Usually, he had only to show himself to give courage to his allies within the walls, to the "good inhabitants" who swept in the others; for sheriffs and magistrates, more circumspect and always men of middle courses, needed to have the people in the streets take part and force their hand. Castres and Montauban were his principal points of support. The Cévennes were favourable to him, and thence he drew his soldiers. The whole was done with accompaniment of assemblies, and the holding of conferences, as befitted a republican enterprise, which rests not only on the consent but the emotion of the people.

Maréchal de Thémines commanded the army of the king; he appeared before Castres, where the Duchesse de Rohan, who had left her husband, with a Council or committee of the Assembly, took upon herself (her councillors being perplexed), to issue orders, and rising, by force of circumstance, above her usual self, that mundane but courageous little person sufficed for all. The maréchal, who had the advantage in numbers, held the country, ravaged the low lands and seized Saint-Paul; the only rather notable action that Rohan in his Memoirs attributes to him; diminishing it however, as much as he can, and representing it as more easy than perhaps it was. On the other hand, Rohan takes delight in extolling the heroic action of seven soldiers of Foix, who, being shut up in a paltry little town near Carlat, stopped the maréchal and his whole army for two days, and after killing forty of his men, made their escape to the number of four; three of the seven, all near relatives, choosing to remain and be sacrificed because one of them was wounded and unable to get away: "The four others," says Rohan, "at the solicitation of the three, under cover of the night, and after embracing one another, fled; and the three that were left stood at the gate, loaded their arquebuses, awaited patiently the coming of daylight, and received their enemies valiantly and, after killing several, died free men." That is the sole flash of emotion in Rohan's narrative; he wanted to secure to the names of those brave soldiers an immortality of which he has not proved the dispenser; for certain special echoes, which are not found twice, have alone given us the glorious names that immortalise Thermopylæ.

After this, he is obliged to relate the defeat of Soubise in a conflict with the forces of the king at the island of Ré, his resistance more or less desperate, and his flight to England with what vessels he could save. A peace was then bargained for and concluded; Richelieu, now at the beginning of his great designs, did not make it too difficult, and the ambassadors from England and Holland, two powers then allied to France, imperiously advised the Reformers to accept it. Rohan in his Memoirs has an air of triumphing more than is becoming. He complains, however, of everybody:

" This is what took place," he says as he concludes, " in that second war, where Rohan and Soubise had against them all the chief nobles of the Religion in France, either from jealousy or want of zeal, all

the kings on account of their avarice, and most of the principal men
in the towns, won over by the enticements of the Court. . . .When
we are no longer men of property God will assist us more powerfully."

By this peace the Reformers obtained what to their
eyes was the essential thing, namely: the maintenance
of the new fortifications which they had constructed
in nearly all the small towns of the South of France;
in other words, facilities for renewing the war.

From this period of his narrative we may note
Rohan's frequent complaints of the versatility, the
impatience, the lack of justice in the common people,
the ingratitude "which is the usual reward for services done to them," and their temper "that leads
them to be as insolent in prosperity as they were
cringing in adversity." He says this again and again
in a score of places. "He who has to do with a
people who find nothing difficult in undertaking an
enterprize but in its execution foresee and provide for
nothing, is greatly hindered." He wishes that those
who come after him "may have as much affection,
fidelity, and patience as he has had, and meet with
peoples more faithful, more zealous, and less miserly."
That proud soul, that energetic Captain, born to command, that aristocratic nature, ambitious of great designs
but shackled at every step, must have suffered much!

Another point must here be mentioned, though
rather delicate and one it seems strange to dwell upon
in speaking of a great warrior who died of wounds
received in battle. Rohan, and also his brother Sou-

bise, have been accused of sparing themselves in military engagements and of not always putting themselves at the head of their troops or into the thick of the battle, sword in hand. At Ré, at the most decisive moment of the effort against the king's troops Soubise appears to have not done with his person and his arm what he might have done; and at Viane, while Maréchal Thémines was attacking and burning a suburb, driving out the troops who opposed him, the Duc de Rohan was seen on a bastion of the town, "whence he was observing the action cane in hand." Nevertheless, to neither should be offered the insult of asking whether they were brave or not brave. They were the leaders of the party; they were bound to preserve themselves for the Cause; moreover, as others have judiciously remarked, they had to fear, not to die the death of a soldier, sword in hand, but to be taken prisoners and finish their days as rebels on a scaffold.

Let us now open the Memoirs of Richelieu where he speaks of the same circumstances. The tone is different, the mists clear away, the flags are hoisted; we feel at every step the advantage of defined situations and of a genius that treads its native way. The XVIth book of the Cardinal's Memoirs thus describes the opening of the second civil war:

"This year (1625) saw at its beginning the outbreak of an infamous rebellion of our heretics, which was plotted by Soubise, from whom no one looked for such treachery.

"He was noted among the rebels as having been the first who dared present himself to forbid an entrance into one of his towns to the king.

"Coming out of Saint-Jean-d'Angely by capitulation, he swore never to take up arms again against His Majesty.

"In defiance of his oath he did not refrain, shortly after, from seizing the dunes of Olonne; but seeing that the king was about to swoop down upon him, he retired to La Rochelle, like those timid birds who hide in the hollows of a rock when an eagle pursues them. There he was pardoned a second time by His Majesty.

"But, as the gratitude of infidels is as faithless as themselves, these favours descended so little into his heart that no sentiment or memory of them remained, and his rebellion, as fruitful as the Hydra, was born again.

"He set fire to the kingdom while the king was engaged in the defence of his allies, as Eratostratus set fire to the temple of Diana while she was giving her attention to promote the birth of Alexander. . . ."

Let us not ask of Richelieu the correct and sober taste that belongs to Rohan: Richelieu has imagination and he shows it; he has literature and he affects it. His style loves the plumed hat, and the plumed hat does not misbecome him, any more than it does the nation that he guides and represents. His bad taste has something in common with that of Châteaubriand; it is a bad taste which seduces and, at moments, carries us away far more than cold reason; it waves the oriflamme.

While Richelieu, already strong in the confidence of Louis XIII, was preparing his grand European design — the lowering of the power of Spain and the house of Austria — for which he expected to use a new and close alliance with England, he found himself suddenly stopped short by this uprising in the interior which cut in two the kingdom.

"This revolt," he says, energetically, " came so unseasonably for the King, at a time when he had many affairs with foreign countries, that most of his Council lost their heads so that sometimes they wanted him to make an ignominious peace with Spain, and sometimes they were willing to grant the Huguenots more than they demanded.

"The cardinal, on the contrary, looking with a firm heart on all this tempest, said to the King. . . ."

Here follows one of those indirect, expounding discourses, such as the cardinal likes to put on paper, in which he develops all considerations in every direction, not without a certain complacency and an ear to his own words, but with clearness, loftiness, breadth, and accuracy. His conclusion is that "so long as the Huguenots have a foothold in France the king will never be master within the Kingdom or be able to undertake any glorious action without"; that there is no way of doing two important things at once; that the internal evil, be it least in itself, is the worst now, and the one to be looked to before all else. He had the idea, very bold and original, to make use for that purpose of the help of allies, and those the very ones who belonged to the Religion of the rebels; for France at that time had no navy; she had not even a single ship to oppose to Soubise, now triumphant on the seas since his capture of vessels. Richelieu resolutely insisted that the number of auxiliary ships which the king was compelled to obtain

for these new wars must be exacted from the English
and Dutch,—twenty from Holland, seven or eight
from England; he also desired to stipulate, so as to
make sure that these vessels should operate efficaciously
and not against the object for which they were obtained, that French captains should be put on board,
and French crews, either wholly or in part. In advising the king to make, imperiously and even with
threats (if necessary), these rather singular demands
on his Protestant allies to defeat his Protestant subjects, the cardinal, whose instinct told him that all
could be obtained, knew very well that he was running a great risk with his master in case of refusal:

"Had he considered himself," he says, with a feeling of noble pride,
"he might not have taken this course which, being the best for
public interests, was not the safest for those who proposed it; but,
knowing that the first condition for him who takes part in the government of States is to give himself wholly to the public and not to
think of himself, he passed over all considerations that might stop him,
liking better to ruin himself than to fail in any necessary thing to save
the State, of which it may be said that the base and cowardly proceedings of the late ministers had changed and tarnished its whole
face."

This naval armament, so boldly collected, to which
England contributed by vessels only, and Holland by
ships and men, had all the success and effect that
Richelieu expected to get from it. In short, and as
we have already seen by Rohan's narrative, after the
defeat of Soubise at the island of Ré, peace was
made, but not altogether such as Rohan desired. The
cardinal, no doubt, knowing, as he says, that "pru-

dent policy consists in taking the most advantageous occasion that can be had to do what we wish," and feeling that the great and various affairs the king then had upon his hands demanded more or less delay, dissimulated and allowed the Reform party to believe that he was not their adversary: "For peace being made," he says, "there was means of waiting for a more convenient time to reduce them to the terms all subjects should be under in a State; that is to say, that no separate body shall be formed within it independent of the will of the sovereign." At any rate, by this treaty of February 5, 1626, the king, already more a king than before, gave peace to his subjects, but did not receive it; on the side of La Rochelle he expressly reserved Fort Louis, as a citadel taken from the town, and the islands of Ré and Oléron, two other fortified places, "which did not make a bad circumvallation."

Rohan in his Memoirs (intended in a way to be read as an apology) asserts that he was satisfied with this provisional peace. His letters and confidential missives, some of which were intercepted and conveyed to the cardinal, show much less satisfaction, and this treaty, so disadvantageous to the Protestants, "threw the two brothers into such despair," says Richelieu, "that Mme. de Rohan, not knowing what other advice to give Soubise, tried to persuade him, in an intercepted letter, to join the Moorish corsairs and retire to the Barbary coast" rather than resign himself

to the law of the victor. It is worth while to read
how Richelieu exclaims, not as a politician only, but
as a theologian and fervent Catholic, at the thought of
such advice.

Such a state of things, in which one part of the
nation was engaged in curbing the other part, which,
in turn, held it in check, could not last without the
greatest detriment to the monarchy and to France,
which, in face of Europe and of the general recon-
stitution of modern political forces then going on,
needed unity and collected strength within its borders.
The honour of Richelieu is that he felt this with
ardent energy and an indomitable genius for execution: the misfortune of Rohan (that of his position) is
not to have been able to feel it; to have been the
natural and as if necessary ally of the foreigner, of whoever was then the enemy of his country; to have
continued to think upon it as an old-fashioned feudal
seigneur become a republican by chance who, stirred
by a peculiar religious conviction, used all means
of defence, unaware of what he was about to shock
in the breast of that other moral and religious sentiment, the patriotic sentiment, then on the point of
becoming universal.

The third war began in 1627; it is useless to seek
for the pretexts or the causes, which each party
bandied with the other; it was certain to break forth;
the peace of 1626 having been submitted to by one
side and conceded by the other with all sorts of men-

tal reservations on both sides and stress of necessity.   A great cabal was formed at Court of which
Monsieur, the king's brother, was the ostensible
head.   England, this time, appeared as an enemy; a
gentleman was sent by the King of Great Britain to
solicit the Duc de Rohan from whom, says the latter,
"the desertions and unfaithfulness he had met with
in the two preceding wars had taken all desire to
renew the game."   Nevertheless, he dared not assume
the responsibility of a refusal, and he joined the party
with that sense of difficulty and non-success which
constituted his fate.   " I considered what a burden I
was taking on my shoulders for the third time; I
reminded myself of the inconstancy of our people,
of the unfaithfulness of the principal men, of the compact parties that the king had in all our communities,
the poverty of the country, the avarice of the towns,
and, above all, the irreligion of every one."

By "irreligion" we must understand merely the
weakening of that exalted religious principle, unknown till the sixteenth century, which drove its
adherents to every sacrifice of life and fortune for the
faith; a weakening derived already from the modern
spirit, in virtue of which many estimable Reformers preferred commerce to war.   This was not the
reckoning of Rohan and the feudal chiefs.   Such
weakening, or gradual relaxing (as much in morals
as in beliefs), made itself more and more felt after
the decapitation of the party by Richelieu; and this

condition of minds, wisely appreciated by Mazarin in
what he called "the little flock," must have been still
further understood by Louis XIV, who followed the
idea and the practice, where possible, of tolerance.

After the perplexities and diversities of mind which
M. de Rohan himself acknowledges that he had at the
beginning of the third war we can understand the
severe and angry judgment that Richelieu pronounced
upon him:

"That miserable Soubise," he cries with indignation (for he never
separates the two brothers), " whose misfortune, capacity, and courage
are equally decried, having no other art to cover his past shames than
to prepare for fresh ones, is soliciting in England. The Sieur de
Rohan, more fitted to be an attorney in a law court than leader of a
party, the benefits of which must be procured by courage in war and
by frankness and ingenuousness in peace . . . continues his
practices, and by a thousand factions makes known to every one that
he is doing as much during peace to bring on war, as he did during
war to bring peace. In peace, his mind has no repose, just as in war
his person was little risked. He keeps up intelligence with all the
factious within the kingdom and all the mischief-makers without."

Let us here allow for passion's share in these words
and free the thought from the insult. Richelieu was
the first to show that at heart he judged better of
Rohan when, later, he intrusted him with an army
corps to enter the Valtelline, and in a letter he then addressed to the victorious general he said: "He would
always very willingly be his surety with the king that
he [Rohan] would preserve all the acquired advantages
and lose no occasion to increase them." But, in this
moment of cruel war, they are two spirits, two rival

and antagonistic souls, struggling against each other, and all the defects, all the complications, all the entanglements in the conduct and rôle of Rohan were uppermost in the cardinal's mind; he imputes them to his character, he expresses them with exaggeration, with injustice, no doubt, but also with discernment of the weak point and in terms unforgettable.   The hour was decisive for the very fortune and grandeur of Richelieu himself.   To suppose that he would have embarked on his great designs for foreign combinations leaving La Rochelle open to the English, and in communication with the Cévennes ill-subdued, and with Languedoc half-rebellious, is not to know him. Rohan, the ablest and most tenacious of the two leaders who were seeking to maintain a sort of federal republic in the heart of the kingdom, was not his least stumbling-block.   The latter had promised the King of England to take up arms again whenever the English army should make its descent on the island of Ré, and he kept his word.

It is not for me to try to write the history of those memorable exploits in the much-disputed channels, or of that siege of La Rochelle and the taking of the place after more than a year's blockade and three naval expeditions of Englishmen powerless to succour it.   The constancy, the obstinacy, the intrepid faith of Richelieu in his own wise counsel and in the fortune of France triumphed over all, even the elements.   On the other hand, the heroism and moral resignation of the besieged and famished population exceeds all that is known of the longest and most trying sieges. This two-fold, conflicting sentiment, as strong in the besieged as in the besiegers, is pictured with fidelity in the pages of Richelieu and Rohan alike; the latter, who at the time was carrying on the campaign in the South and limited to holding the king's troops occupied by a series of skirmishes and small affairs, felt but too well that the brunt of the action was taking place where he was not, and that the fate of the Cause was being decided without him.

Richelieu's ardour in this perilous enterprise, the eagerness that he feels in the affair, and which consumes him, break forth in a thousand fiery flashes in his narrative:

" Nevertheless," he says in one place, " though the Cardinal employed all the mind that God had given him in making the siege of La Rochelle redound to the divine glory and the good of the State, working harder than the bodily strength that God had bestowed upon him warranted, one would have said that the wind and the seas, friends of the English and the Isles, forced themselves into the encounter and opposed his designs."

To take La Rochelle before all else, promptly and without mercy this time, such was his fixed idea; it was, according to him, the best remedy for everything; and all means, all imaginable inventions must be employed, not omitting a single one, to bring it about, because " on the taking of La Rochelle depends the safety of the State, the repose of France, the welfare and authority of the King for ever."

Should there be a State within the State, a natural
and permanent ally of the foreigner among us, a port
and an open door on the flank of the kingdom? that
was the supreme question. He vowed himself to
settle it with a zeal as chivalrous as it was politic.
The spirit of a crusade was in his ardour. The keys
of La Rochelle, when he held them, were worth
in his eyes those of the Cabinets which he could
not force until then, nor drag as he wished into
the sphere of action of the noblest monarchy in the
world. Such were the noble and frank thoughts
that he put in action and pursued beneath his
purple; while Rohan in his Cévennes, not daring
to risk all in a headlong venture (as the great Ven-
déens were to do in their day), exhausts himself in
hurrying from town to town, endeavouring to organise in France a *counter-France*. The disproportion of
the two rôles is seen at a glance, and it is so crushing
for him who does not play the nobler part that it
would be unjust to dwell too much upon it.

The conscience of the vanquished, however, when
sincere feelings and true beliefs are behind it, and also
a portion of the right involved, has inward strength,
deep, invisible springs, of which we must speak only
with respect. Something of that austere and sad-
dened sentiment is reflected in the following words,
in which M. de Rohan, after relating the surrender of
La Rochelle (October 28, 1628), adds in the tone of
firmness and pride that becomes him:

6

" The mother of the Duc de Rohan and his sister [Anne de Rohan, unmarried], refused to be named personally in the capitulation, in order that no one could attribute the surrender to their persuasion in that respect ; believing, however, that they would share like all the others in it. But as the interpretation of capitulations is made by the victors, the Council of the king decided that they were not included, inasmuch as they were not named : unexampled rigour! that a person of her rank, seventy years old (*and over*), coming out from a siege during which she and her daughter had lived for three months on horse-flesh and four to five ounces of bread per day, should be held captives without the exercise of their religion, and so closely that they had but one servant to wait upon them. This, nevertheless, did not shake their courage or their accustomed zeal for the welfare of their party ; and the mother sent word to the Duc de Rohan, her son, that he must not give heed to her letters, for she might be made to write them by force, and that no consideration for her miserable condition ought to make him relax to the injury of his party, no matter what evils they might make her suffer. Truly a Christian resolution, that did not belie the whole course of her life, which, having been a tissue of continual afflictions [her first husband was massacred on the Saint-Bartholomew], had so fortified her with the assistance of God, that she has the benediction of all right-minded persons, and will be to posterity an illustrious example of unexampled virtue and wonderful piety. See how that poor city, formerly the retreat and delight of King Henri IV, has since become the wrath and the boast of his son. Louis XIII. It has been attacked by Frenchmen and abandoned by Englishmen ; it was buried in a bitter and pitiless famine, yet in the end has acquired by its constancy a longer life in fame through centuries to come than those who prosper to-day in this present century."

Here again the Memoirs of Richelieu throw the light of a direct reflection on those of Rohan. In them we find that, during the siege, Mme. de Rohan in a letter which was intercepted, proposed to her son a motto, which she said was that of the Queen of Navarre (no doubt Jeanne d'Albret, Henri IV's mother): *Paix assurée. victoire entière, et mort honnête !* ("Assured

peace, complete victory, honourable death!") Sent a
prisoner to Niort, they tried to work upon her during
the following year to make her write to her son and
induce him to return to his duty; they put forward
third parties, who, without using the name of the king,
exhorted her, as if from themselves, and as if they
were moved solely by consideration for her interests
and those of her children:

"But that woman, malignant to the last degree," says Richelieu,
"would not even condescend to send messages to her son, by letter,
giving as a pretext that such means were not sufficiently powerful and
that it was necessary that she should go herself, which His Majesty
refused, knowing that she desired it only to make the evil more
irremediable, and to strengthen her son and those of his party in
rebellion to the last extremity."

Such was the invincible mother who bore in defence
of her faith the soul of the Portias, the Cornelias, and
the ancient Romans. She it was who could not bring
herself to approve of Henri IV as king, and who resisted, under his reign, the fortune he was desirous of
bestowing on her son.

Our reservations thus made against the methods
and the object of the Duc de Rohan, we have the right
to call attention to his firmness and constancy. The
capture of La Rochelle, which seemed as if it must
surely take all hope from the party, was to Rohan a
reason for redoubling his efforts and his zeal. He was
of those whom adversity inspires. Prince Thomas of
Savoie having sent him word that if he were in the
same humour as in the past, and would come nearer

to him, he, Prince Thomas, would make a diversion into Dauphiné, Rohan replied that he was "in better humour than ever," and ready to march at the first news he should receive of the prince. The politician and the statesman in him (for he was a statesman) contributed at that moment to sustain and embolden the soldier. He told himself that the King of England, after his contracted engagements, could not in honour abandon the Reformers, and that he would bestir himself to support them in war, or, if there were a peace, to have them included therein. He believed that Louis XIII, then about to cross the Alps, had occupation enough in the direction of Savoie and Italy, and other rocks to scale than those of La Rochelle; that Spain's interest in fomenting divisions in the heart of France would lead her before long to assist the Reformers with her gold. At an Assembly convoked at Nîmes, he made his belligerent resolutions prevail, reviving the courage of his adherents. Nothing short of the glories of the Pass of Suza, where it may be said of Louis XIII as of Cæsar, "he came, he saw, he conquered," could convince him of his mistake.

Even then, Rohan would not admit himself cast down; he did not believe, after the victory of Suza, in the peace of Italy, in a solid peace that would allow the king to turn with all vigour upon him. He was not enlightened on the gravity of the situation until he saw the king in person seize Privas, and the King of England at the same moment sign a peace that did not include the Protestants. This last news, together with the taking of Privas and the severities there exercised on the vanquished, made him, at last, begin "to lower his horns," says Richelieu; and then, foreseeing the coming end of the struggle, he brought forth all his resources and expedients, he redoubled in activity and multiplied fine skirmishes to end at least decently, to be reckoned with to the very last, and thus obtain as many guarantees as he could for the bulk of his party. There were no less than six royal armies, in all more than fifty thousand men and fifty cannon, acting against various places in the South at the same time. From all sides came a cry for succour; many places weakened and capitulated; Rohan threw himself on all sides, where he could. He excelled in a war of that kind; at any rate he did enough to compel consent to negotiations for a general peace. "I let the Court (meaning the king's headquarters) know that I would gaily die with the greater part of my people rather than not obtain a general peace; I told them it was dangerous to take all hope of safety from persons with arms in their hand, and that I would never negotiate for myself only. . . ."

The king listened with pleasure to the propositions; but the cardinal confesses in his Memoirs that he hesitated long at this time as to the advice he should give his master; everything convinced him they would soon get the better of the rebels and their

leader by force (which was much more to his taste),
and the latter would then be reduced, after their infallibly approaching defeat, to cry for mercy. Prudence, however, carried the day against temper;
and the idea that Rohan was for once sincere in his
proposals for peace induced the cardinal to consent
to negotiate. Finally, the edicts conformed in all
essential things to what we now call tolerance; but
the bastions and fortifications of the rebellious cities,
those in the Cévennes in particular, which during
the war had been seized with a species of mania
and had, one and all, fortified themselves *à la
Huguenote,* as was then said, were ordered to be
rased at the expense and by the hand of the very
inhabitants who had built them. From that day
forth a belt of little republics across France no longer
existed: there was but one France with subjects under
one king.

The era of war and of rivalry with mailed hand
was over; a new régime began, a régime that ought
to have been one of civil policy, legality, firm reason,
gentle action, and of conquest by speech only. Richelieu, keen as he was on religion, shows that he
was not far from understanding the matter thus in
idea; but, on both sides, how new they were at this
new state of things! how slow and laborious was
the transition that now took place! and before it
was fairly established in our modern order, what
changes, what waverings, what errors still!

The Duc de Rohan, by an article of the treaty, or rather of the "grace" (that was the title given to it), obtained in all that concerned himself a general royal pardon and forgetting of the past; he also obtained the return of his property and 100,000 crowns as indemnity for the losses he had incurred (he owed more than 80,000) and he was made to leave the kingdom. He wrote to the king, who was then at Nimes, asking that a man of rank, authorised by His Majesty, should conduct him to Venice, the place appointed for his retreat, fearing, or pretending to fear some danger on the road from the Italian princes; he probably desired to shelter himself in this way from all suspicion of further intrigues. They gave him M. de La Vallette to accompany him, and he embarked at Toulon, July 20, 1629.

Venice was a place of predilection for Rohan; we have seen how he was struck and as if in love with it in his youth. During the last war he had negotiated with Venice through his wife, who was there in company with the Duc de Candale, recently converted by her to calvinism, and who served her as attendant. The Duchesse de Rohan and her daughter had offered to remain as hostages to give security to Venice that the money furnished should be duly employed as stipulated. The policy of Venice suited Rohan, always full of reflections and views, and, in the matter of a republic, much more likely to accommodate himself to one of an aristocracy than to one of burgher or popular

councils. He was appointed general of the troops of
the republic, with a pension and all sorts of honours.

He passed the first period of his retirement (1630)
in composing his Memoirs on the religious wars,
which were not published until later (1644) under the
supervision of Sorbière. During a stay he made at
Padua he wrote "The Perfect Captain, otherwise an
Abridgment of the Wars of the Gauls and the Commentaries of Cæsar, with some Remarks"; this he dedicated
to Louis XII. Another work: "For the Interests of
Princes and States in Christianity," dedicated to Cardinal Richelieu, seems to have been composed during a
visit of some months to Paris in 1634. These writings,
which were not printed until about the time of his
death, no doubt reached their destination much earlier
in manuscript; they were the visiting-cards the Duc de
Rohan sent to Court to show that he was still capable
of action, and to prove he was no longer an enemy.
These works, much liked when they appeared, the
second of which was translated into Latin, are of little
worth to-day and are not attractive to read.

But a new career was now to begin for Rohan. The
king, by the advice of Cardinal Richelieu, believed
him the right man to conduct his affairs beyond the
Alps, on account of his various qualities as negotiator,
as captain, greatly in renown with foreigners, able to
act as if for himself, his actions not to be acknowledged
until the right time came. The Grisons, allied with
the Swiss cantons, possessed in Italy the Valtelline, a

country of importance from a military point of view,
inasmuch as it forms a passage between Germany and
the Milanais, and might serve as a junction between
the two arms of the House of Austria. Spain had done
her best to get possession of it and had succeeded, the
Valtelline having revolted, hoping to get free from the
yoke. The Imperials thus found the way open for
a descent upon Italy: they built forts to maintain it.

The Grisons complained of France (at all times their
protector) because, by a treaty with Spain, she had
seemed to acquiesce in the situation as it now was.
France, on her side, had an interest in the Grisons
again becoming masters of the Valtelline and of the
keys to the passage. It was important to find a personage to push them on and guide them; "adroit in
managing a populace, and agreeable to the Grisons
(most of whom were Protestants)"; fitted to "recover
this people little by little, and re-engrave on their
minds the devotion they were beginning to lose for
Frenchmen, and one who was of such weight that he
would be regarded in that country as voucher and
surety for his master," without the name of that master being too much put forward at first. Above all, it
was necessary to find some one in whom the republic
of Venice could place confidence, and whom she
esteemed.

Rohan was the living embodiment of the very
complex man who was needed at that moment in
that country. The king wrote to him, and made his

ambassador, M' Avaux, urge him. Rohan was pleased
to see that they were placing confidence in him, and
that coming services might hasten forgetfulness of
the past. He did not leave Venice without making
sure of the Senate's agreement with the mission on
which he was about to embark. Reaching Coire,
the capital of the Grisons, December 4, 1631, he was
very well received and soon declared general of the
three Leagues. It seemed as if he had only to act;
but it was not until the spring of 1635, that is to say,
after three years of delay and ambiguities of all kinds,
and when France at last decided openly for war, that
Rohan had the chance to distinguish himself. He
was sent at first into Upper Alsace, where he held
his own against Duke Charles of Lorraine; but his
real object, which it was important to mask to the
end, was to take possession of the Valtelline. The
manner in which he crossed Switzerland without
notifying the Cantons until the moment came — having already entered that country before it was evident that he meant to go through it; the rapidity
and precision of his march, the accuracy of his plans
and calculations, all were in keeping with his reputation for skill. His army entered the Valtelline April
24, 1635, and the campaign opened under happy
auspices. . . .[1]

---

[1] Then follows a rather minute account of that local war, which has
so little historical interest in the present day that it is here omitted :
— TR.

The last battle of the campaign, that of Morbegno, the most glorious of the four that Rohan fought, crowned to his honour this fine campaign of 1635, in which, thanks to him, the king's arms, less fortunate in all other places, obtained in the Valtelline a steady success. It seemed as though he was about to triumph over fate, that he did so by force of merit, and that fortune at last would smile upon him. Let him obtain a little aid from France, reinforce him with infantry and cavalry to guard the passes, above all, succour him with money, that sinew of war, more needful than ever in the country of the Grisons, let the Duc de Savoie stand ready to back him, and Rohan, at the head of 4000 foot soldiers and 500 cavalry, his ideal of a small army, would have entered the Milanais with plans matured, seized Lecco and Como, made himself master of the whole lake, destroyed the fort of Fuentes, which is the gateway to the Valtelline, and condemned the Germans to have no other road than the pass of the Saint-Gothard by which to enter Italy.

Glorious and too fleeting moment! the secretary of War, des Noyers, writing to d' Eméry, ambassador of France to Savoie, says that it was "indeed a wonderful thing how M. le Duc de Rohan with a handful of soldiers, without cannon or ammunition, did, each day, some signal action and carried terror everywhere, while the army of the Federals, so flourishing, so well fed and well paid, remained inactive." A little

more and history might have cited him as a model of
good fortune. The *Gazette* was filled with bulletins
of his exploits.

But the thwarting star that so many times already
had crossed and darkened Rohan's career, baffled him
again; once more we meet its malign influence which
from this time never ceases. The Duc de Savoie, in
spite of the victory of the Ticino, did not take a single
step toward Rohan, who had then advanced to Lecco
(June 2, 1636), and the well laid plans of the latter
failed. Believing that he had done enough to acquire
honour, he was unwilling to risk more, according to
his maxim that "it is better not to go too fast and
know where one is going, than be obliged to retreat
ignominiously or perish." He returned to the Valtelline, where the difficulties of his situation, without
money and in presence of mutinous populations returned upon him. He sent his private secretary and
confidant, Priolo, to represent them strongly at Court;
but he himself fell seriously ill at Sondrio of an illness
diagnosed as a "profound lethargy," so that the
rumour of his death was noised about, in his own
army, who mourned him, and in that of the enemy,
who rejoiced.

On his revival, and after his convalescence, either
because Rohan was not altogether the same man, or
that matters were growing worse, he saw no means
of reconciling the orders he had received from the king
with imperious necessities that pressed him on all

sides. Pestilence and famine ravaged his troops; the Grison colonels and captains, angry at receiving no pay, quitted their posts; the Council of the Leagues thought of new alliances: no money, no Grisons: "Not a week passes," writes Rohan to M. des Noyers, "since the month of July, that I have not written you about the state of this country, and I am not even told that you have received my letters, which makes me suppose you have never taken the trouble to read them."

These bitter complaints from the depths of the Valtelline reached Paris just as the Spaniards took Corbie and threatened the capital; we can easily conceive, therefore, that they were scarcely heeded. He had no sooner recovered, than he wrote to Richelieu, thanking him for the interest he had shown for him in his illness:

"As for me, monsieur," he says, "I shall hold out as long as I can, according to what I promised you; but it is intolerable to me to see that which I have so far preserved about to perish. In God's name take care that a person who breathes only for your service, may not see the reputation of the king's arms blasted in a region where, until now, he has maintained them glorious; I would rather have died of my illness than see that."

I could not avoid being tedious in dwelling at such length on the details of this sad affair, so brilliantly begun, so badly finished, and in trying to find the clue to the "labyrinth" into which the Duc de Rohan found himself plunged without resource. On Richelieu's part and on his we find nothing but conflicting

recriminations, so grave, so definite, that doubt alone
at this distance of time remains to us: Richelieu reproaches Rohan for having increased the discontent
of the Grisons by his bad government, his extortions,
and his illicit profits, of which he goes so far as to
name the intermediaries and agents; and, in stigma-
tising in the harshest terms the final capitulation of
March 26, 1637, which was consummated May 5, by
which, yielding to the revolted Grisons, Rohan returned to them the Valtelline, contrary to the king's
orders, Richelieu also accuses him of having been
seized with a "panic terror":

"It is certain," says the Cardinal, "that he had, until then, borne
gloriously to a high point the affairs of the King in the Valtelline; but
his last act not only ruined in an instant all that he had well done in
preceding years, but brought more dishonour to the arms of His Majesty
than all the past had given them glory. This shame was such that it
could never be repaired and, whatever excuse he might offer for his
fault, the most favorable name it received from even those who were
most friendly to him was that of a lack of courage."

The Duc de Rohan in his "Apologies" seems to
have strong reasons to refute so harsh a condemnation.
He ought to know better than any one the points of
difficulty. The affair, according to him, was desperate,
and to continue it longer was impossible without exposing himself to disaster. The Comte de Guébriant,
sent at the last moment to the spot, seems to have
been of Rohan's opinion. On the other hand, M. de
Lèques, one of the latter's best lieutenants, was of a
contrary opinion, and wished to try force, having no

doubt it would succeed. I say again, it is best to
doubt and abstain from judging; my only conclusion is
that one of the traits in Rohan's character was circumspection, even in his courage; that is to say, a disposition that is a very little French.   He was not a man to
risk all for all.   He thought of too many things at once.

After this, Rohan, although he still held the position
of general of the king's army, retired to Geneva
and refused to lead the army back through Franche-
Comté; he distrusted the cardinal, whose orders he
had failed to follow.   In this, the Duc de Rohan paid
the penalty of his past; in vain had he behaved during
these last years with all possible loyalty and lustre, his
conscience was not clear, nor his memory free; he
attributed to others designs that those suspicions
on his part may, perhaps, have suggested; and he
could only see France from a distance through a
sombre vista of the Bastille and a scaffold. He always
remembered that the Parliament of Toulouse had condemned him to be drawn and quartered by four horses
and hung in effigy.

Moreover, he belonged, through his female relatives,
to the party of the *dames brouillonnes de la Cour*—
the mischief-making ladies of the Court, as Richelieu
called them (thinking of the Duchesse de Chevreuse);
and he no doubt feared to be implicated in their intrigues more than he wished.   Certainly, pretexts
against him would not have been lacking.

It was while he was in this suspicious frame of mind

that he received a letter from the king commanding him to retire to Venice; he thought it a trap. For greater safety, and distrusting even a group of horsemen who were seen about Versoix at the time, he crossed the lake of Geneva, passed through Switzerland on the Berne side and joined the army of the Duke of Weimar, then besieging Rheinfeldt.   Jean de Welt was preparing to succour the place and a battle was on the eve of taking place.   Rohan decided with a sort of joy to make himself a simple soldier and fight hand to hand—he who until then had fought so long with his head.   Fighting valiantly on the right wing (February 28, 1638) he received two musket balls, one in the foot, the other in the shoulder, and was instantly made prisoner, but rescued before the close of the day.   He died of his wounds, April 13, 1638, at the abbey of Königsfelden, in the canton of Berne.   His body was buried with great pomp in the church of Saint Peter at Geneva.   During the interval between his wound and his death, he received a letter from the king expressing interest in his condition.

The Duc de Rohan was small in height, and, it is said, ill-looking.   The portraits that we have of him indicate a haughty mien.   He had from childhood a lock of white hair which was held to be a family distinction.   Though so often maltreated by fate, leading none of his enterprises to final success, he has, nevertheless, left an illustrious idea of himself.   It was said of Turenne that "he had in all things certain ob-

scurities that were never cleared up except on special
occasions, but which never were cleared up except to
his honour." M. de Rohan often stopped at two-
thirds of his way; and he did not, to our eyes, triumph
over all the obscurities that resulted from the many recesses in his character quite as much as they did from
the conspiring of circumstances. Two or three times
he was obliged to begin his career over again; he had
not that celerity of ardour, that suddenness of decision
that carries a man flying to his end. Still, he was in-
contestably a great personage; negotiator in camp,
man of the sword in council, man of the pen and of
noble words. It has been said of his prose, that it
savoured of his rank and his quality; it is, above all,
excellent in sense, very sound and judicious. We can
see that in daily practice he must have had great
vivacity of mind and eloquence. There is a letter from
him to the Prince de Condé (November, 1628), in
reply to an insulting letter from that versatile prince,
which is a masterpiece of vigour and irony. Skilful
captain rather than great general, his measure in that
respect is difficult to take, and I should prefer to leave
it to the men of his profession. To express it in
modern fashion, which is always hazardous in view of
the extreme difference of methods in use in different
centuries, he gives me the impression of having been,
as a soldier, something between Gouvion Saint-Cyr
and Macdonald, nearer to the former because of his
thoughts.

7

However that may be, he is, by the rare conjunction
of his merits, one of the original figures in our history;
and when, to distinguish him from others of his name,
and to characterise him (the last male of his race), some
people continue from habit to call him "the great Duc
de Rohan," there is nothing to wonder at.   In studying him closely and without bias in his labours and
his vicissitudes, I doubt whether that term would
come to-day to the lips of any one; but, finding it
consecrated we accept it, we respect it, we see the
completion and, as it were, the ideal reflection of his
great qualities in the imagination of his contemporaries;
an exaggeration natural enough, which does justice,
perhaps, to many things that have escaped us in that
far distance, and for which no claim has been made.

III.

Cardinal Mazarin.

III.

Cardinal Mazarin

And His Nieces.

TO Cardinal Mazarin, so fortunate in all things during his lifetime, a very great misfortune happened soon after his death: that man, without friendships, without hatreds, had but one enemy to whom he was not reconciled and whom he never forgave: Cardinal de Retz; and the latter, in writing his immortal Memoirs, has left of his enemy, of him in whom he saw a fortunate rival, a portrait so gay, so keen, so amusing, so withering, that the best historical reasons can scarcely hold their own against the impression conveyed, and will never succeed in triumphing over it.

On the other hand, Mazarin has met with various pieces of good fortune since his death, and it is in our day especially that his reputation as a great statesman has found studious, competent appreciators and avengers. M. Mignet was the first, in the Introduction to his volume on the Spanish Succession (1835), to do him signal justice in a grand, full-length, historical portrait that will last. About the same time (1836)

M. Ravenel published for the Historical Society of
France the "Letters of Mazarin," written during his
retreat out of France, to the queen, the Princess Palatine, and other persons in his confidence, which prove,
at least, that at a time when there were few hearts
truly French among the factious, he was a better
Frenchman than all others in his political views, and
in his wholly reasonable ambition.   Later (1842) M.
Bazin, in the two volumes he devoted to the "History of France under the Ministry of Cardinal Mazarin,"
has taken pains to free the historical account from the
seductive errors cast into it by the pictures of Cardinal
de Retz, even at the risk of quenching a little of its
vivacity and interest.   Last of all comes M. de Laborde,
who has put, as it were, a final touch to the work of
rehabilitation in his *Palais Mazarin,* the palace built
by the cardinal in the rue de Richelieu, where for one
hundred and twenty-five years [dating back from
1850] the Bibliothèque du Roi, now the Bibliothèque
Nationale, has been kept.

It is indeed a fact that Mazarin properly seen, looked
at closely as though we were his contemporaries, possessed those gifts which, as soon as they came into
play, made it difficult to escape his charm.   "He was
insinuating," says Mme. de Motteville; "he knew how
to use his apparent kindness to his own advantage;
he had the art of charming others, and of making himself beloved by those to whom fate subjected him."
It is true that in difficulties where he had the under

CARDINAL MAZARIN.

From an old engraving.

side he used the gifts of flattery and words of honey
with which Nature had provided the cautious and
readily perfidious race of the Ulysses. We never imagine Mazarin to ourselves as other than old, gouty,
moribund under his purple; let us try to see him as
he was in the days when he founded and secured his
fortunes. He was handsome, magnificent in deport-
ment and of cheerful countenance. Born in 1602, he
was only twenty-nine years of age when he gave the
measure of his capacity, his boldness, and his luck
during the war in Italy. Man of the sword, and the
right arm of the Nuncio, the Signore Giulio Mazarini
(as he then was) stopped short, before Casale, the
Spanish and French armies then on the point of attacking each other. Leaving the Spanish camp and bearing the conditions he had wrung from the Spaniards,
he shouted to the French, already advancing: "Halt!
halt! peace!" pushing his horse to a gallop and making signs with his hat to stop. The French army,
already in movement and on the point of firing, answered back: "No peace! no Mazarin!" But he,
redoubling his pacific gestures, came on, passing
through, as he came, a few musket-shots. The
leaders listened to him and suspended the attack.
That wave of the *hat*, by which he stopped and held
spellbound two armies, ought to win him, people
said, the cardinal's hat.

Richelieu valued him from that day and won him
over to the service of France. He seems to have

relished from the first that skilful genius, facile yet
laborious, frank yet insinuating, of a nature other
than his own, of an order in some respects inferior,
but, for that very reason, not unpleasing to him, in
whom he was not sorry to recognise, perhaps on
account of these differences, a successor. The first
time he presented him to the queen [Anne of Austria],
"Madame," he said, "you will like him much; he has
Buckingham's air." If he really permitted himself to
make that speech, he little thought how truly he predicted. As long as Richelieu lived, Mazarin's capacity
was, in a way, buried in the privacy of the cabinet;
he was closely allied with none but Chavigny, who
had the heart and soul of Richelieu, whose son he
was secretly reported to be. On the death of the
great minister and on that of the king there came
a very critical moment for Mazarin: designated by
them for the first place in the Council, he believed
himself rather on the eve of dismissal, and was
already, so it was said, making his preparations to
return to Italy, when his adroitness and his star
carried him, at a stroke, to the summit.

Although there was something of Buckingham
about him, it does not appear that he had any private
relations with the queen before the year 1643. If we
believe La Rochefoucauld, it was during the short
interval that elapsed between the death of Richelieu
and that of Louis XIII, that Mazarin began to open
avenues into the mind and heart of the queen, to

justify himself in her eyes through his friends, and to contrive, perhaps, a few secret conversations of which she herself made mystery to her old servitors. Anne of Austria was about to become queen-regent; but would she be as all-powerful in her own right as she wished, or only through the medium of the Council as the king had intended? Mazarin, who would surely be the soul of that Council, took pains to let the queen understand that it mattered little on what conditions she received the regency provided she had it with the consent of the king; and that afterwards, that point secured, she would not lack for means to free her authority and govern alone. This was letting her feel that henceforth she would have no enemy in him. It is permissible to suppose that in these first approaches Mazarin, still young, only forty years of age, did not neglect to use his personal advantages and put forth those refinements of demonstration of which he was so capable on occasion, and which are sovereign with all women but especially with a queen so much a woman as Anne of Austria.

Brienne has very well narrated the decisive moment when, thanks to the queen, Mazarin tied anew and more tightly than ever the knot of his fortunes. That moment must be long among the first of the regency, or perhaps to the last days of Louis XIII's illness. The Bishop of Beauvais, then the principal minister, was incapable; the queen needed a prime-minister, but whom could she choose? She consulted

two men who had her confidence, President de Bailleul
and the old secretary of State, Brienne. The latter,
who relates the details of the conversation to his son,
spoke after de Bailleul, who gave his opinion first and
began by excluding Mazarin as the creature of Richelieu.
"But I," says old Brienne, " who had more than once
perceived the secret leaning of the queen to his eminence, thought I ought to speak with more reserve."
The fact is, the queen had reached the point where
consultation is held merely to hear advice that is
secretly desired and to prompt it in the direction to
which the heart inclines. The consultation ended, the
queen had made her choice; nothing remained but to
make sure of the cardinal. Calling her head valet-de-
chambre, Beringhen, and telling him what had just
been said: "Go at once," she added, "and repeat it to
the cardinal; pretend to have overheard it by chance.
Spare that poor President de Bailleul, who is a good
servant; praise to the cardinal the good office Brienne
has rendered him; but, above all, discover what the
cardinal's sentiments for me are; and let him know
nothing of my intentions until you know, in the first
place, what gratitude he will show for my kindness."
Beringhen acquitted himself of his errand. He found
the cardinal with Commander de Souvré who had
given him a dinner on that day. The cardinal was
playing cards with Chavigny and some others.
When he saw Beringhen enter the room, he divined a
message, and leaving his cards to be held by Bautur

he passed into the next room. The conversation was long. Beringhen spoke at first with extreme precaution as to the good intentions of the queen. The cardinal, faithful to his habit of dissimulation, showed neither pleasure nor surprise. But when Beringhen, driven at last by the reserve he encountered, said positively that he came from the queen, the effect was that of a magic wand:

" At these words," continued Brienne, " the sly Italian changed his behaviour and language, and passing at once from extreme reticence to extreme effusion of heart: ' Monsieur,' he said to Beringhen, ' I place my career without conditions in the hands of the queen. All the advantages that the king gave me in his declaration I abandon from this moment. I feel troubled in doing so without informing M. de Chavigny; but I venture to hope that her majesty will deign to keep this matter secret, as I will, on my side, religiously.' "

These words were explicit; but Beringhen intimated that he desired some more precise pledge to prove the success of his errand. The cardinal, taking at once a pencil-case, wrote as follows on Beringhen's tablets:

" ' I shall never have any will but that of the queen. I resign, from this moment and with all my heart, the advantages that the king's declaration promised me; I abandon them without reserve, with all my other interests, to the unexampled goodness of her majesty. Written and signed by my own hand.' [Lower down was written]: ' Of her majesty the very humble, very obedient, and very faithful subject, and very grateful creature,

' Jules, Cardinal Mazarini.' "

Mazarin's cleverness consisted in seizing this unique moment ; in divining that, in the instability of things

and alliances at Court, there was for him no plank
safer or more solid on which to launch himself than
the heart of that Spanish princess, romantic and faithful; and that that vessel, reputed so frail by sages,
would, for this once at least, resist all tempests.

From that day forth he was master and might have
taken for his motto: "Whoso has the heart has all."
Chavigny, to whom he owed everything, and with
whom he had been in part allied up to that time, was
sacrificed without regret or shame. Politicians are
not stopped, or, if you choose, were not then stopped
by the trifles that hamper men of honour in the
ordinary walks of life. The first influences of this
mighty rise of Mazarin are admirably depicted by his
enemy, by Retz, who, in an incomparable page,
makes us feel the skill, luck, and hidden prestige, so
to speak, of this insinuating new grandeur. When
Mazarin, to bring to reason the former friends of the
queen who were becoming too importunate and too
important, and claiming her power as a spoil that was
due to them, arrested the Duc de Beaufort, every one
admired and bowed down to him. The moderation
that the cardinal showed on the morrow of that act
of vigour was regarded by all as clemency. The
comparison then made between this power, suddenly
so firm but not terrible, which continued gentle and
even habitually smiling, with that of Cardinal de
Richelieu charmed all minds for a time, and fascinated
imaginations. The cardinal, who had still much to

win, put all his cleverness into seconding his luck. "In short," says Retz, "he managed so well that he found himself on the heads of every one when every one thought him still at their side."

It must not be thought that I am insensible to the persuasive graces of Mazarin; but where I separate a little from his ingenious apologisers is in the general admiration of his personality and character. Why should we admire so vehemently men who have so greatly despised other men, and have believed that the greatest art in governing them was to dupe them? Is it not enough to recognise their merits and be just to their memory? Mazarin was certainly a great minister; but I think it was chiefly as a negotiator with foreign countries, as the man who brought about the treaty of Munster and concluded the Peace of the Pyrenees. It is as a fine diplomatic player that he has his assured place, absolutely beyond attack, in history. As for the interior of France, its administration and finances, he seems to have had no views of general improvement, no thought of the public good; so far from that, he never ceases to sordidly pursue his own gain and profit. Though he knew men so well, there was always a point of French genius that escaped him; a point on which he was not French, either in tone, feeling, or intelligence. I forgive him for being *ignorantissime* in matters of the old magistracy and of the parliaments, but he did not feel that inward, potential mainspring of our monarchy, *honour*, and all that can be drawn from it. He let power debase itself in his hands. He let its noblest prerogative be debased—I mean its favours and benefits; he was liberal in promises, and sometimes in giving; but he gave too visibly to those he feared, and kept back what he promised as soon as he obtained all power. The supreme prosperity of his last years revealed the depths of his heart, and that heart was never either lofty or disinterested. He had not a royal soul: that says all. He mingled petty, almost sordid views with even great projects. No doubt he was fortunate; he succeeded finally in everything; " he died," some one has said, " in the arms of Fortune." Let us respect, to a certain point, that fortune, half-sister of cleverness, but let us not adore it; let us know how to perceive the public contempt that began to glide through it, increasing daily—that contempt which, like a slow fever, undermines all powers and all states. Perhaps a man was needed between Richelieu and Louis XIV to give a certain respite and slacken the tension of spirits; but a single other day of him would have been too much; it was no less necessary for France to have a king who was a king, to raise royalty from its subjection to a minister so absolute and so little royal.

Such is my final and invincible impression after reading all, or nearly all the memoirs and documents on the subject. Mazarin is of the race of ministers such as Robert Walpole, rather than of that of the Richelieus; he is of those (we ourselves have known some) who do not dislike a certain debasement of the spirit of the nation they govern, which, even when they do it true services, cannot rise. What is due to such ministers is justice, not enthusiasm. The son of Robert Walpole, Horace, taking in hand the defence of his father against the enemies who had so insulted him, exclaims:

" Chesterfield, Pulteney, Bolingbroke! those are the *saints* who have vilified my father! . . . those are the *patriots* who have attacked that excellent man known to all parties as incapable of vengeance as any minister ever was, but from whom his experience of the human species wrung on one occasion these memorable words: ' Very few men ought to become prime-ministers, for it is not well that a great number should know how malignant men are.' "

That saying might be applied to Mazarin, except for the words " excellent man," which presuppose a sort of heartiness, which he never had; but it is true to say that Retz Montresor, and many others were singular judges of honour to teach lessons to Mazarin. In his letters to the queen he laughs at them all, at their pretensions and their absurdities, very amusingly.

As for Cardinal de Retz, however, we must come to an understanding; he is too great a writer, too incomparable an author of memoirs, to be left thus without making for him certain reservations, and, in a way, certain conditions. Retz is a man of imagination. Brought up from childhood in the ideas of conspiracy and civil war, he was not sorry to set himself to realise them, then to recount them, like Sallust, and write them down. There is true literature in this fact. He is a man to undertake, not to succeed, but to give himself the emotion and pride of enterprise, the pleasure of the game rather than the winnings and the profit, which never come to him. He is in his element in the midst of cabals; he feels his affinity and swims among them, in idea, all through the vivid description he writes of them. Such men, gifted with the genius of the writer, always have, without fully accounting for it to themselves, an inward reservation, a final resource: that of writing their history and indemnifying themselves for all they have lost on the side of actuality. Those who listened to Retz in his years of retirement remarked that he loved to recount the adventures of his youth, which he exaggerated and embellished with a few marvels: "The truth is," says the Abbé de Choisy, "Cardinal de Retz had a little pea in his head." That "little pea" [*petit grain*] is precisely what made the man of imagination, the writer and the painter of genius, the man of incomplete practicality, who was destined to miscarry against the common-sense and cold patience of Mazarin, but was equally certain to pay him off and take his revenge upon him, pen in hand, before posterity.

I do not answer, and no judicious reader will answer for the historical truth and accuracy of many of the tales offered to us in Retz's Memoirs; but what is evident and strikes the eye at once, is something for us superior to mere accuracy of detail: I mean the moral truth, the fidelity, human and living, of the whole. For example, read that first scene of the Fronde, when, after the imprisonment of Counsellor Broussel, the coadjutor (that is, Retz, bishop's assistant) decides to go to the Palais Royal and represent to the queen the excitement in Paris and the imminent danger of an uprising. He meets on his way the Maréchal de la Meilleraye, a brave soldier, who offers to second him and support his testimony at Court. What a scene of comedy, admirably described, is that at which Retz makes us actually present! The queen, incredulous and angry; the cardinal, who as yet has no fear, smiling maliciously; the sycophants, Bautru and Nogent, cracking jokes; and the others each in his rôle: M. de Longueville, exhibiting sadness, "but in the greatest joy at this beginning of the business"; M. le Duc d'Orléans, playing the eager and ardent in speaking to the queen, "though I never heard him whistle so idly as he did while talking for half an hour in the little grey room with Guerchi"; Villeroy, the maréchal, assuming gaiety in order to pay court to the cardinal, "and owning to me in private, with tears in his eyes, that we were on the brink of a precipice." The scene described by Retz goes on in this way with all sorts of variations until Chancellor Séquier enters the room: "He was so weak by nature that he never until this occasion had spoken a word of truth; but now compliance yielded to fear. He spoke

8

out, and said just that which all he had seen in the streets dictated to him. I noticed that the cardinal seemed much nettled at the liberty taken by a man whom he had never seen take one before." But when, after the chancellor, the lieutenant of the guard came in, paler than an actor in Italian comedy, oh! then it was decisive, and fear, which all had been resisting, came to the surface in every soul. This whole comedy should be read in Retz. The scene is true; it must be, for it is true to human nature, to the nature of kings, ministers, and courtiers in these extremities: it is the scene of Versailles while the Bastille is being taken, or that of the eve of October 5th; it is the scene, so often repeated, of Saint-Cloud, or the Tuileries, on the morning of riots that sweep away dynasties.

These are the aspects that Retz has marvellously caught and comprehended; the characteristics of men, the masking and acting of personages, the general situation, and the instigating influence of events; on all these sides he is superior and beyond attack in the way of thought and moral description, as much as Mazarin himself will ever be in history as the maker of the Peace of the Pyrenees.

When we come to judging great personages, men of action, general family traits will be seen to show out distinctly and are easily identified. For instance, Mirabeau is not well known until we see the source from which he sprang—that original and robust race, already eloquent, of father, uncle, and grandfather. Great as he was, the tribune of '89 only brought to the surface that which his kin had within them, and worked it at will. Napoleon, in the composition of his character, in the combination of primitive elements that were in it and to which his genius gave meaning and a soul, is certainly better known when, before following his whole career, we look around the circle of his brothers and sisters. In the case of Mazarin, although the group of relatives is not in direct line with him, it is by no means useless to look it over in order to define and circumscribe the original nature of the cardinal-minister and make it understood.

The children of his sisters show plainly the strongly constituted race, predestined to action, from which he issued. Nearly all his nieces reveal that race in what it had of unadulterated and *genuine,* as the English say, in the sacred force of blood, as the Greeks would have said, in natural nobleness combined with the terrible instincts of adventurers. These new-comers, whom he risked introducing at the Court of France, where so many malicious taunts and scoffs awaited them, did not shame him, although at times they caused him great embarrassment. The uncle was not obliged to say much to make them take wing; they took it of themselves, they soared, they aimed at thrones and coronets, and lowered their pretensions scarce at all ; they were chips of the old block. Blood never lies. Nearly all of them had beauty, force of character, hardihood, adroitness, and few scruples — although there were among their number (let us not forget it) two virtuous women and one saint.[1]

In bringing them to France their uncle had not ill-speculated for the aggrandisement of the family and for the pleasure of French society. He re-enlivened that fine society (though it did not then stand in much need of it) by this little Roman-Sicilian invasion; with his Olympe, his Marie, his Hortense, he sowed dazzling varieties of splendid existences and furrowed social life with unexpected and fantastic caprices. Among them there was, indeed, one true Christian, an ad-

[1] Mazarin's five most noted nieces were the four daughters of his sister, Mme. Mancini, and one daughter of another sister, Mme. Martinozzi. The names of the first four were (1) Olympe Mancini, married to a prince of the blood, the Comte de Soissons, son of the Duc de Savoie and Marie de Bourbon. Being compromised with her sister, the Duchesse de Bouillon, in the trial of Mme. La Voisin, who sold poisons called *Poudres de Succession* (Inheritance Powders), she fled from France, and after leading with her daughters a wandering life, died at Brussels in 1708. She was the mother of the famous Prince Eugène. (2) Marie Mancini, who was Louis XIV's first love: he fell upon his knees to his mother, imploring to be allowed to marry her. Mme. de Motteville gives all the particulars. She subsequently married the Roman Prince Colonna. (3) Hortense Mancini, married to the son of Maréchal de la Meilleraye, who took the name of Mazarin and was made a duke. After the cardinal's death, the Duchesse de Mazarin lived in England, where she became the devoted friend of Saint-Évremond. (4) Mariana Mancini, married to the Duc de Bouillon, was involved with her sister, the Comtesse de Soissons, in the poisoning case, and was exiled from France.

The daughter of the other sister, Anne Martinozzi, married Armand, Prince de Conti, brother of the Great Condé and of Mme. de Longueville; she is the saint mentioned in the text.—Tr.

MARIE MANCINI, PRINCESS OF COLONNA.
From a steel engraving.

mirable penitent, who seemed to wish to atone for
the others, Anne, Princesse de Conti; but beside her
what pagans were all the rest! They had but one
word, those terrible nieces, a single cry, with which
to deplore the death of that dear uncle, and that heart-
cry is in itself a funeral oration: "He has burst!"
they said: *Il est crevé!*

Their brilliant minds, as soon as developed, were
turned, with instinctive taste, to loving and favouring
the most natural and the least conventional geniuses
of their day; they became their declared inspirers and
patrons. The Duchesse de Mazarin cannot part from
her philosopher, Saint-Évremond, nor the Duchesse
de Bouillon from La Fontaine, her teller of tales.
Their brother, the Duc de Nevers, gives delightful and
easy suppers to Chaulieu and La Fare and the grand-
prior of Vendôme, all libertines in morals and in mind,
who skirted the great century without belonging to
it, awaiting the Regency. France was too small for
the activity of these nieces of Mazarin; some of them
carried to neighbouring Courts and countries their outbreaks and their errors; without, however, forfeiting
the great position to which they seemed born and in
which they had naturalised themselves as semi-sover-
eigns. M. Amédée Renée, in his "Nieces of Mazarin,"
has charmingly strung for us this chaplet of beauties,
violent and volatile, and has pictured, in a series of
quotations, extracts, and rapid observations, the existence and character of the Comtesse de Soissons, the

Duchesse de Mazarin, and the Duchesse de Bouillon. He introduces us to the choice company of the Hôtel de Nevers, that mysterious household "which combined the graces of the Mortemarts with the Mancini imagination."

I shall here permit myself, in my quality of critic, to ask M. Renée in his next edition to mark more distinctly the contrast of one of the figures, that of the Princesse de Conti, the eldest of the Martinozzi, to her brilliant sisters and cousins who lived for pleasure, adventure, folly, and orgies of intellect and wit. She was not only a pure-souled woman, that Princesse de Conti; her life, though clothed with a tinge of severity, has nothing veiled about it; it can be studied in the history of Port-Royal, where she has her place as friend and benefactress. She was born with all the qualities that fit a person of her sex for the world; she had the gift of beauty; with it she was serious, gentle, tranquil from childhood, but always full of feeling; firm, intrepid, but nevertheless cautious, and taking care to establish a reputation beyond attack. But this modesty, this exterior propriety made of her, as she said herself, "only a worthy heathen." She was concerned solely to be happy and glorious on earth and to make a lofty marriage. This ambition, great as it was, seemed more than satisfied when she found herself at the age of seventeen married to Armand de Bourbon, Prince de Conti, who was sincerely enamoured of her. Yet, amid the grandeurs and dignities that now environed her, something was still lacking; her heart felt a void within that remained unfilled.

A deep, internal agitation smouldered within her; at eighteen years of age, beneath a calm exterior, the most contradictory thoughts disturbed her. Rather confusedly instructed in the truths and spirit of Christianity, she had seen enough to make her wish to get rid of it wholly, in order not to be hampered by it. She made efforts to extinguish the feeble remains of her languishing faith, hoping in that way to calm her uneasiness: "but God did not permit her to succeed." She did not find relief from such sadness by affecting doubt and an indifference that she did not feel. Secret infirmities warned her in low tones that the hour of eternity might not be as far from her as her youth seemed to promise. Her converted husband lost no occasion for repeating to her "all that charity could make him say on the greatest of subjects to the person in the world to whom it was most important and whom he loved best." She received with the utmost gentleness what he said to her; but all these persuasions at bottom only importuned her and embittered her against piety, which she regarded as her enemy and her rival in the heart of the prince. It was in this condition of a long-standing inward struggle, that she one day found herself suddenly, and without knowing how, turned to God, convinced of the truths of faith, and burning with a desire to rise upward to the divine source.   Her heart was changed, and not half-changed; in this she showed the greatness of that heart.

From this moment she walked, without ever turning aside, in the paths of practical piety and charity; there was no question henceforth of aught but the degrees by which she grew to the light.   She took a confessor who had been given to the prince, her husband, by the Bishop of Aleth, Pavillon; she guided her whole conduct by the stern principles of the gentlemen of Port-Royal.   It became a question which of the two, she or her beautiful sister-in-law, the Duchesse de Longueville, made most progress in the narrow way. Naturally proud, rather inclined to avarice, she controlled her inclinations, cared for the poor and the sick, gave considerable alms with discernment and intelligence, not forgetting justice even in charity.   Left a widow at twenty-nine years of age, she redoubled her care and vigilance in ruling her household rightly, and in bringing up in a Christian manner her sons, to whom she had given Lancelot, of Port-Royal, as tutor.   Much respected by Louis XIV, she never abandoned to please him those whom he thought too austere.   One Sunday in Advent, 1670, when Bourdaloue had preached on "severity of penitence," making a very cutting allusion to the supposed excessive doctrines of Port-Royal, of M. Arnauld, and of his friends, the princess, who was present at the sermon, expressed her displeasure so loudly that the celebrated

HORTENSIA DE MANCINI, DUCHESSE DE MAZARIN.
From an engraving from her portrait by Sir Peter Lely.

Jesuit thought it best to go and give her an explanation. She listened to him, but did not conceal that she
was far from edified by that part of his discourse. Such
she lived and died. Her sons, those brilliant and dissolute Conti, who answered so ill to her prayers and
to the hopes of their early education, raised a monument to her in the Church of Saint-André-des-Arcs,
with this epitaph, in which is no word that is not true:

" To the glory of God, and to the eternal memory of Anne-Marie
Martinozzi, Princesse de Conti, who, disillusioned of the world at the
age of nineteen, sold all her jewels to feed, during the famine of 1662,
the poor of Berry, Champagne and Picardie ; practised all the austerities her health would allow ; was left a widow at twenty-nine years
of age, and devoted the remainder of her life to bringing up the
princes, her sons, as Christian princes, and in maintaining the laws
temporal and ecclesiastical on her estates : she reduced herself to a very
modest expenditure ; restored property, the acquisition of which
seemed doubtful to her, to the amount of eight hundred thousand
francs ; distributed all her savings to the poor on her estates and elsewhere, and passed suddenly into Eternity, after sixteen years of per-
severance on the 4th of February, 1672, aged thirty-five years."

Here, assuredly, is one of Mazarin's nieces, who, in
her black frame, does not resemble any of her famous
cousins, and who cannot be too carefully distinguished
from them. Let us think for a moment of all there was
so reflective, so profound, so enlightened in the Christian sense, in this piety that felt the need of expiating
and atoning for others—for her husband, the instigator
of civil war and the cause of disaster to so many
villages and cottages; for her uncle, the cardinal, the
grasping and unscrupulous acquirer of countless possessions. From whichever side we look at her we find

ourselves in presence of a rare inspiration, of a noble spirit of sacrifice that fills us with sovereign respect.

What further have I to say of Mazarin that has not been said already ? If I am asked in what manner he loved the queen, and what was the nature of his affection, I answer that there will always be some doubt on that subject; not on the question of love, for love it was, assuredly; true love on her part, and love, more or less simulated so long as he needed her support, on Mazarin's. The letters that we have from him to the queen leave no doubt as to the vivacity of the passionate demonstrations he permitted, or rather, commanded himself to write; but it would appear, if we rely on the testimony of Brienne and his virtuous mother, that this love was restrained to sufficiently platonic terms, that the mind of the queen was especially charmed with the "beauty of the cardinal's mind," and, in short, that it was a love of which she could speak to a confidant in her oratory and on the relics of saints without having to blush too much or to reproach herself.

Such really appears to have been up to a certain day the true state of the queen's feelings. If later Mazarin passed beyond (as is not impossible) and triumphed over the scruples of the queen to complete possession, it was because he saw in that the surest means of government.

The same Brienne who initiates us into these secrets of the cabinet and the oratory has related the last

years and the end of Mazarin in a manner that recalls
the pages of Commines when that faithful historian
relates the end of Louis XI.   Mazarin died at fifty-nine
years of age.   It was time his end came, for the king
as well as for the queen.   In his last years he had
wounded the latter by his harshness and his negligence, after he once felt himself secure from all attack.
According to the testimony of his niece Hortense: "No
one ever had such gentle manners in public or such
rude ones in domestic life."   But Louis XIV, who, as
a child, had little liking for Mazarin and felt galled by
him not only as king but as a son (for sons instinctively
dislike the too-tender friends of their mother), had of
late understood and appreciated the extent of his services, though at the same time he was impatient for
the hour to sound when he should reign for himself.
Mazarin, with his sagacious eye, had divined Louis XIV
from childhood, and was more concerned to retard him
as king than to push him; but the moment came
when delay was no longer possible.   Death then
served the fortunate Mazarin by removing him in the
height of prosperity and the maturity of human power.
After a consultation of physicians, the celebrated
Guénaud declared to him plainly that he was mortally
ill and had barely more than two months to live; he
then began to think seriously of his end, and he came
to it with a singular mixture of firmness, parade, and
pettiness.   He clung to life, holding to it by stronger
ties than those of greater hearts; I mean by the

thousand bonds of the vulgar possessor who clings
to life on account of the property he has amassed:

"One day," relates Brienne, "I was walking through the new
rooms of his palace (I mean the great gallery that runs along the Rue
de Richelieu and leads to his library); I was in the little gallery where
there is a tapestry all in wool representing Scipio and executed from
the designs of Giulio Romano; the cardinal had nothing finer. I heard
him coming by the noise of his slippers, which he dragged along the
ground like a man very feeble and just issuing from a severe illness.
I hid behind the tapestry and heard him say: 'I must leave all that!'
He stopped at every step; he was very feeble and held himself up first
on one side and then on the other; casting his eyes on an object that
met his sight he said again from the depths of his heart: 'I must leave
all that!' Then turning, he added: 'And that! What pains I took
to acquire these things! how can I abandon them without regret? I
shall never see them more where I am going! . . .' I heard those
words very distinctly; they touched me, perhaps more than he was
touched himself. I gave a great sigh which I could not restrain; he
heard it: 'Who is there?' he said, 'who is there? 'It is I, monseigneur, I am waiting the moment to speak to your Eminence.'
'Come here, come here,' he said in a dolorous voice. He was naked
under his camlet dressing-gown, lined with squirrel-skin, and had his
night-cap on his head. He said to me: 'Give me your hand; I am
very weak, I have no strength.' 'Your Eminence should sit down.'
I wished to bring him a chair. 'No,' he said,' no; I am glad to walk
about, and I have something to do in my library.' I offered him my
arm and he leaned upon it. He would not let me speak to him of
business: 'I am no longer in a state to listen to it,' he said; 'speak to
the king, and do what he tells you; I have other things now in my
head.' Then, returning to his thought, he said: 'See, my friend,
that beautiful picture by Correggio, and that Venus of Titian, and
that incomparable Deluge by Annibale Caracci, for I know you love
pictures, and you understand them very well; ah! my poor friend, I
must quit all that! Farewell, dear pictures I have loved so well and
which have cost me so much!'"

Hearing these words and seeing this scene, so
dramatic, so unexpected, reminding us of the Ode of
Horace: *linquenda tellus et domus,* we are touched

like Brienne; but take notice that there is in this regret at quitting beautiful things and beautiful pictures, characteristic of Italian passion and of a noble amateur, still another sentiment: if the first words are those of a lover of art the last are those of a miser.

Is it as an artist, is it that he loves these pictures for themselves that their master regrets them? No; it is because they have cost him dear; he loves them and clings to them because of the price he paid for them: there we reach the depths of Mazarin's soul.

Another trait, that we also owe to Brienne, and which Shakespeare would not have omitted in a *Death of Mazarin,* is of great vigour and of awful truth. One day, Brienne, entering softly into the cardinal's chamber at the Louvre, found him dozing in his arm-chair by the fire; his head swayed forward and back with a sort of mechanical swing, and he was murmuring, as he slept, unintelligible words. Brienne, fearing he might fall into the fire, called the valet-de-chambre, Bernouin, who shook his master rather roughly: "What is the matter, Bernouin?" he said, waking up, "what is it? *Guénaud said so!*" "The devil take Guénaud and his saying!" replied the valet; "you are always talking of it." "Yes, Bernouin, yes; *Guénaud said it!* he said but too true, I must die! I cannot escape! *Guénaud said it — Guénaud said it!*" Those words he had been saying mechanically in his sleep, though Brienne at first did not distinctly hear them.

A complete and anecdotal life of Mazarin would
be very curious and interesting to make; nearly all
the elements are at hand.   M. de Laborde has collected a great number in his Notes to the *Palais
Mazarin*.   He often quotes from Mazarin's *Carnets*
and gives several of the notes written by him, in
Italian as well as in French, on subjects that preoccupied his mind and about which he intended
to speak to the queen.   We find in these *Carnets*
maxims of State, excellent judgments on men, the
minor topics of the day; in short, everything, I imagine,
except things of grandeur.   M. de Laborde succeeds
in his apology for Mazarin in the sense that, after
reading him, we have obtained a very vivid idea of
the mind of the cardinal-minister and of his amiable
and potent qualities which is quite equal to what we
already thought of him.   Nevertheless, I could desire
that in another edition he would confine his quotations and notes to signifying no more than they
can prove; and that he would never advance anything that impartial and strict criticism cannot justify.
I could also desire that he had treated Retz, Saint-
Évremond, and all the cardinal's adversaries with less
levity; also that he did not despise so heartily what
he calls the "silly Memoirs" of La Porte.   La Porte
was a valet-de-chambre who left Memoirs not by any
means those of a man of intellect, but certainly those
of an honest man; and no Memoirs of a valet are ever
silly for posterity.

IV.

The Duc de La Rochefoucauld.

IV.

François, Duc de La Rochefoucauld.

Author of the Maxims.

A MAN should know how to catch the spirit of his age and the fruit of his season. There comes a moment in life when La Rochefoucauld pleases us, and in which we think him more true than perhaps he really is. The disappointments of enthusiasm bring disgust. Mme. de Sévigné thought it would be charming to hang the walls of her cabinet with the backs of cards; her amiable thoughtlessness saw only the amusing and piquant side of it. But the fact is that on a certain day all those beautiful queens of hearts, those noble and chivalrous knaves of diamonds, with whom we were playing so confidently, turn about; we fell asleep trusting in Hector, in Bertha, in Lancelot; we wake up in Mme. de Sévigné's cabinet and their backs alone are visible. We feel beneath our pillow for the book of the night before; it was Elvire and Lamartine, and lo! in its place we find La Rochefoucauld. Well, let us open him; he consoles, for the reason that he is gloomy like ourselves; he amuses. These thoughts of his which, in days of

9

youth revolted us as too false, or annoyed us as too true, and in which we saw nothing but book-morality, now appear to us, for the first time, in all the freshness of novelty on the uphill of life, they, too, have their spring-tide; we discover it: " How true that is!" we cry. We cherish the secret insult; we suck the bitterness with pleasure. But this very excess has something reassuring. Enthusiasm for those thoughts is a sign that already we are passing beyond them and beginning a cure.

It is permissible to conjecture that M. de La Roche-foucauld himself softened toward the end, and cor-rected in his heart certain too positive conclusions. During the course of his delicate and lasting intimacy with Mme. de la Fayette it can be said that he often seemed to abjure them, certainly in practice; and his noble friend had some right to congratulate herself on having reformed him, or, at any rate, in having comforted his heart.

The life of M. de La Rochefoucauld, before his great intimacy with Mme. de la Fayette, falls naturally into three divisions, of which the Fronde is only the second: his youth and his first exploits antedate it. Born in 1613 and entering the world at the age of sixteen, he never studied, and merely added to his vivacity of mind a natural good sense, masked, how-ever, by a great imagination. Before the discovery, in 1817, of the true text of his Memoirs, which gives on this early period a mass of particulars withheld by

FRANÇOIS, DUC DE LA ROCHEFOUCAULD.
From a steel engraving.

the author in the version known until then, no one suspected the degree of romantic chivalry to which the young Prince de Marsillac was carried. Buckingham and his royal adventures seem to have been the object of his emulation, just as Catiline was that of the young de Retz. Such early misleadings bar many a life. All La Rochefoucauld's noble fire was then consumed in his devotion to the unhappy queen (Anne of Austria), to Mlle. d'Hautefort, and Mme. de Chevreuse. In taking this path of devotion he turned, without thinking of it, his back to fortune. He displeased the king, he irritated the cardinal: what matter? the fate of Chalais, of Montmorency, of all those illustrious beheaded-ones seemed only to spur him on. At a certain moment (in 1637, when he was twenty-three or twenty-four years of age) the persecuted queen,

" abandoned by every one," he tells us, " and daring to confide in none but Mlle. d'Hautefort and me, proposed to me to abduct them both and take them to Brussels. Whatever difficulty and danger I saw in the project I can truly say it gave me more joy than I had ever had in my life. I was at an age when one delights to do extraordinary and dazzling things, and I thought nothing could be more so than to carry off the queen from her husband and from Cardinal de Richelieu who was jealous of her, and take Mlle. d'Hautefort from the king who was in love with her."

All these fabulous intrigues ended for him, on the flight of Mme. de Chevreuse, by eight days in the Bastille, and an exile of two or three years at Verteuil (1639–1642). This was getting off on easy terms with Richelieu; and the rather weary exile was agreeably diversified, he owns, by family joys (he had married Mlle. de Vivonne), the pleasures of country life, and, above all, the hopes of the coming reign, when the queen-regent would surely reward his faithful services.

This first part of the Memoirs is essential, it seems to me, to throw light on the Maxims, and to enable us to measure the height from which this chivalrous ambition had fallen before it burrowed into human nature as a moralist; the Maxims were the revenge of the Romance.

From this first period (now better known) it appears that Marsillac, who was in fact over thirty-three years old when his alliance with Mme. de Longueville began, and thirty-five at his entrance into the Fronde, was already at this latter period a disappointed man, irritated, and, to tell the truth, much perverted. This, without excusing him, does explain in part the detestable conduct he then exhibited. We see him tainted from the start. He does not conceal from himself the motives that cast him into the Fronde. "I did not hesitate," he says; "I felt great pleasure that in whatever position the harshness of the queen and the hatred of Cardinal Mazarin had placed me, I still had the means of revenging myself upon them." Ill-rewarded for his early devotion, he was fully resolved not to be caught in that way again.

The Fronde is therefore the second period of La

Rochefoucauld's life; the third comprises the ten or a dozen years that followed the Fronde, during which he recovered as best he could from his bodily wounds, and avenged himself, amused himself, and raised his tone to the moral plane of the Maxims. His intimate friendship with Mme. de la Fayette, which softened and truly consoled him, came later.

We may give to each of the four periods of M. de La Rochefoucauld's life the name of a woman, just as Herodotus gave to each of his books the name of a muse. These four women were Mme. de Chevreuse, Mme. de Longueville, Mme. de Sablé, Mme. de la Fayette; the first two, heroines of intrigue and romance: the third, a moralising and converting friend; the last, reverting, though unconsciously, to the heroine type by a tenderness tempered with reason, blending their tints and illuminating them as if by a last sun.

Mme. de Longueville was the brilliant passion: was she a sincere passion? Mme. de Sévigné writes to her daughter (October 7, 1676): "As for M. de La Rochefoucauld, he went, like a child, to revisit Verteuil, and the places where he had hunted with so much pleasure; I do not say where he had been in love, for I cannot believe that he has ever been what is called *in love.*" He himself (according to Segrais), said he had never found love except in novels. If his Maxim is true, "There is only one sort of love, but a thousand different copies of it," that of M. de La

Rochefoucauld and Mme. de Longueville may very well be thought merely a flattering copy of the real thing.

Marsillac, at the moment when he attached himself to Mme. de Longueville, was anxious, above all, to advance himself at Court and avenge the neglect in which he had been left, and he judged her suitable for his purpose. He has told us how he negotiated for her, as it were, with Miossens, afterwards Maréchal d'Albret, who had precedence in her regard:

"I had reason to think that I could make better use of the friendship and confidence of Mme. de Longueville than Miossens; I made him admit this himself. He knew the position in which I stood at Court; I told him my views, but added that consideration for him would always hold me back, and that I would not attempt to take up an intimacy with Mme. de Longueville, unless he permitted it. I own that I embittered him against her in order to obtain her, but without telling him aught that was not true. . . . He gave her up to me wholly—but he repented it."

Attraction counted for something, no doubt, imagination and desire assisting. M. de La Rochefoucauld loved great passions and thought them necessary to the making of a man of honour. What more noble object could there be on which to practise them! Nevertheless, all this, in its origin at least, was done in cold blood.

On the side of Mme. de Longueville, there is not less to reason about and discriminate. We do not fear to subtilise on sentiment with her, for she herself was subtile beyond measure. In the matter of devotion we have her secret examinations of conscience at

Port-Royal, in which the refinements of her scruples pass all conception. In love, in gallantry, the same thing—less the scruples. But her life and portrait must not be lightly touched in passing; she deserves a place apart, and she shall have it. Her fate has such contrasts and such harmonies throughout its whole tissue that it would be a profanation to diminish its lights and shades. She is of those, moreover, of whom it is in vain to speak ill; reason loses all rights; it is with her heart as it was with her beauty, which, in spite of many defects, had a radiancy, a languorous habit, in short, a *charm* that attached every one.

Her twenty-fifth year had already passed when her *liaison* with M. de La Rochefoucauld began. Until then she had mingled very little in politics ; though Miossens had tried to initiate her. La Rochefoucauld applied himself to the task, and succeeded in giving her activity rather than skill, to which, indeed, he himself only half attained.

The natural taste of Mme. de Longueville was for that which has been called the style of the Hôtel de Rambouillet. She liked nothing so well as gay and gallant conversations, discussions on sentiments, delicate distinctions that testified to the quality of the mind. She sought, above all things, to show the refinement within her, to detach herself from whatever was common, and to shine in all that was exquisite. When she came to believe herself a political personage she was not displeased to be thought less sincere, imagining that it made her seem the shrewder. Petty considerations of this kind decided her on great occasions. Chimeras, fancies, notions of false glory, and also what we baptise by the name of poesy, were in her; she was always outside of the real. Her step-daughter, the Duchesse de Nemours, who was never, herself, out of it, an Argus of little charity but very clear-sighted, shows her to us in Memoirs so just that we could wish them at times less rigorous. La Rochefoucauld, in his turn, does not say otherwise, and he, well placed as he was to know her, complains of the ease with which she allowed herself to be governed—a weakness he used too much and of which he did not continue the master. "Her fine qualities were less brilliant," he says, "because of a blemish that was never before seen in a princess of her merit, which was, that far from giving the law to those who had a particular adoration for her, she transformed herself so completely into their sentiments that she no longer recognised any of her own." At all times it was M. de La Rochefoucauld, or M. de Nemours, or (at Port-Royal) M. Singlin who governed her. Mme. de Longueville used her own mind less than she did that of others.

In order to guide her in politics M. de La Rochefoucauld was not firm enough in them himself. "There was always a something I know not what in M. de La Rochefoucauld," says Retz. And in a wonderful page, where the old enemy effaces himself and seems to be only the malignant friend, he develops that "I know not what" into the idea of something irresolute, insufficient, incomplete in action amid so many great qualities. "He was never a warrior, though very soldierly. He was never of himself a good courtier, though he had full intention to be one. He was never a man of party, though all his life he was bound to party." He dismisses him, however, as the most honourable of men in private life. On one single point I venture to contradict Retz, he denies imagination to La Rochefoucauld who, as I think, had a very great one. He began by practising romance in the days of Mme. de Chevreuse; under the Fronde he tried history, politics, and failed. Vengeance and vexation drove him into them more than serious ambition, and the noble remains of romance came back with ill-fortune; private life and its peaceful idleness, in which his days were to end, already called him. He was hardly embarked on an enterprise before he showed his impatience to be out of it; his inmost thought was not there. Now, with Mme. de Longueville's disposition to be swayed, let us reflect on what her course would naturally be as soon as this "something I know not what" in M. de La Rochefoucauld became her guiding star; and grouped around that star, like so many moons, were her own caprices.

It would be undertaking too much to follow the pair. With regard to M. de La Rochefoucauld it would often be too painful and too humiliating for those who admire him to accompany him. The outcome with him is better than the way to it. Let it suffice to say here that during the first Fronde and the siege of Paris (1649) his ascendency over Mme. de Longueville was complete. When, after the arrest of her brothers (the Prince de Condé and the Prince de Conti) she fled by sea to Holland and thence to Sténay, she was weaned from him somewhat. After her return to France and the struggle was renewed we find her still ruled by M. de La Rochefoucauld, who now gives her better advice in proportion as he himself becomes more disinterested. But she finally escapes him altogether (1652) and lends her ear to the amiable Duc de Nemours; who made himself especially pleasing by sacrificing to her claims the Duchesse de Châtillon.

"Persons have great difficulty in breaking apart when they no longer love each other." They had reached that difficult point: M. de Nemours cut through it, and M. de La Rochefoucauld joyfully seized the opportunity to be free by playing the injured party: "When we are weary of loving we are very glad when the other side is faithless to us and so releases us from our fidelity."

He was very glad, but not without some mixture and return of bitter feelings. "Jealousy," he says, "is born with love, but does not always die with it." The punishment of such alliances is that it is equal suffering to bear them or break them. He wanted to

avenge himself, and manœuvred so well that Mme.
de Châtillon recovered M. de Nemours from Mme.
de Longueville, and, flushed with triumph, she also
made the latter lose the heart and confidence of the
Prince de Condé. Between Mme. de Châtillon, M.
le Prince, and M. de Nemours, La Rochefoucauld,
who was the soul of the intrigue, congratulates
himself cruelly. Sight and wound of threefold bitterness to Mme. de Longueville!

Shortly after, M. de Nemours was killed in a duel
with M. de Beaufort, and (whimsicality of heart!)
Mme. de Longueville mourned him as if she still
possessed him. Her ideas of repentance followed
closely on his death.

M. de La Rochefoucauld was soon punished for his
vile action; he received, at the battle of the Faubourg
Saint-Antoine, that musket-shot in the face which
blinded him for some time. For him it was the end
of his active errors. He was nearly forty years old,
gout had already gripped him, and now he was nearly
blind. He retreats into private life and buries himself
in the easy-chair he was never again to leave. Assiduous friends surround him and Mme. de Sablé pays
him every attention. The accomplished man of honour begins; the moralist declares himself.

M. de La Rochefoucauld makes it felt that he is a
wise man from the moment that he becomes disinterested. Such are men: wisdom on one side, action
on the other. Good sense is at the summit when

they have nothing more to do than to judge those who have none.

The "something, I know not what," of which Retz sought the explanation, reduces itself, so far as I can define it, to this: that La Rochefoucauld's true vocation consisted in being an observer and a writer. This was the end to which all the rest of his life served him. With his divers attempted callings as warrior, statesman, and courtier he was never wholly in any of them: there was always an essential corner of his nature that kept aloof and displaced the equilibrium. His nature, without his then suspecting it, had an *arrière-pensée* in all enterprises, and that hidden thought was an instinct to reflect upon the enterprise when it was over. All adventures were to finish with him in maxims. What would seem to be fragments collected by experience after shipwreck, composed the true core, found at last, of his life.

A slight but very singular sign seems to me to indicate still further in M. de La Rochefoucauld this particular destination of nature. For a man so much in the world he had (Retz tells us) a strange air of shyness and timidity in civil life. He was so embarrassed in public that if he had to speak on official matters before six or seven persons his courage failed him. The dread of a solemn harangue kept him always from entering the French Academy. Nicole was the same, and could never have preached or maintained an argument. A characteristic of the moralist is secrecy

of observation, communication with others in a low
voice.   Montesquieu says of him, somewhere, that if
he had had to get his living as a professor he could
not have done it.   Maxims are things that cannot be
taught; half a dozen persons before whom to recite
them are too many; the maker of them will be admitted to be right only in a tête-à-tête.   Mankind in
the mass need a Jean-Jacques or a Lamennais.

The *Réflexions ou Sentences et Maximes Morales*
appeared in 1665.   Twelve years had elapsed since
the adventurous days of M. de La Rochefoucauld, and
the musket-shot, his last misfortune.   In that interval
he had written his Memoirs, which an indiscretion
had divulged (1662), and to which he was forced to
give a denial that proved nothing.   A copy of the
Maxims also got about and was printed in Holland.
He parried this by giving them to Barbin to publish
in Paris.   This first edition, without the author's
name, although he is plainly indicated, contains a
Note to the Reader very worthy of the book, and
a discourse, much less worthy, attributed to Segrais,
which replies to objections already current by many
quotations from classical philosophers, and from
Fathers of the Church.   The short Note to the Reader
makes a far better answer in a single sentence: "Take
care; there is nothing more fitted to establish the truth
of these *Réflexions* than the heat and subtlety shown
in combating them."

Voltaire, judging La Rochefoucauld's Maxims in his

light-hearted and charming way, says that no book had contributed more to form the taste of the nation: "People read the little volume eagerly; it accustomed them to think, and to inclose their thoughts in a lively, precise, and delicate form. This was a merit no one had had before him in Europe since the renascence of letters." Three hundred and sixteen thoughts, forming one hundred and fifty pages, had this glorious result. In 1665, it was nine years since the appearance of the *Lettres Provinciales ;* Pascal's *Pensées* were not published until five years later, while La Bruyère's *Caractères* came twenty years later still. The great prose monuments, the eloquent oratorical works which crowned the reign of Louis XIV, did not issue until after 1669, beginning with the funeral oration over the Queen of England. In 1665 France was on the very threshold of the great century, on the first landing of the portico, on the eve of *Andromaque ;* the staircase of Versailles was inaugurating the fêtes: Boileau, accosting Racine, was mounting the steps; La Fontaine, in sight, was forgetting to mount; Molière was already at the top, and *Tartuffe,* under its original form, was producing itself clandestinely. At this decisive moment of universal ardour, M. de La Rochefoucauld, who had little love for lofty discourse and liked only brilliant talk, said his word: a great silence fell; he found he had spoken for all the world, and each word was lasting.

Here was a courteous, insinuating, smiling misanthrope, preceding by very little and delightfully preparing the way for that other *Misanthrope*.

In the history of the French language and literature, La Rochefoucauld comes in date in the first rank after Pascal, and even precedes him as a pure moralist. He has the clearness and conciseness of phrase that Pascal alone, in that century, had before him; which La Bruyère caught; which Nicole could not keep; which was destined to become the sign-manual of the eighteenth century, the perpetually easy triumph of Voltaire.

Though the Maxims may seem at their inception to have been merely a relaxation, a social game, a sort of wager of men of wit playing at proverbs, how completely they detach themselves by their result and assume a character above their occasion! Saint-Évremond, Bussy, who have been compared to La Roche-foucauld for wit, bravery, and loss of favour, are also writers of social quality: at times they charm, and yet they have I know not what that is corrupt; they foretell the Regency. The moralist in La Rochefoucauld is stern, grand, simple, concise; he attains to the noble; he belongs to the pure Louis XIV period.

La Rochefoucauld cannot be too highly praised for one thing: in saying much he does not express too much. His manner, his form is always honourable to the man, even when the matter is little so.

In correctness he belongs to the school of Boileau, but far in advance of the *Art Poétique*. Some of his

Maxims he rewrote thirty times, until he reached the necessary expression; nevertheless, there seems no torturing effort. The original little volume in its primitive arrangement (afterwards broken up) offering its three hundred and sixteen thoughts, so brief, and framed between general considerations of *self-love* in the beginning and reflections on *contempt of death* at the end, expresses to me even better than succeeding editions an harmonious whole in which each separated detail arrests the eye. The modern perfection of style is there: it is aphorism sharpened and polished. If Racine is to be admired after Sophocles, La Rochefoucauld may be read after Job, Solomon, Hippocrates, and Marcus Aurelius.

So many profound, solid or delicate intellects have spoken in turn of the Maxims that it is almost temerity in me to add my word. None have so far better treated of their philosophy than M. Vinet in his *Essais de Philosophie Morale*. He is rather of the opinion of Vauvenargues, who says: "La Bruyère was a great painter and was not, perhaps, a great philosopher. The Duc de La Rochefoucauld was a great philosopher and no painter." Some one else has said, with the same meaning: "In La Bruyère thought often resembles a woman who is better dressed than beautiful; she has less person than style." But, without detracting at all from La Bruyère, we shall find in La Rochefoucauld an angle of observation that is wider, a comprehensive glance

that goes deeper.   I even think that he had more system and unity of principle than M. Vinet is willing to
allow, and that in this way he fully justifies the title
of philosopher which that ingenious critic so expressly
grants him.   The "often," "sometimes," "nearly
always," "usually," with which he moderates his
grievous conclusions, may be taken for polite precautions.   While putting his finger on the mainspring
he pretends to step back a little; it is enough, he
thinks, not to let go.   After all, the moral philosophy
of La Rochefoucauld is not much opposed to that of
his century; he profits by the propinquity to dare to
be frank.   Pascal, Molière, Nicole, La Bruyère, can
hardly be said, I imagine, to flatter mankind; some
tell the evil and its remedy; others tell the evil only;
there lies the whole difference.

Vauvenargues, who was one of the first to begin
the rehabilitation of the race, has remarked this very
well.   "Mankind," he says, "is just now in disgrace
with all those who think; they vie with one another
to load it with vices; but perhaps this only shows
that it is on the point of rising again and compel-
ling the restitution of all its virtues . . . and far
more."   Jean-Jacques took upon himself the "far
more"; he pushed it so far, that we might consider
it exhausted.   But no; there can be no stopping in so
good a road; the proud stream flows and swells; man
is so rehabilitated in our day that we scarcely dare to
say or write the things that passed for truths in the

10

seventeenth century. This a characteristic trait of our times. Many a rare mind when talking is not less satirical than La Rochefoucauld; the same men as soon as they write or speak in public put on a tone of sentiment and begin to exalt human nature. They proclaim in the tribune the noble and the grand at which they laugh in the recess of a window, or sacrifice to a flash of wit around a green table. Philosophy practises self-interest, and preaches a pure ideal.

La Rochefoucauld's Maxims do not in any way contradict Christianity, although they do without it. His man is precisely the fallen man, if not as François de Sales and Fénelon understood him, at any rate such as Pascal, Du Guet, and Saint-Cyran consider him. Take from the Jansenist doctrine *redemption* and you have pure La Rochefoucauld. If he seems to forget in man the exiled king that Pascal recalls, and the broken particles of his diadem, what is that but the insatiable pride that he denounces, which, by force or craft, seeks still to be sole sovereign? But he limits himself to satire; it is not enough, says M. Vinet, to be mortifying, he should be useful. La Rochefoucauld's misfortune is to think that men do not correct themselves. "We give advice," he said, "but we cannot inspire behaviour." When it was a question of finding a tutor for the dauphin, he was thought of for a moment; I cannot but think that M. de Montausier, less amiable and more doctoral, was better suited to the place.

La Rochefoucauld's moral reflections seem true, exaggerated, or false, according to the humour and the situation of the reader. They please whoever has had his Fronde and a musket-shot between the eyes. The soured celibate treasures them. The fortunate worthy man, father of a family, attached to life by sacred and prudent ties, cannot accept them without qualifying them, or he thinks them odious. A mother suckling her child, a grandmother whom all revere, a noble, pitying father, devoted and upright hearts not subtilised by analysis, the lifted foreheads of young men, the pure and blushing foreheads of young girls,—these direct recalls to frank, generous, and healthy nature bring back the vivifying hour in which all subtlety of reasoning disappears.

In La Rochefoucauld's own time, and around him, the same objections and the same replies were made. Segrais and Huet thought he had more sagacity than equity; and the latter even remarked, very acutely, that the author had brought certain accusations against mankind for the sole purpose of not losing some witty or ingenious expression he meant to apply to them. However little of an *author* we may pique ourselves in being as we write, we are always one at some point. If Balzac and the "academists" of that school had ideas only through phrases, La Rochefoucauld himself, the strict thinker, sacrifices to the word. His letters to Mme. de Sablé during the time when the Maxims were in making, show him to us full of ardent imagination, but of literary preoccupation as well; there was rivalry between her and himself and M. Esprit and the Abbé de La Victoire. "I know that they dine with you without me," he writes to her, "and that you show them maxims I have not made, about which they will not tell me anything. . . ." And again, from Verteuil, not far from Angoulême, where he was staying: "I do not know if you have noticed that the desire to make phrases is as catching as a cold in the head; we have here some disciples of M. de Balzac who have caught the infection and will do nothing else." The fashion of "maxims" was succeeding that of "portraits." Later, La Bruyère took both and united them.

The postscripts of La Rochefoucauld's letters are filled and seasoned with these "sentences," which he jots down, retouches, and inclines to keep back even when sending them; "for I may regret them," he says, "as soon as the postman has gone." "I am ashamed to send you such works," he writes to a person who has just lost a quarter of his income from the Hôtel-de-Ville. "In earnest, if you find them ridiculous, return them to me without showing them to Mme. de Sablé." But the friend did not fail to show them, as he knew very well. Put thus into circulation before printing, these "thoughts" excited contradiction and criticism. There was one on Mme. de Schomberg, formerly Mlle. d' Hautefort, the object of Louis XIII's chaste love, of whom Marsillac, in the days of his early chivalry, had been the devoted friend and servitor: "Oh! who would then have believed it," she may have said to him, "Can it be that you have grown so perverted?"

These "thoughts" were also blamed for obscurity; Mme. de Schomberg does not think them obscure; she complains instead of understanding them too well. Mme. de Sévigné writes to her daughter in sending her the edition of 1672: "Some of them are divine, and, to my shame, there are some that I cannot understand." Corbinelli commented on them. Mme. de Maintenon, to whom they went earlier, writes in March, 1666, to Mlle. de l'Enclos, "Offer, I beg you, my congratulations to M. de La Rochefoucauld, and tell him that the book of Job and the book of Maxims form my sole reading."

Success, opposition, and praise were not confined to social interviews and correspondence; the newspapers took part in them. When I say "newspapers," I mean the *Journal des Savants,* the only one then founded, which had been in existence for only a few months. The matter here becomes piquant and I shall venture to divulge it all. In turning over, myself, the papers of Mme. de Sablé I came upon the draft of an article intended for the *Journal des Savants* and written by that witty lady. Here it is:

"This is a treatise on the emotions of the heart of man, which we may say was unknown until now even to the heart that felt them. A seigneur as great in mind as he is by birth is the author. But neither his mind nor his rank has prevented very different judgments being formed of it.

"Some think it an outrage on men to make so terrible a picture of them, and that the author can have found the original only in himself. They say that it is dangerous to bring such thoughts to the light, and that having been so plainly shown that good actions are only done from bad motives, most persons will believe that it is useless to look for virtue, inasmuch as it is impossible to have any except in idea; that, in short, it is upsetting morality to show that the virtues it teaches us are mere chimeras because they come to none but bad ends.

"Others, on the contrary, find the treatise very useful because it reveals to men the false ideas they have of themselves, and shows them that without religion they are incapable of doing right; it is always well, they say, to know ourselves as we are, even though there may be no other advantage in doing so than that of not being deceived in the knowledge of ourselves.

"However that may be, there is so much wit in this work, and such great penetration in perceiving the true state of man, in considering only his nature, that all persons of good sense will find here an infinity of things of which they might, perhaps, have remained ignorant all their lives if this author had not drawn them from the chaos of the heart of man and set them in the light, where all the world may see them and comprehend them without difficulty."

In sending this draft of her article to M. de La Rochefoucauld, Mme. de Sablé adds the following little note, dated February 18, 1665:

"I send you what I have been able to draw out of my head to put into the *Journal des Savants.* I have put in the side to which you are so sensitive. . . . I did not fear to put it in, because I am certain that you will not allow it to be printed even if the rest pleases you. I assure you, also, that I shall be more obliged to you if you will use it as a thing of your own, by correcting it, or by throwing it into the fire, than if you did it an honour it does not deserve. We great authors are too rich to mind the loss of our productions."

Let us note all this carefully: Mme. de Sablé, now

devout, who, for several years, had had a lodging in the Faubourg Saint-Jacques, rue de la Bourbe, in the buildings of Port-Royal of Paris,—Mme. de Sablé, greatly occupied, even at this time, with the persecutions to which her friends the nuns and the recluses were subjected, is not less concerned in the cares of the world and the interests of literature. These Maxims, known to her in advance, which she had caused to be copied, and had lent, under the rose and with great mystery, to a number of persons, gathering for the author the various opinions of society, she is now to aid before the public in a newspaper; she *works* at their success. On the other side, M. de La Rochefoucauld, who dreads of all things to play the author and allows it to be said of him in the Discourse at the beginning of the book: "He would not feel less vexation in knowing that his Maxims were made public than he felt when the Memoirs attributed to him were published"—M. de La Rochefoucauld, who had meditated so long on man, is now to review his own praise written for a newspaper and take out those parts which displease him! The article was inserted in the *Journal des Savants* of March 9, and if compared with the draft, we shall see that the part to which Mme. de Sablé thinks M. de La Rochefoucauld will be "sensitive" has disappeared; nothing remains of the second paragraph, beginning "Some think it an outrage on men." At the end of the first paragraph, where it is a question of the different judgments formed on the book, the article, as printed, skips suddenly to the third paragraph, with these words: "We may nevertheless say that this treatise is very useful, because," etc. M. de La Rochefoucauld left all as it was, except the least agreeable paragraph. The first literary journal that ever appeared had existed only three months, but already authors were arranging their articles themselves! As journals improved, the Abbé Prevost and Walter Scott wrote theirs at greater length.

The part that Mme de Sablé had in the composition and publication of the Maxims, that rôle of moralising and semi-literary friendship which she filled during those important years to the author, would give us the right to speak of her here more fully, if it were not that we ought above all to study her in connection with Port-Royal: a charming, coquettish, yet solid mind; a rare woman, in spite of some absurdities, to whom Arnauld sent the manuscript of his Discourse on Logic, saying to her: "It is only persons like yourself whom we desire to judge us"; and to whom, almost at the same moment, M. de La Rochefoucauld wrote: "You know that I trust none but you on certain subjects and especially on the recesses of the heart." She forms the true link between La Rochefoucauld and Nicole.

I shall say only one word on her own Maxims, which are printed; they serve to measure the little that belongs to those of her illustrious friend. She was his counsellor, but nothing else: La Rochefoucauld remains the sole author of his work. In the eighty-one thoughts of Mme de Sablé that I have read I could scarcely quote one that stands out in relief; their base is either Christian morality, or pure civility and usage of the world; but the form is especially defective; it is lengthy, long-drawn-out; nothing comes to a conclusion, nothing fastens on the mind. The mere comparison makes us better understand the manner in which La Rochefoucauld is a *writer*.

Mme. de La Fayette, of whom there is little question until now in the life of M. de La Rochefoucauld, became his intimate friend immediately after the publication of the Maxims, and applied herself, in a way, to correct them in his heart. Their two existences were never, henceforth, separated. I will relate elsewhere, in speaking of her, the grave comfort given, the afflictions tenderly consoled, during those last fifteen years. Fortune as well as friendship seemed at last to smile on M. de La Rochefoucauld: he had fame; the favour of his fortunate son raised him at Court, and even brought him back there; there were times when he never quitted Versailles, detained by the king whose childhood he had spared so little. Family joys and sorrows found him incomparable. His mother did not die until 1672: "I have seen him weep," writes Mme. de Sévigné, "with a tenderness that made me adore him." His great grief, as we know, was that "hail of fire" at the passage of the Rhine, where he had one son killed and the other wounded. But the young Duc de Longueville, another of the victims, born during the first Fronde, was dearer to him than all else. The youth had made his entry into society about the year 1666, the year of the Maxims: the bitter book, the young hope —two children of the Fronde! In the well-known letter in which Mme. de Sévigné relates the effect of this death on Mme. de Longueville, she adds immediately: "There is a man in the world who is not less moved. I have it in my head that if the two could meet in these first moments, with no one present, all other feelings would give way to sobs and tears, shed, and doubly with all their hearts: this is a vision."

No death, so say all the contemporaries, ever caused so many tears, and such noble tears, as that of this young man. In M. de La Rochefoucauld's room in the hôtel de Liancourt, above a door, hung a portrait of the young prince. One day, shortly after the fatal news, the beautiful Duchesse de Brissac, coming to pay a visit and entering by a door opposite to the portrait, recoiled at the sight; then, after standing a moment motionless, she made a little curtsey to the company and went away without a word. The unexpected sight of the portrait had wakened all her sorrows, and being no longer mistress of herself she could only withdraw.

In his advice and solicitude about the graceful loves
of the Princesse de Clèves and the Duc de Nemours
La Rochefoucauld doubtless thought of that flower of
his youth mown down; finding, perchance through
tears, something not quite imaginary in the portrait.
But were it not so, the sight of the now aged moralist bending with tenderness over the story of those
romantic and charming beings is more fitted to touch
us than surprise us.   When minds are upright and
hearts are sound at their source, after many experi-
ments in taste men revert to the simple; after many
aberrations in morality they come back to virginal
love, if only to contemplate it.

It is from Mme. de Sévigné that we obtain an
account of his fatal illness and his supreme last moments, his sufferings, the anguish of all around him,
and his constancy; he looked *fixedly* at death.

He died March 17, 1680, before the end of his
sixty-seventh year.   Bossuet assisted him in his last
moments; from which fact one of his biographers, M.
de Bausset, has drawn certain religious deductions
very natural in such a case.   Another, M. Vinet,
seems less convinced: "Persons," he says, "can
make what they like of the following passage from
Mme. de Sévigné, a witness of his last moments":

"I fear," she writes, "that we must lose M. de La Rochefoucauld;
his fever continues; he received Our Lord yesterday; but his state
is a thing worthy of admiration.   He is well settled as to his
conscience; *that is done.*   .   .   .   Believe me, my daughter, it
was not useless that he made reflections all his life; he approached

his last moments in such a way that they have brought nothing new
or strange for him."

" It is permissible to conclude from these words,"
adds M. Vinet, " that he died, as was said later, with
decency."

V.

The Duchesse de Longueville.

V.

Anne=Geneviève de Bourbon.

Duchesse de Longueville.

THE name of Mme. de Longueville, as well as that
of Mme de La Fayette, is bound to that of M. de
La Rochefoucauld by all sorts of attractive relations, conventions, and reverberations more or less
mysterious. Her life, divided into two opposing parts,
one of ambition and gallantry, the other of repentance
and devotion, too often had witnesses who were solely
concerned with one aspect of it. Mme de Sévigné
alone, in a memorable letter, has thrown light upon
her portrait at its most pathetic moment. To me,
who have met her at the very centre and heart of a
subject on which I was writing [the "History of
Port-Royal"] the opportunity has been given to follow her and to have the honour of frequenting her
presence in hours of retreat and through her hidden
experiences. She came before me as the most illustrious penitent and protectress of Port-Royal during
many years. On her, and on her presence in that
monastery, depended solely, towards the end, the

preservation of "the peace of the Church"; her death broke it up. Without pretending to paint a life so varied and so elusive, there was duty and pleasure for me in rightly catching the expression of a countenance to which an immortal enchantment clings, and which, even beneath its doubled veils, came smiling to me from the depths of that austere monastery. I detach it to place it here.

Anne-Geneviève de Bourbon, daughter of a very beautiful mother, Charlotte de Montmorency, whose beauty, so coveted by Henri IV, came near causing a war, was very young when she appeared at Court beside her mother, Mme. la Princesse [de Condé] still loftily brilliant, bringing with her, says Mme. de Motteville: "the first charms of that angelic face, which later had such dazzling lustre, a lustre followed by so many grievous events and salutary sufferings."

Her earliest and tenderest thoughts turned to piety; her end only recovered and realised the mystical dreams of her childhood. She often accompanied Mme. la Princesse to the Carmelite convent in the Faubourg Saint-Jacques; there she spent long hours that later were painted with an ideal halo in her azure imagination, and revived in living colours at last when the whirlwind had gone by. She was thirteen years old (1632) when her uncle Montmorency was immolated at Tours to the vengeance and the policy of Richelieu; the young niece, wounded in her pride as much as in her tenderness by so sharp a blow, would fain have

ANNE-GENÉVIÈVE DE BOURBON, DUCHESSE DE LONGUEVILLE.

imitated the august widow, and vowed herself to mourn in conventual perpetuity. Her mother began to fear this marked inclination for the worthy Carmelites; she thought she saw that the blonde, angelic face was not making ready to smile upon the brilliant world which was about to judge it on its first appearance. To this, Mlle. de Bourbon replied, with an instinctive flattery that already belied such fears: " You have such touching graces, Madame, that as I go out only with you and am seen after you, no one finds any in me." The turn of Mme. de Longueville's spirit and mind is early seen in that one saying.

It is told that on the occasion of her first ball, to which she went in obedience to her mother, a great council was held among the Carmelites, at which it was decided, in order to conciliate matters, that before exposing herself to the danger, she should be armed beneath her ball dress with a little cuirass, called a hair-shirt. That done, all was felt to be safe, and Mlle. de Bourbon might think only of making herself beautiful. She had hardly entered the ball-room before a murmur of universal admiration and flattery rose around her; her smile, which her mother had doubted for a moment, responded, and ceased no more; delightful perversion! the prickles of the hair-shirt were blunted, and from that day those good Carmelite sisters were in the wrong.

But she thought of them still, at intervals; in the midst of her greatest dissipations she kept up an

intercourse of letters; she wrote to them after each
blow, each sorrow; she returned to them in the end
and divided her time between their convent and Port-
Royal.   She was with them in the Faubourg Saint-
Jacques when she died; she was there when Mlle.
de la Vallière came, and among the agitated spectators
of that arrival she was remarked for the abundance of
her tears.   The life of Mme. de Longueville is full
of those harmonious symmetries, those returns upon
herself that make her easily poetical, and by which
the imagination allows itself, in spite of everything,
to be seduced.   It was thus (I omitted to say) that
she was born in the castle of Vincennes during the
imprisonment of her father, the Prince de Condè
(1619); in that Vincennes where her brother, the
Great Condé, a captive, was one day to cultivate
pansies; in that Vincennes of Saint-Louis fated to
bear upon its stones in after days the stains of the
blood of the last Condé.

She frequented, with her brother, at that time Duc
d'Enghien, the hôtel de Rambouillet, then in its first
prime; and we have letters to her from M. Godeau,
Bishop of Grasse, all full of myrtles and roses.   This
sort of influence was serious upon her, and her
thoughts, even after her repentance, always felt it.
At this period, and before politics came into her life,
she and her brother and the young cabal (already decided to be a cabal) merely aimed, it is said, to show
off the brilliancy of their wits in gay and gallant con-

versations, in discussing and refining till point was lost on the delicacies and intricacies of the heart. That was the test, to their minds, of men of honour. Whatever had an air of solid conversation seemed to them coarse and vulgar. With them it was a resolution and a pledge to be *distinguished,* as it was called sixty years later; *superior,* as we should say to-day: but then they called it *précieux.*

Mlle. de Bourbon was twenty-three years old when they married her (1642) to the Duc de Longueville, then forty-seven, and widowed of a princess of more virtue than mind who was closely allied with the Mothers of Port-Royal during the period called that of the Institution of the Holy Sacrament and of M. Zamet. The duke had a daughter, seventeen years old at the time of his second marriage who, before she was Duchesse de Nemours, lived for some time with her young step-mother, noted all her transgressions, and finally, in her Memoirs, spares her the record of none of them.

The Duc de Longueville was the greatest seigneur of France, but, coming after the princes of the blood, he was somewhat beneath Mlle. de Bourbon. Her father, M. le Prince, forced her into the marriage; on which, however, she put a good face. In the first days of it a great scandal excited and also flattered her passionate pride and brought out the vanities of her heart.

One day, during a "circle" at the Duchesse de

Montbazon's, some one picked up a dropped letter, without address or signature, but in a woman's hand, writing tenderly to some one she did not hate. The letter was read and reread, they all tried to guess the writer, and soon decided that it must be the Duchesse de Longueville, and that the letter had undoubtedly fallen from the pocket of the Comte de Coligny, who had just left the room. It seems that really, whether intentionally or not, they were mistaken. This attack was the first yet brought against the reputation of the young duchess. The malicious tale was told everywhere, without much credence being given to it. At the first rumour that reached the ears of the insulted lady, she, knowing that the story was false (though she may have intended to make it true), thought it best to keep silence. But her mother, Mme. la Princesse, would not allow her to do so, and in the tone of a person proud of having entered the House of Bourbon she exacted formal reparation. Her complaint became a State affair. This was in the first year of the regency [of Anne of Austria]; Mazarin tried his power; it was his first opportunity to disentangle Court intrigues, and to set aside the friends of Mme. de Montbazon, Beaufort, and the "Importants." Mme. de Motteville tells all this to perfection.

The composition of the words of apology was debated and decided in the little cabinet of the Louvre, in presence of the queen, and written down on the tablets of the cardinal, who was playing his own game under cover of this comedy. The apology was then copied on a little piece of paper which Mme. de Montbazon fastened to her fan. At a fixed hour she went to Mme. la Princesse and read the paper; but she did so in a haughty tone that seemed to say: "I ridicule it." Soon after this, Coligny, in consequence of this pretended letter, "called out" the Duc de Guise, who took the part of Mme. de Montbazon. They fought on the Place-Royal; Coligny received a wound, of which he died; it was said at the time that Mme. de Longueville was hidden behind a window to watch the fight. At any rate, all this uproar about her delighted her; it was the hôtel de Rambouillet in action. Coligny might have found his reward had he lived.

Was it before or after this event that Mme. de Longueville was attacked by the smallpox? Probably before; she had it the year of her marriage, and her beauty came out of it with little damage; the eclipse was transient. "As for Mme. de Longueville," says Retz, "the smallpox took away the first flavour of her beauty but left her nearly all its brilliancy; and that brilliancy, joined to her rank, her wit, and to her langour, which in her was a peculiar charm, made her one of the most charming persons in France." M. de Grasse thought himself more faithful to his character as bishop in writing to her, as soon as she recovered:

"I praise God for preserving your life. . . . As for your face, others than I will rejoice with more seemliness that it is not injured;

Mlle. Paulet sent me word of this. I have such good opinion of your wisdom that I think you would have been easily consoled if your illness had left its marks. They are often marks engraven by the divine Mercy, to show to persons who love their complexion too well that it is a flower liable to fade before it fully blooms, and consequently does not deserve to be placed in the rank of things that may be loved."

The courteous bishop dwells so complacently on these marks of mercy only because Mlle. Paulet has assured him they do not exist!

Mme. de Motteville goes farther; after the illness she describes to us this beauty, which consisted more in certain incomparable tones of the complexion than in any perfection of feature; those eyes, less large than soft and brilliant, of an admirable blue, the blue of turquoise; and the silvery blonde hair, like that of an angel, adding its profusion to the other charms. And with them all a perfect figure, the nameless something that is called "air," elegance in her whole person, and at every point a style supreme. No one approaching her ever escaped the desire to please her; her irresistible charm extended even over women.

The Duc de Longueville, descendant though he was of Dunois, had little that was chivalrous about him; he was a great seigneur, magnificent and pacific, without humour, rather clever in negotiations, as much so as an undecided man can be. They sent him to complete those of Munster; Mme. de Longueville did not join him there for two years (1646), by which time the Prince de Marsillac had made upon her the impression that he himself had received.

The diplomatic world and the honours of which she was the object left her indifferent and rather reflective; she thought then, as she did on another occasion when she yawned over Chapelain's *Pucelle* which she was asked to admire: "Yes, it is very fine, but it is very wearisome."

"Would it not be better, Madame," writes the careful M. de Grasse, "if you returned to the hôtel de Longueville, where you are even more plenipotential than you are at Munster? Every one wishes for you there this winter. Monseigneur, your brother, has returned, laden with palms; return yourself covered with roses and myrtles, for it seems to me that olive branches are not sufficient for you."

She reappeared in Paris in May, 1647. That year of absence had increased her value; her return put the crown to her success. All desires sought her. Her *ruelle* it is said, became the scene of choice discussions, of the famous duel of the two sonnets, and also of graver preludes. To speak the language of M. de Grasse, myrtles hid blades.

Her brother the victorious, hitherto so united with her in feeling, now, little by little, separated from her; this irritated her. On the other hand, her second brother, the Prince de Conti, became more and more bound to her, and Marsillac seized the tiller of her heart decisively.

To follow the life of Mme. de Longueville at this epoch, through budding rivalries, through intrigues, through the wars of the Fronde, would be to condemn ourselves to winnow the Memoirs of the time (pleasant as that task might be); but especially should we have to register the caprices of an ambitious yet tender soul in which the heart and mind were incessantly duping each other. One might as well attempt to follow step by step the airy foam on each mocking wave : *in vento et rapida scribere oportet aqua.* Let us rather concern ourselves with her character.

La Rochefoucauld, who more than any one was qualified to judge her, has told us his judgment, and I give the passage because it is too essential to her portrait to be omitted here :

" This princess had all the advantages of mind and beauty in so high a degree and with such charm, that it seemed as if Nature had taken pleasure in forming in her person a perfect and complete work; but these fine qualities were less brilliant because of a blemish which was never before seen in a person of her merits; namely, that instead of giving the law to those who had a particular adoration for her, she transferred herself so completely into their sentiments that she no longer recognised her own."

La Rochefoucauld could not at first complain of this defect inasmuch as he led her into it.

It was love that awakened ambition in her soul, but awakened it so quickly that henceforth the two were indistinguishable. Singular contradiction! The more we consider the political career of Mme. de Longueville, the more it blends and is confounded with the caprices of her love; yet if we search closely into that love it seems (and she herself avows it later) it was only the disguise of ambition, the desire to shine anew.

Her character, therefore, lacked stability and a will of her own.   And her mind,—note this well,—brilliant and acute as it was, had nothing that opposed itself directly to this weakness of character.   We may see the right thing, and yet not have the force to do it.   We may have reason in the mind but not in the conduct; between the two the character gives way.   But here the case was different.   Mme. de Longueville's mind was not pre-eminently reasonable; it was delicate, quick, subtile, ingenious, full of recesses; it followed her nature, which was fluctuating; it shone in evasions and in the tangle of cross-purposes before it consumed itself finally in scruples.   There was much of the hôtel de Rambouillet in a mind like hers.

"The minds of most women serve to strengthen their folly rather than their reason."   The author of the Maxims said so, and Mme. de Longueville with all her metamorphoses must have been present to his mind when he said it.   She, the most feminine of women, could offer him the best epitome of womankind.   On the other hand, while he observed, evidently through her, she, in turn, seems to have drawn her conclusions from him.   Mme. de Longueville's final confession, which we shall presently read, will seem to us little else than a Christian translation of the Maxims.

Retz, less involved in this subject than La Rochefoucauld, but who would fain have been as much so, has spoken marvellously of Mme. de Longueville; my own portrait has no other glory than to gather and present these several pictures:

"Mme. de Longueville," he says, "has by nature, a solid foundation of mind, but she has even more subtlety and cleverness. Her capacity, which is hampered by her laziness, has not been carried into those affairs to which her hatred for M. le Prince [her brother, the Great Condé] enticed her, and in which gallantry maintained her. She had a languor of manner, more affecting than the brilliancy of others who were more beautiful; she had the same in her mind, which charmed, because of its surprising and luminous awakenings. She would have had few defects if gallantry had not given her many. As her passion compelled her to make public affairs secondary in her conduct, from being the heroine of a great party she became the adventuress. The Grace of God restored what the world could not give back to her."

As, in the Fronde, we see Mme. de Longueville superior in mind to Mme. de Montbazon, for example, or to Mlle. de Chevreuse (which is saying too little), or even to La Grande Mademoiselle, so we find her inferior to her friend the Princess Palatine [Anne de Gonzague], a true genius, firm, possessing the secrets of all parties, and ruling all, advising them with loyalty and coolness; not the adventuress, no! but the statesman of the Fronde: "I do not believe that Queen Elizabeth had greater capacity to guide a State," says Retz, speaking of the Princess Palatine.

Why did not Bossuet do honour to Mme. de Longueville as he did to that other repentant princess, whose funeral oration he pronounced in the church of these very Carmelites in the Faubourg Saint-Jacques? The Prince de Condé, who had asked for his eloquent services in memory of La Palatine, never thought, it

ANNE DE GONZAGUE, PRINCESS PALATINE.

From a steel engraving.

appears, of expressing the same wish, some years earlier, in regard to his sister. Did he consider its accomplishment impossible from those resounding lips? The difficulties, in fact, were great; even in her repentance Mme. de Longueville retained something that seemed rebellious. Bossuet could not say as he did of the Princess Palatine: " Her faith was not less simple than artless. In the famous questions that have troubled, in so many ways, the peace of our times, she openly declared that she took no other part than that of obeying the Church." Port-Royal would have been a more perilous rock to strike than the Fronde; vague allusions might have been allowed in the dim distance to M. de La Rochefoucauld or to M. de Nemours, but never to M. Singlin.

But consider how a few words of the potent orator would have fixed for ever, in its gracious majesty, that figure of dazzling languor, that character of seductive and skilful weakness—weakness that was never more actively effectual than when it was most subjugated! How admirably would he have drawn her upon that background of tempests and civil whirlwinds, on which he first threw and then detached the other princess! We all know that grand page on the Fronde, which cannot be read too often; I refer my readers to it. He would not have written it less grandly for this lacking oration on Mme. de Longueville which is one of my regrets.

In default of that magnificent painting, the chronicle

of Memoirs is here to help us.　In using the key that those of La Rochefoucauld supply, I have already told (in my portrait of the latter) how the influences directing Mme. de Longueville were quite other before the imprisonment of the princes to what they were after it.　During the first period, that is to say, during the siege of Paris (1648), having quarrelled with the Prince de Condé, she followed only the interests and sentiments of M. de La Rochefoucauld; she followed them still after peace was signed (April, 1649), when, she urged and obtained for him patents and privileges at Court, and when, after the arrest of her brothers (January, 1650), she fled, through all sorts of perils in Normandy, by sea to Holland, arriving at last, very proud of herself, at Sténay, where she negotiated with the Spaniards and troubled Turenne.

On her return to France, after the release of the princes, and during the preliminaries of the return to arms, she seemed to follow the same sentiments though with a less decided yielding to them.　We see her in council with the Prince de Condé at Saint Maur, when she seems to wish sometimes for peace, because La Rochefoucauld desired it, and sometimes for rupture, because war would keep her away from her husband, "whom she had never loved," says Retz, "but was now beginning to fear."　And he adds, "this constitution of minds with which M. le Prince had to do would have hampered Sertorius." Strange and sorry omen ! aversion to the husband

struggling against the interests of the lover, while
for the latter not to triumph was to forfeit all.   Before long M. de La Rochefoucauld's sentiments ceased
to be Mme. de Longueville's compass; she seemed
to accept without reluctance the homage of M. de
Nemours; losing it not long after through the intrigues of Mme. de Châtillon, who recovered that
homage as her own property and at the same time
found means to obtain that of the Prince de Condé,
then escaping once more from intimate relations with
his sister.

It was M. de La Rochefoucauld whose policy and
vengeance plotted this thrice irritating revenge on
Mme. de Longueville.   She had already openly quarrelled with her second brother, the Prince de Conti,
whom, up to that time, she had governed absolutely,
and even subjugated.   She lost before long the last
remains of hope to recover M. de Nemours, who
was killed in a duel with the Duc de Beaufort; and
from that moment her anger, her hatred against him
turned to tears, as if he were just torn from her.
About this time peace was finally concluded (October, 1662); the Court and Mazarin triumphed; youth
had fled; doubtless beauty was beginning to follow;
all things failed at once, or were about to fail for
Mme. de Longueville.   Being at Bordeaux in a convent of the Benedictines where she had gone to lodge
when peace was evidently approaching, she wrote
to her dear Carmelites in the Faubourg Saint-Jacques,

with whom, even in the midst of her greatest dissipations, she had never quite broken:

"I desire nothing with so much ardour now as to see this war
at an end, that I may fling myself among you for the rest of my
life. . . . If I have had attachments in this world, of whatever
nature you can imagine, they are now broken off and even shattered.
This news will not be disagreeable to you. . . . I desire, in
order to give me sensibility towards God (which I have not as yet,
but without which I shall still do as I have told you if peace comes)
that you will do me the favour to write to me often and confirm me
in the horror that I have for this age. Send me word what books you
advise me to read."

Anterior to this time we have letters from her to
the same sisters; every misfortune, as I have said,
brought her thoughts involuntarily back to them; she
wrote to them when she lost a little daughter, and
when her mother, the Princesse de Condé, died. The
latter death occurred while the duchess was at Sténay.
From there, in answer to a letter of condolence from
the convent, she writes a touching request to the
Mother-superior for particulars about the death:

"It is in being afflicted that I ought to find comfort," she writes.
"The tale will have a sad effect, and that is why I ask you for it;
for you see plainly that it is not repose that ought to follow a sorrow
like mine, but secret and eternal torture: for which, indeed, I prepare
myself, to bear it in the sight of God and in view of those of my
crimes that have laid His hand upon me. Perhaps He will find acceptable the humiliation of my heart and the long series of my
deep miseries. . . . Adieu, my dear Mother; tears are blinding
me; if it were the will of God that they should cause the end of
my life they would seem to me more the instruments of my good
than the effects of my evil."

M. de Grasse. also, continued to write to her, and

he did so on the occasion of this death with a sort of eloquence. Thus were preserved, even through periods of prodigal delirium, the secret heart-treasures of Mme. de Longueville; her tears, abundant and renewed from time to time, kept them from drying up at their source.

Nevertheless, a new life was about to begin. She was thirty-four years of age. She quitted Bordeaux under an order from the Court and went to Montreuil-Bellay, a domain belonging to her husband in Anjou, and from there to Moulins. In the latter town she stayed with the Filles de Saint Marie, and visited the tomb of her uncle, the Duc de Montmorency, whose tragic death had so moved her at the age, still pure, of thirteen, and was now a solemn lesson to her, coming, vanquished herself, from civil factions. Her aunt, the widow of M. de Montmorency, was superior of the convent. The example of such chaste and pious consistency acted more than all else on her imagination, always so easily stirred, on her soul still adrift, still drenched by the shipwreck. One day, at Moulins, in the midst of some religious reading,

" a curtain was drawn back " [it is she herself who is speaking] "from the eyes of my mind; all the charms of truth, gathered into one object, came before me; Faith, which had remained as it were dead and buried beneath my passions, awoke. I felt like a person who, after a long sleep in which she had dreamed that she was great, fortunate, honoured, and esteemed by all the world, wakens suddenly to find herself loaded with chains, pierced by wounds, weary with languor, and locked in a dark prison."

After ten months' stay at Moulins she was joined by the Duc de Longueville, who took her, with all sorts of attentions, to his government of Normandy. New trials were added daily to the old ones; the mere announcement of some success of the Prince de Condé, who had gone over to the Spaniards largely at the suggestion of his sister, revived her remorse and prolonged the ambiguity of her relations to the Court. She was reconciled during these years to her brother, the Prince de Conti, and was closely allied with her sister-in-law, Anne Martinozzi, Princesse de Conti, niece of Mazarin, who redeemed that suspicious blood by noble virtues; these three, the brother and sister and the former's wife, soon became the envy of all emulators in the path of conversion.

Nevertheless, Mme. de Longueville was still in need of direction; with her style of character, with that habit of following adopted sentiments and of ruling herself only by some chosen will, she, above all others, needed a firm guide. She wrote from Rouen to ask advice of her aunt, Mme. de Montmorency, and from an intimate friend, Mlle. du Vigean, sub-prioress of the Carmelites of Paris,[1] also of others. She questioned the Abbé de Camus, afterwards Bishop of Grenoble and a cardinal, recently

[1] Mlle. du Vigean had been beloved by the then Duc d'Enghien, before the Fronde; he even wished to break his marriage in order to marry her. Their love, thwarted by Mme. de Longueville, who warned M. le Prince, her father, had, on the lady's side, the cloister for a tomb.

converted himself, who replied: "God will lead you farther than you think, and will ask of you things of which it is not yet time to speak to you. When we examine our conduct by the principles of the Gospel we find fearful voids." But the enlightened physician who could take in hand this vacillating and aching soul did not appear. Then it was that the advice of M. de Bernières, possibly of M. le Nain (head of Mme. de Longueville's council), given very certainly at the instigation of Mme. de Sablé, turned the mind of this anxious inquirer to Port-Royal and its directors.

Under date of April, 1661, we find a letter from Mère Angélique to Mme. de Sablé, telling her that she had seen Mme. de Longueville, and found her mind more solid, more natural, than she had been led to expect: "All that I saw of the princess in that short time seemed to me pure gold." M. Singlin, [director of Port-Royal] already obliged to conceal himself to evade the Bastille, consented to go and see Mme. de Longueville; he was the first to enlighten and regulate her repentance.

I find a letter from Mlle. de Vertus to Mme. de Sablé, which is as follows (I give it because, to my mind, all details relating to persons so lofty, so delicate, and finally so worthy, have a value):

"I received last night a note from the lady" [Madame de Longueville]. "You are entreated to do what you can to induce your friend, M. Singlin, to come here to-morrow. In order that he may have no uneasiness lest he be seen in the quarter, he can come in a chair and send away the porters; I will lend him mine to take him back where he pleases. . . . If he would like to come to dinner they shall put him in a room where no one whom he knows can see him; and it would be better, I think, that he should come rather early, that is to say between ten and eleven at the latest. . . . I am very anxious that this should be done, for this poor woman has no peace. Have many prayers offered to God I entreat you. If I could see her in such good hands I should, I own, be very joyful; it seems to me I should be like those persons who see their friend provided for and have no more to do than to rest in that. The truth is, this lady makes strange troubles for herself which she will not have when her mind is settled. I am much afraid that your friend will be too harsh. However, we must pray to God and commend the affair to him."

M. Singlin, once introduced, returned frequently. He paid his visits disguised as a physician, with the enormous wig then worn by that profession; he said, in justification of this disguise, that he was indeed a physician of souls. He remained for some time hidden at Méru, an estate belonging to the princess. Is it refining too much to think that these mysteries, these various concerted precautions in behalf of repentance had for Mme. de Longueville a last charm of romantic imagination at the entrance of the narrow way?

We possess her Examination of Conscience, written by herself after her first confession to M. Singlin, November 24, 1661. It is a document to put beside that other confession of the Princess Palatine, written by her on the advice of the Abbé de Rancé, and so magnificently paraphrased by Bossuet. They should be read without scorn and with a simple heart; in the papers themselves there is nothing agreeable or flattering. But considered humanly, so to speak, and from the single point of view of psychological observation, such papers merit consideration—*respectus*. If they reveal to us the human heart in its most minute pettiness, it is because pettiness is the ordinary foundation of it; they follow it, they prove its smallness, its meanness, through all degrees of its depth. Mme. de Longueville regarded this new birth as the first step for her in a truly penitent life:

> " I had long been searching (so it seemed to me) the path that led to life; but I always felt I was not in it, without knowing precisely what my obstacle was; I felt that there was one between myself and God, but I did not know it, and I felt as though I were not in my right place. I had a certain anxiety to be there, without knowing where it was, nor where I ought to seek it. It seems to me, on the contrary, since I have put myself under the guidance of M. Singlin that I am in the right place which I was seeking, namely: the true entrance to the path of Christian life, on the outskirts of which I have hitherto been."

It is to be remarked in this Examination of Mme. de Longueville, and also in her manuscript letters, of which I have seen a quantity, that the style is superannuated and much less elegant than we might have expected; much less vivid and clear, for instance, than that of the divine letters and Reflections of Mme. de La Vallière, published in one volume by Mme. de Genlis. This is chiefly because there is twenty-five years' difference in the ages of the two illustrious women: Mme. de La Vallière was the exact contemporary of La Bruyère, almost of Fénelon; Mme. de

Longueville's style was formed before the period of Louis XIV. But go to the depths and end of her long-drawn-out sentences, and delicate refinement will be found. Moreover, Mme. de La Vallière's style has been slightly corrected in the later editions.

Before listening to her general confession and thus engaging himself to direct her conduct, M. Singlin wished to know, from her, whether she felt willing to quit the world in case she was one day able to do so. She answered in all sincerity, "Yes." This acknowledgment and this pledge obtained, he exacted that she should continue to occupy herself with external affairs as long as it was necessary to do so, and without permitting herself to call them "miserable."

Skilful physician and practitioner of the soul that he was, M. Singlin showed her, after his first glance, her capital defect, namely: that pride of which she herself, she says, was quasi-ignorant for so many years. This pride is also what the Duchesse de Nemours, in her Memoirs, denounces in a hundred ways. It is curious to see how the denunciations of the latter, the indications of M. Singlin, and the sincere avowals of Mme. de Longueville fit into one another and agree:

"The things that it" [her pride] "produced," she writes, "were not unknown to me, but I dwelt only on its effects, which I thought great imperfections; but now, from what has been shown to me, I see that I did not go to their source. It was not that I did not recognise that pride was the principle of my errors, but I did not think it as living as it is; I did not attribute to it all the sins that I committed; yet I now see plainly that they *all* drew their origin from it."

She recognises that in the days of her most criminal errors the pleasures that touched her were those of the mind, which come of self-love; "the others naturally did not attract her." These two miserable emotions, pride and pleasure of the mind, which are but one, entered into all her actions and were the soul of her conduct:

"I have always found my pleasure, which I sought so much, in that which flattered my pride and offered to me what the Devil offered to our first parents: 'You shall be as gods!' And that saying, which was an arrow that pierced their hearts, so wounded mine that the blood still flows from that deep wound and will flow ₁ong, if Jesus Christ by his grace does not stanch its flux. . . ."

The discovery, which she first owed in its full extent to M. Singlin, of this vast stratum in her nature, on which he made her lay her finger and follow in all its ramifications, and which now seemed to her to comprise the whole substance of her soul, alarmed her and led her to "the very edge of the temptation to discouragement." She fears henceforth to find pride in all things; and even this docility, apparently the only sound spot in her soul, becomes suspicious to her; she dreads lest she be docile in appearance only, and merely because by obeying she pleased others and regained the esteem she had lost. In a word, she seems to see in this docility her pride "transforming itself, if I may say so, into an Angel of light, in order to have something to live upon." Terrified, she stops short, and can only cry to God, with her face to earth and after long silence: *Sana me et sanabor.*

But a letter from M. Singlin which she receives and reads after praying, comforts her by proving that this servant of God does not despair of her nor of her trials. I might, if this were the place, multiply extracts and reveal without sparing her, in all their naïve subtilty and old-fashioned negligence of style, these delicacies of conscience in a mind once so elegant and haughty, now so humble and, so to speak, engulfed. She knows herself henceforth; she bares her soul and analyses it. In one place her description falls in with that of Retz and responds to it precisely. We remember how he describes to us her laziness and languor, interrupted suddenly by flashes of light. Here follows her Christian and rigorously moral representation of that apparently charming trait. Once more I ask pardon for the carelessness of its style; poor as it is, when we plunge to the depths of what it says, we are tempted to exclaim with Bossuet (speaking of the dream of the Princess Palatine), "I take pleasure in repeating these words, in spite of fastidious ears; they eclipse the most magnificent discourses; I would I spoke only such language ":

"On receiving the letter of M. Singlin, which seemed to me very thick and on that account made me hope for many things on the subject which now occupies me, I opened it rapidly, for my nature leads me always to follow whatever fills my mind; just as, on the contrary (I say this to make myself known), it gives me great coldness and negligence for whatever is not my then occupation, which is always very strong and single in me. This is what makes some persons think me vehement and impetuous, because they have seen me in my passions, or merely in my petty inclinations and tendencies; while to others I seem slow and lazy, even dead, if I may use the word, because they have never seen me moved by what I once was either in evil or in good. That is also why I have been defined as if I were two persons of opposite tempers; so that sometimes I was called sly and sometimes fickle in humour; which was not so, neither the one nor the other; but it came from the different situations in which they saw me. For I was dead, dead as death, to all that was not in my head, and all alive to the slightest atom of things that touched me. I still have the diminutive of this humour, and I let myself be ruled by it too much. So it was this that made me open the letter so rapidly."

She goes on in this strain, and adds many avowals of her hasty dislikes, her mobility of temper, her brusque asperity to others if she did not guard herself against it. I find therein an incredible number of testimonies to that spirit, so acute, so unfettered, which now has only its own labyrinth to unravel. She says in closing:

" A thought has come to me about myself, which is that I am very glad, from self-love, that I have been ordered to write all this; because I like above everything to occupy myself and occupy others about myself; for self-love makes us like better to say evil of ourselves than to say nothing at all. I expose this thought, and submit it in exposing it, as I do all the rest."

I have copies of several manuscript letters written by Mme. de Longueville, all equally full of scruples and anxieties over some action that she thinks had a worldly motive, over some forgotten sin, over an absolution received with a clouded conscience. She practised repentance and mortification by continual vigilance and anguish of mind, even more than by hair-shirts.

By the advice of M. Singlin, Mme. de Longueville concerned herself especially with restitutions and the giving of alms in the provinces ravaged, through her fault, by civil war. On the death of M. Singlin, she passed under the direction of M. de Saci. When the latter was sent to the Bastille, she had M. Marcel, rector of Saint-Jacques, and others equally safe. She wrote very assiduously to the saintly Bishop of Aleth (Pavillon) and followed his replies in detail as though they were oracles.

The Duc de Longueville having died in May, 1663, she was henceforth free to enter without delay upon the path of penitence that claimed her wholly. The troubles of the Church at this period alone kept her in the world. She was very active in behalf of Port-Royal during those difficult years. The revision of the New Testament, called that of Mons, was completed at the conferences held at her house. After 1666, she kept Arnauld, Nicole, and Lalane hidden there. Several anecdotes are told, with an appearance of truth, which must have enlivened the weariness of that retreat.

Arnauld was one day attacked by fever. The princess sent for Dr. Brayer and asked him to take particular care of a nobleman who had lately come to stay with her, Arnauld having assumed the secular garments, wig and sword, and other paraphernalia of a noble. Brayer went up to see him, and after feeling his pulse, began to tell him about a new book that

was making a great noise and was attributed to the
gentlemen of Port-Royal: " Some," he said, " give it
to M. Arnauld, others to M. de Saci; I don't think it
is by the latter, for he can't write so well." On
which Arnauld, forgetting the rôle of his coat and
shaking his ample wig, cried out: " What's that you
say, monsieur ? my nephew writes better than I do."
Brayer came down laughing and said to Mme. de
Longueville: " Your nobleman is not very ill; nevertheless, I advise you to keep him from seeing people, and above all, not to let him talk." Such in truth,
with his simple ingenuousness, was the great plotter
and leader of a party, Antoine Arnauld.

We see (in the " History of Port-Royal " by Racine)
that Nicole was more to Mme. de Longueville's taste
than Arnauld, as being more polished, more attentive.
In their evening meetings, the worthy Arnauld, preparing to go to sleep beside the fire and going head-
foremost into Christian equality, would gently " untie
his garters before her; which made her suffer a little."
Nicole had more of the customs of the world, but
even he, coming in one day with an absent mind,
laid his hat, gloves, cane, and muff on the princess's
bed! She accepted all such things as part of her
penance.

Mme. de Longueville contributed more than any of
the prelates to the Peace of the Church. Those conflicting negotiations, so often broken off and resumed,
their secret activities, at the centre of which she was,

renewed for her the Fronde, the only Fronde now permissible, and gave her back a few of the same emotions for a good purpose, and in all security of
conscience. Learning one morning (about 1663) of
one of the ruptures, which was imputed to the
Jesuits, she said, with a flash of her old wit: "I
was simple enough to believe that the Reverend
Fathers were acting sincerely — it is true I have only
believed it since last night." Finally, however, serious negotiations began. M. de Gondrin, Archbishop
of Sens, concerted everything with her. She wrote
to the Pope to justify the accused persons and guarantee their faith; she wrote also to Cardinal Azolini,
secretary of State, to interest him in bringing matters
to a conclusion. She deserves, with the Princesse de
Conti, to be saluted by the title of Mother of the
Church.

Peace concluded, she caused to be built at Port-
Royal-des-Champs a detached building, or small
house, communicating by a gallery with the church.
From the year 1672 she divided her time between
this retreat and that of her faithful Carmelites in the
Faubourg Saint-Jacques; where she already had an
apartment. Very sorrowful trials from without
pushed her finally into these two havens: first, the
death of her sister-in-law, the Princesse de Conti,
then the imbecility and misconduct of her eldest son,
the Comte de Dunois; but, above all, the death of
her cherished son, the Comte de Saint-Paul, then

Duc de Longueville. She never quite left the hôtel de Longueville until after this last cruel death, so well known to us through the admirable letter of Mme. de Sévigné. The young duke was killed immediately after the passage of the Rhine by flinging himself with imprudent valour upon a body of the flying enemy; and with him perished a crowd of young noblemen. The news had to be told to Mme. de Longueville. Lest I tell it incompletely I repeat here the whole of that immortal page:

"Mlle. de Vertus," writes Mme. de Sévigné, June 20, 1672, "had returned two days earlier to Port-Royal where she usually is; they sent to fetch her with M. Arnauld to tell this terrible news. Mlle. de Vertus had but to show herself; her sudden return was sign enough of something fatal. As soon as she entered: 'Ah! mademoiselle, how is my brother?' [the Great Condé]. Her thoughts dared not go farther. 'Madame, he is recovering from his wound.' 'Then there has been a battle! and my son?' They made her no answer. 'Ah! mademoiselle, my son, my dear child! answer me, is he dead?' 'Madame, I have no words to answer you.' 'Ah! my dear son! did he die instantly? did he not have a single moment? Ah! my God! what a sacrifice! And with that she fell upon her bed, and all that the sharpest sorrow could do, by convulsions, faintings, by deathly silence and by stifled cries, by bitter tears, by appeals to heaven, by tender plaints and pitiful—all these she underwent. She sees certain persons, she takes some broth, because God wills it; she has no rest; her health, already very bad, is visibly failing. For my part, I wish her death, not comprehending how she can live after such a loss."

And seven days after the above letter she writes again:

"I have at last seen Mme. de Longueville; chance brought me near to her bed; she sent for me to come nearer and spoke to me first; as for

me, I knew not what words to say on such an occasion.   She told
me that she did not doubt that I felt pity for her; that nothing was
lacking to her misfortune; she spoke of Mme. de La Fayette and of M.
d'Hacqueville as those who would pity her most; she spoke to me of
my son, and of the friendship her son had for him.   I will not repeat
my answers; they were what they ought to have been, and, in truth,
I was so touched that I could not speak amiss.   The crowd drove me
away.   But the circumstance of the peace is a sort of bitterness that
wounds me to the heart when I put myself in her place; when I keep
in my own I praise God, since it preserves to me my poor Sévigné and
all my friends."

It was discovered (compliantly perhaps) that before
starting for the war M. de Longueville was secretly
converted: he had made a general confession (the
gentlemen of Port-Royal had brought it about), he had
distributed immense alms, and, in short, that, in spite
of his mistresses and a natural son, he was a quasi-
saint.   This was a sort of final comfort, very permissible under the circumstances; the inconsolable mother
was credulous.   As soon as the first flood of condo-
lences had abated, Mme. de Longueville went to Port-
Royal-des-Champs, where her house was ready, and
there she lived in solitude; leaving it from time to
time and returning to stay with the Carmelites.   In
the latter convent she saw the passing, like a funeral
procession, of the grandeurs of her time: Mme. de
La Vallière taking the veil, and, shortly after, the
arrival of Turenne's heart—that heart which she had,
alas ! so troubled.

Her austerities, joined to her pangs of mind, hastened her end; a change took place in her during

her last illness, and she had, as it were, a foretaste
of calm. She died at the Carmelites' on the 15th
of April, 1679, aged fifty-nine years and six months.
Her body was buried in the convent, her entrails at
Saint-Jacques-du-Haut-Pas; her heart was taken to
Port-Royal. One month after her death, the Archbishop of Paris, M. de Harlay, went to Port-Royal in
person to command the nuns, by order of the king,
to send away their pupils and postulants, and forbid
them to return in future. The death of the princess
had been awaited to begin the final blockade under
which the celebrated nunnery was fated to succumb.
There was no longer a Palladium in Ilion.

The funeral oration of Mme. de Longueville was
pronounced one year after her death, not by Bossuet,
I regret to say, but by the Bishop of Autun, Roquette,
supposed to be the original of Tartuffe, and of whom
it was said that his sermons were undoubtedly his
own, inasmuch as he bought them. Mme. de Sévigné, in a letter dated April 12, 1680, praises in a
singular manner, and not without sharp points of
irony, this oration which was never allowed to be
printed. What was far more eloquent than the
words of the Bishop of Autun on this anniversary
of Mme. de Longueville's death, was the presence of
the Mlles. de La Rochefoucauld in mourning for their
father, of Mme. de La Fayette, whom Mme. de
Sévigné went to see after the ceremony and found
in tears; for Mme. de Longueville and M. de La

Rochefoucauld died in the same year: "There was much to dream of in those two names."

Our worthy historians of Port-Royal have said many commonplaces and much pettiness about Mme. de Longueville; the title of Serene Highness dazzled them.   When they speak of her, or of Mlle. de Vertus, or of M. de Pontchâteau they are inexhaustible; in the very legitimate plenitude of their gratitude we must not ask them for discernment of character. We see by a little fragment at the end of Racine's Abridgment, which he did not have time to recast and conceal in his narrative, that if Mme. de Longueville kept, into the last years of her life, the grace, elegance, and what Bossuet calls "the insinuating manners" of those who have retired from the world, she had also kept her touchiness, her dislikes, her readiness to take umbrage; "she was sometimes jealous of Mlle. de Vertus, who was more equable and winning."   But why be surprised? even to the cold shelter of a cloister, even to the funeral slabs on which she pressed her face she brought *herself;* the sphere was purer, but the enemies were the same, and the same inward struggles continued.

The true crown of Mme. de Longueville during those years, that which we must the more revere because she did not perceive it, covering it with both hands,—hiding it, as it were, in a tabernacle, is the crown of humility.   That is her Christian glory which inevitable defects ought not to obscure.   Many touching traits are told of it. She had her enemies, persons who were jealous of her; wounding and even insulting speeches came to her ears; she bore them all, saying to God: "Strike on!" Once, going in a chair from the Carmelites' to Saint-Jacques-du-Haut-Pas, she was approached by an officer who asked her for some favour—I know not what. She answered that she could not do it, and the man thereupon flew into a passion and spoke in the most insolent terms. Her servants were about to fling themselves upon him. "Stop!" she cried, "do nothing to him; I have deserved much more." If I point out beside this grand chief trait of humility some persistent pettinesses it is far less to invalidate a repentance so deep and so sincere than to expose to their end the obstinate hidden failings and evasions of these elegant natures.

Lemontey, in a witty notice, but flimsy and sharp, did not fear to call her a "theatrical and conceited soul." Who will dare, after having gone with me so near to her repentance, to call her aught else than a poor, delicate, anguished being?

Nicole, that spirit also so delicate, who frequented her presence for many years, has judged her very well. He had always had a good understanding with her. She thought him right in the various little quarrels of Port-Royal. He said pleasantly that after her death he had sunk in public estimation; "I have even" he said, "lost my abbey; for no one now

calls me M. l'Abbé Nicole, but simply M. Nicole."
In vol. xii of the *Ouvrages de Morale et de Politique*
by the Abbé de Saint-Pierre, we find the following
testimony as to the class of mind and intellectual
capacity of Mme. de Longueville; a place where we
should little have thought of looking for it; its quaint-
ness is none the less piquant.

"I asked M. Nicole one day what was the character of Mme. de
Longueville's mind; he told me she had a very keen and very delicate
mind in knowledge of the character of individuals, but that it was
very small, very weak, very limited on matters of science and reasoning, and on all speculative matters in which there was no question of
sentiment. 'For example,' added he, 'I told her one day that I could
bet and prove that there were in Paris at least two inhabitants who
had the same number of hairs upon their head, though I could not
point out who were those two persons. She said I could not be certain of it until I had counted the hairs of the two persons. Here is
my demonstration,' I said to her: 'I lay it down as a fact that the
best-furnished head does not possess more than 200,000 hairs, and the
most scantily furnished head is that which has only 1 hair. If, now you
suppose that 200,000 heads all have a different number of hairs, they
must each have one of the numbers of hairs which are between 1 and
200,000; for if we suppose that there were 2 among these 200,000 who
had the same number of hairs, I win my bet. But suppose these
200,000 inhabitants all have a different number of hairs, if I bring in a
single other inhabitant who has hairs and has no more than 200,000
of them, it necessarily follows that this number of hairs, whatever it is,
will be found between 1 and 200,000, and, consequently, is equal in
number of hairs to one of the 200,000 heads. Now, as instead of one
inhabitant more than 200,000, there are, in all, nearly 800,000 inhabitants in Paris, you see plainly that there must be many heads
equal in number of hairs, although I have not counted them.' Mme.
de Longueville still could not understand that demonstration could be
made of this equality in number of hairs, and she always maintained
that the only way to prove it was to count them."

This proves to us that Mme. de Longueville who

had such affinity with Mme. de Sablé in refinements and titillations of the mind was very different from her on one point. Mme. de Sablé liked and could follow dissertations and was a good judge of them; but Arnauld would never have thought of making Mme. de Longueville read his " Logic of Port Royal " to interest her and to obtain from her a competent opinion.

She belonged by nature to those *esprits fins* which Pascal contrasts with the geometric minds: "those delicate, refined minds that are only refined; which, being accustomed to judge of things by a single and rapid glance, are quickly repelled by detailed definitions seemingly sterile, and have no patience to come down to the first principles of speculative things, and things of the imagination, which they have not seen in the world and in its customs."

But, geometry apart, her knowledge of the world and her rapid *coup d'œil,* her subtlety, her elegance, the blood of a princess in all her veins, a soul feminine in its every recess, her vocation, the point of honour to please, which is victory in itself, great passions, great misfortunes, the halo of a saint in dying, the supreme intertwining around her of those consummate names: Condé, La Rochefoucauld, Port-Royal—all this suffices to bestow on Mme. de Longueville a lasting distinction, and to secure to her in French memory a very flattering part that no renown of heroine can surpass; no fame, even that of superior women, can efface.

13

What more shall I say? If, from the bosom of that world which she has entered, she can smile at the effect, the charm her name produces on those who judge her, she is smiling now.

VI.

Cardinal de Retz.

VI.

Cardinal de Retz.

Instigator of the Fronde.

THE Memoirs of Cardinal de Retz appeared for the first time in 1717, under the regency of Philippe d'Orléans. When it was known that a copy of them was furtively being printed and about to appear, the Regent asked the lieutenant of police, d'Argenson, what effect the book would produce.

" None that need trouble you, monseigneur," replied d'Argenson, who knew the work; " the manner in which Cardinal de Retz speaks of himself, the frankness with which he exhibits his own character, admits his faults, and informs us of the ill-success of his imprudent actions, will encourage no one to imitate him. On the contrary, his misfortunes are a lesson to all mischief-makers and rash minds. I cannot conceive how that man could have left behind him that confession in writing. . . ."

Nevertheless the effect was wholly different from the one foretold by d'Argenson. One might as well have said on the eve of the production of the *Confessions* of Jean-Jacques Rousseau, that they would ruin the authority of philosophy. Errors and wrongdoings may be so well confessed that they instantly

197

become contagious for the human imagination. "This book," said the honest Brossette (the most pacific of men), speaking of the Memoirs of Retz, "makes me a leaguer, a frondeur, and almost seditious by contagion." The Regent knew something of this shortly after the publication; the conspiracy of Cellamare in 1718 was in its way a counterfeit and summary of the Memoirs of Retz. In all the periods of our civil struggles they have been emergent and have roused fresh interest. Benjamin Constant said, during the Directory, that he could no longer read any books but two: Machiavelli and Retz. We are to-day [1837] at a propitious moment to re-read these Memoirs and draw from them a few lessons—if lessons of this kind are ever useful. In speaking of them to-day, I do not seek to make any political application, nor to work out any perspective according to the views of the moment; I prefer to consider them in a more general, more impartial manner; more in themselves only.

Retz belongs to that great and strong generation before Louis XIV, of which were also, more or less, and a few years apart, La Rochefoucauld, Molière, Pascal, a generation which Richelieu had found too young to crush; which revived, or rose on the morrow of his death, and signalised itself in thought and language (when action was denied it) by a free, bold outpour, to which the distinguished men who came through the long régime of Louis XIV were too much unaccustomed. This is so true as to the

CARDINAL DE RETZ.

thought and the language that when the Memoirs of
Retz appeared one of the reasons alleged or stam-
mered against their authenticity by a few fastidious
minds was the language itself of those admirable
Memoirs—that vivid, familiar, superlative, and negligent touch that betrays the hand of a master and
shocks those it does not enrapture. Our language
under Louis XIV acquired many fine qualities, and
fixed them at the beginning of the eighteenth century
with a seal of conciseness and precision, but it lost
I know not what of breadth and the air of grandeur.

It was precisely that air of grandeur that Retz prized
most, and of which, from the start, he was ambitious
in everything, in his words, his actions, carrying it
into all his projects. But if he sought for glory he had
in him many qualities of the first order well calculated
to form its basis. Born in October, 1614, of an illustrious family, destined against his will for the Church,
"with a soul as little ecclesiastic as was ever, perhaps, in the universe," he tried to get out of the profession by duels and affairs of gallantry; but the
obstinacy of his family, and his star, prevented these
first scandals from producing their effect and casting
him back into secular life. He then chose his course,
and set himself to study with vigour, determined, like
Cæsar, to be second in nothing, not even at the Sorbonne. He succeeded; he held his own in the final
competitions and in the *Actes* of the great School,
against an abbé protected by Richelieu, and carried

off the victory in a signal manner, not caring whether he provoked the powerful cardinal, who "wanted to be master everywhere and in everything." About this time, a copy of the "Conspiracy of Fiesque," the first secular work of the Abbé de Retz, came into the hands of Richelieu, who saw in it to what point the young man caressed the ideal of a grandiose and seditious conspirator, and he said: "There's a dangerous mind." It is asserted that he said on another occasion to his groom of the chambers, speaking of Retz: "There's a face for the gibbet."

Retz was short, ugly, dark, rather ill-made and near-sighted; qualities little fitted to make a man of gallantry, though they did not hinder his being one, and with success. Sober in eating and drinking, he was extremely licentious ; but being, above all, ambitious, he led everything abreast—his passions, his views, even his schemes, into which there entered, in some degree, regard for the public weal. Possessed by a burning desire to make himself talked of, and to reach the grand, the extraordinary, at a time when he entered the world under the reign of a despotic minister he had no resource except in the idea of conspiracy ; and to that side he turned his first predilections ; just as, in other times, he might have turned them elsewhere. In spite of his turbulence and his impetuosity, Retz was very capable of self-control when the interests of his ambition required it. In Italy, at Rome, during a journey that he made there in 1638, when twenty-four years of age, he resolved to give no cause for complaint against him and to acquire at all risks a good name at the ecclesiastical Court. Retz tells us this, and Tallemant des Réaux, who accompanied him, expressly confirms it: " We must praise him for one thing," he says : "neither in Rome nor in Venice did he see a woman ; or if he did, it was so secretly that we could discover nothing of it." At the same time he took pains to relieve the modesty of the journey by great expense, fine liveries, a very jaunty equipage ; and one day, to maintain the point of honour and not yield the ground in a game of tennis, he came very near drawing swords with his handful of friends against the whole escort of the Spanish ambassador.

He was much to the fore in all the conspiracies against Richelieu, in fact, he staked his head during the last years of that minister. He details the scheme of one of these conspiracies, in which it was proposed that at the first news of a victory by the Comte de Soissons, Paris should be stirred to insurrection, and a sudden attack made in combination with the principal prisoners in the Bastille, Maréchal de Vitry, Cramail, and others. The scheme was novel. The governor of the Bastille was made prisoner by his own garrison, of which the conspirators had made sure. They also seized the Arsenal which was close by. In short, it was " Mallet's Conspiracy," organised by Retz against Richelieu. It all failed ; but it might

have succeeded.   How many great things in history
hang by a thread !

Richelieu dead, and Louis XIII having followed
him closely, the Regency came ; certainly at first the
most easy-going ever seen.   Retz obtained, in a trice,
the appointment of coadjutor [assistant to a bishop
or archbishop, with the right to succeed him] to his
uncle, the Archbishop of Paris ; and henceforth, to
use his own language, he ceased to "be in the pit, or
even in the orchestra playing and joking with the
violins" ; he mounted the *stage*. We may observe
throughout his Memoirs, where he speaks of himself
with so little concealment, that he perpetually uses the
expressions and images of the "stage" the "comedy";
he seems to consider everything in the light of a play,
and there are moments when, speaking of the principal personages with whom he has to do, he takes
account of them and arranges them absolutely as
a stage-manager would do with his star-actors.
In relating one of the first scenes of the Fronde, in
Parliament (January 11, 1649), and telling of the
manner in which he managed to take away the command of the troops from the Duc d'Elbeuf to bestow
it on the Prince de Conti, he shows us M. de
Longueville, then M. de Bouillon, then the Maréchal
de la Mothe, entering the hall, one after the other,
each, in turn, beginning anew to declare adhesion to
the choice of the Prince de Conti, and joining hands
in what concerned them :   "We had arranged," he

says "to bring these personages on the stage one after the other, because we considered that nothing so touches and stirs the people, and even the Companies, who always stand by the people, as variety in the scene." In all such passages Retz openly shows himself as a dramatic author or a skilful *impresario* who mounts his piece. He was even then of the race of those who in the matter of turmoils and revolutions like the play better than the *dénouement;* great artists in intrigues and influences take delight in them ; whereas, the more ambitious men, the more true, the more practical, look to the object and aspire to results. There are places where, while reading these Memoirs of Retz through the charming scenes so well marshalled under his pen, he seems less at war with Mazarin than in harmony with Molière.

Nevertheless, let us not exaggerate this view to the point of overlooking what there was of real and serious policy in the projects and views of Retz. And let us never forget this: Retz, after all, did not triumph; he failed in the purpose he pursued, which was to drive out Mazarin and himself replace him beside Anne of Austria. We know him to the full as agitator, frondeur, conspirator; but we do not know what he might have been as minister, or what he would have done in that new rôle. It would not have been the first time that a superior nature transformed itself on obtaining power and in using it; and it may even be that such a nature is not wholly

superior unless it has in it that which transforms and
renews it, that which suffices for great situations.
In Retz, as in Mirabeau, we see only the ardent struggle, the vast intrigue, and the plot that is torn in
twain. The man of the second epoch had, in both
of them, no career in which to develop himself.
Retz, in this comparison, has the disadvantage of
having survived; of being, as it were, present at the
miscarriage of all his hopes,—present as the de-
moralised, lowered, and defeated party, as may well
happen to the strongest natures who let their aim
escape them. Seeing the battle lost, base diversions
lay hold upon them in their hours of exile. It is in
his last years only that Retz recovers some dignity in
a retirement nobly borne; that he conveys an idea of
honesty by the complete payment of his vast debts;
and redeems himself to our eyes in the realm of mind
by the composition of his incomparable Memoirs. But,
in his Memoirs, Retz abandons action and practica-
bilities, and is, more and more, simply a writer, a
painter, a great artist; it is impossible for him henceforth to be anything else; and we arm ourselves easily
against what he was or might have become in other
days, with this last quality, which will for ever make
his fame.

I wished to slip in this observation because I always
wonder at the way that narrow and negative natures
hasten to say to all superior genius: "Thou hast never
done more than this in thy life, up to the present;

fortune has prevented thee from trying thyself in a
broader and freer career, consequently, thou couldest
not have done more than thou hast done." Such
persons have need to receive, from time to time,
a few flat contradictions, like that, for instance,
given them by Dumouriez in the defiles of the
Argonne.

As for Retz, there are, unfortunately, too many
reasons to assume that in him the adventurer, the
audacious *téméraire,* as Richelieu called him, was the
essential part and even the foundation of his nature;
and that it would at all times have compromised the
statesman, whose ideas he entered into with his mind
only. He belongs to those in whom humour rules
character; love of his own pleasure, licentiousness,
intrigue for intrigue's sake, a taste for disguises
and masquerades, a little too much Figaro, if I may
so express it, corrupted his serious aims, and destroyed, in practice, designs that his fine and impetuous genius was so capable of conceiving. Many
a time, he recognised this himself, he lacked good
sense in his purposes; there were times when he
blamed himself for not having "a grain of it"; he
was liable to be dazzled, to have flights of imagination from which men whose thoughts are to guide
and govern empires know how to protect themselves.
His contemporaries tell us this, and he himself says
it was so. When a La Rochefoucauld paints Retz,
and Retz agrees with him by recognising the chief

features of the portrait, we can only be silent, poor observers from afar, and bow low.

The second volume of Retz's Memoirs is the one that shows him to most advantage in the elevation of his political thought and in the charm of his pictures. There is no finer and no more truthful painting (I say truthful, for it is redolent of life itself) than that of the opening of the Regency of Anne of Austria and of the establishment, almost imperceptibly and by means of insinuation, of the power of Mazarin. The gentleness and facility of the first four years of the Regency, followed suddenly, and without apparent cause, by smothered discontent and the growl of a tempest, are described and interpreted on these pages in a manner to defy and baffle all future historians. I do not understand why M. Bazin, in reading them, did not instantly recognise and salute Retz as a master, confuting him, of course, in many cases where there was necessity. But any historian who meets at the start, on the subject of which he is treating, with such an observer and painter in a predecessor, and only finds ground to belittle and obliterate what he has left behind him, seems to me to give proof of an aggravating and cavilling spirit which excludes him from the broad road of the vocation. Observe that Retz, while painting, explains; the political and profound reason of things glides into the stroke of his brush.

After those first four years of the Regency, during

which the impulsion given by Richelieu continued to
send onward the vessel of State without the necessity
arising for any fresh instigation,—after those four years
of perfect quiet, of smiles and indulgence, they entered, without at first perceiving it, new waters;
a new breeze little by little made itself felt: the gust
of reforms, of revolutions. Whence came it? What
occasioned it? What were the slender grounds that
brought about so violent a shaking up? This is
what Retz excels in telling us, and those pages of
his Memoirs (which could well be entitled "How
Revolutions begin") remind us, by the elevation of
their tone and their firmness, both of Bossuet and of
Montesquieu.

"It is more than twelve hundred years that France
has had kings," says Retz, "but these kings have
not always been absolute to the point at which they
now are." Then, in a rapid and brilliant summary,
he seeks to show that, although the French monarchy
was never ruled and limited by written laws, or by
charters, like those of England and of Aragon, there
had always existed in former times a "wise medium" [*sage milieu*] "placed by our forefathers between the license of kings and the licentiousness
of peoples." That wise and golden mean, which in
France has always been more a condition of desire,
of regret or hope, than a state of actual reality, had a
certain shadow and effect of custom in the power
attributed to Parliament; and Retz shows all the wise

kings — Saint-Louis, Charles V, Louis XII, Henri IV,
— seeking to moderate their own power and surround it by the limits of law and justice. To the
contrary of this: all that we now call in the language
of to-day tendency to centralisation, all the efforts
of Louis XI, of Richelieu which were about to be
consummated under Louis XIV, all that would render
the monarchy sole master, seemed to Retz the road
to despotism. We cannot deny that it was pure
despotism until oneness in administration was joined
and combined, after '89 and after 1814, with a constitutional régime and liberty.

When the work was only half way, and done on
one side only, as in the time of Retz on the morrow
of Richelieu's death, this invasion without check of
the royal and ministerial power was surely despotism if ever there were any; and there is nothing
surprising that, in the interval of respite between
Richelieu and Louis XIV, the thought occurred to
oppose it and build, as it were, a dam with a sort
of constitution. That was the first serious thought
from which issued the Fronde; a thought which produced itself in the Parliaments only on occasions of
special grievance, and was then quickly swept aside
in the whirlwind of intrigues and personal ambitions. But Retz expresses it clearly in the beginning,
and Parliament confirmed it formally in its Declaration
of October 24, 1648 (a true Charter in embryo) which
it would be frivolous to misunderstand.

A man of much intelligence, and, what is even better, of sound and judicial mind, M. de Sainte-Aulaire, has made this view the leading idea of his "History of the Fronde." He has sought to disengage, in a way, the constitutional element, too often masked and perverted at the pleasure of factions. It seems sometimes as if M. Bazin had constructed his work on the same period of our history with the sole purpose of counteracting, step by step, the point of view of M. de Sainte-Aulaire. The opinions the two historians express on Retz are diametrically opposite. While M. Bazin leads us to see in him merely the wittiest, most selfish, and boastful of plotters, M. de Sainte-Aulaire seeks in his conduct and through all the tangle of detail a clue that is not solely that of a frivolous and factious ambition:

" Although," says M. de Sainte-Aulaire, " in writing his book Retz did not escape the influences I have just pointed out " [the reigning influences and the changes introduced into opinion by the establishment of Louis XIV's regime] " we find, nevertheless, the proof that he had seen all and comprehended all; that he had measured the dangers to which despotism was about to expose the monarchy, and that he sought to prevent them. My admiration for this great master has increased in copying the pictures drawn by his hand. . . ."

If this favourable judgment has its justification, it is more especially at the beginning of the Memoirs, at the origin of the Fronde.

Richelieu's rule had been so strong and so absolute, the prostration which it caused in the whole

14

body-politic was such, that no less than four or five years were needed for the *reaction* to be felt, for the public organs he had repressed to resume their office and seek to recover strength; and even then they did so, as usually happens, only on occasions of special measures that irritated them personally. Mazarin, a foreigner in France, a skilful negotiator outside of it, but with no idea of our political rights and maxims, followed, with slow steps, the path marked out by Richelieu; but he followed it without suspecting that it was "edged with precipices on all sides." He believed, above all else, in French levity, and saw nothing logical or consistent in it. He did not perceive that the peace of the first four years of the Regency was not real health; instead of husbanding means and preparing by remedies for the morrow, he continued in the old course; which aggravated disturbances and the sufferings of the interior of France: "The ill grew worse and worse," says Retz; "the head awoke; Paris felt itself, and sighed; no notice was taken of its sighs; it fell into frenzy. Let us now come to details." Do you not admire this opening, worthy of Bossuet, or, if you prefer it, of Montesquieu ?

There are, as we know, certain moments when physical diseases of like nature break forth at once in various lands; this is true of moral epidemics as well. The news of the revolution at Naples, that of the revolution in England, sent, as it were, a wind

of sedition to French minds. The vague humours of
public discontent are very quick, in hours of crises,
to be caught by emulation, letting the example of
a neighbour decide them, and taking the particular
form of malady that reigns and circulates. Retz understands and makes us understand all that admirably. Do not suppose that he understands seditions
and riots only; he comprehends and divines revolutions. He describes as an observer gifted with an
exquisite sensitiveness of tact, their period of on-
coming, so brusque sometimes, so unforeseen, and
yet so long in preparation. I know no finer page
of history than that in which he paints the sudden
passage from the discouragement and supineness of
minds, making them believe that present evils can
never end, to the contrary extreme where, far from
considering revolutions as impossible, they think
them, in a moment, simple and easy:

" And this disposition alone," he adds, " is sometimes capable of
making them. . . . Whoever had told us three months before
the *little dawn of troubles,* that a revolution could be born in a
State where the royal family was perfectly united, where the Court
was the slave of the minister to whom the provinces and the capital
were equally submissive, where the armies were victorious, where
the Guilds appeared at all points to be impotent — whoever had told
us that would have been thought insane, I do not say in the minds
of common people, but in those of the Estrées and the Seneterres " —

that is to say, the ablest of those who stood high
at Court.

That which follows takes us, as though we were
present, through all the degrees of that unexpected

awakening, soon to change to terror, consternation, and fury. He is like an inquiring physician writing down all the symptoms of the disease, the very disease he has always desired to study closely: evidently he would rather watch it than cure it.

" There seems a little sentiment," he says, in speaking of the depressed condition of the State, " a gleam, or rather a spark of life; and that sign of life, almost imperceptible in its beginnings, is not given by *Monsieur,* is not given by M. le Prince, is not given by the Nobles of the Kingdom, is not given by the Provinces; it is given by Parliament, which, until our day, had never begun a revolution, and which certainly would have condemned the bloody Decrees it made itself, if any others than itself had made them. It grumbled over the Edict of the Tariff (1647); and no sooner had it merely murmured than everybody waked up. They searched about, groping, as they woke, for the laws; they could not find them; they were alarmed, they shouted, they demanded them; and, in this agitation, the questions to which their excitement gave birth, from obscure as they were and venerable through their obscurity, became problematical; and hence, in the opinion of half the country, odious. The people entered the sanctuary; they raised the veil which should always cover whatever can be said and whatever can be believed about the rights of the people and the rights of kings, which never accord so well together as they do through silence. The hall of the Palais profaned these mysteries. Let us now come to particular facts that will make you see this matter with your eye."

Those are the exordiums that count for much in history. The man who under Louis XIV, at the age of fifty-eight, wrote these things in solitude, in privacy, addressing them by way of pastime to a woman among his friends, had certainly in his mind and in his imagination serious ideas of the essence of societies, and a grandeur of political conception. He had too often changed them and tarnished them in practice; but pen in hand, as often happens to writers of genius, he grasped them again with clearness, brilliancy, and amplitude.

With all historical personages we should fasten first upon their great aspects; I know not if I shall have time to note all the weaknesses, all the infirmities, all the shames even, of Retz and brand them; but I should blame myself if I did not from the start point out in him the manifest signs of superiority and force which capture admiration the more we approach him. I have not yet reached the end of them.

Retz, who to us, because we know his life and his confessions, seems a most scandalous ecclesiastic, did not seem such in his lifetime to those of his cloth, or to his flock. He explains, with a frankness that nothing equals, the means he took to procure respect among the clergy and favour among his people, not only as a man of party but in his quality as archbishop, without in the least retrenching his secret vices and weaknesses. Astonishing as this may seem, we are forced to recognise that respect and consideration remained with him as long as he lived and in spite of all he did to impair it. Learned man, or skilful enough to make himself appear so, careful administrator, always ready to defend the rights and prerogatives of his Order, excellent and eloquent preacher, prodigal in alms for all purposes, he had a dual reputation, and his adventures of every kind, in politics and intrigues, were never able, thanks to the incomplete publicity of those days, to shake his good fame in the Île-Saint-Louis nor yet in the quarter of Saint-Jacques. The Jansenist party, then flourishing, was very favourable to him: "I had much esteem for devout persons," he says, "and in their eyes, that is one of the great points of piety." There was no hypocrisy properly so called in this; for that is a degrading vice; but he profited by the disorder of the times, the dispensations of an extraordinary situation, relying at the same time on prejudices that walled in minds. It may even be believed, as he has very well explained to us, that in peaceful times, his reputation of archbishop would have been more damaged, for he would then have found it difficult to conceal his vices and irregularities, whereas they were lost in the inevitable confusion of civil war.

The fact from which we augur that Retz could never have been any thing than what he was, is the enthusiasm with which he allowed himself to be swept, from the very first days of the troubles, into the rôle of popular leader. He was persuaded "that greater qualities are needed to form a good leader of a party than to make a good emperor of the universe." That title "Leader of a party" was what he had always most honoured in "Plutarch's Lives"; and when he saw that matters were becoming embroiled to the point of allowing him to come naturally into the rôle, he felt a tickling of his feelings, an emotion of vainglory, which seem to indicate that he conceived of nothing nobler or more delightful. He was about to swim in his element.

When Saint-Simon, in his day, describes to us the delights and thrillings he experienced in being able to observe the faces and expressions of the courtiers under the great circumstances that lay bare secret passions and intentions, he does not express himself with a keener sense of delectation than does Retz when he shows us his joy at the thought of seizing the rôle so coveted. We may well conclude that one was in his element as observer, the other as agitator; both artists in their own way, and consoled, after all, by their imaginations when the opportunity came to them to relate their past pleasure and describe it.

In the second volume of the Memoirs there is an admirable conversation between Retz and the Prince de Condé who, returning victorious from Lens, was really the arbiter of the situation. The double rôle of restorer of the public weal and preserver of the royal authority tempted, at first, the lofty and luminous mind of Condé; but Retz, in a wonderful manner, makes us understand how the prince could not hold to it, being too impatient. "Heroes have their defects; that of M. le Prince was that there was not enough persistency in one of the finest minds in the world." Then, going farther, Retz points out to us in what that lack of persistency consisted. On the return of the army, finding Parliament in a struggle with the Court, the glory of "restorer of the public weal" was the first idea of the Prince de Condé, that of "preserver of the royal authority" was the second. But, while seeing both things equally, he did not feel them equally. Balancing between the two ideas, and even seeing them together, he could not weigh them together. He passed from one to the other: thus, that which seemed to him on one day to be the lightest seemed the weightiest on the morrow. The exalted manner in which Retz estimates the Prince de Condé at that moment and his first intentions before they deflected and were embittered in the struggle deserves that we apply the same form of judgment to himself. He says at every turn enough evil of that self to make us believe in his sincerity when he shows himself in another light.

Wishing to convince the Prince de Condé that there was a great and incomparable rôle to play in this crisis between the magistracy and the Court, wishing to temper his impatience and his wrath in regard to Parliament, and to prove to him that, prince of the blood and victor as he was, he could, with a little address, handle and insensibly govern the great Assembly, Retz in a conversation he held with him at the hôtel de Condé (December, 1648) rises to the highest views of statesmanship, to views which outran the times, while at the same moment he keeps in sight that which was practicable then. The Prince, irritated by the opposition he meets at every step in the deliberations and resolutions of the Assembly, was

returning to his instincts, that were very slightly parliamentary, and threatening to bring to reason those
"square caps," as he did the populace, with mailed
hand and force. To which Retz replied, with a pro-
phetic instinct of '89:

" Is not Parliament the idol of the people? I know that you count
them for nothing because the Court is armed; but I beg you to let me
tell you that *they ought to be counted for much each time that they
count themselves as all. They are now at that point.* They are
beginning themselves to count your armies for nothing; and the *misfortune is that their strength consists in their imagination: and it
may with truth be said that, unlike all other powers, they can, when
they have arrived at a certain point, do all they think they can do.*"

Cardinal de Retz, we see, knew as much and as far
on the strength of Tiers-État as the Abbé de Sieyès.
Looking back to former ages and to the spirit that then
existed, he defines in singularly happy terms the ancient and vague Constitution of France which he calls
"the mystery of the State." "Each monarchy has its
own" he says, "that of France consists in the religious and sacred silence in which is buried, while
obeying, nearly always blindly, the kings, the right
the people will not believe they have to dispense with
kings, except on occasions when it is not their duty
even to please them." He makes us see how latterly,
on the Court side, they had, with signal clumsiness,
put Parliament under the necessity of defining the
cases in which it might disobey, and those in which
it could not do so. " It was a miracle that Parliament did not at last lift that veil, and did not lift it

formally and by Decree; which would have been far more dangerous and more fatal in its consequences than the freedom of the people have taken of late to look through it."

The conclusion of this memorable speech is an endeavour to reconcile Condé with the Parliament, without absolutely separating him from the Court, and the proposal of a useful, innocent, and needed rôle, which should make him the protector of the public and of the sovereign guilds, and would infallibly eliminate Mazarin: in this he reckoned without the queen's heart. However that may have been, it was a noble dialogue carried on with frankness by the two speakers, about to become adversaries. The parts of the two men, the characters and language are kept distinct. Condé and Retz parted, each holding his own opinion but with esteem for the other; one, for the Court, deciding, after weighing all, to defend it; the other remaining Coadjutor and, above all, the defender of Paris.

Many quarrels, treacheries, insulting outrages happening later lowered the nobleness of this first explanation and soiled its memory; nevertheless, one takes pleasure, when reading it, in thinking that those great minds, those impetuous and misguided hearts, were not originally as evil-intentioned nor as given over to their selfish and perverse ends as they seemed to be later, when the passions and cupidities of each were unchained. One of the greatest evils of civil war is to corrupt even the best and most generous of those who enter upon them. That was true of the Prince de Condé; that was true of even Retz.

He himself has taken care to point out to us the precise moment, very near to this conversation, when he determined to deliver himself wholly up to his passion and to his hatred of Mazarin (January, 1649): "When I saw," he says, "that the Court would not accept even good except in his way, which was never good, I thought of nothing but of how to do him harm; and it was not until this moment that I made a full and complete resolution to attack Mazarin personally." From that day, all means were good to him to win success — arms, pamphlets, calumnies. Here begins the gala; henceforth, he thinks of nothing but of continuing "master of the ball" as Mazarin himself very aptly said.

It was at this moment that Retz, artist that he is pen in hand, considering that he has issued from the preamble or vestibule of his subject, gives himself free way, and, having up to that time sketched his personages only in profile, he now shows them full face and full length, as if in a gallery. He makes no less than seventeen portraits in a series, all admirable for life, brilliancy, delicacy, and resemblance; even impartiality is there when he paints his enemies. Among these portraits, of which not one is less than a masterpiece, we note, above all, those of the queen, of Gaston, Duc d'Orléans, of the Prince de Condé,

M. de Turenne, M. de La Rochefoucauld, Mme. de Longueville and her brother the Prince de Conti, Mme. de Chevreuse, Mme. de Montbazon, and finally, Mathieu Molé. This gallery, the portraits of which, repeated and reproduced a hundred times, fill all our histories, are the glory of the French brush; and we may say that, before Saint-Simon, nothing else had been written more vivid, more striking, more marvellously lifelike. Even in comparison with Saint-Simon, nothing pales in this gallery of Retz; we admire the difference of manner, something more concise, more clear, freer perhaps in colour, but not less penetrating into the quick of souls: M. le Prince, to whom "nature had given a mind as great as his heart, but whom Fortune did not allow to show the one to its full extent as plainly as he did the other, and who was *never able to fulfil his own merit*"; M. de Turenne, to whom no fine qualities were lacking "but those he had never thought of," and to whom we should deny none, "for who knows? he had in everything, even in his speech, *certain obscurities* which only developed as opportunity offered, and then developed only to his glory"; Mme. de Longueville, whose "languor of manner touched more than the brilliancy of those who were more beautiful. She had the same in her mind, which charmed, *for it had awakenings both luminous and surprising.*" I should like to quote all, to repeat all in these pictures of a touch both strong and captivating.

Coming after the fine and statesmanlike conversation with the Prince de Condé, after the marvellous scenes of comedy in the first days of the Barricades, after the grand and lofty considerations that precede them, these portraits form an introduction to his subject, and a unique exposition which will last even if the rest of the pieces fade.

Retz's style is that of our finest language; it is full of fire, and the spirit of everything circulates through it. The language itself is of that manner, slightly anterior to Louis XIV, which unites to grandeur a supreme air of elegance that makes its grace. The expression is readily gay, picturesque as it flows, always true to French genius, yet full of imagination, and sometimes of magnificence. Speaking of an imprisoned magistrate whose release the insurrectionists demanded from the Court, and who was set at liberty: "They would not lay down their arms," says Retz, "till their object was secured; even Parliament did not give a Decree to lay them down, until it saw Broussel in his place. He returned to it on the morrow, or rather he was borne to it on the heads of the people with incredible acclamations." I do not inquire whether the expression is proportioned to Broussel's importance; but how faithfully it renders the impression, the enthusiasm of the moment! Retz, as you can well suppose, is not the dupe of it; and immediately showing us Paris after its Broussel is restored to it, as "more tranquil than

I ever saw it on a Good Friday" he makes us feel the contrasting absurdity without expressing it.

"The Court felt itself hit in the very pupil of its eye," he says, àpropos of the suppression of intendants, discussed in the collective assembly of the Courts of Parliament; he is full of such lively and perceptive expressions. At other times he expands his images agreeably. He excels in giving to words their full value of meaning, all their quality, and he sometimes makes it better felt in thus developing it. After having said that President Molé was " all of a piece," a good but common expression, he adds: " President de Mesmes, who was at least as well intentioned to the Court as he, but who had more insight, more *jointure,* whispered in his ear. . . ." There is an instance of how a new expression is legitimately created, how it is drawn from some ordinary term. Retz's pen does many such things without taking heed of them, without even thinking of them. He had the gift of speech, and that which pictured itself in his mind made but one bound on to his paper. I ought to add that there are many inequalities in his volumes. The last are languid; the first are strewn, even to affectation (the only instance of it) with political maxims that Chesterfield said were the only just and the only practical ones he had ever seen printed. They would teach experience, if experience were ever learned from books. They at least recall it, and sum it up in a striking manner for those who have seen and lived.

I am astonished that many persons find in these Memoirs of Retz instigations to civil disorders and seditious intrigue. Rightly read, they are more likely to give a disgust for them. But every man reads with his own humour and his own imagination even more than with his judgment. What is well told is seductive, though the thing told may be detestable, and the relator, after the first moment of enthusiasm is past, may not attempt to embellish it.

We will not confine ourselves to the opening of the Memoirs, as so many people do; let us go farther and follow the skilful rebel beyond that honeymoon of the Fronde. What hindrances! what impossibilities! what meannesses! what shame! On the morrow of the Barricades, the queen-regent, the young king, with Mazarin and the Court having fled from Paris (January, 1649), what will the Coadjutor, the tribune of the people, the master of the pavements do? he, having for ally on one side Parliament, that machine so little easy to guide, and on the other those princes of the blood and the nobles of the kingdom (the Bouillons, the Contis, the Longuevilles), who had joined the faction with personal objects only.

Among the numerous pamphlets published at this date, one is rather curious, with an official character, and has for its title: "Contract of Marriage between

Parliament and the City of Paris." It is a species of
Charter under the form of contract and in the style of
a notary. We read in it the aspiration and the programme of the opening moments of the Fronde: "In
the name of God the Creator," it is declared that "the
wise and illustrious seigneur, the Parliament of Paris,
takes for wife and legitimate spouse the powerful and
good dame, the City of Paris, as likewise the said dame
takes etc., etc., to be, the said seigneur and dame,
joined and united perpetually and indissolubly." The
couple pledge themselves to be henceforth "one and
in common as to all their desires, actions, passions,
and interests whatsoever," for the greatest good of the
State and for the preservation of the king and the
kingdom. Then follows a list of the principal clauses
agreed upon by the contracting parties:

"That God shall be always served and honoured, feared and loved
as he should be.

"That all atheists, ungodly, licentious and sacrilegious persons shall
be punished in an exemplary manner, and exterminated wholly.

"That vices, crimes, and scandals shall be corrected as much as possible, etc.

"That the good of the State and the preservation of the king and
the kingdom shall be," etc.

I abridge. But behind these first articles which are
merely for show and blazon, come others far more
essential, for instance: that in view of the tender age
of the young king the Parliament of Paris shall select
for the government of the State illustrious persons,
drawn from the three classes, clergy, nobles, and mag-

istrates, who shall be, after the princes of the blood, the natural councillors and ministers of the Regency. In short, the effect of all the articles is, that Parliament should govern during the minority; that when it demanded the dismissal of any minister or councillor there should be no opposition; that an exemplary reform be introduced into the management of the finances, into the distribution of benefices, into appointments to the various offices, into the levying and collecting of taxes; in short, that "the poor people shall be effectively and really relieved, that order in all things shall be restored, and the reign of justice fully re-established in all the provinces of the kingdom."

The conclusion and the end to which the whole necessarily comes is that Cardinal Mazarin was incompatible with this golden age, this reign of Justice upon the earth, and that "he shall be incessantly prosecuted until he be brought under the arm of the Law to be publicly and exemplarily executed."

The final clause is thus worded :

"For thus have promised and sworn the said seigneur Parliament and the said dame City of Paris on the Holy Gospels and before the church of Notre-Dame, in the month of January in the year one thousand six hundred and forty-nine, and is signed," etc.

It was Retz himself who, in his character of Coadjutor, gave the benediction to this famous marriage which presented itself under such magnificent auspices. But what did he think of it himself?

During the first weeks we can see the idea he had

15

of the real state of affairs in the shrewd and very serious conversations he held with the Duc de Bouillon, Turenne's elder brother, and the best head among the nobles who had joined the faction. Retz, who knows his Paris better than any one, lays bare to the Duc de Bouillon all the divisions and the probable causes of ruin: "The bulk of the people that are firm," he says, "keeps us from perceiving as yet the dislocation of parties." But he himself feels this dislocation, *disunion,* to be very near if care is not taken, and he lays his finger upon it better in his words than by his acts. Less than six weeks after the breaking out of the first Fronde, he said, energetically:

"A people are weary some time before they perceive that they are so. The hatred against Mazarin sustained and covered that weariness. We divert their minds by our satires, our verses, our songs; the blare of trumpets, drums and cymbals, the sight of flags and banners rejoice the shops in the streets, but, after all, are the taxes paid with the same punctuality as at first?"

The taxes — there 's the delicate point to which one must always return if one wants to organise any kind of order on the morrow of a revolt; and the first cry of a revolt is that it is made in behalf of a relief that is often impossible to grant.

Retz reveals to the Duc de Bouillon his whole policy under the first Fronde, and we must do him this justice: if he was seditious, he was only half so. In concert with the Duc de Beaufort, he made himself master of the populace, he held it in his hand

and it proved but a phantom; he is the idol of the
churches as the duke was of the markets.   But he
will not abuse "this mania of the people," he says,
"for M. de Beaufort and for me."   He resists firmly
the idea of doing without the Parliament, of crushing
it by the people, of "purging it" violently, as some
advised.   Such proceedings of the days of the League
horrify him; he leaves such things to the Seize and
to sanguinary ambitions.   He has no less horror of
them than of Cromwell, whose advances he repulsed,
just as he objected at all times to a close and complete
union with Spain.

It was not that he concealed from himself the
hidden intentions of Parliament or the proceedings of
its companies; in spite of the fine words that are said
on great occasions, "the foundation of the spirit of
Parliament is peace, and it never gets far from it
except by fits and starts," which are quickly followed
by returns.   He knows that that Assembly, the slave
to rules and formulas, understands no way of making
war except by Decrees and by bailiffs; that the loudest thunders of its eloquence end in nothing more
than inquests and edicts; that nothing can prevent it
from adjourning when midday and five o'clock, the
sacramental hours for dinner and supper, strike.   In
vain may Retz have "the lanterns" (the tribunes of
those days) for him; in vain does he have the young
heads in Parliament, and the bench of Inquests at his
feet; that "holy mob," as he calls it, which knows

so well how to shout when the word of command is
given, can do nothing in Parliament, where President
Molé is not to be led.

What Retz would fain have had, to act upon the
mind of that Assembly, to excite it sufficiently without oppressing it, was an army, not in Paris but outside of Paris; an army, a veritable army in the service
of the Fronde; he could have cried, like the Abbé
Sieyès: "Oh for a sword!" At one moment he
thought he had that of M. de Turenne; he might
have chosen worse; but it failed him. According to
his idea, an army at some distance and a general of
renown would act upon Parliament and give him
needed energy without threatening it; whereas the
action of the populace of Paris is too dangerous, too
immediate. Retz, who has it at his disposal, fears to
employ it, for such blind forces are apt to strike without warning. "That is the fate and the misfortune
of popular powers," he remarks; "they are not believed in till they make themselves felt; and it is very
often to the interest and even to the honour of those
in whose hands they are to make them less felt than
believed in."

The other evils of the civil war that he himself had
lighted Retz confesses without reserve. One of the
first articles of the Contract of Marriage between
Parliament and the City of Paris was, as we have
seen, that atheists and licentious persons should be
repressed and punished; but one of the actual effects

of the Fronde was to let loose licentiousness, a mortal injury to any state of things that seeks to establish and consolidate itself. Speaking of the debauchery of Fontrailles, Matha, and other free-thinkers:

"Their table songs," he says, "did not always spare the good God; I cannot express to you the trouble such follies gave me. President Molé knew very well how to put them in evidence, the people did not really think them good in any way, the clergy were scandalised to the last degree. I could not cover them, I dared not excuse them, and the odium fell, of course, on the Fronde."

Farther on he says: "We had an interest in not stifling the libels and ballads that were made against the cardinal, but we had no less an interest in suppressing those against the queen, and sometimes against religion and the State. No one can imagine the trouble the heated minds of the people gave us in this matter." This was how they kept to the first article of their Contract of Marriage! In short, every page of the Memoirs only confirms this truth: "the greatest misfortune of civil war is that we are responsible for the evil that we do not do."

But, once committed, they are compelled to do it. In more than one case, Retz finds himself compromised and just escapes being discredited with the people and with the hot-heads in Parliament by opposing absurd measures or acts of rapine and vandalism, such as the sale of Cardinal Mazarin's library. He is quickly obliged to repair these good promptings by himself proposing some folly; this is what shows very naturally, he says, "the extravagance of such

periods, when all the fools go mad and it is no longer
possible for people of sense to speak or act wisely."

After the first Fronde was pacified and before the
second broke out, Retz seems to have had, at moments, a sincere intention to reform and become once
more an honest man and a faithful subject; but his
past reputation weighed upon him, also his acquired
habits, and before long he was again involved in
the ways of sedition.   They distrusted him at Court,
and this suspicion provoked him in the end to justify
anew that distrust.   In all his relations with Queen
Anne of Austria there happened to Retz what happened to Mirabeau in his relations with Queen Marie
Antoinette.   He felt there was no reliance placed
upon him; that he was taken solely from a necessity
of the occasion.   He was a man who would have
felt a wholly generous treatment by the queen, or
even by Mazarin, and one of his keenest grievances
against the latter was that, with plenty of mind, he
was absolutely lacking in generosity and soul, and
that, supposing others to be like himself, he never
believed they would give him advice with good
intentions.

Like Mirabeau, Retz could render services to the
queen only by maintaining his credit with the multitude; and to maintain that credit he had to do os-
tensibly certain acts and make certain speeches that
savoured of sedition, and seemed the exact opposite
of the engagements he had just taken.   It was only

too easy to make cause against him at Court and to present him as a traitor and renegade, at the very moment when he was merely employing the means at his command for a secret end that was honourable.

At the time of the multiplied conferences that he had at night with the queen in the Palais-Royal and elsewhere, it is to be supposed that in those mysterious oratories where she received him in order to confer more freely, he tried to interest the woman in the queen; that he looked often at her beautiful hands, of which Mme. de Motteville tells us, that at times he replied with a dreamy, abstracted air to questions of even policy; but the queen's coquetry was not caught by such wiles; her heart was fixed. Retz felt he could never displace Mazarin. But he was not, it would seem, quick enough in feeling it, and he continued to act outside as if he still had hope of getting the cardinal finally sent away. A jest which he allowed to escape him against the queen and which came to her ears (he called her *Suissesse*) irritated her as a woman and contributed more, perhaps, to her final vengeance than the political infidelities of the man could have done.

He always denied that he aspired to the ministry, and the reasons he gave are energetic enough to strike us, if not to convince us. To one of these advances, true or false, that were made to him, he replied that "he was very incapable of the ministry for all sorts of reasons, and that it was even not for the queen's dignity to raise to that post a man who was *still hot and smoking, so to speak, with faction.''* Elsewhere, he opens himself on this point with a tone of sincerity even more fitted to convince us; this was at the close of the second Fronde, in which he pursued a very different line of conduct from that he followed in the first; nevertheless that first reputation as an ambitious man with a mailed hand followed him always.

" Is it possible," people said, ascribing to him a yearning for the ministry, " is it possible that Cardinal de Retz is not content with being at his age " (he was thirty-seven) " cardinal and archbishop of Paris ? And how did he get into his mind that the first place in the king's council is to be conquered by force of arms ? " — " I know," he adds, " that even to-day the miserable gazettes which treat of that period are full of these ridiculous ideas "; and he speaks of those ideas as being very far from his; " I do not say this by force of reason only, but I say it from my own inclination, which leads me with such eagerness to pleasure and to fame. . . ." And he concludes that the ministry was even less to his taste than within his reach: " I do not know if I am making my excuses to you," he writes, addressing Mme. de Caumartin; " at any rate, I do not think that I am writing you my eulogy."

This fame, this point of honour, of which Retz speaks so often, and which he felt after his fashion, lay in winning a certain popular reputation, the favour and love of the public; in being faithful to his promises to friends; in seeming never to yield to direct self-interest. Towards the end, his whole doctrine of resistance seems to have been little more than a wager of honour against Mazarin.

The second Fronde (1650–1652) broke out, as we

know, in the name of the princes of Condé, whom
Mazarin had put in prison and was presently obliged
to release. In this second period of the troubles Cardinal de Retz, far from being an agitator and a firebrand,
as too generally believed, was rather a negotiator and
moderator, barely listened to. *Monsieur*, Gaston, Duc
d'Orléans, lieutenant-general of the kingdom, was
seized with a sudden confidence in him, and made
him his intimate counsellor. But when we reflect on
what *Monsieur* was, timid, distrustful, dissimulating,
changing his opinion many times a day, whistling
when he did not know what to say, and employing
his whole mind in hiding his cowardice by inventing
creep-holes, we can readily explain to ourselves the
perplexity and daily embarrassments of Retz. The
weakness of *Monsieur* had various degrees and
"stages," he tells us, and he makes us measure and
count them, one by one. "In him, *fancies* and *will,
will* and *resolution, resolution* and *choice of means,
choice of means* and their *application* were very far
apart. But what was more extraordinary, it happened
quite often that he stopped short in the *middle of the
application.*"

Placed between a prince of this nature and Parliament (that other complicated machine, not less dis-
heartening to influence) ranked in the party by the
Prince de Condé, then his enemy, and whose triumph
he could not desire, Retz consumed himself during
two years in parleys, expedients, the perpetual

attempts of an impotent third party to come to birth, resulting always in miscarriage. What wise maxims he strews, to no purpose, along the way! What penetrating glances on the truths of the situation and the wretchedness of parties! How many times did he not have occasion to cry out as he quitted the sessions of Parliament: "Nothing is more *mob* than these Assemblies! . . . The wisest among them seem as mad as the populace, and the populace seems to me more mad than ever." The gaiety of certain parts of his narrative covers very incompletely his disgust at this anarchic, inconsistent régime, which those who had plunged into it could not, from a too common optical illusion, perceive.

Retz, whom nothing escapes, is nauseated by it, again and again. We ask ourselves, in reading him, how it was that some fine morning, a good sentiment, a rush of energetic sound sense, of integrity, were it even no more than a fit of impatience and weariness, did not decide him to break, once for all, with that inextricable complication of intrigues, henceforth without object and without issue. Here it is that the vices of the man come into line and find their profit. Retz, while judging the depth of the things he despises, did not dislike the game nor the gambling. He had brought himself to a disorderly and licentious manner of living. Every evening, the hôtel de Chevreuse, or some other clandestine amusement, consoled him for his daily annoyances and for the ruin of the

State. Such, in men of superior minds, is the evil of
vices; they quench good aspirations at their source
and prevent them from coming to birth. The time
came at last when Retz, retiring, toward the end of
the troubles, into his cloister of Notre-Dame, withdrawn into the shadow of his cathedral towers,
sheltered, as he says, by the hat, hesitated, with all
his lights and his worldly generosities, to do a public
act that would hasten the issue and put an end to
the universal suffering. He brought himself to do it,
however, and was one of the chief negotiators for the
return of the Court to Paris.

For this he was poorly thanked; his past reputation
clung to him, not without cause, and he was treated
solely on political grounds; that is to say, having
used him in the first moments they imprisoned him
in the next.

His imprisonment, his flight, his stay in Rome, his
journeys, his career of dissipation in divers regions,
his obstinacy to the last in retaining his see of the
archbishopric of Paris, supply us with too many
aspects of his frailties and the weaker side of his
nature. One of his counsellors and servants, Gui
Joly, has given us in his Memoirs very shameful
details, which may be true as to material facts, but
which are false inasmuch as they are solely base,
which Retz was not. He had in him certain generous parts that never perished, and of which he gave
proof in his old age, after his return to France. His

peace made, and his pardon obtained, he had permission, after a rather long stay in his seigneurie in Lorraine, to reappear in Paris and at Fontainebleau (1664). There he once more met all his friends and many of his enemies, with whom he reconciled himself frankly. We now find a Cardinal de Retz quite different (save for beauty of mind) to what he had hitherto appeared. "If he lived like a Catiline in his youth," says Voltaire, "in his old age he lived like Atticus."

It is Mme. de Sévigné who best enables us to know Cardinal de Retz after his return and makes us like him.   She is inexhaustible on that subject.   Retz had won her by showing an especial affection for Mme. de Grignan.   If he came to Paris without seeing her he was not to be comforted: "You make him wish for the Pope's death," writes Mme. de Sévigné. When the Pope died, Cardinal de Retz did not fail to go to the Conclave to sedulously serve the interests of Louis XIV, and, as he passed through Provence, he was able to see Mme. de Grignan.   Though not of advanced age, being still under sixty, he was much worn out in health.   Mme. de Sévigné worked with all her might to entertain him:

"We try to amuse our good cardinal," she writes (March 9, 1672). "Corneille read him a play that is to be acted before long; it reminded him of the classics; Molière is to read him *Trissotin* on Saturday, which is a very amusing thing; Despréaux [Boileau] is to give him his *Lutrin* and his *Poétique ;* that is all we can do to serve him."

Incomparable and for ever blessed age, in which the

illustrious shipwrecked in politics had, by way of consolation, in one week a Corneille, a Boileau and a Moliére in the flesh, their works in hand, and Mme. de Sévigné above all to tell of it!

This man who, as I have said, had never been more than half-seditious, and by no means a Catiline, as Voltaire calls him, and who, in his greatest rebellion, had always respected (in all that regarded the royal authority) what he called "the claim of the sanctuary," had now become the most reconciled and the most zealous of the French cardinals for the interests of Louis XIV. In spite of his increasing infirmities, he made three journeys to Rome (in 1667, 1669, and 1676) to support and make effective in the Conclave the intentions of the king.

In 1675, he was seized with an idea which seemed extraordinary, and caused great wonder among his contemporaries: it was to renounce the hat, and strip himself of the dignity of cardinal, to go and live in Lorraine in absolute solitude. The policy of Rome and that of France united to oppose a sort of renunciation which might have become a precedent and, in the future, a political means in the hands of the powers. Retz was forced to resign himself to keep the hat and to remain for his friends the "very good cardinal." He reduced his expenses by a great deal with the laudable object of paying all his debts, on which he staked his honour. This last and brusque idea of a solemn humility which looked like repentance, gave rise to much talk and various opinions:

"I see none, thank God," writes Mme. de Sévigné (July 24, 1675), "but those who view his action in all its beauty, and who love him as we do. His friends do not wish him to nail himself at Saint-Mihiel; they advise him to go to Commercy and sometimes to Saint-Denis. He will keep his equipage for the honour of the purple; and I gaily persuade that his life is not ended."

Every one, on this occasion, wrote to him to compliment him on the grandeur of his action. The exiled Bussy-Rabutin, who judged that action more philosophically, wrote him, nevertheless, a letter full of eulogy. Mme. de Sévigné advised her daughter to write to him on the subject and renew their correspondence by that means: "In writing to him this first letter, do not, believe me, feel too constrained; if some nonsense flows off the tip of your pen he will be as charmed as with things more serious: the solid foundation of religion does not forbid such little *trimmings.*"

Better or worse than *trimmings* were the Memoirs in which the cardinal took secret delight, and which, at this date, he had just completed in obedience to Mme. de Caumartin, who asked him for the narrative of his life. It is difficult to admit that the man who wrote them was the least in the world touched by a single religious thought. And yet, as it is supposed that the last parts were written towards this period, 1675–1676, it would be rash to say that thoughts of that kind did not end by germi-

nating in the soul of Cardinal de Retz. Suffice it
that several of his contemporaries, those who approached him closely, seem to have believed in his
final persuasion of Christianity and a future life,
enough, at any rate, to impose upon us respect and
reserve on that vital point.

Towards the end, Retz amused his leisure at Commercy by conversing and discoursing on the philosophy of Descartes, then in its greatest vogue. A
certain Dom Robert Desgabets, prior of the abbey
of Breuil, situated in a faubourg of Commercy, was
a semi-emancipated Carthusian who assumed to
rectify nature. Dom Hennezon, abbé of Saint-Mihiel,
three leagues distant, disapproved of these pretended
rectifications of Dom Desgabets. Hence a regular
philosophical dispute, in which the disputants took
the good cardinal as umpire. M. Cousin has published the very judicious and prudent decision of
Retz. His conclusion on the fundamental question
of this metaphysic was, all points being carefully examined, that " *no one knew anything about it.*" This
great *frondeur* who, in his youth, had tried in vain to
hold the scales between all parties, between *Monsieur,*
the Parliament and the Court, and who, in default
of scales had taken the sword, and taken it even
against the Prince de Condé, came in his old age to
this innocent arbitrament.

The retirement of Cardinal de Retz into Lorraine did
not last long; he returned to his abbey of Saint-Denis.

The scoffers tattled, and tried to see in this return an infraction of his great design. Mme. de Sévigné has amply justified him:

"You know," she writes to Bussy, who asked nothing better than to be one of the scoffers (June 27, 1678), "you know that he has paid off eleven hundred thousand crowns. He received from no one this example, and no one will follow it. In short, we must trust him in order to maintain our wager. He is much more regular than he was in Lorraine. Those who want to be rid of him can be so as much at Saint-Denis as if he had stayed at Commercy."

He died August 24, 1678, tenderly regretted by Mme. de Sévigné, and praised by her in terms that are the finest of funeral orations, leaving us an idea of the most amiable of men, of easy intercourse, a delightful and perfect friend. Thus ended, with sweetness and dignity, one who never had within him that which was necessary to make him a complete revolutionist; and one who, in his boldest schemes, always stopped half-way on this side of Cromwell or Machiavelli. I mark this as being at once a defect and a claim to eulogy.

An idea has entered my mind within the last few minutes,—I cannot resist expressing it. We are reaching an epoch of desires and prayers; I will offer mine—

May all factious persons, all agitators, all those who have passed their lives in stirring up parliaments and people, end them as sweetly and decently as did Cardinal de Retz; may they range themselves, as he did, under the law of necessity and of their period; play,

like him, at whist when growing old, at the philosophy of their time (if there be still a philosophy);
continue, or become again, perfectly amiable; converse
with the Sévignés, if they meet any; and, in writing
their Memoirs, fill them, as he did, with the maxims
of experience, rendering them piquant, amusing, instructive, but not so captivating that they instil a
desire to imitate and renew their follies.

16

VII.

Mademoiselle de l' Enclos.

VII.

Mademoiselle de l'Enclos.

" Ninon."

THERE is no better introducer to Ninon than
Saint-Évremond, an amiable wise man, a
mind of the first quality for good sense, and
one that can enter into all the graces. His natural
character is one of easy superiority; I cannot define
him better than by calling him a sort of softened
Montaigne. His mind is distinguished alike for its
firmness and its delicacy; his soul is never forced out
of itself or its habits. He felt the passions, he let them
come to birth; up to a certain point, he nurtured
them, but he never blindly gave way to them; even
in yielding he did so with discernment and restraint.
In his youth he had been, like all the flower of the
Court, in Ninon's train, her lover a little, and much her
friend; he corresponded with her at times throughout
his long exile; the small number of authentic letters
that we have by Ninon are addressed to Saint-Évremond, and they make us know her on the mental
side, the only side on which she deserves to survive.

245

Saint-Évremond requires a Study on himself alone; to-day all I ask of him is the favour of being introduced into the intimacy of a woman, who, through a long life, renewed her charm so many times, and whose mind continued to perfect itself even to the end.

Saint-Évremond, born in 1613, was three years older than Ninon, who was born in 1616; he died in 1703 at an age of over ninety, and she in 1705 at the same age, less a few months. His life divides itself into two very distinct halves. Until he was forty-eight he led, in France, at Court, with the army, a brilliant and active existence, esteemed by all the great generals, and on the road to some distinguished military fortune. A long letter of his, very witty and very malicious, on the Treaty of the Pyrenees and against Cardinal Mazarin, found among the papers of Mme. Duplessis-Bellière at the time of Fouquet's arrest, irritated Louis XIV, who gave orders to put the writer in the Bastille. Warned in time, Saint-Évremond left France, took refuge in Holland, then in England, where he lived, forty-two years longer, the life of an observer and philosopher; much enjoyed and sought by the highest society, seeing all that was best in foreign lands, and bearing his exile with real pride and apparent indifference. A thing that contributed much to soften it was the arrival in England of the beautiful Duchesse de Mazarin, Hortense Mancini, the niece of the very man who was the original cause of his misfortune. He attached himself to her, and loved

MADEMOISELLE DE L'ENCLOS.
From a steel engraving.

her for her mind and her solid qualities as much as for her beauty. All the nieces of the cardinal had the singular gift of charm; a magic, as it were. "The source of their charm is in the Mazarin blood," said Ninon. The Duchesse de Mazarin was an essential part of Saint-Évremond's life; more essential than Ninon herself.

The greatest pleasure of Saint-Évremond, that which he most delighted in from his youth, during the age of passions, and which grew dearer to him daily as he aged, was conversation: "Whatever pleasure I take in reading," he said, "that of conversation will always be to me the keenest. Intercourse with women would be to me the sweetest if the pleasure we find in their amiability did not involve the pain of forbidding ourselves to love them." And he points out of what sort and in what spirit the ordinary intercourse with women should be in order to please them:

"The first merit in the eyes of women, is to love them; the second is to enter into the confidence of their inclinations; the third, to ingeniously put all they have that is most charming in its best light. If nothing leads us into the secret places of the heart, we must at least win their minds by praises; for, in default of lovers to whom all is yielded, he will please best who gives them the means of pleasing themselves most."

The precepts that he lays down for pleasing and interesting women in conversation are the result of the most consummate experience:

"In conversation, remember, never allow women to become indifferent; their soul is inimicable to such languor; either make yourself loved, or flatter them on what they love, or lead them to find within them something that shall make them love themselves more; for, after all, what they want is love, of whatever nature it may be; their heart is never void of that passion."

If that is the ordinary condition of women, even the most intellectual, their merit is all the greater when they are able to emancipate themselves from the habitual moving springs of their sex, without losing anything of their grace. Saint-Évremond had met with such rare women, and we can readily divine that he thought of them when he wrote:

"Some we find, truly, who gain esteem and tenderness even without love; some are as capable of secresy and strict confidence as the most faithful of our male friends. I have known some who have not less mind and discretion than charm and beauty; but they are exceptions that nature, by design or caprice, takes pleasure in sometimes giving us. . . . These unusual women seem to have borrowed the merit of men; perhaps they do a species of infidelity to their sex in passing thus from their natural condition into the true advantages of ours."

In an ideal Portrait that he makes of "the Woman who is never found," he finds pleasure in uniting on the head of an Émilie of his own invention all the qualities most difficult to combine and most opposite:

"This is the Portrait," he says, as he ends, " of the Woman who is never found and never will be found, if a portrait can be made of a thing that is not. It is, rather, the idea of a perfected being. I do not look for it among men, because there always lacks in their intercourse a something, I know not what, of gentleness, which we find in that of women. I think it less impossible to find in a woman the sound, strong reason of men, than to find in men the charm and the natural graces of woman."

That sound reason, that sensible mind, joined to sportiveness and charm, he had found in Ninon, and this feature in the Portrait of Émilie was not by any means a purely imaginary idea.

Let us now see what this Ninon, so celebrated, was; and let us look at her on the side that gives her, justly, a place in the history of Letters and of French society. Let us see her—profane that I am, I was about to say, let us study her—in the species of influence by which she corrected the tone of the hôtel de Rambouillet and the *Précieuses,* and seconded the judicious action of Mme. de La Fayette.

I have sometimes heard it asked why I like to busy myself so much about these amiable and clever women of the past, and take such pains to put them in their true light. Without counting the disinterested pleasure there is in resuscitating for a while in idea that choice company, I shall make answer in the words of Goethe, the great critic of our age:

"It would be," he said, speaking of Mme. de Tencin, "most interesting to follow her history and that of the celebrated women who presided over the different societies of Paris in the eighteenth century: such as Mme. Geoffrin, Mme. du Deffand, Mlle. de Lespinasse, etc.; we should gather details useful to a knowledge of the French character and mind in particular, and of human nature in general; for such details would connect themselves with other times equally honourable to both."

I try, according to my capacity, to carry out, in a way, this programme of Goethe; for if he said that of the eighteenth century, I can say it with even stronger reason of the seventeenth, in which there was, on the part of the celebrated women who influenced it, still more initiative and personal originality. In the matter of polite society and conversation the eighteenth century had only to expand, regulate, and perfect that which the seventeenth had previously founded and established.

Before coming to be, in the end, a personage almost respectable, Ninon had one or two anterior epochs on which I shall merely touch. Mlle. Anne de l'Enclos (for Ninon is only a diminutive), born in Paris, May 15, 1616, of a father who was a nobleman, duellist, intriguer, free-thinker, musician, and man of pleasure, and of a mother strict and severe, was left an orphan at fifteen years of age, and much inclined to enjoy her liberty with a boldness, seasoned with wit and tempered by taste, which was soon to recall the existence of the courtesans of Greece.

There was in France at that period a school of epicureanism and scepticism represented in science by Gassendi and La Mothe Le Vayer; in Letters and in society by Des Yveteaux, Des Barreaux, and many others. Montaigne and Charron were the authors in vogue, and their spirit aided this liberty of opinion. Ninon was among the first of the women to emancipate herself, to profess that there is at bottom one and the same morality for men and women; that in reducing, as was done by society, all the virtues of women to one single virtue, her sex was depreciated,

and wrong and injury were done to it by seeming to
exclude it totally from the practice of integrity — that
male and universal virtue which combines all others;
also that integrity is compatible in a woman with the
infraction of what society agrees to call the one virtue.
"The virtue of women is the finest invention of
men"; that singular saying of a witty muse of our
day seems stolen from Ninon. We can take in at
a glance that whole code of morality, which is much
less novel in these days when it has become a rather
vulgar commonplace. In the days of Ninon, it was
still only an audacity, an exception wholly individual,
a daring wager she made it a duty to sustain, all the
while giving herself up to inconstancy and variety in
her likings. What did she, or rather what did she
not do in those days? What did she not permit herself in those wild moments? What caprice did she
ever deny herself? The list of her conquests goes
everywhere, and however long we make it, it still is
left incomplete.

That Ninon, rival and heiress of Marion Delorme, is
not to detain us here. I send inquirers to history, to
legends, to all that was said, invented, and embroidered upon that topic. "If this mania continues," wrote Voltaire, "we shall soon have as many
Histories of Ninon as of Louis XIV." Tallemant des
Réaux gives the chronicle in its nudity, and with very
circumstantial details. M. Walckenaer, in volumes
i and iv of his excellent Memoirs of Mme. de Sévigné,

has very well established what may be called the
"Chronology of Ninon." The succession of her lovers has been discussed and regulated very much as
that of the Assyrian or Egyptian kings. What is
certain is, that in the midst of this license, where she
allowed the passions to have so large a part, she
imposed certain limits upon herself, and governed
herself up to a certain point. Her reason gave proof
of its solidity in her judgments; her wildest sallies
often covered a sound good sense. She reflected at
an age and in a way of life where others are scarcely
able to think at all; and she, who remained young to
old age, through her mind, was matured by that mind
in her youth.

Nevertheless, there were moments when very little
hindered her capricious and violent existence from
running upon the rocks on which her sisterhood are
usually shipwrecked and from which the most skilful
find no return. The time came, under the Regency
of Anne of Austria, when Ninon's laxity, encouraged
by that of the times, passed all bounds and was on
the point of causing a public scandal. In those days
nothing was needed but a pretext, a chance event, for
society and public morality, defied in its principles,
its most respectable prejudices, to rise at last and
begin reprisals, often brutal but in part deserved.
The queen-regent was solicited to take severe action
against the sinful woman. It was no small service to
Ninon that in this conjuncture the Prince de Condé,

once her lover and her friend always, interposed in person to give her at Court and elsewhere public proofs of interest. On one occasion, meeting her in her carriage, he stopped his own, got out, and went, hat in hand, to salute her in presence of the astonished crowd. Such marks of consideration were still all-powerful.

Ninon was said about this time to be on the eve of departure for Cayenne, where a great number of emigrants of all classes were induced to go. It is permissible to suppose that in her case this was only a pretence to quiet the anger of her enemies and give a signal to her friends to assist her. She did not go; she continued the same life, slightly moderating its tone. From the Marais, where she lived at first, she had moved to the Faubourg Saint-Germain, where she spent the period of her greatest license. She now returned to the Marais, and there, surrounded by friends, lived as she pleased; but, warned by the air from without and the reigning influence of Louis XIV, she regulated her life and reduced it, little by little, to the honourable footing on which it ended, so that even the severe Saint-Simon said of her:

"Ninon had illustrious friends of all sorts, and so much intelligence herself that she kept them all, and held them united with one another, or at any rate without clashing. Everything at her house was conducted with a respect and outward decency that many of the highest princesses rarely sustained without failure. She had in this way as friends the choicest and most distinguished persons at Court; so that it became the fashion to be received by her; and people had reason to desire it on account of the intimacies there formed. Never any cards, or loud laughter, or disputes, or discussions of religion or government; much wit and graceful talk, news of the past and modern news, social news of gallantries, etc., but always without opening the door to malice or evil-speaking; all was delicate, lightsome, restrained, forming conversations she knew well how to sustain by her wit and by what she knew of events of all periods. The consideration — strange fact! — which she had acquired, the number and distinction of her friends and acquaintance, continued to attract society to her when charms were past and when the proprieties of life forbade her from any longer mingling body with mind. Her conversation was charming; Disinterested, faithful, discreet, safe to the last degree; and, frailty apart, she may be said to have been virtuous and full of integrity. . . . These things gave her reputation, and a respect that was altogether singular."

To use a comparison that is not disproportionate, and to which that term *integrity* so often applied leads naturally, we may say that Ninon kept, throughout her intrigues and gallantries, something of that frankness, that uprightness, which the Princess Palatine was able to preserve through the Fronde in the midst of so many political factions.

Tallemant des Réaux says a remarkable thing about Ninon, —that " she never had much beauty, but, above all, she had *charm.*" Somaize in his *Dictionnaire des Précieuses* says about the same thing: " As for beauty, though we know she has enough to give love, we must admit that her mind is more charming than her face, and that many would escape her chains if they merely saw her." As soon as she spoke all were captured and enchanted; it was her mind, her wit that completed her beauty and gave it its expression and power. The same in music when she played the lute; she preferred a touching expression to the most scientific execution: "Sensibility," she said, "is the soul of song."

So many Portraits have been written of Ninon that I shall content myself with mentioning one that shows her to us in her youth, in her most favourable and decent light. It is that of Mlle. de Scudéry who, in her novel of *Clélie*, must surely have painted Ninon under the mask of Clarice. The resemblance in many of the essential features makes me believe that the true key of this Portrait, so little known, is the one I indicate:

" The amiable Clarice is, undoubtedly, one of the most charming persons in the world, whose spirit and humour have a very particular character; but before engaging myself to depict them to you, I must tell you something about her beauty. Clarice has a very beautiful figure, of agreeable height, capable of pleasing every one by a certain free and natural air which gives her good grace. She has hair of the finest chestnut ever seen, her face is round, the complexion bright, the mouth agreeable, the lips rosy, a little dimple on her chin becomes her well, the eyes are black and brilliant, full of fire, smiling, and the countenance refined, gay, and very intelligent. . . . As for mind, Clarice undoubtedly has much, and she has even a certain style of it of which few persons are capable ; for with her it is gay, diverting, and accommodates itself to all classes of people, principally to people in society. She speaks readily ; she laughs easily; she makes a great pleasure of a trifle; she likes to make innocent war upon her friends. . . . But, amid all this inclination that she has for joy, we must say that this amiable, sprightly being has the good qualities of melancholy persons who are well brought up ; her heart is feeling and tender; she knows how to weep with afflicted friends ; she knows how to quit her pleasures when friendship requires it ; she is faithful to her friends ; she is capable of secrecy and discretion ; she never makes a quarrel with any one, no matter who ; she is generous and constant in her feelings;

and she is so lovable that she is beloved by all the best persons of
the Court of both sexes, by persons who do not resemble one another
in condition, in temper, in spirit, in interests, but who all agree,
nevertheless, that Clarice is very charming, that she has intellect,
veritable kindness, and many other qualities worthy of being infinitely esteemed."

There is Ninon young; such as she may have
appeared to friendship in the days when she frequented the society of the *Précieuses;* she, who was
so little like them; she who, talking with Queen
Christina, defined them so well in a word: "The
Précieuses" she said, "are the Jansenists of love."
But, with a mind all the more apart from theirs because it was her very own, she knew how to accommodate herself to all, so that she found grace,
at need, and favour even in the eyes of the hôtel de
Rambouillet, and paid Molière in his own coin when
he consulted her about Tartuffe.

Mlle. de Scudéry's Portrait of Ninon may give us,
perhaps, too softened and weakened an idea of her;
she had, on the contrary, great animation, gushes of
wit and piquancy. Joy was the basis of her soul,
and the expression, as it were, of the health of her
mind; it was she who wrote to Saint-Évremond:
"The joy of the spirit shows its strength." They
said of her that at table she "was drunk from the
soup" so gay and merry was she, drunk with bright
humour and sallies, for she herself drank nothing but
water, and drunkards, even though their names were
Chapelle or Vendôme, were never welcomed in her

house. It was one of her maxims that "in life we should make provision for food only, never for pleasures, but take them day by day as they came"; and she used to declare that "wrinkles would be much more in place under heel than on the face." She had a keen sense of the ridiculous, she caught people at a glance and described them in a word. She said of Mme. de Choiseul who dressed her hair absurdly: "She is as like the spring-time of an inn as two drops of water."[1] She said of the poor little Chevalier de Sévigné who, between Ninon and the actress Champmeslé, had engaged himself to more than he could well perform: "He is a pumpkin fricasseed in snow." And her merry exclamation: *"Oh! le bon billet qu'a la Châtre!"* has passed into a proverb. To the Comte de Choiseul, who annoyed her a little and whom she saw one day after a Court promotion, admiring himself with all his orders in a mirror, she said, before the whole company: "Take care, M. le comte, if I catch you at that again I will name to you your comrades"; the promotion of unworthy persons at the same time with him having

[1] *Printemps d'hôtellerie.* These jokes are incomprehensible in English. The one that follows is based on the following story: Her lover, the Marquis de la Châtre, being obliged to leave her and go abroad on a mission, insisted that she should give him, in writing, a promise to be faithful to him. Ninon signed the paper, and then forgot it ; but something bringing it to her mind later, she exclaimed: *"Oh! le bon billet qu'a la Châtre!"* and the saying has passed into the Fr nch language, meaning a worthless guarantee.— Larchey's *Dictionnaire d'argot.*

17

been deplorable. Attacked in her youth by a serious
illness, and her life being despaired of, lamentations
were made around her; every one declared that he
wished to die, and she, teasing them a little even while
trying to comfort them, exclaimed: " Bah! I shall leave
only dying men behind me." Her gift of repartee was
quick, irresistible; it was delicate, sparkling, piquant.
She never quoted for the sake of quoting, but only
what came into her mind at the moment, applying
it with freshness to the circumstance. Imagination
was even in her memory; it showed itself in her
narratives: " what were called tales from the lips of
others, from hers were perfect scenes, to which, for
resemblance of characters and witty turns, nothing
was lacking."

It was by all these amiable and brilliant qualities,
borne upon a strong foundation of solidity and security
in friendship, that she won the suffrages of those who
knew her; making some forget that she was growing old, and others that she once was young without
ever ceasing to be so. La Fare, that fastidious volup-
tuary, said:

"I never saw Ninon in her beauty ; but at the age of fifty, and
even till she was over sixty she had lovers who adored her, and
the most honourable men in France for friends. Until she was
ninety she was sought by the best society of her time. She died
with all her senses, and with the charms of her mind, which was
the best and most lovable I have ever known in a woman."

Mme. de Maintenon, very intimate with Ninon in her

youth, but now on a footing at Court and in the highest favour, writes to her (Versailles, November, 1679) recommending her brother: " Continue, Mademoiselle, to give good advice to M. d'Aubigné; he has great need of lessons from Leontium " [friend of Epicurus: a philosophic nickname given to Ninon] " the advice of an amiable friend persuades better than that of a stern sister."

The letters of Ninon, simple, original, and quite in the tone of her conversation, are very few in number; I know of only a dozen that are authentic, and those are addressed to Saint-Évremond. When he left France in 1661 she seems to have owed him one hundred pistoles. Eight years later she still owed them. Saint-Évremond, then in Holland, seems annoyed at the delay: " Her good faith is strong " (he writes to a M. d'Hervart whom he had seen at The Hague and who had since returned to Paris), " but my absence is long, and after eight years nothing is easier than not to remember people when remembrance would cost a hundred pistoles. Perhaps I am wrong to suspect her of that human weakness." He was wrong. Ninon had proved her integrity by returning to Gourville, after many years, the famous strong-box that the latter had left in her care, interference with which she denied to more than one lover, successor to Gourville, who would have been glad enough to be his heir in all things. At the first reminder of her debt Ninon sent word to Saint-Évremond that he could have fifty pistoles whenever he pleased. Fifty pistoles instead of one hundred were not the reckoning of the exiled philosopher; he thought it was treating him too like a lover,—that is to say, with semi-unfaithfulness,—and not as a friend. He made some joke on the subject which was not very well received. There was, in fact, a misunderstanding, Ninon having promised to pay the rest of the sum at a certain date. Before the time expired she paid the whole, and plumed herself on being more punctual than Marcus Aurelius, emperor and philosopher, who never paid his debts in advance: "That spurs courage," she wrote to Saint-Évremond; "and when you have thought it all over you will see that you should not be sarcastic with a blameless banker. . . . I told you my charms were changed into solid and serious qualities, and you know it is not permissible to joke with such a personage."

This was just at the moment when Ninon, ceasing to be the Ninon of the Fronde, of the Regency, and of her first gallantries, was becoming Mlle. de l'Enclos and passing into the "personage" she perfected more and more and sustained thenceforth to the end of her life.

Saint-Évremond, proved in the wrong, and a little ashamed, no doubt, of his unfair jest, hastens to atone for it, and writes Ninon a letter in which he praises her as she deserves, and shows her natural self to us at this moment of transition and metamorphosis. I will

quote a part of this letter, which is very little known
and is not to be found in his "Works :"

"In spite of that old dreamer who thought no one happy till after
death, I hold you, full of life as you are, to be the happiest creature
that ever was. You have been loved by the most honourable men in
the world, and you have loved as long as was needed to leave no
pleasure untasted, and just so far as was needed to prevent the dis-
gusts of a wearisome passion. Never has happiness been carried farther
by your sex. There are few princesses in the world whom you do
not cause to feel the hardness of their fate through jealousy of yours;
there are few saints in convents who would not willingly change the
tranquillity of their minds for the charming troubles of your soul. Of
all the tortures, you have felt none but those of love, and you know
better than any one that in love no other pleasures are worth 'its
pains.' To-day, when the flower of your great youth has passed (the
words are rough, but you have written them to me so often, that I
only quote them) you retain such good looks on your face and such
charms in your mind that, if it were not for the fastidiousness of your
choice as to the persons you receive, there would be as great a crowd
without selfish interests in your house, as there are Courts where
fortunes are made. You mingle virtues with your charms, for at the
moment when a lover reveals to you his passion, a friend may confide
to you his secrets. Your word is the safest bond on which we
can rely. . . ."

Ninon's correspondence with Saint-Évremond
through such divers events and wars was not very
punctual or well sustained, and the few letters that
have been preserved belong to only the last years of
their life. They are then decidedly old, very old both
of them, and their greatest pleasure is to talk of the
past with regret, and to jest of old age very pleasantly. Ninon regrets her friend and wishes he were
near her: "I should have liked to pass what remains
to me of life with you; if you had thought as I do

you would be here now." At that date, nothing pre-vented Saint-Évremond from returning to his own country if he chose. But she says pleasantly that per-haps it is a finer and more meritorious thing to re-member the absent after so many years of separation. "Perhaps this separation of bodies is intended to embellish my epitaph," she says.

Saint-Évremond gives a letter of introduction to Ninon to a M. Turretin, a very distinguished Gene-vese minister and preacher. Ninon at once pro-cures for the learned Calvinist all the resources at her command: "He has found here a number of my friends who think him worthy of the praises you gave him. If he will profit by the worthy abbés who remain to us during the absence of the Court, he shall be treated as a man whom you esteem." These abbés of distinction were, in fact, very numerous, toward the last in Ninon's circle. She adds: "I read your let-ter before him with spectacles; but they are not unbe-coming to me; I have always had a grave face. If he loves the merit that they call here *distinguished* per-haps your wish will be accomplished; every day people try to console me for my losses with that fine word." Since then the word *distinguished* has been much abused; we catch it here at its origin, or at least in its earliest acceptation. To console Ninon for old age they told her she was a woman of *distin-guished merit*. In the seventeenth century the word had not hitherto been employed so absolutely. Persons were said to be distinguished *for* one quality or *for* another; but to *be distinguished* was left for the eighteenth, and especially the nineteenth century to bring into general circulation. Everybody nowadays is *distinguished,* just as everybody wears the ribbon of the Legion of Honour in his buttonhole.

The few letters exchanged between Ninon and Saint-Évremond give occasion for many remarks both literary and ethical. They are perfectly sincere, and human nature is under no disguise, and affects nothing; one might, indeed, wish at moments for a few efforts to keep its tone higher. In vain does Saint-Évremond tell Ninon: "Nature will begin to show by you that it is possible never to grow old," in vain he tells her: "You are of all countries,—as much esteemed in London as in Paris; you are of all times, and when I cite you to do honour to mine the young men claim you instantly as the honour of theirs; thus you are mistress of the present as of the past. . . ." In spite of all these fine words Ninon grows old; she has her moments of sadness, and her manner of evading them seems saddest of all:

"You used to say in other days," she writes, "that I should die of reflections; I try to make no more, and to forget on the morrow the day that I have lived to-day. Every one tells me that I have less reason to complain of time than others. However that may be, had any one foretold me such a life I would have hung myself. And yet one clings to a vile body as if it were an agreeable one; one likes to feel ease and repose; appetite is a thing that I still enjoy. . . ."

That idea of *appetite* often comes up between them,

and mingles rather naïvely with the warm tenderness of friendship. "How I envy those who go to England!" writes Ninon; "what pleasure I should have in dining with you once more! Is it not coarseness to wish for a dinner? The mind has great advantages over the body, and yet the body supplies us with various little tastes that reiterate themselves and soothe the soul under sad reflections."

To hold to life only by the body and to feel that body shrinking and withering day by day is the main idea that pervades the correspondence of these two old persons, and it ends in painfully affecting the reader. We feel more than they did what is lacking to them in the order of higher hopes. They perceive it themselves at the moment when they lose their friends. Ninon sees Charleval die, her old and most faithful friend; Saint-Évremond loses the Duchesse de Mazarin, his sole resource and prop. Ninon tries to comfort him by a letter of feeling and good sense, which she cannot prevent herself from ending with these words: "If one could think like Mme. de Chevreuse, who believes that by dying she will go and converse with all her friends in another world, it would be sweet to think it."

In reading these pages one cannot help desiring some other motive, some other impulse, be it only an illusion, in these two amiable old people. Their grovelling ethics distress us, their horizon lowers at every step. Saint-Évremond does not believe in a future, and all his hopes, like all his joys, end for him in the next or the present moment: "I do not regard reputation," he says. "I look to a more essential thing; I mean life; eight days of which are worth far more than eight centuries of fame when dead. . . . There is no one who thinks more of youth than I do. . . . Live; life is good when it has no pain."

But, as there must always be a motive more or less near and a recompense, in default of posterity and a future the two friends gave each other praises and compliments letter after letter.

"Would to God that you thought of me as you say you do!" writes Ninon, "and I will do without the praise of other nations. Your last letter is a masterpiece. It has made the subject of every conversation held in my rooms for a month. You have returned to youth; you do right to love it. Philosophy goes well with charms of the mind. It is not enough to be wise, one must also please; and I see that you will always please so long as you think as you do. Few persons resist age. I believe I have not yet allowed mine to crush me."

It was thus that they gave themselves, through intellect at least and by delicate flattery, their last pleasures.

It is time to sum up my remarks upon Ninon and to mark distinctly the only side on which I have viewed her. Her salon collected a far greater variety of personages than the hotel de Rambouillet, and it comprised many sorts. It united with the best of the great world the best of the good Parisian *bourgeoisie*. Mme. de La Fayette had attempted for a moment the same rôle (in which Mme. de Sablé had preceded her), "to whom," says Gourville, "all the young men were accustomed to show great attentions, because, having trained them a little, she gave them a claim to enter society. But Mme. de La Fayette's health and her inclination to take her ease kept her from continuing this rôle very long. In a great measure it was that of Ninon. For it, she had much more gaiety than Mme. de La Fayette, and more solidity than that other brilliant woman of the same date, Mme. de La Sablière. It was therefore in her salon and through her that young men made their entrance into society. In her rooms people conversed: cards were not played. Mothers sought to introduce their children. Mme. de Sévigné, who had such reason earlier in life to complain of Ninon in respect to her husband and her son, saw, without anxiety, her grandson, the Marquis de Grignan, pay her much attention. Fashion joined in, and, public consideration covering all, the women ended by seeking Ninon sedulously. "The women are all running after Mlle. de l'Enclos," said Mme. de Coulanges, "just as other people used to run after her formerly." Whereupon Mme. de Sévigné wrote to M. de Coulanges: "Corbinelli tells me marvels of the good company of *men* he meets in the house of Mlle. de l'Enclos; so, in her old days, she gathers them all in, men *and* women, whatever Mme. de Coulanges may say."

No book shows us better what the salon of Mme.

de l'Enclos really was than the "Dialogue on the Music of the Ancients" by the Abbé de Châteauneuf; it gives a conversation at her house, in which we find her speaking with taste, with judgment and accuracy, excellent musician that she was. Leaving her salon the interlocutors continue to talk of her and they recount to one another her various good qualities. The Abbé Fraquier has also painted her on a very true page; and the Abbé d'Olivet — (good heavens! what a collection of abbés àpropos of Ninon!) — in a Eulogy in Latin on Fraquier, representing the latter at the moment when he wished to write in French and to train himself to the best style of our language, says:

"For this purpose, he put his education into the hands of two Muses; one was the celebrated La Vergne (Mme. de La Fayette) and the other was called Leontium (Ninon). Both of them held at that time the sceptre of intellect and were thought the arbiters of elegance . . . The latter was so fashioned by nature that she seemed a Venus in beauty, and a Minerva in mind. But when Fraquier first knew her, age had long withdrawn what was dangerous in her, assuring him of that only which was profitable and salutary."

"Do you know," said a merry jester to whom I read the above passage in Latin, "that from the the way in which your Abbé d'Olivet writes, I conclude that in the seventeenth century Mme. de La Fayette and Mlle. de l'Enclos, through their function of oracles of taste to the world, were the two first vicars of Boileau." It was in terms such as these, or approaching them, that the later contemporaries of

Ninon spoke of her. Is it necessary to recall the fact that the Abbé de Châteauneuf presented to her one day his godson, François Arouet (Voltaire) then thirteen years old and already a poet? She seems to have foreseen what that child would become, for she bequeathed him 2000 francs in her will to buy books.

From Montaigne and Charron to Saint-Évremond and Ninon, and from Ninon to Voltaire there is but a hand's-breadth, as we see. Thus it is that in the stretch of time certain spirits make a chain.

And now, when one has spoken of Ninon and her charm with justice and without too deeply entering into what was shameful, even debased at a certain period, and baneful during the disorders of her early life, we must never forget that such a career, singular and unique as it was, cannot be run twice; that it came of incomparable luck. aided by a quite peculiar genius for conduct; but that all women who, following her example, should attempt to treat love with license and afterwards turn it into sacred friendship, would run great risk of being left by the wayside, and of withering the one sentiment within them without rendering themselves worthy of the other.

VIII.

Tallemant des Réaux
and
Bussy=Rabutin.

VIII.

Tallemant des Réaux and Bussy=Rabutin.

The Bourgeois Scandal=monger and the Scandal= monger of Quality.

WITHOUT aiming at a parallel, I am tempted to bring together the names of these two writers, and to say something of their class of Memoirs, wholly anecdotical, which, under different forms, succeed still in making themselves read and in pleasing, after the lapse of many years.

The *Histoires amoureuses* of Bussy and the *Historiettes* of Tallemant, though belonging, each of them, to the class of chronicles more or less scandalous, cannot be ranked on the same line, nor ascribed to the same spirit. Bussy is a satirist, Tallemant is merely a teller of tales. In Bussy himself there are various personages who complicate and foil one another, while at the same time they mar the perfect candour of his words. We have the lover and the man *à bonne fortunes,* the wit and the academician, the ambitious soldier and the man who will miss the marshal's bâton: all these conflicting

271

elements may impair his sincerity a little, even in backbiting, and turn his sharp pen one way or another; he is susceptible of envy, or of bitterness; he has his secret leaven, he is affronted, he takes revenge.

Tallemant has nothing of all this; he obeys a single taste, a single humour. Witty after the style of our fathers, inquisitive as no man should be, on the watch for all that is said and done about him, informed to the lowest detail of the incidents and the tittle-tattle of society, he registers everything, though not so much the foul things as the drolleries and gaieties. He writes what he hears for the pleasure of writing it with the salt of his language, which is always good, and joining thereto his judgment, which is natural and shrewd. Such as he was and thus trained he is, in his line, inimitable and incomparable. Whoever had told Bussy, the wit, the brilliant pen of the army and the Court, that he had, in his own day, a rival and a master of pungent and naïve narration in that bourgeois scandal-monger, encountered everywhere in society and out of place nowhere, he would certainly have been much astonished and would not have believed it.

From all that we read, especially from things already classic, we may draw certain serious remarks, or, at any rate, a few notions on the manners and customs of a time that is no more. I open the *Histoire amoureuses des Gaules,* and at once I am struck with what gave the author the idea of writing such a

COMTE DE BUSSY-RABUTIN.
From a steel engraving of the period.

book. Bussy, forty-two years old, lieutenant-general and commander of the light-horse cavalry, having twenty-six years of good and glorious service behind him, aspiring to the *cordon bleu* and to the office of marshal of France, falls in love with Mme. de Montglat, and during a month's absence sets about writing down, in order to amuse her, the histories of Mesdames so-and-so, which she had asked him to tell her. Mme. de Montglat, a brilliant and graceful beauty, loved music and poetry; she even composed rather prettily herself, and could sing better than any woman in France of her rank; also she spoke and wrote with surprising facility and all the naturalness in the world. She admired intellect; much admired just then, little as they had of it, for society was in process of freeing itself from a brutality and coarseness of manners still prevalent and with which comparison was readily made. Mme. de Montglat had in Bussy a man of intellect all her own, and she wished to employ him as she chose. The result was the ruin of his career.

For us, speaking frankly, the first pages of Bussy's chronicle respond very little to the expectation given by his much-vaunted reputation. There is no art of composition in the book; nothing is connected; all is successive and haphazard. We come upon the name of a man or a woman, quick, a portrait ! The portrait begins with a description that reminds us of a passport: face round, nose well formed, etc. Patience ! the finer traits are coming; they do come. But all this

18

gives the impression of very elementary art. Something of the same kind appears in regard to the toilet of the personages about whom Bussy remarks that they are " clean " or they are " dirty " ; which does not always tell us whether persons dressed well or not; it means that they took care, or did not take care of their person, and we are left to suppose there was a certain medium of cleanliness which was not the common and required usage There was no middle course between delicacy and neglect. So with the mind; some had it wholly refined: others, at their elbow, were still coarse or barbarous. At the beginning of the reign of Louis XIV, and before the fusion of manners and tone was completed, we are very much struck by these contrasts and this crudity side by side with refinement. We see the remains of barbarism still existing in the beautiful morning, already begun, of civilisation; we might think ourselves, from certain details, in a land of savages, when, suddenly, we are in the midst of exquisite things. Bussy's book gives this mingled impression very plainly.

How did a gentleman on service live in those days ? The king spent the summers on the frontier, where the armies fought hard. He then returned, usually, to Paris, where amusements were in season: cards, billiards, tennis, hunting, theatres, masquerades, lotteries, whatever complete idleness engenders, but above all love. One might say that such is, more or less, the history of all periods; but love at that period had its own particular stamp.   Speaking of M. de Candale, one of the *beaux* who was most in vogue at that time, Bussy defines him thus:

"His mind was mediocre ; but in his first love he fell into the hands of a lady who had infinite intelligence, and as they loved each other very much, she took such pains to form him, and he such pains to please the beauty, that art surpassed nature, and he was really a better appearing man [*plus honnête homme* [1]] than a thousand others who had more mind than he."

Mme. de Châtillon, receiving with marked favour the declaration of M. de Nemours and letting him see she had a good opinion of his merits, drew forth the reply: "Ah, madame, it rests with you to make me seem the best-bred man in France."   The Marquis de Sévigné, who left his charming wife for Ninon, was convinced "that a man could not be an *honnête homme* [civil, polished, well-appearing man] unless he were always in love."

That which took place at Court during the winters was not merely the noisy and heedless amusements of young warriors; there was much emulation among those who piqued themselves on being men of good breeding, and many wagers like the following:

"The Duc de Candale," says Bussy, "who was the best-trained man at Court, thought that nothing was wanting to his reputation than to be loved by the handsomest woman in the kingdom.   He

---

[1] The term *honnête homme* did not then mean exclusively or chiefly, a man of integrity and honesty — but a man who conformed to good-breeding, good manners, propriety and honour.—Tr.

therefore resolved at the army, three months after the campaign,
that he would be in love with her (Mme. d'Olonne) as soon as
he met her; and he showed by the great passion he then had for
her, that they [such passions] are not always strokes of heaven
or fate."

Both sexes embarked by fixed intention with some
man or some woman, in order to do honour to themselves in society and be talked about, " because women gained for men as much esteem as arms." They
owed it to themselves, therefore, to make love in some
place of renown. Vanity in love, and as the principle
of love, became a sign of the times, and it is still, in
a general way, that of French gallantry, into which
passion, at the beginning, enters for very little. " To
embark " was the consecrated term habitually employed. Thus the Chevalier de Grammont takes a
fancy to attach himself to Mme. d'Olonne " about the
same time that Marsillac *embarked* with her." Beu-
vron, formerly in love with the same lady, now keeps
aloof from her because " the levity she showed in all
things made him fear to *embark* himself with her."
The Abbé Fouquet, brother of the Superintendent,
intriguer of the first water, man of the sack and rope,
whose conduct was the farthest possible from his
profession, " *embarked* at first on loving more for
fame than for love "; but the taste came to him by
degrees, and soon we hear of nothing but his " embarkations." During the time that he tyrannised
over Mme. de Châtillon, a friend of the latter, Vineuil,
wrote to her as follows, to shame her: " You have

become the continual subject of all conversations. Your embarkation is described as the lowest and most abject ever seen in a person of your quality. It is said that your friend exercises a tyrannical empire over you and over all that you approach. . . ."

Thus they embarked; and are said sometimes to "re-embark" with the same person, to repair, if possible, the injury done to their reputation by a first rebuff. In this quantity of embarkations, most of them are made from points of honour, or from "reason," rather than from inclination; from the head far more than from the heart. The heart, however, sometimes ends in taking part in the affair. We look in vain for *charm* in Bussy's narrative; there is neither sweetness nor ardour; but he has the art of keen, delicate, and piquant malice.

In two places Bussy betrays both bad taste and inexperience. He quotes letters, and inserts them in his narrative. These letters apparently seem to him piquant. To understand how they could seem so to him or to others, we must remember that the period was one when the art, the epistolary genius, that was about to shine and sparkle in the correspondence of Bussy's charming cousin, Mme. de Sévigné, was still to be essayed and formed. The letters that he quotes, and perhaps fabricates, were not worth the trouble of invention; they are those of a writing-master. Bussy also loves to quote, on occasion, verses, couplets, madrigals of his own making, and such verses!

Many of the writers of his century and of the next, distinguished for intellect and very agreeable in their prose writings, had a species of infirmity for believing that they added to the charm of a thought by composing, and putting in some place where it was least to be expected, a worthless couplet. They wrote well, they jested with grace, with point, they shot their well-aimed, well-steeled arrows, and then, all of a sudden, without any one's knowing why, a little mania, self-styled poetical, seizes them, they catch up a village violin and make, for a minute or two, a dreadful fiddling that rasps the ears. False taste in wit, in epigram, in cold gallantry, derived from the last troubadours and utterly opposed to true imagination and the genius of poesy! How far the classics were from work like this! In Petronius, whom Bussy imitates and translates now and then (the model of a style he affects too much), there are verses also, mingled with the prose and making a conglomerate composition; but they are the verses of a poet, they sparkle, they are white as Parian marble, they have the cool greenery of Italian groves:

> " Emicuere rosæ violæque et molle cyperon,
> Albaque de viridi riserunt lilia prato;
>
> Candidiorque dies secreto favit amori."

The classics were licensed for poesy and for the painting of natural objects. Even at the period when corruption began, they kept the measure of great things and the clear sight that saw all beauty; they had Virgil before their eyes and Homer on the horizon. As for Bussy, he thinks he is a poet when he makes a wretched couplet to a jig tune.

It is not known whether all is Bussy's own in this satirical painting, which he partly disavowed. If the conversation between Mme. Cornuel and Mme. d'Olonne is by him, he has not escaped one of the improprieties and defects of his day: pedanticism and dogmatism in gallantry. It was not worth while to introduce Mme. Cornuel, that person of so much spice and sarcasm, merely to make her profess a code of decent love, and preach a sort of sermon under three heads. The passage is very little worthy of Mme. Cornuel and would come better from the pen of the Chevalier de Méré than from that of Bussy.

But now, all being said, and the wrongs done by betrayal and indiscretion having long passed away, we are, involuntarily, grateful to Bussy (at this distance) for showing us in action all this fine society, nobles, gentlemen, and great ladies; for producing them to us in a state of nature, as it were, in an originality of disorderly living which makes one reflect on the degree of civilisation and decency that belongs to different ages and might serve to bring to reason the enthusiasm of historians and the makers of funeral orations. Bussy's polite diction, his simplicity of phrase, brings out distinctly certain fundamental points. There are, however, charming traits, and delicate, in his narrative; his portrait of Mme. de Sévigné is one of the most lifelike and most carefully worked-up in its malignity; in it he actually sur-passed himself and summoned all his treachery against such a model. He makes us think, by this malignant portrait, of those of Hamilton, although he has not the light touch of the latter n)r his almost imper-ceptible fine irony. However that may be, Bussy has given in the *Histoire amoureuse des Gaules* a dish of his own concoction, a *rabutinade,* which has a particular relish for palates that want something else than the meats of the golden age.

Saint-Évremond judged Bussy well when he said of him:

" What are we to think on the subject of M. de Bussy that every-body has not already thought? He is a man of quality; he has al-ways had much wit, and in former days I saw him in a position to hope for high fortune, to which have since succeeded many men who were his inferiors.

" He preferred to his advancement in life the pleasure of writing a book and making the public laugh; he has chosen to make a merit of his liberty; he affects to speak frankly and undisguisedly, but he has not always sustained that character to the end.

" After twenty years of exile he returned to a humiliating situation, without office, without employment, without consideration among courtiers, and without any reasonable grounds for hope.

" When one has renounced fortune by one's own fault, and when one has chosen to do what M. de Bussy did deliberately, one ought to pass the rest of one's days in retirement, and support with a sort of dignity the sorry rôle with which one burdened oneself."

I ought to quote all that follows. Saint-Évremond, in speaking thus of a man who had more than one affinity with himself in talents as well as in exile, enables us, nevertheless, to perceive their differences. Both destroyed their fortunes by an indiscretion, by indulging a wit more satirical than propriety allowed; their military careers were broken, and both were driven into a long exile, to which Bussy could never reconcile himself, while Saint-Évremond bore his to the end with fortitude, even disdaining at the last to return to France when he might have done so. Saint-Évremond at bottom is an epicurean, and he is that before all. Had circumstances turned otherwise, he would doubtless have been a very different personage, but he had in him, essentially, the stuff of a philosopher of indifference and pleasure, of a smiling and firm observer, who appreciates the real value of things and detaches himself from them as much as possible. Provided he spent his afternoons and evenings in talking with Mme. de Mazarin he felt he had not lost his day and was content.

Bussy, on the contrary, was an ambitious man, and a courtier who had imprudently barred his own fortune, who felt it and suffered from it; his was a vain, uneasy soul which did not find within itself resources of consolation. Imagine a soldier of courage and talent, who has in him, perhaps, the stuff to win ten battles, to make himself illustrious when he reached the highest post, but who, by an incurable perversity, has created for himself all sorts of shackles and impossibilities. Man of war, lieutenant of Turenne, but

complicated with the spirit of a Maurepas, he found
means to give umbrage to his general and to alienate
him by the fear he had of his squibs. A courtier, all
ready, if need were, to crawl before Louis XIV provided he were employed, he found means, at the
opening of the glorious reign, by a scandalous folly to
get himself treated as a libellist and his pen broken,
he, whose sword was eager for action and impatient
of the scabbard. To give himself the pleasure of
writing a book worthy of the Regency and the Directory, and which was wholly of the date when
Fouquet made a collection of his *billets-doux* and
wrote out a list of the great ladies who were his
mistresses, Bussy missed the great century, missed
the war in Flanders, missed that in Franche-Comté,
when the army passed almost before his windows,
all his former companions in arms being with it.
"Ten thousand men have just passed my gates"
(the gates of his château de Bussy), he writes; "there
was not an officer however little out of the common,
who did not come to see me; many of the Court
people slept here." Quick! he writes to the king,
asking to serve in this campaign; and the impassible
king replies: "Let him have patience; not yet, not
this time." And the other time never comes. This
was enough, we must allow, to enrage a gentleman of
good family and lead him to eat his heart out; and
that, in fact, was what Bussy spent the rest of his life
in doing.

In Tallemant we have to deal with a man of another nature, another condition, another temperament. He thinks himself well off where he is; he has found his level at once, he is angry with no one. If he permits himself a grain of malice, he at least puts no rancour into it, nor any secret bitterness. Of the same age as Bussy (Tallemant was born about 1619, and Bussy in 1618), son of a rich financier, nurtured in bourgeois joviality and opulence, he keeps us informed about all the fine passions of his youth; he, too, writes his *histoire amoureuse,* but how different its tone! While still a schoolboy he had read "Amadis" and adored it. When he went from the Place Maubert to the rue Montorgueil to see a certain widow who had favours for him, and, in order to arrive less muddy before her (sedan-chairs and galoshes, a resource some years later, were not yet invented) he hired a horse, people cried out, when they met him, "Where are you going, Sir Knight?" But what sort of knight was he? there was much of Sancho in his chivalry.

At one time he came very near entering, for one of his girl-cousins, into grand sentiments and languishing airs: "A fool of a comrade whom I had in college," he remarks, "who was a bit romantic, managed to spoil me; we took sentiment askew, both of us." This crookedness did not last long. Even when he was melancholy, it was "gentle melancholy which never prevented him from being gay when he wished."

He began again, at the first chance, to jump, and joke, and play tricks and laugh. At eighteen years of age he and two brothers were sent with the Abbé de Gondi (the future Cardinal de Retz) to make a journey into Italy; passing through Lyons, he fell in love with the daughter of a friend with whom they lodged, and he carried away with him the promises, and the bracelets, of his beauty with the intention to be sad; he believes himself a lover after the fashion of Amadis. He, a hero of romance, the deuce!—he does n't support that rôle very long: "This did not prevent me," he says, "from diverting myself much in Italy— so fine a thing is youth."

Tallemant's father would have liked to make him a counsellor at the Parliament of Paris; but the young man did not feel the slightest vocation for the magistracy. To set himself completely at liberty he married his cousin-german, a Rambouillet. Tallemant's mother was a Rambouillet of the financial family of that name which had no connection with the noble Rambouillet d'Angennes but, together with money, had wit and intellect for its patrimony. We know very little of Tallemant's life. He seems to have filled some financial office—controller-provincial of regiments in Lower Brittany, they called it. He bought the estate of Plessis-Rideau in Touraine about the year 1650, and obtained the right to change its name to "des Réaux," which henceforth became his own name. He distinguished his identity in this way from that of his

younger brother, the Abbé Tallemant, the academician; just as Boileau *des Préaux* distinguished himself from his elder brother Gilles Boileau.   That Abbé
Tallemant, known to us as the dry translator of the
French of Amyot, did not like our Tallemant and was
envious of him.   Between them there may have been
family jars and no doubt antipathies of taste; Tallemant is certain to have sneered at purists.   Also he
made verses equal to those of his brother; but those
we have of him are insipid enough, or very flat.   We
have an epistle of his in verse to Père Rapier, in which
there is not the least little word to raise a smile.

Born and brought up in the Reformed religion Tallemant was converted in old age; we are not told if this
took place on the revocation of the Edict of Nantes.
He reached his seventy-third year and died in Paris in
his own house, rue Neuve Saint-Augustin, November
10, 1692.

But what need is there for insignificant details as to
the life of this easy-going, happy man? He shows
himself to us in his *Historiettes;* there we see him
naked and undisguised.   He finished writing them
in 1657, during the years when Bussy's pen was taking its license.   Tallemant took his, but without paying much heed to it.   Going everywhere in society, on
good terms with persons of the highest rank, and
specially allied with men of intellect; loving to hear
all, record all, and make good stories out of it; a born
anecdotist, as La Fontaine was a born fabulist, his

friends were constantly saying to him: "Write that down." He did so, and we profit by it. Without Tallemant and his indiscretions, many special studies on the seventeenth century would to-day be well-nigh impossible. Through him we belong to all coteries, all quarters; we know all the masks, even to their stripping off. Are we to pin our faith on what Tallemant tells us? By no means. He tells what he hears; he records current talk; he does not lie, but he gossips with delight and joy of heart. Nevertheless, what he tells is always very worthy of consideration, because he is natural and judicious, veracious and shrewd, without any conceit or any pretension. Of Henri IV, Sully, Richelieu, of all who were older than himself and were beyond his reach in every way, he picked up only the crumbs (yet they fell from good tables); he should in their case be listened to as an echo and collector of rumours; but on the persons he has seen and frequented, whose measure he had himself taken, he counts for as much as any one; he has read physiognomies, and he imparts them to us. He holds the red pencil, brusque, expressive, violent in colour, of our old sketchers lodging near the Halles. He makes a speaking sketch. We must not treat Tallemant lightly, nor contradict him without proof. Burrow into many places and you will find confirmation of what he said as he ran. And it is not only in the *bourgeois* class that he excels; not only when he exhibits and spreads before us Mme. de. Cavoye, Mme. Pilou, or Mme. Cornuel in all the originality and copiousness of their sallies; Tallemant is also the best witness we have to the hôtel Rambouillet and its refined society; he judges it with the French spirit of the good old times, as becomes a friend of Patru and a man who has in him something of La Fontaine in prose, and something of Maucrois in Gallic atticism that has passed through the Place Maubert.   Much has been said of M. de Montausier; but in truth, his portrait was made long ago.   What could give it better than this page of Tallemant ?

" M. de Montausier is a man all of a piece; Mme. de Rambouillet said he was crazy by dint of being wise.   Never was there any one who had more need to sacrifice to the Graces.   He shouts, he is rude, he attacks everyone to his face, and when he grumbles at a man he sets before his eyes his past iniquities.   No man ever helped me so much to cure myself of a humour for disputing.   He wanted two citadels built in Paris, one above and one below the river, saying that a king, provided he made good use of them, could not be too absolute — as if that 'provided' were an infallible thing!   Unless he were convinced that a man's life depended on it he would not keep his secret.   His wife helps him mightily in the provinces; without her, the nobles would not visit him.   He rises at eleven o'clock, as he does here, and shuts himself up to read; for he does not like hunting, and has nothing popular about him.   She is just the reverse of him.   He makes wit and intellect too much of a profession for a man of rank, or, at any rate, he does it too seriously.   He goes to the Saturdays very often [Mlle. de Scudéry's day for receiving].   He makes translations; but just see the fine author he has chosen!   He turns Persius Flaccus into French verse!   He talks of almost nothing but books, and sees M. Chapelain and M. Conrart more regularly than any one.   He takes fancies, and of pretty bad taste; he likes Claudian better than Virgil.   He wants pepper and spice.   Nevertheless, as we have said elsewhere, he relishes a poem that has neither salt nor sage, 'La Pucelle'; and that is solely because Chapelain wrote it. He has a fine library at Angoulême."

If that is not a masterpiece of truth and likeness, where shall we find one? We have a choice of such pages in Tallemant; open him anywhere; all is gay, clear-cut, smiling, well set-up; never involved or twisted. I much prefer the good Tallemant to Bussy. When Bussy has said a pretty thing he is afraid of losing it. Of the two, it is always the nobleman whose inkstand we see the most.

Tallemant continues without effort the race of tale-tellers and authors of *fabliaux;* a vein of Rabelais runs through him. He uses excellent language, of great precision of meaning, full of idioms, familiar, Parisian in its essence. His style agrees very ill with the true reign of Louis XIV; we cannot imagine Tallemant at Versailles. The scandal-monger of those coming years will have their amplitude and grandeur: that scandal-monger of genius is to be Saint-Simon. The social world that Tallemant shows us is that of the Town, properly so called; of Paris in the days of Mazarin, before and after the Fronde, and under the minority of Louis XIV (corresponding more or less to the period of the first satires of Boileau); the Paris in which was stirring in all directions a rich, bold, and free *bourgeoisie,* the types of which are in Molière, the physician of which is Gui Patin, and, at a future period, Regnard. That is the framework within which Tallemant plays his play. He swims in his element.

After this we need not be surprised if writers profit by Tallemant's pages but do not cite him honourably, or if they often rob him without saying much about it, and even with an air of saying, "Fie"! A Tallemant is not a Tacitus. He writes in a style that is little elevated, that seems easy, and is only moderately honourable. But every man gives what he can.

19

IX.

The Abbé de Rancé.

IX.

The Abbé de Rancé.

Reformer of La Trappe.

WHO and what was Rancé in the world? A wonderful mind, brilliant, eager for all knowledge and all diversions, seeking ever the honey of the poets; eloquent and winning of speech, generous and magnificent of heart; an ardent soul, impatient, intemperate, exhausted with fatigue yet never in repose; a soul that nothing could fill, grasped in the midst of successes and pleasures by an infinite melancholy, obsessed at times by the idea of death, the image of eternity; rejecting, at a certain moment, that which seemed to it incomplete, and immolating itself finally at the foot of the Cross in a "passionate hatred of life." For it is with life as it is with one beloved—there is no great distance between passionate love and passionate hatred; it is precisely because we have loved too much, dreamed too ideally of this passing life, clasped, in rare and unique moments, too much, that the soul, when it is great, gives itself obstinately to disgust and to relinquishment.

With Rancé the sacrifice was complete, was lasting; the gleam from on high not only fell, but the lightning fell with it, and consumed the holocaust: the forehead of the repentant man beneath the ashes remains for ever stamped with the sacred stigmata.

Armand-Jean Le Bouthillier de Rancé, born in 1626, son of a president of the Cour des Comptes, nephew of a superintendent of finance, nephew also of the Bishop of Aire and the Archbishop of Touraine, cousin-german of Chavigny, minister of State, was tonsured while still a child, loaded with benefices, and destined to receive the ecclesiastical heritage of his uncle of Tours. Meantime, he was put to studies both sacred and profane, and delivered, still a youth, to the whirl of society. At twelve years of age (1639) he published an edition of Anacreon, with table-songs [*scolie*] and comments in Greek of his own making. Much has been said of the contrast between this precocious edition and the future destiny of the child. A visitor to La Trappe mentioned it one day to the abbé:

" He answered me that he had burned all the copies that remained except one, and that one he had given to M. Pellisson when the latter came to La Trappe after his conversion; not, he said, as a good book but merely as a very clean and well-bound volume: he said, also, that during the first two years of his retreat, before he became a monk, he had wished to re-read the poets; but it only served to recall his old ideas; for there was in such reading a subtle poison hidden beneath the flowers that was very dangerous; so that finally he had to quit all that."

The most conflicting studies excited the restless curiosity of young Rancé; at one time he gave himself

ARMAND JEAN LE BOUTHILLIER DE RANCÉ.
From a steel engraving.

up to astrology. Theology, however, was not neglected; he did well in it, obtained his degree, and
preached eloquently.   If not in politics, at least in the
variety of his dissipations he seemed to follow closely
in the footsteps of Retz, his elder by twelve years, and
he, too, in his way, was a *roué* of the first Regency;
never stirring, Saint-Simon tells us, from the hôtel
de Montbazon, a friend of all the personages of the
Fronde, and sharing the great hunting parties of the
Duc de Beaufort, the leader of the "Importants." An
elegant biographer, the Abbé de Marsollier, pictures
him to us at this time with a sort of complacency:

"He was in the flower of his age, being then about twenty-five
years old.   His figure was above middle height, well set up and
well proportioned; his countenance was happy and intellectual; he
had a lofty forehead, a large nose, well defined but not aquiline; his
eyes were full of fire, his mouth and all the rest of his face had
every charm one could wish for in a man.   With it all, a certain air
of gentleness and of grandeur which predisposed in his favour and
made him both beloved and respected."

Compare this portrait of the young man with that
of the old man given to us by Saint-Simon forty years
later, when the latter tricked him into posing unconsciously for his portrait by Rigaud:

"The resemblance [of the portrait] is absolutely exact," Saint-
Simon says: "the gentleness, the serenity, the majesty of his face;
the noble fire, keen and piercing, of his eyes (so difficult to render),
the delicacy, the intellect and the grandeur expressed in his countenance; that candour, that wisdom, that interior peace of a man who
possesses his soul—all was rendered, even to the charm which had
not left his attenuated face, worn by penance, age, and suffering."

All the visitors of that day agree in speaking of the "refined and delicate countenance" and the "noble air" of M. de La Trappe which contrasted with the harshness of his life.

With a very delicate constitution people hardly understood how he could suffice for his various exercises; for at that time his activity about incongruous things had the same excessive and indefatigable ardour that afterwards impelled him along a single furrow. Often, after hunting all the morning, he would come twelve or fifteen leagues by post to preach at the Sorbonne at a given hour, as if the effort were a mere nothing. "His speech," says his biographer, M. de Châteaubriand, "had *torrent,* like that of Bourdaloue later, but Rancé's touched more, and he spoke less rapidly." His violence of passion was, at all times, masked by a perfect politeness. He knew Bossuet in early youth and was intimate with him while both were at school, and Bossuet, as we shall see later, claims for himself the happiness and honour of sitting beside Rancé, that man of whom he never spoke without betraying a reverent admiration.

Ardent, active, practical, Rancé was ever going forward, never turning back. When he was in the world, as later, when he was out of it, he did nothing by halves. Hunting, sermons, pleasures, business, intrigues, he was equal to all. Closely in touch with the Coadjutor de Retz, that most stirring of party leaders, tenderly allied with the Duchesse de Montbazon, the most beautiful woman of her day and by no means a dreamer, Rancé boldly played his part as a man-of-the-world-abbé, and a man of gallantry.

But this tumultuous life received at times certain warnings that struck his mind and caused him to think. One day, for example, he had gone with his gun to a barren piece of land behind the church of Notre-Dame, intending to fire at some bird of passage, when the steel buckle of his game-bag was struck by a ball fired from the other side of the river; the buckle deflected the shot, but he keenly realised the danger, and exclaimed: "What would have become of me alas! had God called me to him at this moment!" Thus, at that epoch (more fortunate in this respect than ours), and even in those dissipated souls in the height of their license, belief existed; whatever may have been the surface of the waves or the swelling of the storm, below was faith: souls returned in time, and the great souls rose high. To-day, almost universally, even when the appearance is of honourable and philosophically avowable belief, the undercurrent is doubt, and our great souls make no return upon themselves, they think there is no need of it. In a word, there was faith even in the license of those days; in ours, scepticism has glided into our philosophical beliefs and — why not add?— into our Christian professions; I speak of those that are sincere.

Before the moment of his conversion Rancé was

deputy of the second order to the Assembly-general of the Clergy held in the years 1655–1657. He took a somewhat active part and one of opposition to the Court, at any rate in all that concerned the interests of Cardinal de Retz, his friend, whom Court and clergy were trying to dispossess. He mingled less in the other conflicts of that day, and remained aloof from the Jansenist strife, although he was one of those who refused to sign the censure of Arnauld at the Sorbonne. In all these affairs, even the ecclesiastical ones, his conduct was that of a gallant man of the world who makes it a point of honour to be faithful to his friends in misfortune.

This was the state of his affairs when the death of Mme. de Montbazon (1657) struck him the blow of which so much has been said, which the public imagination has delighted to adorn with a romantic legend,—as it did for the history of Abelard and Heloise,—but about which he himself was more silent than the grave. It was told that, being in the country when the death of this most beautiful woman who preferred him to all others took place, he returned without being informed of it, and going to her apartment, to which he had secret access, he found his idol not only dead but headless; for the surgeons had, so it was said, detached that beautiful head to put the body into the coffin which was too short for it. The imagination of the tellers of this tale did not stop in so romantic a path, and it cost nothing to add

DUCHESSE DE MONTBAZON.
From a steel engraving.

that the head, that dear head, carried away by Rancé,
became in after years the object of his meditations at
La Trappe, the sign transformed and present at all
hours of his repentant worship.

The facts are (as Saint-Simon being well-informed
relates them, and I see no reason to doubt him) that
Mme. de Montbazon died of measles after a very few
days' illness, that M. de Rancé was beside her, never
left her, made her receive the sacraments and was
present at her death.   Shortly after, he started for his
beautiful estate of Véretz in Touraine, where he began to think more and more seriously of his irrepara-
able loss; but retirement only increased his sorrow
and a black melancholy took the place of his former
joy.   His pious biographers are extremely chary of
details at this crisis; at most they risk a few veiled
statements that "one cause or another, such as the death
of certain persons of consideration who were among
his best friends, struck him and recalled him to God."

But Rancé was a strong soul, a great soul; he
comprehended from the first day that he had lost
something he could never recover; that to begin a
maimed life on the ruins of the past was unworthy
of even a noble human ambition.   While he said
these things to himself aloud an inward voice spoke
to his soul in lower tones, and that voice had for him
a name.   Happy those for whom that voice preserves
its name, distinct and efficacious, calling itself simply
the grace of Jesus Christ!

The death of Gaston, Duc d'Orléans, whose chaplain he was, came, soon after, to impress upon him still more strongly the nothingness of man and the one existing truth of Eternity. All the lesser reasons that have been given from time to time, and even down to our day, to lower in its essence the resolution of this repentant man vanish before this one idea of Eternity fully comprehended. Where hidden springs and secondary motives escape us it is right to dwell on the dominant and manifest inspiration. That inspiration rose and resulted from the whole life and the whole soul of Rancé, and we should do wrong to ourselves if we did not perceive it in considering him. "What have you done during these forty years?" was once asked of a Chartreux in the hour of his death: "*Cogitavi dies antiquos, et annos æternos in mente habui,*" he replied,—"I have had in my thoughts the eternal years."

That was Rancé's object, his overmastering occupation from the hour of his awakening, the aim that gave him fortitude and led him, more and more, into the steep and rocky paths of repentance. That idea of Eternity — (let us think upon it!) is such that if a man looks upon it fixedly without having any gleam of immortal hope, there is enough in it to make him rush headlong to the abyss and kill himself in despair! What did Lucretius in his delirium? What did Empedocles on Etna? What might not Pascal have done had he set himself to consider (as he did, but without result) "the short duration of his life absorbed in the Eternity that preceded and followed it"— measuring with terror the two infinities without believing or hoping anything?

Rancé was thirty-one years old at the time of Mme. de Montbazon's death in 1657. Six years elapsed before he took the cowl and began his novitiate in 1663, during which time his purpose widened, strengthened and attained maturity. Living secluded, nearly the whole time on his estate of Véretz, he employed himself in breaking his many ties, in selling his patrimony for the benefit of the poor, in evading the ecclesiastical ambitions of his uncle, the Archbishop of Tours; and, so doing, he passed six years in slowly advancing towards the cloister. "My thoughts," he says in one of his letters, "went at first no farther than to lead an innocent life in the country-house which I had chosen for my retreat; but God made me know that more was needed, and that a gentle, peaceful state, such as I had pictured to myself, did not become a man who had spent his youth amid the ideas, the errors, and the maxims of the world."

He felt at first a great repugnance to the cloister; he kept his prejudices as a man of the world and a man of rank against the frock. The most respected men whom he consulted (Choiseul, Bishop of Comminges, the Bishop of Châlons, and the saintly Pavillon, Bishop of Aleth) did not advise it; on the contrary, they urged him to follow, even in his repentance, "that wise medium course which is always the character of true virtue." But a medium course was precisely that which was most contrary to his nature and most intolerable to his thoughts. The scruple of expiation in view of eternity, the ardent desire for penance were upon him; in vain did moderate reason seek to mitigate them; in great repentant hearts something else cries aloud; conscience seeks its punishment and cannot be consoled so easily. Such souls, once captured, cannot away with a sweet, false happiness in the bosom of which they would feel themselves eternally desolate.

Having decided to become a regular abbé instead of the secular one he already was, it does not appear that Rancé ever looked back. Closing his ears to clamour and even to advice, he entered the monastery of Perseigne, under the strict Cistercian rule, June 13, 1663; and the following year, July 13th, he was consecrated abbé in the church of Saint Martin, at Séez. On the 14th he went to La Trappe, the one poor benefice he had retained for himself; crossing thus the threshold of that high career in which he was henceforth to advance untrammelled, guiding others. He was thirty-eight and a half years old, and God granted him thirty-six years more of life — the time to accomplish many designs.

The poor abbey needed repairs and reformations of every kind. Already, in a stay which he made there the previous year (1662), Rancé had been forced to purge the place of the presence of the monks, six in number, who had merely the name and titles of religion and were living in the utmost debauchery. Threatened by them and at the risk of being stabbed or thrown into a pond, he held firm, even refusing the assistance offered by M. de Saint-Louis, a cavalry colonel living in the neighbourhood, an honourable soldier whose character Saint-Simon has transmitted to us. The bad monks finally consented to retire on payment of a pension, and six monks from Perseigne were brought to take their place. Besides this, materials had to be provided; the buildings, falling into ruins, needed to be rebuilt, the cattle and night-birds driven away, the fences set up. At last, thanks to these first efforts, the Abbey of Notre-Dame of the Maison-Dieu of La Trappe became a house of prayer and silence, in that valley made for it, as it seemed, expressly; encircled by forests and hillsides and watered by its nine ponds.

The history of the Monastery of La Trappe during the following years is that of gradual, silent, and hidden progress; the rumours that came to the outside world told of the least part of its work and often of the part that was least worth being known. The austerity of the rule became erelong an irresistible attraction to some; they came from neighbouring monasteries as to a hive of more celestial honey. Rancé might call himself a winner of souls, and sometimes he had to dispute for them with other monasteries that sought to get them back. Such were the chief events, the quiet contentions, that brought diversion to the early simplicity of the work. About the year 1672 La Trappe had reached its highest perfection, its full monastic fame, and one original monument the more was added, in shadow, to the wondrous splendour which illumined that period of Louis XIV.

If it is permissible, without profaning anything, to grasp the ensemble and place all things at their true value in the picture, I must say that this period of 1672 was, beyond a doubt, the most complete of a marvellous reign. Never did maturity more brilliant, more fruitful, offer more diverse masterpieces, or bring more considerable personages into view. The group of poets had not diminished: Boileau celebrated the passage of the Rhine; Racine in mid-career, was taking breath with *Béjazet;* La Fontaine mingled with new fables certain tales that were decorous. This was the year of the " Femmes Savantes " before the last hours of Molière; Lulli took in hand the Opera; M. de Pomponne was entering as minister on Public affairs, and lending to the noble good sense of the monarch the elegance of an Arnauld's pen. Bossuet, glorious orator through his first Orations, and proved a learned man by his " Exposition of Faith," was devoting himself to the Dauphin's education. Port-Royal, in these sincere years of the " peace of the Church," was flowering and fructifying afresh with the abundance of a late autumn. And afar, in the hidden byways of the

Perche, something angelic, I scarce know what, was operating like an early springtide. "People perceived," says M. de Chateaubriand, "that fragrance was coming from an unknown land and they turned to inhale it."

It was Bossuet who induced Rancé to publish his book on "The Holiness and Duties of Monastic Life." Reading the book in manuscript on his return from the Assembly of 1682, he writes to Rancé: "I own that, coming from the shameful laxities and impurities of casuists, I need to be comforted by these heavenly ideas of the life of hermits and solitaries." Rancé's style, when he is not engaged in a simple discussion which he wants to cut short and finish (as often happens to him), and when he applies it to treatises on doctrine and edification, has compass and beauty: "I know of none," says a contemporary, "more equal, more natural, more polished. The thoughts are full, the images well managed, the words appropriate and choice, the expressions clear, and the periods harmonious."

As the century advanced, the Abbey of La Trappe gained more and more authority in the eyes of the world; also it inherited the influx and concourse of postulants no longer divided among other saintly houses now suspected and inaccessible. Rancé became the sole oracle of the desert; converts and the virtuous of other lands went to him. The Princess Palatine [Anne de Gonzague] consulted him and followed

20

his directions; the King of England, to console himself for the loss of a throne, came to him yearly to talk of God; the Duchesse de Guise, daughter of Gaston d'Orléans, made retreats to La Trappe two or three times a year, lodging in the neighbourhood; the Maréchal de Bellefonds was always within reach, having a house near by. We know of the frequent visits of the Duc de Saint-Simon, who has given us much private information about that austere interior, on which he throws so vivid a light that he makes us enter it. He never mentions that rigorous penitent without tenderness.

Feeling, more and more, the weight of years, Rancé desired to give up his office as head of the monastery and see with his own eyes his successor. Louis XIV consented. Dom Zozime, whom Rancé had designated, was appointed, but died in a few months (1696). His second choice was unfortunate. Dom Gervaise came near ruining everything. Saint-Simon has related the details, long kept secret and truly singular, which led the new abbé to a forced resignation; Saint-Simon was himself too long employed at Court in this affair to allow us to doubt the circumstances he affirms, and which he had no interest, it would seem, in exaggerating. At last, however, Rancé had the satisfaction of seeing the abbey placed in good hands under the management of Dom Jacques de La Cour (1698), and from that moment he thought only of death. He died in the arms of his bishop,

M. de Séez, on the 27th of October, 1700, in the seventy-fourth year of his age.

Shortly after his death, Bossuet laid down certain rules and traced a course for Rancé's biographer such as he himself conceived to be necessary; after doing homage to him living he gave this judgment on him dead:

"I shall state my feeling on the monastery of La Trappe with much frankness, as a man who has no other view than that God be glorified in the most saintly House there is in the Church, and in the life of the most perfect director of souls ever known in monastic life since Saint-Bernard. If the history of this saintly personage is not written by an able hand and a head as much above all human views as heaven is above earth, all will go ill. In some directions they would want to pay court to the Benedictines, in others to the Jesuits, in others again to Monks in general. . . . All parties wish to draw to themselves the saintly abbé. . . . If he who undertakes so great a work does not feel strong enough to have no need of counsel, the mixture is to be feared, and through it a species of degradation in the work. . . . Simplicity ought to be its sole ornament. I should prefer a simple narrative, such as Dom Le Nain could make, to laboured eloquence. . . ."

It had been proposed to Bossuet to write the life himself; he alone, under the conditions he laid down, was strong enough to do it; but he was unable on account of his multifarious occupations. His chief thought was that every party would seek "to draw the saintly abbé to itself"; whereas, on the contrary, his own conduct in holding himself, as he had done, aloof from all parties should be imitated.

To-day things are changed: we are more prepared to accept, such as he offers himself, that sublime abbé, that monk worthy of Syria, or of the primitive Clairvaux, ardent, impetuous, impatient, man of action and of deeds rather than of discussion or doctrine, but a great intellect all the same; a true monk by *race,* as de Maistre would say; indomitable to all but God himself. We might even be disposed to take him too much in this sense only, and to create a Rancé of a single pattern, which no man ever was, not even he. To picture to ourselves the true Rancé an atom of the world must be introduced, a moral spring must be touched, a secret fibre reached, which the orthodoxy of contemporaries never sought and would not have admitted.

In the "Letters of Rancé" collected and published by M. Gonod, librarian of Clermont-Tonnerre, we have the veritable man himself, speaking in person, simply, gravely, with monotonous sadness or with a smileless joy that resembles sadness and never brightens. We feel, in reading those equable words and in approaching closer to the individual, how little there was, in the very real and practical religion then prevailing, of the poesy which we have since introduced to adapt religion to the taste of to-day and to recover belief by imagination. Even in Rancé's time there were men of the world zealous enough and inquiring enough to go of their own volition and spend twenty-four hours at La Trappe simply as an act of piety. They would be very ready to do so in our day; men would willingly make a pilgrimage that would long be talked-of, and about which they could tell the public the slightest circumstances and "impressions"; but in the mere idea of duration attached to such a life there is something that alarms them, chills and repulses them. Now, that *something* is felt inevitably on every page of the letters of the reformer of La Trappe. Nothing could be less poetic, I assure you, nothing less literary in the modern sense of the word, and I will add, almost as an immediate consequence, nothing more truly humble and sincere.

The letters collected by M. Gonod are of different dates and are addressed, excepting a very small number, to three persons: the Abbé Favier, his former tutor; the Abbé Nicaise, of Dijon, one of the most active correspondents of the seventeenth century, who took the place to Rancé of a gazette or the *Journal des Savants;* and lastly, the Duchesse de Guise, daughter of Gaston d'Orléans one of the souls from without who placed themselves under the guidance of the austere abbé.

Though the letters addressed to the Abbé Favier are, at least in the beginning, of a much earlier date than the conversion and reform of Rancé, we may search them in vain for any trace of his worldly dissipations and his brilliant errors. The young abbé was contented, during those fiery years, to obey his passions without parading them in letters; moreover, they are not the things that a young man is accustomed to relate to a former tutor. The latter had left his pupil on the path of hard study and theological discussion, and he always thought of him under that aspect: "You have too good an opinion of my vocation in the theological way," Rancé writes to him; "provided it has been pleasing to God, that is all that I desire." In vain do we reread and sift the letters of that date; we find kind and respectful feelings for his old tutor, a tone of true modesty when he speaks of himself and his first appearance in the schools or the pulpit, much gravity, much propriety but not the least little ear-tip of the lover of Mme. de Montbazon.

The period of his retreat at Véretz is marked by a softened tone and a few expressions of contentment, if that word is applicable to a nature like that of Rancé. "I live in my house much alone," he writes, "I am seen by very few persons, and all my application is given to my books and to what I imagine to belong to my profession. I feel enough liking for it to believe that I shall not weary of the life I lead. . . . " But after this stage, as it may be called, this first period of repose, Rancé rises, he sets forth in search of a repentance unwearying and almost pitiless; he faces it humanly: "I assure you, Monsieur," he writes to the Abbé Favier (January 24, 1670), "that as soon as a man wills to belong entirely to God and be separated from man, life is good for nothing except to be destroyed; and we ought not to consider ourselves other than *tanquam oves occisionis.*" Beside these stern and almost savage words we cannot help feeling the constant proofs of affection, always grave, always reserved, but deepening more and more as the years went on, which he gave to the worthy old man, his former master; there are days of effusion and tenderness, when instead of calling him "Monsieur" it escapes him to say: "My very dear Monsieur."

An historical thought comes out clearly in reading these letters of Rancé, even in the midst of the reform which he is undertaking with such heroic energy: it is, that the time of monks was past, that the world wanted them no longer, did not understand them, and would not permit their existence. This appears by the confession of Rancé himself; he expresses it, in his own manner, when he says (October 3, 1675): "Inasmuch as you wish to know the news of our affair, I will tell you that, however just it was, the judgment has gone entirely against us; and, to speak frankly to you, my thought is that the Order of the Cistercians is rejected of God; that having reached the summit of iniquity it is no longer worthy of the good we have striven to do to it, and that we ourselves who seek to procure its re-establishment do not deserve that God should protect our designs or cause them to succeed." He returns in many places to this despairing idea; his judgment on his Order is decisive: "The very ruins," he exclaims, "are not repairable!" He had resigned his abbey of Saint-Symphorien-lez-Beauvais to the Abbé Favier, who did not know what to do with it, for the

few monks who remained there were living scanda-
lously. " To put reformers there," wrote Rancé, " is
no longer possible; reformers are so decried; and,
partly from the bad conduct of the monks, people will
not allow them to be introduced where they are not
already. It is our sins that have caused this." Thus
the great century, the century of Louis XIV, which we
at a distance imagine to be so devout, had done with
monks, and that, by the confession of the saintliest and
purest monastic reformer of the age.

"We live," he writes to the Abbé Nicaise, "in times
more prudent and wise—I speak of the wisdom of
this world and not of that of Jesus Christ." Since
then, two centuries and over have only increased that
human prudence and wisdom, and the anachronism of
the saintly reformer is not less crying. This is a reflection that cannot be stifled in reading him, and it
leads to many others.

The letters of Rancé to the Abbé Nicaise, without
being of much interest to read, have a very real value
for the literary history of that time. The Abbé Nicaise
was, as everybody knows, the most undefatigable
writer of letters, the newsmonger *par excellence*, and
the officious go-between of the learned men of all
countries. He could not resist the idea of knowing so
celebrated a man as M. de La Trappe, and of keeping
up an intercourse with him. Once in relation with
the recluse he never let him go, and the latter was
compelled to continue a correspondence in which curi-

osity did violence to charity. However, if the Abbé
Nicaise drew his grave and sombre correspondent into
more than one difficulty by the indiscretions he committed, he did him in return a variety of good offices;
if Rancé, for instance, wished to inform the world of
his true sentiments on such or such a point in litiga-
tion, he had only to state them to the abbé.

Nevertheless, that worthy man, always on the watch
with his nose to the wind, puts the patience of the
saint to the proof, and tries again and again to excite
his curiosity. Most of the news on which he comments and the books he extols, wishing to know
Rancé's opinion of them, never reach La Trappe, and
Rancé exhausts himself in saying, gently and quietly:
"We have neither seen nor heard of any of the books
you mention. The republic of letters does not spread
to places where it knows it has none but enemies,
who are incessantly occupied with unlearning and forgetting what curiosity made them know, that they
may give all their application and their study to the
one book of Jesus Christ." Each time that the incor-
rigible Nicaise returns to the charge Rancé reiterates
this profession of forgetfulness: "None of the books
of which you speak to me reach us; we regard them
as lost and flung into a pit whence nothing ought ever
to return." But the good abbé is not discouraged; in
default of the works of others he sends his own, hoping at least to hear what is thought of them. On
one occasion he takes it into his head to compose a

"Dissertation on Syrens, a Discourse on their Face and Form," and straightway sends his manuscript to La Trappe. Oh! this time Rancé cannot restrain a smile; we catch that movement on his countenance (in him so rare) through the simple lines of his answer: "I have cast my eyes over your work on Syrens, but I own to you that I have not dared go farther into the matter. All the fabulous species feel themselves awakened, and I recognise that I am not as dead as I ought to be. That is a thought which has been followed by many reflections — this is how we may profit by everything."

The letters to the Duchesse de Guise are all edifying, noble, sufficiently expansive, but sober nevertheless. This last characteristic is found everywhere in Rancé's correspondence; even when he takes a pen he goes straight to his object, he cuts mere phrases short. Speaking of the death of M. de Nocé, a penitent of rank and one of the hermits living near La Trappe, he writes to Mme. de Guise, who has questioned him: "There were no brilliant circumstances, Madame, in the death of that hermit. His passing was peaceful and tranquil. Struggle he had none, and we only perceived that he had ceased to live because he breathed no longer. God willed that he should say nothing remarkable in order to abridge the Record." *Abridge, shorten* all passing things; that is Rancé's permanent sentiment; he never sees a useless branch without instantly producing his axe or his shears.

Though the mere reading of these letters of Rancé may, if we are not on our guard, seem monotonous, all of them being more or less alike, yet we may draw from them a great quantity of beautiful and noble thoughts. I have already given some, detaching them intentionally, because they are so imbedded on a sombre background that it is almost necessary to present them alone in order to have them noticed. What more lofty thought, for instance, than this, which might serve as the epigram and the motto of the life of the great reformer: "We should do those works and those actions which exist independently of the different passions of men." And what delicacy in this other saying, which reveals a tenderness of soul surviving beneath the hard exterior: "It would be a very sweet thing to be so entirely forgotten that we lived only in the memory of friends." Notice that this profound forgetting on the part of the world, joined to faithful recollection on the part of friends, is the perfect concordance embraced by the hermit's hope.

X.

La Grande Mademoiselle.

Anne—Geneviève de Bourbon.

La Grande Mademoiselle.

ONE of the most original figures, the most singular, and at the same time the most natural of the seventeenth century is certainly La Grande Mademoiselle, daughter of Gaston, Duc d'Orléans, niece of Louis XIII and cousin-german of Louis XIV. In every epoch, a certain type is in fashion, a certain romantic phantom occupies imaginations and floats, as it were, upon the clouds. At the close of the reign of Louis XIII and at the beginning of that of Louis XIV this type, this model, was chiefly formed from the heroes and heroines of Corneille, also from those of Mlle. de Scudéry. La Grande Mademoiselle, a person of imagination, fancy, and high temper, with little judgment, embodied much of this type in herself; to it she added all that belonged to the prejudices of her race and to the superstitions of her royal birth. The result was the most fantastic of compositions, the most vainglorious,

319

the least reasonable, and her whole life showed the effects. Though she held the sword for some time as an amazon, she also produced, pen in hand, a great deal; for not only did she leave interesting and very truthful Memoirs (of which it was said that "they are sufficiently ill-written to assure us they were written by herself"), but we also have, of her making, Portraits, Letters, and short Romances. In short, Mademoiselle was not only a very extraordinary princess, she was an author as well. As such, she belongs to us of right, and it is justice to assign to her the place and date she ought to occupy in the series of literary fashions and varieties.

She was born in the Louvre, May, 1627. Having lost her mother in infancy, she was brought up by an estimable and pious governess but with all the respect due to a granddaughter of Henri IV. Naturally, she grew accustomed to consider herself of different blood from that of other men, even noblemen, and on a par with kings and queens. This idea, which to her was a religion, dictated to her on all occasions speeches of the frankest and most naïve vanity, and imposed upon her sentiments that aimed at grandeur and certainly did not derogate from dignity. Her father, Gaston, Duc d'Orléans, endowed with a thousand fine qualities of the mind and not one of the heart or character, was the soul of all the intrigues against Richelieu, compromising incessantly his followers and friends, whom he

LA GRANDE MADEMOISELLE.
From a steel engraving.

afterwards abandoned. Mademoiselle from her earliest childhood showed more pride and more honour. Having witnessed at Fontainebleau the ceremony of degrading two knights of the Order (the Duc d'Elbeuf and the Marquis de La Vieuville) she asked the reason; being told it was because they had been of Monsieur's party, she burst into tears and wished to withdraw, declaring that she could not witness that act with decency.

In a period when Richelieu ruled and "tyranny reigned so haughtily over even royal personages" she kept intact within her a worship and lofty idolatry of her race. Her childhood and her first youth were passed in frivolities, in a round of Court, of ceremonial and idle amusements, balls, comedies, collations, with no one to tell her there was anything in life more serious. She went one day on a visit to the convent of Fontevrault, the abbess of which was her aunt, a natural daughter of Henri IV, and began by getting tired of it at once. But the young girls of her suite having discovered a crazy woman locked up in a dungeon, quick! they called Mademoiselle to amuse her with the sight of her antics: "I took my course to the dungeon," she says, "and did not leave it till evening." The next day the abbess, seeing her taste for it, "regaled her with another crazy woman"; "as there was not a third for the next day," she adds amusingly, "it was all so wearisome that I went away, in spite of my aunt's entreaties." This is the

tone in which human wretchedness was treated by
one who was kind at heart; but no one, I say again,
was there to warn and enlighten her. When the
Fronde began, the same thing happened. Mademoiselle at first saw nothing in it but a subject of curiosity
and amusement: "All these novelties delighted me
. . . no matter what importance an affair might
have, if it served only to amuse me I thought of
nothing else all the evening." Such was Mademoiselle at ten years of age, such at twenty, such at
thirty, such nearly all her life, until a tardy passion
taught her what it was to suffer.

The first pages of her Memoirs are filled with exterior details only. She went to all the hunting
parties of Louis XIII in the days of his amour with
Mlle. de Hautefort. Enumerating the young ladies she
had in her suite: "We were all dressed in colour,"
she says, "and mounted on fine ambling horses richly
caparisoned; and to guard us from the sun each had
a hat trimmed with quantities of feathers." That
paints her to us already, proud and of haughty mien,
tall of her age and wearing the white plumes from
the helmet of her grandsire of Navarre. What matters it that Mademoiselle, at this period, was only ten
years old? her mind, in many respects, remained at
that age, and never matured. They began even then
to talk of marrying her, either to the king, or to the
cardinal-Infant, brother of the queen-mother, or to
the Comte de Soissons; they amused her with it.

For thirty years more they talked to her of such
projects *ad infinitum;* she talked about them herself
incessantly, but like a child, unable to resolve upon
the step, without perceiving that in the end that
eternal indecision would become a jest. She, who
called herself MADEMOISELLE *par excellence* could not
bring herself to cease to be so, and this lasted until
nature, so long set aside, recovered its rights and
spoke, once for all, in her heart. But we have not
reached that point as yet.

She showed at an early date a taste for things of
the mind, wit, spirit, shrewdness, all that serves for
conversation. Her father excelled in this; she relates
how at Tours, every evening, she loved to listen to
Monsieur, who told her his past adventures, "and
that very agreeably, like the man in the world who
had most grace and natural faculty for talking well."
It is rare to find a child so perceptive of that sort of
charm. Mademoiselle, in the letters she addressed to
Mme. de Motteville in 1660, speaks to her of conversation as being "to your taste and mine, the
greatest pleasure in life and almost the only one I care
for." It was by that means, even more than by his
fine air that Lauzun first insinuated himself into her
confidence: "I found in him," she says, "methods
of expression that I heard from no one else."

Richelieu dead, Gaston, whom his last intrigues
had sent into exile, made peace with the Court; he
returned to Paris and went to his daughter's residence:

"He supped with me, where we had twenty-four violins," says Mademoiselle: "he was as gay as if MM. de Cinq Mars and de Thou had not been left by the way. I own I could not see him without thinking of them, and in my joy I felt that his gave me pain." Mademoiselle's good qualities show already; she has humanity in spite of her pride of race, fidelity to friends through their varied fortunes, and dignity. Her father laughs more than once at her pretensions to chivalry and heroism, but in those respects as in others she was worth more than he.

The time that elapsed between the death of Louis XIII and the first Fronde (1643–1648) was a brilliant moment for Mademoiselle. She was sixteen to twenty years of age, and shone at Court in the first rank and in all the pride of hope. There was no alliance that did not seem worthy of her. Not at all gallant in temperament, in no way coquettish, so cold that she was long compared to the virgin Pallas, she saw nothing in marriage but the means to reach a great part and a glorious destiny; and, romantic as she was, she liked almost as well to nurse the idea as to accomplish it. Should she be Queen of France by marrying the young King, Louis XIV, eleven years younger than herself? Should she be Queen of England by marrying the Prince of Wales, then in exile but who could not fail to be restored? Or should she be an empress by marrying the Emperor of Germany, lately become a widower? It seemed as if she had

only to choose; and no one can show her proud
perversity better than she does herself àpropos of a
fête given at the Palais-Royal during the winter of
1646, for which the queen-mother was anxious to
adorn her:

" They were three whole days arranging my attire; my gown was
loaded with diamonds, and scarlet and black and white tassels; I had
upon me all the crown-jewels, and those of the Queen of England,
who still had some left in those days.   No one was ever seen better
nor more magnificently adorned than I was that day, and I did not
fail to find many persons to tell me, rather apropos, that my fine
figure, my good countenance, the whiteness of my skin and the splendour of my blonde hair did not adorn me less than all the riches that
shone upon my person. . . ."

They danced in the great theatre, brilliantly lighted.
At one end was a throne raised three steps and sur-
mounted by a dais:

" The King (Louis XIV) and the Prince of Wales (afterwards
Charles II), would not seat themselves on the throne; I sat there alone,
so that I saw at my feet those two princes and all the princesses who
were then at Court.   I did not feel embarrassed in that position
. . .   All present did not fail to tell me that I had never seemed
less constrained than I did on that throne, and that, as I came of a
race to occupy it, when I was in possession of one on which I should
sit longer than merely at a ball, I should do so with more ease still.
While I was there and the prince was at my feet, my heart looked
down upon him as well as my eyes; I had it in mind just then to
marry the emperor. . . .   I no longer regarded the Prince of
Wales as anything but an object of pity."

Such was this romantic princess, who tells everything about herself naturally, sincerely, with a sort of
bravura in her sincerity, and a frankness which at
times is hearty even in her pride.

The beauty, to which she is the first to do justice, was real at that period of her first youth. Brilliancy, freshness ''which, of Lilies, kept their candid innocence,'' said the poets, fine eyes, blonde hair, a beautiful figure, all this concealed what was wanting in her of delicacy and grace; ''she had the air of a great beauty,'' says Mme. de Motteville. Nevertheless, her teeth, that were not good, and her large, aquiline nose showed the rather common defects of the Bourbon race. Years gave to her features and to her shape more stiffness, without taking from her the quickness and petulance of movement, which never allowed her to have dignity.

When the Fronde broke out, and the good sense inclosed in each head was put to the roughest proof in that brusque civil tempest, Mademoiselle was already known for impetuosities and caprices of temper, which sometimes thwarted and overcame her real feelings to the point of injuring her fortune and even of lessening the consideration paid to her. She could not decide on her choice of a husband and, in her desire for a crown, she allowed opportunities that were under her hand to escape her in order to grasp at distant impossibilities. She was on particularly bad terms with the queen [Anne of Austria] and with Cardinal Mazarin; and for that reason as little disposed to be wise and sensible in the dawning troubles as any one at Court.

The first Fronde, that of 1648, gave her no occasion

to come forward herself; her action was limited to
giving way to prejudices that she did not take the
pains to conceal: "As I was not much satisfied with
the queen, or with Monsieur at that time," she says,
"it gave me great pleasure to see them embarrassed."
When the queen and the Court left Paris, by Mazarin's
advice, and went to Saint-Germain during the night
of January 6, 1649, she made it her duty to accompany them, though she was very far from sharing their
thoughts and intentions: "I was all excited with
joy at seeing they were about to commit a blunder,
and in being spectatress of the troubles it would cause
them; this avenged me a little for the persecutions I
had suffered." The levity, disorder, and bustle of
the Court at Saint-Germain are painted to admiration
by a person as thoughtless and frivolous as any of
them, but who is veracious and tells all. Mademoiselle had great satisfactions to self-love during that
sojourn. "The people of Paris," she says, "have
always loved me because I was born and brought
up there; that has given them a respect for me, and
a greater inclination than that they usually feel for
persons of my quality." It resulted from this exception in her favour on the part of the Parisians, that
they allowed her carriages and horses to leave for
Saint-Germain; and while the queen and king lacked
everything, she had all she wanted and lacked nothing.
All this, however, was but a prelude to the part she
was to play in the second Fronde: "I did not then

foresee," she says, "that I should find myself concerned in a considerable affair, where I could do my
duty and avenge myself at the same time; nevertheless, in doing that sort of vengeance we sometimes
avenge ourselves much against ourselves."

That little final touch of repentance does not hinder
Mademoiselle from being very proud and very vainglorious of what she did in 1652, when she was able
both to obey her father and to give herself up to her
instincts for adventure. She was twenty-five years
old at this second epoch, the finest age for an amazon.
The idea of marriage, which was always flitting in
perspective before her eyes, was then suggesting to her
a possible union with either the Prince de Condé in
case he became a widower (she never shrank from that
species of supposition), or with the king if she made
herself formidable and necessary. Meanwhile she
obeyed, without much consistency, her romantic and
grandiose tastes, and, converting her former aversion
for the Prince de Condé into sudden friendship, she
was fired with a desire to signalise herself for the
common cause by some dazzling service.

An occasion presented itself. Her father, Monsieur,
was in Paris, which he thought he could not quit
without serious inconvenience. He was much
needed at Orléans, which belonged to his appanage,
and where a rather considerable party wished to open
the gates to the royal army, then advancing from
Blois. Hence it became of the utmost importance that

the city of Orléans should stand firm for the Fronde, otherwise the whole line of the Loire was cut, and the Prince de Condé, coming from Guyenne, would find the enemy master of the position. Mademoiselle offered to go in person to Orléans and hold the town. Her father distrusted her and her judgment: "Such chivalry would be very ridiculous," he said on the day she started, "if the good sense of Mmes. de Fiesque and de Frontenac did not support her." Those were the two ladies who accompanied her and who were called, partly in courtesy and partly in derision, her "field-marshals."

So Mademoiselle started, with joy in her heart on finding herself, at last, on the way to do some extraordinary action and achieve fame. An astrologer predicted it to her on the morning of her departure, and she made no manner of doubt that he was right. As soon as she reached the plains of Beauce, she mounted her horse and put herself at the head of the armies of the Fronde, which were then in that neighbourhood. A council of war was held before her at which it was agreed that nothing should be done except by her order. The difficulty was to enter Orléans; for, pressed hard on either side between the summons of the Keeper of the Seals, Molé, on the part of the king, and that of the Frondeurs, the gentlemen of the Hôtel-de-Ville had a strong desire to remain neutral. Impatient at the parleys, which were much prolonged, Mademoiselle marched up and down before the ramparts, exciting the people behind them by her gestures and words. Then, finding she could rely more on the populace than on the comfortable *bourgeois*, she sprang into a boat which some sailors offered her, crossed the moat and ordered a gate that opened on the quay and was ill-guarded to be battered in. When two planks were down, she passed through the hole, and there she was! followed afar by her ladies, carried in triumph by the people, and mistress of the place in the twinkling of an eye: "for," she says to the governor and sheriffs, who were not a little astonished, "when persons of my quality enter a town they are its mistresses, and with justice: I ought to be so here, as the place belongs to Monsieur—on which, a good deal frightened, they made me their compliment. . . . When I reached my house, I received the harangues of all the public bodies and the honours that were due to me." Not content with being harangued, she improvised a speech before the Hôtel-de-Ville, and acquitted herself no worse than other orators and public speakers in a like crisis.[1]

These first days were the finest. People did not fail, of course, to compare Mademoiselle to the Maid of Orléans. The Queen of England, whose son she

[1] Mademoiselle's insatiable vanity led her in after years to have her portrait painted in military costume, to commemorate this glorious taking of Orléans, and also her really splendid conduct on the day of the battle of Saint-Antoine, when she saved the life of the Prince de Condé and turned the guns of the Bastille on the king's army—an exploit that Louis XIV never, in his heart, forgave. The picture is a small one painted on vellum, and is now in the collection of the " Portraits Nationaux. "—Tr.

had refused for a husband, said of her, satirically, that it was "very right for her to save Orléans like the Maid, having begun by driving away the English." The Prince de Condé, hurrying from Agen, incognito and disguised, arrived at this crisis, fortunately, and took command of his army near Orléans. Thence he writes a letter to Mademoiselle to thank her and congratulate her on her prowess: " It is a deed the glory of which belongs to none but you, and it is of the utmost importance." A report having been rendered to him of a council of war at which she was present and gave her opinion, she remarks: " M. le Prince says that the resolutions taken at the council at which I was good enough to be present ought to be followed, even if they were not wise, but in fact they were such that the King of Sweden (Gustavus Adolphus) could not have taken better, and that he himself would have done so even if I had not ordered them." Mademoiselle accepts and repeats such praises in solemn earnest. When she returned, shortly after, to Paris, all the people came out to meet her; she was the heroine of the moment. The Prince de Condé assured her that he wished for nothing so passionately as to see her queen of France, and that he would make no terms of peace in which she was not included. In her credulous exaltation she was, indeed, at the most brilliant moment of her existence.

Reverses came, and she took part in them valiantly. Aloof from intrigues, incapable of politics, the affairs of the Fronde were already in dissolution, and negotiations were begun on all sides before she suspected it. On the 2nd of July, 1652, when the bloody battle of the Faubourg Saint-Antoine was fought, where the Prince de Condé, after prodigies of valour, was about to be crushed with all his men by Turenne if the gates of Paris were not opened to his exhausted army, it was Mademoiselle who, wrenching consent from Monsieur, already half a traitor, flew to the Hôtel-de-Ville and forced the undecided and unwilling municipals to open them. To the Maréchal de l' Hôpital, who resisted as long as he could, she said these noble words: "Reflect, monsieur, that while you are all amusing yourselves by disputing over useless things M. le Prince is in peril within your suburbs. What sorrow and what shame it will for ever be to Paris if he perishes for want of succour! You can give it to him; then give it to him quickly!" It is told, that as he still hesitated she said to him that if he did not hasten she would "drag him by the beard and he should die by no hand but hers." Hastening from there to the Bastille, armed with full powers, she gathered up as she went the wounded, nearly all men of mark, whom she recognised with pity. She paints to us with expressive strokes the moment when, in one of the intervals of the action, she met the Prince de Condé:

" He was in a pitiable state ; he had a mass of dust upon his face, his hair was thick with it ; his collar and his shirt were full of blood, though he had not been wounded ; his cuirass was dented with blows, and he held his naked sword in his hand, having lost the scabbard ; he gave it to my equerry. He said to me : ' You see a man in despair ; I have lost all my friends ; Messieurs de Nemours, de La Rochefoucauld, and Clinchamps are mortally wounded.' I assured him they were in better condition than he thought. . . . That rejoiced him a little ; he was deeply afflicted. When he entered he flung himself on a chair and wept ; he said to me : ' Pardon the grief in which I am.' After that, let no one tell me that he loves nothing ; for my part, I have always known him tender for his friends and for those he loves."

It is to be remarked here that Condé loved and wept as a soldier for friends whom he might have seen die in other ways without much regret, perhaps. On a day of battle he recovered his good qualities, his humanity, and his other virtues; he was in his element, and, like all great hearts at such times, he was kind.

Mademoiselle ordered a few volleys from the cannon of the Bastille, which manifested plainly the attitude of the people of Paris and warned the troops of the king that the hour had not come to enter the city. Mazarin said that those cannon-balls, fired by order of Mademoiselle, had " killed her husband," meaning that she could never henceforth hope to marry the king; but it is very doubtful if she could ever have married him. However that may be, she had, on this day of the Bastille, the satisfaction of having done, not, as at Orléans, a dashing stroke, but an act of courage and humanity. She blushed for her father and for the prolonged indecision from which she had been compelled to wrench him; she tried to excuse him as well as she could, and to save him the shame of not having mounted his horse and done the deeds that she did; but heart and courage were hers, not his.

On a third occasion she again supplied his deficiency. Two days later (July 4th) during the massacre at the Hôtel-de-Ville, by which the Prince de Condé repaid so grievously his welcome by the Parisians, and which Gaston, according to his habit, favoured, to say the least, by his inaction, Mademoiselle offered to go and save those who were being massacred and curb the populace. Starting from the Luxembourg she could not at first enter the Hôtel-de-Ville; she was more fortunate on a second attempt and reached the place very late, much too late, but soon enough, nevertheless, to do some acts of protection and humanity.

The Fronde was at an end and every one was seeking to make his peace. The rumour ran that Gaston had come to terms with the Court by separating his interests from those of the Prince de Condé. President Viole spoke of it to Mademoiselle, who was reduced to replying: ."You know him; I will not answer for what he does." When she went to her base father to ask if he had orders to quit the Luxembourg, and, if so, what she was to do herself, he replied that he should not mix himself up in what concerned her; and he disavowed all that she had done in his name:

"Do you not think, Mademoiselle," he said, with the cowardly and contemptuous irony that was common with him, "that the affair of

Saint-Antoine must have injured you at Court ? You have been very pleased to play the heroine, and to be told you were that of our party; that you saved it twice. Whatever happens to you, you will console yourself by thinking of the praises people gave you."

She answered proudly and with dignity:

"I do not think I did you ill-service at the Porte Saint-Antoine, any more than at Orléans. Those two irreproachable actions I did by your order; if they were to do over again, I should do them again, because my duty would oblige me to do so. It is better to do as I did than be humiliated for having done nothing. I do not know what being a heroine is. I am of a birth that does nothing that is not great and lofty. People can call that what they choose; as for me, I call it following my inclination and going my way; I was born not to take that of others."

There is, of course, some pomposity and a little swagger in that utterance, we feel it of course; but we cannot fail to recognise also an echo, as it were, of the "Cid," and certain Corneillian accents. Mademoiselle, during the Fronde, was in love with false grandeur, she sought a false glory; but at least she remained disinterested, generous, and put no stain upon her name.

In the years that followed she had to make the king forgive her, and in the long run she succeeded. During the sojourns, more or less enforced, that she made on the estates of her appanage she acquired a taste for literature and its cultivation. She began at that time to write her Memoirs, which have lately been re-edited by M. Chéruel from the autograph manuscript in the Bibliothéque Nationale. The modern editors (M. Petitot and M. Michaud) neglected to consult that manuscript and have continued to print their editions in which the text has been much touched up, and where various mistakes occur in proper names, and some omissions. All such errors have been repaired in M. Chéruel's edition. The Abbé Terrasson said of a Jansenist translation of the Bible that "the scandal of the text was preserved in all its purity." We may equally say that in this good edition of Mademoiselle's Memoirs her style is given in all the purity of its natural incorrectness.

One of her gentlemen and household attendants was the poet Segrais. Through him she knew Huet (the future bishop) who, then young, served her sometimes as reader during her toilet. She liked novels above all else. She composed one or two about this period (1658), also society Portraits, the fashion of which had just been introduced. She had a whole volume of them printed at Caen in 1659, under the supervision of Huet, with a small number of copies; nearly all these Portraits being written by herself. In short, she made literature much as she had made civil war and played the amazon, at a venture, heedlessly, offhand, but not without a certain capacity.

We find her again in 1660, making part of the Court during the Conferences of the Peace of the Pyrenees, and giving herself up once more to her imagination, no longer under the form heroic; now it was the form pastoral. One day, being at Saint-Jean-de-Luz in the chamber of Cardinal Mazarin, and standing at a window with Mme. de Motteville, admiring the beauty of

the scenery, Mademoiselle began to imagine a plan of
retirement and solitude, and to moralise on the happy
life it would offer. Coming away, full of her project, she wrote a long letter to Mme. de Motteville,
who replied in turn. This correspondence, which is
quite agreeable to read, marks very well a certain
moment in French literature. It represents and characterises the Spanish pastoral element that was in
vogue from the novels of d'Urfé to those of Mlle. de
Scudéry, and to which the good sense of Louis XIV,
aided by Boileau, put an end.

Mademoiselle imagined, in a meadow, near a forest,
in view of the sea, a society of the two sexes, composed wholly of amiable and perfect beings, delicate
and simple, who watched their flocks on sunny days
and for their pleasure, and visited the rest of the time,
from one hermitage to another, in chair, calèche or
coach; who played the lute and the harpsichord, read
poesy and new books, united the advantages of civilised life with the easy habits of rural life (not forgetting the virtues of Christian life); and who all, celibates
and widowers, polite without gallantry and even
without love, lived honourably together, and felt
no need to have recourse to the vulgar remedy of
marriage. Observe that a convent of Carmelites is at
hand in the forest, and the company does not fail to
go there for edification at stated times; for one must,
even when leading the gentle life, think also of
salvation.

22

Mme. de Motteville, while replying with all sorts of compliments, and calling Mademoiselle in turn the "illustrious princess" and the "beautiful Amelinta," laughs at her slily for the article interdicting matrimony, which was meant to be the great novelty of this Code of the Sheepfold, and she tries to insinuate a little reality, a little common sense into the scheme of this platonic, Christian, and, withal, gallant republic. She points out that as it would be difficult to suppress gallantry and love altogether, it might perhaps be better to "return to the very common error that an old custom has made legitimate, which is called marriage." The pair expatiate on that topic from one to the other, and Mademoiselle gives proof in the discussion of a romantic spirit rather elegant and distinguished, even elevated now and then. But, on the whole, here, as in the Fronde, it is the sentiment of reality, it is common sense, a sense of the fitness of things, that is always lacking in her.

I shall not follow her through her various compositions and literary rhapsodies (Portraits, Romances of Society, and what not), but come at once to the great event of her life which completes her picture. Mademoiselle was forty-two years of age; she had missed so many and such great marriages that there seemed nothing else for her but to continue in the free and independent position of the richest princess of France, when she began to notice M. de Lauzun, a favourite of the king, and younger than herself by several years. Still cold

and pure, never having loved until then, she now, for
the first time, felt love with an extreme youth-
fulness, or, as one might say, childlikeness of heart;
she describes it to us with the naïveté of a shepherdess.

She perceived one day that this little man, captain
of the guards, a Gascon with haughty mien and satirical, witty air, had a nameless something about him
that she had never yet remarked in any one.   The first
time he went on duty as captain of the guards, and
"took his baton," as they say " he did his functions
with a grand and easy air, full of attentions without
eagerness.   When I made him my compliment," she
relates, "he replied that he was very sensible of the
honour I did him in taking part in the kindness that the
king had for him."   That simple speech enchanted
her: "I began from that time to regard him as an *extraordinary* man, very agreeable in conversation, and
I sought very willingly for occasions to speak to him."
She began to be vaguely annoyed when she did not
see him.   "That winter," she says (1669), "without
quasi knowing why, I could not endure Paris nor to
leave Saint Germain."   Every day that she succeeded
in conversing with him in the embrasure of a window
(a thing not so easy to do because of etiquette and her
rank) she found more and more intellect and accom-
plishments in him.   When she held him thus, she forgot herself for hours. She took pleasure in discovering
all sorts of distinctions about him, an elevation of

soul above the common, and "a million singularities" that charmed her.

After dreaming thus for some time, she ended by fixing her mind resolutely; and as she was very honourable and very lacking in foresight, and as, moreover, the idea of love without marriage never entered her head, she thought that the shortest way would be to make the grandeur of the gentleman and wed him. The difficulty was to make him understand this, for the respect behind which Lauzun intrenched himself left her no access to him. It has been remarked that "in friendship as in love princesses are condemned to take all the first steps, and that the respect which surrounds them often obliges the proudest and most virtuous to make advances that other women would not dare to permit themselves." Mademoiselle was compelled to take all these steps. Lauzun's strategy consisted in adding to and raising higher these barriers of respect, already so high, in still further intrenching himself behind them, and getting out of sight. It was all low bows, assurances of submission without end, but he turned a deaf ear to every tender word; and not only did he persistently follow this course , but Baraille, officer of his company and his confidential man, did the same ; " Every time I met him (Baraille)," says Mademoiselle, " I bowed to him, to give him a desire to appro me; he always pretended to think I was bow some other person, and while he made me bows on one side he was going away on the other; at which I was in despair." These were Lauzun's tactics and order of the day. If Mademoiselle had not had any idea of marriage in her head he would have led her and constrained her to it by his conduct; so careful was he not to lend himself to any overture that was simply tender and wooing. The man of *bonnes fortunes* became for the nonce a man of principle; he played the virtuous and the chaste to get himself married.

Poor Mademoiselle, as much of a novice as a school girl, and without a confidant, did not know what to invent to reveal to this conceited coxcomb what he knew very well already. She sent for the Works of Corneille and re-read them, looking for images of her own fate in order to take lessons; she counted on the secret sympathy of souls: Lauzun would see nothing. She pretended to consult him on the various marriages proposed to her, hoping that he would declare himself and give her the opportunity to make her own confession. But Lauzun was strictly, cruelly respectful, respectful to excess. Always homage, never presumption. She had made him, as if in spite of himself, her counsellor, her confidant; she wished to marry, she told him,—to marry in France, to make the fortune of some one who deserved it; to live with that honourable man and friend in perfect esteem, with sweetness and tranquillity; it was only a question of finding some one worthy of that choice.

Lauzun discussed the matter with her at length; he weighed the advantages and the disadvantages of such a step, taking very good care not to seem to divine that he himself was in question. There were days, however, when he seemed to be beginning to understand; but he always escaped in time "by respectful manners full of witty sense," which only inflamed the innocent princess more and more.

She loved like Dido, like Medea, like Ariadne, but twenty years too late. She did things that would have been quite charming in a very young girl. During a journey into Flanders where M. de Lauzun commanded as general, on a day when it poured with rain he came often to the side of the king's carriage, bareheaded and hat in hand. Mademoiselle at last could not contain herself and said to the king: "Make him put on his hat!" At Saint-Germain, where the Court then was, being, for the hundredth time, on the point of naming to Lauzun the man she had chosen to render happy, about whom she consulted him perpetually, without having the courage to articulate the name, she said to him: "If I had an inkstand and paper I would write it down for you"; then pointing to a mirror beside her, she added: "I have a mind to breathe upon it and write the name in big letters that you might read it plain."

One thing is remarkable, and it is, as it were, a stamp of the times; namely that the idea of the king, the official worship and idolatry vowed to him, forms

a third in the whole affair.   It is in the king's name
and as if under his invocation that they love each
other and dare, in the end, acknowledge it: "The
king has always been and is my first passion, M. de
Lauzun the second," writes Mademoiselle; and Lauzun, on his side, says he would not flatter himself
to have pleased Mademoiselle definitely and have
touched her heart, except by reason of the respect
and "true tenderness" that he felt for the person
of the king.   As soon as the marriage is decided we
find him stipulating that he is not to leave the king
for a single instant, that he is to continue to do all
the duties of his office, first at the *lever* and last at the
coucher; and quite resolved not to give up sleeping
in the Louvre.   The first use he intends to make of
Mademoiselle's enormous wealth is to put his company of the guards into new uniforms to " pay court
to the king."   In her letter to the king, asking permission to marry Lauzun, Mademoiselle is careful
to clang very loud that chain of servitude, which, to
her eyes, is more honourable than all else and in
which she claims her share: "I say this to Your
Majesty," she writes, "to prove to you that the more
we have of grandeur the more worthy we are to be
your servants [*domestiques*]."   There was one thing
for which Lauzun cared more than to be the husband
of Mademoiselle, Duc de Montpensier, and the greatest noble of the kingdom, and that was to stand well
with his master.   I note expressly the reigning form

of grovelling in those days: let us not flatter ourselves that we escape it in ours.

The rest is well known. Louis XIV consented, at
first, to the marriage. They were very unwise not
to profit by the permission within twenty-four hours,
and give him no time for reflection. The marriage,
consented to the evening before, was announced on
Monday, December 15, 1670, and held good till the
following Thursday. The king then withdrew his
permission abruptly. Mademoiselle was thrown into
a state we can well suppose, but without daring, as
yet, to blaspheme against the king. Lauzun received
the blow like an accomplished courtier and as if he
had said: "The king gave, and the king has taken
away, I can only thank and bless him." He seemed
for a moment, on the point of increasing in favour.
Nevertheless, for reasons that have always remained
obscure, he was arrested a year later (November 25,
1671) and imprisoned in the castle of Pignerol. His
captivity lasted no less than ten years.

Mademoiselle, during those years, had no thought
that was not of him; she did everything she could to
obtain his deliverance, and she bought it at the price
of enormous sacrifices of property, the gift of which
Mme. de Montespan drew out of her in behalf of her
son, the Duc du Maine, the king's bastard. She
passed through all they put upon her in order to see
once more the man she loved. She was ill-rewarded.

When Lauzun left prison he was no longer the

honourable man, the gallant man, the polished man who had so charmed her; the courtier alone survived, the rabid courtier, who had no peace because he did not recover footing and a patching up of favour with the master; in other respects, hard, openly selfish, covetous, daring to reproach Mademoiselle for the sacrifices of property she had made to deliver him! Imprisonment had only brought out defects of character and of heart which he had known how to hide in his splendid years. Besides which, marriage (for it seems that a secret marriage really took place at this time) relieved him henceforth from the necessity of restraining himself.

Mademoiselle came late to a knowledge of life, but she ended by knowing it and by passing, too, through all stages of trial; she had the slow suffering that wears out love in the heart, the contempt and indignation that break it, and she came at last to the indifference that has no cure and no consolation other than God. It is a sad day that, on which we discover that the one person we have delighted to adorn with all perfections and crown with all gifts is so worthless a thing. Mademoiselle had several years to meditate on that bitter discovery. She died in March, 1693, at sixty-six years of age.

Her obsequies, celebrated with great magnificence, were disturbed by a singular accident. The urn that contained her embalmed entrails, which were badly embalmed, exploded in the middle of the ceremony with a loud noise and sent all present flying. It was written above that a little absurdity should mingle in all that concerned Mademoiselle, even her funeral.

What was lacking in her life, in her character, and in her mind was grace, reasonableness, fitness (*justesse*), those qualities, in short, which were to mark the best epoch of Louis XIV. With her ten years more than the king, Mademoiselle was always a little behind the age and an echo of the old Court. She belonged, by her turn of imagination, to the literature of the last years of Louis XIII and the Regency, to the literature of the hôtel Rambouillet, a literature that did not come under the reform of Boileau nor that of Mme. de La Fayette. There was always a sort of pell-mell in her admirations; she valued Corneille highly; she had Tartuffe played before her, but she received the Abbé Cotin: "I like verses, no matter what kind they are," she said. But, above all, she loved grandeur, she loved glory; she often mistook it, but at all times she had emotions of pride, honour, and goodness that were worthy of her race. The days on which she is at her best she is conscious of the neighbourhood of Corneille. Her conduct on the day of Saint-Antoine ought to be reckoned in her favour. Her Memoirs, also, have most durable claims; they are truthful and faithful Memoirs, in which she tells everything about herself and about others, naïvely, and openly, and according to what comes into her mind. Persons of good sense who read them and who enjoy, as a lost singularity, such amazing confessions and her princely fashion of seeing things, can supply without effort the reflections and the morality that she herself does not put into them.

XI.

The Comtesse de La Fayette.

XI.

Marie Madeleine de La Vergne.

Comtesse de La Fayette.

IN the time of Mme. de Sévigné, beside her, and in
her most cherished intimacy was a woman whose
history was closely interwoven with that of her
amiable friend. It is she whom Boileau described
as "the woman of most mind in France and the
best writer." She wrote, however, very little, at
her leisure, for amusement, and with a sort of negligence that had nothing of the professional about it;
above all, she hated to write letters, so that we have
but a very small number of hers, and those very
short; it is in the letters of Mme. de Sévigné rather
than in her own that we shall know her. But she
had in her day a rôle apart, serious and elegant, solid
and charming; a rôle that was, in fact, considerable
and, in its class, on a level with the highest. To
tenderness of soul and a romantic imagination she
added a natural precision and, as her witty friend said
of her, "a divine reason" that never failed her; she
had them in her writings as well as in her life; they
belong to the models that ought to be studied in that

351

century, where they present, one with another, so balanced a mixture.

A recent attempt has been made, in rehabilitating the hôtel Rambouillet, to show its perfected and triumphant heiress in the person of Mme. de Maintenon; a saying of Ségrais decides the matter far more in favour of Mme. de La Fayette; showing the direct affiliation, from which all the *précieux* has disappeared. After a rather prolonged portrait of Mme. de Rambouillet, he adds incontinently: "Mme. de La Fayette had learned a good deal from her, but Mme. de La Fayette's mind was more solid." This perfected heiress of Mme. de Rambouillet, this friend for ever of Mme. de Sévigné, and of Mme. de Maintenon for many years, has her rank and her assured date in our literature, inasmuch as it was she who reformed the novel, and applied a part of the "divine reason" that was in her to treating gently and fixing within its due limits a school of tenderness, the excesses of which had been great, but which she had only to touch to make it find grace once more in minds of serious mould who seemed disposed to abolish it.

For, this secondary class of literature where elegance and a certain interest sufficed, but where no genius (if any there be) is out of place; a class that the *Art Poétique* does not mention, which Prevost, Le Sage, and Jean-Jacques have consecrated, and which, in the days of Mme. de La Fayette, was confined, at least in its higher reaches, to the affecting

MARIE MADELEINE DE LA VERGNE,
COMTESSE DE LA FAYETTE.

parts of Berenice or Iphigenia—for this class Mme.
de La Fayette has done what her illustrious contemporaries strove with rivalry to do in the graver and
more respected walks of literature. *L'Astrée,* by im-
planting, so to speak, the novel in France, had served
as stock to those interminable grafts, *Cyrus, Cleo-
patre, Polyxandre,* and *Clélie.* Boileau, with his
satire, cut them short, as he did that long line of
epic poems, *Moïse Sauvée, Saint-Louis, La Pucelle.*
Mme. de La Fayette, without apparent satire, and
seeming merely to come after and under cover of
her predecessors (from whom Ségrais and Huet have
very ill-distinguished her, enveloping them all in the
same praises), dealt them a heavier blow than any one
by her *Princess de Clèves.* And she knew very well
what she was doing, and what she meant to do.
She was accustomed to say that a sentence cut out of
a work was worth a gold louis, and a word left out,
twenty sous; that saying has great value in her
mouth when we reflect on the novels in ten volumes from which it was so necessary to escape.
Proportion, sobriety, decency, simple methods, and
heart, substituted for great catastrophes and grand
phrases, those were the features of the reform, or, to
speak less ambitiously, the retouching she gave to
the novel; in that, she belonged to the purer period
of Louis XIV.

The long and inviolable friendship of Mme. de
La Fayette with M. de La Rochefoucauld makes her

own life resemble a novel, a virtuous novel, but a novel all the same; more out of rule than the life of Mme. de Sévigné, who loved no one but her daughter, less schemed and calculated than that of Mme. de Maintenon, whose sole aim was the sacrament with the king. We like to see a tender heart allying itself with a bitter and disillusioned mind to soften it; a tardy passion, but faithful, between two serious souls, where the one that feels corrects the misanthropy of the other; where delicacy, tenderness, reciprocal consolation and sweetness reign rather than illusions and fire: Mme. de Clèves, in short, ill and a little sad beside M. de Nemours, grown old and a maker of maxims. Such was the life of Mme. de La Fayette and the exact relation between her person and her novel. The lack of illusion that we remark in her, the melancholy reason that formed the basis of her life, passed a little into the ideal of her novel and also, it seems to me, into all those other novels that, in a way, emanated from her and which are her posterity: *Eugène de Rothelin, Mademoiselle de Clermont, Édouard.* Whatever tenderness there may be in those charming creations, reason is there too, the breath of human experience blows from a corner and cools passion. Beside the loving soul that is ready to yield there is something that warns and restrains. M. de La Rochefoucauld with his maxims is ever there.

If Mme. de La Fayette reformed the novel in France, the chivalrous and sentimental novel, and gave to it the particular tone that conciliates to a certain point the ideal with the actual and the observed, it may also be said that she was the first to give an example altogether illustrious of those attachments, lasting, decent, legitimate, and sacred in their constancy of every day, every minute, through years till death, that came of the manners and morals of the old society and were well-nigh extinguished with it. The *Princesse de Clèves* and her attachment to M. de La Rochefoucauld are the two almost equal titles of Mme. de La Fayette to serious and touching fame; they are two points that mark the literature and the society of Louis XIV.

I should have left the pleasure of recomposing this existence, so simple in events, to the imagination of the readers of Mme. de Sévigné if a little unpublished document, but a very private one, had not invited me to make a frame in which to set it.

The father of Mme. de La Fayette, a general and the governor of Havre, had, it is said, some merit, and he took great pains with the education of his daughter. Her mother (*née* de Péna) came from Provence, and counted a certain troubadour-laureate among her ancestors. Mlle. Marie-Madeleine Pioche de La Vergne had, at an early age, more reading and study than many persons of the preceding generation, even intellectual ones, ever had in their youth. Mme. de Choisy, for example, had amazing natural wit in conversation or in letters, but she could not spell correctly.

Mme. de Sévigné and Mme. de La Fayette, the latter younger by six or seven years than her friend, added to an excellent foundation a perfect culture. We have for direct testimony as to their education the raptures of Ménage, who ordinarily, as we know, fell in love with his beautiful pupils. He celebrated, under every form of Latin verse, the beauty, the grace, the elegance in speaking well and writing well of Mme. de La Fayette or rather Mlle. de La Vergne, Laverna, as he called her. Later, he presented to her his friend, the learned Huet, who became to her a literary counsellor. Ségrais, who, with Mme. de Sévigné, suffices to make Mme. de La Fayette known to us, says:

"Three months after Mme. de La Fayette began to learn Latin she knew more of it than M. Ménage and Père Rapin, her masters. One day, in making her translate, they had a dispute themselves about the meaning of a passage, and neither would give way to the sentiment of the other. Mme. de La Fayette said to them: 'Neither of you understands it,' and she gave them the right explanation of the passage; they agreed then that she was right. It was a poet she explained, for she did not like prose, and had never read Chéron; but she took great pleasure in poesy, reading Virgil and Horace specially; and as she had a poetic mind and knew all that belonged to that art, she entered without difficulty into the meaning of those authors."

A little farther on he refers again to the merits of M. Ménage: "Where shall we find such poets as M. Ménage, who can make good Latin verses, good Greek verses, and good Italian verses? He was a great personage, whatever jealous people chose to

say.   Yet he did not know all the delicacies of poesy;
but Mme. de La Fayette knew them well." The woman
who preferred poets to all other writers and felt their
truth, was she who proved herself "true" *par excellence* as M. de La Rochefoucauld told her, using that
expression, which has lasted until now, for the first
time: "Poetic spirit, true spirit! — her merit, like her
charm, is in that alliance."

She lost her father when fifteen years of age.
Her mother, a good woman, Retz tells us, but rather
foolish and very bustling, remarried, soon after, with
the Chevalier Renaud de Sévigné, much mixed up
in the intrigues of the Fronde, and who was one
of the most active in rescuing the cardinal from the
castle of Nantes.   We read in the cardinal's Memoirs,
àpropos of that imprisonment at Nantes (1653), and
the amusing visits he received there:

"Mme. de La Vergne, who had married for her second husband
M. le Chevalier de Sévigné, and who lived in Anjou with her husband, came to see me and brought her daughter, Mlle. de La Vergne,
now Mme. de La Fayette.   She was very pretty and very amiable,
and had much the air of Mme. de Lesdiguières.   She pleased me
much, and the truth is, I did not please her at all, either because she
had no inclination for me, or because the distrust that her mother
and step-father had sedulously put into her, even in Paris, on account
of my various amours and inconstancies, had put her on her guard
against me.   I consoled myself for her cruelty with the ease that was
natural to me.   . . ."

Mlle. de La Vergne, then twenty years old, needed
nothing more than her own good sense to take small

account of this idle and trivial caprice of the daring prisoner, so quickly consoled.

Married in 1655 to the Comte de La Fayette, what was probably the most interesting fact about the marriage and the most in accordance with imagination, was that she thus became the sister-in-law of Mère Angélique de La Fayette, superior of the convent of Chaillot, formerly maid of honour to Anne of Austria, whose perfect love with Louis XIII made so chaste and simple a romance, resembling those described in the *Princesse de Clèves*. Her husband, after giving her the name that she was to make illustrious, effaces himself and disappears, so to speak, from her life; we hear nothing more by which to distinguish him. She had two sons by him, whom she deeply loved; one, a soldier, whose advancement in life occupied her greatly, and who died shortly after her, and another, the Abbé de La Fayette, provided with good abbeys, of whom we chiefly know that he carelessly lent his mother's manuscripts and lost them.

Mme. de La Fayette was introduced while young to the hôtel Rambouillet and learned a great deal from the marquise. M. Roederer, who is anxious that none of Molière's mockery shall touch the hôtel Rambouillet, depopulates it and brings it to a close much sooner than is accurate. Mme. de La Fayette went there before her marriage and profited by its intercourse, as did Mme. de Sévigné. M. Auger, in the notice, correct

and interesting but dry in tone, that he gives to Mme.
de La Fayette, says: "Introduced early to the society
of the hôtel Rambouillet the natural correctness and
solidity of her mind might not, perhaps, have resisted the contagion of bad taste of which that house
was the centre, if her reading of the Latin poets had
not given her a preservative."

The preservative ought to have acted on Ménage
first of all. The above is most unjust to the hôtel
Rambouillet, and M. Roederer is completely right in
protesting against that manner of speaking ; but he,
himself, is assuredly misled when he makes that hotel
the cradle of good taste and shows us Mlle. de Scudéry as being more tolerated there than extolled and
admired. He forgets that Voiture, as long as he
lived, ruled the roast in that company, and we know
very well, in the matter of taste, as well as of intellect, what Voiture was. As for Mlle. de Scudéry,
it is enough to read Ségrais, Huet, and others to see
what was thought at the hôtel Rambouillet of that
incomparable spinster, of her *Illustre Bassa* and
Grand Cyrus, and of her verses "so natural, so
tender," disparaged by Boileau but to which, nevertheless, "he could never attain himself." What Ségrais and Huet admired in such terms as these was
not likely to be judged more severely in a company
of which they were the final oracles.

Mme. de La Fayette, whose mind was solid and acute,
came out of that intercourse, as did Mme. de Sévigné, by

simply taking its best. In age she belonged wholly
to the young Court; even with less solidity of mind
she would not have failed to possess its appropriate
elegancies. From the first days of her marriage she
had occasion to see frequently at the Carmelite convent of Chaillot the young Princess of England with
her mother, Queen Henrietta, who, being in exile,
had retired there. When the young princess became Madame [Henrietta Anne, Duchesse d'Orléans]
and the most lively ornament of the Court, Mme. de La
Fayette, though ten years her elder, was still admitted
to their old familiarity, had her private *entrées,* and might
have passed for Madame's favourite. In the charming sketch she has drawn of the brilliant years of the
princess, speaking of herself in the third person, she
judges herself thus:

> " Mlle. de La Trémouille and Mme. de La Fayette were of this
> number " (the number of those who frequently saw Madame). " The
> first pleased her by her goodness and by a certain ingenuousness in
> telling all that was in her heart, which had something of the simpli-
> city of early youth ; the other was agreeable to her by her happi-
> ness, for, although she thought she had merit, it was a sort of merit
> so serious in appearance that it seemed hardly likely to please a
> princess as young as Madame. "

So, at thirty years of age, Mme. de La Fayette was
at the centre of the politeness, good-breeding, and
gallantry of the flourishing years of Louis XIV; she
was present at all Madame's parties at Fontainebleau;
a spectator rather than an actor; having no share,
she tells us, in Madame's confidence on certain affairs;

but after those affairs had taken place and were a little noised abroad she heard them from her lips and wrote them down to please her. "You write so well," Madame said to her: "write, and I will supply you with good memoirs."—"It was rather difficult work," says Mme. de La Fayette, "to turn the truth of certain matters in a way to make it known and yet not let it be offensive or disagreeable to the princess."

One of these "certain matters," among others, which set Mme. de La Fayette's delicacy on edge and excited Madame's laughter at the pains the amiable writer was giving herself, must have been, I fancy, the following:

"She [Madame] became intimate with the Comtesse de Soissons . . . and thought only of pleasing the king as a sister-in-law. I think that she pleased him in another way; I think also that she thought he pleased her as a brother-in-law, though, perhaps, he pleased her much more; in short, as they were both infinitely charming and both were born with dispositions to gallantry, and as they saw each other daily in the midst of pleasures and diversions, it appeared to the eyes of every one that they felt for each other that attraction that usually precedes great passions."

Madame died in the arms of Mme. de La Fayette, who did not leave her in her last moments. The narrative she has left of this death equals the finest that we have of the most affecting deaths; it has expressions, as it were by the way, that light up the whole scene:

"I went up to her. She told me she was vexed; but the ill-humour of which she spoke would have made the good-humour of

other women, so much natural sweetness had she, and so little
was she capable of bitterness or anger. . . . After dinner she
lay down upon the floor . . . she made me sit beside her, so
that her head was partly on me. . . . During her sleep she
changed so considerably that I felt much surprised, and I thought
it must be that her mind contributed greatly to embellish her face.
. . . I was wrong, however, in making that reflection, for I
had seen her asleep many times, and never did I see her less lovely."

And, farther on:

"Monsieur was beside her bed; she kissed him, and said gently,
with an air capable of wooing the most barbarous heart: 'Alas!
Monsieur, you ceased to love me long ago; but that is
unjust; I have never wronged you.' Monsieur seemed much
touched, and all who were in the room were so affected that nothing was heard but the noise of persons weeping. . . . When
the king had left the room, I was beside her bed and she said to
me: 'Madame de La Fayette, my nose is already sunken,' I answered her only by tears. . . . She failed steadily."

On the 30th of June, 1673, Mme. de Lafayette wrote
to Mme. de Sévigné: "It is three years to-day since
I saw Madame die; I received yesterday many of
her letters; I am all full of her."

For the space of ten years in the midst of that
brilliant and gallant society, was Mme. de La Fayette,
still young, with nobility and charm of face, if not
beauty,—was she only an attentive observer, without
active interest of heart other than her attachment to
Madame? was she without any single and secret
choice of her own? Towards the year 1665, as I
conjecture and will explain farther on, she had chosen
out of the vortex M. de La Rochefoucauld, then about
fifty-two years of age, to be her friend for life.

Mme. de La Fayette wrote while still young from taste, but always with sobriety. It was the day of "Portraits." She wrote one of Mme. de Sévigné, (1659), supposed to be written by a stranger: "It is better than myself," said the latter, finding the Portrait, in 1675, among the old papers of Mme. de La Trémouille: "but those who loved me sixteen years ago might find some resemblance." It is under these youthful features, for ever fixed by her friend, that Mme. de Sévigné still appears to us immortal. When Madame, inviting Mme. de La Fayette to set to work, said to her: "You write well," she had doubtless read the *Princesse de Montpensier*, the first short novel of our author, printed in 1662. For elegance, and vivacity of narration, it detaches itself from all the other novels and historiettes of its day, and shows a spirit of correctness, accuracy, and reform. Mme. de La Fayette's imagination in composing turned willingly back to the polished and brilliant epoch of the Valois, to the reigns of Charles IX or Henri II, which she idealised a little, and embellished in the same direction as that in which the graceful and discreet tales of Queen Marguerite shows them to us. The *Princesse de Montpensier,* The *Princesse de Clèves*, and *La Comtesse de Tende* do not belong to those reigns, whose vices and crimes have, perhaps, too much eclipsed to our eyes their intellectual culture. Madame's Court, for wit, for intrigues, for vices also, was not without affinity to that of the Valois; and the history Mme. de La Fayette has made of it recalls more than once the Memoirs of Queen Marguerite, so charming in her day, but who is not to be believed at all times. The perfidious Vardes and the haughty de Guiche are figures that have their counterparts at the Court of Henri II; and at Madame's Court the Chevalier de Lorraine was not wanting. Mme. de La Fayette held in that society a rôle of authority, as it were exercising on its tone a sort of wise criticism. Two months before the unhappy death of Madame, Mme. de Montmorency wrote to M. de Bussy, by way of a joke (May 1, 1670):

" Mme. de La Fayette, Madame's favourite, has had her skull broken by a chimney cornice that did not respect a head so brilliant with the glory given by the favours of a great princess. Before this mishap I read a letter from her, which has been given to the public, in ridicule of what are called words à la mode, the use of which is worthless. I send it to you."

Here follows the letter, which is composed in a burlesque jargon by which she meant to correct the absurdities of the great world; it purports to be from a jealous lover to his mistress. Boileau, in his line, could not have done better. In fact she is, by one degree softened, a species of Boileau to the manners of the Court.

Mme. de La Fayette never knew, I think, those passions that rend the soul with violence; she gave her heart voluntarily. When she made choice of M. de La Rochefoucauld and allied herself with him she was, as I have said, thirty-two or thirty-three years old; he was fifty-two. She had seen him and known him no doubt for a long time, but it is of their particular intimacy that I now speak. We shall see by the following letter, hitherto unpublished, which is one of the most confidential ever written, that about the time of the publication of the Maxims and of the Comte de Saint-Paul's first entrance into society, there was talk of the liaison of Mme. de La Fayette and M. de La Rochefoucauld as of something quite recently established. Mme. de La Fayette writes the letter to Mme. de Sablé, an old friend of M. de La Rochefoucauld, the same who had so much share in the making of the Maxims, and who, for some time past, was wholly given up to Port-Royal, more, it would seem, from intention to reform and in fear of death than from any complete conversion. Here is the letter:

" Monday evening; I could not reply to your note yesterday, because I had company; and I think I may not reply to it to-day, because it is too kind. I am ashamed of the praises you give me; on the other hand, I like you to have a good opinion of me, and I wish not to say anything to contradict what you think. Therefore, I will only answer by telling you that M. le Comte de Saint-Paul has just left me, that we talked of you for one hour, as you know well I should talk.

" We also talked of a man that I always take the liberty of putting on a par with you for charm of mind. I do not know whether that comparison will offend you; but if it would offend you on the lips of others, on mine it is great praise, if all *they say is true*. I saw plainly that the Comte de Saint-Paul had heard talk of those sayings, and I entered slightly into the matter with him. But I fear he may take too seriously what I said to him. I conjure you, the first time you see him, speak to him yourself about those rumours. It can come about easily, for I gave him the Maxims, of which he will speak to you no doubt. But I beg you to speak to him in the right way to put into his head that the whole thing is merely a jest. I am not certain enough of what you think yourself to be sure that you will say the right thing; and I believe I must begin by convincing my ambassadress. Nevertheless, I must rely on your skill; it is above all ordinary maxims. But do convince him. I do hate like death that young men of his age should think I have gallantries. They think those who are older than themselves a hundred years old, and they are quite astonished that there should still be any question of them; besides which, he will believe more readily what is told him about M. de La Rochefoucauld than about others. In short, I do not want him to think anything, unless it is that he is one of my friends; and I beg you also not to forget to get it out of his head, if it is in it, that I forgot your message. It is not generous to remind you of one service by asking another.

(On the margin.) "I must not forget to tell you that I found a terribly clever mind in the Comte de Saint-Paul."

To add to the interest of this letter, the reader must kindly remember the exact situation: M. de Saint-Paul, son of Mme. de Longueville and, probably, of M. de La Rochefoucauld, coming to see Mme. de La Lafayette, who is thought to be the object of a last tender passion, and who wants to have him undeceived —or deceived—on that score. The "terribly clever mind" of the young prince went straight, I imagine, to the heart of Mme. de Longueville, to whom the postscript at least, and the rest of the letter probably, was certain to be quickly shown. There is a charming sentence in the letter that all belated lovers should meditate upon: "I do hate like death that young men of his age should think I have gallantries." It is the counterpart of the following thought in the *Princesse de Clèves:*

"Mme. de Clèves, who was at that age when it is not believable that a woman can be loved if she is more than twenty-five years of age, regarded with extreme astonishment the king's attachment to the Duchesse de Valentinois." That idea, as we see, was familiar to Mme. de La Fayette. She feared above all to seem to inspire, or feel, the passion that at that age others affect. Her delicate reasonableness became a chastity.

I hold the more to the conclusion that the intimate and declared relations between M. de La Rochefoucauld and herself did not begin until this period, because it seems to me that the influence of this affectionate friend upon him was directly contrary to the Maxims; that she would have made him correct and cut out some of them if she had influenced him before as she did after their publication; and that La Rochefoucauld, the misanthrope, who said he had never found love except in novels and that as for himself he had never felt it, is not the man of whom she said later: "M. de La Rochefoucauld gave me a mind, but I have reformed his heart."

In a little note written by her to Mme. de Sablé, (unpublished), who had herself already composed Maxims, she says:

"You will cause me the greatest vexation in the world if you do not show me your Maxims. Mme. Du Plessis has given me an extreme desire to see them; and it is just because they are virtuous and reasonable that I have that desire; they will convince me that all persons of good sense are not so sure of the general corruption as M. de La Rochefoucauld is."

It is this idea of general corruption that she set herself to combat in La Rochefoucauld, and which she rectified. The desire to enlighten and soften that noble spirit was, no doubt, an allurement of reason and beneficence leading her to the borders of the closer relation.

The former Knight of the Fronde, now become bitter and gouty, was not in other respects what might have been expected from his book. He had studied little, Segrais tells us, but his marvellous perception and his knowledge of the world stood him in place of study. Young, he had plunged into all the vices of his time, and had come out of them with more health of mind than of body, if one can call anything healthy that was so soured. This did not interfere in any way with the sweetness of his intercourse and his infinite charm. He was good-breeding itself, perfect, unfailing; he gained more and more each day by being better known; but he was a man for private intercourse and conversation; a wider audience did not suit him; if he had been obliged to speak before five or six persons rather solemnly strength would have failed him; the harangue that must be made before the French Academy deterred him from seeking to enter it. One evening in June, 1672, when word was brought to him of the death of the young Duc de Longueville (Comte de Saint-Paul) that of the Chevalier de Marsillac, his grandson, and of the wound of the Prince de Marsillac, his son,

when all this hailstorm fell upon him, he was wonderful, says Mme. de Sévigné "in his sorrow and his
firmness. . . . I saw his heart uncovered," she
adds, "at that cruel moment; he is in the front rank
of all that I have ever seen of courage, merit, tenderness, and reason." Not long after this she said of
him that he was patriarchal, and felt almost as
strongly as she did the parental feeling. There is
the real La Rochefoucauld as Mme. de La Fayette
reformed him.

It was not until after the death of Madame, and
after Madame de La Fayette's health had begun to
fail, that the *liaison*, such as Mme. de Sévigné shows
it to us, was completely established. The letters of
that incomparable friend, which continue uninterrupt-
edly precisely from that period, permit us to follow
all its circumstances, even to the happy monotony of
its tender and rooted habit:

"Their ill health," she writes, "made them necessary to each
other, and . . . and gave them leisure to taste their good qualities,
which is not the case in other *liaisons*. . . . At Court, people
have no leisure to love; that vortex, so violent for others, was peaceful for them, and gave great space to the pleasure of an intercourse
so delightful. I believe that no passion can exceed in strength such
an intimacy. . . ."

I shall not quote all that could be extracted from, I
might say, every letter of Mme. de Sévigné, for there
are few in which Mme. de La Fayette is not mentioned, and many were written or closed in her house,
with the compliments of M. de La Rochefoucauld

15

"now present." On the good days, the days of tolerable health and of dinners *en lavardinage ou bavardinage,* all is graceful enjoyment, roulades of mischievous gaiety on that goose of a Mme. de Marans, on the manœuvring of Mme. de Brissac and M. le Duc. Some days are more serious but not less delightful, when, at Saint-Maur for instance, in the house that the Prince de Condé had lent to Gourville, and which Mme. de La Fayette willingly enjoyed, the *Poétique* of Boileau was read to a choice company who declared it a masterpiece. Another time, in default of Boileau and his *Poétique* they took to Lulli, and at certain parts of the opera of "Cadmus" they wept: "I am not alone in being unable to bear them," writes Mme. de Sévigné, "Mme. de La Fayette is much agitated." That agitated soul was sensitiveness itself.

There were also days when Mme. de La Fayette went to pay little visits at Court; and the king took her in his calèche with other ladies to show her the beauties of Versailles, as any private individual might have done; and such a trip, such success furnished Mme. de La Fayette on her return, wise as she was, with a topic for very long conversations and even, though she did not like to write them, for letters less short than usual; Mme. de Grignan at a distance is a little jealous; so she is again, àpropos of an inkstand in mahogany that Mme. de Montespan presents to Mme. de La Fayette. But Mme. de Sévigné smooths such matters over by compliments and sweet messages, which she arranges and exchanges constantly between her daughter and her best friend.   Even when Mme. de La Fayette no longer went to Versailles and no longer embraced the king's knees, weeping with gratitude, even when M. de La Rochefoucauld was dead, she maintained her influence and the consideration shown to her.   "Never did a woman without leaving her own place," says Mme. de Sévigné, "manage so many good affairs."   Louis XIV liked her always as the favourite of Madame, a witness of her touching death, and of the beautiful years with which she was associated in his memory.

But Versailles, and Boileau's *Poétique*, the operas of Lulli, and the gaieties on Mme. de Marans are often interrupted by the wretched health which with its tertian fever never allowed itself to be forgotten and became, little by little, their principal occupation.   In her fine and vast garden of the rue de Vaugirard, so verdant, so balmy; in Gourville's house at Saint-Maur, where she made herself frankly at home as a friend; at Fleury-sous-Mendon, where she went to breathe the air of the woods, we can follow her, ill and melancholy; we see that long and serious face grow thinner, consuming its own vitality.   Her life, for twenty years, was converted into a little fever, more or less slow; and the bulletins read thus:

" Mme. de La Fayette goes tomorrow to the small house at Mendon where she has been already.   She will spend a fortnight there, to be, as it were, suspended betwixt earth and heaven; she will not think, speak, answer, or listen; she is weary of saying good evening and good morning; she has fever every day and repose would cure her; repose therefore she must have. I shall go and see her sometimes. M. de La Rochefoucauld is in that chair that you know. He is unutterably sad; one understands very well what is the matter with him."

What was, no doubt, the matter with M. de La Rochefoucauld, besides the gout and his ordinary ailments, was missing Mme. de La Fayette.

The sadness that such a state naturally nurtured did not prevent the return of smiles and pleasures at slight intervals. Among the various nicknames that society bestowed,—Mme. Scarron being "Thaw" Colbert "North," M. de Pomponne, "Rain,"—Mme. de La Fayette was called "Mist"; the mist rose sometimes and then there were charming horizons. A gentle, resigned, melancholy reason, attracting yet detached, reposeful in tone, strewn with striking and true sayings easily remembered, such was the habitual course of her conversation and of her thought. "It is enough to be," she said of herself, accepting her inactive existence. That saying, which describes her fully, is from the woman who said also, àpropos of Montaigne, that it would be a pleasure to have a neighbour like him.

An extreme sensitiveness, often full of tears, appeared at moments and suddenly athwart this steady reason, like a spring gushing from a tract of level land. We have seen her "agitated" by the emotion of music. When Mme. de Sévigné leaves Paris for

Les Rochers or for Provence she must not bid her
farewell or let the visit appear to be the last; Mme.
de La Fayette's tenderness could not support the departure of such a friend.   One day, when they were
talking before her, M. le Duc [de Bourbon] being present, of the campaign that was to open in another
month, the sudden idea of the dangers M. le Duc was
about to run brought tears to her eyes.   These effusions of feeling had the greater charm and the more
value as coming from so judicious a woman and so
calm a mind.

Her attention, in the retirement of her feeble life,
was none the less given to essential things; without
stirring from her place she watched over all.   If she
reformed the heart of M. de La Rochefoucauld she
also improved his business affairs.   She was well
informed as to lawsuits; she prevented him from
losing the finest part of his property by supplying him
with the means of proving that it was entailed.   We
can conceive from that why she wrote few letters and
those only necessary ones.   This was her one stormy
point with Mme. de Sévigné.   The few letters that
she did write to her friend are nearly all to say that
she can say only two words, and would say more
only she has a headache.   Even M. de La Fayette
makes his appearance one day in person, arriving
from I know not where, as an excuse for not writing.
The pretty letter should be read: " There! there! my
dearest, why are you screaming like an eagle?" etc.,

to understand fully Mme. de La Fayette's way of life, and to catch the difference in tone between her and Mme. de Sévigné. Here we find those words so often quoted: "You are in Provence, *ma belle;* your hours are free, your head still more so; the taste for writing to everybody still lasts with you; with me it has gone by; if I had a lover who wanted a letter from me every morning, I should break with him."

Mme. de La Fayette was very "true" and very frank; "her word was to be believed." "She would not have given the slightest freedom to any one if she had not been convinced that he deserved it; and this made some persons say that she was stiff; she was only upright." Mme. de Maintenon, with whom Mme. de La Fayette had close relations, was also marvellously upright in mind, but her character was less frank; as judicious but less true; and this difference must have contributed to the cooling of their friendship. In 1672, when Mme. Scarron was secretly bringing up Louis XIV's bastards in the Faubourg Saint-Germain near to Mme. de La Fayette's house, the latter was still intimate with her; she heard from her, as did Mme. de Coulanges, and she must have visited her. But Mme. Scarron's confidence being withdrawn by degrees, there resulted the usual words reported and conjectures made that cause trouble between friends: "The idea of entering a convent never came into my mind," writes Mme. de Maintenon to the Abbé Testu; "pray reassure Mme.

de La Fayette." Giving her brother a lecture on economy, she writes in 1678: "If I had fifty thousand francs a year, I would not keep up the style of a great lady, nor have a bed trimmed with gold lace like Mme. de La Fayette, nor a valet-de-chambre like Mme. de Coulanges; is the pleasure they get out of it worth the ridicule they incur?" I know not if Mme. de La Fayette's gold-lace bed did lend itself to ridicule, but lying in it, as too often happened, she was, by all odds, more simple than her friend in that "dead leaf" mantle she affected to wear to the very end.

All friendship finally ceased between them, Mme. de Maintenon declares it: "I am not able to preserve Mme. de La Fayette's friendship; she puts its continuation at too high a price. I have at least shown her that I am as sincere as herself. It is the Duke who brought about our quarrel. We had others formerly about trifles." In Mme. de La Fayette's Memoirs, àpropos of the "Comedy of Esther," we find:

"She (Mme. de Maintenon) ordered the poet to make a comedy but to choose a pious subject: for, as things are now, outside of piety there is no salvation at Court, nor in the other world. . . . The comedy represents, in some sort, the fall of Mme. de Montespan, and the rise of Mme. de Maintenon; all the difference being that Esther is a little younger and less affected in the matter of piety."

In quoting these words of two illustrious women, I certainly take no pleasure in bringing out the bitterness that spoiled a long affection. In truth, Mme. de

Maintenon and Mme. de La Fayette were powers too considerable, and the claims of each were too high, not to produce in the end a coolness between them. Mme. de Maintenon, coming last to grandeur, must have changed by degrees to Mme. de La Fayette, who remained what she ever was; it was, perhaps, this uniformity of conduct that Mme. de Maintenon would fain have changed a little when her own fortunes changed.

In July, 1677, one year before the appearance of the *Princesse de Clèves,* we see that Mme. de La Fayette's health was at its worst, although she was to live fifteen years longer, dying by degrees without a respite, being of " those who drag their miserable existence to the last drop of oil." Nevertheless, it was in the following winter that M. de La Rochefoucauld and she busied themselves finally with the charming novel which was published by Barbin, March 16, 1678. Segrais tells us, in one place, that he has not taken the trouble to reply to criticisms made on the book; and in another place he says that Mme. de La Fayette disdained to reply to them, so that a doubt might be raised, if we chose, about the degree of his co-operation. But, as to that, I shall not discuss it; the novel is too superior to all that he ever wrote to admit of hesitation. No one, moreover, mistook the author; confidential readings had spread the news and the book was received by society as the work of Mme. de La Fayette alone.

As soon as the *Princesse* thus heralded appeared, she became the subject of all conversations and correspondences. Bussy and Mme. de Sévigné wrote to each other; everywhere persons were on the *qui-vive* to discuss her; they met in the great alley of the Tuileries and questioned one another. Fontenelle read the novel four times over. Boursault turned it into a tragedy, as nowadays we should make it into vaudevilles. Valincourt wrote, quite incognito, a little volume of criticism which was attributed to Père Bonhours, and an Abbé de Charnes replied by another little volume that was attributed to Barbier d'Ancourt, a noted critic and adversary of the witty Jesuit. The *Princesse de Clèves* has survived the vogue she well deserved and still remains among us as the first in date of interesting novels.

It is touching to think of the peculiar situation in which were born these beings so charming, so pure, these noble, spotless personages, their sentiments so fresh, so perfected, so tender; to think, too, how Mme. de La Fayette put into them all that her loving and poetic soul held in reserve of early dreams long cherished; how M. de La Rochefoucauld took pleasure, doubtless, in finding in M. de Nemours that flower of chivalry that he himself had misused, an embellished reflection, as it were of his own romantic youth. Thus the two friends, grown aged, went back in imagination to the first beauty of their youth when they did not know, but might have loved each

other.   The ready blush of Mme. de Clèves, which at
first is almost her only language, marks well the
thought of the writer, which is to paint love in all
it has of freshest, purest, most adorable, most troub-
lous, most undecided, most irresistible, — most *itself,*
in short.   At every moment we are made to see
"that joy which first youth joined to beauty gives,
that sort of trouble and embarrassment in every action
that love produces in the innocence of early youth,"
in short, all the emotions that are farthest from her
and from her friend in their tardy union.

In the tenor of her life, she was, above all, sensible;
she had a judgment greater even than her wit, so they
told her, and that praise flattered her more than all
the rest.   But here, in her novel, poesy, inward sensibility, recovered their rights, though reason was not
wanting either.   Nowhere have the contradictions
and the delicate duplicities of love been so naturally
expressed as in the *Princesse de Clèves.*   We love
even its colour, a little faded; the moderation of its
paintings that touch so lightly; the manner, everywhere restrained, that gives so much to dream of;
a few willows beside a brook where the lover passes;
and all description of the beauty of the princess:
"her hair loosely knotted "; " eyes enlarged by tears
a little "; and, at the last, " a life that was short
enough," a final impression, itself moderated.   The
language is equally delightful, exquisitely choice, with
negligences and irregularities that have their grace,

and which Valincourt notes in detail as being de-
nounced by a grammarian, though with some shame
at putting too direct a blame on the author.

As she advanced in the composition of the *Princesse de Clèves* the thoughts of Mme. de La Fayette,
after this first flight backward toward youth and its
joys, return to gravity.   The idea of duty increases
and bears her along.   The austerity of the end shows
us that "sight so far and yet so near of death which
makes the things of this world and of these present
eyes seem so different from those we see in health."
She herself had felt this from the summer of 1677,
when, as Mme. de Sévigné indicates, she turned her
soul toward the end.   Her disillusion as to all things
is shown in the fear she gives to Mme. de Clèves
that marriage will be the grave of the prince's love,
and open the door to jealousies; these fears turn the
princess's mind against a marriage with her lover as
much as the scruple of duty.   In completing their ideal
romance, it is clear that the two friends, M. de La
Rochefoucauld and she, came to doubt what there
would have been of imaginary bliss for their dear
personages, and so turned to their own gentle and
real relation as the most consoling and the safest.

They did not enjoy it long.   On the night of March
16, 1680, two years to a day after the publication of
the *Princesse de Clèves* M. de La Rochefoucauld died:

"I have had my head so full of this misfortune, and of the affliction
of our poor friend," writes Mme. de Sévigné, "that I must tell you

of it all. . . . M. de Marsillac is in a state of affliction that cannot be described; and yet, my daughter, he will return to the king and Court; all the family will return to their place in the world, but where will Mme. de La Fayette find another such friend, such society, such gentleness, pleasantness, confidence, and consideration for her and for her son? She is infirm, she is always in her chamber, she never goes into the streets. M. de La Rochefoucauld was sedentary also; this made them necessary to each other, and nothing could be compared to the confidence and charm of their friendship. Think of it, my daughter, and you will see it was impossible to have met with a greater loss and one that time can less console. I have not quitted my poor friend through all these days; she did not go into the crowd around that family, so that she needed some one to have pity on her. Mme. de Coulanges has done well also; and together we shall continue it for some time longer. . . ."

And in all her following letters she says again: "Poor Mme. de La Fayette does not know what to do with herself. . . . Every one will be consoled, except her. . . . That poor woman cannot draw the threads together so as to fill the place." Mme. de La Fayette did not seek to fill it; she knew that nothing could repair such ruins. Even the tender friendship of Mme. de Sévigné did not suffice,—she felt this but too well; too many shared it. If we need to be convinced of the insufficency of such friendships, even the best and the dearest, we have only to read Mme. de La Fayette's letter to Mme. de Sévigné, dated October 8, 1689, so perfect, so imperious, so, from its very tenderness, without ceremony, and then read Mme. de Sévigné's comments upon it in writing to her daughter, and we shall comprehend that too much must not be asked of friendships that are not single and unshared, inasmuch as the most delicate of

women judged thus.   After love, after absolute friendship without reservation, without change, a friendship *entire,* in which the other is *the same* as ourselves,
there is nothing but death or God.

Mme. de La Fayette lived thirteen years longer;
the slender details of her exterior life during those
desert years will be found in Mme. de Sévigné's
letters.   A lively beginning of intimacy with young
Mme. de Schomberg awakened some jealousy in
other and older friends; but it does not appear that
this effort of a soul to recover its hold on something
lasted long.   Perhaps it was from the same restless
need that she built, during the first months after her
loss, an addition on the garden side to her house,
already too vast, alas! in proportion to her diminishing existence.   Also, to fill the hours, Mme. de La
Fayette spent her time on various writings, some of
which went astray and were lost.   The *Comtesse de
Tende* dates from that period.   The severest criticisms of Bussy and society in general on the *Princesse
de Clèves* turned on the extraordinary confession that
the heroine makes to her husband: Mme. de La
Fayette, by inventing another analogous situation
which led to a still more extraordinary confession,
thought that she thereby justified the first.   She succeeded in the *Comtesse de Tende,* though with less
development than was needed to give the *Princesse
de Clèves* a sister comparable to herself.   We feel
that the writer had her object and rushed upon it.

Mme. de La Fayette had, as I said, more than one affinity with Boileau in uprightness of mind and irrefutable criticism, and she was, in her way, an oracle of good sense in her society. Her sayings *à la Boileau* that have been preserved are numerous; I have quoted several, but others should be added, for instance: "Whoso puts himself above others, no matter what his mind may be, puts himself beneath himself." Boileau, conversing one day with d'Olivet said:

"Do you know why the classics have so few admirers? It is because at least three fourths of those who have translated them are fools. Mme. de La Fayette, the woman who had the most mind in France and wrote the best, compared a foolish translator to a footman whom his mistress sends to give her compliment to some one. What she gave him in terms polite, he offers in a vulgar way, he maims it; the more delicacy there was in the compliment the less well the footman acquits himself. And there, in a word, is the most perfect image of a bad translator."

Boileau seems, in this remark, to certify himself to the resemblance, the harmony between them that I have indicated. M. Roederer is a thousand times right when, speaking of the relations of Molière to the social word of Mmes. de Sévigné and de La Fayette, he shows that *Les Femmes Savantes* did not relate to them in any way. As for La Fontaine, it is certain that at one time he was on terms of much familiarity with Mme. de La Fayette; we have some very affectionate verses that he addressed to her on sending her a little billiard table. This must have

been about the time that he dedicated a fable to the
author of the Maxims, and another to Mme. de Sévigné.

After the death of M. de La Rochefoucauld Mme.
de La Fayette's thoughts turned more and more to
religion; we have a precious testimony to this in a
long and beautiful letter to Du Guet, written by her.
She had chosen him as her director.   Without being
actually connected with Port-Royal, she inclined that
way, and the hyprocrisy of the Court drove her more
and more into it.   Her mother, as we have seen,
gave her for step-father the Chevalier Renaud de
Sévigné, uncle of Mme. de Sévigné, and one of the
benefactors of Port-Royal-des-Champs, the cloisters
of which he had rebuilt.   He did not die ·till 1676.
Mme. de La Fayette knew Du Guet, who was beginning to take a great spiritual part in the direction
of consciences, and had, in connection with the decadence of Port-Royal, very just and well-informed
views on that subject, in which there was nothing
contentious or narrow.   Here are a few of the stern
words this priest of the mind addressed to the repentant woman who had asked for them:

"I have thought, madame, that you ought to employ usefully the
early moments of the day when you cease to sleep, and begin to dream
or muse. I know that such are not connected thoughts, and that often
you have striven not to have them; but it is difficult to keep from
yielding to our nature when we are willing it should be our master;
and we return to it without difficulty, having had so much in quitting
it.   It is important, therefore, that you be fed on food more solid than
thoughts that have no aim, the most innocent of which are useless;
and I believe you cannot better employ such tranquil moments than

in rendering account to yourself of a life already very long, of which nothing now remains to you but reputation, the vanity of which you know better than any one.

"Until now the clouds with which you have tried to cover religion have hidden you from yourself. As it is in relation to religion that we ought to examine and know ourselves, by affecting to ignore it you have merely ignored yourself. It is time to leave everything in its place, and to put yourself in yours. Truth will judge you; you are in the world solely to follow it, not to judge of it. In vain do we defend ourselves against it, in vain do we dissimulate; the veil is torn from our eyes as life and its cupidities vanish, and we become convinced that we must lead a new life just as we are not permitted to live longer. We must therefore begin by a sincere desire to see ourselves as we are seen by our Judge. The sight is crushing, even to those persons who are the most outspoken against concealment. It takes all our virtues from us, and even all our good qualities and the self-esteem they had acquired for us. We feel that we have lived until then in illusions and falsehood; that we have nourished ourselves on painted flesh, have judged virtue by its garments and its jewels, neglecting the foundation because that foundation is the ascription of all to God and to his salvation; it is to despise self in all things, not from a wiser vanity, not from pride more enlightened and of better taste, but from a feeling of its wrongfulness and its misery."

The rest of the letter is equally admirable and in the same suitable and pressing tone: "Therefore, you who have dreamed, cease your dreams. You who esteem yourself *true* among others, and whom the world flatters that you are so, you are *not* so; you are only half so and falsely so; your virtue without God was only good taste." And farther on I find a sentence on those years "for which you have not yet sincerely repented because you are still astray enough to excuse your weakness and to love that which caused it."

One year before her death, Mme. de La Fayette

wrote Mme. de Sévigné a little note which describes her illness without repose night or day and her resignation to God, ending with these words: " Believe, my very dear one, that you are the person I have most truly loved." The other affection that she did not name and counted no longer, was it buried, consumed at last in sacrifice ?

Her life harmonises to the end and is then consummated. Mme. de Sévigné writes to Mme. de Guitand, June 3, 1693, two or three days after the fatal day, deploring the loss of a friend of forty years:

" Her infirmities for the last two years had become extreme; I defended her always, for people said she was crazy in not being willing to go out. She was deathly sad. ' Another folly ! ' they said, for was she not the luckiest woman in the world ?   But I said to those people so hasty in their judgments: ' Madame de La Fayette is not crazy '; and I kept to that.   Alas ! madame, the poor woman is more than justified now.   .   .   .   She had two polypuses in her heart, and the point of her heart was withered.   Was not this enough to cause the desolations of which she complained ?   She was reasonable in her life, she was reasonable in her death, never was she without that divine reason which was her principal quality.   .   .   . She was unconscious during the four days of her last illness.   .   .   .   God did her, for our consolation, a special grace which shows a true predestination: it is that she confessed on the day at the little Fête-Dieu, with scrupulous exactitude, and with a sentiment that could come only from him, and received our Lord in the same manner.   Therefore, my dear madame, we regard this communion, which she was accustomed to make on Whit-Sunday as a mercy of God, who desired to console us for her not being in a state to receive the viaticum."

Thus lived and died, in a mingling of sad sweetness and sharp suffering, of wisdom according to the world and of repentance before God, the woman

25

whose ideal production still enchants us.   What more
can be added as matter for reflection and instruction?
The letter to Mme. de Sablé, the *Princesse de Clèves,*
and the letter of Du Guet, are they not the whole record
of a life?

XII.

Madame, Duchesse d'Orléans.

XII.

Henrietta Anne of England.

Madame, Ducbesse d'Orléans.

TWO volumes written by Daniel de Cosnac, a man of Louis XIV's century and of whom Mme. de Sévigné said, "He has much intelligence," cannot be read with too much attention. At first, these Memoirs please but slightly, and seem to respond imperfectly to the reputation of the author: it is only little by little, as we advance, and after we have finished them, that we perceive how much they have increased our knowledge and enriched our judgment on many points. To-day, I take pleasure in detaching their most beautiful and most interesting figure, that of MADAME, to whom Cosnac had the honour of devoting himself of his own free choice, and for whom he had the glory to suffer. The portrait he makes of her does not pale beside even the greatest and the most affecting that we possess; it can be read with pleasure after Bossuet's Funeral Oration, and it adds much to what Mme. de La Fayette, Choisy, and La Fare have said of her.

Mme. de La Fayette has given a most charming history of Madame Henriette such as every woman of delicacy, a born princess in heart, must desire. It is a narrative written down from a confidence, and intended for her who gave it, who smiled at seeing herself so justly, so airily painted, and took, at moments, pen in hand to retouch the sketch. Madame, after her dinner, liked to lie upon the floor, near to Mme. de La Fayette, so that her head was almost upon the latter's knees; and in that familiar and charming position, she related the details of her heart, or listened to those already written, looking at herself in the mirror that her friend offered her. Reading to-day this history so delicate, so flowing, so lightly touched, so timely stopped, we have need of some gift of imagination to catch all its grace and recreate its enchantment. Something is there, like the light down on fruits in their first freshness, which melts if you touch it.

The young Princess of England, daughter of Charles I and granddaughter of Henri IV, brought up in France during the troubles of her family, was destined to marry MONSIEUR, the king's brother, as soon as the young king, Louis XIV, had married the Infanta of Spain, which took place about the time that Charles II was restored to the throne of his fathers. Going with her mother to London on a visit to her brother during the first days of his Restoration she inflamed all hearts and made essay of her charms,

HENRIETTA ANNE OF ENGLAND.   MADAME, DUCHESSE D'ORLÉANS.
From a steel engraving.

being then, at most, seventeen years old. "She had," says Choisy, "black eyes, lively and full of contagious fire, that men could not fixedly look at without feeling the effect; her eyes seemed themselves affected with the desire of those who looked into them. Never was there so touching a princess." On her return to France, she became the object of all imaginable assiduities, including those of Monsieur, "who paid her, until their marriage, attentions in which only love was lacking; but the miracle of inflaming the heart of that prince was granted to no woman in the world."

Near to Monsieur, was a young seigneur who, in those days, was his favourite. This was the Comte de Guiche, the handsomest young man at Court, the best-made, bold, proud, with a certain air of assumption that is not displeasing to young women, and perfects to their eyes a hero of romance. The Comte de Guiche, in all respects, was perfect. Monsieur, without being in love, was jealous, which is not rare. But he was not so at first of the Comte de Guiche, whom he introduced into the privacy of the young princess, making him admire charms that of themselves were sufficiently felt and irresistible. Those years (1661–1662) were unique seasons of freshness and youth which may properly be called the springtide of Louis XIV's reign. All things opened themselves to joy, to gallantry, to thoughts of glory and of love; and intellect also bore its part; for, no

sooner was Madame married and separated from the
queen, her mother, who had kept her until then at
her side, than "a new discovery was made of her
mind which was as lovable as all the rest."

Sometime after her marriage, Madame came to live
with Monsieur in the Tuileries, which she did not
quit until she went some years later to the Palais-
Royal; so that she became in reality a Parisian princess.   Monsieur himself, indolent as he was, piqued
himself on being liked in Paris.   When the Court was
elsewhere, he was fond of making little trips and
sojourns in the capital; he even put a sort of malice
to the king, whom he thought these trips displeased,
into making them:

"But the truth is," says Cosnac, "they gave him the joy of having
a Court of his own; he was enchanted when he saw a great influx of
fine people at the Palais-Royal, coming there for love of him, he said,
though it was wholly for Madame.   He neglected nothing to cajole
each one, and it was visibly remarked that he was more or less gay
according as a small or a large Court appeared at his house.   Nevertheless, as I could not see that these trips produced the effect he desired, on the contrary, I judged from what he himself told me, that
though in the beginning they might have vexed the King, His Majesty
ended by laughing at them.   I did not have the compliance to applaud
such conduct.   I told Monsieur I did not think it was prudent to give
small displeasures to those who could so easily give him great ones.
But Monsieur was so pleased at being able, every time he went to
Paris, to ask ten or a dozen persons privately, 'Well, did you see
what a large company I had to-day?' that it was only opposing one's
self to his pleasures to tell him these truths; and his pleasures always
carried the day in his mind over the most important matters."

Thus Monsieur, that father of the Orléans branch,
a father so feeble and so little worthy, had this in

common with his successors, that he liked to hold his
Court in the Palais-Royal, to be well thought of in
Paris, and to make a sort of rivalry to the king;
nullity that he was, vanity in him forestalled and divined policy.

But I leave this forward glance and presage, which
would be an anachronism in all that concerns Madame
and the wholly ideal charm of her beginnings (1661).
She installed herself in the Tuileries and made choice
of her ladies and her friends, whom Mme. de La Fayette
enumerates:

"All these persons," says the pleasant historian, "passed their afternoons with Madame. They had the honour to follow her on her
drives; returning, the party supped with Monsieur; after supper, all
the men of the Court arrived, and the evening was passed in the
pleasures of cards, comedies, violins ; in short, they amused themselves with every imaginable diversion, and without the slightest
mixture of grievances."

On a trip to Fontainebleau that was made soon after,
Madame carried joy and pleasure with her. The
king who, previously, had not smiled upon the idea
of marrying her, "found when he came to know her
better how unjust he had been in not thinking her the
most beautiful person in the world." Here begins
the romance, or rather many romances in one. Madame became the queen of the moment, and that moment lasted till her death; she gave the tone to the
young Court, was the cause of all parties of pleasure,

"which were made for her, and it seemed as if the King had no
pleasure in them except through that which they gave to her. It was

then the middle of summer. Madame went to bathe every day; she started in a coach on account of the heat and returned on horseback, followed by all her ladies gracefully dressed, with many feathers on their heads, and accompanied by the King and all the young nobles of the Court. After supper, they entered calèches, and to the music of violins, drove, for a part of the night, around the canal."

Mme. de La Fayette, who gives us thus the frame-work of the novel, puts also into our hands some of the threads that entangled and agitated these young hearts: the king, more touched than a brother-in-law should be; Madame, more affected, perhaps, than a sister-in-law should be; La Vallière dawning, and coming at the right instant to break the spell; the Compte de Guiche, at the same moment, making as much way with Madame as La Vallière was making with the king. Jealousies, suspicions, rivalries, con-cealments, confidants thrusting themselves forward and playing the traitor — in short, the eternal his-tory of all groups young and amorous when left to themselves at leisure beneath the leafage. But here it was royal youth, glittering in the morning of a splen-did reign; history has crystallised them; literature, in default of poesy, has consecrated them; a woman's pen has told their tale in polished language full of per-missible negligences; posterity glances back upon them with envy.

To explain to ourselves how, in the midst of the pitfalls and perils among which she played, Madame did not succumb and could say sincerely to Monsieur on her death-bed: " *Monsieur, je ne vous ai jamais manqué* '' [I have never wronged you], we must remember her situation, always so watched, also her youth with the sort of innocence that accompanies the imprudence of early years. To me, all these great and these semi-passions, such as Mme. de La Fayette shows them to us in her History, and such as I believe them to have been, can be explained by first youth only. When the Comte de Guiche was exiled in 1664, Madame, just twenty, had become more prudent: "Madame," says Mme. de La Fayette, "did not choose that he should bid her farewell, because she knew she should be observed, and she was no longer at the age when that which is dangerous seemed to her so agreeable." Therefore, all her amiable pledges, adventures, entanglements of fancy and intrigues of heart belong to those early years before she was twenty

These amours and the exile of the Comte de Guiche gave rise to scandal, and the result was one of those libels printed in Holland to which Bussy-Rabutin has the sad honour of having set the example by his *Histoires Amoureuses.* Madame, informed in time, and dreading the effect on Monsieur, requested Cosnac to inform the prince and forestall his displeasure. What particularly distressed her was the printing of the libel; Cosnac undertook to stop it. He sent an intelligent man to Holland, M. Patin, son of Gui Patin, with orders to go to all the publishers who might have the book in hand.

" So well did he accomplish his errand," says Cosnac, " that he
obtained from the State's government a prohibition to print it, and
withdrew eighteen hundred copies already printed, which he brought
to me in Paris, and I gave them, by Monsieur's order, to Merille,
head valet-de-chambre.   This affair cost me much trouble and
money, but far from regretting either I considered myself too well
paid by the gratitude Madame showed to me."

This affair bound Cosnac more closely than before
to Madame, and from that moment we see him on
all occasions espousing her interests and serving them.
This was the period when he acted zealously on the
mind of Monsieur to induce him to become a prince
worthy of esteem and of his lofty birth.   He failed.
The influence of the Chevalier de Lorraine at the close
of the campaign of 1667 ruined all his efforts; and
that unworthy favourite, who saw in Cosnac a natural
enemy, neglected nothing to destroy and send him
into exile.

I shall say nothing of the miserable domestic intrigues through which, at this epoch, the soul of
Madame, so delicate, so elevated, was forced to
struggle.   Cosnac fills up here a gap left unfilled in
Mme. de La Fayette's History, and he takes us into
all the wretchedness, while the latter gives us only
the romance.   This attachment to Madame is certainly
the finest and most honourable part of Cosnac's life.
When he was exiled to his diocese (he was Archbishop of Aix) Madame never ceased to write to him
and wish for him; she asked for his recall, and her
insistence even went contrary to the king's will:

"The king," says Cosnac, "thought Madame could not preserve so violent and constant a desire for my return unless we
had some great bond together which made me necessary to
her; and this bond, from ideas that were given to him, seemed
to him some fixed cabal, which could not be too carefully destroyed."

There was no cabal, but Madame, had discovered
among the persons attached to her husband one
capable man, a generously ambitious man of merit,
and she acquired him for herself; she wished to make
him serve in the accomplishment of her own views,
which were becoming more serious with age. In
the wicked libel that Cosnac recovered in Holland,
there was one phrase, among others, that was not
ill-turned: "She has," it was said of Madame, "a
certain languishing air, and when she speaks to any
one, as she is very amiable, she seems to be asking
for their heart no matter what indifferent thing she
may be saying." This tenderness in Madame's look
had operated on the rather insensible soul of Cosnac,
and, without mingling therewith the slightest tinge of
gallant sentiment, he had let his heart be captured by
her who asked for it so sweetly and so sovereignly.

While Cosnac was in exile at Valence, Madame
found herself chosen by Louis XIV, who appreciated
her more and more, as mediatrix with her brother,
King Charles II, whom it was desirable to detach from
the alliance with Holland, and also to induce him to
declare himself a Catholic. Louis XIV, however, held
much less to the second point than to the first. The

affair was so advanced, and even on the most delicate
point, the declaration of catholicity, Madame supposed
it so near conclusion, that she thought she could inform Cosnac of a great present and surprise she was
preparing for him.   He received a letter from her
dated at Saint Cloud, June 10, 1669, which said:

"In the sorrow you surely feel at the injustice done you, there
must be some comfort in thinking that your friends are devising consolations which might aid you in bearing your misfortunes.   Mme.
de Saint-Chaumont " (governess to the Orléans children), "and I have
resolved, in order to do this, that you shall have a cardinal's hat.
That thought, I am certain, will seem to you visionary at first, seeing
that those on whom such favours depend are so far from giving them
to you; but, to clear up the enigma, you must know that, among
the multiplicity of matters that are treated of between France and
England, this last one will, in a short time, be made of such consequence in Rome, where they will be so glad to oblige the king my
brother, that I am quite certain they will refuse him nothing; and I
have made advances to him so that he would ask for a cardinal's hat
without naming for whom; the which he has promised me; and it
will be for you; therefore you can count upon it."

This cardinal's hat, which she shows thus unexpectedly as about to fall upon the head of a man in disgrace, has an odd effect, and we remain convinced,
even after reading her letter, that there was something
a little visionary and fanciful about it, such as women
of the best minds are apt to mingle with their politics.
We must do Cosnac the justice to say that he did not
allow himself to be dazzled by it; and that he chiefly
saw in the idea, what we see to-day, a noble testimony to Madame's esteem for him: "However ambitious the world may have thought me," he says, "I

can say with sincerity that what flattered me the most
in this letter, was to see the increase of Madame's
friendship. This was, speaking with truth, the one
honour that I felt the most." He was on these terms
of friendship and close correspondence with the noble
princess in the spring of 1670, and was receiving from
her all sorts of new proofs of affection and of sympathy for his unfortunate misadventure in Paris.
During a journey to Dover, whither she went to see
the king, her brother, and bring him to sign the treaty
with Louis XIV (June 1st) she thought of "that poor
M. de Valence." On her return from that journey,
four days before her death on the 26th of June, she
wrote to him:

" I am not surprised at the joy you tell me you feel at my journey
to England; it has been very agreeable; and however much I was convinced of the friendship of the king my brother, I found it greater than I
could have hoped. Also, I found in all the things that depended on
him as much willingness as I could wish. The king also, on my
return, showed me a great deal of kindness; but as for Monsieur, nothing can equal his implacable determination to complain of me. He
did me the honour to tell me that I was all-powerful and that I could
do what I choose; and, consequently, if I did not bring back the
Chevalier" (the Chevalier de Lorraine, then exiled by order of the
king) " I did not care to please him, and to that he added threats for
the time to come. I represented to him how little that return depended on me; and how little I could do what I wished inasmuch as
you were where you are. Instead of seeing the truth of what I said
and being softened by it, he took this occasion to do you harm with
the king, and to do me an ill turn also."

This letter also gives expression to a sorrow that to
a mother was very keen. Cosnac had written a little
letter to Madame's daughter, then about eight years

old, for whom he had taken a fancy when seeing her with Mme. de Saint-Chaumont, her governess. This letter, which was delivered with a sort of mystery, had produced a bad effect, and Madame adds to the above letter :

"I have several times blamed the tenderness you have for my daughter; in God's name give it up. She is a child who is incapable of feeling about it as she ought; and she is being brought up to hate me. Content yourself with loving those who are as grateful as I am, and who feel as keenly as I do the grief of not being in a position to draw you from that in which you are."

Three days after the writing of this letter, on the 29th of June, about five in the afternoon, Madame, being at Saint-Cloud, asked for a glass of iced chicory water; she drank it, and nine or ten hours later, at half-past two in the morning of June 30th, she died in all the agony of a violent colic. We have the details of her slightest actions and words during that interval. Throughout this sudden attack, when death took her, as it were, by the throat, she kept her presence of mind, thought of essential things, of God, of her soul, of Monsieur, of the king, her family, her friends; addressing to all simple and true words, charming in restraint and, if I may say so, supreme in their decorum.

In the first moments they sent for the learned Feuillet, canon of Saint-Cloud, a stern rigorist; he did not spare the princess; he spoke to her harshly; let us listen to his own account of it: "At eleven o'clock at night she sent to call me in a great hurry. Having arrived at her bedside, she made all present retire and said to me: 'You see, Monsieur Feuillet, the state in which I am.' 'In a very good state Madame,' I replied, 'for now you will confess that there is a God, whom you have known very little during your life.'" He goes on to tell her that all her past confessions counted for nothing, that her whole life had been nought but sin; he helped her, as much as time permitted, to make a general confession. She made it with feelings of great piety. A Capuchin, her usual confessor, being with M. Feuillet beside her bed, the good man wished to speak to her, and wandered into long discourse. She looked at Mme. de La Fayette, who stood by, with a mixture of pity and distress; then, turning to the Capuchin: "Let M. Feuillet speak, my father," she said with wonderful gentleness (as if she feared to hurt him), "you shall speak in your turn." Nevertheless, M. Feuillet said to her, in a loud voice, the harshest words: "Humble yourself, Madame; behold all your deceitful grandeur annihilated beneath the heavy hand of God. You are nought but a miserable sinner, an earthen vessel, about to fall and be broken to pieces; of all this grandeur not a trace will remain." "It is true, O my God!" she exclaimed, accepting all with submission from the lips of a deserving but rough priest, giving in exchange, what was unalterable in her, something kind and gentle.

26

They had sent to Paris in all haste for M. de Condom, Bossuet. The first messenger could not find
him: they sent a second, then a third. She was
dying, and had just taken a last potion when he arrived. Here the account of the stern Feuillet changes
in tone and is sensibly affected: "She was as glad to
see him," he says, "as he was afflicted at finding her
at the last gasp. He prostrated himself upon the
ground and made a prayer which charmed me; he
mingled in it acts of faith, of confidence, and of love."

Prayer of Bossuet prostrate by the death-bed of Madame, natural and instant effusion of that great, tender
heart ! you were the inward treasury whence he drew
the touching grandeurs of his Funeral Oration; that
which the world admires is but the echo of the accents
that gushed forth then and were lost in the bosom of
God with groans from the plenitude of the spirit.

As Bossuet ceased speaking, the head waiting-
woman came forward to give the princess something
that she needed; taking advantage of the occasion,
Madame said to her in English, so that Bossuet could not
understand, keeping until death all the delicacy of her
actions and the courtesy of her spirit: "Give M. de
Condom, when I am dead, the emerald I have had
made for him." This was what Bossuet remembered
in his Funeral Oration when he said: "That art of
giving agreeably, which she had practised throughout her life, followed her, as I know, into the arms of
death."

Was Madame poisoned? It is agreed to-day to deny it; and it seems to be a settled thing to say that she died of cholera-morbus. The official autopsy, required, in part, by policy, appears to declare it; much stress was also laid on constitutional lesions which were covered by that graceful exterior. The feeling, or rather the inward sensation of Madame, was that she had been poisoned. She said so before Monsieur, requesting that the water she had drunk should be examined. Mme. de La Fayette says:

"I was in the alcove, near to Monsieur, and, though I thought him very incapable of such a crime, a bewilderment as to human malignity made me observe him with attention. He was neither moved, nor embarrassed by Madame's opinion; he said the water must be given to a dog; and he agreed with Madame that oil and counter-poison should be sent for, to take from Madame's mind so painful a thought."

It is in such temperate and circumspect words that Mme. de La Fayette justifies Monsieur. The letter written to Cosnac in June showed us Monsieur more "implacable" than ever against Madame, and "threatening her in the future." In another letter, written on the eve of her journey to England, April 28, 1670, Madame expressed her fears and her sad forebodings in very energetic and very precise language: "Monsieur is still too bitter about me, and I must expect many troubles when I return from this journey. . . . Monsieur insists that I shall have the Chevalier brought back, or he will treat me as the lowest of creatures." Observe that as soon as she was dead

the Chevalier reappeared at Court. But it does not
appear that Cosnac drew any precise induction from
the letters addressed to him, or that he gave them
any evil meaning. He expresses no suspicion of his
own. He simply let his sorrow find vent, and here
I ask permission to quote at length a page that does
honour to him who wrote it, and which nobly completes the circle of funeral orations of which Madame
was the subject.

"I shall not attempt," he says, "to express the state in which I
was on hearing of her death. Inasmuch as there have been persons
who died of grief, it is shameful in me to have survived mine. All
that respect, esteem, gratitude, ambition, self-interest could inspire of
dreadful reflections passed a thousand times through my mind. My
constitution resisted it, I was not even ill; but my mind became so
grieved, so languid, that I was hardly better than if I had been dead.
As for the loss of my fortunes, I was not very conscious of that; I
had never been able to persuade myself that the hopes held out
to me were solid, though, to judge by all appearances, success was
indubitable; but to lose so great, so perfect, so good a princess,
a princess who could repair the harm my fall had done me — no,
if I had had a truly delicate and feeling heart it must have cost me
my life. To justify my devotion to this princess, and for my own
consolation, I trace here a slender idea of her virtues. . . ."

Here follows a formal Portrait in the style of the
day :

"Madame's mind was solid and delicate; she had good sense,
knowledge of choice things, a soul lofty and just, enlightened on
all she ought to do, but sometimes not doing it, either from natural
indolence, or from a certain haughtiness of soul, which came of
her origin and made her look upon duty as a degradation. She
mingled with all her conversation a gentleness that is never found
in other royal personages; it was not that she had less majesty,
but that she knew how to use it in an easy and touching manner;

so that with qualities that were wholly divine she never ceased to be the most human of beings. One might say that she appropriated hearts instead of leaving them in common; and it was that that gave rise to the belief that she liked to please everybody and to win the liking of all sorts of persons.

"As for the features of her face, we seldom see any so complete; her eyes were keen without being rude, the mouth admirable, the nose perfect,— a rare thing! for nature, to the contrary of art, makes nearly all eyes well and nearly all noses badly. Her skin was white and smooth beyond expression, her figure mediocre, but refined. One might say that her mind as well as her soul animated her body; she had it even in her feet and danced better than any woman in the world.

"As for that *je ne sais quoi* so talked about, and given in pure wantonness to so many unworthy persons, that ' I know not what ' which goes at once to the bottom of all hearts, persons of delicacy agreed that while in others it was copy, in Madame it was original. Whoso approached her remained convinced that no one more perfect could be seen.

"I have nothing more to say of this princess, except that she would have been the glory and the honour of her century, and that her century would have ad red her, had it been worthy of her.

"With this princess I lost the desire and the hope of my return, and, utterly disgusted with the world, I turned all my aims to my ministry."

The event of Madame's death brought a crisis to many lives. La Fare relates that on that day he brought back from Saint-Cloud M. de Tréville, a particular friend of Madame, one of those she most appreciated for his elegant mind, somewhat subtile and extremely accomplished: "Tréville, whom I brought back that day from Saint-Cloud and kept to sleep at my house, so as not to leave him a prey to his sorrow, left the world and gave himself up to devotion, which he has always continued ever since." Mme. de La Fayette herself, after losing Madame, retired from the

Court, and lived with M. de La Rochefoucauld that
more private life which she never afterwards quitted.

Dying at twenty-six years of age, having been for
nine years the centre of charm and of pleasures,
Madame marks the finest, or at least the most graceful period of the Court of Louis XIV. After her, at
that Court, there was, perhaps, more splendour, more
imposing grandeur, but less of distinction and refinement. Madame loved intellect, distinguished it for
itself, went in search of it, awakened it in the older
poets, Corneille, for instance, favoured it and embold-
ened it in the younger, such as Racine; she wept at
Andromaque, when the young author first read it to
her: "Pardon me, Madame," wrote Racine in the
preface to his tragedy, "if I dare to boast of that fortunate beginning of its destiny." In all the Courts
which had but recently preceded that of Madame, at
Chantilly, at the hôtel Rambouillet and its surroundings, there was a mingling of taste already past and
about to become superannuated: with Madame begins, properly speaking, the modern taste of Louis
XIV's reign; she contributed to fix it in its purity.

Madame naturally calls for comparison with that
other interesting princess of the last years of Louis
XIV, the Duchesse de Bourgogne. Without pretending to sacrifice the one to the other, let us merely
note some differences. The Duchesse de Bourgogne,
cherished pupil of Mme. de Maintenon, whom she
sometimes distressed by disobedience, belonged to

the generation of young women who loved pleasure,
cards, and at times the table, immoderately; in short,
she was well fitted to be the mother of Louis XV.
Madame who, had she come in the days of the
Duchesse de Bourgogne, might, perhaps, have loved
all those things, did, in point of fact, love the things of
the mind; solidity and good sense mingled insensibly with her graces; decency and good manners
never deserted her.   Louis XIV, in allying himself to
her with a true friendship that conquered love, seems
to have desired to regulate that happy nature and to
give it some of his own good qualities; "he made
her in a short time one of the most finished persons
in the world."   In the few days she spent at Saint-
Cloud, on her return from England, and just before
her death, La Fare pictures her to us enjoying the
beauty of the weather and the conversation of her
friends, "such as M. de Turenne, M. de La Rochefoucauld, Mme. de La Fayette, Tréville, and several
others."   That is not, I imagine, the circle that the
Duchesse de Bourgogne, more giddy and frolicsome,
would have chosen and grouped around her.

The letters of Madame, written to Cosnac, are
short, friendly, sufficiently well-turned, but with nothing remarkable; evidently she had not the imagination that can reach to a distance; hers was one of
those light and blessed spirits that we must catch and
adore at their source.   Literature has nothing here to
do except to record the testimony of contemporaries

and, in a way, to cut them out from the pages of other days. That is what I have tried to do with as much simplicity and as little effort as possible, asking indulgence of my readers, for we too, servants of the public, are sometimes tired out ourselves.

XIII.

Louis XIV.

XIII.

Louis XIV.

His Memoirs by Himself.

U NDER the improper title of "Works," there
exist six most interesting and most authentic
volumes which it would have been more correct to entitle the "Memoirs of Louis XIV." They are
in reality true memoirs of his reign and of his principal
actions, which he undertook to write for the instruction of his son. The narrative is often interrupted by
moral and royal reflections that are very judicious.
The six or seven years after the death of Cardinal
Mazarin, which constitute the first epoch of Louis
XIV's reign (1661–1668) are exhibited and related consecutively in almost uninterrupted detail. The following years, till 1694, are represented in a series of letters
which concern, more especially, the campaigns and
military operations. A number of private letters,
relating to all the epochs of his reign are added
thereto; the whole forming a body of documents,
notes, and instructions emanating directly from Louis
XIV himself, and casting the strongest light both on his
actions and on the spirit that presided over them.

411

One day, in 1714, the old king, near his end, sent the Duc de Noailles to his desk to bring him the papers that were written by his own hand: "At first he burned several that concerned the reputations of various persons; he was then about to burn the rest, notes, memoirs, fragments of his own composition on war or policy. The Duc de Noailles begged him earnestly to give them to him, and obtained that favour." The originals, deposited by the Duc de Noailles in the Bibliothèque du Roi, are preserved there. From those manuscripts the publication was made, in 1806, of the six volumes of which I speak; to which, I know not why, the public has never done justice or given them the attention they deserve. The volumes have long been for sale at a very cheap price. It is but a few years since the same could be said of the nine volumes of Napoleon's authentic Memoirs. As for those of the great Frederick, there is such mixture in them that it is not surprising the fine historical parts that form their basis should long have been hidden under the literary rubbish that at first sight covers and compromises them. Nothing of the kind appears in the Memoirs of Louis XIV, nor in those of Napoleon; they are pure history, the reflections of men who speak of their art, and the greatest of arts, that of reigning. Our levity shows here: the worst frivolous political pamphlets were read by everybody, yet many distinguished and serious minds never troubled themselves even to know

LVDOVICVS XIIII DEI GRATIA FRANCIÆ
ET NAVARRÆ REX CHRISTIANISSIMVS.

LOUIS XIV. IN 1661.
From an illustration, based on an old print, in Philippson's
Das Zeitalter Ludwigs XIV.

whether it would be well to read those writings,
attached to great names, where, on every page, they
could have verified the stamp of their genius or their
good sense.

Louis XIV had nothing more than good sense, but
he had a great deal of it. The impression made by
the reading of his writings, especially those that date
from his youth, is well fitted to double our respect
for him. The smile that we cannot restrain in certain
places, where he superabounds with the idea of his
glory, soon dies upon our lips and gives place to a
higher feeling when we remember that an inward
spring is necessary to all souls, and that a prince who
doubted himself, a king sceptical of his greatness
would be the worst of kings. The wheel of history,
ever turning, has brought us back to the point of view
that is necessary to comprehend better what a royal
and sovereign nature is, and of what use it is in a society. Let us give ourselves the pleasure of considering it in Louis XIV, in its purity and its hereditary
exaltation, and before the days of Mirabeau.

From childhood Louis XIV was remarkable for
peculiar traits and serious graces that distinguished
him from others of his age. The virtuous and sensible Mme. de Motteville has drawn some charming
portraits of him in his early years; of a ball that took
place in Cardinal Mazarin's apartments while he was
still a child, she says:

"The king wore a coat of black satin with gold and silver

embroidery of which the black showed only enough to set off to advantage the embroidery. Carnation-coloured plumes and ribbons completed his adornment; but the beautiful features of his face, the gentleness of his eyes joined to their gravity, the whiteness and brilliancy of his skin, together with his hair, then very blond, adorned him much more than his clothes. He danced perfectly; and though he was then only eight years old, one could say of him that he was the one of the company who had the best air, and assuredly the most beauty."

Speaking elsewhere of his intimacy with the young Prince of Wales (afterwards Charles II) who was then in France, she says: "The king, whose beauty had charm, though young, was very tall. He was grave; in his eyes we saw a serious look that marked his dignity. He was even prudent enough to say nothing for fear of not speaking well."

About this time (1647) the king fell ill of the small-pox; his mother felt the keenest anxiety, for which he showed her a tender and touching gratitude:

"In this illness he showed himself to all who approached him a prince full of gentleness and kindness. He spoke humanely to all who served him, saying witty and obliging things to them, and was docile to all that the doctors desired. The queen received from him marks of affection that touched her keenly."

These first traits are essential to remark. One of the severest contemporaries of Louis XIV, Saint-Simon, who never saw or knew him till the last twenty-two years of his life, says, in the midst of the penetrating analyses he made of him on all sides:

"He was born virtuous, moderate, discreet, master

of his motions and of his tongue.   Will it be believed ?
he was born good and just; God had given him
enough to be a good king, perhaps, even a fairly
great king."

That there was in Louis XIV an early foundation of
kindness, gentleness, and humanity, which disappeared
too often in the idolatry of supreme rank, Saint-Simon
recognises and, surprised though he was, bears witness to it.   Mme. de Motteville makes us see it as
the natural character of the child-king, and more than
one saying of Louis XIV in the sincere pages of his
youth will confirm it to us.

Gravity and gentleness, all contemporaries agree to
note those two manifest traits, though the gentleness
gave place more and more to gravity.   "I often
noticed with astonishment," says Madame de Motteville "that in his games and in his amusements the
king never laughed."   We have a letter of his in
which he asks the Duke of Parma (July, 1661) to send
him a Harlequin for his Italian troop; he asks it in
terms of the utmost seriousness, without the least
little word of gaiety.   If he was at a ball, if he danced,
Mme. de Sévigné, who watched him with anxiety
during Fouquet's trial, applied to him Tasso's words,
showing that even in a ballet he had, like Godefroy de
Bouillon "a countenance that induced more fear than
hope."   "He was," she says, "amiable in his person,
civil and easy of access to every one, but with a grand
and serious air that impressed respect and fear on the

public, and prevented those whom he most esteemed from feeling free with him even in private; although he was familiar and lively with ladies." The gentleness that mingled in his speech is singularly certified and depicted to us in this fine passage of Bossuet:

" Whoso would like to know how far reason presides in the councils of this prince has only to lend an ear when it pleases him to explain his motives. I could here call to witness the wise ministers from foreign Courts, who found him as convincing in his discourse as he was formidable in arms. The nobleness of his expressions came from the nobleness of his sentiments, and his precise words are the image of the accuracy that reigns in his thoughts. While he speaks with so much force, a surprising gentleness opens to him all hearts and gives, I know not how, a new splendour to the majesty it tempers."

That passage would be the best epigraph to put at the head of the writings of Louis XIV; it would be found, in part at least, justified as we read them.

In choosing, at twenty-three years of age, to reign wholly by himself, Louis XIV placed in the number of his necessary occupations and duties that of noting down in writing his principal actions, rendering an account of them to himself, and, later, making them the ground of instruction to his son in order to train him in the art of reigning. The idea of glory, inseparable from Louis XIV, mingled in this work, and as history would some day concern itself with his actions, as the passion and genius of many writers would be exercised upon them, he wishes that his son should find in his work that which would correct history wherever it might be mistaken.

Louis XIV, with little knowledge of Letters, and whose early education was much neglected, had, nevertheless, received that far superior instruction which a just and upright mind and a lofty heart derive from events the play of which they have known from childhood. Mazarin, who during his last years understood the king, gave him in conversing the counsels of a statesman, which the young man grasped and comprehended better than minds reputed more cultivated and more acute might have done. Mazarin declared to some who seemed to doubt the future of the young king, that "they did not know him; for he had the stuff in him to make four kings and one honest man."

In these Papers or Memoirs, Louis XIV has exhibited the first idea that he himself had of things, and the first interior education that gradually worked through his mind, his first doubts in view of difficulties, and his reasons for waiting and deferring, "because," he says, "preferring, as I do, to all things and to life itself a lofty reputation, if I can acquire it," he comprehended at the same time that his first proceedings would lay its foundations or else make him lose for ever even the hope of it; so that the sole and same desire for glory which urged him forward restrained him almost equally:

"Nevertheless," he says, "I did not cease to practice and test myself, in secret and without a confidant, reasoning alone and within myself on all the events that happened; full of hope and joy when

27

I discovered sometimes that my first thoughts were the same as those arrived at in the end by able and accomplished persons; and convinced in my heart that I had not been put and preserved upon the throne with so great a passion for doing right without being able to find the means of doing it."

Mazarin dead, there was no longer any motive for Louis XIV to delay:

" I began, therefore, to cast my eyes upon the different parties in the State; and not with indifferent eyes, but with the eyes of a master, keenly touched by not seeing one that did not invite me and urge me to lay my hand upon it; but observing carefully what time and the arrangement of things might permit me."

Louis XIV, religious as he is, believes that there are lights proportioned to situations, and particularly to that of kings: "God who will make you king," he tells his son, "will give you the lights that are necessary to you, so long as you have good intentions." He believes that a sovereign sees, by nature, the objects that present themselves in a more perfect manner than the common run of men. Such a conviction we feel is dangerous; it will soon mislead him. Nevertheless, reduced and understood in a certain sense, that idea is a just one: "I do not fear to tell you," he writes, "that the higher the position the more it has objects that cannot be seen or known until we occupy it."

Saint-Simon, whom I shall venture to contradict and refute on this point, says:

" Born with a mind below mediocrity, but a mind capable of forming itself, correcting and refining itself, of borrowing from oth-

ers without imitation, and without awkwardness, he profited im-
mensely by having, all his life, lived with persons who, of all
the world, had the best minds, and the most varied sorts of minds,
both men and women, of all ages, all styles, all characters."

He returns quite frequently to this idea, that Louis
XIV's mind was "below mediocrity," but that he
was very capable of acquiring, and of forming himself and appropriating what he saw in others. There
was one thing, however, that Louis XIV did not need
to borrow from any one, and which is very original
to himself, I mean *state;* that true function of sovereignty, which no one at that time about him had
any idea of, which the troubles of the Fronde had
allowed to perish in the minds of all, and which
Mazarin, even after the restoration of power, had very
poorly restored to public reverence. Louis XIV had
the instinct within him, and revealed, perceptibly to
all, its character. Nature had made him for it physic-
ally by giving him a unique mixture of decorum and
majesty. Wherever he might be, he would at once
have been distinguished and recognised as we recognise "the queen among the bees." His solid
qualities, the laborious application of his mind, the
feelings of his heart, responded to this intention of
Nature and to the rôle of his destiny. Later, and
soon, he overpassed it; but in the beginning he
simply fulfilled it to perfection and with majestic
propriety.

Saint-Simon, who came toward the close of the

reign and at an epoch when the spirit of opposition was reappearing, has not sufficiently recognised this first period of pure and integral royal originality in Louis XIV. His long reign was beginning to weary the people of France; everywhere they were aspiring to some respite. But the true answer to Saint-Simon is that of Louis XIV himself in terms that are worthy of both of them:

"We scarcely notice," says the sensible king, "the wonderful order of the universe, and the course, so regulated and useful, of the sun until some irregularity of the seasons, or some disorder apparent in the system, obliges us to give it a little more reflection. So long as everything prospers in a State we may forget the infinite blessings produced by royalty, and envy only those that royalty possesses: man, naturally ambitious and proud, never finds in himself why another should rule him until his personal need makes him feel it. But to that need, as soon as it has a constant and regular remedy, custom renders him insensible. It is only extraordinary events that make him consider how much that is useful he daily derives from it, and that without such rule he would be a prey to the strongest, and find in this world neither justice, nor reason, nor security for what he possesses, nor resource for what he may lose; and it is in this way that he comes to love obedience as much as he loves his life and his tranquillity."

That is what Louis XIV wrote. Saint-Simon has related to us at great length two or three audiences that he obtained with him, and has vividly conveyed to us the impression of respect, submission, and grateful joy that he brought away with him. Superior as he himself is as an observer, he felt his master on approaching him, and the detail with which he relates the matter proves it. The page I

have just quoted leads me to believe that if (by im-
possibility) a political conversation had taken place
between them, Louis XIV, simple in tone and with
easy good sense, would have kept, on all essential
points, his sovereign superiority. Let us give to each
the name that correctly designates him: Saint-Simon
was a great painter and a great moralist; Louis XIV
was a king. He wished to show to the whole earth
(and it is he himself who says it) that "there was
still a king in the world."

In the reforms of all kinds that Louis XIV undertook and carried on, in finances, in law and justice, in military regulations, in affairs with foreign
countries, he never shows undue eagerness. He
examines, he listens, he consults; then he decides
for himself: "Decision," he says, "needs the mind
of a master." This last point was always the great
concern of Louis XIV: not to let himself be governed; to have no prime minister. It has been remarked that this was more an appearance than a
reality; he had head-clerks who, by art and flattery,
were able to make him adopt as if by his own
impulse what they themselves desired. But at the
start, and during the first seven or eight years of
his youth, Louis XIV certainly escaped that reproach.
The form of his mind was judicial and reasoning; it
was a practical mind, liking business, finding pleasure
in utility, and taking account of facts in the greatest
detail. "Every man who is illinformed," he remarks,

"cannot prevent himself from arguing badly"; and he adds shrewdly in a conclusion worthy of a moralist: "I believe that whoso should be well informed and well convinced of things as they are would do only as he ought to do."

He takes true pleasure in diligent application and in gaining information; he enjoys unravelling matters that are obscure. "I have already begun," he writes on the day of Fouquet's arrest, "to taste the pleasure there is in working oneself at the finances; having, in the little application I have given to them this afternoon, observed important things of which I had previously seen nothing; and it cannot be doubted that I shall continue to do so." He makes us feel at every moment the sort of charm there is in the exercise of good sense. He thinks that good sense, put to the test of practice and experience, is the best counsellor and the surest guide; and he is sometimes tempted to regard written counsel as useless, and hold to that only which he gives his son. But he instantly revises that opinion, and considers it profitable for all good minds to be put on their guard in advance and be cautioned against error. Regretting that he came so late to the study of history, he considers that "the knowledge of the great events produced by the world through many centuries, digested by solid and active minds, will serve to fortify the reason in all important deliberations."

Note the words, "solid and active minds," clothe

them with majesty and splendour, and there you have the best definition that can be given of him in the days of his youth. His wholly royal soul kept its equilibrium even when it soared the highest; his greatest heights have something that is moderate in their principle. He seeks to elevate the heart of his son, not to swell it; he says: "If I can explain to you my thought, it seems to me that we ought to be humble as to ourselves and, at the same time, proud for the place we occupy."

Some of these first pages set forth dispositions of mind more extended, more varied than he was able to maintain. "He had a soul greater than his mind," says Montesquieu. He desires that princes who are really able should know how to transform and re-make themselves to fit conjunctures. It does not suffice a prince, in order to be great, that he be born àpropos. "There are several in the world," he says, "who have obtained a reputation for ability through the sole advantage of having been born at a time when the general state of public affairs was in exact proportion to their capacity," but as for him, he aspires to something better; he desires to be of those who suffice through their minds for all situations, even contrary ones: "For it is not an easy thing to transpose oneself at all times into the right way," and "the face of the world is subject to such different revolutions that it is not in our power to keep long to the same measures." In reading this passage it

seems as though Louis XIV foresaw the rock on
which, in after years, his pride was to strike. He
was not of those whose minds can grasp the renewals
of the age, and his final policy was only an exaggeration of his first policy in the midst of public circumstances that were incessantly being modified.

When we read these notes, written day by day,
these reflections drawn from each event, when we
join to that a reading of the diplomatic instructions he
was, at the same time, addressing to his ambassadors
and agents at various Courts, we cannot help admiring, in the midst of his *carrousels* and fêtes, the industrious, solid, prudent, and persevering character of
this ambitious young man. How little levity, how
little rash enthusiasm he has! How he reasons out a
thing! how he disputes the ground foot by foot, and
argues each advantage bit by bit! Then, too, how
much secretiveness and discretion he possesses—royal
qualities as necessary to success as they are to respect
and reverence, the mere absence of which casts so
many men in politics aside: "for great talkers," he
remarks, "often talk great nonsense." He prefers,
as he does in everything, the slowest but the safest
course. In treaties, above all, he thinks there should
be no spurring on:

"He who tries to go too quickly," he says, "is liable to make many false steps. It is no matter in how
much time, but with what conditions a negotiation
ends. Better conclude an affair much later than ruin

it by haste; and it happens often that we retard by our own impatience what we tried to hurry on."

This procedure served him at the peace of Aix-la-Chapelle (1668). The young king has those precepts of safe, deliberate slowness that belonged to Philippe de Commynes, and come naturally to the pupil of Mazarin.

I think I find a wonderful relation between Louis XIV's manner of seeing and doing and that of the distinguished men of his time. Boileau advised doing work over and over a score of times, and he taught Racine to make with difficulty very easy verses. Louis XIV gives to his son precisely the same, or analogous precepts on politics; he advises him to turn a thing over in his mind twenty times before proceeding to execute it; he wishes to teach him to find slowly the easy method in each affair. Also, in many a moral reflection that he mingles with his policy, Louis XIV shows himself a worthy contemporary of Nicole and of Bourdaloue.

Even in affairs of war and in the sieges that he undertook, he yielded to the difficulties put before him, "convinced," he says, "that whatever desire one may have to signalise oneself, the safest road to glory is always that which shows the most reason." I do not say that in his conduct he did not, many a time, derogate from this early resolution; it suffices me, in order to characterise him, that he proposed it to himself amid the first fire of his ambition.

When he feels a leading and ruling passion, how-ever noble it may be, Louis XIV endeavours not to listen to it alone, but to counterbalance it by others which shall be equally for the good of the State: "Variety is needed in glory, as in all things else, and more in the glory of princes than of private persons; for whoso says 'great king,' says nearly all the talents of his most excellent subjects com-bined." There are talents, however, in which he thinks a king ought not to excel too much; it is good and honourable in him to be surpassed in them by others; but he ought to appreciate them all. Knowledge of men, discernment of minds, the selection of each for the employment for which he is best fitted and can be most useful to the State, that is properly the great art and perhaps the chief talent of a sovereign. Some princes have good reason to fear allowing themselves to be approached too closely, and communicating freely with others; he believes that he is not of them; sure as he is of himself and lending himself to no surprise, he thinks he gains by this easy communication the power to penetrate more deeply into those with whom he speaks, and to learn for himself who are the honest men of his kingdom.

It has been said that Louis XIV made the monarchy despotic and Asiatic: that was never his thought. Having recognised that "liberty, gentleness, and, so to speak, facility of the monarchy had passed all

proper limits during his minority, and the troubles
of the State, and had become license, confusion and
disorder," he believed it his duty to restrain these
excesses by endeavouring in the first place to preserve to the monarchy its humane and affectionate
character, to gather persons of quality about him
in an "honourable familiarity," and to keep in communication with the people by pleasures and spectacles conformed to their minds. In this, Louis XIV
only half succeeded; evidently, he forced the character of the French monarchy in his pomps and glories,
and, as he grew an old man, he ceased to be in
harmony with the public spirit of the nation. Nevertheless, he did not see it thus in his youth.

He thought, and he expressly says it to his son,
that "empires are preserved only as they are acquired, that is to say, by vigour, by vigilance, by
toil." When a wound is inflicted on the body of
the State "it is not enough to repair the evil if
we do not add more good than there was before."
He wishes that his son, instead of stopping on the
road and looking around him and beneath him on
those who are worth least, should turn his eyes higher:

"Think rather of those whom we have most reason to esteem and
admire in past ages; who from private life or very moderate power, by
the sole force of their merit, have founded great empires, passed like
lightning flashes from one half of the world to the other, charmed all
the earth by their great qualities, and left, through many long ages,
an eternal memory of themselves, which seems, instead of being destroyed, only to increase and strengthen with the lapse of time."

The misfortune of Louis XIV's descendants is never to have meditated on that thought. The condition of hereditary kings was about to become more and more like that of founders of empires; they needed, for preservation, the same genius and the same courage which had been needed to create and to acquire. I leave aside Louis XV and the base unworthiness of his reign; but it may be said that the good, honest, moderate, respectable Bourbons who succeeded him were not any more at the height of their circumstances; they did not know how to fulfil the hope and the counsel of their great ancestor. Therefore, the empire went to those " who passed like lightning flashes from one part of the world to the other."

Judicious and sensible as Louis XIV usually was, and desirous as he showed himself to foresee all and apply his reason to all, he felt there were moments when, as king, it was absolutely necessary to risk and devise at a venture, under pain of failing in wisdom itself. The religious thought that was joined to this in his mind adds rather than takes away from what this royal maxim has that is politically remarkable; it is in such parts as these that we recognise in Louis XIV the true man of talent in the difficult art of reigning:

" Wisdom," he says, " requires that in certain junctures we leave much to chance; reason itself then counsels us to follow I know not what blind instincts or impulse, above reason, which seem to come from heaven, known to all men, and more worthy of consideration in those whom heaven itself has placed in the first rank. To say when we ought to deny them and when abandon ourselves to them, no one is able; neither books, nor rules, nor experience will teach it; a certain exactitude, a certain boldness of mind will always find it, and, without comparison, more freely in him who owes account of his action to no one."

"Exactitude and boldness of mind"; do you not admire the excellent choice and happy conjunction of those words and the grand and noble style he carries naturally into simple sayings?

It may be said that the text of these Memoirs was written out by a secretary from the king's notes, but whoever that secretary may have been, Pellisson or some other, I find nothing in these pages that does not show, from beginning to end of them, the presence and dictation of the master. All is simple and worthy of him who said: "We notice almost always a difference between the letters which we give ourselves the trouble to write, and those that our secretaries, even the most skilful, write for us; we discover in the latter a something, I know not what, that is less natural, and the uneasiness of a pen that fears eternally to say too much or too little." I find nothing of that uneasiness, nothing of that rhetoric, or that affected simplicity in the pages that form the historic Memoirs of Louis XIV. All is there unfolded with calmness, continuity, and perfect clearness, which answers completely to what contemporaries (Mme. de Caylus, Mme. de Motteville, Saint-Simon) have told us of the unique appropriateness, the easy nobility of the king's words: "His commonest speech was never without a natural and obvious majesty." One day, during Louis XIV's youth, Brienne was reading to the queen-mother in her chamber a draft of the Letters-patent for the removal of the relics of Sainte-Madeleine. He had made M. d'Andilly, well known for his piety, write them. The king chanced to enter the room, requested that the reading might begin again, and then interrupted it by saying: "You make me talk like a saint and I am not one." Brienne told him the Letters were written by one of the ablest men in France for style and eloquence. "Who is that able fool?" asked the king. Being told it was M. d'Andilly, "Very well," he said, "but all that does not suit me at all," and tearing up the Letters he threw them to Brienne, saying: "Write others, and make me speak like a king, not a jansenist."

Louis XIV's style has not the quick, brusque brevity that characterises the original writings of Napoleon, what Tacitus calls *imperatoria brevitas*. That incisive character of the conqueror and the despot, that short, hasty, staccato rhythm, beneath which we feel the genius of action and the demon of battles palpitating, differs wholly from the more tranquil style, the fuller and, in a way, hereditary style of Louis XIV. When this monarch forgets himself and is negligent his sentences are long, like those that have since become the appanage of the Younger Branch, and of which we see no end: it is there that Louis XIV comes when he slumbers. But usually, in his habitual manner, his style has the good proportions, the accuracy, the golden mean of the sanest of languages. Henri IV, the first Bourbon king, had in his vivid style something warlike and Gascon which Louis XIV was without. The pitiable Louis XIV, who was not without intelligence, a few pregnant sayings of his being quoted, was, in his habitual conversation, long-winded and given to eternal repetitions; that was the Bourbon style in what was already its weakness and enervation. Louis XIV alone presents to us that style in its true plenitude and perfection, its veritable and regal stature.

It was said of Louis XIV that no one related things better than he: "he could tell a story better than any man in the world, and also a narrative." He put into it "infinite grace and a noble or shrewd turn of phrase that was all his own." We have a specimen of his manner of describing and painting in his letter written from Montargis to Mme. de Maintenon on the arrival in France of the Duchesse de Bourgogne, but narrative, properly so called, or tale of his we do not possess.

Pellisson, who was a little the Fontanes of those days, and whom Louis XIV took out of the Bastille [he had been Fouquet's secretary] to attach him to his service and make him his rhetorician in ordinary, transmits to us a conversation, or rather a discourse, which he took down from the lips of the king himself at the siege of Lille, August 23, 1667. It is a discourse

on glory, and on the motives that filled the king's soul
at that moment. He had exposed his life in an affair
two days earlier, and, being reproached for it, he gives
his reasons with naive solemnity. This course lays
bare to us the young king in his first magnificence
of ambition: "It seems to me," he says, "that they
strip me of my glory when they can have any without
me." That word "glory" is ever on his lips, and he
ends by perceiving this himself: "But it would ill-
become me to say more of my glory to those who
witness it." In this beginning of exultation and
apotheosis we find him better and more worthy than
he is later; he has certain words of sympathy for the
friends, the servitors, who expose and devote themselves before his eyes: "There is no king," he says,
"provided his heart is in the right place, who can see
so many brave men throwing away their lives like
refuse in his service, and yet remain with his arms
crossed." That is why he decided to leave the
trenches and expose his life under fire in the open;
above all, on an occasion, he says: "When all appearances were that we should have a fine action
where my presence should do all, I believed that
I ought to make visible in open daylight something
more than buried valour."

Louis XIV was little of a soldier; but he had the
pretension of being one; and nothing shows his foible
better than this discourse, this extraordinary apology
which he thinks he ought to make because he went

once into the trenches, and another time in front
of them.

If we pursue him in the direction of vain-glory
it would be only too easy to grow frivolous and
irreverent towards him. In his own discourses we
find him, from time to time, stopping short to congratulate himself with reason and reflection; he takes
himself to be naturally the type and figure of the perfect prince; he sees himself in that attitude and at
full length before posterity. But it is more useful
to insist on the lofty impulses that underlaid this faith
and this royal consciousness and made him say, in the
midst of political dangers: "But at least, whatever
be the outcome, I shall always have within me all the
contentment that a brave soul should have when it has
satisfied its own virtue."

Speaking of these six volumes of Memoirs when
they appeared, M. de Chateaubriand judged them very
rightly in saying:

"The Memoirs of Louis XIV increase his renown: they disclose no
meanness, they reveal none of those shameful secrets that the human
heart too often hides in its abysses. Seen more closely and in the
privacy of life, Louis XIV does not cease to be Louis the Great; one
is charmed to find that so fine a bust has not an empty head, and
that the soul responds to the exterior nobleness."

This feeling is that which rules the reader and
triumphs over all criticisms and all restrictions that a
just mind may rightly make.

Since it is here a question of Louis XIV as a writer and
one of the models of our speech, I shall, in concluding,

28

point out a direct benefit affecting the whole order
of literature which we owe to him. I have enumer-
ated elsewhere the men of letters grouped around
Fouquet and flourishing in rivalry under his auspices.
If we suppose for an instant that Fouquet had remained in power and firmly established, Louis XIV
leaving him to do as he would, we cannot help perceiving the elements and spirit of the literature that
would then have prevailed; it would have been a
literature freer in every sense than it actually was
under Louis XIV; the eighteenth century would have
been in part forestalled. We should have had La
Fontaine without restraint, Saint-Évremond, Bussy,
the Scarrons, the Bachaumonts, the Hesnaults; many
libertines and epicureans would have glided into the
front rank. This first literature of the morrow of the
Fronde and before Boileau and Racine, not being
restrained by the eye of the master, would have developed, and become more and more emancipated
under a less rigid Mæcenas. It was all ready, as we
can now see; licentiousness and wit would have been
the double danger; a foundation of corruption was
already laid. The young king came, and he brought,
he gave rise to his young literature, he put a corrective
to the old and, save for certain shining infractions,
he impressed upon the body of the productions of
his time a character of solidity and finally of morality,
which is also that which reigns in his own writings
and in the habit of his thought.

XIV.

The Duchesse de La Valliere.

XIV.

Louise de La Baume Le Blanc.

The Duchesse de La Vallière.

MME. DE LA VALLIÈRE is one of those subjects
and those names that are ever youthful, ever
fresh; she represents the ideal of the loving
woman, with all the qualities that we delight in giving to it — unselfishness, fidelity, unique and delicate
tenderness; and no less does she represent in its
perfection a touching and sincere repentance. Seen
close by and in its actuality her life answers well to
the idea we formed of it from a distance and through
its halo; the person herself resembles at all points the
charming memory she has left to us. Without pretending to discover anything new about her, let us
give ourselves the pleasure of considering her for a
moment.

Françoise-Louise de la Baume Le Blanc de La Vallière was baptised in the parish church of Saint-
Saturnin at Tours August 7, 1644, having probably
been born on the preceding evening. She lost her
father early; her mother, who married for her second
husband a man who had an office at Court, placed her

as maid of honour to Madame, daughter of Cnarles II,
when the latter married Monsieur, brother of the king
(1661). The Court of Madame was all youth, wit,
beauty, amusement, and intrigue. Mlle. de La Vallière, then seventeen years old, seemed at first merely
"very pretty, very gentle, and very artless." The
young king was more occupied than he should have
been with Madame, his sister-in-law. The queen-
mother, Anne of Austria, jealous of her son's friendship
which Madame was taking from her, found much to
say, in the name of propriety, against that intimacy.
In order to carry it on and cover it it was agreed between Madame and the king that he should feign to
be in love with some one of Madame's maids of honour, and thus have a pretext for being at all her
parties and for going to see her at all hours. They
chose to take three of these make-believe loves, the
better to hide their own game; and the three selected
were Mlle. de Pons, Mlle. de Chemerault, and Mlle.
de La Vallière. The latter was particularly the one
whom the king chose to seem in love with. But
while in bringing forward the pretty young girl he
thought only of putting society on the wrong scent
and of dazzling the eyes of the public with her, he
dazzled himself and became in love with her seriously.

Mlle. de La Vallière's beauty was of a nature, a
quality, tender and exquisite, about which there is
but one voice among contemporaries. The engraved
portraits and the painted portraits give us no just idea

LOUISE DE LA BAUME LE BLANC, DUCHESSE DE LA VALLIÈRE.
From a steel engraving.

to-day of the sort of charm that belonged to her. Freshness and brilliancy, a delicate brilliancy with shaded tones and sweet, made an essential part of it. "She was lovable,"writes Mme. de Motteville, "and her beauty had great charm from the whiteness and rosiness of her skin, from the blueness of her eyes which were very gentle, and from the beauty of her flaxen hair [*cheveux argentés*] which increased that of her face." These charms were accompanied by a touching tone of voice that went to the heart; all things blended in her harmoniously.   Tenderness, which was the soul of her person, was tempered, visibly, by a foundation of virtue.   Modesty, grace— a simple, ingenuous grace—an air of chastity that won respect, inspired and controlled all her motions delightfully: "Though she was slightly lame she danced extremely well."   A little slow in walking, she could suddenly, when necessary, find wings.   Later, in the cloister, one of her greatest annoyances and mortifications concerned her shoes, which were made, in the world, to fit her slight infirmity.   Very slender, and even a little thin, a riding-habit became her well. The close-fitting corsage showed to advantage the slimness of her waist, while "cravats made her seem rather fatter."   On the whole, it was a touching, rather than a triumphant beauty, one of those beauties that are not complete in themselves, that are not demonstrated to the eye solely by the perfections of the body, but need that the soul be mingled in them (and with her the soul was ever mingled); she was of those of whom no one could keep from saying at once and at a glance: "There is a face and soul to charm."

The king loved her, and during several years solely and very warmly. As for her, she loved nothing in him but himself, the king not the royalty, and the man still more than the king. Born modest and virtuous, she had great distress in her love even while yielding to it; and she resisted as much as she could all the testimonials of distinction and favour that tended to declare it. Louis XIV lent himself to this and conspired in the secrecy as long as the queen-mother lived. We have in a note from Colbert a circumstantial account of the birth of Mme. de La Vallière's first two children. Colbert was charged to provide for everything in the greatest secrecy. These children, two boys, lived only a short time, and were presented for baptism by old servants, poor people, one a parish pauper. But what is more surprising is that in October, 1666, at the time of the birth of Mlle. de Blois (afterwards Princesse de Conti) Mme. de La Vallière, who was then at Vincennes in attendance upon Madame, concealed everything so carefully up to the last moment, that she passed almost from the salon of the princess into the hands of the midwife, who was in hiding close by, and on the very evening of her confinement she reappeared in Madame's apartment before all the company, in ball-dress, as if nothing had happened. We may conjecture from this what she morally suffered, since shame compelled her to put such constraint upon herself. As the queen-mother was dead at that time, nothing subjected her to this degree of suffering but her own shame. The mistresses of the king who succeeded her did not constrain themselves as much.

Referring one day to Mlle. de Fontanges, that rather silly and boastful mistress, Mme. de Sévigné wrote, comparing her to Mme. de La Vallière: "She is always languid, but so affected by grandeur that you must imagine her the very opposite of *that little violet hiding under the leaves,* who was so ashamed of being mistress, mother, and duchess; there will never be another of that mould."

From the very first period of her connection with the king Mme. de La Vallière had thoughts of the cloister; twice she took refuge there before her last retreat which was final. The first time she fled to it was during the early and most beautiful days of her love. The Court of Madame was, as I have said, a labyrinth of intrigues and tangled gallantries. Mme. de La Vallière had learned, through a friend's confidence, something about the manœuvres of Madame with the Comte de Guiche; she said nothing of it to the king. But, being too simple and too naturally straightforward to be able to dissimulate long, the king perceived that she was hiding something from him, and he flew into a passion. La Vallière was frightened, but, having promised secrecy to her friend, she continued to keep silence, on which the king left her, more and more irritated. " They had agreed many times," says Mme. de La Fayette, " that whatever quarrel they might have together they would never sleep without writing to each other and being reconciled." The night passed without news or message; in the morning, Mme. de La Vallière, who thought that all was over, left the Tuileries in despair and went to hide herself in a convent, not at Chaillot this first time, but at Saint-Cloud. The king was beside himself when told that no one knew what had become of her. He instituted a search in person, and, soon learning where she was, he rode at full speed to Saint-Cloud to bring her back instantly; ready to burn the convent down if she was not restored to him.

Such efforts were not needed; he found La Vallière lying on the ground, broken-hearted, in the parlour outside of the convent, to which she had been refused admittance. The king said to her, bursting into tears: " You do not love me; you do not care for those who love you." Louis XIV at this period was madly in love with her, to the point of being jealous of the past and of making himself uneasy lest he was not the first to have a place in her heart, fearing that she might have had in the provinces some early inclination for a M. de Bragelonne.

The second flight of Mme. de La Vallière to a convent took place under very different circumstances. The years of happiness had passed. Mme. de Montespan, witty, haughty, dazzling, had taken her place and was enthroning herself more and more in the heart of the master; the poor La Vallière paled. On the Shrove-Tuesday of 1671, there was a ball at Court, at which she did not appear. It was learned that she had gone for refuge to the convent of Sainte-Marie at Chaillot. This time the king did not fly to bring her back himself; he sent Lauzan and Colbert to do so. It is said that he wept, but his tears were few, and the last. Mme. de La Vallière returned, no longer in triumph, but as a victim. The three years longer that she stayed at Court were to her mind only a long trial and punishment.

She often said to Mme. de Maintenon, during this interval when she was nerving herself and arranging all for her last retreat: "When I have painful things to bear at the Carmelites I shall remember what those people" (the king and Mme. de Montespan) "have made me suffer here."

She suffered, from a rival, what she herself, gentle and kind as she was, had made another suffer. The queen, Marie Thérèse, wife of Louis XIV, had felt very keenly the favour shown to Mme. de La Vallière, which began so little time after her marriage; and she shed more tears than persons thought possible from her apparent coldness. "Do you see that girl with the diamond earrings?" she said one day to

Mme. de Motteville, pointing to Mlle. de La Vallière, who was just then crossing the room. "It is she whom the king loves." The queen's heart, at that moment, was only suspicious of the king's infidelity; but when she was informed of it later beyond a doubt the certainty made her shed many bitter tears. In May, 1667, the king, before departing for the army, had sent an Edict to parliament, with a preamble (said to have been written by the fine pen of Pellisson) by which he acknowledged a daughter he had had by Mme. de La Vallière and conferred upon the mother the title and honours of a duchess. The queen and the ladies of the Court went to pay a visit to the king, then in camp with the army in Flanders. Mme. de La Vallière, though confused and distressed by her new grandeur, was carried away by her love; she arrived at the same time as the queen, almost in spite of herself and without being summoned by her Majesty. When the party came in sight of the camp, Mme. de La Vallière, in spite of the queen's express command that no one should precede her, could restrain herself no longer, but ordered her carriage to be driven at full speed across the fields. "The queen saw it, was tempted to have her arrested, and flew into a frightful passion." That the modest La Vallière allowed herself to do such an act in view of the whole Court, shows how true it is that the shyest and most timid are so no longer when their passions, once unchained, get the better of them.

Did she not have good reason to say in after years, accusing herself in her "Reflections on the Mercy of God," that her glory and her ambition (we must understand here her ambition and joy in being loved and preferred) had been "like furious horses dragging her soul to the precipice." That sentence has been thought too strong for the gentle La Vallière. I think I see its justification in the above circumstance.

Among the ladies who proclaimed themselves scandalised by this unusual audacity of Mme. de La Vallière one, especially, was remarked, who said: " God preserve me from ever being mistress of the king! but if I were so unfortunate I should never have the effrontery to present myself before the queen." That scrupulous lady who talked so loudly was Mme. de Montespan, she, who from that moment, sought in every way, by all the charms of coquetry and the sallies of her brilliant wit to supplant the poor La Vallière in the master's favour.

It is time to come to the feelings of sorrow and repentance which have purified the passion of Mme. de La Vallière and given to the thirty-six last years of her life a consecration, without which she would have been no more than a mistress of a king, rather touching, but ordinary.

When she returned to Court in 1671, after her flight to the convent of Chaillot, there was much jeering. All the women in society, all the women of wit and intelligence, even Mme. de Sévigné herself, thought she lacked dignity. The fact is, dignity and love will not go together; and so long as we love, so long as we hope, small as that hope may be, all the rest counts for nothing. So society laughed at Mme. de La Vallière and her religious fancies that came to nought: "With regard to Mme. de La Vallière," writes Mme. de Sévigné to her daughter, February 27, 1671, " we are in despair at not being able to get her back to Chaillot; but she stands better at Court now than she has for a long time; so we must bring ourselves to leave her there." We read in the Memoirs of Canon Maucroix, on the occasion of a journey he made to Fontainebleau in August, 1671:

" Having seen the carriages of His Majesty in the Oval Court, I waited nearly an hour; and at last I saw the king get into his calèche; Mme. de La Vallière was placed first, then the king, and then Mme. de Montespan; all three sat on the same seat, for the calèche was very wide. The king was very well dressed in a brown stuff with much gold trimming; his hat was edged with the same; he was rather red in the face. La Vallière seemed to me very pretty, and fatter than I had been told she was. I thought Mme. de Montespan very handsome, especially her complexion which was wonderful. They all disappeared in a moment."

Again Mme. de Sévigné writes (December 15, 1673):
"Mme. de La Vallière no longer talks of retreat; it was enough to have talked about it." We see the poor immolated woman figuring not only at Court but in the train of her rival: " Mme. de Montespan, abusing her advantages," says Mme. de Caylus, af-

fected being served by her, gave her many praises,
declaring that she could not be satisfied with her
toilet unless she put the last touches to it.   This
Mme. de La Vallière did with all the zeal of a waiting-
maid whose fortune depends on the charms she can
give to her mistress."

Such was the talk of society which loves to humble and disparage all that once was brilliant, ready to
pity later the very object of its rigour, and thus play
all the chords of emotion for the benefit of conversation.   Must we believe what Madame, mother of the
Regent says, when she tells us with her Germanic
frankness:

" The Montespan, who had more wit, ridiculed her publicly, treated
her very badly, and obliged the king to do the same.   It was necessary to go through La Vallière's room to reach that of the Montespan.
The king had a pretty spaniel named Malice.   At the instigation of
the Montespan he took the little dog and tossed it to the Duchesse de
La Vallière, saying: ' There, Madame, there is your company, and it
is enough.'   This was all the harder, because, instead of remaining
with her, he only passed through to go to the Montespan.   However,
she bore it patiently." [1]

What was passing, during that time, in the sincere
and tender soul, the repentant soul, which drank thus
willingly the bitterness of the cup that she might let
herself be punished in the way that she had sinned?

[1] No; for it is to be remembered that Madame, in her delightfully
amusing daily letters to her German relatives, wrote down all the
malicious Court gossip and news that was brought to her.   The
present incident is not characteristic of Louis XIV, one of whose
strongest personal points was decorum and a sense of what was outwardly due to others.—TR.

She herself has recorded the secret feelings of her heart in a series of "Reflections on the Mercy of God," which she wrote during these years, after her recovery from a serious illness.

That little writing, which appeared for the first time in 1686, during Mme. de La Vallière's lifetime, has often been reprinted; but I warn all readers who think they know it from any of the later editions, that the style has been continually altered and weakened, so that they have not in their hands the true and pure con-confession of Mme. de La Vallière.

She compares herself, in the beginning, to three great sinners, the Canaanitish woman, the woman of Samaria, and the Magdalen. Speaking of the first, she cries out: "Lord help me, look upon me sometimes as I approach thee like that poor stranger, that poor dog, who thinks herself too fortunate to gather of the crumbs that fall from the table where thou dost feed thine elect." The expression is frank to crudity, but it is sincere, and in reproducing the text of Mme. de La Vallière, nothing should be suppressed.

Side by side with this we find sweet thoughts more in keeping with the idea that we form of this delicate and shrinking soul: "For, alas! I am so weak, so changeable, that my best desires are like the flowers of the field of which thy Prophet-king has said that they blossom in the morning and are withered before night." To save herself from these relapsings, these weaknesses, "from the sweet poison of pleasing this world and loving it," she invokes the bestowal of one of those "blows of mercy" that afflict, humiliate, and, at the same time, turn back the soul to God. That word "mercy," which is on the title-page, recurs at every instant; it overflows her lips, it is her cry; it is also the name under which she entered the religious life: Sœur Louise de la Miséricorde — Sister Louise of God's mercy.   Lately, there has been some attempt to doubt if the little paper was really written by Mme. de La Vallière, but that one word Mercy, thus placed with manifest intention does it not become, as it were, her signature ?

We find, and we divine allusions more or less covered to her sufferings, her humiliations:

" If to impose upon me," she says, " a penance in some way suited to my offences thou willest, O my God ! that, for indispensable duty, I remain in the world to suffer on the scaffold where I have so much offended thee, if thou wilt draw from my sin itself my punishment, in making those I had made idols my torturers: *Paratum cor meum, Deus*—My heart is ready, Lord."

While awaiting the great stroke she hopes for, she makes a resolution to profit by the slightest internal succour to advance in the path of return:

" I will not wait, O my God, till I come out of my dangerous slothfulness, till the full sun of thy righteousness be risen.   So soon as the dawn of thy grace begins to break I will begin to act, to labour at the work of my salvation. . . . Contenting myself to advance and grow in thy love, like the dawn, softly and imperceptibly."

It is natural to compare these words with those of

29

Bossuet writing on the subject of Mme. de La Vallière on the eve of her complete conversion: "It seems to me," he says, "that she advances a little in her own manner, quietly and slowly." Thus her habitual bearing and progression, even in the path of salvation, was gently slow, and as if with an air of soft indifference until the moment came when love, the divine love, gave her wings to rise.

"Whoso loves, runs, flies, and rejoices; he is free, nothing can stop him." The "Imitation of Jesus Christ" says that. Mme. de La Vallière, who had so deeply felt it in the order of human feelings, was now to say them to herself in the path of her heavenward progress.

We perceive, toward the end of the "Reflections," eager soarings of a tender love about to transform itself into a divine passion, and into charity. The "semi-repentant woman," as she calls herself, is wholly occupied in persuading her soul to transport, to *transpose* her love; that soul must turn and render to God alone that which it had wasted on a god of earth: "It loves thee, O Lord, with a keen and loving sorrow for its past unfaithfulness, and with all the respect and religious trembling that is due to thy sovereign Majesty."

In estimating a writing of this simplicity, talent and imagination, properly so-called, cannot fairly be brought into the question. Two or three passages alone give a rather figurative and vivid impression:

" If it is true, Lord, that the prayer of a Carmelite who has retired into solitude and no longer does ought but fill herself with thee, is like a sweet perfume-box which needs only to be held to the fire to give forth its fragrant odour, that of a poor creature who is still attached to earth, and who can only creep in the path of virtue is like those muddy waters that must be distilled little by little to make a useful liquor of them."

The letters of Mme. de La Vallière to the Maréchal de Bellefonds, and those of Bossuet to the same maréchal on the subject of Mme. de La Vallière, complete the interior picture of her conversion. The Maréchal de Bellefonds, a man of worth and piety, had a sister who was a nun in the Carmelite convent of the Fauboug Saint-Jacques, where Mme. de La Vallière had a project of retiring. He exhorted and strengthened, as best he could, that poor distressed soul, as Bossuet sustained and incited it on his side:

" I have seen M. de Condom [Bossuet] and I have opened to him my heart," writes Mme. de La Vallière to the maréchal, November 21, 1673; " he admires the great mercy of God to me, and urges me to execute at once his holy will; he is even convinced that I shall do it sooner than I think. For the last two days the report of my retreat has been so spread about that my friends and relatives now speak of it to me. They are very pitying, in advance, upon my fate. I know not why they speak of it, for I have not done anything to show it. I believe it is God who permits this talk to draw me to him more quickly."

We do not find in her letters one word that is not natural, humble, and kind; with lively gratitude to those who wish her well, and perfect indulgence for all others. "My affairs do not advance," she writes (January 11, 1674), "and I find no help in persons from whom I might expect it: I must have the mortification of importuning *the master;* and you know what that is for me. . . ." And elsewhere she says: "To quit the Court for the cloister does not cost me anything; but to speak to the king, oh! that is my torture." The sight of her daughter, Mlle. de Blois, moved her, but did not shake her: "I own to you that I felt joy in seeing how pretty she is; but at the same time I had a scruple; I love her, but she cannot hold me back a moment; I see her with pleasure and I shall leave her without pain; make that accord as you please; but I feel it just as I tell it to you." These struggles, these last difficulties dragged on, and were prolonged for some time, until persevering resolution prevailed and one morning the tone of deliverance breaks forth:

" At last I quit the world," she cries, March 19, 1674, " without regret, but not without pain; my weakness has kept me here long without pleasure, or, to speak more truly, with a thousand griefs. You know the greater part of them; you know how sensitive I am; that feeling has not diminished; I am conscious of it daily; I see that the future will not give me any more satisfaction than the past and the present. You judge rightly that according to the world I ought to be content, and according to God I ought to feel transported. I do feel myself warmly urged to respond to the grace that He has done me, and to abandon myself wholly to Him.

" Everyone leaves here the last of April; I leave too, but it is to take the surest way to heaven. God grant that I may advance in it, as I must, if I would obtain the pardon of my sins. I feel within me inclinations so sweet and so cruel and, at the same time, so decided (accord that opposition that is within me as you can) that the persons to whom I open my heart admire more and more the extreme mercy that God is showing to me."

Speaking of Bossuet she says: "As for M. de Condom, he is an admirable man for his mind, his goodness, and his love of God." And, in truth, when we read at the same time Bossuet's letters relating to Mme. de La Vallière, we are struck with the qualities of kindness, perfect charity, and even humility in the great director and the sublime orator. He had begun by thinking that she advanced rather slowly: "A nature a little stronger than hers would have made more way," he writes, "but we must not bind her to more than she is able to carry on." Her final resolution, when declared, did not lack opposition and, above all, ridicule. Mme. de Montespan, particularly, scoffed at the project of the Carmelites, and it was feared that the king would forbid it: it was necessary to conduct the matter cautiously. Bossuet followed the alternations of delay and progress with fatherly solicitude. "It seems to me," he said of the humble convert, "that without her making any movement her affair is advancing. God never quits her, and, without violence he is breaking her bonds." Then, suddenly, when the last tie is worn through and breaks, when the dove takes her flight, he is full of the joy of triumph, of wonderment in his turn:

"I send you," he writes to the Maréchal de Bellefonds, "a letter from Mme. la Duchesse de la Vallière, which will make you see that by the grace of God, she is about to execute the intention that the Holy Spirit put into her heart. The whole Court is edified and astonished at her tranquillity and her joy, which increase as the time approaches. In truth, her feelings have in them something so divine that I cannot think of them without being in a state of continual thanksgiving. The mark of the finger of God is in the strength and the humility which accompany all her thoughts; that is the work of the Holy Spirit . . . that transports me, and confounds me; I speak, she acts; I discourse, she does the work. When I consider these things I feel a desire to be silent and hide myself . . . poor channel through which the waters of heaven pass, and which can hardly retain a few drops."

Thus spoke and thought about himself with touching simplicity the great bishop, the oracle of his times, the greatest of mankind through his talent.

The evening before the day on which she quitted the Court Mme. de La Vallière supped with Mme. de Montespan; she chose to drink the cup to its last dregs and to "taste the rejection of the world," as Bossuet said, to the last remains of its bitterness. The next day, April 20, 1674, she heard the mass of the king who was starting for the army; leaving the mass she went to ask pardon on her knees of the queen for her offences; then she got into her carriage and went to the convent of the Carmelites in the Faubourg Saint-Jacques, where a great crowd of people lining the way awaited her. Entering, she threw herself on her knees before the superior and said: "My mother, I have always made so bad a use of my will that I come to place it in your hands." Without waiting for the end of her novitiate, on the very day of her entrance into the Cloister, she made them cut off her hair, "the admiration of all those who have spoken of her person," making haste to despoil herself of her last earthly crown. Mme. de La Vallière, when she entered the Cloister, was thirty years old.

Bossuet could not preach the sermon for the *véture,* or taking of the habit, which took place in June, 1674; but he did for that of the *profession,* that is to say, the irrevocable vow, which was taken in June of the following year.   Mme. de La Vallière, then become Sister Louise de la Miséricorde, solemnly received the black veil from the hands of the queen.   We can judge of the strain of such an occasion: " That beautiful and courageous person," writes Mme. de Sévigné, "did this action, like all the others of her life, in a noble and winning manner; her beauty surprised every one ; but what will astonish you is that the sermon of M. de Condom [Bossuet] was not as divine as was hoped for."   When we read that sermon to-day we comprehend and, I must own, share a little in the impression of Mme. de Sévigné; we say to ourselves that we expected something else.   So much the worse for those who had that expectation, and for us! Bossuet, before being an orator was a religious man, a true bishop, and, on the present occasion, he felt to what a point it behoved him to be grave and not lend himself in any way to a smile, nor to an illusion, nor to the secret malice of hearts that would have taken pleasure in certain memories, certain descriptions.   He transported his audience at once into higher and purer regions.   He took for his text the words of Him who is seated on the throne in the Apocalypse: " Behold, I make all things new," and he applied it to the present case.   The more he had

seen of Mme. de la Vallière during the time of her
novitiate the more he had been struck with her
strength, with the soaring of her spirit, and her entire
renewal of heart. What he desired above all in
preaching before her was to bear to that soul a *good
word,* and not to shine in the eyes of worldlings by
one of those miracles of eloquence which were to
him so easy and so familiar:

> " Take notice, Messieurs, that we must here observe more carefully
> than ever the precept given us by the Preacher: ' The wise man
> listens to the wise word, lauds it, and applies it to himself.' He looks
> neither to the right nor to the left to see whom it may fit; he applies
> it to himself, and finds his profit in it. ' My sister,' " he added, turn-
> ing toward the new nun, " ' from among the things I have to say to
> you, you will know how to distinguish those that apply to you.
> Do you likewise, Christians. . . ."

It was in these simple terms, cutting short all vain
and alien curiosity, that Bossuet approached his subject and applied himself to describe the two loves,
profane and divine; "the love of self pushed to contempt of God," and "the love of God pushed to
contempt of self."

Having entered the path of prayer and penitence,
Mme. de La Valliére never looked back for a single
instant. She was visited sometimes by the queen,
and by Mme. de Montespan herself; but she withdrew
as much as possible from communication with the
outside. When Mme. de Montespan asked her one
day, whether, really and truly, she was as glad as
people said she was, she replied, with a tact that the

mind borrowed from the heart, "No, I am not glad, I am content." *Content* is, in truth, the Christian word, the one that expresses tranquillity, peace, submission, joy without effusion, something *contained* withal.

Mme. de La Vallière on entering the convent had two children living. Her son, the Comte de Vermandois, died in the flower of his age (*1683*), tainted already by the vices of the young Court. Bossuet was charged with announcing to the mother her painful loss. At first she could answer only with tears, but as soon as she was in a fit state to reply, the penitent within her rose above all, and she said : "I have wept enough for a son whose birth I have not mourned enough." Her daughter, Mlle. de Blois, who married the Prince de Conti, was a model of grace; it was of her that La Fontaine said, describing her light and as it were aërial step : " A blade of grass could bear her; a flower would scarce have bent beneath the imprint of her feet." When she married the Prince de Conti people hastened from all parts to congratulate the mother, who bore this last homage of the world, which to her was humiliation, with a modesty, a good grace, and a perfect decorum, which have been much celebrated. Mme. de Sévigné began by jesting about it, as even the best persons in society did not refrain from doing: "They say that she [Mme. de La Vallière] has adapted her style to her black veil perfectly, and seasons her tenderness as a mother with that of the spouse of Jesus Christ." But when she went herself to the convent grating and saw with her own eyes Mme. de La Vallière, she has only a cry of admiration for a simplicity so truly humble and yet so noble:

"What an angel appeared to me at last! . . . To my eyes, there were all the charms we used to see in other days; I found her neither bloated nor yellow; she is less thin and more content; she has the same eyes, the same glance; austerely bad food, and little sleep have not hollowed nor dulled them; that strange garb takes nothing from her grace, nor from her elegance; as for modesty, it is no greater than when she gave birth to a Princesse de Conti, but that is enough for a nun. She said many kindly things to me, and spoke to me of you [Mme. de Grignan] so well, so appropriately, all that she said was so in keeping with herself that, as I think, nothing could be better."

And she ends this strain of eulogy by the following very mundane reflection: "In truth, that garb and that retreat give her great dignity."

Mme. de La Vallière was certainly not thinking of making them into a dignity. Completely given up to the calmness and the consolations of her hidden life, she thought she could not sufficiently purchase them by austerities and mortifications which she imposed upon herself with ardour and a species of subtlety. Those who have written the narrative of her penitent life have taken pleasure in producing some singular examples of it, which would move us very little to-day; but the principle that inspired them, the end that she approached by such means, are forever worthy of respect in all ages and from whatever point of view we look at them: "I hope, I believe, I love," she said; "it is for God to perfect his gifts." "Faith and hope are two great virtues; but those who have not charity have nothing; they are like sterile plants that the sun never shines upon."

This beautiful soul, realising henceforth in her own being the qualities of divine love, considered herself to the end one of the lowest in God's eyes. "I do not ask him," she said, "for those great gifts which are only put into the great souls he sends into the world to enlighten it; I could not contain them: but I do ask him to incline my heart, according to his promise, to seek his law and meditate upon it night and day." Such desires of the soul, no matter in what form they wrap themselves, are for ever precious; they lead in all ages to the great moral heights.

Mme. de La Vallière died on the 6th of June, 1710, after thirty-six years of cloistered life. Louis XIV had seen her enter the convent with a dry eye. He retained for her, Saint-Simon says, "esteem and a dry consideration." Here is dryness enough, but, even so, it tells too little. He had long ceased to love her; but when she proved to him that she could tear herself from him and prefer another to him, even though that other were God himself, she entirely detached and alienated him from her, and he never forgave it. "She has often said to me," relates Madame, mother of the Regent, "that if the king came to the convent she should refuse to see him and would hide herself where he could not find her. She has been excused from that trial, for the king has never gone there.   He has forgotten her as much as if he had never known her."

Of the three women who veritably occupied the mind of Louis XIV and divided his heart and his reign among them, Mme. de La Valliére, Mme. de Montespan, and Mme. de Maintenon, the first remains by far the most interesting; the only one truly interesting in herself.   Much inferior to the two others in mind she is incomparably their superior in heart: one may say that in this respect she inhabits another sphere which those two women of intellect (the latter, moreover, a woman of judgment) could never reach.   Whenever we try to make for ourselves the image of a perfectly loving woman, we think of La Vallière.   To love for the sake of loving, without pride, without coquetry, without arrogance, without one secret thought of ambition, of self-interest, of narrow calculation, without a shadow of vanity—and then to suffer, to make herself of no account, to sacrifice even her dignity so long as there was hope, to allow herself, when hope was gone, to be humiliated as an expiation; and, when the hour came, to immolate herself courageously in a higher hope, to find in prayer and in the presence of God treasures of energy, of a new tenderness; to persevere, to ripen and strengthen at every step, to arrive at the plenitude of her soul by her heart — *such was her life,* the last part of which developed resources of vigour and

Christian heroism which were not to have been expected from her early fragility. As a loving woman she recalls Heloise, or even the Portuguese Nun, but with less violence and flame; for they had not only the genius of passion but also its transports and its madness; La Vallière had its tenderness only. Soul and beauty delicate and sweet, she had more of Berenice than the other two. As a nun, a Carmelite, daughter of Saint Teresa, it is not for us to seek comparisons for her here. Let us only say, in our least profane tone, that when we read that wonderful fifth chapter of the Third Book of the " Imitation " in which are shown the effects of divine love, which in that chapter is the ideal of the other love, Mme. de La Vallière is one of the living figures that explain it to us in their person, and are its best commentary.

FRANÇOIS DE SALIGNAC DE LA MOTHE FÉNÉLON. *Frontispiece.*
From a steel engraving.

Portraits

of the

Seventeenth Century

Historic and Literary

Part II

History of the French Academy — Corneille — Mademoiselle de
Scudéry — Molière — La Fontaine — Pascal — Madame de Sé-
vigné — Bossuet — Boileau — Racine — Madame de Caylus —
Fénelon — Comte Antoine Hamilton — The Princesse des Ursins

Contents of Part II

iii

Illustrations to Part II

v

I.

History of the French Academy.

I.

History of the French Academy.

THE short history that M. Pellisson has given of the beginning of this Association, in the form of a "Letter to a Friend," is in reality one of the most finished and most agreeable essays in our language, a rare and perfect example, that shows better than all definitions what it is to write with elegance and purity in French. There are, and there were in the days of Pellisson, two sorts of elegance and urbanity in conversing and in writing: one lively, more natural, easier, more familiar, also more coloured; derived from commerce with the great world and the Court by those who were born and bred to them from infancy, that, for instance, of Saint Évremond, Bussy, Clérembault, La Rochefoucauld, Retz:—the other more studied, formed in the library and by reading, or by assiduous attendance in certain brilliant circles, and by intercourse with the best-qualified literary personages; this last form of urbanity is that of Conrart and Vaugelas; in it Pellisson excels, and is, above all others, the perfect model of his time.

If, after reading some natural and living work of that period, the Memoirs of Cardinal de Retz for example,

3

Pellisson is immediately taken up, what I mean to say will be understood. We have to do with an excellent writer in him, but a writer of another species, of a wholly different stamp, of another origin and genus. He is not of those who, like Retz, have seen all and essayed all in action, and, daring all, risk saying all, making to themselves a language in their own likeness, which they alone can speak with a certain air, well assured as they are of being always of a good school and a good race. Pellisson is one of those authors by profession who, having begun by the pen, never lose it from sight, and would prefer to cut themselves short, like Fontanes, of ideas or incidents to relate, if they thought they could not gather and present them with absolute correctness and perfect elegance.

Born at Béziers in 1624, of a Protestant family very distinguished in the law, he was educated in the South, and was twenty-six years of age when he came to Paris, where he was introduced into the literary world under the auspices of Conrart. It was then that he composed, under the form of a "Letter to a Friend," this Narrative, or History of the French Academy, which he was admitted to read before it in full assemblage. The approbation the paper won was so great that the first vacant place in the Association was voted to Pellisson, and, meanwhile, he was allowed to be present at the meetings in the capacity of "supernumerary"; which has never happened except to him. He thus found himself the object of a unique exception; he was the only man of letters to whom the Academy did not fear to make a promise in advance.

He was thus placed under the very best conditions to write this narrative; beside the Academy but not as yet of it, and in the confidence of the best-informed witnesses. It is thanks to him that we are able to know the Golden Age, the Evander age, of this much-lauded Association, which was soon to have its Louvre and its Capitol.

During the first half of the seventeenth century numerous efforts were made in France for the culture and perfecting of the language, natural and spontaneous efforts of little societies, or coteries, grammatical and literary. After the coming of Malherbe a general impulse in this direction was felt. One of these little societies, that of MM. Conrart, Godeau, de Gombauld, de Malleville, de Serisay, de Cerisy, Habert (Chapelain came a little later), assembled weekly at Conrart's, whose lodging was the most central. They read to one another the works they composed; these they criticised or encouraged. "The conferences were followed sometimes by a promenade, sometimes by a collation." During three or four years the meetings continued thus in perfect obscurity and freedom.

"When they talk to-day of that first period of the Academy," says Pellisson, "they speak of it as a Golden Age during which, in all the innocence and freedom of the first centuries, without noise or pomp,

without other laws than those of friendship, they enjoyed together all
that association of minds and reasonable living can give that is sweetest
and most charming."

Secrecy was pledged and kept: *Qui sapit in tacito
gaudeat ille sinu.* One of them (M. de Malleville)
was the first to infringe it; he spoke rather indis-
creetly of the conferences and of what was there
discussed to Faret, author of the *Honnête Homme,*
who brought his book to him, then just printed.
Faret talked to others. Des Maretz and Boisrobert
were informed of the meetings, and asked to be
admitted. The members could not refuse Boisrobert,
a great favourite of Cardinal Richelieu and his chief
amuser. As the latter well knew that rather jovial
tales and literary news were most likely to amuse his
patron, he did not fail to entertain him with the
proceedings of the little company; and gave him so
favourable an idea of it, that Richelieu conceived a
scheme to adopt the association and constitute it into
a formal body, for use as the literary decoration of
the reign.

For Richelieu (let us in our turn and after so many
others, do him this homage), had in him that flame,
that religion of Letters which Pericles, the Augustuses,
and the Mæcenases had in their day to so high a
degree; he believed that truly noble and great things
would not continue to be regarded as such for ever,
except in so far as they were consecrated by that
religion; and that the genius of Letters is the neces-

sary and indirectly auxiliary ornament, the magnificent and most honourable decoration of the genius
of States. If he had less taste than the great men of
Greece and Rome whom I have just cited, that came
of the hindrances of his epoch, of his education, and
of a vice of his mind which was given to a species of
pedantry; but though he transgressed in the minor
detail he was not mistaken in his public view of literature, nor in the value of the institution he sought to
establish for the service and pleasure of all.

After having subdued and decapitated the nobles,
checkmated the Protestants as a party in the State,
foiled and humbled the factions in the royal family;
after making head throughout all Europe against the
House of Austria, counteracting its prominence by
several armies in the field and on the sea, he had the
intelligence to comprehend that there was something
to do for the French language, to polish, adorn, au-
thorise it, render it "the most perfect of modern languages," transport into it that empire, that universal
ascendancy once possessed by the Latin language, and
which, since then, other languages had seemed to
usurp transiently, rather than actually possess. The
Spanish language at that time was usurping this semblance of authority; so that even on that ground he
would still combat the House of Austria. But for the
execution of such an idea he needed choice auxiliaries;
a happy chance threw them, already collected, in his
way. He stretched forth his hand and said to that

little gathering which thought itself so obscure: "I adopt you; belong to me, belong to the State!"

On the other side, it is piquant and almost touching to see how this offer of protection and aggrandisement alarmed, at first, those worthy men, sincere lovers of private life and studious leisure; they were strongly tempted to decline so great an honour. But the wise and prudent Chapelain remarked that inasmuch as, unfortunately, their conferences had come to light, they no longer had liberty of choice; that this honourable offer of protection, coming from such a height, was an order; and to withdraw from the good intentions of the Cardinal would be to incur his enmity: *Spretæque injuria formæ.* The reasons presented on this occasion, and those produced in other and private discussions are given by Pellisson in little indirect discourses imitated from those of Livy, and not less suitable. The Cardinal was therefore thanked, surprise and gratitude mingling in the reply, and the little company placed itself at his disposition. This took place early in 1634.

It is unfortunate that the history of the Academy has not been continued on the plan and in the detail of Pellisson. That history, as I conceive it, is now rather difficult to write, for want of sufficient private documents; nevertheless, I do not think it impossible. I speak, of course of the old Academy, destroyed in 1793; as to the new Academy, documents and recollections abound. The important point would be

to mark carefully the different periods, the different
ages, and the various influences which the Association
has undergone or has exercised, the currents of mind
that have reigned within it, and through which it has
found itself more or less in harmony and in communication with the tone and opinion of the outside.

It has proved an almost general rule that the Academy, after a period when it was completely on the
level of exterior literary opinion, and represented the
aspects most in view and most flourishing, has lowered its level or retarded its progress.   This came of
the duration and longevity of its members.   For example, under Richelieu and from its origin, it was
composed, naturally, of all that was best and most
highly considered among men of letters, Balzac at
their head, and Chapelain.   But, by the very fact that
Chapelain lived on and survived himself, there came a
moment under Louis XIV, and at the finest period of
his reign, when we note in the breast of the Academy a slightly old-fashioned and behind-the-age spirit.
Not only were Molière and La Fontaine not of it, but
Boileau was not, until Louis XIV, having asked him a
question on the subject, heard with amazement of his
absence.

For the very reason that the school of Chapelain
and Des Maretz lived out its course of nature and
prolonged itself by its choice of successors, Boileau
was never completely at home in the Academy;
he was never satisfied with it, and could not speak

of it without an epigram ; he was almost of the opinion of Mme. de Maintenon, who was reproached for not regarding it as "a serious body." The fact is, the old academicians, against whom Boileau in the beginning had contended, lived long enough to admit much younger academicians who, from the start, were opposed in their turn to Boileau, already old and mature. I know, of course, that there were grand classic days, when Racine solemnly eulogised Corneille, when La Bruyère was received ; but the ordinary routine of the Academy was the reading of a poem by Perrault, a dissertation by Charpentier, an idyll by Fontenelle, and, after a while, a fable or a translation in verse by La Motte. The latter, as soon as he belonged to the Academy, became, by his assiduity, his politeness, his amiable, social spirit, one of the most essential members, and the dearest to the heart of the company. Through him, and through Fontenelle, the Academy found itself once more well in advance, and at the head of all literary questions under the Regency.

But after that, and until the middle of the eighteenth century, time and effort were needed to raise the Academy from the selections made under the stagnating influence of Cardinal Fleury, and to bring it once more into harmony and true alliance with the literary and philosophical powers active in the world. Voltaire did not belong to the Academy until 1646, that is, very late, like Boileau ; but once in it, though

absent and living out of the country, he ruled and
governed it, which Boileau never did.   Duclos first,
and then d'Alembert were his chief prime-ministers.

M. Paul Mesnard, in a "History of the Academy,"
(which has no other fault than that of being too much
abridged), has sketched these epochs and these interior divisions very well.   He indicates a chapter
that ought to be written about the influence of
women on the elections to the Academy—Mme. de
Lambert, Mme. de Tencin, Mme. Geoffrin, Mlle. de
Lespinasse, etc.—there is another that ought also to
be written, on the imperceptible directing influences
of the perpetual secretaries.   A good perpetual secretary, without making much stir in its interior, gives
motion to the machine and enables it to go as if of itself.
We still have some of that kind; and we notice very
quickly when, by chance, they are absent or lacking.
The saddest period of the Academy in the eighteenth
century was that of the insignificant perpetual secretaries Dacier, Du Bois, Houtteville, Mirabaud.   In
their day the company slumbered or drifted.

In spite of the brilliant rôle that the Academy was
able to play in the second half of the eighteenth century,
which made it a sovereign organ of opinion, especially
about the time of the accession of Louis XVI until
1788, I do not think that it has ever, altogether and at
all points, fulfilled the hope of its founder, Richelieu;
it has done both more and less than he desired.   Let
me explain:

It is not on the Letters Patent of his institution that I lay the blame; and besides, I do not assume to lay any blame at all, but merely to state facts accurately and draw conclusions. The Letters Patent of 1635 and the project which preceded them explained, in very clear terms, the name of the studies and the object of the work of the Academy, namely:

" The hope that our language, more perfect already than any other living language, may succeed to Latin, as Latin did to Greek, if more care be taken than has been hitherto of *elocution ;* which is not, in truth, the whole of eloquence, but a very good and very important part of it "; and, for that object, it was necessary " to establish certain rules, and, primarily, to establish a certain usage of words, and to regulate terms and phrases by an ample Dictionary and a precise Grammar, which would give to the language a part of the ornaments that it lacked, so that later it might acquire the rest through a *Rhétorique* and a *Poétique,* that should be composed to serve as regulators to those who wished to write in verse or prose: that, in this way, the French language might be rendered not only elegant, but capable of treating of all Arts and Sciences, beginning with that most noble of all the arts, eloquence," etc., etc.

Of all this and of the other articles of its first programme, the Academy accomplished nothing but its Dictionary. Add to that, if you like, Vaugelas's *Rémarques* which the Academy publicly adopted, and perhaps also the French grammar of Regnier Desmarais, its perpetual secretary, who made it semi-officially. This was enough, rightly viewed ; and in that direction the Academy has done, in course of time, what it was commissioned to do. As for the *Rhétorique* and the *Poétique,* it prudently confined itself to the Letter of Fénelon, which it could show to friends and enemies as a charming series of questions and projects, every one being allowed to build and dream as he chose on the engaging words of the least dogmatic of masters.

But Richelieu meant that his French Academy should be something more; he meant to make it the judge of all the noted works that appeared; to constitute it a grand jury, as we say now, a high literary tribunal, expected to give its judgment on all the important current productions that came before the public. I imagine to myself a living and ever-present Richelieu: he would ask the Academy its opinion on *Phèdre* for example, on *Athalie* the morning after the first representation of those famous plays, in the very quick of the discussions they excited. He would ask the same on all the great poetic works that led to schism and controversy (I am supposing a permanent and immortal Richelieu); he would, in short, exact that learned men should speak out; not waiting for the verdict of time, but forestalling it, regulating it to some extent, and giving their reasons; leading the tide of public opinion and not following it. Was this possible? was it desirable? That is another question, and when I say that the Academy in this has not fulfilled its vocation and has not acted in the direction indicated by its founder, I am not blaming it. No one does things of that sort unless they are not only authorised but forced and constrained to do them.

No one plunges, from mere gaiety of heart, into the mêlée of contemporaneous discussions, even if he flatters himself he can rule them. Men are not so ready to confer upon themselves such extraordinary commissions, always thorny, and which look like usurpation, if they are not imposed as a duty. I shall merely remark in defence of Richelieu's idea (of which there are others to tell the objections and difficulties), that it was a truly French idea in the mind of the great minister, like all the many others that came to him in the course of his glorious patriotic tyranny.

For in France—note this well—we are not, above all, desirous of being amused or pleased by a work of art or intellect, nor even of being touched by it; we want to know if we are right in applauding and in being amused and touched. We fear to be compromised, to make ourselves ridiculous; we turn about, we question our neighbour; we like to meet an authority, to find some one, man or Association, before whom we can lay our doubts. In this is a double process of the French mind. It has impulse, ardour, a dashing spirit, but criticism is close beside it, rules and regulations are felt on the morrow of what has seemed rashness. I therefore suppose that the Academy, which began by giving its judgment rather pertinently on the "Cid," might have kept fairly well to its opening promise if it had found itself obliged to do so. Let us suppose a judgment, with reasons assigned, pronounced by the Academy within six months on

every leading work in literature; which judgment
(due allowance being made for difference of periods
and customs) should not be inferior for sound sense,
impartiality, and moderation to that early verdict on
the "Cid." Such judgments would to-day form a
very memorable series, and a critical jurisprudence, so
to call it, that would certainly not be without its
action on the vicissitudes and variations of the public
taste. But I perceive that this view presupposes and
demands a series, or at least a frequent recurrence of
Richelieus historically impossible.

In all this, I have only tried to make it felt in a
rather salient way, what the great founder intended
on this point. The Academy, I repeat, has done less
and has done more than he expected of it; and, on the
whole, if he could reappear on one of our fête-days,
he would not blush too much for his creation; he
might grumble a little, but he would also quiver
with fatherly pride at the sight of his emancipated
offspring.

Since I am on the subject of the Academy, one of
the most national subjects in France, and about which
everybody talks, I ask to be allowed to recall a few
facts, and make a few observations without much
connection as they occur to me.

People always speak of the academic *fauteuils*
(arm-chairs). Originally, and when the Academy
held its sessions at the Louvre, there were but three,
for the officers of the company, the director, chancellor,

and perpetual secretary. It was on the election of
La Monnoye (December, 1713) that this feature was
changed. La Monnoye was a man of letters, witty,
educated, commonplace as to talent, but universally
liked and esteemed in person; a laureate grown grey
in competitions, one of those happy medio-critics
that make a desirable candidate; he was unanimously
received; Louis XIV, whom he had celebrated many
a time in verse, showing special satisfaction. La
Monnoye, writing to a friend, relates his reception by
the Academy as follows :

" There is no example of an Academician received with greater distinction. I am careful not to attribute this to my own merit, which
is slight; it is due solely to the influence of Cardinal d' Estrées and his
nephew. . . . Something quite memorable happened at the
Academy on this occasion. None but the three officers of the Company had *fauteuils ;* the cardinals who were not allowed any unless
they were one of the officers, refused in consequence to be present at
the sessions. The embarrassment of Cardinal d'Estrées was great, he
being unable to give me his vote without going in person to the
Academy; but this he could not resolve to do on account of not having
a *fauteuil.* The two other cardinals who were members of the
Academy, Cardinal de Rohan and Cardinal de Polignac, having conferred with him, laid the matter before the King, who ended the difficulty by ordering that henceforth all the Academicians should have
fauteuils."

Such is the authentic history of the academical arm-
chairs. Now those forty *fauteuils* of the old Academy were not transmitted to the new. To satisfy
inquisitive persons and those who want to know by the
card what is real in a metaphor, I will state that at our
sessions there are no *fauteuils* only comfortable seats.

Sometimes a list of academicians is given by *fauteuils;* on the election of each new member it is customary to say that he occupies the *fauteuil* of such and such illustrious men, going back to the origin of the Academy.   All that is chimerical.   The old Academy having been suppressed in 1793, its affairs became muddled and confused.   Later, when the Institute was created, and in the bosom of that Institute a class that corresponded fairly well to the original French Academy was formed, there was no direct relation established from one to the other; those of the old academicians who were appointed were so under new rights, and not as a recovery of possession. The genealogy of the *fauteuils* coming down to our day, which was invented some thirty [now eighty] years ago, by a certain professor of history, who thought it had a good effect in a synoptical table, is as false as most genealogies.   Nevertheless, the public believes in it and, in spite of what I say, will probably continue to believe in it.

The Dictionary of the French Academy, not that in common use, which is already in the hands of every one, and which will suffice awhile longer until newly revised, but an *historical* Dictionary, begun about fifteen years ago—an important addition very complete, very rich in citations, and very interesting to read (a rare thing in a dictionary)—is about to appear with a preface by the learned editor, M. Patin; this first addition, important as it is, is only preliminary, and will be presented in a few days to the Minister of Public Instruction. On this side the Academy shows itself faithful in extending rather than limiting its first mission.[1]

What is a classic?—a delicate question to which divers answers might be given according to ages and seasons. A man of intellect put it to me to-day, and I will try, if not to solve it, at least to examine and sift it before my readers, to induce them to answer it themselves, and throw light, if I can, on their idea and mine. Why not, from time to time, risk treating critically subjects that are not personal, which concern, not some one, but some thing; subjects of which our neighbours, the English, have succeeded so well in making a whole category under the modest title of Essays. It is true that to treat such subjects, which are always a little abstract and moral, we need to speak in tranquillity, to be sure of one's own attention and that of others, to seize, in short, one of those half-hours of silence, moderation, and leisure that are so rarely accorded to our lively France, whose

[1] Since the above was written (1859), M. Émile Littré, of the French Academy, was charged with the duty of revising and enlarging the original Dictionary, until now it stands as a great monument to the French language in many volumes. An historical, biographical, geographical, mythological section has been added by M. Beaujean, inspector of the French Academy, and the collaborator of M. Littré. An abridged edition of the whole, in one small volume, has been published, under the sanction of the Minister of Public Instruction, by Hachette et Cie., which is quite invaluable for daily and constant use.—Tr.

genius is impatient of them, even when she tries to be wise and to make no more revolutions.

A classic, according to the ordinary definition, is an ancient author, already consecrated by admiration, and an authority in his own class. The word *classic,* used in this sense, first appears among the Romans. They termed *classici* not all citizens of diverse classes, but those of the first class only, who had a revenue of, at least, a certain specified sum. All who possessed an inferior revenue came under the denomination of *infra classem,* beneath *the* class *par excellence.* Figuratively, the word *classicus* is used in Aulus Gellius, and applied to writers: a writer of value and note, *classicus assiduusque scriptor,* a writer of account, who has property, and is not to be confounded with the crowd of proletaries. Such an expression supposes an age advanced enough to have something like a census and classification of literature.

As for moderns: in the beginning, the true and only classics were, naturally, the ancients. The Greeks, who, by singular good fortune and an easy buoyancy of mind, had no other classics than themselves, were, at first, the only classics of the Romans, who took pains and strove to imitate them. The Romans, after the noble ages of their literature, after Cicero and Virgil, had classics of their own, which became, almost exclusively, those of the succeeding centuries. The Middle Ages, which were not as ignorant of Latin antiquity as was thought, but which lacked both judgment and taste, confounded ranks and orders: Ovid was treated on a better footing than Homer; Boetius was thought a classic equal, at the least, to Plato.   The renascence of Letters, in the fifteenth and sixteenth centuries, cast light into this long confusion, and then at last admirations were graduated.   The true and classic authors of the double antiquity were henceforth detached upon a luminous background, and grouped themselves harmoniously on their respective heights.

Meantime, the modern literatures were born, and a few of the most precocious, the Italian for instance, had already an antiquity of their own.   Dante had appeared; and posterity had early saluted him as a classic.   Italian poesy may since have dwindled, but when it chooses it can recover and preserve the impulsion and the echo of that high origin.   It is no indifferent thing for a poesy to have such a point of departure, a classic source in such high regions, and to come down from a Dante rather than issue lamely from a Malherbe.

Modern Italy had its classics and Spain had every right to feel that she had hers, while France was still without them.   A few writers of talent gifted with originality and exceptional warmth of fancy, a few brilliant efforts, isolated and without sequence, immediately broken off and needing ever to be renewed, did not suffice to endow our nation with the solid and imposing foundation of literary wealth.   The idea of a *classic* implies, in itself, something that has sequence and consistency, which makes a traditional whole, which creates itself, transmits itself, and lasts. It was not until after the great years of Louis XIV that the French nation felt, with a quiver of pride, that such happiness had come to her. All voices told it then to Louis XIV with flattery, with exaggeration and emphasis, and yet with a certain assured feeling of its truth. A singular and piquant contradiction then appeared: the men who were most enchanted by the marvels of this age of Louis the Great, and who even sacrificed the ancients to the moderns, these men, of whom Perrault was the leader, brought about the exaltation and consecration of the very ones who were their most ardent adversaries and opponents. Boileau avenged and angrily maintained the ancients against Perrault, who extolled the moderns, that is to say: Corneille, Molière, Pascal, and the eminent men of his day, including among the first of them Boileau himself. The kind La Fontaine, taking part in the quarrel on behalf of the learned Huet, did not perceive that he himself, in spite of his careless habits, was about to wake up and find himself a classic.

The best definition is example: as soon as France possessed its Louis the Fourteenth century, and could consider it from a little distance, she knew what a classic was, better than any statements could tell her. The eighteenth century added to this idea by noble

works due to its four great men.   Read the " Age of
Louis XIV " by Voltaire, the " Grandeur and Decadence of the Romans " by Montesquieu, the " Epochs of
Nature " by Buffon, the " Savoyard Vicar," and certain
fine pages of revery and description of nature by
Jean-Jacques, and say if the eighteenth century did
not, in those memorable works, combine tradition
with freedom of development and independence.
But at the beginning of the last century (the nineteenth) and under the Empire, in presence of the first
attempts of a literature decidedly novel and rather
adventurous, the idea of the classic shrank and
narrowed strangely in certain resisting minds, more
grieved than severe.   The first Dictionary of the
Academy (1694) defined a classic author simply as
"an ancient author much approved, who has authority
in the matter of which he treats."   The Dictionary
of the Academy of 1835 takes that same definition and
makes it, from being rather vague as it was, precise
and even narrow.   It defines classic authors as those
" who have become *models* in any language "; and
in the articles that follow, the expressions, " model "
— " rules established for the composition of style " —
" strict rules of the art to which writers must con-
form," recur continually.   This definition of the
classic was evidently made by the respectable Academicians, our predecessors, in presence and in view
of what was then called the *romantic,* that is to say,
in view of the enemy.   It is time, I think, to re-

nounce such restrictive and timid definitions, and to enlarge our minds.

A true classic, as I should like to hear it defined, is an author who has enriched the human mind, who has really augmented its treasury, who has caused it to take a step in advance, who has discovered some moral truth that is not equivocal, or some eternal passion in the heart where all seemed known and explored; who has rendered his thought, observation, or invention under any form, no matter what if it be broad and grand, refined and rational, healthful and beautiful in itself; who speaks to all in a style of his own, which is felt to be that for all the world, a new style without neologisms, new yet ancient, easily contemporaneous with all epochs.

Such a classic may be for a moment revolutionary; or rather, he may seem so at first, though he is not so; he has never violently attacked that which was around him, he has overthrown that which hindered him only to re-establish, as soon as possible, the equilibrium to the profit of the orderly and the beautiful.

My readers can put, if they like, many names under this definition, which I have tried to make grandiose and plastic, or, to express it better, open and generous. I should put there, in the first instance, Corneille, the Corneille of *Polyeucte, Cinna*, and *Horace*. I should put Molière, the most complete, the fullest poetical genius we have had in France.

"Molière is so great," said Goethe, that king of critics, "that he astounds us each time that we read him. He is a man apart; his comedies touch the tragic, and no one has the courage to try to imitate them. . . . In a play for the stage each action must be important in itself, and lead up to an action more important still. Tartuffe is, in this respect, a model . . . it is all that there is of finest. Every year I read a play of Molière, just as, from time to time, I contemplate some engraving from the great Italian masters."

I do not conceal from myself that the definition I have just given of the classic is rather outside of the idea that usually accompanies that title. Conditions as to regularity, wisdom, moderation, reason, dominating and controlling all else, prevail in that idea. In this sense the classics *par excellence* must be writers of the second order; correct, intelligent, elegant, always clear and precise; of noble passion still, but its force slightly veiled. The characteristic of this theory, which subordinates imagination and sensibility to reason (of which Scaliger gave perhaps the first signal among moderns), was, properly speaking, that of the Latin theory, and it long remained the preference of the French theory. It has truth, if used only in the right way, and provided that word *reason* is not abused. It is evident, however, that it is abused, and that if reason is to be confounded with poetic genius, and to make one with it in a moral homily, it cannot be the same thing as that genius so varied, so diversely creative in its expression of passions in the drama or the epic. Where will you find reason in the fourth book of the Æneid and in the transports of

Dido? Where will you find it in the madness of Phédre? The spirit that dictated that theory leads to putting in the first rank writers who control their imagination, rather than those who yield themselves up to it; who put Virgil before Homer, Racine before Corneille. The masterpiece that this theory loves to quote, which unites, in truth, all its conditions of prudence, force, gradual audacity, moral elevation and grandeur, is *Athalie*. Turenne in his last two campaigns and Racine in *Athalie*—those are the great examples of what the prudent and the wise can do when they take possession of the full maturity of their genius.

Racine's *Athalie* and Bossuet's "Discourse on Universal History," are the highest masterpieces that the rigorously classic theory can offer in France to its friends as to its enemies. But in spite of what is admirably simple and majestic in the accomplishment of such unique productions, we ought, in practising the art, to broaden that theory a little, and show that there are ways of widening it without going so far as relaxing it. Goethe, whom I like to quote on such a matter, says:

"I call the classic *healthy* and the romantic *sickly*. To me the poem of the 'Niebelungen' is as classic as Homer; both are healthful and vigorous. The works of the present day are not romantic because they are new, but because they are feeble, sickly, or diseased. The works of the ancients are not classic because they are old, but because they are energetic, fresh, buoyant. If we consider the romantic and the classic from these two points of view we shall soon agree."

In France we have had no great classic anterior to the age of Louis XIV; the Dantes and the Shake-speares, those primal authorities, to whom sooner or later we return in days of emancipation, are lacking to us. We have had mere skeletons of great poets, like Mathurin Regnier, like Rabelais, without ideal of any kind, without passion or serious aim to conse-crate them. Montaigne was a species of premature classic, of the genus of Horace, but he gave himself like a prodigal, for want of worthy surroundings, to the libertine fancies of his pen and his temperament. It results that we, less than all other nations, have among our ancestral authors that which enables us boldly to lay claim to literary liberties and franchises. Still, with Molière and La Fontaine among our classics of the great century, we have enough that nothing legitimate can be refused to those who will dare and know all.

The important thing to-day seems to me to main-tain the idea and the worship of the classic, while enlarging both. There is no receipt for making clas-sics; that point at least ought to be evident. To believe that by imitating certain qualities of purity, sobriety, correctives, and elegance, independently of nature and its plane, we can become classic, is to believe that after Racine himself there is room for Racine's sons. More than that; it is not good to appear too soon and to contemporaries as a classic; such men stand great chance of not remaining so to

posterity. Fontanes, in his day, seemed a classic to
his friends; and see the pale colour that he has at
a distance of twenty-five years! How short a time
these precocious classics, made so by the moment, last!
We turn about some morning and we are amazed not
to find them erect behind us — they were only for a
"breakfast in the sun," as Mme. de Sévigné would
gaily say. In the matter of classics the most unexpected are always the best and the greatest; ask
those virile geniuses born immortal and perennially in
vogue. The least classic, apparently, of the four
great poets of Louis XIV's era was Molière; he was
applauded then far more than he was rightly esti-
mated; people enjoyed him without knowing his
value. Next to him, the least classic seemed to be La
Fontaine; and see, after two centuries and a half,
what has happened for both of them! Much before
Boileau, before even Racine, are they not unanimously
recognised to-day as the richest, the most fruitful, in
their gift of universal moral truth? Let us content
ourselves with feeling them, penetrating them, admiring them; as for us, coming at this late day, let
us at least try to be ourselves; let us have the sincerity and the natural instinct of our own thoughts,
our own feelings. This can always be attained; add
to it (which is more difficult) elevation, direction, if
possible, toward some high-placed aim; and while
we speak our language, and are subject to the conditions of the age in which we live and from which we

derive our strength as well as our defects, let us ask ourselves, from time to time, looking upward to the summits, and fastening our eyes upon those venerated groups: "What would they say of us?"

But why speak always as an author, and of writing? There comes an age, perchance, when we write no more. Happy they who read, who re-read; they who can follow their free inclinations among their books! There comes a season in life when, all work done, all experiences over, the keen joys remain of studying, of going to the depths of the things we know, the things we feel, just as we see, and see again with relish the friends we love: pure delights of the heart and of the taste in their maturity! Then it is that the word *classic* takes its true meaning, and defines itself for every man of taste by his own irresistible predilection and choice. The taste is formed by that time, formed and definite; good sense, if it ever comes, has come, and is consummate. There is no time now to make trials, no desire to start out upon discoveries. We hold fast to our friends, to those whom we have tested by long intercourse — old wine, old books, old friends!

II.

Pierre Corneille.

II.

Pierre Corneille.

AS a matter of criticism and literary history, there is no reading, it seems to me, more entertaining, more delectable, and at the same time more fruitful of instruction of all kinds than good biographies of great men: not shallow and dry biographies, scanty yet pretentious notices, in which the writer thinks only of shining, and of which each paragraph is sharpened with an epigram; I mean broad, copious, and sometimes even diffuse histories of the man, and of his works: biographies that enter into an author, produce him under all his diverse aspects, make him live, speak, move, as he must have done in life; follow him into his home, into his domestic manners and customs, as far as possible; connect him on all sides with this earth, with real existence, with those every-day habits on which great men depend no less than the rest of us; in short, the actual foundation on which they stand, from which they rise to greater heights at times, and to which they fall back constantly.

31

The Germans and the English, with their complex nature of analysis and poesy, understand and take great pleasure in these excellent biographies. Walter Scott declares that, for his part, he knows no more interesting work in English literature than Boswell's "Life of Johnson." In France we are beginning to esteem and to require studies of this sort. In our time, the great men of Letters, if they were even less eager than they are to come forward with personal revelations in their memoirs and poetical confessions, may be very certain that they will not lack after death for demonstrators, analysts, and biographers. It was not always thus; so that when we come to inquire into the life, especially the childhood and the first beginnings of our great writers and poets of the seventeenth century, it is with difficulty that we discover a few traditions, little authentic, a few doubtful anecdotes dispersed among the *Ana.* The literature and the poesy of those times were not personal; authors did not entertain the public with their own sentiments or their own affairs; biographers imagined, I know not why, that the history of a writer was wholly in his writings, and their superficial criticism never went to the man below the poet. Moreover, as in those days reputations were very slow in making, it was not until much later, in the old age of the great man, that some ardent admirer of his genius—a Brossette, a Monchesnay—bethought him of making his biography. Or perhaps this biographer

CORNEILLE.
From an engraving of the painting by Lebrun.

was a pious and devoted relative, too young to have known the youth of his author—like Fontenelle with Corneille, and Louis Racine with his father. Hence, in the nephew's history of Corneille, and the son's history of Racine, much ignorance, many inaccuracies catch the eye at once; and, in particular, we find a rapid hurrying over of the first literary years, which are, nevertheless, the most decisive.

When we begin by knowing a great man in the full force of his genius only, we imagine that he has never been without it; and this seems to us so natural that often we never trouble ourselves to explain to our own minds how it came about; just as, on the other hand, when we know such a man from the first, and before his fame, we usually do not suspect what he will some day become; we live beside him without thinking to watch him; we neglect to take account in him of that which it was most important we should know. Great men themselves often contribute to strengthen this twofold illusion by their manner of acting; young, unknown, and obscure, they efface themselves, keep silence, elude attention, and affect no position because they want but one, and the time is not ripe to lay their hand upon it; later, bowed down to by all, and famous, they cast into the shade their beginnings, usually rough and bitter; they do not willingly relate their own formation, any more than the Nile reveals its sources.

And yet, the essential point in the life of a great

writer, a great poet, is just this: to seize, grasp, analyse the whole man at the moment when, by a concurrence more or less slow or easy, his genius, his education, his circumstances accord in such a way that he has given birth to his first masterpiece. If you comprehend the poet at this critical moment, if you unravel the knot to which all within him will henceforth be bound, if you find, so to speak, the key to that mysterious ring, half iron, half diamond, which links his second existence, radiant, dazzling, and solemn, to his first existence, obscure, repressed, and solitary, the very memory of which he would often-times fain destroy, then it may be said of you that you possess and know your poet to the depths; you have entered with him the darksome regions, as Dante with Virgil; you are worthy to accompany him, side by side and without fatigue, through his other marvels. From *Andromaque* to *Athalie,* from the " Cid " to *Nicomède,* the initiation is easy: the thread of the labyrinth is in your hand; you have only to unwind it.

It is a glorious moment for the critic and for the poet when each, in his own special meaning, can exclaim with the old philosopher: "I have found!" The poet has found the region where he can henceforth live and develop; the critic has found the inspiration and the law of that genius. If the sculptor, who, in his way, is a noble biographer, fixing for the eye in marble the idea of the poet,—if he could always choose the

moment when the poet is most like unto himself,
there is no doubt that he would seize it at the day
and hour when the first ray of fame and glory came to
illumine that powerful and sombre forehead.   At that
unique moment in life, genius, for some time past
adult and virile, existing uneasily, sadly, within its
own consciousness, restraining itself with difficulty, is
suddenly called forth by the voice of acclamation,
and expands to the aurora of triumph.   With time,
that man of genius may become more calm, more
reposeful, more mature; but also he will lose in
naïveté of expression; he will make himself a veil
which must be lifted before we can reach him; the
freshness of personal sentiment will be dimmed on his
forehead; the soul will be careful not to reveal itself;
a studied countenance, or at least a more mechanical
one, will have taken the place of that first free, eager
attitude.

Now what the sculptor would do if he could, the
critic-biographer, who has under his hand the whole
life and all the moments of his author, ought, with
still greater reason, to do; he ought to turn into living
reality, by his sagacious and penetrating analysis, that
which the artist instinctively figures under the form
of symbol.   The statue once erected, the type once
found and expressed, nothing remains to do but to
reproduce it, with slight modifications, during the
successive developments of the life of the poet, as if
in a series of bas-reliefs.

I know not if this theory of mine, half poetic, half
critical, is here made clear; but I believe it to be very
true; and so long as the biographers of great poets do
not keep it before their mind, they will make useful
and correct books, estimable no doubt, but not works
of the higher criticism and of art; they will collect
anecdotes, determine dates, lay bare literary quarrels;
but readers will be left to extract the essence, to
breathe vitality into the men; they will be chroniclers,
not sculptors; they will keep the records of the
temple, but they will not be the priests of the god.

The general state of literature when a new author
appears, the special education that author has received,
and the individual genius which nature has bestowed
upon him, those are three influences which it is important to distinguish in his first masterpiece, giving
to each its part and determining clearly what belongs
of right to pure genius.   Now, when Corneille, born in
1606, reached the age when poesy and drama began
to occupy his mind, when he saw things at first in
the bulk, and at a distance in the depths of his province, the names of three great poets (to-day very unequally famous) appeared to him above all others:
Ronsard, Malherbe, and Théophile: Ronsard, long
dead, but still in possession of a vast renown, and
representing the poesy of an expired century; Malherbe, living but already old, opening the poesy of the
new century, and placed beside Ronsard by those
who do not look closely into the details of literary

disputes; Théophile, young, adventurous, ardent; seeming, in the splendour of his advent, about to equal his predecessors. As for the stage, that was already occupied for a score of years by a single man, Alexandre Hardy, who never even signed his plays on the posters, so notoriously was he the dramatic poet *par excellence*. His dictatorship, it is true, was about to cease; Théophile, by his tragedy of *Pyrame et Thisbé* had struck the first blow, and Mairet, Rotrou, and Scudéry were just appearing on the scene. But all these lesser reputations, scarcely born as yet, which made the pedantic topic of the fashionable alcoves, of that crowd of *beaux esprits* of the second and third class, who swarmed around Malherbe below Maynard and Racau, were lost upon the young Corneille, who lived in Rouen, and there heard only the echoes of the loudest public fame. Ronsard, Malherbe, Théophile, and Hardy composed, therefore, the whole, or nearly so, of his modern literature.

Brought up at a Jesuit college, he had there obtained a sufficient knowledge of antiquity; but the study of the law, to which his father destined him, and which he pursued until his twenty-first year (1627), must have retarded the development of his poetic tastes. Nevertheless, he fell in love; and without admitting here an improbable anecdote related by Fontenelle, and especially rejecting that writer's ridiculous conclusion that to this love we owe the great Corneille, it is certain, by Corneille's own avowal, that this first

passion awoke him, and taught him to make verses.
It seems not unlikely that some special circumstance
of this affair incited him to compose *Mélite,* though
we can scarcely see what part he could have played in
it. The object of his passion was, we are told, a
young lady of Rouen, who became Mme. Du Pont
by marrying an official of that city. Extremely beautiful and clever, known to Corneille from childhood, it
does not appear that she ever responded to his respectful love otherwise than by an indulgent friendship. She received his verses, and sometimes asked
him for them; but the growing genius of the poet was
ill-contained in the madrigals, sonnets, and gallant
songs with which his career thus began. He found
himself "imprisoned"; he felt that "to produce he
needed a free wing—*le clef des champs.* A hundred
verses cost me less," he said, "than two lines of
song." The stage tempted him; the counsels of his
lady contributed, no doubt, to encourage him in this.
He wrote *Mélite,* and sent it to the old dramatist,
Hardy. The latter thought it "a rather pretty farce,"
and the young lawyer, just twenty-three years old,
started from Rouen to be present at the success of his
play in Paris (1629).

The principal part of these first years of Corneille's
life is undeniably his passion, and the original nature
of the man is revealed in it. Simple, pure-minded,
shy, and timid of speech, rather awkward, but very
sincere and respectful in love, he adored a woman

whom he failed to win, and who, after giving him
some hope, married another man. He tells us, himself, of a "misfortune which broke the current of their
affections"; but this ill-success never embittered him
against his "beautiful inhuman one," as he calls her:

> "My love for her must still remain the same;
> I feel myself still shaken by her name.
>
> .   .   .   .   .
>
> All love in me by her was so consumed,
> That nought seems lovable now that is doomed;
> So love I nought—no later conquering art
> Has since possessed my genius or my heart."

It was fifteen years before this sad and tender
memory, guardian of his youth, weakened sufficiently
to allow him to marry another woman; and then he
began the life of a burgher household, from which no
dissipation distracted him, even amid the licence of
the stage world in which he was forced to mix. I
know not if I mistake, but I think that I already see in
that sensitive, resigned, and sober nature, a touching
naïveté that reminds me of the worthy Ducis and his
loves, a virtuous awkwardness, full of integrity and
openness of heart, such as I admire in the Vicar of
Wakefield: and I take the more pleasure in seeing,
or, if you choose, in dreaming all this, because I perceive the genius below it, the genius of our great
Corneille.

From 1629, the period when Corneille first came to
Paris, to 1636, when "The Cid" was first acted, he
completed his literary education, which was merely

sketched-out in the provinces. He put himself into connection with the wits and poets of his time, especially with those of his own age, Mairet, Scudéry, Rotrou: he learned then what he had not known hitherto, that Ronsard was a little out of fashion, that Malherbe, dead within a year, had dethroned him in public opinion; that Théophile, also dead, had disappointed all hopes and left but a questionable memory behind him; that the stage was growing nobler and purer under the care of Cardinal de Richelieu; that Hardy was no longer by any means its sole supporter, for a troop of young rivals were judging him, to his great displeasure, rather freely, and disputing his heritage. Above all, Corneille learned that there were rules of which he had never dreamed in Rouen, but about which the brains of Paris were keenly excited: such as keeping five acts in one place or getting out of it; to be, or not to be within the space of twenty-four hours, etc. The learned men and the rule-lovers made war on these points against the lawless and the ignorant. Mairet held with the former; Claveret declared against them; Rotrou cared little; Scudéry discussed emphatically.

In the various plays that Corneille composed during this space of five years, he applied himself to understand thoroughly the habits of the stage and the taste of the public; I shall not try to follow him in this tentative course. He was quickly accepted by the city and the Court; the cardinal took notice of him, and attached him to his service as one of five authors; his comrades cherished and extolled him. With Rotrou, in particular, he contracted one of those friendships, so rare in literature, which no spirit of rivalry could ever chill. Younger than Corneille, Rotrou had, nevertheless, preceded him on the stage and, in the beginning, had helped him with advice. Corneille was grateful to the point of calling his young friend "father"; and certainly, if we must indicate at this period of his life the most characteristic trait of his genius and his soul, we should point to this tenderly filial friendship for the worthy Rotrou, just as, in the preceding period, it was his pure and respectful love for the woman I have mentioned. In it there was, as I think, truer forecast of sublime greatness than in *Mélite, Clitandre, La Veuve, La Galérie du Palais, La Place Royale, L'Illusion;* and fully as much as in *Medée.*

During this time, Corneille made frequent excursions to Rouen. In one of these journeys he visited the house of a M. de Châlons, former secretary of the queen-mother, now retired from old age:

"Monsieur," the old man said to him, "the style of comedy which you have taken up can give you only ephemeral fame. You can find among the Spaniards subjects which, if treated according to our taste by hands like yours, would produce great effects. Learn their language, it is easy; I offer to teach you all I know of it, and, until you are able to read for yourself, I will translate to you parts of Guillen de Castro."

This meeting was great good luck for Corneille;

no sooner had he set foot into the noble poesy of Spain than he felt at ease, as if in a country of his own. Loyal spirit, full of honour and morality, walking with uplifted head, he could not fail to feel a sudden and deep affection for the chivalrous heroes of that brave nation. His impetuous warmth of heart, his childlike sincerity, his inviolable devotion in friendship, his melancholy resignation in love, his religion of duty, his nature wholly unveiled, naïvely grave and sententious, noble with pride and *prud'homie* — all inclined him strongly to the Spanish style. He embraced it with fervour, adapted it, without much considering how, to the taste of his nation and his age, and created for himself a unique originality in the midst of the commonplace imitations that were being made around him. No more tentatives, no slow progressive advance, as in his preceding comedies. Blind and rapid in his instinct, he went at one stroke to the sublime, the glorious, the pathetic, as if to things familiar; producing them in splendid, simple language that all the world can understand, and which belongs to him alone. From the night of the first representation of "The Cid" our theatre was truly founded; France possessed the great Corneille; and the triumphant poet, who, like his own heroes, spoke openly of himself as he thought, had the right to exclaim, without fear of denial:

"I know what I am; I believe what is said of me."

The dazzling success of "The Cid" and the very le-

gitimate pride felt and shown by Corneille raised all his
past rivals and all the authors of tragedy, from Claveret to Richelieu, against him. I shall not dwell here
on the details of this quarrel, which is one of the best-
illuminated spots in our literary history. The effect
produced on the poet by this outbreak of criticism
was such as might be expected from the character of
his talent and his mind. Corneille, as I have said,
was a pure, instinctive, blind genius, of free, spontaneous impulse, and well-nigh devoid of those medium
qualities which accompany, and second efficaciously,
the gift divine in a poet. He was neither adroit nor
skilful in details, his taste was little delicate, his judgment not sure, his tact obtuse, and he gave himself
small account of his methods as an artist; he piqued
himself, however, on his shrewdness and reserve.
Between his genius and his good sense there was
nothing, or nearly nothing; and that good sense,
which did not lack subtlety or logic, had to make
strong efforts, especiall ʲᶜ provoked, to goad itself up
to the level of the genius, to grasp it in hand, comprehend it, and train it. If Corneille had come earlier,
before the Academy and Richelieu, in place of Alexandre Hardy, for example, he would doubtless not
have been exempt from falls, errors, and mistakes;
perhaps, indeed, other enormities might be found in
him than those against which our present taste revolts
in certain of his worst passages; but at least his failures would have been solely according to the nature

and trend of his genius; and when he rose out of them, when he obtained sight of the beautiful, the grand, the sublime, he would have rushed to it as into his own region, without dragging after him the baggage of rules, cumbersome and puerile scruples, and a thousand petty hindrances to a vast and soaring flight. The quarrel of " The Cid," arresting him at his first step, forcing him to return upon himself and confront his work with rules, disturbed for the future that prolonged growth, full of chances, that sort of potent, unconscious vegetation, so to speak, for which nature seemed to have destined him. He took umbrage, he was indignant at first at the cavillings of criticism; but he inwardly reflected on the rules and precepts imposed upon him, and ended, finally, by adapting himself to them, and believing them.

The mortifications that followed closely on the triumph of " The Cid " carried him back to his family in Rouen, which place he did not leave again until 1639, when he returned to Paris with *Horace* and *Cinna* in hand. To quit Spain the instant he had set foot in it, to push no farther that glorious victory of "The Cid," to renounce, in gaiety of heart, all those magnanimous heroes who stretched their arms to him, and turn aside to fasten upon a Castilian Rome on the faith of Lucan and Seneca, Spanish burghers under Nero, was, for Corneille, not to profit by his advantages and to misinterpret the voice of his genius at the very moment when it spoke so clearly. But at that time fashion, vogue, carried minds more toward ancient Rome than toward Spain. Besides the amorous gallantries and noble, conventional sentiments attributed to those old republicans, special occasion was given, by producing them on the stage, to apply the maxims of State, and all the political and diplomatic jargon that we find in Balzac and in Gabriel Naudé, and to which Richelieu himself gave currency. Probably Corneille allowed himself to be seduced by these reasons of the moment; nevertheless, out of his very error came masterpieces.

I will not follow him through the various successes that marked his career during its fifteen finest years. *Polyeucte, Pompée, Le Menteur, Rodogune, Héraclius, Don Sanche,* and *Nicomède* are its enduring landmarks. He returned to imitation of the Spanish in *Le Menteur,* a comedy in which the comic (which Corneille did not understand) is much less to be admired than the *imbroglio,* the movement, and the fancy. Again he returned to the Castilian genius in *Héraclius,* but above all in *Nicomède* and *Don Sanche,* those two wonderful creations, unique upon our stage, which, coming in the midst of the Fronde, with their singular mixture of romantic heroism and familiar irony, stirred up innumerable malignant or generous allusions, and won universal applause. Yet it was shortly after these triumphs, in 1653, that Corneille, wounded by the non-success of *Pertharite,* and touched perhaps by Christian sentiments and remorse, resolved to renounce the theatre. He was then forty-seven years of age ; he had just translated in verse the first chapters of the " Imitation of Jesus Christ," and he desired henceforth to devote the remainder of his vigour to pious subjects.

Corneille had married in 1640, and in spite of his frequent journeys to Paris he lived habitually in Rouen with his family. His brother Thomas and he had married two sisters, and lived in adjoining houses. Both took care of their widowed mother. Pierre had six children; and as in those days plays brought more to the actors than to their authors, and as, moreover, he was often not upon the spot to watch his interests, he scarcely earned enough to support his numerous family. His nomination to the French Academy did not take place till 1647. He had promised, before he was appointed, to arrange to live in Paris the greater part of the year; but it does not appear that he did so. He did not establish himself in the capital till 1662, and until then he derived none of the advantages that assiduous attendance at the sessions procures for academicians.

The literary morals of the time were not like ours: authors felt no scruple in asking and receiving gratuities from princes and seigneurs. Corneille, on the title-page of *Horace,* says that he " has the honour to belong to his Eminence; gentlemen in those days boasted of being the *domestiques* of a prince or a seigneur. This explains to us, and excuses in our illustrious poet, his singular dedications to Richelieu, to Montauron, to Mazarin, to Fouquet, which so unfairly scandalised Voltaire. About the same period in England the condition of authors was no better, and we find very curious details on this subject in Johnson's "Lives of the Poets" and Samuel Pepys's "Diary." In Malherbe's correspondence with Peiresc there is hardly a letter in which the famous lyric poet does not complain of receiving from King Henri more compliments than money. These morals still existed in Corneille's time; and even if they were passing a little out of usage, his poverty and his family burdens must have prevented his emancipating himself from them. No doubt he suffered at times; and he somewhere deplores "this feeling, I know not what, of secret abasement" to which a noble heart can scarcely stoop; but with him necessity was stronger than delicacy. Let me say it again: Corneille, outside of his sublimity and his pathos, had little skill and tact. He carried into all the relations of life something awkward and provincial; his speech on his reception at the Academy, for instance, is a model of bad taste, insipid praise, and pomposity. Well! we must judge in the same way his dedication to Montauron, much attacked and ridiculed even at the time it appeared. The worthy Corneille lacked the sense of fitness and propriety; he persisted heavily where he ought to have glided; he—like in heart to his heroes, solid in soul, but broken by fate — he bowed too low in salutation, and struck his noble forehead on the earth.

Corneille imagined, in 1653, that he renounced the stage. Pure illusion! That withdrawal, could it have been possible, would no doubt have been better for his peace of mind, and perhaps for his fame. But he had not the kind of poetic temperament that could impose upon itself at will a continence of fifteen years — as Racine did later. Encouragement and a gratuity from Fouquet sufficed to bring him back to the stage, where he remained a score of years longer, till 1674, waning, day by day, under numberless mistakes and cruel griefs. Before saying a few words of his old age and death, let us pause a moment to sum up the chief traits of his genius and his work.

Corneille's dramatic form has not the freedom of fancy that Lope de Vega and Shakespeare gave themselves; neither has it the exactly regular severity to which Racine subjected himself. If he had dared, if he had come before d'Aubignac, Mairet, or Chapelain, he would, I think, have cared very little for graduating and marshalling his acts, connecting his scenes, concentrating his effects on a single point of space and duration; he would have written haphazard, tangling and untangling the threads of his plot, changing the locality as it suited him, delaying on the way, and pushing his personages pell-mell before him to marriage or death. In the midst of this confusion beautiful scenes, admirable groups

would have detached themselves here and there; for
Corneille understands grouping very well, and, at
essential moments, he poses his personages most
dramatically. He balances one against the other,
defines them vigorously with a brief and manly saying, contrasts them by cutting repartees, and presents to the spectator's eye the masses of a skilful
structure. But he had not a genius sufficiently artistic
to extend over an entire drama that concentric con-
figuration which he has realized in places; at the same
time, his fancy was not free or alert enough to create
for itself a form, moving, undulating, diffuse, multiplied, but not less real, less beautiful than the other,
such as we admire in certain plays of Shakespeare,
such as the Schlegels admire so much in Calderon.
Add to these natural imperfections the influence of
a superficial and finical poetic art, about which
Corneille overconcerned himself, and you will have
the secret of what is ambiguous, undecided, and
incompletely reckoned in the making of his tragedies.

His *Discours* and his *Examens* give us numerous
details on this point, in which we find revealed the
most hidden recesses of his great mind. We see
how the pitiless unity of place frets him, and how
heartily he would say to it: " Oh! you hamper me! "
and with what pains he tries to combine it with
" decorum." He does not always succeed. " Pauline," he writes, " comes to an antechamber to meet
Severus whose visit she ought to await in her private

apartment." Pompey seems to disregard the prudence of the general of an army, when, trusting to Sertorius, he goes to confer with him in a town where the latter is master; "but it was impossible," says Corneille, "to keep the unity of place without making him commit this blunder." But when there was absolute necessity for the action to be carried on in two different places, the following is the expedient that Corneille invents to evade the rule:

"These two places have no need of different scenery, and neither of the two should ever be named, but only the general region in which both are situated, such as Paris, Rome, Lyons, Constantinople, etc. This will help to deceive the audience, who, seeing nothing to mark the diversity of place, will not perceive it — unless by malicious and critical reflection, of which few are capable ; most of them attending eagerly to the action they see represented before them."

He congratulates himself like a child on the complexity of *Héraclius* because "that poem is so involved it requires marvellous attention"; and requests us to notice in *Othon* that "never was a play seen in which so many marriages were proposed and none concluded."

Corneille's personages are grand, generous, valiant, frank, lofty of head, and noble of heart. Brought up for the most part under austere discipline, the maxims by which they rule their lives are for ever on their lips; and as they never depart from those maxims we have no difficulty in recognising them; a glance suffices: which is almost the contrary of Shakespeare's personages and of human beings in life. The morality of his heroes is spotless: as fathers, lovers, friends, or enemies, we admire and honour them ; in pathetic parts their tone is sublime, it lifts the soul and makes us weep. But his rivals and his husbands have sometimes a tinge of the ridiculous: so has Don Sancho in "The Cid," also Prusias and Pertharite. His tyrants and his step-mothers are all of a piece like his heroes, wicked from one end to the other; nevertheless, at sight of a fine action it sometimes happens that they face about suddenly to virtue, like Grimoald and Arsinoé.

Corneille's men have formal and punctilious minds: they quarrel about etiquette; they argue at length and wrangle loudly with themselves, even in their passions. There is something of the Norman in them. Auguste, Pompée and others seem to have studied logic at Salamanca, and to have read Aristotle with the Arabs. His heroines, his "adorable furies," nearly all resemble one another; their love is subtle, over-refined, with a purpose; coming more from the head than the heart. We feel that Corneille knew little of women. Nevertheless, he succeeded in expressing in Chimène and Pauline that virtuous power of self-sacrifice that he himself had practised in his youth. Strange as it may seem, after his return to the theatre in 1659; and in all the numerous plays of his decadence — *Attila, Bérénice, Pulchérie, Suréna,*— Corneille had a mania for mingling love in everything, just as La Fontaine had for introducing Plato. It

seems as though the successes of Quinault and Racine
enticed him to that ground, and that he wanted to
read a lesson to "those tender ones" as he called
them. He imagined that in his day he had been still
more gallant and amorous than those "young flaxen
wigs," and he never spoke of other times without
shaking his head like an elderly swain.

Corneille's style is, to my thinking, the merit by
which he excels. Voltaire, in his commentary, exhibits on this point, as on others, a sovereign injustice, and also what may be called great ignorance of
the origins of our language. He blames his author at
every turn for having neither grace nor elegance nor
clearness; he measures, pen in hand, the height of
the metaphors, and when they exceed somewhat he
calls them gigantic. He translates and disguises in
prose Corneille's lofty and sonorous phrases, which
suit so finely the bearing of his heroes, and asks if
that is speaking and writing French. He churlishly
calls "solecism" what he ought to describe as
"idiom"—namely the construction, or form of speech
peculiar to a special language; a thing that is completely lacking to the narrow, symmetrical, abbrevi-
ated French language of the eighteenth century.
Corneille's style, with all its negligences, seems to
me one of the greatest manners of the century that
had Molière and Bossuet. The touch of the poet is
rough, severe, vigorous. I compare him to a sculptor,
who, working the clay to express heroic portraiture,

employs no instrument but his thumb, and, kneading thus his work, gives it a supreme character of life itself with all the jostling incidents that accompany and complete it; but all such proceeding is incorrect, it is not polished, not "proper," as they say. There is little painting or colour in Corneille's style; it is warm rather than brilliant; it turns willingly to the abstract; imagination and fancy give way to thought and to reasoning. It ought to please statesmen, geometricians, soldiers, and others who enjoy the styles of Demosthenes, Pascal, and Cæsar.

In short, Corneille, pure genius but incomplete, with his lofty aspects and his defects, gives me the impression of those great trees that are bare, rugged, sad, monotonous as to their trunk, with branches and sombre foliage at their summit only. They are strong, powerful, gigantic, with little verdure; sap in abundance rises; but expect neither shelter, shade, nor bloom. They leaf out late, their leaves fall early, yet they live on, half-despoiled; but when their hoary brow has cast its last leaves to the autumn wind their perennial nature puts out, here and there, belated branches and green twigs. And when at last they die, their groans, the cracking of their fissures, remind one of that armoured trunk to which Lucan compared the great Pompey.

Such was the old age of our great Corneille; a ruined, furrowed, bald old age, dropping piece by piece, but of which the heart was the last to die. He had put his whole life and all his soul into the theatre. Outside of it he was worth but little; brusque, heavy, taciturn, and melancholy, his grand wrinkled forehead was never illuminated, his dulled, veiled eye never sparkled, his voice, harsh and toneless, had no emphasis unless he spoke of the drama, and especially his own. He did not know how to converse, he was out of place in society, and only saw M. de La Rochefoucauld, Cardinal de Retz, and Mme. de Sévigné for the purpose of reading to them his plays. He became with age more unhappy and morose. The success of his younger rivals troubled him; he seemed distressed and nobly jealous of it, like a vanquished bull or an old athlete. When Racine parodied this line in " The Cid "

" The wrinkles on his brow engrave his deeds "

Corneille, who could not understand a jest, exclaimed, naïvely: "Is it a young man's business to come here and turn people's verses into ridicule?" On another occasion he said to Chevreau: "I have taken leave of the drama; my pocsy has gone with my teeth."

Corneille had lost two sons, and his poverty scarcely enabled him to provide for his other children. A delay in the payment of his pension brought him almost to want on his deathbed: we know the noble conduct of Boileau on that occasion. The old man died on the night of September 30, 1684, in the rue d'Argenteul, where he lodged. Charlotte Corday was the great-granddaughter of one of Pierre Corneille's daughters.

III.

Mademoiselle de Scudéry.

Mademoiselle de Scudéry.

THIS is not a rehabilitation that I am about to attempt; but it is well to put correct ideas to certain names that recur frequently. The books of Mlle. de Scudéry are no longer read; but her name is still cited; she serves to designate a literary class, a fashion of intellect, and the cultivation of *belles-lettres* at a celebrated period: it is a medal that has almost passed into circulation and become a coin. What is its value and its charm? Let us do with Mlle. de Scudéry as she herself was so fond of doing with others: let us examine, distinguish, and analyse.

This young woman, "of extraordinary merit," as they said of her, was born at Havre, in 1607, under Henri IV; she did not die until 1701, at ninety-four years of age, toward the close of the reign of "Louis quatorzième," as she liked to call him. Her father was from Provence; he removed to Normandy and married there, not without transmitting to his children something of his southern temperament. The son, Georges de Scudéry, is celebrated for his pompous

verses, his braggadocio, and his rhodomontades, in
which he one day had the misfortune to meet and
affront Corneille; for which posterity has never for-
given him.   Mlle. Madeleine de Scudéry was far more
sensible than her brother; Normandy, if I may venture to say it, was much more apparent in her; she
reasoned, she discussed, she argued on matters of
mind like the cleverest lawyer or pettifogger.   But
she, too, had her share of family vanity; she always
said: "Since the overthrow of our house"; "You
would really think she was talking of the overthrow
of the Greek empire," says the malicious Tallemant
des Réaux.   The Scudérys claimed, in fact, to have
issued from a very noble, very ancient, and "ever
warlike" family of Neapolitan origin, but established
for centuries in Provence.   In transforming into her
novels the persons of her acquaintance under the
guise of heroes and princes, Mlle. de Scudéry felt herself among her own kind.

Having lost her parents while very young, she was
brought up in the country by an uncle, a well-informed and worthy man, who gave great care to her
education, which was, in fact, much better than
young girls were accustomed to receive in those days.
Writing, spelling, dancing, drawing, painting, needle-
work, she learned them all, says Conrart, and she
divined for herself what they did not teach her.

"As she had," continues Conrart [first secretary of the French
Academy], "a prodigious imagination, an excellent memory, an ex-

MADEMOISELLE MADELEINE DE SCUDÉRY.
From an old print.

quisite judgment, a lively temper, naturally inclined to understand all she saw done that was curious, and all she heard said that was laudable, soon taught herself other things: such as related to agriculture, gardening, household management, country life, cookery, the causes and effects of illness, the composition of many remedies, perfumes, fragrant waters, and useful or delectable distillations for necessity or pleasure. She had a fancy to know how to play the lute, and took some lessons with fair success."

But the lute took too much time, and, without renouncing it wholly, she preferred to turn more particularly to occupations of the mind. She learned Italian and Spanish perfectly; her principal pleasures were reading and choice conversation, of which she was not deprived in her neighbourhood. The picture that Conrart gives us of her early education reminds us of that of Mme. de Genlis in Bourgogne; and I will say at once that in studying Mlle. de Scudéry closely, as I have just done, she seems to me to have had much of Mme. de Genlis in her, with virtue added. To learn all, to know all, from the properties of simples and the making of preserves to the anatomy of the human heart; to be, from her earliest years, on the footing of a marvel of perfection; to draw from all she saw in society matter for novels, portraits, moral dissertations, compliments, and lessons; to combine a mass of pedantry with extreme delicacy of observation and a perfect knowledge of the world,—these are traits common to both of them; the differences, however, are not less essential to note. Mlle. de Scudéry, who had "a very good appearance" and a rather grand air, had no beauty:

"She is a tall, thin, dark person, with a very long face," says Tallemant. She was gifted with moral qualities which have never been denied. Respect and esteem were, to her, inseparable from the idea of celebrity and fame. In a word, she was a Genlis of the date of Lous XIII, full of force and virtue, who stayed a virgin and an old maid until she was ninety-four years of age.

We should hear her speak of herself, whenever she can do so under a slight disguise. In most of the dialogues in which her personages converse, she finds means to make the one who replies remark after each pretty thing she produces: "All that you say is so well said"—"That is marvellously thought out." Or, to use a word she affects: "That is admirably distinguished [démêlé]." This indirect compliment is addressed to herself again and again; she is inexhaustible in formulas for self-approval. In the tenth volume of *Le Grand Cyrus* she partly pictures herself in the personage of Sappho, and the name stayed by her, "The illustrious Sappho"; those who had read *Le Grand Cyrus* never called her otherwise. There are some passages of that Portrait, for which Mlle. de Scudéry had certainly examined herself. After speaking of the long line of ancestors of which her heroine could boast, she says:

"Sappho has also this advantage, that her father and mother had, both of them, much mind and much virtue; but she had the misfortune to lose them so early that she could receive from them

only the first inclinations to good, for she was six years old when
they died. It is true that they left her under guidance of a female
relative. . . ."

The uncle is here changed to a female relative, but
the rest refers plainly to herself:

"In fact, madame," [this is a narrative which one of the personages is supposed to address to the Queen of Pontis], "I think that
in all Greece there is no one to be compared with Sappho. I will not
stop to tell you, madame, what her childhood was, for she was so
little of a child that at twelve years of age people began to speak of
her as a person whose beauty, intellect, and judgment were already
formed and were causing admiration to every one. I will merely tell
you that never did persons observe in any one, no matter who, nobler
inclinations or greater facility in learning all that she wished to know."

Facing courageously the question of beauty, she is
still thinking of herself when she says:

"Though you hear me speak of Sappho as the most marvellous and
most charming person in all Greece, you must not imagine that her
beauty is one of the greatest beauties on earth . . . As for *complexion,* hers is not of the utmost whiteness ; but it has such a fine
glow that you may say that it is beautiful; but what Sappho has
that is sovereignly agreeable is that her eyes are so fine, so lovely, so
loving, so full of intelligence, that one can neither sustain their brilliancy nor detach one's own eyes from them. . . . That which
makes their *greatest* brilliancy is that never was there *greater* contrast
than that of the white and the black of her eyes. Nevertheless this
great contrast has nothing harsh about it. . . ."

We remark here the negligence of her style, the
repetitions, etc. I abridge much (which Mlle. de
Scudéry herself never did); I leave out as I go along a
great many "but's," and "for's," and "even so's." But
from these few traits we can do more than merely

perceive the ideal she wishes to present of her beauty,
or, if you choose, the corrective of her plainness.
Such the Sappho of the Marais may have appeared to
friendly eyes when Chapelain, passing in those days
for a great epic poet, compared her, intrepidly, to La
Pucelle; and Pellisson, ugliest of *beaux esprits,* made
her his passionate declaration.

In this same portrait of Sappho, which is precious
to us, she comes at last to charms of mind, on which
she enlarges with redoubled complacency:

"The charms of her mind surpass by far those of her beauty.   In
truth, she has it" [mind] "of such vast extent that we may say that
what she does not understand cannot be understood by any one; and
she has such a faculty to learn easily all she wants to know that, although one has seldom heard it said that Sappho ever learned anything,
she nevertheless knows all things."

Then follows the enumeration of her talents—poesy,
prose, impromptu songs:

"She even expresses very delicately sentiments that are most difficult to express, and she knows so well the *anatomy of an amorous
heart* (if it is permissible to speak thus) that she can describe exactly
all the jealousies, all the anxieties, all the impatience, all the joys, all
the dislikes, all the murmurings, all the despair, all the hopes, all the
rebellions, and all those tumultuous feelings that are never well known
except by those who feel them or have felt them."

It was one of Mlle. de Scudéry's claims that she
knew and could describe the most secret emotions of
love without ever having felt them otherwise than by
reflection; and it is true that she often succeeded in
whatever was delicate and refined, in short, in all that
was not the actual flame.   "You explain that so ad-

mirably," we might say to her, like a person of one of her dialogues, "that if you had done nothing all your life but be in love you could not express it better."—"Though I never was in love," she would answer with her prettiest smile, "I have friends who have been so for me, and they have taught me how to speak of it." That is wit, and Mlle. de Scudéry had a great deal of it.

In this Portrait of Sappho she insists strongly that Sappho not only knows to the depths whatever relates to *love,* but that she does not know less all that concerns *generosity;* and this marvel of knowledge and nature is crowned, according to her, with modesty:

> "In fact, her conversation is so natural, so easy, so polite, that she is never heard to talk in general conversation of any but those things that a person of intelligence might say without having learned all that she knows. It is not that persons who understand things do not know very well that nature alone could not have opened her mind as it has been opened; but it is that she takes such care to remain always in the proprieties of her sex, that she almost always speaks only of that which ladies should speak of."

I leave the faults of grammar. But here we see a Sappho, both wise and modest, wholly of the seventeenth century, and in accordance with the last good taste of the Place-Royale and the hôtel Rambouillet.

Mlle. de Scudéry made no delay in appearing there; provinces could not keep her long. Having lost her uncle, she hesitated between Paris and Rouen; but her brother, who was taking rank among dramatic

authors and whose plays were succeeding at the hôtel
de Bourgogne, persuaded her to settle in the capital.
She appeared to advantage from the start; was
greeted and extolled by the best society, and began
to write novels; without, however, putting her name
to them, but hiding behind that of her vainglorious
brother. *Ibrahim ou l'Illustre Bassa* began to appear in 1641; *Artamène ou Le Grand Cyrus,* in 1650;
and *Clélie,* in 1654.

The true date of Mlle. de Scudéry is in those years,
the period of the Regency, the fine years of Anne of
Austria, before and after the Fronde; and her fame
lasted without check of any kind until Boileau attacked
it, like the kill-joy that he was: "That Despréaux,"
said Segrais, "thinks of nothing but talking of himself and criticising others; why should *he* speak ill of
Mlle. de Scudéry as he does?"

To understand fully the success of Mlle. de Scudéry
and the direction that she gave to her talent, we must
picture to ourselves the higher society of Paris such as
it was before the period when Louis XIV began to
reign for himself. For some years a taste for things
of the mind, for literary *bel esprit* had existed; into
which entered more zeal and emulation than discernment and knowledge. The novel of d' Urfé, the
Letters of Balzac, the great success of plays, those of
Corneille and other writers in vogue, the protection,
slightly pedantic, but real and efficacious of Cardinal
de Richelieu, the foundation of the French Academy

—all these causes had developed a spirit of inquiry, especially among women, who felt that the moment had come to bring society to their own level. People were freeing themselves from antiquity and the learned languages ; they wanted to know their mother-tongue, and they looked to the grammarians by profession. Men of the world made themselves intermediaries between scholars, properly so-called, and the salons: they desired to please as well as to instruct. But mingled with these first efforts of a serious and polished society was great inexperience. To do Mlle. de Scudéry all the justice that is her due, and to assign her her true title, we ought to consider her as one of the *instructors* of society at this moment of transition and formation. It was her rôle and, in a great measure, her design.

In the Portrait and history of Sappho, which can be read toward the end of the *Grand Cyrus,* she shows to what a point she was filled with this design, and she brought to it more discrimination and tact than we, judging her afar off from her reputation, might have expected. Do not think her a professed *bel esprit ;* she repudiates it from the start: "There is nothing more annoying," she thinks, "than to be a *bel esprit,* or to be treated as being one when our heart is noble and we are of certain birth." She feels more than any one the impropriety of clever persons, especially women, being received by society on that footing; and she exposes it like a young woman of good sense and a lady who has suffered from it. One of the greatest of these inconveniences, and the one that gives her the most annoyance, is that persons in society fancy they cannot approach *bel esprits* as they would other people but speak to them always in the grand manner:

"For I find men and women speaking to me sometimes with strange embarrassment, because they have taken it into their heads that I must not be talked to like other persons. In vain do I speak of the fine weather, the news of the day, and all the other things that make ordinary conversation; they always return to their point; they are so convinced that I compel myself to speak thus, that they compel themselves to talk of other things that weary me so that I would gladly not be Sappho when this happens to me."

I beg pardon of my readers for all these "that's" in favour of the idea, which is a right one. Mlle. de Scudéry makes many objections addressed to herself on the inconveniences of being a female *bel esprit* and a *femme savante*. Long before Molière she said more than one very sensible thing on this subject. But let us not forget the moment of social life and the sort of difficulties with which she had to do. She discusses very carefully the question of whether it would be well for women, in general, to be taught more than they then knew: "Though I am the declared enemy of all women who play the learned, I nevertheless think the other extreme very condemnable, and I am often shocked to see many women of rank so grossly ignorant that, in my opinion, they dishonour our sex."

There, indeed, was a defect that needed remedy
at once.   The education of persons of rank was at
that date, 1641–1654, most defective.   What ignorance, what strange negligence even in women of
intelligence and fame!   Mme. de Sablé, the wise and
witty friend of La Rochefoucauld could not spell.

"It is certain," says Mlle. de Scudéry, "that there are women who
speak well and write ill, and who write ill purely through their own
fault .   .   .   It is, as I think," she adds, "an intolerable error in
women to wish to speak well and yet be willing to write badly .   .   .
Most ladies seem to write with the intention not to be understood, so
little connection is there between their words, and so fantastic is their
spelling.   Yet these very ladies, who boldly make such gross blunders
in writing and lose all their minds when they begin to write, will laugh
a whole day at some poor foreigner who may have said one word for
another."

One of the corrections that Mlle. de Scudéry urged,
and to which she contributed most, was that of
bringing harmony between the manner of speaking
and that of writing.   She made persons of her own
sex blush at their inconsistency.   All her ideas on the
education of women are very just and well-considered
in theory:

"Seriously," she writes, "can there be anything more whimsical
than the way the education of women is usually carried on?   They are
not to be coquettish or gallant, yet they are permitted to learn carefully all that appertains to gallantry, without allowing them to know
anything that might fortify their virtue or occupy their mind.   All
those reprimands made to them in early youth, about not being clean,
not dressing in good style, not attending sufficiently to the lessons
that their dancing or their music-master gives them, do they not prove
what I say?   And what is singular is, that a woman who can dance
with propriety only five or six years of her life, spends ten or a dozen

in continually learning what she can use for only five or six; but this same person is obliged to have judgment till she dies, and to talk to her last breath, yet she is never taught anything to make her speak more agreeably and act with more decorum."

Her conclusion, which she gives with some reserve, (for in a matter, she says, that touches "diversity of minds" there cannot be "universal law"), her conclusion, I say, is that in asking that women should know more than they do she does not wish that they should act or speak as learned women:

"I want it to be said of a person of my sex that she knows a hundred things of which she does not boast; that she has an enlightened mind, that she comprehends fine books, that she speaks well, writes correctly, and understands society; but I do not wish it to be said of her: 'She is a learned woman'; for the two characters are so different that they do not resemble each other in any way."

This is reason; of which there is a great deal in Mlle. de Scudéry's books; mingled, it is true, with far too much argument and dissertation, and drowned in what seems in these days romantic extravagance.

That which to us is extravagance was, nevertheless, the very thing that caused instruction to pass from hand to hand, and reach more surely those to whom it was addressed. Tallemant tells us that in speaking she had a masterful and preaching tone that was not agreeable: this tone was disguised in her novels by passing through the lips of her personages, and to-day it requires some study to find her didacticism. Of real imagination and invention Mlle. de Scudéry had none at all; when she wanted to construct or invent a tale she took some plot in use at the moment; she supplied herself freely from the shops and the wardrobes in vogue; she copied the plot of d'Urfé in *Astrée*. So doing, she flattered herself she allied fiction with history, art with actuality: "It is never permissible in a wise man," she said, "to invent things that cannot be believed. The true art of falsehood is to resemble truth." This was part of a conversation in *Clélie* where they discussed the "manner of inventing a tale and composing a novel." A little more and Mlle. de Scudéry would have preached observation of nature: she makes the poet Anacreon utter almost as good rules of rhetoric as we find in Quintilian. It is a pity she did not put them into practice.

To speak to-day of Mlle. de Scudéry's novels, and to analyse them would be impossible without calumniating her, so ridiculous would they seem. Too much of what was really the absurdity of the times would be attributed to her. To rightly appreciate her novels as such, we must go back to the models that were set before her, and write the history of a whole section. What strikes us most at a first glance is the way she takes the personages of her acquaintance and her society and transforms them into Greeks, Romans, Persians, and Carthaginians, and makes them perform in the principal events very nearly the same rôle that is assigned to them in history; all the while making them think and talk precisely as she saw them in Paris. *Hamilcar* is the poet Sarasin; *Herminius* is Pellisson; Conrart becomes *Cléodamas* and has, near Agrigentum, a pretty country-house, described at length, which is no other than that of Athys, near Paris. If she meets an historical personage, she at once puts him on a level with the men of her acquaintance; she tells us of Brutus, for instance, he who condemned his own sons and drove out the Tarquins; that he was born with "the most gallant, gentlest, and most agreeable mind in the world"; and of the poet Alcæus she remarks that he was "a clever lad, full of wit and a great intriguer." The actions and behaviour of all these personages (as she travesties them) are almost in keeping with her factitious method of presenting them; a glaze of falsity covers them all.

But how, you will ask, could such novels obtain so much vogue and credit? How could the youth of Mme. de Sévigné and Mme. de La Fayette have fed upon them? In the first place, persons in those days had no real idea of the spirit of divers times, or of the profound differences in manners and morals throughout history. Besides which, nearly all the personages who figured in Mlle. de Scudéry's novels were living and contemporary beings, whose names were known, whose portraits and characters were recognised, from *Le Grand Cyrus,* thought to be the Great Condé, to *Doralise,* who was Mlle. Robineau. All these personages, even the most secondary, were known in society; the key was passed round, the masks were named; and even to-day, when we know the real names, we are not entirely without curiosity as we glance through her pages.

"You could not believe," says Tallemant, "how pleased the ladies are to appear in her novels, or, to speak correctly, to have their Portraits seen there; for nothing but the *character* of the personages will be found, their actions not at all. Some, however, have complained of them. . . ." Among those who complained was one of the wittiest women of that period, who said many a good thing that has since come down to us. In the fourth volume of *Le Grand Cyrus* Mlle. de Scudéry gives the portrait of Mme. Cornuel under the name of Zénocrite, making her one of the most agreeable and most formidable satirists of Lycia. The Portrait is very exact. Mme. Cornuel justified the reputation given her of a bold satirist by saying of Mlle. de Scudéry, who was very dark-skinned, that "anybody could see she was destined by Providence to blot paper, for she sweated ink from every pore." Molière's Dorine could not have said more.

What is remarkable, and really distinguished in Mlle. de Scudéry's novels is the Conversations they contain, for which she had a singular talent, a true vocation. She made later, after her novels had gone out of fashion, extracts from these Conversations, which appeared successively in ten little volumes (ten

was her number and she did not go beyond it). "Mlle.
de Scudéry has just sent me two little volumes of
'Conversations,'" wrote Mme. de Sévigné to her
daughter, September 25, 1680. "It is impossible
that they should not be good when no longer submerged in her great novel." These little volumes,
and others of the same kind which survive and do
credit to Mlle. de Scudéry's old age, are still sought
for by inquiring minds, and those to whom nothing
that concerns the great century is indifferent. It is
not uncommon to hear it said that Mlle. de Scudéry's
novels are unreadable and detestable; but it is not so
with her "Conversations." It is well to know, however, that the "Conversations," certainly the first of
them, are taken verbatim from *Cyrus, Clélie,* and her
other novels.

One of the first subjects that she treats of is conversation itself :

"As conversation is the social bond of all men, the greatest pleasure of honourable persons, and the usual means of introducing not
only politeness into society, but also the purest morality, and a love
of fame and virtue, it seems to me that the company cannot more
agreeably or more usefully entertain itself" says Cilenie, one of her
personages "than by examining what is called Conversation."

Whereupon they begin to inquire what conversation
should be in order to be agreeable and worthy of a
company of well-bred persons: it must not, they
think, be too limited to family topics and servants,
nor turned to futile subjects and to dress, which so

often happens when women are by themselves. "Are you not compelled to own," says one of the interlocutors, "that whoever would write down what fifteen or twenty women say to each other would make the worst book in the world?" And this, even when, among the fifteen or twenty, many were intelligent. But let a man enter,—a single one and not even a distinguished man,— and the conversation at once rises and becomes, all of a sudden, more connected, more witty, more agreeable. In short,

"the most charming women in society, when they are together in great numbers, without men, seldom say anything that is worth hearing, and feel more bored than if they were alone. But with men it is not so. Their conversation is, no doubt, less lively when no ladies are present, but, as a usual thing, though it may be more serious, it is also more reasonable; they can do without us better than we can do without them."

Those are shrewd remarks, which show experience of the world and almost of the heart. This whole chapter "On Conversation" is very well thought out; after going over the different defects of conversation, Cilénie or Valérie, or rather the author, in a summary that has no other drawback than being too precise and methodical, concludes that in order not to be wearisome, but to be both charming and reasonable, conversation ought not to be confined to one object but to be made up of all:

"I conceive," she says, "that, speaking generally, it ought to consist more frequently of ordinary and gallant things than of great things; but I also think that there is nothing that may not enter it; that it ought to be free and diversified according to the time, place and persons about us; I think that the secret is to speak nobly of low things, simply of high things, and very courteously of courteous things, without too much forwardness and without affectation."

But what was still more necessary to render it charming is that "there be a spirit of politeness that shall banish absolutely all sharp and bitter jesting, and also all those things that may, ever so little, be offensive to modesty. . . . Also I desire that a *certain spirit of joy* may reign there." All that is well said, and as charming as it is judicious—as one of the personages of the Conversation did not fail to remark.

Read, after that chapter, the one that treats of "The manner of writing Letters" (partly extracted from *Clélie*), and you will understand how it is that beneath this novel-writing that seems to us so extravagant, there was in Mlle. de Scudéry a serious Genlis, a Miss Edgeworth; in short, shall I say it? an excellent *schoolmistress* for high society and the young ladies of rank of the seventeenth century.

On every possible social subject she proceeds thus: she gives a complete little course, too complete sometimes, in which she combines the historical examples she has collected with the anecdotes she gathers in the society of her day. She analyses all, expatiates on everything; on perfumes, on pleasures, on desires, on qualities and virtues; once, she even makes observations as a natural philosopher on the colour of wings and the flight of butterflies. She conjectures, she

refines, she symbolises; she seeks and gives reasons
for everything.   Never was so much use made of the
word *car* [for, because].   There are days when she is
a grammarian, an academician, when she discourses
on synonyms, and carefully elicits the meaning of
words; in what, for instance, do *joy* and *enjoyment*
differ; whether *magnificence* is not an heroic and
royal quality rather than a virtue; for magnificence is
suitable for certain persons only, whereas virtues are
suitable for all; how *magnanimity* includes more
things than *generosity,* which usually has narrower limits, so much so that we may at times be very generous
without being truly magnanimous.   Some of her little
Essays are charmingly headed, such as "Ennui without cause."   In some of these "Conversations" Mlle.
de Scudéry seems to us a Nicole among women; with
more refinement, perhaps, but with a background of
pedantry and stiffness, which that ingenious theologian never had.   And, besides, Nicole sums up all in
God and by thoughts of the final end; whereas Mlle.
de Scudéry goes no farther than the laudation and
apotheosis of the king; into which she puts an adroitness and special ingenuity that Bayle remarks upon,
and which is slightly displeasing.

The fact is, this estimable woman, long ill-used by
fortune, had early accustomed herself to pay compliments which were useful to her; a little wordly wisdom was at the bottom of all her bad taste.   More
vapid laudation was never combined with a mania

for correcting the little faults of the society around
her. But what of that! She needed to sell her books
and to place them under illustrious patronage. Besides
which, to describe her friends and acquaintances at
full length, their town-houses and their country-
houses,—all that served, while flattering their vanity,
to fill pages and swell a volume. Sappho was not
above these little reasons of trade. "Upon my word,"
says Tallemant, "she needs to set all stones to work;
when I think of it I forgive her." Little gifts, emolu-
ments, pensions, she liked to add such positive proofs
to the consideration she received, which never failed
her. All this contributed to lower the moralist in her
somewhat, and to restrict her sight to the narrow
circle of the society of her day.

At certain points, however, we think we feel a firm
and almost virile mind, which approaches lofty subjects with subtle reasoning, which comprehends their
diverse aspects, and which, faithful always to consecrated opinions, is, above all, guided by considerations of decorum.

Mlle. de Scudéry was approaching her sixtieth year
when Boileau appeared, and began, in his first Satires
(1665) to ridicule the great romances, and relegate
Cyrus to the class of admirations no longer permissible to any but country gentlemen. The war boldly
declared by Boileau against a false style which had
had its day, and existed only as a remains of superstition, gave it a mortal blow, and from that day Mlle.

de Scudéry was to the new generation a superannuated writer.   Mme. de La Fayette reduced her still further to the rank of venerable antiquities by publishing her little novels, especially that of the *Princesse de Clèves,* in which she showed how it was possible to be succinct, natural, and delicate.   In vain might we try to-day to protest against the irrefragable verdict, and to enumerate all the testimonials of consolation given to Mlle. de Scudéry, the letters of Mascaron, Fléchier, Mme. de Brinon, the directress of Saint-Cyr, the eulogies of Godeau, of Segrais, of Huet, Bonhours, and Pellisson.   The latter, who distressed and supplanted Conrart, became, as we know, the proclaimed lover of Mlle. de Scudéry, her platonic adorer, whom he celebrated in a score of gallant verses under the name of Sappho.   But if anything proves to me that Pellisson, in spite of his elegance and the purity of his diction, was never a true classic and for ever ignored the real Graces, it is precisely his declared taste for such an idol.   We cannot conclude anything from the compliments addressed by Mme. de Sévigné and Mme. de Maintenon to Mlle. de Scudéry, then an old woman; those women of gracious demeanour and high breeding continued to respect in her, when they spoke to her, one of the admirations of their youth.   As for the other names I have quoted (I except none) it is not, the reader will kindly remark, by good taste or sound and judicious taste that they shine; they have all kept, more or less, a marked tinge of the hôtel Rambouillet, and they are, in some respects, behind the age. The admiration for Mlle. de Scudéry is a touchstone which tests them all and judges them.

The French Academy awarded for the first time in 1671 the prize for Eloquence, founded by Balzac. This prize, in its origin, was to be given to a discourse or species of sermon on some Christian virtue. The first subject designated by Balzac was "On Praise and Fame." Mlle. de Scudéry wrote for it and obtained the prize, to the great applause of all that were left of the veteran academicians of the days of Richelieu. The Muse who thus carried off at a stroke the first crown, leading the procession of future laureates, was at that time sixty-four years of age.

She continued to grow old and to survive her renown, being literally annihilated in the outside world, though still enjoying fame in her chamber behind closed doors. Her worth and her estimable qualities won her, to the last, a little court of friends, who spoke of her as "the first unmarried woman of the world" and "the marvel of the age of Louis-le-Grand." When she died, June 2, 1701, the *Journal des Savants* of the following month registered these pompous eulogies. About the same time, in the same quarter of the Marais, lived and grew old, though nine years less aged than herself, a woman who was truly marvellous, who had really the grace,

the easy urbanity, the freshness and virility of mind,
the gift of rejuvenation — all, in short, that Mlle. de
Scudéry had not: I mean Ninon de l'Enclos.   There
is a lesson in taste in the juxtaposition of those
names.

However that may be, Mlle. de Scudéry deserves
that just ideas should be attached to hers.   Her novels
obtained a vogue that marks a precise date in the
history of manners and morals, and in the education
of society.   We shall always remember that a volume
of *Cyrus* was sent to the Great Condé, when a
prisoner at Vincennes, to amuse him; and to M.
d'Andilly, hermit of Port-Royal, a volume of *Clélie*,
to flatter him with a description of his desert.   With
her false apparatus of imagination and false historical
paraphernalia, Mlle. de Scudéry was, after all, not
more absurd than Mme. Cottin a few years ago.
The masquerading attire was merely borrowed: what
was really and essentially her own was her method
of observing and painting the society about her, of
seizing on the fly the persons of her acquaintance,
and putting them, all alive, into her books, where
she makes them converse with wit and shrewdness.
It is on this side that I judge her, and while recognising much distinction and ingenious sagacity of
analysis, much moral anatomy, I must add that the
whole is abstract, subtile, the reasoning overdone,
with too much of the thesis about it; lacking in
buoyancy, without illumination, dry to the core, and

not agreeable. It resembles La Motte and Fontenelle, but with much less ease and freedom than either of them. She "distinguishes," she divides, she subdivides, she classifies, she teaches. Never any freshness; the delicacy itself soon becomes didactic and far-fetched. Even in her little summer-houses, amid the parks and gardens she describes, she is careful to put an inkstand. Such appears to me, in spite of all my efforts to represent her to myself as more agreeable, the geographer of the *Pays de Tendre,* the Sappho of Pellisson. If, therefore, I must come to some conclusion and reply to the question with which we started, I am compelled to attach to the name of Mlle. de Scudéry an idea, not of ridicule, rather of esteem, a very serious esteem, but not in the least an idea of attractiveness or grace.

A spinster of such great worth and no grace is, nevertheless, unsatisfactory to paint, and even painful to point out; one would so much rather put in all that was lacking in her!

M. Cousin has lately attempted to make a complete revolution in honour of Mlle. de Scudéry, and in favour of her *Grand Cyrus.* By the help of a printed key, known to exist in the Bibliothèque de l'Arsenal, and of another key, in manuscript, in the Bibliothèque Mazarine, he has endeavoured to give to the novel a serious historical value in relation to the actions and deeds of arms of the Prince de Condé. The Abbé Lambert in his *Histoire Littéraire du Regne de Louis XIV,* speaking of the immense vogue of Mlle. de Scudéry's writings, gives the following explantion of it:

> "It is true that these novels, if we can call them by that name, must be regarded as a species of epic poems and true histories under disguised names. Such is *Artamène ou Le Grand Cyrus,* in which we find a considerable part of the life of Louis de Bourbon, Prince de Condé ; while *Clélie* contains a quantity of traits relating to all the illustrious personages then in France."

M. Cousin has given new and piquant and very precise proofs of the truth of this statement in all that concerns *Le Grand Cyrus,* but he goes too far when he attempts to make a military authority of Mlle. de Scudéry, and to attribute to her an importance she could not have in such matters. The fact is, that as soon as we see her Persian or Scythian personages unmasked, and their true names given by the help of a key, as M. Cousin has done with ease, but as no one had had the idea or the patience to do before him, we are convinced that Mlle. de Scudéry, to whom all was fish that came into her net, had received documents from the hôtel de Condé which, under a slight disguise, she introduced bodily into her book: the battle of Rocroy, that of Lens, the siege of Dunkerque under the name of the siege of Cumæ, are described with all their particulars; she printed her notes and extracts as she made them: this flattered the Condés, and spared her the trouble of invention; it "made copy" for the printer, a consideration we must never forget in speaking of Mlle.

de Scudéry. She little thought she would some day furnish arguments for the military discussions of future Jominis, and become herself a staff authority! But the fact remains that, through her, we have the version of the Prince de Condé and his friends on his great deeds of arms, some points of which have been subjects of controversy. She is the faithful echo of the hôtel de Condé in such matters, just as she was the echo of the hôtel de Rambouillet in matters of taste.

NOTE: Sainte Beuve omits to do justice to Mlle. de Scudéry on a point that gives true glory to her name. She was one of a small band who did a work for which France and the world can never be too grateful.

At the beginning of the seventeenth century France had no standard of national language ; spoken language was chiefly a variety of dialects; written language was chiefly a learned jargon. Polite manners and personal refinement did not exist. The nobles, who were the sole arbiters of manners, morals, and language, were soldiers trained to war and to the coarse habits of a camp. Women had little influence ; there was no such thing as the *home ;* the only places for social meeting were dark bedrooms so ill-furnished that the company sat on the floor, or vast halls, like those at Blois, where half a regiment could be quartered.

Such was the state of society when a woman, quietly and without pretension, opened the way to as great a revolution and reform as history can show. In 1608, Mme. de Rambouillet resigned a distinguished place at Court to devote herself to her family, to study, to the cultivation of her mind by intercourse with other choice minds of men and women whom she attracted to her house in the rue Saint Thomas du Louvre. Such was the beginning of the far-famed hôtel de Rambouillet, where the art of conversation was born, where women devoted themselves to the pleasures of the intellect, where men of learning were sought and honoured, where persons of intelligence were received on equal terms without regard to their condition in life, where great lords learned to respect writers, while women held an ascendency over all which powerfully contributed to refine and polish both writers and warriors. The possibilities of the French language, and of a future literature were the chief topics of conversation but not the only ones; social manners, religion, politics were also discussed. Among the men who frequented that salon we find the Prince de Condé, Cardinal Richelieu, La Rochefoucauld, Corneille, Bossuet; among women, Mme. de Longueville, Mme. de La Fayette, Mme. de Sévigné, Mlle. de Scudéry, who may be called the historian of the coterie, for her novels are really a portrait-gallery of all these choice persons. It is true that her books are unreadable now and exasperating to literary taste; but we should remember that she made part of a great pioneer work, in which all the actors laid stepping-stones by which social life, literature, manners, refinement, the status of women, were to rise, and rise rapidly to higher things. With this before our minds we can overlook the Carte du Tendre (Map of the Country of Tenderness)— which, by the way, was only a bit of private nonsense which her friends unwisely persuaded her to put into *Clélie*—and turn to her solid advice to women, given in her *Grand Cyrus:*

"I leave you to judge whether I am wrong in wishing that women should know how to read, and read with application. There are some women of great natural parts who never read anything; and what seems to me the strangest thing of all is that those intelligent women prefer to be horribly bored when alone, rather than accustom themselves to read, and so gather company in their minds by choosing such books, either grave or gay, as suit their inclinations. It is certain that reading enlightens the mind so clearly and forms the judgment so well that without it conversation can never be as apt or as thorough as it might be. . . . I want women to be neither learned nor ignorant, but to employ a little better the advantages that nature has given them. I want them to adorn their minds as well as their persons. This is not incompatible with their lives; there are many agreeable forms of knowledge which women may acquire thoroughly without departing from the modesty of their sex, provided they make good use of them. And I therefore wish with all my heart that women's minds were less idle than they are, and that I myself might profit by the advice I give to others."

These words, be it remembered, were written by a woman in the dawn of "culture."

In the history of the hôtel de Rambouillet the reader is referred to M. Charles Livet's *Précieux et Précieuses;* M. Victor Cousin's *La Société Française au XVIIᵉ Siècle*; also to M. Auguste Brachet's *Histoire de la Langue Française.*—Tr.

IV.

Moliere.

IV.

Molière.

IN poesy, in literature, there is a class of men
beyond comparison, even among the very first;
not numerous, five or six in all, perhaps, since the
beginning, whose characteristic is universality, eternal humanity, intimately mingled with the painting of
manners and morals and the passions of an epoch.
Facile geniuses, strong and fruitful, their principal
trait lies in this mixture of fertility, firmness, and
frankness; it is knowledge and richness at the foundation; true indifference to the employment of means
and conventional styles, every framework, every
point of departure suiting them to enter upon their
subject; it is active production multiplying through
obstacles, the plenitude of art, obtained frequently
without artifices or retarding apparatus.

In the Greek past, after the grand figure of Homer,
who begins this class so gloriously and gives us
the primitive genius of the noblest portion of humanity, we are puzzled to know whom to take next.
Sophocles, fruitful as he seems to have been, human
as he shows himself in the harmonious expression o*

sentiments and sorrows,—Sophocles stands so perfect in outline, so sacred, if I may use the word, in form and attitude, that we cannot take him in idea from his purely Greek pedestal. Famous comedians are lacking; we have only the name of Menander, who was perhaps the most pleasant in that class of genius; for with Aristophanes a marvellous fancy, so Athenian, so charming, injures his universality. In Rome I see no one but Plautus; Plautus ill-appreciated still, profound and varied painter, director of a troop of actors, actor and author himself like Shakespeare and like Molière, whose legitimate ancestor we must count him. But Latin literature was too directly imported, too artificial from the first, copied as it was from the Greek, to admit of much unfettered genius. The most prolific of the great writers of that literature are also "literary men" and rhymers in soul—Ovid and Cicero for instance. Nevertheless, it has the honour of having produced the two most admirable poets of all literatures of imitation, study, and taste—those chastened and perfected types, Virgil and Horace.

It is to modern times and the Renaissance that we must turn for the men whom we are seeking. Shakespeare, Cervantes, Rabelais, Molière, with two or three later of unequal rank, and that is all; we can characterise them by their resemblances. These men had divers and thwarted destinies; they suffered, they struggled, they loved. Soldiers, physicians, comedians, captives, they found it hard to live; poverty,

MOLIÈRE.
From a steel engraving.

passions, impediments, the hindering of enterprises,
—they endured all. But their genius rose above their
shackles and, without resenting the narrowness of the
struggle, kept its neck from the collar and its elbows
free. You have seen true, natural beauty force itself
to the light amid poverty, unhealthy air, and mean life;
you have, though rarely, perhaps, encountered young
girls of the poorer classes who seem to you formed
and illumined, heaven knows how, with a grand perfection of body, whose very finger-nails are elegant;
such beings keep the idea of the noble human race,
the image of the gods, from perishing. And thus
these rare geniuses, of grand and plastic beauty,—
beauty inborn and genuine,—triumph with an easy
air under the most opposing conditions; they develop,
they assert themselves invincibly. They do not develop merely by chance and at the mercy of circumstances, like such secondary geniuses as Ovid,
Dryden, or the Abbé Prévost, for instance. No: their
works, as prompt, as numerous as those of minds
that are chiefly facile, are also entire, strong, cohering
to an end when necessary, perfected again and again,
and sublime. But this perfection is never to them the
solicitude, sometimes excessive, the constantly chastened prudence of the studious and polished school of
poets, the Grays, Popes, and Boileaus, poets whom I
admire and enjoy as much as any one, and whose
scrupulous correctness is, I know, an indispensable
quality, a charm, and who seem to have taken for

their motto, Vauvenarque's admirable saying: "Clearness is the varnish of masters." In the very perfection of the superior poets there is something freer, bolder, more irregularly born, incomparably more fertile, more independent of ingenious fetters; something that goes of itself, that sports; something that amazes and disconcerts the distinguished contemporary poets by its inventive resources, even in the lesser details of their profession. It was thus that Boileau, among his many natural causes for surprise, cannot refrain from asking Molière where he "found rhymes."

Rightly understood, these excellent spirits hold a middle place between the poesy of primitive epochs and that of the civilised and cultivated centuries; between the Homeric and the Alexandrine periods. They are the glorious, still mighty representatives, the distinct and individual continuators of the first epochs in the bosom of the second. In all things there comes a first blossom, a first and full harvest; these happy mortals lay their hand upon it and fill the earth, once for all, with millions of germs; after them, around them, others strive and watch and glean. These teeming geniuses, no longer the divine old men, the blind of fable, read, compare, imitate like others of their day, but are not thereby prevented from creating as in the dawning ages. Their productions are, no doubt, unequal, but among them we find masterpieces of the combination of the human

with art: they know art by this time; they grasp it
in its maturity and to its full extent, but without
reasoning upon it as others do around them; they
practise it night and day with an admirable absence
of consciousness and literary fatuity. Often they die
(a little as it was in the primitive epochs) before their
works are all printed, or at any rate collected and
made lasting, unlike their contemporaries the poets
and *littérateurs* of the salons, who attend to such
matters early. Such is their negligence and their
prodigality. They abandon themselves completely,
especially to the good sense of the people, to the decisions of the multitude; of which, however, they
know the chances and risk as well as any of the poets
who scorn the common people. In a word, these
grand individuals seem to me to come down from the
very genius of poetic humanity, and to be tradition
living and perpetuated—an irrefutable embodiment.

Molière is one of these illustrious witnesses. Although he chiefly grasped the comic side, the dis-
cordances, vices, deformities, and eccentricities of
mankind, seldom touching the pathetic side, and then
only as a passing accessory, yet, when he does so,
he yields to none, even the highest, so much does he
excel in his own manner and in every direction from
freest fancy to gravest observation, so amply does he
occupy as king all the regions of social life that he
chooses for his own.

Molière belongs to the age in which he lived by his

picturing of certain peculiar oddities and the presentation of customs and manners, but he is, in fact,
of all ages; he is the man of human nature. To obtain the measure of his genius nothing serves better
than to see with what facility he fastens to his century
and detaches himself from it; how precisely he adapts
himself to it and with what grandeur he can issue
from it. The illustrious men, his contemporaries,
Boileau, Racine, Bossuet, Pascal, are far more specially
men of their time, of Louis XIV's epoch, than Molière.
Their genius (I speak of the greatest of them) bears
the hall-mark of the moment when they came, which
would, probably, have been quite other in other times.
What would Bossuet be to-day? What would Pascal
write? Racine and Boileau fitted marvellously the
reign of Louis XIV in all its youthful, brilliant, gallant, victorious, sensible parts. Bossuet dominated
that reign at its apogee, before bigotry set in, but
during a period already loftily religious. Molière,
who would, I think, have felt oppressed by that religious authority, growing more and more stringent,
and who died in good time to escape it,—Molière, who
belonged like Boileau and Racine (though much older
than they) to the first period, was far more independent of it, although he paints it more to the life than
any one. He adds to the lustre of that majestic aspect
of the great century; but he is neither stamped by it,
nor confined to it, nor narrowed to it; he proportions
himself to it, he does not inclose himself within it.

The sixteenth century had been, as a whole, a vast decomposition of the old religious, Catholic, and feudal society; the advent of philosophy into minds, and of the middle classes into society. But this incoming was done amid disturbances, disorders, an orgie of intellects and the fiercest material anarchy, chiefly in France and by means of Rabelais and the League. The mission of the seventeenth century was to repair this disorder, to reorganise society and religion; from the time of Henri IV it thus proclaimed itself, and in its highest monarchical expression under Louis XIV its mission was crowned, and with pomp. I shall not attempt here to enumerate all the stern efforts that were made, from the beginning of the seventeenth century, in the centres of religion, by communities, endowed congregations, by reformed abbeys, and in the bosom of the University and of the Sorbonne, to rally the legions of Jesus Christ and reconstitute doctrine. In literature it is evident, and readily explained.

To the Gallic, jovial, indecent, irreverent literature of Marot, Bonaventure, Desperiers, Rabelais, Regnier, etc., to the pagan literature, Greek, epicurean, of Ronsard, Baif, Jodelle, etc., philosophical and sceptical of Montaigne and Charron, succeeded one of a very different and opposite character. Malherbe, man of form, of style, of a caustic, even cynical mind (like M. de Buffon in the intervals of his noble work), — Malherbe, a freethinker at heart, has nothing

Christian about his Odes except their exterior; but the genius of Corneille, father of Polyeucte and Pauline, was already profoundly Christian. So was that of d'Urfé. Balzac, vain and pompous *bel esprit,* learned rhetorician busy with words, has forms and ideas that hold firmly to orthodoxy. The school of Port-Royal was founded; the antagonist of doubt and of Montaigne, Pascal, appeared. The detestable poetic school of Louis XIII—Boisrobert, Ménage, Costar, Conrart, d' Assoucy, Saint-Armant, etc., did not enter the path of reform; that school is not serious, scarcely moral, quite Italian, a mere insipid repetition of the literature of the Valois. But that which succeeds and smothers it under Louis XIV comes, by degrees, to faith and the observance of law — witness Boileau, Racine, Bossuet. La Fontaine himself, in the midst of his good-humoured frailties and wholly of the sixteenth century as he was, had fits of religion when he wrote the *Captivité de Saint-Malc* and the epistle to Mme. de La Sablière, and he ended by repentance. In a word, the farther we advance in the period called that of Louis XIV the more we find literature, poesy, the pulpit, the stage, taking on a religious and Christian character; the more they evidence, even in the general sentiments they express, a return to belief in revelation, to humanity as seen *in* and *by* Jesus Christ. This is one of the most characteristic and most profound features of that immortal literature. The seventeenth century rose *en masse* and made a dike between the sixteenth and the eighteenth centuries, which it separates.

But Molière,— I say it without conveying either praise or moral blame, and simply as a proof of the freedom of his genius,—Molière does not come within this point of view. Although his figure and his work appear and stand forth more than all others in this admirable frame of the great epoch of Louis the Great, he stretches and reaches forward, backward, without, and beyond; he belongs to a calmer thought, more vast, more unconcerned, more universal. The pupil of Gassendi, the friend of Bernier, of Chapelle, and of Resnault is directly connected with the philosophy and literature of the sixteenth century; he had no antipathy against that century and what remained of it: he entered into no reaction, religious or literary, as did Bossuet, Racine, Boileau, and three-fourths of Louis XIV's century. He is of the posterity of Rabelais, Montaigne, Larivey, Regnier, of the authors of the *Satyre Menippée;* he has, or would have had, no difficulty in coming to an understanding with Lamothe-le-Vayer, Naudé, or even Gui Patin, that carping personage, doctor of medicine though he was.

Molière is naturally of the society of Ninon, of Mme. de Sablière before her conversion; he welcomes at Auteuil Des Barreax and a number of young seigneurs not a little libertine.

I do not, by any means, intend to say that Molière, in his work or in his thought, was a decided free-

thinker; that he had any system on such subjects, or
that (in spite of his translation of Lucretius, his free
jesting, and his various *liaisons*) he did not have a
foundation of moderate, sensible religion, such as accorded with the custom of the times, a religion which
reappeared at his last hour, and had already burst
forth with such strength from Cléante's lips in *Tartuffe*. No; Molière the wise, an Ariste of calm propriety, the enemy of all excesses and absurdities of
mind, the father of that Philinte whom Lélius, Eras-
mus, and Atticus would have recognised, had nothing
of the licentious and cynical braggadocio of the Saint-
Amants, Boisroberts, and their kind. He was sincere
in being indignant at the malicious insinuations which,
from the date of the *École des Femmes,* his enemies
cast upon his religion.

But what I want to establish, and which characterises him among his contemporaries of genius, is that
he habitually saw human nature in itself, in its universality of all periods; as Boileau and La Bruyère saw
and painted it often, I know, but Molière without
mixture such as we see in Boileau's *Épitre sur
l'Amour de Dieu,* and La Bruyère's discussion on
Quietism. He paints humanity as if it had no growth;
and this, it must be said, was the more possible to
him, painting it, as he did especially, in its vices and
blemishes: tragedy evades Christianity less easily.
Molière separates humanity from Jesus Christ, or rather
he shows us the one to its depths without taking

much account of the other.   In this he detaches himself from his century.   In the famous scene of the
Pauper he gives, without a thought of harm, a speech
to Don Juan which he was forced to suppress, such
storms did it raise: "You spend your life in praying
to God and you are dying of hunger; take this money;
I give it you from love of humanity."   The beneficence and the philanthropy of the eighteenth century,
that of d'Alembert, Diderot, and Holbach, are in that
saying.   And it was Molière who said of the Pauper
when he brought back the gold piece that other saying, so often quoted, so little understood, it seems to
me, in its gravest meaning,—a saying that escaped
from a habit of mind essentially philosophical: "Where
must virtue needs go niche itself!"—*Où la vertu va-
t-elle se nicher!*   No man of Port-Royal or its con-
geners (note this well) would have had such a
thought; the contrary would have seemed to him
more natural, the poor man being, in the eyes of the
Christian, an object of special mercies and virtues.   It
was he, too, who, talking with Chapelle of the philosophy of Gassendi, their common master, said,
while disputing as to the theory of atoms, "Never
mind the morality of it."   Molière belongs simply, as
I think, to the religion, I do not say of his Don Juan
or of Epicurus, but of Chremes in Terence: *Homo
sum*.   We may apply to him in a serious sense Tartuffe's speech: "A man   .   .   .   a man, in short!"
This man knew frailties and was not surprised by

them; he practised good more than he believed in it; he reckoned upon vices, and his most burning indignation was uttered by a laugh. He considered this sad humanity as an old child now incurable, to be corrected a little, but, above all, to be soothed by amusing it.

To-day, when we judge of things from a distance and by clear results, Molière seems to us much more radically aggressive against the society of his time than he thought he was: this is a danger we should guard against in judging him. Among the illustrious contemporaries I cited just now, there is one, only one, the one whom we should be least inclined to connect with our poet, but who, nevertheless, like him, and more than him, brought into question the principal foundations of the society of those days, and who looked in the face, without prejudices of any kind, birth, rank, and property. Pascal (for he is that audacious man) made use of the ruin he proclaimed of all things about him solely to cling with terror to the pillar of the temple, to clasp more convulsively the Cross. They both, Pascal and Molière, seem to us to-day the most formidable witnesses against the society of their times. Molière, in a vast space reaching to the edge of the religious inclosure, foraging with his troop every corner of the field of the old society, delivering, pell-mell, to laughter and ridicule, titled conceit, conjugal inequality, captious hypocrisy, often alarming, by the same stroke, righteous subordination, true piety, and marriage: Pascal, at the very heart of orthodoxy, making the very arches of the edifice tremble, after his fashion, with the cries of anguish that he utters, and putting the strength of Samson into grasping the sacred pillar. But while accepting this connection, which has, I think, both novelty and accuracy, we must not ascribe to Molière more intention to overthrow than to Pascal; we must even grant him less calculation of the whole bearing of the matter. Had Plautus a systematic reservation in his mind when he laughed at usury, prostitution, slavery, and all the other vices and motives of ancient society ?

The moment when Molière came upon the scene was exactly that which suited the liberty that he had, and that which he gave himself. Louis XIV, still young, supported him in all his bold and free endeavours, and protected him against whoever attacked him. In *Tartuffe,* and also in the tirade of Don Juan against advancing hypocrisy, Molière foresaw with his divining eye the sad end of a noble reign, and he hastened, when it was with great difficulty possible and when it seemed to be useful, to denounce with pointed finger the growing vice. If he had lived till 1685, till the declared reign of Mme. de Maintenon, or had he lived from 1673 to 1685, during that glorious period of the ascendancy of Bossuet, he would no doubt have been less efficaciously protected, and he might have been persecuted at the last. We ought fully to compre-

hend — through understanding that universal, free,
natural, philosophical mind, indifferent, at the least,
to what they were seeking to restore—the anger of
the religious oracles of those days against Molière, the
cruel severity of expression with which Bossuet scoffs
and triumphs over the actor dying on the stage, and
even the indignation of the wise Bourdaloue in his
pulpit after the production of *Tartuffe*—Bourdaloue,
friend of Boileau that he was! We can even conceive
the naïve terror of the Jansenist Baillet, who in his
Jugements des Savants begins his article on Molière
with these words: " Monsieur de Molière is one of the
most dangerous enemies to the Church of Jesus Christ
that this century or the world has produced," etc.
It is true, however, that some of the clergy, more
liberal, more men of the world, were less severe upon
him. Père Rapin praised him at great length in his
Reflexions sur la Poétique, and cavilled only at the
carelessness of the winding up of his plots. Bonhours
made him an epitaph in French verse both agreeable
and judicious.

Molière was so thoroughly *man* in the freest sense,
that he obtained, later, the anathemas of the haughty
and so-called reforming philosophy just as he had first
won those of the ruling episcopacy. On four different counts—*l'Avare, Le Misanthrope, Georges Dan--
din,* and *Le Bourgeois Gentilhomme*—Jean Jacques
will not listen to wit, and spares him no more than
Bossuet did.

All this is simply to say that, like Shakespeare and Cervantes, like three or four superior geniuses through the course of ages, Molière is a painter of human nature to its depths, without acceptance or concern about worship, fixed dogma, or formal interpretation; that in attacking the society of his time he represented the life of the greater number; and that in the midst of established manners and morals, which he chastised to the quick, he is found to have written of mankind.

Jean-Baptiste Poquelin was born in Paris, January 15, 1622, not, as was long thought, under the columns of the Market, but in a house in the rue Saint-Honoré, at the corner of the rue des Vieilles-Étuves. He belonged, through mother and father, to families of upholsterers. His father, who, besides his trade, held the office of "valet-upholsterer" to the king, intended that his son should succeed him; and young Poquelin, apprenticed when a mere child in the shop, knew nothing at fourteen years of age but how to read, write, and cipher, the necessary knowledge for his trade. His maternal grandfather, who loved the theatre, took him sometimes to the hôtel de Bourgogne, where Bellerose played high comedy, and Gautier-Garguille, Gros-Guillaume, and Turlupin played farce. After each evening at the theatre young Poquelin was more sad, more absent-minded at his work in the shop, more disgusted with the prospect of his trade. We can imagine what those dreamy mornings following a play were for the adolescent genius before whom, in the novelty of apparition, human life was beginning to unroll itself like a perpetual stage scene. He at last confided in his father, and, supported by his grandfather who "spoiled" him, he obtained permission to study. He appears to have been boarded out and to have attended as a day-scholar the college of Clermont, afterwards that of Louis-le-Grand, managed by Jesuits.

Five years sufficed him to complete the whole course of the studies, philosophy included; moreover, he made useful acquaintances in the school who had great influence on his future fate. The Prince de Conti, brother of the Great Condé, was one of his schoolmates and remembered him ever after. That prince, though at first, and as long as he remained under the direction of the Jesuits, ecclesiastically inclined, loved the theatre and endowed it magnificently. When converted later to the Jansenist side, he retracted his first liking to the point of writing against the theatre, but seems to have transmitted to his illustrious elder brother the care of protecting Molière to the last. Chapelle was also a student friend of Poquelin and procured him the acquaintance and the lessons of Gassendi, his tutor. These private lessons by Gassendi were likewise shared by Bernier, the future traveller, and by Hesnault, known for his invocation of Venus; they must have influenced Molière's manner of viewing things, less by the details of the instruction than by the spirit that emanated from it, which all the young hearers shared. It is, in truth, remarkable how free and independent of spirit were all the men who came from this school — Chapelle, the frank speaker, the practical and lax epicurean; Hesnault, the poet, who attacked the powerful Colbert and delighted in translating all that was boldest in the choruses of Seneca's tragedies; Bernier, who roamed the world and came back knowing how, under diverse customs and costumes, man is everywhere the same, replying to Louis XIV, when he asked him in which country life seemed to him best, that it was Switzerland, and deducing on all points philosophic conclusions in the select little circle of Mlle. de L'Enclos and Mme. de La Sablière.

It is also to be remarked how those four or five leading minds came of the pure *bourgeoisie* and of the people: Chapelle, bastard son of a rich magistrate; Bernier, a poor boy, associated out of charity in the education of Chapelle; Hesnault, son of a baker in Paris; Poquelin, son of an upholsterer; and Gassendi, their master, not a gentleman (as Descartes stated), but the son of simple villagers. Molière took the idea of translating Lucretius from these conferences with Gassendi; he did it partly in verse and partly in prose, according to the nature of the topic; but the manuscript is lost. Another comrade who forced himself into these lessons of philosophy was Cyrano de Bergerac, suspected, in his turn, of impiety by certain verses on Agrippina, but convicted, above all, of bad taste. Molière took, in after years, two scenes from Cyrano's *Pédant joué* which certainly did not disfigure *Les Fourberies de Scapin;* it was his habit, as he said on this occasion, to take his property wherever he found it.

On leaving school Poquelin had to take the office of his father, then too old for service, as valet-upholsterer to the king. For his novitiate, he followed Louis XIII on the journey to Narbonne, in 1641, and witnessed on his return the execution of Cinq-Mars and De Thou; bitter and bloody sarcasm on human justice! Instead of continuing in the paternal office during the years that followed he seems to have studied law at Orléans, where he was admitted to the bar. But his taste for the theatre drew him to Paris, where, having haunted, it was said, the harlequin booths on the Pont Neuf and followed the Italians and their Scaramouche, he put himself at the head of a group of young actors in society, which became before long a regular and professional troop.

The two brothers Béjart, their sister Madeleine, and Duparc, called Gros-René, formed part of this strolling company which called itself " The Illustrious Theatre." Our poet broke away at this time from his family and the Poquelins, and took the name of Molière. He went with his troop through all the different quarters of Paris and then into the provinces. It is said that he played at Bordeaux a *Thébaïde,* an attempt at serious drama, which failed. Farces, Italian plots, and impromptus he did not spare, such as the *Médecin volant* and the *Jalousie du Barbouillé* — the original sketches of the *Médecin malgré lui* and *Georges Dandin,* which have been preserved. He travelled about haphazard; well received by the Duc d'Épernon at Bordeaux, by the Prince de Conti wherever they met, hired by d'Assoucy, whom he afterwards received and entertained like a prince himself; hospitable, liberal, a good comrade, in love often, trying all the passions, playing on every stage, leading his train of youth like a joyous Fronde through the land, with a fine stock in his mind of original human characters. It was in the course of this wandering life that, in 1653 at Lyons, he brought out *L'Étourdi,* his first regular play. He was then thirty-one years old.

Molière, as we see, began his career by the practice of life and passions before painting them. But it must not be thought that his inward existence had two separate and successive parts, like that of many eminent moralists and satirists — a first part, active and more or less ardent; then, the fire subsiding from excesses or from age, a second part of sour, biting observation, disillusion, in short, which harks back to motives, scrutinises, and mocks them. That is not at all the case with Molière, or with any of the great men endowed, to his degree, with the genius that creates. Distinguished men who go through this double phase, reaching the second quickly, acquire, as they advance, only a shrewd, sagacious, critical talent,

like M. de La Rochefoucauld, for example; they have
no animating impulse nor power of creation. Dramatic genius, that of Molière in particular, has this
that is singular about it: its method of proceeding is
wholly different and more complex. In the midst of
the passions of his youth, of hot-headed, credulous
transports like those of the mass of men, Molière had,
even then, in a high degree, the gift of observing and
reproducing, the faculty of sounding and seizing hidden springs which he knew how to bring into play to
the great amusement of every one; and later, in the
midst of his complete, sad knowledge of the human
heart and its divers motives, from the height of his
melancholy as a contemplative philosopher, he still
preserved, in his own heart, the youth of active impressions, the faculty of passions, of love and its
jealousies—a sacred heart indeed! Sublime contradiction, and one we love to find in the life of a great
poet; an indefinable assemblage which corresponds
with what is most mysterious in the talent of dramatic
comedy; I mean the painting of bitter realities by
means of lively, easy, joyous personages who all have
natural characters; the deepest probing of the heart
of man exhibiting itself in active and original beings,
who translate it to the eye by simply being themselves!

It is related that during his stay at Lyons Molière,
who was already rather tenderly allied with Madeleine
Béjart, fell in love with Mlle. Duparc (or the person

who became so by marrying the comedian Duparc) and also with Mlle. de Brie, who were both members of another troop of actors. He succeeded, in spite, it is said, of the Béjart, in engaging the two actresses for his own troop, and, repulsed by the haughty Duparc, he found consolations in Mlle. de Brie, to which he afterwards returned during the miseries of his married life. Some have even gone so far as to find in the scene between Clitandre, Armande, and Henriette, in the first act of *Les Femmes Savantes,* the reminiscence of a situation anterior by twenty years to the writing of the comedy. No doubt between Molière, much inclined to love, and the young actresses whom he managed ties were formed, variable, tangled, often interrupted, sometimes resumed; but it would be rash, I think, to try to find any definite trace of them in his works, and what has been said on this particular point, forgetting the twenty years' interval, seems to me not justified.

The Prince de Conti, who was not yet Jansenist, had made Molière and his troop of the *Illustre Théâtre* act on several occasions at his house in Paris. Being in Languedoc, he summoned his former schoolmate, who came with his actors from Pézénas to Montpellier, where the prince was. There he made use of his most varied repertory, and of his last play, *L'Étourdi,* to which he added the charming comedy of the *Dépit amoureux.* The prince, enchanted, wanted to engage him as his secretary in place of the poet Sarazin, lately dead. Molière refused out of attachment to his troop, love of his profession, and of an independent life. After several more years of strolling in the South, where we find him bound by friendship to the painter Mignard at Avignon, he came nearer to the capital and settled for a time at Rouen, where he obtained permission not, as some have conjectured, through the protection of the Prince de Conti (who became a penitent under the Bishop of Alet in 1665), but through that of Monsieur, Duc d'Orléans, to act in Paris before the king. This event took place, October 24, 1658, in the guard-room of the old Louvre, in presence of the Court and of the actors of the hôtel de Bourgogne, a perilous audience, before whom Molière and his troop risked representing *Nicomède.* That tragi-comedy over, Molière, who liked to speak as orator for the troop, and who could not on so decisive an occasion yield that rôle to any one, advanced to the footlights and after

" thanking his Majesty in very modest terms for the kindness he had shown in excusing his defects and those of his troop, who had trembled in appearing before so august an assembly, he said that his desire to have the honour to amuse the greatest king in the world had made them forget that his Majesty had in his service most excellent originals of which they themselves were feeble copies; but, inasmuch as his Majesty had been able to endure their country manners, he entreated him very humbly to allow him to give one of those little farces by which he had acquired a certain reputation in the provinces."

The *Docteur amoureux* was the piece he selected. The king, pleased with the performance, allowed

Molière's troop to establish itself in Paris under the name of the "Troop of Monsieur," and to act alternately with the Italian comedians on the stage of the Petit-Bourbon. When the building of the colonnade of the Louvre was begun, in 1660, on the site of the Petit-Bourbon, the Troop of Monsieur removed to the Palais-Royal. It became the Troop of the King in 1665; later, at Molière's death, it was united first with the Troop of the Marais, then with that of the hôtel de Bourgogne and became the *Théâtre Français*.

After the installation of Molière and his company, *L'Étourdi* and the *Dépit amoureux* were given for the first time publicly in Paris, succeeding there no less than in the provinces. Though the first of those plays is only a comedy of intrigue imitated from the Italian imbroglios, what fire already in it! what flaming petulance! what reckless activity thrilling with imagination in Mascarille! whom the stage up to that time had never known. No doubt Mascarille, such as he first appears, is only the son in direct line of the valets of Italian farce and ancient comedy, one of the thousand of that lineage anterior to Figaro: but soon, in the *Précieuses Ridicules,* he will individualise himself, he is Mascarille the marquis, a wholly modern valet in the livery of Molière alone. The *Dépit amoureux,* in spite of the unlikelihood and commonplace conventionality of its disguises and recognitions, presents, in the scene between Lucile and Éraste, a situation of heart eternally young, eternally renewed from the dialogue of Horace and Lydia; a situation that Molière himself renews in *Tartuffe* and in the *Bourgeois Gentilhomme* with success always, but never surpassing in excellence this first picture; he who knew best how to scourge and ridicule shows how well he knew love.

The *Précieuses Ridicules,* acted in 1659, attacked modern manners to the quick. In it Molière abandoned Italian plots and stage traditions to see things with his own eyes, to speak aloud and firmly, according to his nature, against the most irritating enemy of all great dramatic poets at their outset — affected and finical pedantry, the shallow taste of the alcove, which is mere distaste. It is related that on the night of the first representation of the *Précieuses*, an old man in the pit, delighted with this novel frankness, an old man who had doubtless applauded Corneille's *Menteur* seventeen years earlier, could not restrain himself from calling out, apostrophising Molière, who was playing Mascarille: "Courage! courage, Molière! that is good comedy!" At this cry, which he divined to be that of the true public and of fame, at the universal and sonorous applause that followed, Molière felt (Segrais tells us) his courage swell, and he uttered that saying of noble pride that marks his entrance upon his great career: "No longer need I study Plautus and pluck at the fragments of Menander; I have only to study the world."

Yes, Molière, the world is opening before you; you

have discovered it, and it is yours; henceforth you have only to choose your pictures. If you imitate still, it will be that you choose to do so, that you take your own wheresoever you find it; you will do it as a rival who fears no competitor, as a king to enlarge your empire. All that you borrow becomes for ever embellished and honoured.

After the rather coarse, but honest, spice of the *Cocu imaginaire,* and the pale but noble essay of *Don Garcie,* Molière returned, in the *École des Maris,* to the broad road of observation and truth with gaiety. Sganarelle, whom the *Cocu imaginaire* showed us for the first time, reappears and is developed in the *École des Maris;* Sganarelle succeeds Mascarille in Molière's favour. Mascarille was still young and a bachelor; Sganarelle is essentially a married man. Derived probably from the Italian stage, employed by Molière in the farce of the *Médecin volant,* introduced upon the regular stage in a rôle that has a little of the Scarron about it, he naturalises himself there as Mascarille had done. The Sganarelle of Molière in all his varied aspects, valet, husband, father of Lucinde, brother of Ariste, tutor, poetaster, doctor, is a personage who belongs to Molière, as Panurge to Rabelais, Falstaff to Shakespeare, Sancho to Cervantes; he is the ugly side of human nature embodied; the aged, crabbed side, morose, selfish, base, timid, by turns pitiful or humbugging, surly or absurd. At certain joyous moments, such as that when he touches the

nurse's bosom, Sganarelle reminds us of the rotund
Gorgibus who, in turn, brings back the goodman
Chrysale, that other jovial character with a paunch.
But Sganarelle, puny like his forefather, Panurge, has
left other posterity worthy of both of them, among
whom it is proper to mention Pangloss, not forgetting
Victor Hugo's Gringore. In Molière, facing Sganarelle at the highest point of the stage, stands Alceste:
Alceste, in other words, all that there is most serious,
most noble, loftiest in comedy; the point where ridicule comes close to courage, to virtue. One line
more, and the comic ceases; we reach a personage
purely generous, almost heroic and tragical. Sganarelle possesses three-fourths of the comic ladder, the
lower by himself alone, the middle he shares with
Gorgibus and Chrysale; Alceste holds the rest, the
highest—Sganarelle and Alceste; in them is all of
Molière.

Voltaire says that if Molière had written nothing
but the *École des Maris* he would still be an excellent
writer of comedy. Boileau cannot witness the *École
des Femmes* without addressing to Molière (then attacked on all sides) certain easy stanzas in which he
extols the "charming naïveté of the comedy, which
equals those of Terence supposed to be written by
Scipio." Those two amusing masterpieces were
separated in their production by the light but skilful comedy-impromptu called *Les Fâcheux,* written,
learned, and represented in fifteen days for the famous

fête at Vaux. Never did the free, quick talent of Molière for making verse show more plainly than in this satirical comedy, especially in the scenes of the piquet and the hunt. The scene of the hunt was not in the play at its first representation; but Louis XIV, pointing with his finger to M. de Soyecourt, a great huntsman, said to Molière: "There is an original you have not yet copied." The next day the scene of the huntsman was written and acted. Boileau, whose own manner of writing the play of the *Fâcheux* preceded and surpassed, thought of it, no doubt, when he asked Molière, three years later, where he "found his rhymes." The truth is, Molière never sought them; he did not habitually make his second line before the first, nor did he wait half a day or more to find in some remote corner the word that escaped him. His was the rapid vein, the ready wit of Regnier, of d'Aubigné, never haggling about a phrase or a word even at the risk of a lame line, a clumsy turn, or, at worst, an hiatus—a Duc de Saint-Simon in poesy; with a method of expression always looking forward, always sure, which each flow of thought fills out and colours.

During the fourteen years that followed his installation in Paris, and to the hour of his death in 1673, Molière never ceased to produce. For the king, for the Court, and for fêtes, for the pleasure of the public at large, for the interests of his company, for his own fame, and for posterity, Molière multiplied himself, as it were,

and sufficed for all.　Nothing hypercritical in him,
nothing of the author in his study.　True poet of
drama, his works are for the stage, for action; he does
not write them, so to speak, he plays them.　His life
as a comedian of the provinces had been somewhat
that of the primitive popular poets, the ancient rhap-
sodists, the minstrels and pilgrims of Passion; these
went about, as we know, repeating one another, taking the plots and subjects of others, adding thereto as
occasion demanded, making little account of themselves and their own individual work, and seldom
keeping "copy" of that which they represented.　It
was thus that the plots and improvisations in the
Italian manner which Molière multiplied (we have
the titles of a dozen) during his strolling years in the
provinces were lost, with the exception of two, the
Médecin volant and the *Barbouillé. L'Étourdi* and
the *Dépit amoureux,* his first regular plays, were not
printed until ten years after their appearance on the
stage (1653–1663); the *Précieuses* was printed during
its first success, but in spite of its author, as the
preface indicates, and this was no sham pretence of
gentle violence, such as so many others have practised
since.　Molière's embarrassment in going reluctantly
into print for the first time is plainly visible in that
preface.　The *Cocu imaginaire,* having had nearly
fifty representations, was not to be printed, when an
amateur of the stage, named Neufvillenaine, finding
that he had learned the play by heart, wrote it down,

published it, and dedicated the work to Molière.
That M. de Neufvillenaine knew with whom he had
to do. Molière's carelessness was such that he gave
no other edition of the play, so that the copyist admitted (what would have been plain enough without
his admission) that perhaps, in his copy, made from
memory, a quantity of misplaced words might have
slipped in. O Racine! O Boileau! what would you
have said if a third party had thus presented to the
public your cautious work in which every word has
its value? In this we can see the inborn difference
there is between Molière and the sober, careful race,
rather finical but with reason, of the Boileaus and La
Bruyères.

To guard against other thefts like that of Neufvillenaine, Molière was forced to think of publishing
his plays himself in the height of their success on the
stage. *L'École des Maris,* dedicated to his protector,
the Duc d'Orléans, is the first work he published of
his own free will; from that moment (1661) he came
into constant communication with readers. Nevertheless, we find him continually distrustful in that
direction; he feared the bookstalls in the gallery of the
Palais-Royal; he preferred to be judged "under the
candles," on the stage, by the decision of the multitude. It has been thought, from a passage in the
preface to the *Fâcheux,* that he intended to print his
remarks and almost his poetic theories with each
play; but if that passage is better understood, it will

be seen that his promise, wholly out of keeping with the cast of his genius, is not serious, but rather on his part a jest against the great logicians after Horace and Aristotle. Besides which, his poetic theory, as actor and author, will be found complete in the *Critique de l'Ecole des Femmes* and in the *Impromptu de Versailles,* where it is in action. In scene seventh of the *Critique,* is it not Molière himself who says to us through the lips of Dorante:

" You are pretty people with your rules, by which you hamper ignorant folk and bewilder us daily! It seems, to hear you talk, as if the rules of art were the greatest mysteries in the world; and yet they are only certain easy observations that good sense has made on what might mar the pleasure taken in this kind of poem: and the same good sense that formerly made those observations can make them again without the help of Horace and Aristotle. . . . Leave us to go in good faith to the things that take us by the soul, and don't seek to reason us out of finding pleasure."

To finish with this literary negligence which I have shown in Molière, and which contrasts so strongly with his ardent prodigality as a poet, and his extreme care as actor and manager, I must add that no complete edition of his works appeared during his lifetime. It was his comrade and fellow-actor, La Grange, who collected and published the whole in 1682, nine years after his death.

Molière, the most creative and the most inventive of geniuses, is the one, perhaps, who has imitated the most, and on all sides; this is still another trait which he has in common with the primitive popular poets

and the illustrious dramatists who followed them.
Boileau, Racine, André Chénier, poets of study and
taste, imitate also; but their method of imitation is
much more ingenious, circumspect, and disguised, and
it chiefly bears on details. Molière's method of imitating is far freer, fuller, and at the mercy of his memory. His enemies attacked him for stealing half his
works from the old bookstalls. He lived, during his
first manner, on the traditional Italian and Gallic farce;
after the *Précieuses* and the *École des Maris* he became
himself; he governed and overtopped his imitations,
and, without lessening them much, he mingled them
with a fund of original observation. The river continued to float wood from its banks, but the current
was wider and more and more powerful. What we
must carefully recognise is that Molière's imitations
are from all sources and infinitely varied; they have a
character of loyalty, free and easy as they are, something of that primitive life where all was in common;
although usually they are well worked-in, descending sometimes to pure detail: Plautus and Terence
for whole tales, Straparolo and Boccaccio for subject matter, Rabelais and Regnier for characters,
Boisrobert, Rotrou, and Cyrano for scenes, Horace,
Montaigne, and Balzac for simple phrases—all are
there; but all is transformed, nothing is the same. In
a word, these imitations are for us chiefly the fortunate
summary of a whole race of minds, a whole past of
comedy in a new, superior, and original type, as a

child beloved of heaven who, with an air of youth, expresses all his forbears.

Each of Molière's plays, following them in the order of their appearance, would furnish matter for a long and extended history; this work has already been done, and too well done by others for me to undertake it; to do so would be merely copying and reproducing. Around the *École des Femmes,* in 1662, and later around *Tartuffe* battles were fought as they had been round "The Cid" and were to be around *Phèdre;* those were the illustrious days for dramatic art. The *Critique de l'École des Femmes* and the *Impromptu de Versailles* sufficiently explain the first contest, which was chiefly a quarrel of taste and art, though religion slipped in àpropos of the rules of marriage given to Agnes. The *Placets au Roi* and the preface to *Tartuffe* show the wholly moral and philosophical character of the second struggle, so often and so vehemently renewed afterwards.

But what I wish to dwell on here is that, attacked by bigots, envied by authors, sought by nobles, valet to the king, and his indispensable resource in all his fêtes, Molière, troubled by passion and domestic jars, consumed with marital jealousy, frequently ill with his weak lungs and his cough, director of a company, an indefatigable actor himself while living on a diet of milk,—Molière, I say, for fifteen years was equal to all demands; at each arising necessity his genius was present and responding to it, keeping, moreover, his

times of inward inspiration and initiative. Between
the duty hurriedly paid at Versailles and at Chantilly,
and his hearty contributions for the laughter of the
bourgeoisie, Molière found time for thoughtful works
destined to become immortal. For Louis XIV, his
benefactor and supporter, he was always ready ;
L'Amour médecin was written, learned, and acted in
five days; the *Princesse d'Élide* has only the first act
in verse, the rest is in prose, for, as a witty contemporary of Molière said, "Comedy had time to fasten
only one buskin, but she appeared when the clock
struck, though the other buskin was not laced." In
the interests of his company he was sometimes obliged
to hurry work; as he did when he supplied his theatre
with a *Don Juan,* because the actors of the hôtel de
Bourgogne, and also those of Mademoiselle, had theirs,
and the statue that walked was a town marvel. But
these distractions did not keep him from thinking of
Boileau, of strict pledges, of himself, and of the human race, in the *Misanthrope,* in *Tartuffe,* in the
Femmes Savantes. The year of the *Misanthrope* is,
in this sense, the most memorable and the most sig-
nificant in Molière's life.

Boileau, let us recognise it, although we may blame
his reserves in his *Art Poétique* and his innocent and
quite permissible surprise at Molière's rhymes,—Boileau was sovereignly equitable in all that concerned
the poet, his friend, whom he called the Contemplator.
He understood and admired him in the parts most

foreign to himself; he delighted in being his assistant in the Latin macaronics of his merriest comedies; he furnished him with the malicious Greek etymologies of the *Amour médecin;* he measured in its entirety that manifold and vast faculty; and the day when Louis XIV asked him who was the rarest of the great writers who had honoured France during his reign, the rigorous judge replied without hesitation: "Molière, sire." "I did not suppose it," said Louis XIV, "but you understand the matter better than I."

Molière has been lauded in so many ways, as painter of manners and morals and human life, that I wish to indicate more especially a side which has been brought too little into light, or, I may say, ignored. Until his death, Molière was continually progressing in the *poesy* of comedy. That he progressed in moral observation and in what is called high comedy—that of the *Misanthrope, Tartuffe,* and the *Femmes Savantes*—is too evident a fact, and I shall not dwell upon it; but around and through that development, where reason grew firmer and still firmer, and observation more and more mature, we ought to admire the influx, every rising and bubbling, of the comic fancy, very frolicsome, very rich, very inexhaustible, which I distinguish strongly (though the boundaries be difficult to define) from the rather broad farce and the Scarronesque dregs in which Molière dabbled in the beginning. How shall I express it? it is the difference between some chorus of Aristophanes and certain rash outbreaks of Rabelais. The genius of ironical and biting gaiety has its lyric moments also, its pure merriment, its sparkling laugh, redoubled, almost causeless in its prolonging, aloof from reality, like a frolic flame that flutters and flits the lighter when the coarse combustion ceases — a laughter of the gods, supreme, inextinguishable. This is what many minds of fine taste, Voltaire, Vauvenargues, and others, have not felt in appreciating what are called Molière's latest farces; and Schlegel should have felt it more. He who mystically celebrated the poetic final fireworks of Calderon ought not to have been blind to these rockets of dazzling gaiety, these auroras at an opposite pole of the dramatic universe. *Monsieur de Porceaugnac,* the *Bourgeois Gentilhomme,* the *Malade imaginaire,* witness in the highest degree to this sparkling, electrifying gaiety which, in its way, rivals in fancy the " Midsummer Night's Dream " and the " Tempest." Pourceaugnac, M. Jourdain, Argant, they are the Sganarelle element continued, but more poetic, freer from the farce of the *Barbouillé,* often lifted, as it were, above realism.

Molière, compelled by Court amusements to combine his comedies with ballets, learned to run riot and display in these dances, made to order, his droll and petulant choruses of lawyers, tailors, Turks, apothecaries; genius makes of each necessity an inspiration. This issue once found, Molière's inventive imagination rushed headlong through it. The comedy-ballets of which I speak were not at all (we should be careful not to think it) concessions to the vulgar public, direct provocations to the laughter of the *bourgeoisie,* although that laugh was promoted by them; they were conceived and produced for the Court fêtes. But Molière soon took delight in them; he even made ballets and interludes to the *Malade imaginaire* of his own free will, without order from the king or intention to produce the play at Court. He flung himself into them, the great man, with a mixture of irony and gaiety of heart, in the midst of his daily sorrows, as if into an acrid and dizzy intoxication. He died in the midst of it, to the sharpest sounds of that gaiety rising to delirium. I find in Cizeron-Rival the following incident which illustrates this point:

" Two months before Molière died, M. Despréaux [Boileau] went to see him and found him much troubled with a cough, and making efforts with his lungs that seemed to threaten approaching death. Molière, rather cold naturally, showed more friendship than usual to M. Despréaux. This encouraged the latter to say : ' My poor M. Molière, you are in a pitiable state. The continual application of your mind, the continual straining of your lungs upon the stage, ought to make you resolve to give up acting. Is there no one but you in your troop who can play the leading parts ? Content yourself with composing, and leave the stage work to some of your comrades; this will do you more honour with the public, who will regard the actors as your agents; moreover, your actors, who are not any too tractable with you, will feel your authority more.' ' Ah, monsieur,' replied Molière, ' it is a matter of honour with me not to quit the stage.' ' A pretty point of honour,' said the satirist to himself, ' which consists in blackening his face to make a moustache for Sganarelle and devoting his back to the bastinades! Think of it! this man, the first of our day for wit and for the sentiments of true philosophy, this skilful censor of human follies, has a folly more extraordinary than those he scoffs at daily! That shows us how small men are.'"

Boileau did not advise Molière to abandon his comrades nor to abdicate the management, which the leader of a troop of actors might well have refused out of humanity, and for many other reasons; he urged him only to quit the boards; it was the obstinate old comedian in Molière that refused to do so.

Posterity feels otherwise; far from blaming, we love these weaknesses and contradictions in a poet of genius; they add to Molière's portrait and give to his personality an air more in keeping with that of the mass of men. Again we see him such, and one of us all, in the passions of his heart, in his domestic tribulations. The comedian Molière was born tender and easily moved to love, just as the tragedian Racine was born caustic and inclined to epigram. Without going outside of Molière's works, we find proofs of this sensibility in the tendency he always shows toward the noble and the romantic. Plautus and Rabelais, those great comic writers, show also (in spite of their reputation) traces of a sensitive, delicate faculty which surprise us joyfully in them, but especially do they delight us in Molière. There is all of Terence in him.

About the time when he was so gaily painting Arnolphe dictating the rules and regulations of marriage to Agnes, Molière, then forty years old (1662), married the young Armande Béjart, younger sister of Madeleine, and not more than seventeen years old. In spite of his passion for her, and in spite of his genius, he did not escape the misery of which he had given so many sportive descriptions. Don Gavere was less jealous than Molière, Georges Dandin and Sganarelle less deceived. After the infidelity of his wife became apparent to him his domestic life was one long torture. Warned of the success attributed to the Duc de Lauzun in his wife's good graces, he came to an explanation with her. Mademoiselle Molière fooled him as to Lauzun, by avowing an inclination for the Comte de Guiche, and got herself out of the crisis, says the chronicle, by tears and a fainting fit. Bruised and wounded by his misfortune, Molière returned to his early love for Mlle. de Brie, or rather he went to her with the tale of his sorrows, as Alceste is driven back to Éliante by the treatment of Célimène. At the time when he played the *Misanthrope,* Molière, having quarrelled with his wife, met her only on the stage, and it is difficult to suppose that between Armande, who played Célimène, and himself, representing Alceste, some allusion to their feelings and real situation did not occur. Add, by way of complicating the vexations of Molière, the presence of the elderly Béjart, an imperious creature, it appears, with little compliance. The great man made his way among these three women, often as much harassed, Chapelle says of him, as Jupiter at the siege of Ilion between the three goddesses. But I will let a contemporary of the poet speak on the chapter of his domestic sorrows:

" It was not without doing great violence to himself that Molière resolved to live with his wife in a state of indifference. His reason made him regard her as a person whose conduct rendered her unworthy of the affection of an honest man; his tenderness made him dwell on the pain he should feel in seeing her daily without making use of the privileges of marriage. He was reflecting on this one day in his garden at Auteuil, when a friend of his, Chapelle, who chanced to be walking there, came up to him and, finding him more troubled than usual, asked him several times the reason. Molière, who felt some shame at having so little firmness under a misfortune that was much in vogue, resisted as long as he could; but being in one of those fulnesses of heart so well known to persons who love, he yielded at last to the desire of relieving himself, and he owned in good faith to his friend that the manner in which he was forced to treat his wife was the cause of the depression in which he found him.

" Chapelle, who thought himself above all such things, laughed because a man like him, who knew so well how to paint the weaknesses of others, fell into the very one he was ridiculing every day; and he showed him that the most ridiculous thing of all was to love a woman who did not respond to the tenderness felt for her. ' As for me,' said Chapelle, ' I own to you that if I were so unlucky as to be in such a position, and was convinced that the woman I loved granted favours to others, I should have such contempt for her that it would infallibly cure me of my passion. Besides, you have a greater satisfaction at hand than you would have if she were your mistress; vengeance, which usually succeeds love in an outraged heart, will pay you for all the grief your wife has caused you, inasmuch as you have only to lock her up; that will be a sure means to set your mind at rest.'

" Molière, who had listened to his friend with some tranquillity, here interrupted him, and asked him if he had ever been in love. ' Yes,' answered Chapelle, ' I have been in love as a man of good sense should be; but I never should make a great trouble out of a thing my honour required me to do; and I blush for you to find you so vacillating.'—' I see plainly that you have never loved,' said Molière, ' you have taken the name of love for love itself. I will not detail to you an infinity of examples that would make you see the power of that passion; I will merely give you a faithful account of my trouble,

to make you understand how little a man is master of himself when
love has obtained a certain ascendancy over him.   To answer you as
to the perfect knowledge that you say I have of the heart of man, and
the portraits that I make of it daily, I grant that I have studied myself
as far as I could to learn its weakness; but if my knowledge teaches
me that peril should be shunned, my experience shows me only too
plainly that it is impossible to escape it; I judge daily by myself.   I
was born with the utmost disposition to tenderness, and as I thought
that my efforts would inspire my wife, through habit, with feelings
that time could not destroy, I neglected nothing to succeed in doing
so.   As she was very young when I married her, I did not perceive
her evil inclinations, and I thought myself less unfortunate than others
who make such marriages.   Marriage did not lessen my eager attentions to her; but I soon found such indifference that I began to see
that all my precautions were useless, and that what she felt for me was
very far from what I had desired in order to be happy.   I blamed myself for a sensitiveness which seemed to me ridiculous in a husband,
and I attributed to her temper what was really the effect of her want
of affection for me.   But I soon had too much reason to perceive my
error, and the passion which she had, shortly after, for the Comte de
Guiche made too much noise in the world to leave me in my apparent
tranquillity.   Finding it impossible to change her feelings, I spared
nothing, from the first, to conquer myself.   For that I employed all
the strength of my mind; I summoned to my help all that could contribute to my consolation.   I considered her as a person whose whole
merit had been in her innocence, and who, for that reason, had none
after her infidelity.   I then took the resolution to live with her as an
honourable man who, having a light-minded wife, is convinced that,
no matter what may be said, his reputation does not depend upon her
bad conduct.   But I have had the grief to find that a young woman
without beauty, who owes the little intelligence men find in her to
the education that I gave her, has been able in a moment to destroy
my philosophy.   Her presence makes me forget all my resolutions,
and the first words she says to me in her defence leave me so convinced that my suspicions are ill-founded, that I beg her pardon for
having been so credulous.   And yet, all my kindness does not change
her.   I have therefore determined to live with her as if she were not
my wife; but if you knew what I suffer you would pity me.   My
passion has reached such a point that it even enters with compassion
into all her interests.   When I consider how impossible it is for me to

conquer what I feel for her, I tell myself that she may have the same difficulty in conquering her inclination to be coquettish, and I find myself more disposed to pity her than to blame her. You will tell me, no doubt, that a man must be a poet to feel this; but, for my part, I think there is but one kind of love, and that those who have not felt these delicacies of sentiment have never truly loved. All things in the world are connected with her in my heart. My idea is so fully occupied with her that, in her absence, nothing can divert it from her. When I see her, an emotion, transports that may be felt but not described, take from me all power of reflection; I have no longer any eyes for her defects; I can see only all she has that is lovable. Is not that the last degree of madness? and do you not wonder that what I have of reason serves only to make me know my weakness without enabling me to triumph over it?'—'I confess to you,' replied his friend, ' that you are more to be pitied than I thought; but we must hope for better things in time. Continue to make efforts; they will take effect when you least think it; as for me, I will offer ardent prayers that you may soon obtain contentment.' He withdrew, leaving Molière to muse still longer on the means to allay his grief."

This touching scene took place at Auteuil, in that garden more celebrated for another affair which the literary imagination has endlessly embroidered, the gaiety of which is more in keeping with the usual ideas evoked by Molière's name. I mean the famous supper at which, while the amphytrion was ill in his bed, Chapelle did the honours of the feast and the cellar so well that all the guests, Boileau at their head, were rushing to drown themselves in the Seine in pure gaiety of heart, when Molière, brought down by the noise, persuaded them to put off the immolation till the morrow and perform it under a glowing sky. Observe that this joyous tale obtained its vogue only because the popular name of the great comedian was

mingled in it. The literary name of Boileau would
not have sufficed to make it national property in this
way; such anecdotes would never be told about
Racine. Legends of this kind obtain currency only
when connected with truly popular poets.

Though Molière did not, after the fashion of several
great poets, leave sonnets on his personal feelings, his
loves, his sorrows, the question arises, did he indirectly convey something of them into his comedies?
and if he did, to what extent? We find in his Life,
by M. Taschereau, several ingenious connections
made between his domestic circumstances and parts
of his plays with which they correspond.

"Molière," says La Grange, his comrade and the first editor of his
complete works,—"Molière made admirable applications in his comedies, in which, we may say, he made game of every one, inasmuch as
in various places he jested about himself and his family affairs, and
what happened in his own home; this was often noticed by his intimate friends."

Thus in the third act of the *Bourgeois Gentilhomme*
he has given a speaking likeness of his wife; in the
first scene of the *Impromptu de Versailles* he puts a
piquant reference to the date of his marriage; and in
the fifth scene of the second act of the *Avare* he
laughs at himself for his cough and his catarrh. It is
very probable, also, that in Arnolphe, in Alceste, he
thought of his age, his situation, his jealousy; and
that under the mask of Argan he gave vent to his
antipathy to the Faculty.

But an essential distinction must be made here, and we cannot reflect upon it too much because it reaches to the very bottom of dramatic genius. The traits above-mentioned bear only on rather vague and general conformities, or very simple details; in reality, none of Molière's personages are *himself*. The greater part of those very traits should be taken only as the tricks and little-by-plays of an excellent actor, customary with comedians of all epochs and which incite to laughter. No less may be said of the so-called copies which Molière is said to have made of certain originals. Alceste is said to be the portrait of M. de Montausier, the Bourgeois that of Rohault; the Avare that of President de Bercy, and so on: here it is the Comte de Grammont, there the Duc de La Feuillade who takes the honours of the play. Dangeau, Tallemant, Gui Patin, Cizeron-Rival, all those amateurs of *ana,* plunge into discourse with ingenuous zeal, and keep us informed of their anecdotical discoveries. It is all futile: Alceste is no more M. de Montausier than he is Molière, than he is Boileau, of whom he reproduces certain features. Even the huntsman of the *Fâcheux* is not M. de Soyecourt solely, and Trissotin is the Abbé Cotin only for a moment in his verse. Molière's personages, in a word, are not copies but creations. He invents, he engenders them; they may have an air, here or there, of resemblance to such or such an individual, but they are, as a total, themselves only. To view them otherwise is to ignore what is multiform and complex in that mysterious dramatic physiology of which the author alone has the secret; he alone knows the point to which the copy goes and where creation begins; he alone can distinguish the sinuous line, the knitting together, — more learnedly, more divinely accomplished than that of the shoulder of Pelops.

In that order of minds which includes, through divers ages and in divers ranks, Cervantes, Rabelais, Le Sage, Fielding, Beaumarchais, and Walter Scott, Molière is, with Shakespeare, the most complete example of the dramatic and, properly so-called, creative faculty. Shakespeare has, above Molière, pathetic touches and flashes of the terrible—Macbeth, King Lear, Ophelia—but Molière redeems in some respects this loss by the number, the perfection, the continual and profound weaving together of his principal characters. In all these great men evidently, but in Molière more evidently still, the dramatic genius is not an outside extension, expansion of a lyrical and personal faculty, which, starting from its own interior sentiments, toils to transport them outwardly and make them live, as much as possible, under other masks (Byron in his tragedies, for instance); nor is it the pure and simple application of a faculty of critical, analytical observation, which carefully exhibits in the personages of its composition the scattered traits it has collected. There is a whole class of true dramatists who have something lyrical, in one sense almost blind, in their inspiration; a warmth, a glow, born of an inward vivid sentiment, which they impart directly to their personages. Molière said of Corneille: "He has an elf that comes from time to time and whispers excellent verses in his ear; then it leaves him, saying: 'Let us see how he will get on without me': he does nothing good and the elf makes merry at him."

In truth, Corneille, Crébillon, Schiller, Ducis, old Marlowe, were each and all subject to elves, to sudden, direct emotions, in the crises of their dramatic impulse. They did not govern their genius with the fulness and consistency of human freedom. Often sublime and magnificent, they obeyed some mysterious cry of instinct, or some noble warmth of blood, like generous animals, lions or bulls; they knew not fully what they did. Molière, like Shakespeare, does know; like that great forerunner, he moves in a sphere more freely broad, and thus superior; he governs himself, he rules his fire, ardent in his work but lucid in his ardour.

This lucidity, nevertheless, his habitual coldness of nature in the midst of so stirring a work, do not aspire to the predetermined, icy impartiality, such as we have seen in Goethe, that Talleyrand of art—such critical subtleties in the bosom of poesy were not as yet invented. Molière and Shakespeare are two brothers of the primitive race; with this difference, as I conceive, that in common life Shakespeare, poet of tears and terror, would readily develop a more smiling and happier nature, while Molière, the joyous comedian, would yield himself more and more to melancholy and silence.

Mlle. Poisson, wife of the comedian of that name, has left the following portrait of Molière, which those painted by Mignard do not contradict as to physical traits, and which satisfies the mind by the frank, honest image it suggests:

"Molière," she says, " was neither too fat nor too thin; his figure was tall rather than short, his bearing noble, his leg handsome. He walked gravely, had a very serious air, a big nose, a large mouth, thick lips, a brown skin, black, heavy eyebrows, and the movements he gave to them made his countenance extremely comical. With regard to his character: he was gentle, obliging, generous ; he liked to harangue; and when he read his plays to the comedians he wanted them to bring their children, that he might make conjectures from their natural emotions."

What is shown in these few lines of Molière's manly beauty reminds me of a tale told by Tieck of the "very human face" of Shakespeare. Shakespeare, young, and then unknown, was waiting in the parlour of an inn for the arrival of Lord Southampton, who was about to become his protector and friend. He was listening silently to the poet Marlowe, who, without taking notice of the unknown youth, was giving vent to a noisy enthusiasm. Lord Southampton, having arrived in the town, sent his page to the inn: "You are to go," he said, "into the common room; there, you must look attentively at all the faces; some, remember this, will look to you like the faces of less noble animals, others will have the faces of more noble animals; but search on farther till you find a face that seems to you to resemble nothing but a human face.   That is the man I want; salute him, and bring him to me." The young page hastened away; he entered the common room and examined the faces; after a slow examination, finding the face of the poet Marlowe the handsomest of all, he thought he must be the man and took him to his master. Marlowe's countenance was not without resemblance to the head of a noble bull, and the page, child that he still was, was struck by it.   But Lord Southampton afterwards showed him his mistake, and explained to him how the human and fitly proportioned face of Shakespeare, less striking when first seen, was, nevertheless, the more beautiful.   What Tieck says of faces he means to apply, we feel sure, to the inward genius.

Molière never separated dramatic works from their representation; he was equally director, excellent actor, and fine poet.   He loved, as I have said, the boards, the stage, the public; he clung to his prerogatives as director, he liked to harangue on certain solemn occasions, and to face an audience that was sometimes stormy.   It is told how he pacified by a speech a party of angry *mousquetaires,* whose right of entrance to the theatre had been withdrawn.   As actor, his contemporaries agree in according him great perfection in comedy, but a perfection acquired through study and by force of will:

"Nature," says Mlle. Poisson, "had denied him those external gifts so necessary for the stage, especially for tragic rôles. A muffled voice, harsh inflections, a volubility of tongue that made his declamation precipitate, rendered him on this side very inferior to the actors of the hôtel de Bourgogne. But he did himself justice and confined his acting chiefly to a style in which his defects were more bearable. He had much difficulty, however, in succeeding, and he did not conquer his volubility, so contrary to fine articulation, without continual efforts that caused him a hiccough which he never lost to the day of his death and of which he knew well how to make use on occasions. To vary the inflections of his voice, he was the first to use certain unusual tones, for which, in the beginning, he was accused of affectation, but to which people soon accustomed themselves. He gave pleasure not only in the rôles of Mascarille, Sganarelle and Hali, but he excelled in those of the highest comedy, such as Arnolphe, Orgon, Harpagon. It was then that by truth of sentiment, by intelligence of expression, by all the delicacies of his art he fascinated the spectators to the point of no longer distinguishing the personage represented from the comedian who represented him. He always took for himself the longest and most difficult parts."

Molière was grand and sumptuous in his manner of living, possessing thirty thousand *livres* a year, which he spent in liberalities, receptions, and benefactions. His domestic service was not confined to the good Laforest, the celebrated confidant of his verses, and people of rank, to whom he always returned their hospitalities, found nothing bourgeois and *à la* Corneille in his home. He resided, during the latter part of his life, in the rue de Richelieu, facing the rue Traversière, about where No. 34 stands to-day.

Having reached the age of forty, at the summit of his art and apparently of his fame, strong in the king's regard, protected and sought by the nobles, frequently sent for by the Prince de Condé, going to the Duc de

La Rochefoucauld to read his *Femmes Savantes,* and to
the old Cardinal de Retz to read the *Bourgeois Gentilhomme* — was Molière (independently of his domestic
discords), I will not say happy in his life, but satisfied
with his position in the world? or must we assert
that he was not? Stifle, attenuate, disguise the fact
under all imaginable reserves, there was ever in Molière's position, in spite of the brilliancy of his talent
and his favour, something from which he suffered.
He suffered in lacking at times a certain serious and
lofty consideration; the comedian in him detracted
from the poet. Every one laughed at his plays, but
all did not esteem them enough; too many people
took him as their best means of amusement, and he
felt it deeply. Mme. de Sévigné speaks of sending
for him to tickle and enliven "that good old cardinal."
Chapelle called him "great man," but his chief
friends, Boileau among them, regretted in him a mixture of the buffoon. After his death, de Visé, in a
letter to Grimarest, contests his right to be called
"Monsieur"; and while his funeral procession was
passing along the streets, a woman of the populace
being asked whose it was, answered: "Only that
Molière." Another woman, who was at her window
and overheard the remark, cried out: "How! You
miserable woman! He is *monsieur* for such as you!"
Molière, clear-sighted and inexorable observer that he
was, could have lost nothing of a thousand such mean
and petty affronts which he swallowed with outward

contempt. Certain honours were a poor compensation, and sometimes a bitter one, I fancy; such as the honour of making, in the capacity of a servant, Louis XIV's bed. And again, when Louis XIV made him sit at his own table and said aloud, offering him the wing of a chicken: "Here am I giving supper to Molière, whom my officers do not think good enough company for them."

Ten months before his death, Molière, by the mediation of mutual friends, was reconciled to his wife, whom he still loved, and even became father of a child which did not live. The change of habits, caused by this resumption of married life, increased the inflammatory state of his lungs. Two months before his death he received the visit from Boileau of which I have spoken. On the day of the fourth representation of the *Malade imaginaire* he felt more ill than usual; but here I will let Grimarest speak, he having received from the actor Baron the details of the scene, the plain *naïveté* of which seems to me preferable to the more concise correctness of others who have reproduced it:

"Molière, feeling more oppressed in his lungs than usual, sent for his wife, to whom he said in presence of Baron: 'My whole life has been equally mingled with pleasure and pain; I have thought myself happy; but to-day, when I am so overwhelmed with sufferings that I cannot count on a single instant of relief, I see that I must give up the game; I can bear up no longer against sufferings and vexations which give me not one moment's reprieve. But,' he added, after reflecting awhile, 'how much a man can suffer without dying! Still, I feel that I am coming to my end.' Mlle. Molière and Baron were deeply

touched by this address, which they did not expect, in spite of his
condition, and they implored him, with tears in their eyes, not to act
that evening, but to take some rest and recover. 'How can you wish
me to do so?' he said; 'there are fifty poor workmen who have only
their daily wages to live on; what would they do if I did not act?
I should reproach myself for having neglected to give them bread unless
I were absolutely unable to do so.'"

But he sent for the comedians and said to them that,
feeling more uncomfortable than usual, he could not
play that day unless they were ready to act at four
o'clock precisely. "Otherwise," he said to them, "I
cannot act and you must refund the money." The
comedians had the chandeliers lighted and the curtain
raised at four o'clock precisely. Molière acted with
great difficulty, and half the spectators noticed that in
pronouncing the word *Jure,* in the ceremony of the
Malade imaginaire, a convulsion seized him. Observing himself that the audience had perceived it, he
made an effort, and concealed by a forced laugh what
had happened to him.

"When the play was over he took his dressing-gown and went into
Baron's box and asked him what was said of the piece. M. Baron
replied that his plays always had good success the closer they were examined, and the more they were acted the more they were liked. 'But,'
he added, 'you seem to us more ill than you were.' 'That is true,' replied Molière, 'I am chilled to death.' Baron, after touching his
hands, which he found like ice, put them in his muff to warm them; he
then sent for Molière's porters to take him home as quickly as possible,
and did not himself leave the side of the chair, fearing that something
might happen between the Palais-Royal and the rue de Richelieu, where
Molière lived. When he was in his room Baron wanted him to take
some bouillon, of which Mlle. Molière always had a provision for herself, for no one could take more care of themselves than she did.

'Eh! no,' said Molière, 'my wife's bouillons are strong as brandy to me; you know all the ingredients she puts into them. Give me instead a little bit of Parmesan cheese.' Laforest brought him some; he ate it with a bit of bread, and had himself put to bed. He had not been there more than a minute when he sent to his wife for a pillow filled with a drug she had promised him to make him sleep. 'All which does not enter the body,' he said, 'I try willingly; but remedies taken internally frighten me; it would take very little to make me lose what remains to me of life.'

"An instant later he was seized with an extremely violent cough. After spitting, he asked for a light. 'Here,' he said, 'is a change.' Baron, seeing the blood he had just thrown up, cried out in terror. 'Don't be frightened,' said Molière, 'you have seen me throw up much more. Nevertheless,' he added, 'go and tell my wife to come up.' He remained in the care of two sisters of charity, of those who come to Paris to beg for the poor during Lent, and to whom he was in the habit of giving hospitality. They gave to him in this last moment of his life the edifying succour to be expected of their charity, and he made apparent to them the sentiments of a good Christian, and all the resignation that he owed to the will of the Lord. He rendered up his soul in the arms of these two good sisters; the blood that flowed in abundance from his mouth suffocated him, so that when his wife and Baron came up they found him dead."

It was Friday, February 17, 1673, at ten in the evening, one hour at the most after leaving the stage, that Molière breathed his last sigh, at the age of fifty-one years, less a few days. The rector of Saint-Eustache, his parish church, refused him Christian burial, as not having been reconciled with the Church before death. Molière's widow addressed a petition on the 20th of February to the Archbishop of Paris, Harlay de Champvallon. Accompanied by the rector of Auteuil, she went to Versailles and threw herself at the king's feet; but the good rector seized the occasion to free himself of a suspicion of Jansenism, and the king silenced him. Besides which, if all must be told, Molière, being dead, could no longer amuse Louis XIV, and the immense selfishness of the monarch, that hideous, incurable selfishness laid bare to us by Saint-Simon, resumed the upper hand. Louis XIV sent the widow and the rector abruptly away, at the same time writing to the archbishop to find some middle course. On the 21st of February Molière's body, accompanied by two priests, was carried by night to the cemetery of Saint-Joseph, rue Montmartre. Two hundred persons followed it, each bearing a torch; no funeral anthem was allowed to be sung. On the day of the obsequies the crowd, always fanatic, assembled around Molière's house with apparently hostile intentions; it was dispersed by flinging money to it. The same Parisian crowd was less easily dispersed on the occasion of the funeral of Louis XIV.

Hardly was he dead, before Molière was appreciated on all sides. We know the magnificent lines of Boileau, who rose in them to eloquence. Molière's reputation has since shone ever higher and incontestable. The eighteenth century did more than confirm it,—it proclaimed it with a sort of philosophical pride. Our own young century, accepting that fame and never calling it in question, made use of it, at certain times, as an auxiliary, as an arm of defence or condemnation. But later, comprehending it in a more equitable manner, comparing it, according to philosophy and art, with other renowns of neighbouring nations, it has better understood and respected it. Constantly enlarging in this way, Molière's reputation (marvellous privilege!) has reached its true measure, has equalled truth, but has not passed beyond it. His genius is henceforth one of the ornaments, one of the claims of the genius of humanity itself. Among the great world-fames that survive and last there are many that maintain themselves afar, so to speak; whose names last better than their works in the memory of mankind. Molière is of a smaller number, whose life and works are sharers in all the possible conquests of the new civilisation. Reputations, future geniuses, books, may multiply; civilisations may transform themselves hereafter, but five or six great works have entered inalienably the depths of human thought. Every coming man who can read is one reader the more for Molière.

V.

La Fontaine.

La Fontaine.

IN these rapid essays, by which I endeavour to recall the attention of my readers and myself to pacific memories of literature and poesy, I have imposed no law upon myself ; I have simply certain principles of art and literary criticism which I seek to apply, without violence and in a kindly spirit, to the illustrious authors of our two preceding centuries. Moreover, the impression that a recent and fresh reading of their works leaves upon me—a simple, frank impression, quick and naïve—is that which, above all, decides the tone and colour of my remarks; it is that which impels me to severity against Jean-Jacques, to esteem for Boileau, to admiration for Mme. de Sévigné, Regnier, and others. To-day it is La Fontaine. Coming to him after so many panegyrists and biographers, I find myself condemned to say nothing fundamentally new and to do no more than reproduce in my own way, assigning other reasons at times, the same conclusions of praise, the same homage of a disarmed and loving criticism.

It must be said, however, that if La Harpe and Chamfort praised La Fontaine with intuitive sagacity, they detached him far too much from his century, which was much less known to them than to us. The eighteenth century, in fact, knew little of Louis XIV's epoch, except that part of it that continued and was prevalent under Louis XV. It ignored or disdained one whole portion, by which that reign looked back to precedents; a portion certainly not less original, which Saint-Simon unveils for us to-day. Those wonderful Memoirs, which until now have been thought to ruin the glorious prestige and grandeur of Louis XIV, seem to us in these days to restore to that memorable epoch a character of grandeur and power, hitherto unsuspected, and to rehabilitate it loftily in public opinion, along the very lines that destroy the notions of superficial admiration. There will come, I think, as great variation in our judgment of Louis XIV's epoch as there has been in our ways of seeing and judging the things of Greece and the Middle Ages. For instance, men studied little, or, at any rate, they little understood the Greek theatre; they admired it for qualities it did not have; then, casting a rapid glance upon it and perceiving that those qualities they considered indispensable were often lacking to it, they treated it lightly,—witness Voltaire and La Harpe. Finally, studying it better, like M. Villemain, men began to admire it precisely for not possessing those qualities of false nobleness and stilted dignity which they thought they saw in the first instance, and, later, were disappointed not to find.

LA FONTAINE.

From a steel engraving.

Opinions have followed the same course on the Middle Ages, on chivalry, on the Gothic. To the golden age of fancy succeeded sterner studies, which cast some trouble into that first romantic region; then those studies, becoming stronger and more intelligent, came at last to an age, not of gold but of iron, yet marvellous still; an age of simple priests and monks more powerful than kings, of mighty barons whose enormous bones and gigantic armour frighten us; an art of granite and of stone, learned, delicate, aërial, majestic, mystical. In like manner the monarchy of Louis XIV, admired at first for the ostentatious and apparent regularity and order that Voltaire extols, then revealed in its real infirmity by the Memoirs of Dangeau and the Princess Palatine, and belittled intentionally by Lemontey, reappears to us in Saint-Simon vast, impeded, fluctuating, in a confusion that is not without grandeur and beauty; with the running-gear of the old abolished constitution more and more useless, but with all that habit retains of form and motion even after the spirit and meaning of things have passed away; already subject to despotic good pleasure, but ill-disciplined for the supreme etiquette that was about to triumph.

This being clearly laid down, it becomes easy to put in their right place, and to see in their true light, the men native to the time who, in their conduct and in their works, have done much besides fulfilling the programme of the master. Without this general knowledge we run some risk of considering them too much apart, as beings aloof and accidental. This is what the critics of the last century did in speaking of La Fontaine; they isolated him, and they exaggerated him in their portraits; they gave him a far more complete personality than was needed in regard to his works, and they imagined him, out of all proportion, a jovial fellow and fable-maker. They could explain to themselves Boileau and Racine far more easily, because they belonged to the regular and visible portion of the epoch and were its purest literary expression.

There were men who, following the general movement of their century, retain none the less a deep, indelible individuality: Molière is, perhaps, the most striking example. There are others who, without going in the direction of the general movement, and showing consequently a certain originality of their own, have less of it than they seem to have. In the style or manner that discriminates them from their contemporaries there is much imitation of the preceding age; and in this striking contrast which they present to what surrounds them we ought to recognise and allow for what belongs of right to their predecessors. It is among the men of this class that La Fontaine must be ranked; he was, in fact, under Louis XIV, the last and the greatest of the poets of the sixteenth century.

Born in 1621, at Château Thierry in Touraine, his

education was much neglected, and he early gave
proof of his extreme inclination to let himself go in
life and to obey the impressions of the moment. A
canon of Soissons having one day lent him a few
books of piety, the young lad fancied he had a leaning to the clerical profession, and he entered the
seminary. He was not long in leaving it; and his
father, having married him, made over to him his
office of Director of Waters and Forests. But La
Fontaine, with his natural forgetfulness and laziness,
accustomed himself by degrees to live as if he had
neither office nor wife. He was not as yet a poet,
however, or, at any rate, he did not know that he was
one. Chance put him in the way of knowing it. An
officer who was in winter quarters at Château
Thierry read to him one day an ode by Malherbe, the
subject of which was an attempt on the life of Henri
IV; and La Fontaine, from that moment, thought he
was destined to write odes. He composed a number,
it is said, and very bad ones; but one of his relations,
named Pintrel, and a schoolmate, Maucroix, dissuaded
him from that style and urged him to study the
classics. It was also about this time that he began to
read Rabelais, Marot, and the poets of the sixteenth
century, the basis of a provincial library at that period.
In 1654 he published a translation in verse of the
"Eunuch" of Terence; and one of his wife's relations, Jannart, friend and deputy of Fouquet, took him
to Paris to present him to the Superintendent himself.

This journey and presentation decided La Fontaine's fate. Touquet took a liking to him, attached him to himself, and gave him a salary of one thousand francs on condition of his producing every quarter a piece of poetry, ballad or madrigal, *dizain* or *sizain*. These little pieces with the *Songe de Vaux* [Vaux being Fouquet's country-seat] are the first original productions of La Fontaine that we possess; they belong wholly to the taste of that day, the taste of Saint-Évremond and Benserade, and to the *marotisme* of Sarasin and Voiture; but the inexpressible *something* of easy indolence and voluptuous revery characteristic of the delightful writer is already perceptible, though much overloaded with insipidity and *bel esprit*.

Fouquet's poet was greeted from his start in Paris as one of the most delicate ornaments of the polished and gallant society of Saint-Mandé and Vaux. He was very agreeable in company, especially that of private life; his conversation, free, easy, and naïve, was seasoned now and then with roguish wit, his absence of mind being checked in time to be only a charm the more. He was certainly less of the *good-man* in society than Corneille. Women, slumber, and the art of doing nothing shared in turn his homage and his devotion. He boasted of this sometimes, and talked readily of himself and his tastes to others without ever wearying them, though making them smile. Intimacy, especially, brought out his charm; he gave it an affectionate turn, a tone of familiar good-breeding: he let himself go to it like a man who forgets all else, and who takes seriously or with easy jesting every passing caprice. His acknowledged liking for the fair sex did not make him dangerous to women unless they wished it. In fact La Fontaine, like Regnier, his predecessor, liked best all "easy and little-defended loves." While he was addressing Climène, Iris, and the goddesses, on his knees with respectful sighs, employing what he thought he had learned from Plato, he was seeking elsewhere, and far lower, for less mystical pleasures which helped him to bear his fictitious martyrdom with patience. Among his *bonnes fortunes* soon after his arrival in Paris was the celebrated Claudine, third wife of Guillaume Colletet and his cook (Colletet always married his servant-women). Our poet often visited the good old rhymer at his house in the Faubourg Saint-Marceau, and courted Claudine while discussing the authors of the sixteenth century at supper with her master, who could give him good counsel thereon and reveal to him riches by which he profited.

During the first six years of his residence in Paris and until the fall of Fouquet, La Fontaine produced little; he gave himself up wholly to the pleasures of a life of enchantment and festivity, to the delights of a choice society which enjoyed his ingenuous talk, and appreciated his gallant trifling. But this dream vanished on the downfall of the enchanter. Matters were thus, when, the Duchesse de Bouillon, niece of Mazarin, having asked the poet for some tales in verse, he hastened to satisfy her, and the first collection of *Contes* appeared in 1664. La Fontaine was then forty-four years old. Critics have sought to explain this tardy first appearance of so facile a genius; and some have gone so far as to attribute his long silence to secret studies, to a laborious and prolonged education. But in truth, while La Fontaine never ceased testing and cultivating his talent in his leisure moments from the day Malherbe revealed it to him, I much prefer to believe in his laziness, his somnolence, his absent-mindedness, all, in short, that was naïve and forgetful in him, rather than admit that he ever went through the wearisome novitiate to which those critics have condemned him. Instinctive, heedless genius, fickle, volatile, ever the sport of circumstances, we have only to recall certain features of his life to know him and comprehend him: On leaving college, a canon of Soissons lends him a pious book— behold him in the seminary; an officer reads him an ode of Malherbe, and lo! he is a poet; Pintrel and Maucroix turn him to antiquity, and he dreams of Quintilian and dotes on Plato while awaiting Baruch; Fouquet orders *dizains* and ballads, and he makes them; the Duchesse de Bouillon, tales, and he tells them; another day it is fables for Monseigneur the dauphin, a poem on quinine for Mme. de Bouillon; again, an opera of *Daphne* for Lulli, the *Captivité de Saint-Malc* at the request of Port-Royal; or else it may be letters, long, flowery, negligent letters, mixtures of verse and prose, to his wife, to M. de Maucroix, to Saint-Évremond, to the Contis, to the Vendômes, to all, in short, who demand them. La Fontaine spent his genius, as he did his time and his fortune, without knowing how, and in the service of every one. If up to the age of forty he seems less prolific than he was later, it is because occasions were lacking to him, and his natural laziness needed to be overcome by gentle violence from without. No sooner did he meet at forty-three years of age with the style and manner that suited him—that of *conte* and *fable*—than it was quite natural he should give himself to it with a sort of effusion, and return to it again and again, of his own accord, from liking as well as from habit.

La Fontaine, it is true, was, in some respects, a little mistaken about his gifts; he piqued himself much on correction and labour; and his poetic art, which he mainly derived from Maucroix, and which Boileau and Racine completed for him, accorded ill with the natural character of his work. But this slight inconsistency, which he has in common with other great, ingenuous minds of his day, is not surprising in him, and confirms, far more than it contradicts, the opinion I have of the facile and accommodating nature of his genius.

What La Fontaine is in *tale,* all the world knows; what he is in *fable,* the world also knows and feels;

but it is much less easy to explain it.   Authors of intelligence have tried the same style and failed; they
have put in action, according to precept, animals, trees,
men; hiding a sly meaning, a healthy moral under
their little dramas; and then, to their surprise, they are
judged inferior to their illustrious predecessor.   The
reason is that La Fontaine understood Fable in a different way.   I except his first books, in which he shows
timidity, holds closer to his little tale, and is not yet
wholly at his ease in this form, which adapted itself less
immediately to his mind than did the elegy or the *conte*.
When the second collection appeared, containing five
books (from the sixth to the eleventh included), contemporary critics cried out, as they always do, that it
was much below the first.   Yet it is in that collection
that we find, in its perfection, Fable, such as La Fontaine invented it.   He had ended, evidently, by finding
in it a framework suited to thoughts, to sentiments,
and to *talk ;* the little drama at the base is made more
important than before; the moral, four lines at the end,
is still there from force of habit, but the Fable, freer in
its course, turns and gathers on its way, now from
elegy or idyll, anon from epistle or tale, here an anecdote, there a conversation, a theme rising to fancy —
a mixture of charming avowals, gentle philosophies,
and dreamy plaints.

Nevertheless, in his first manner, at the close of the
first book, in the *Chêne et le Roseau,* he attained the
perfection of the Fable, properly so-called; he found

means to introduce into it grandeur and the higher poesy, without exceeding its limits by an iota; he was master already. In *Le Meunier, son Fils et l'Âne,* he jokes, he talks, he makes the masters, Malherbe and Racan, talk, and the apologue is merely an adornment of the discourse. But his second manner begins more distinctly and declares itself, as I have said, in the second collection, seventh book, which opens with the fable of the animals ill of the plague. In his preface the poet himself acknowledges that he has diverged a little from the pure fable of Æsop, and has "sought for other enrichment and has extended farther the circumstances of his tale."

When we take up the seventh book of the Fables and read it consecutively, we are enraptured; it has truly "a charm," as the poet says in his Dedication; little masterpieces succeed one another: *Le Coche et la Mouche, La Laitière et le Pot au lait, Le Curé et le Mort;* scarcely one that we can call mediocre steps in (such as *La Tête et Queue du Serpent).* The Fable that ends Book VII, *Un Animal dans la Lune,* discloses in La Fontaine a philosophical faculty that his native *naïveté* would scarcely allow us to suspect; the simple man, who might be thought credulous when you argued with him, because he always had an air of listening to your reasons without thinking to give you his, proves a rival of Lucretius and of that élite of great poets who have thought. He treats of things of Nature with elevation of mind and firmness. In the physical world, not less than in the moral world, appearances do not mislead him. Speaking of the sun, he says in language that Copernicus or Galileo would not disavow:

> "I see the sun: what figure doth it bear?
> Its great mass here below seems scarce three feet;
> But did I see it at its own great height,
> 'T would seem to my eyes like the Eye of Nature.
> Distance enables me to judge its size,
> By angle and by outline I determine it:
> Ignorance thinks it flat; but round I deem it;
> I make it motionless; 't is earth that moves."

Pascal himself, geometrician that he was, would not have dared to say more on the movement of the earth. Again, in his Fable of *Démocrite et les Abdéritains,* his thought is far above vulgar prejudices. No one in his day refuted more wittily than he Descartes and the Cartesians on the souls of animals, and those pretended mechanisms which the haughty philosopher knew no better than he knew the human being he flattered himself he explained. In the Fable, *Les deux Rats, le Renard et l'Œuf,* addressed to Mme. de La Sablière, La Fontaine discusses and reasons on these subtle matters; he even offers his own explanation, but, wise man that he is, he is careful not to venture a conclusion. In *Les Souris et le Chat-Huant* he returns to that philosophic subject; in *Les Lapins,* addressed to M. de La Rochefoucauld, he returns again and argues it, but he enlivens his arguments with gaiety after his fashion, sending through them, as it were, a fragrance of heather and of thyme.

At the end of the fable, *Un Animal dans la Lune,* La Fontaine enlarges on the happiness of England, which was then escaping the risks of war ; and in speaking of that first, full glory of Louis XIV, he gives voice to words of peace; he does it with delicacy and recognition of the exploits of the monarch, admitting that "peace is our desire, though not our prayer." Whenever he has to speak of the masters of earth, of the Lion, which represents them in his Fables, La Fontaine shows plainly that he is neither seduced nor dazzled by them. But in all that he has written against monarchs and lions it would be a mistake to conclude that he did it with a purpose, or was hostile to them in any way. To interpret him thus would be narrow and unpoetic; if, speaking of the great and the powerful, he did not withhold the lesson that escapes him, still less did he intend to flatter the people, that people of Athens that he somewhere calls an "animal with frivolous heads."

I shall not presume here to classify La Fontaine's Fables; it would be to misunderstand their spirit and hamper their diversity. But foremost in the order of beauty we must place those grand moral fables, *Le Berger et le Roi* and *Le Paysan du Danube,* in which there is an eloquent sentiment of history and almost of statesmanship. Next come other fables which, taken together, form a complete picture, a rounded whole, and are equally full of philosophy: *Le Vieillard et les trois Jeunes Hommes ; Le Savetier et le Financier ;* the latter as perfect in itself as some grand scene, some compact comedy of Molière. There are elegies, properly so-called, such as: *Tircés et Amaranthe,* and other elegies less direct but more enchanting,— *Les Deux Pigeons,* for example.

Though human nature is often treated with severity by La Fontaine, though he flatters the species in no way, though he says that childhood is "without pity," and that old age is "pitiless," still, in spite of all, he is not the calumniator of mankind; on the contrary, he will ever remain its consoler in one respect, namely: that friendship has found in him so constant and so tender an interpreter. His *Deux Amis* is the masterpiece of that topic; but on all the other occasions when he speaks of friendship, his heart opens, his mocking observation dies; he has words of feeling that he feels, tones either tender or generous, as when he lauds in Mme. d'Hervart

> "Nobility of soul, the talent to conduct
> Affairs and men;
> A temper frank and free, the gift to be a friend
> In spite of Jupiter and stormy skies."

It is when we have read in a single day a chosen quantity of La Fontaine's Fables that we feel our admiration for him renewed and refreshed, and that we say with an eminent critic [Joubert], "There is in

La Fontaine a plenitude of poesy that is found nowhere else among French authors."

La Fontaine is our only great personal, pensive,
musing poet before André Chénier. He puts himself
knowingly into his verse, he tells us about himself, his
soul, his caprices, his weaknesses. Usually his tone
breathes gaiety, roguish malice, mischief, and the jolly
conteur laughs to us from the corner of his eye, wag-
ging his head. But often, also, he has tones that
come from the heart, a melancholy tenderness that
brings him close to the poets of our own time. Those
of the sixteenth century had already had some foretaste
of revery; but with them its individual inspiration was
lacking. La Fontaine restored to it a primitive character of vivid and discreet expression; he freed it of
all it had contracted of commonplace and sensual; on
this side Plato did him the good he once did to Petrarch; and when La Fontaine exclaims in one of his
delightful fables:

> "Shall I feel no more the charm that holds me?
> Have I passed the time to love?"

The word *charm,* thus employed in a sense indefinite
and wholly metaphysical, marks a progress in French
poesy that was, later, taken up and followed by André
Chénier and his successors.

Friend of retirement, of solitude, and painter of the
fields, La Fontaine has the additional advantage over
his predecessors in the sixteenth century of giving to

his pictures faithful colours that render the region truly
and, so to speak, the soil itself. Those vast plains of
wheat, where the master walks early and the lark
hides her nest; those bushes and copses and bracken
where a whole little world is swarming; those pretty
warrens, whose giddy inhabitants pay court to Aurora
in the dew and perfume their banquet with thyme —
all is Beauce, Champagne, Picardy; I recognise the
farms with their ponds, their poultry yards, their dove-
cotes. La Fontaine had well observed those regions,
if not as Director of Waters and Forests, at least as
poet. He was born there, he lived there long; and
even after he was settled in Paris he returned every
autumn to Château Thierry to visit his property and
sell it piecemeal, for Jean, as we know, "spent capital and revenue."

When all La Fontaine's property was dissipated, and
the sudden death of Madame [Henriette, Duchesse
d'Orléans] deprived him of the office of gentleman-
in-waiting which he held in her household, Mme. de
La Sablière invited him to her house and took care
of him for twenty years. Abandoned in his habits,
ruined in fortune, without abode or hearth, it was for
him and for his genius an inestimable blessing to find
himself maintained, under the auspices of an amiable
woman, in the heart of a witty and well-bred society,
and with all the comforts of opulence. He keenly
felt the value of this benefit; and his inviolable friend ·
ship, familiar yet respectful, which death alone could

break, is one of the natural sentiments he succeeded
best in expressing.

At the feet of Mme. de La Sablière and of other distinguished women whom he celebrated and respected,
his muse, soiled at times, resumed a sort of purity
and freshness, which his rather vulgar tastes, growing
less and less scrupulous with age, tended too much to
weaken. His life, thus orderly amid disorder, became
dual; he made it into two parts: one elegant, animated, intelligent, and open to the light; the other
obscure and, it must be said, shameful, given over to
those prolonged dissipations which youth embellishes
with the name of "pleasures," but which are vices
on the forehead of old age. Mme. de La Sablière
herself, who rebuked La Fontaine, had not always
been exempt from human passions and frailties; but
when the unfaithfulness of the Marquis de La Fare
left her heart free and empty, she felt that no other
than God could henceforth fill it, and she devoted her
last years to the most active exercise of Christian
charity. This conversion, as sincere as it was glittering, took place in 1683. La Fontaine was moved to
think it an example he ought to follow; his frailty,
and other intimacies that he contracted about that
time, deterred him; and it was not until ten years
later, when the death of Mme. de La Sablière gave
him a second and solemn warning, that this seed of
good thoughts sprang up within him to wilt no more.
But, even in 1684, the year after her conversion, he

wrote an admirable *Discours en Vers,* which he read
before the French Academy on the day of his reception, in which, addressing his benefactress, he shows
her with candid truth the state of his soul:

> "Of solid joys I follow but the shadow;
> I have abused the dearest of our boons—
> Amusing thoughts, gay dreams, and vague discourses,
> Delights chimerical, vain fruits of leisure,
> Novels and cards, the curse of all republics,
> By which e'en upright minds may be misled,
> A foolish madness scoffing at the laws,
> With other passions by wise men condemned,
> Have plucked, like thieves, the flower of my years.
> To seek true good would still repair these ills;
> I know it—yet I turn to false gods ever."

This is, as we see, a grave, ingenuous confession,
in which religious unction and lofty morality do not
quite prevent a lingering, loving glance toward those
"chimerical delights" from which he was ill-detached.
A simplicity of exaggeration enters into it; novels and
cards that entice the sinner are "the curse of republics, a madness that laughs at laws"!

> "What profit in these lines with care composed?
> Need I no other fruit than praise for them?
> Little their counsels if I heed them not,
> And, at the close of life, do not begin to live.—
> For live I have not; I have served two masters,
> An empty fame and love have filled my years.
> What, then, is living? Iris, you could tell me!
> Your answer promptly comes; I seem to hear it:
> 'Enjoy true good in sweet tranquillity,
> Make use of time, and of thy leisure hours;
> Pay honour where 't is due—to God alone;

Renounce thy Phyllises in favour of thyself;
Banish those foolish loves, those impotent desires,
Like Hydras in our hearts incessantly reborn.' "

Sincere, eloquent, sublime poesy, of a singular turn, where virtue contrives to make terms with idleness, where Phyllis and the Supreme Being are side by side; poesy that gives birth to a smile in a tear! Alas! why did La Fontaine never know the "God of good men"? It would have cost him less to be converted.

At first sight, and judging only by his works, art and labour seem to have had but little place in La Fontaine, and if the attention of critics had not been awakened on this point by a few words in his prefaces, and by certain contemporaneous testimony, we should probably never have thought of making a question of it. But the poet "confesses" in the preface to *Psyche* that "prose costs him as much trouble as poesy." In one of his last Fables, written for the Duc de Bourgogne, he complains of "manufacturing under stress of time" verses that have less sense than the prose of the young prince. His manuscripts are full of erasures and changes; the same pieces are copied several times, and often with very happy alterations. It is amusing to see the care that he gives to errata. "Several errors in printing have slipped in," he says in the preface to his second collection: "I have made them make an errata, but that is a small remedy for a considerable defect. If the reader is to have any pleasure in this work he must correct those errors with his own hand in his copy according as they are given in each erratum, as much for the first two parts as for the last."

La Fontaine read much, not only the moderns, French and Italian, but the classics, in the original or in translation; he plumes himself repeatedly upon it. His erudition, however, makes singular blunders and is charmingly confused in places. In his *Vie d'Esope* he says: "As Planude lived in a century when the memory of things that happened to Æsop had not yet faded, I think he knew by tradition what the latter left behind him." In writing thus he forgot that nineteen centuries had elapsed between the Phrygian and his editor, and that the Greek monk lived barely two centuries before the reign of Louis the Great. In an epistle to Huet in favour of the ancients over the moderns, and in special honour of Quintilian, he reverts to Plato, his favourite topic, and declares that among modern sages not one can approach that great philosopher:

"All Greece is swarming in his smallest corner."

He attributes the decadence of the ode in France to a cause that one would never have imagined:

" . . . the ode, which doth expire,
Needs patience, and our men have only fire."

In this remarkable epistle he protests against servile imitation of the ancients, and tries to explain the nature of his own imitation. I advise all those who are curious in such matters to compare this passage with the end of the second epistle of André Chénier; the idea at bottom is the same, but the reader will see, on comparing the two expressions of it, the profound difference that separated a poet-artist like Chénier from a poet of instinct like La Fontaine.

That which is true up to this time of nearly all our poets except Molière and perhaps Corneille,—that which is true of Marot, Ronsard, Regnier, Malherbe, Boileau, Racine, and André Chénier,—is true also of La Fontaine: when we have surveyed his various merits we must end by saying that it is in style that he excels. With Molière, on the contrary, with Dante, Shakespeare, and Milton, the style equals the invention, no doubt, but never surpasses it; the manner of utterance reflects the depths below, but never eclipses them. As to La Fontaine's special manner, it is too well known and too well analysed elsewhere for me to recur to it here. Let it suffice to remark that there is in it quite a large admixture of gallant insipidities and false pastoral taste, which we should blame in Saint-Évremond and Voiture, but which we love in La Fontaine. In fact, those insipidities and that false taste cease to exist from the moment that they flow from his bewitching pen. La Fontaine needs longer breath and more consecutiveness in his compositions; he has, as he goes along, frequent distractions which hamper his style and swerve his thought; his delicious verses, flowing like a rivulet, slumber at times, or they wander away and lose themselves; but that, in itself, constitutes a manner; and it is with that manner, as with those of all men of genius, — what would elsewhere seem poor and even bad, in them becomes a trait of character or a piquant grace.

The conversion of Mme. de La Sablière, which La Fontaine had not the courage to imitate, left him solitary and unoccupied. He continued to live in her house; but she no longer received the company of other days, and she absented herself frequently to visit the poor and the sick It was then, more especially, that, to relieve his tedium, he gave himself up to the society of the Prince de Conti and of MM. de Vendôme, whose morals we all know; and thus, without losing any of his powers of mind, he exposed to the eyes of every one a cynical and dissolute old age, ill-disguised under the roses of Anacreon. Maucroix, Racine, and his true friends were grieved at such licence without excuse; the austere Boileau ceased to see him. Saint-Évremond, who tried to attract him to England and to the Duchesse de Mazarin, received from Ninon a letter in which she said: "I have heard that you are wishing for La Fontaine in England; here, in Paris, people enjoy him no longer; his head is much weakened. That is the fate of poets: Tasso and Lucretius met with it. I doubt if there is any philter of love for La Fontaine; he has never loved women who could pay the cost."

La Fontaine's head was not weakened as Ninon thought; but what she says of his vile loves is only too true; he often received from the Abbé de Chaulieu gifts of money of which he made a melancholy use. Fortunately, a rich and beautiful young woman, Mme. d'Hervart, attached herself to the poet, offered him the attractions of her house, and became to him, by care and kind attention, a second La Sablière. At the death of the latter, she took the old man to her home and surrounded him with friendship to his last moments. It was in that home that the writer of *Joconde,* brought at last to repentance, put on the sackcloth and ashes he never again put off. The details of that repentance are touching: La Fontaine consecrated it publicly by a translation of the *Dies Iræ,* which he read before the Academy, and he formed the design of paraphrasing the Psalms before he died.

But, apart from the chilling of old age and sickness, we may doubt if that task, often attempted by repentant poets, would have been possible to La Fontaine, or to any one else in those days. At that epoch of ruling and traditional beliefs, it was the senses, not the reason, that led men astray: they had been licentious, they made themselves devout; they had passed through no philosophical pride or arid impiety; they did not linger in the regions of doubt, they were not made to feel a hundred times their failure in the search for truth. The senses charmed the soul for

themselves, for their own sake, and not as a be-
wildering and fiery emotion, not from ennui or
despair. Then, when licence and errors were exhausted, and men returned to the one supreme truth,
they found a haven all ready for them, a confessional,
an oratory, a hair-shirt that subdued the flesh; they
were not, as in our day, pursued into the very bosom
of reviving faith by fearsome doubts, eternal obscurities, and an abyss ever yawning:—I am wrong; there
was one man, even in those days, who experienced
all this and it well-nigh drove him mad: that man
was Pascal.

VI.

Pascal.

Pascal.

IN writing a few pages upon Pascal, I am under the disadvantage of having formerly written a large volume *(Histoire de Port-Royal)* of which he was, almost exclusively, the subject. I shall endeavour, in speaking on this occasion of a book that ranks among our classics, to forget what I have hitherto written of it that was too minute for my present purpose, and limit myself here to what is likely to interest the generality of readers.

Pascal had a great mind, and a great heart — which great minds do not always have; and all that he has done in the domain of mind and the domain of heart bears a stamp of invention and of originality which testifies to strength, profundity, and an ardent, even rabid, pursuit of truth. Born in 1623, of a family full of intelligence and virtue, brought up without close restraint by a father who was himself a superior man, he had received great gifts from Nature; a special genius for mathematical calculations and concepts, and an exquisite moral sensibility which made him passionate for good and against evil, eager for happiness, but a happiness that was noble and everlasting. His discoveries in childhood are famous; wherever he turned his eyes he sought and found something new; it was easier to him to find for himself than to study from others. His youth escaped the frivolities and licence which are its usual perils; his nature, however, was very capable of storms; he had them, those storms, and he spent their force in the sphere of knowledge, but, above all, in that of religious sentiment.

His excess of intellectual toil had early made him subject to a singular nervous malady, which still further developed a naturally keen sensibility. His meeting with the gentlemen of Port-Royal furnished food for his moral activity, and their doctrine, which was something new and bold, became to him a point of departure, whence he sprang forward with his native originality towards a complete reconstruction of the moral and religious world. A Christian, sincere and impassioned, he conceived an apology, a defence of religion by a method and by reasons that no one had so far found, but which, as he believed, would carry defeat to the very heart of unbelief. At thirty-five years of age he turned to this work with the fire and precision that he put into everything; new and more serious disorders appearing in his health prevented its steady execution; but he returned to it in every interval of his sufferings; and he cast on paper his ideas, his perceptions, his inspirations. Dying at thirty-eight years of age, in 1662, he could not put them into order as a whole, and his *Pensées sur la Réligion* did

BLAISE PASCAL.
From a steel engraving.

not appear till seven or eight years later, under the
care of his family and friends.

What was that first edition of the *Pensées?* What
must it have been? We can easily conceive it, even
if the original manuscripts were not in existence to
show it. The first edition did not contain all that
Pascal left; only the principal parts were given; and
of those, scruples of various kinds, either of doctrine
or of grammar, caused corrections, modifications, explanations in certain places, where the excitability and
impatience of the author were shown in statements
too brusque, or too concise, or in a decisive manner,
which on such subjects might be compromising.

In the eighteenth century Voltaire and Condorcet
seized upon some of Pascal's *Pensées* very much as
in war-time generals try to profit by the premature
advance of an audacious and rash enemy. Pascal was
audacious only, he was not rash; but since I have
compared him to a general, I will add that he was
a general. Killed in the very moment of his enterprise, it was left unfinished, and in part unprotected.

In our day, by restoring Pascal's true text, giving
his sentences in all their simplicity, their firm and precise beauty, their boldness in challenging, and their
familiarity, which is sometimes singular, we are
brought back to a point of view that is far more
just, and in no way hostile. M. Cousin was the first
to suggest (in 1843) the work of completely restoring
Pascal; M. Fougère has the merit of executing it in

1844. Thanks to him, we now have Pascal's *Pensées* in precise conformity with the original manuscripts. This is the text that a young professor, M. Havet, has just published, surrounding it with much necessary help in the way of explanations, comparisons, and commentaries; he has given us a learned edition, truly classic, in the best acceptation of that word.

Being unable, in this essay, to enter fully into an examination of Pascal's method, I wish merely to insist on a single point, and show how, in spite of all changes that have come about in the world and in ideas, in spite of the repugnance that is more and more caused by certain views peculiar to the author of the *Pensées,* we are to-day in a better position to sympathise with Pascal than they were in the days of Voltaire; that which shocked Voltaire shocks us much less than the beautiful and heartfelt parts, which are one whole side of him, touch and transport us.

It is because Pascal is not merely a reasoner, a man who presses his adversary closely from every direction, who flings a challenge to him on all the points that are commonly the pride and glory of the understanding; he is at the same time a soul that suffers; he has felt, and he expresses, in himself, the struggle and the agony.

There were unbelievers in Pascal's time; the sixteenth century gave birth to quite a number, especially among the lettered classes; these were pagans, more or less sceptical, of whom Montaigne is for us the

gracious type, and we see the race continued in Charron, La Mothe Le Vayer, and Gabriel-Naudé. But these
men of doubt and erudition, or others, the mere libertines of wit and society, such as Théophile and Des
Barreaux, took things little to heart. Whether they
persevered in their unbelief, or were converted in the
hour of death, we feel in none of them that deep uneasiness that marks a moral nature of a high order,
and an intellectual nature sealed with the signet of the
Archangel: in a word, and to speak after the manner
of Plato, they are not royal natures. Pascal is of that
primal and glorious race; he has upon his heart and
on his brow more than one sign of it; he is one of the
noblest of mortals, but he is ill, he seeks a cure. He
was the first to bring to the defence of religion the
ardour, the anguish, the lofty melancholy that others
have since carried into scepticism.

"I blame equally," he says, "those who take the
side of praising man, those who take the other side of
condemning him, and those who merely divert themselves; I can approve of those only who *seek with
groans.*"

The method he employs in his *Pensées* to combat
unbelief, and, above all, to stir the indifferent and put
desire into their hearts, is full of originality and unex-
pectedness. We know how he starts. He takes man
in the midst of nature, in the bosom of the infinite;
he considers him, by turns, in his relation to the im-
mensity of the heavens and in his relation to atoms;

he shows him alternately grand and petty, suspended between two infinities, two abysses. The French language has no finer pages than the simple and se-· vere lines of that incomparable picture. Then, following man within himself, as he has followed him without, he strives to show that in the soul are two abysses, one straining upward towards God, towards a noble morality, a movement of return to man's illustrious origin; on the other a descent, an abasement towards evil, a sort of criminal attraction towards vice. That is, undoubtedly, the Christian idea of original corruption and the Fall; but by the manner in which Pascal lays hold of it he makes it his own in a way, so far and so hard does he drive it to a conclusion: he makes man in the beginning a monster, a chimera, something incomprehensible; he forms the knot and ties it indissolubly, in order that God alone, descending upon it like a sword, can cut it.

To vary my reading of Pascal, I have given myself the satisfaction of re-reading, side by side, certain pages of Bossuet and Fénelon. I took Fénelon in his treatise on the *Existence de Dieu,* and Bossuet in his treatise on the *Connaissance de Dieu et de Soi-même ;* and without seeking to fathom the difference (if there be any) in doctrine, I have felt, more especially, the difference in their value and their genius.

Fénelon, as we know, begins by obtaining his proofs of the existence of God from the general aspect of the universe, from the spectacle of the wonders that start forth in all orders — the stars, the various elements, the structure of the human body; all are to him a path by which to rise to the contemplation of the work, and to admiration of the art and knowledge of the workman. There is a plan, there are laws, therefore there must be an architect and a legislator. There are defined purposes, therefore there must be a supreme intention. After accepting with confidence this method of interpretation by external things, and the demonstration of God by Nature, Fénelon, in the second part of his treatise, takes up another class of proofs; he admits philosophic doubts on things external, and turns inward to man's self, reaching the same end by another road, and demonstrating God by the very nature of our ideas. But, while admitting the universal doubt of philosophers, he is not alarmed by the state of things; he describes it slowly, almost kindly; he is neither hurried, nor impatient, nor distressed, like Pascal; he is not what Pascal in his researches seems to us at first sight to be — a bewildered traveller longing for shelter, who, lost without a guide in a dark forest, takes many a wrong path, returns upon his steps discouraged, sits down at a crossways in the forest, utters cries that no one answers, starts again in grief and frenzy, and, still lost, flings himself to earth, wanting to die, and attains his goal at last through terror and bloody sweat.

Fénelon has nothing of all this in his easy, gradual, circumspect advance. It is very true that at the moment when he asks himself whether all Nature is not a phantom, an illusion of the senses, and when, to be logical, he assumes this supposition of absolute doubt — it is very true that he says to himself: "This state of suspension surprises and alarms me; it casts me into my inward self, into a deep solitude that is full of horror; it impedes me, it holds me, as it were, in air; it cannot last, I know that; but it is the only reasonable state."

At the moment when he says that, we feel very plainly, by the manner in which he speaks and his levity of expression, that he is not seriously alarmed. A little farther on, addressing reason and apostrophising it, he asks it: "How long shall I remain in this doubt, which is a species of torture, and yet is the only use I can make of reason?" This doubt, which is a "species of torture" for Fénelon, is never admitted as a gratuitous supposition by Pascal; it is its reality that seems to him cruel torture, the most revolting and intolerable to Nature itself. Fénelon, in putting himself into this state of doubt under the example of Descartes, makes sure previously of his own existence and the certainty of several primary ideas. He continues in this path of broad, agreeable, and easy deduction, mingled here and there with little gusts of affection, but without storms. We feel, as we read him, an airy, angelic nature, which has only to let itself go, and it will rise of itself to its celestial origin. The whole is crowned by a prayer addressed to a God who is, above all else, infinite and kind; a God to whom he abandons himself with confidence, even if at times his words deny it: "Pardon my errors, O Kindness, that is not less infinite than all the other perfections of my God; pardon the stammerings of a tongue which cannot abstain from lauding thee, and the failures of a mind that thou hast made to admire thy perfection."

Nothing can be less like Pascal's method than this smooth and easy way. Nowhere do we hear the cry of distress; Fénelon, in adoring the Cross, never clings to it, like Pascal, as to a mast in shipwreck.

Pascal, in the first place, begins by rejecting all proofs drawn from Nature of the existence of God: "I admire," he says ironically, "the boldness with which these persons undertake to speak of God, addressing their discourse to unbelievers. Their first chapter is to prove Divinity by the works of Nature." Continuing to develop his thought, he insists that such discourse, tending to demonstrate God from natural works, can have their true effect only on the faithful, and on those who already worship him. As for the others, the indifferent, and those who are destitute of living faith and grace,

"to say to these that they have only to look at the least things that surround them and they will see God plainly, and to point them, for all proof on this great and important subject, to the course of the moon or the planets is to give them good reason to think that the proofs of our religion are very weak; and I see, by reason and from experience, that nothing is more fitted to give birth to contempt."

We can judge clearly from that passage to what point Pascal neglected and even rejected with disdain all semi-proof; and yet in this he shows himself more critical than Scripture, which says in a celebrated psalm, *Cœli enarrant gloriam Dei:* "The heavens declare the glory of God, and the firmament showeth his handiwork." It is curious to notice that Pascal's rather contemptuous sentence: "I admire the boldness with which," etc., was printed in the first edition of his *Pensées,* and the Bibliothèque Nationale possesses a unique copy, dated 1669, in which the sentence appears verbatim. But presently friends, or the examiners and censors of the book, alarmed at so exclusive a proceeding, which was actually in contradiction to Holy Scripture, cancelled that passage before the book was offered for sale; they softened the language, and presented Pascal's idea with a precaution that that vigorous writer never took, even with regard to his friends and auxiliaries. The only point on which I desire to insist here, is the open opposition of Pascal to what was soon to be Fénelon's method. Fénelon, serene, confident, and without anxiety, beholds the wonderful system of the starry night, and says with the Magi, or the Prophet, or the Chaldean shepherd: "How almighty and wise must he be who made worlds as innumerable as the sands on the seashore, and who leads throughout the ages those wandering worlds as a shepherd his flock!" Pascal considers the same brilliant night, he feels beyond it a void that the geometrician cannot fill, and he cries out: "The eternal silence of that infinite space terrifies me." Like a wounded eagle he flies from the sun, and seeks, without attaining, a new and eternal dawn. His plaint and his terror come of finding nought but silence and night.

With Bossuet the contrast of method is not so striking. Even if, in his treatise on *Le Connaissance de Dieu,* the great prelate were not addressing his pupil, the young dauphin, if he spoke to any reader whatever, he would not write otherwise than as he does. Bossuet takes the pen, and states with lofty tranquillity the points of doctrine — the dual nature of man, his noble origin, the excellence and the immortality of the spiritual principle within him, his direct linking with God. Bossuet lectures like a truly great bishop, seated in his pulpit and leaning on it. He is not an anxious, sorrowful soul in search of something; he is a master, indicating and warranting the way. He demonstrates and develops the whole line of his discourse and conception without contest or effort. He makes no struggle to prove; in a way, he only recognises and promulgates the things of the spirit, like a man convinced who has not fought inward battles for a length of time; he speaks as a man of all authorities and all stabilities, who takes pleasure

in beholding order everywhere, or in re-establishing
it instantly, by his speech. Pascal insists on the discord and disorder inherent, as he thinks, in all nature.
Where the one extends and develops the august advance of his instruction, the other exhibits his wounds
and his blood; but in all that Pascal has which is over-
strained and excessive, he is like ourselves, and he
touches us.

Not that Pascal puts himself completely on a par
with those he reclaims and directs. Without being
either bishop or priest, he is sure of his fact, he knows
his object, he lets us see, plainly enough, his certainty, his scorn, his impatience; he chides, he jeers,
he handles roughly whoso resists or does not understand him; then, all of a sudden, charity or natural
frankness gets the better of him; his despotic airs
cease; he speaks in his own name, and in the name
of all; he associates himself with the soul in trouble,
making it his living image and ours also.

Bossuet does not reject the light or the help of ancient philosophy; he never insults it; according to
him, all that moves onward to the idea of the intellectual and spiritual life, all that aids the exercise and
development of that higher portion of ourselves by
which we are allied to the Supreme Being — all is
good; and every time our "illustrious truth" is made
apparent to us, we gain a foretaste of that higher
existence to which the reasoning human creature is
predestined. Bossuet, in his magnificent language,

loves to associate himself, to unite himself with great names; to link, as it were, a golden chain by which the human understanding can attain to the highest summits. I must quote one passage of sovereign beauty:

"He who beholds Pythagoras transported at having found the squares of the sides of a certain triangle with the square of its base, and sacrificing a hecatomb in thank-offerings; — he who beholds Archimedes, watchful of every new discovery, forgetting to eat or drink; — he who sees Plato extolling the happiness of those who contemplate the good and the beautiful, first in the arts, then in nature, and lastly in their source and essence, which is God; — he who sees Aristotle lauding those happy moments when the soul is possessed solely by the perception of Truth, judging such life to be the only one worthy to be eternal, the life of God;—but (above all) he who sees all saintly persons so transported with this divine exercise of knowing, praising, and loving God that they never quit it, and, in order to continue it, extinguish throughout the whole course of their lives every sensual desire;—whoso, I say, sees all these things, recognizes in their intellectual operations the principle and the exercise of the blessed eternal life."

That which carries Bossuet to God is the principle of human grandeur rather than the sentiment of man's misery. His contemplation rises gradually from truth to truth, it does not bend incessantly over each abyss. In the above words he has painted for us a spiritual enjoyment of the first order, which, beginning with Pythagoras and Archimedes, and passing Aristotle, rises to the saints on earth; he, himself, viewing him in this example, seems only to have mounted one step more to the altar.

Pascal never proceeds thus. He holds to marking

distinctly, in an insuperable manner, the differences
of the spheres. He refuses to see what there was of
gradual advancement towards Christianity in the
ancient philosophies. The learned and reasonable
d'Aquesseau said, in the plan of a work he proposed
to make from the *Pensées:* "If any one should undertake to make actual use of the *Pensées* of M. Pascal,
he would have to rectify in many places the imperfect
ideas he gives of pagan philosophy; true religion
does not need to attribute to its adversaries or its
rivals defects they have not." Brought into comparison with Bossuet, Pascal may at first sight show a
harshness and narrowness of doctrine that shock us.
Not content to believe with Bossuet and Fénelon, and
all other Christians, in an unseen God, he wants to
insist on the mysterious nature of that obscurity; he
takes pleasure in expressly declaring that God "has
chosen to blind some and enlighten others." At times
he "obstinately strikes" (I use his own words) on
rocks which it would be much wiser, from reason and
even from faith, to go round, rather than discover and
denounce them. He says, for example, of the prophe-
cies quoted in the Gospels: "You believe they are
quoted to make you believe—No, it is to prevent you
from believing." He says of miracles: "Miracles do
not serve to convert, but to condemn." Like a too
intrepid guide in mountain climbing, he skirts intentionally the precipices and crevasses; one would think
he was braving vertigo.

Pascal, unlike Bossuet, has an affection for small churches, little flocks of the elect, which leads in the end to sect. "I like," he says, "worshippers unknown to every one and to the Prophets themselves." But, beside and through the hard asperities of his way, what piercing words! what cries that move us! what truths felt by all who suffer, all who desire, all who have lost and then refound the way, never willing to despair of it! "It is good," he cries, "to be tired and weary from the fruitless search for the true good, for then we stretch out our arms to the Liberator." No one has ever made it better felt than Pascal what faith is, perfect faith, "God felt in the heart, and not by reason." "What distance there is," he says, "between the knowledge of God and loving him!"

This affectionate side of Pascal, in breaking through what is sour and stern in his doctrine and methods, has all the more charm and empire. The emotional manner in which that great, suffering, and praying spirit speaks to us of what is most private in religion, of Jesus Christ in person, is fitted to win all hearts, to inspire them with deep, mysterious feeling, and impress upon them for ever a tender respect. We may remain sceptical after reading Pascal, but we find it not permissible to jest or to blaspheme; and, in that sense, it is true that he has vanquished, on one whole side, the spirit of the eighteenth century and of Voltaire.

In a fragment, lately published for the first time,

Pascal meditates on the death of Jesus Christ; on the tortures which that soul, absolutely heroic and firm when it chooses to be so, inflicted on itself in the name and for the sake of all men; and in these few verses, alternately of meditation and of prayer, Pascal penetrates into the mystery of Christ's suffering with a passion, a tenderness, a piety to which no human soul can remain insensible. He supposes a dialogue, in which the divine Sufferer says to his disciple:

" ' Console thyself; thou wouldst not seek me if thou hadst not found;—thou wouldst not seek me if thou didst not possess me; therefore, be not anxious.

" ' I think of thee in my agony; I have shed my blood for thee. Wilt thou that the blood of my humanity be for ever shed whilst thou givest me no tears ? ' "

This writing should be read as a whole and in its place. Jean-Jacques Rousseau could not have heard it, I venture to believe, without breaking into sobs, and, perhaps, falling on his knees. It is by such pages, burning, passionate, in which the love divine is instinct with human charity, that Pascal has more hold upon us to-day than any writer of his time. In this trouble, this passion, this ardour, there is something that redeems his harshness and his extravagances of doctrine. Pascal is for us more violent than Bossuet, but more sympathetic; he is more our contemporary in feeling. We can read him on the same day that we read "Childe Harold" or "Hamlet," "René" or "Werther," and he holds his own against them; or, rather, he makes us comprehend and feel a moral ideal and a beauty of heart that is lacking in all of them, and which, once perceived, is the despair of others. It is an honour to mankind to have despairs that come of such high objects.

Some searchers and erudites will continue to study Pascal; but the conclusion that to-day seems good and useful for simply serious minds and upright hearts, the counsel that I give them after a fresh reading of the *Pensées* in this last edition is not to attempt to penetrate too deeply into the personal and Jansenist Pascal; to be satisfied with divining him on that side and understanding him on certain essential points, and to limit themselves to the sight of the moral struggle, the storm and stress of that passion which he felt for Good, and for deserved happiness. Taking him thus, we can sufficiently resist his rather narrow, stubborn, and arbitrary logic; but our souls will open to that flame, that upward soaring, and to all else that is so tender and so generous in him; we shall grasp without difficulty the ideal of moral perfection which he embodies in Jesus Christ; we shall feel ourselves lifted up and purified in the hours we spend tête-à-tête with this athlete, this martyr, this hero of the invisible moral world — Pascal for us is all that.

The world goes on: it develops more and more in ways that seem the most opposed to those of Pascal; in the ways of practical self-interests, of physical nature trained and subdued, and of human triumphs through industry. It is well to find somewhere a counterpoise; well that in some solitary chambers firm minds, generous, not bitter, and not assuming to protest against the movement of the age, should tell themselves what that age lacks, and in what way it might perfect and crown itself. Such reservoirs of high thoughts are necessary, that the habit of them be not wholly lost, and that the positive, the practical, may not consume the whole man. Human society, and, to take the clearest example, French society, seems to me sometimes like an indefatigable traveller, who takes his way and follows it under more than one costume, changing his name and coat repeatedly. Since '89 we stand on our feet and we walk: whither? who can say? but on we go, ceaselessly. Revolution, at the moment when, under one form, we thought it stopped, rises and appears under another: sometimes it wears the military uniform, sometimes the black coat of the deputy; yesterday it was the proletary, the day before it was the bourgeois. To-day it is industrial before all else; the engineer is he who has the right of way and who triumphs. Let us not complain, but, at the same time, let us remember that other part of ourselves, that part which was so long the most precious honour of humanity. Let us go to London, and visit and admire the Crystal Palace and its marvels; let us enrich it and add to its pride with our products — yes, but on the way, on our return, let us repeat these words, which should be carved upon its frontal:

" All bodies, the firmament, the stars, the earth and its kingdoms, are not equal in value to the lowest human mind; for that knows all things and itself, too; but the bodies know nothing. All bodies together, and all minds together, and all their productions are not equal in value to the smallest impulse of charity: that is of an order infinitely higher.

" From all bodies put together not the slightest little thought can be obtained; that is impossible, and is of another order. Of all bodies and minds not a single impulse of true charity can be obtained; that, too, is impossible, it is of another order, the supernatural."

It is thus that Pascal expresses himself in his brief, curt *Pensées,* written for himself only, rather abrupt, and issuing with a gush, as it were, from the living spring.

VII.

Madame de Sévigné.

VII.

Madame de Sévigné.

THOSE critics, and especially foreign critics, who, in these latter days, have judged our two literary centuries with severity, agree in recognising their ruling qualities, qualities that were reflected by them in a thousand ways, which gave them their brilliancy and distinction, namely: the spirit of conversation and of society, knowledge of the world and of men, a quick, acute sense of proprieties and absurdities, subtile delicacy of sentiment, grace, piquancy, and a perfected politeness of language. And, in truth, it is there—with the reserves that we all make, and two or three names, like those of Bossuet and Montesquieu, understood—it is there that, until about the year 1789, the distinctive characteristics, the signal traits of French literature, among the other literatures of Europe, will be found. That glory, which has been made almost a reproach to our nation, is fruitful and beautiful enough for whoso knows how to understand and interpret it.

At the beginning of the seventeenth century our civilisation, and consequently our language and our literature, had nothing mature, nothing fixed. Europe,

issuing from the religious troubles and passing through
the phases of the Thirty Years' War, was laboriously
giving birth to a new political system; France, within
her borders, was working off the remains of her civil
discords.   At Court, a few salons, a few *ruelles* [al-
coves [1]] of wits and *beaux-esprits* were already in
vogue; but nothing was yet born of them that was
great or original; people were fed to satiety on Spanish novels and the sonnets and pastorals of Italy.   It
was not until after Richelieu, after the Fronde, under
the queen-mother and Mazarin, that suddenly, amid the
fêtes of Saint-Mandé and Vaux, from the salon of
the hôtel de Rambouillet or the antechambers of the
young king, there issued, as if by miracle, three
choice minds, three geniuses diversely endowed, but
all three of pure and naïve taste, perfect simplicity,
easy productiveness, fed by their own native graces
and delicacies, and destined to open a brilliant era of
glory, in which none have surpassed them.

Molière, La Fontaine, and Mme. de Sévigné belong
to a literary generation which preceded that of which
Racine and Boileau were the leaders, and they are distinguished from the latter by various traits, derived
from the nature of their genius and the date of
their coming.   We feel, from the turn of their minds
as much as by their circumstances, that they are nearer

---

[1] Social life went on chiefly in dark, half-furnished bedrooms, until
Mme. de Rambouillet instituted her famous blue salon; hence the use
of the word *ruelles*, applied to social meetings.—Tr.

MADAME DE SÉVIGNÉ.

to the France that preceded Louis XIV, to the old French language and spirit; more commingled in them, so to speak, by education and study; and that if they are less appreciated by foreigners than certain later writers, they owe it to what is precisely more inward, more undefinable, more charming for Frenchmen in their tone and manner. So that if to-day we attempt (and with reason) to revise or call in question many judgments delivered, twenty years ago, by scholastic professors; if we declare war pitilessly against a number of exaggerated fames, we cannot, on the other hand, venerate too much and uphold too firmly these immortal writers, who were the first to give to French literature its original character, and to secure for it to this day its unique place among the literatures of other nations. Molière drew from the spectacle of life, from the living play of human eccentricities, vices, and absurdities, all that we can conceive of strongest and highest in poesy. La Fontaine and Mme. de Sévigné, on a less wide stage, had so delicate and true a sense of the things and the life of their time, — La Fontaine nearer to nature, Mme. de Sévigné to society, — and this exquisite sense they have expressed so vividly in their writings, that they find themselves placed, without effort, beside, and very little below, their illustrious contemporary.

It is of Mme. de Sévigné only that I have now to speak. It seems as if all had been said about her; certainly the details are nearly exhausted; but I believe that she has been until now regarded too much as isolated, which was long the case with La Fontaine, to whom she bears much resemblance. To-day, when the society of which she represents the most brilliant aspect in receding from us becomes more distinctly defined to our eyes as a whole, it is easier, and at the same time more necessary, to assign to Mme. de Sévigné her rank, her importance, and her affinities. Doubtless it is through not making these remarks, and not allowing for difference of periods, that several distinguished minds in our day seem inclined to judge with as much levity as rigour one of the most delightful geniuses that ever existed. I shall be glad if this article can help in removing some of those unjust prejudices.

The excesses of the Regency have been greatly stigmatised; but before the regency of Philippe d'Orléans there was another, not less dissolute, not less licentious, and more atrocious from the cruelty that mingled in it—a species of hideous transition between the debauchery of Henri III and that of Louis XV. The bad morals of the League, which lay low under Henri IV and Richelieu, revived, being no longer repressed. Debauchery became as monstrous as it had been in the days of the *mignons,* and as it was later in the days of the *roués;* but that which brought this period nearer to the sixteenth century and distinguished it from the eighteenth was, especially, assassinations, poisonings (Italian habits due to the Medici), and a frenzy for duels, inherited from the civil wars. Such appears, to the impartial reader, the regency of Anne of Austria; such was the dark and bloody background upon which appeared, one fine morning, the Fronde, which people have agreed to call "a jest of mailed hands." The conduct of the women of those times, the women most distinguished for birth, beauty, and intelligence, seems fabulous; we need to believe that historians have calumniated them. But, as excess leads always to its opposite, the little band of those who escaped corruption flung themselves into sentimental metaphysics, and became *précieuses;* hence the hôtel de Rambouillet. Here was the haven, the asylum of good morals, in the midst of the highest society. As for good taste, it found its place there, in the end, inasmuch as Mme. de Sévigné was of it.

Mlle. Marie de Rabutin-Chantal, born in 1626, was the daughter of the Baron de Chantal, a frantic duellist, who, on an Easter Sunday, left the holy table to serve as second to the famous Comte de Bouteville. Brought up by her uncle, the good Abbé de Coulanges, she received early in life a solid education, and was taught, under Chapelain and Ménage, Latin, Italian, and Spanish. When eighteen years of age she married the Marquis de Sévigné, a man little worthy of her, who, after greatly neglecting her, was killed in a duel in 1651. Mme. de Sévigné, freed at that age, and left with a son and daughter, never thought of remarrying. She loved her children to excess, especially

her daughter; all other passions were unknown to
her. She was, personally, a smiling blonde, not at all
sensual, very gay and frolicsome; the flashes of her
wit sparkled in her changeful eyes and, as she expressed it, in her "mottled eyelashes." She made
herself *précieuse;* she went into society, was loved,
sought, courted; sowing around her hopeless passions, to which she paid little attention, but retaining
generally as friends those whom she would not take
for lovers. Her cousin, Bussy, her master, Ménage,
the Prince de Conti (brother of the great Condé), the
Superintendent Fouquet, wasted their sighs upon her;
but she remained inviolably faithful to the latter in
his overthrow; when she relates his trial to M. de
Pomponne it is worth while to notice with what
tender feeling she speaks of "our dear unfortunate
one."

Young still and beautiful, without pretension, she
placed herself in society on the footing of devotion to
her daughter, wishing for no other happiness than
that of presenting her, and watching her shine. Mlle.
de Sévigné figured, after 1663, in the brilliant ballets
at Versailles, and the official poet, Benserade, who
filled at Court the place that Racine and Boileau were
to hold after 1672, made more than one madrigal in
honour of that "shepherdess," and that "nymph,"
whom an idolising mother called "the prettiest girl
in France." In 1669 M. de Grignan obtained her in
marriage, and sixteen months later he took her to

Provence, where he commanded in the absence of M. Vendôme. Separated henceforth from her daughter, whom she never again saw except after long and unequal intervals, Mme. de Sévigné sought comfort for her loneliness in a daily correspondence, which lasted till her death in 1696, a period of twenty-five years, except for a few interregnums, when mother and daughter were briefly reunited. Before this separation, in 1671, we have only a few letters of Mme. de Sévigné, addressed either to her cousin Bussy, or to M. de Pomponne on Fouquet's trial. It is, therefore, from that date only that we know thoroughly her private life, her habits, the books she read, and even the smallest movements of the society in which she lived and of which she was the soul.

From the very first pages of this correspondence we find ourselves in a wholly different world than that of the Fronde and the Regency; we perceive that what is called French society was at last constituted. No doubt (and, in default of the numerous memoirs of that time, the anecdotes related by Mme. de Sévigné would prove it),—no doubt horrible disorders, disgraceful orgies were prevalent among that young nobility on which Louis XIV imposed, as the price of his favour, dignity, politeness, and elegance; no doubt, under that brilliant surface, that gilded glory, there were vices enough to overflow into another Regency, especially when the bigotry at the close of the reign set them all to fermenting. But at least a conventional decorum was observed; public opinion had begun to blast whatever was ignoble and debauched. Moreover, while disorder and brutality were becoming less scandalous, decency and the employment of the intellect were gaining in simplicity. The qualification of *précieuse* had passed out of date; people remembered, with a smile, that they had once been that, but they were so no longer. No one descanted interminably, as they formerly did, on the sonnet of Job or of Uranie, on the Carte de Tendre, or the nature of the novel; but they talked, they *conversed* — on Court news, recollections of the siege of Paris, or the war in Guienne; Cardinal de Retz related his travels, M. de La Rochefoucauld moralised, Mme. de La Fayette made heartfelt reflections, and Mme. de Sévigné interrupted them to quote a clever saying of her daughter, a prank of her son, an aberration of the worthy d'Hacqueville or of M. de Brancas.

We find it difficult in these days, with our habits of practical occupation, to represent to ourselves faithfully this life of leisure and of talk. The world now moves so fast, so many things are brought upon the stage, that we find we have not the time to examine and grasp them. Our present days are spent in studies, our evenings in serious discussions; of agreeable conversations, interesting talks, we have few or none. The noble society of our day, which has preserved to some extent the leisure habits of the two preceding centuries, seems to have done so on condition of keeping aloof from the ideas and the manners and morals of the present.

At the period of which I speak, conversation had not yet become, as it did in the eighteenth century in the salons under the rule of Fontenelle, an occupation, a business, an exaction; wit was not made necessarily an aim; display, geometrical, philosophical, and sentimental, was not demanded: but they talked, they conversed, of themselves and others, of little or of nothing. It was conversation, as Mme. de Sévigné herself says, *ad infinitum:* "After dinner," she writes somewhere to her daughter, "we went to talk in the most agreeable woods in the world; we were there till six o'clock, engaged in various sorts of conversation so kind, so tender, so amiable, so obliging, both for you and for me, that I am touched to the heart by it." Amid a course of society so easy, so simple, so desultory, and so gracefully animated, a visit, a letter received, insignificant in itself, was an event in which all took pleasure and related eagerly. The least things became of value from the manner and form of telling; it was art which, without perceiving it, and very negligently, they put into life.

It is often said that Mme. de Sévigné gave minute care to her letters, and that in writing them she thought, if not of posterity, at least of the social world of her day, whose suffrages she sought. That is false: the days of Voiture and Balzac were past. She wrote usually offhand, as the pen ran, and of all the things

she could; if time pressed, she scarcely read over hei
letters. "In truth," she says, "between friends one
ought to let the pens trot as they like; mine always
has the rein on its neck." But there are days when
she has more time, or else she feels in better humour
for writing; then, very naturally, she takes pains, she
arranges, she composes very much as La Fontaine
composed a fable: such, for instance, as her letter to
M. de Coulanges on the marriage of Mademoiselle; or
the one about poor Picard, dismissed because he would
not spread the hay. Letters of this sort, brilliant in
form and in art, in which there were not too many
little secrets or slanders, made talk in society and
every one desired to read them. "I must not forget
to tell you what happened this morning," writes Mme.
de Coulanges to her friend; "I was told: 'Madame, a
lacquey from Mme. de Thianges is here'; I ordered
them to bring him in. This is what he had to say to
me: 'Madame, I am sent by Mme. de Thianges, who
begs you to send her the *horse* letter of Mme. de Sévigné, and also that of the *meadow.*' I told the lacquey
that I would take them to his mistress, and I have
done so. Your letters make all the noise they deserve; it is certain that they are delightful; and you
are as much so as your letters."

Correspondence at that time had, like conversation,
great importance; but neither was composed; people
simply put all their minds and all their souls into
them. Mme. de Sévigné praises her daughter con-

tinually in the matter of letters: "You write incomparable thoughts and effusions," and she adds that she reads "here and there" certain choice passages to persons who are worthy of them: "sometimes I give a little bit to Mme. de Villars, but she wants the tender parts, and tears fill her eyes."

If some deny to Mme. de Sévigné the spontaneousness of her letters, no one has ever questioned the sincerity of her love for her daughter; and there again they forget the period in which she lived, and how in that life of luxurious idleness persons may resemble fancies, just as manias may often become passions. She idolised her daughter, and had early established herself on that footing in society. Arnauld d'Andilly called her, in that respect, "a pretty pagan." Separation had only increased her tenderness; she had scarcely any other thing to speak of; the questions and compliments of those she met always brought her back to it; that dear and almost single affection of her heart ended, in the long run, by becoming her status, her posture, her demeanour, which she used as she did her fan. Mme. de Sévigné was perfectly sincere, frank, and an enemy to all pretence; to her, among the first, do we owe the saying that a person is *true;* she might have invented that expression for her daughter if M. de La Rochefoucauld had not already found it for Mme. de La Fayette; she takes pleasure in applying it to those she loves. When we have analysed, and twisted, and turned in all ways that inexhaustible

mother-love, we come back to the opinion and explanation of M. de Pomponne: "It seems, you say, that
Mme. de Sévigné loves Mme. de Grignan passionately;
and you want to know what is at the bottom of it.
Shall I tell you? It is that *she loves her passionately.*"
It would, indeed, be very ungrateful to cavil at Mme.
de Sévigné for this innocent and legitimate passion, to
which we owe the opportunity to follow the wittiest
and most intellectual of women through twenty-five
years of the most charming period of the most delightful French society.

La Fontaine, painter of fields and animals, did not
ignore society, and has often pictured it with dainty
and malicious touches. Mme. de Sévigné, on her
side, loved the fields; she made long stays at Livry
with the Abbé de Coulanges, or on her own estate of
Les Rochers in Bretagne; it is piquant to learn under
what aspects she saw and has pictured Nature. We
at once perceive that, like our good fabulist, she had
early read *Astrée,* and had dreamed in her youth
beneath the mythological shades of Vaux and Saint-
Mandé. She loves to walk "by the rays of the beautiful mistress of Endymion"; to pass two hours
"alone with the Hamadryads"; her trees are deco-
rated with inscriptions and ingenious devices, such as
passages from the *Pastor fido* and the *Aminta: "Bella
cosa far niente,* says one of my trees; another answers: *Amor odit inertes.* " And elsewhere she says:
"As for our sentences, they are not defaced; I go

often to look at them; they are even increased, and two trees side by side sometimes contradict each other: *La lontananza ogni gran piaga salda;* and then: *Piaga d'amor non si sana moi.''*

These rather insipid reminiscences of pastorals and romances come naturally from her pen, and bring out very agreeably many fresh and novel descriptions that are wholly her own:

> "I came here (Livry) to end the summer and say farewell to the leaves; they are still on the trees, they have only changed colour; instead of being green they are now aurora colour, and so many sorts of aurora that they compose a brocade of gold, very rich and magnificent, which we try to think lovelier than green—if only by way of change."

And when she is at *Les Rochers* she cries out: "I should be very happy in these woods if I only had a leaf that sings: ah! the pretty thing a singing leaf would be!" How she pictures for us "the triumph of the month of May"! when the "nightingale, the cuckoo, the white-throated warblers in the forest herald the spring." How she makes us feel and almost live in "those beautiful crystal days of autumn, which are no longer hot and yet not cold"! When her son, to pay for some foolish extravagance, cuts down the ancient woods of Buron, she is roused to emotion, she weeps with all those fugitive dryads, those evicted wood-nymphs.

Because we often find her in a gay and frolicsome humour, we should do wrong to consider Mme. de Sévigné either frivolous or shallow. She was serious, even sad, especially during the sojourns she made in the country; revery held a great place in her life. But here it is necessary to come to an understanding: she did not dream in her long and sombre avenues like Delphine, or the mistress of Oswald; that style of revery was not invented in her day; it needed, as a preliminary, that Mme. de Staël should write her admirable book on the *Influence des Passions sur le Bonheur*. Until then, dreaming was a much easier, much simpler, much more personal thing; yet it was one of which the dreamer rendered little account to herself: it was thinking of her daughter in Provence, of her son with the armies of the king, of her friends far away or dead; it was saying: "As for my life, you know it; it is passed with five or six friends whose society pleases me, and in duties to which I am compelled and which are no small matter. But what vexes me is, that in doing nothing the days go by, and our poor life is made up of such days, and we grow old and die. I think that hard."

Formal and precise religion, which governed life in those days, contributed much to temper the licence of sensibility and imagination, which, since then, has felt no curb. Mme. de Sévigné guarded herself carefully from those thoughts over which she believed it "best to glide." She expressly desires that morals be Christian, and more than once she jokes her daughter on being tainted with Descartism. As for her, amid the chances and changes of this world, she bows

her head, and takes refuge in a sort of providential
fatalism, which her relations with Port-Royal and her
readings of Nicole and Saint Augustine had inspired
in her.   This religious and resigned tendency in her
increased with age, without altering in any way the
serenity of her temper; but it often communicated to
her language something more strongly wise and a
greater tenderness.   In a letter to M. de Coulanges, on
the death of the minister Louvois, she rises almost to
the sublimity of Bossuet, just as at other times and in
other places she attains to the comedy of Molière.

M. de Saint-Surin, in his excellent work on Mme.
de Sévigné, has lost no occasion to contrast her with
Mme. de Staël, and to place her above that famous
woman.   I believe there is interest and profit in thus
comparing them; but it ought not to be done to the
detriment of either.   Mme. de Staël represents a completely new society; Mme. de Sévigné a vanished
society; hence vast differences, which one might be
tempted at first sight to explain solely by the different
turn of their minds and natures.   Without pretending
to deny the profound divergence of their two souls —
one of which knew only maternal love, the other
knowing every passion, the most generous and even
the most virile — I find in both, looking closely at
them, many weaknesses, many ordinary qualities,
the divers developments of which were solely the
result of the diversity of periods.   What natural ease
full of gracious light-heartedness, what dazzling pages

of pure intellect in Mme. de Staël when sentiment
does not interfere and she allows her philosophy and
her politics to slumber! And Mme. de Sévigné, does
she never descant and philosophise? Why else should
she make her daily reading in Saint Augustine?—for
this woman, called frivolous, read all and read well:
"It gives," she said, "such pale colours to the mind
not to enjoy solid reading." She read Rabelais, Montaigne, and Pascal, the "Cleopatra" of Quintilian,
Saint John Chrysostom and Tacitus, and Virgil, "not
travestied, but in the grandeur of Latin and Italian."
When it rained, she read folios in twelve days. During Lent she made it a joy to give herself up to Bourdaloue. Her conduct toward Fouquet in his overthrow
lets us imagine what devotion she would have been
capable of in times of revolution. If she shows herself a little vainglorious when the king, one evening,
dances with her, or when, at Saint-Cyr, he pays her a
compliment after the acting of *Esther,* who else of
her sex would have been more philosophical? Did
not Mme. de Staël put herself to great cost and trouble
to obtain a word or a glance from the conqueror of
Egypt and Italy? Certainly a woman who, mingling
from youth with Ménage, Godeau, Benserade, and
their like, preserved herself by the sole force of her
good sense from their insipidities and punctilios; who
evaded, as if playfully, the more refined and seductive pretensions of Saint-Évremond and her cousin
Bussy; a woman, friend and admirer of Mlle. de

Scudéry and of Mme. de Maintenon, who kept herself
equally distant from the romantic sentiments of the
one and the strait-laced reserve of the other; who,
allied with Port-Royal, and feeding on the works of
ces Messieurs, valued none the less Montaigne, and
quoted none the less Rabelais, and who wished no
other inscription on what she called her convent than
the words: "Sacred Liberty," or "Do what you like,"
as at the Abbey of Thélème—such a woman may frolic
and sport and "glide over thoughts," and choose to
take things by their familiar and diverting side, but,
all the same, she gives proof of an inward energy, an
originality, that was rare indeed.

There is one single instance in which we cannot
help regretting that Mme. de Sévigné gave way to her
light-hearted, bantering habit; an instance in which
we absolutely refuse to share her jest, and for which,
after seeking all its extenuating reasons, we find it
hard to forgive her: it is when she relates so gaily to
her daughter the revolt of the Bas-Breton peasantry,
and the horrible severities that repressed it. So long as
she confined herself to laughing at the Assemblies, at
the country-gentlemen and their giddy galas, at their
enthusiasm for voting everything "'twixt midnight
and one o'clock," and the other after-dinner follies of
her Breton neighbours, it is all very well; it is, in fact,
a merry and legitimate pleasantry, recalling in places
the touch of Molière; but from the moment that M. de
Forbin arrives with six thousand troops against the

malcontents, and those poor devils, perceiving from afar the soldiers, disperse among the fields or fall upon their knees, crying out, *Mea culpa* (the only French words they know); when, to punish Rennes, its parliament is transferred to Vannes; when they take, haphazard, twenty-five men and hang them; when they drive out and evict a whole street-full of people, women in childbed, old men and children, and forbid that any succour be given them on pain of death; when they torture on the wheel; when they quarter; and when, weary themselves of torturing and quartering, they hang — in the midst of such horrors perpetrated upon innocent persons or poor, misguided creatures, we suffer in seeing Mme. de Sévigné jesting almost as usual; we wish she had shown indignation, a burning, bitter, heartfelt indignation; above all, we would like to erase from her letters such lines as these:

" The real rioters at Rennes ran away long ago, so the good have to suffer in place of the wicked; but I think it all very right, provided the four thousand soldiers who are at Rennes under MM. de Forbin and de Vins do not prevent me from walking in my woods, which are of a height and beauty that is marvellous. . . . They have captured sixty of the burghers, and begin to hang them to-morrow. This province will be a fine example to all the others; it will teach them to respect their governors and not to insult them and fling stones into their gardens. . . . You speak very humorously of our troubles; but we have no longer so many broken on the wheel; only one a week to keep justice going; the *hangings* seem to me now a refreshment."

The Duc de Chaulnes, who instigated all these cruelties because stones were thrown into his garden

COMTESSE DE GRIGNAN.

and insults were shouted to him (the most personal of
them being "fat pig"), was not lowered one iota
thereby in Mme. de Sévigné's estimation; he remained
for her and for Mme. de Grignan "our dear duke,"
and later, when he is appointed ambassador to Rome
and leaves Bretagne, she says the whole region is
"left to sadness." Certainly there is matter here for
reflection on the morals and the civilisation of the
great century. We regret that on this occasion Mme.
de Sévigné's heart did not rise above the prejudices of
her time; it was fitted to do so, for her kindness and
goodness equalled her beauty and her grace. There
were times when she recommended galley-slaves to
the mercy of M. de Vivonne or to M. de Grignan.
The most interesting of her *protégés* was a gentleman
of Provence, whose name has not been preserved.
"The poor young fellow," she says, "was attached
to M. Fouquet; he has been convicted of having been
the means of conveying a letter to Mme. Fouquet
from her husband, for which he is condemned to the
galleys for five years; it is a rather extraordinary case.
You know that he is one of the most honourable
young men you could find, and as fit for the galleys
as to catch the moon by his teeth."

The style of Mme. de Sévigné has been so often
and so intelligently judged, analysed, admired, that it
would be difficult to-day to find eulogy both novel and
suitable to apply to it; on the other hand, I do not
find myself disposed to revive a worn-out topic by

cavilling criticism. A single general observation will
suffice: it is that we may connect the grand and
beautiful styles of the Louis XIV period with two
different systems, two opposite manners. Malherbe
and Balzac founded in our literature the learned,
polished, chastened, cultivated style; in the composition of which they came from thought to expression,
slowly, by degrees, and by dint of tentatives and
erasures. This is the style that Boileau advised for
all purposes; he would fain have a work returned
twenty times to the stocks to be polished and re-
polished constantly; he boasts of having taught
Racine to write easy verses in a difficult manner.
Racine is, in fact, the most perfect specimen of this
style in poesy; Fléchier was less successful in his prose.
But, by the side of this style of writing, always somewhat uniform and academic, there is another, widely
different, free, capricious, variable, without traditional
method, and wholly conformed to diversities of talent
and genius. Montaigne and Regnier gave admirable
samples of it, and Queen Marguerite a most charming
one in her familiar memoirs, the work of her *après-dis-
nées:* this is the broad, untrammelled, abundant style
that follows the current of ideas ; the style of the
first thought, the *prime-sautier*, as Montaigne himself
would say; it is that of La Fontaine and Molière, that
of Fénelon, of Bossuet, of the Duc de Saint-Simon, and
of Mme. de Sévigné. The latter excels in it; she lets
her pen "trot with the reins on its neck," and, as it

goes along, she scatters in profusion colours, comparisons, images, while wit and sentiment escape her on all sides. She is thus placed, without intending or suspecting it, in the front rank of the writers of our language.

I ask myself how Mme. de Sévigné issues from a fresh study of her: She issues such as a first sight of her suggested, and more than ever like unto herself. I am confirmed, after study and reflection, in the idea that a first frank impression had given me. of her. In the first place, the more we think of it the better we explain to ourselves her mother-love; that love which, for her, represented all the others. Her rich, strong nature, a nature sound and blooming, in which gaiety was chiefly the temperament with serious thought beneath it, never had a passion properly so-called. Left an orphan early, she never felt filial tenderness; she never spoke of her mother; once or twice she even jested about the memory of her father, whom she never knew. As for conjugal love, she tried it loyally; it soon became bitter to her, and she had no chance to give herself up to it. Left a young and beautiful widow, with a free, intrepid spirit, had she, in that dazzling rôle of Célimène, some hidden weakness that lay concealed? Did a spark ever fall upon her heart? Was she ever in danger of an instant's forgetfulness with her cousin Bussy? We never know what to expect of these smiling, brilliant creatures, and we should often be finely duped if we fastened upon words which, said by others, would mean a great deal. The fact is that she resisted Bussy, her greatest peril, and though she may have liked him a little, she never loved him with passion. Passion she never felt for any one until the day when the accumulation of her treasures of tenderness fell upon the head of her daughter to be nevermore displaced. An elegiac poet has remarked that a love which comes late is often the most violent; all the arrears of feelings and emotions are paid at once:

" Sæpe venit magno fænore tardus amor. "

So of Mme. de Sévigné. Her daughter inherited all the savings of that rich and feeling heart, which had said to itself until that day, "I wait." There is the true answer to those hypercritical minds who have chosen to see in Mme. de Sévigné's love for her daughter an affectation and form of posing. Mme. de Grignan was the great, the one only passion of her mother; and this maternal tenderness had all the characteristics of passion, enthusiasm, prejudice, and slight absurdity (if I may apply that word to such persons), with a *naïveté* of indiscretion that makes us smile. Let us not complain of it. Mme. de Sévigné's whole correspondence is illumined by this passion which came, at last, to add itself to the brilliancy, already so varied, of her imagination and her delightful humour.[1]

[1] Mme. de Grignan's merits have been much discussed; her mother has done her some wrong in our eyes by praising her too much. The

On this latter point, I mean temperament and
humour, let us try to understand Mme. de Sévigné
thoroughly. In speaking of her, we are speaking of
grace itself, not a soft and languid grace, but a lively,
overflowing grace, full of wit and intellect, and without the least touch of pale colour.   She has a vein of
Molière in her.   There 's a Dorine in Mme. de Sévigné,
a Dorine of the great world and the best company, with
very nearly the same vigour and raciness.   A few
words of Tallemant have very well characterised that
charming and powerful feminine nature, such as it
showed itself, quite young, in its abounding life.
After saying that he thinks her one of the most
amiable and most honourable women in Paris, he
adds: "She sings, she dances, she has a very lively
and agreeable wit; she is *brusque* and cannot keep
herself from saying what she thinks pretty, although
quite often they are things rather free."   That is a
saying we should not lose sight of in thinking of
her, covering it, however, with all the delicacy and
courtesy that we like.   There was joy in her.   She
verified in her person Ninon's saying: "The joy of
the spirit shows its strength."   She was of the race

---

son, who was somewhat of a libertine, appears to us more agreeable.
It would seem as if Mme. de Sévigné's reason and gaiety, so charmingly mingled in her, were divided between her children; the son
having all his mother's grace but not her reason; the daughter having
the reason only, and with it a certain crabbedness, not tempered, and
without either piquancy or charm.   Certain tales of her insolence and
ill-temper have come down to us.

of minds to which belonged Molière, Ninon herself,
Mme. Cornuel somewhat, and La Fontaine; a generation slightly anterior to Racine and Boileau, and more
full-blooded, more vigorously nourished. "You
seem born for pleasures," Mme. de La Fayette said to
her, "and pleasures seem made for you. Your presence increases all amusements, and amusements increase your beauty when they surround you. In
short, joy is the true state of your soul, and grief is
more contrary to you than to any one else in the
world." She said herself, recollecting an old friend:
"I have just seen M. de Larrei, son of our poor friend
Lenet with whom we laughed so much; for never
was any youth so full of laughter as ours, and of all
kinds."

Her rather irregular but real beauty became radiant
at moments when she grew animated; her countenance was lighted by her mind, or, to quote a saying
literally, "her mind even dazzled our eyes." One of
her friends (the Abbé Arnauld), who had as little imagination as it was possible to have, must have found
some in order to describe her when he tells us : "I
seem to see her still as she appeared to me the first
time I had the honour of seeing her, seated in her carriage all open, between monsieur her son and mademoiselle her daughter: all three such as the poets
represent Latona with the young Apollo and the young
Diana, such charm shone forth from the mother and
children." We see her there, in her natural frame and

full expansion: beauty, mind, and grace unveiled and glowing in the sunshine.

I must note, however, one shadow. Her joyousness, real as it was, was not for all seasons, nor out of season, and as the years went on it lessened, though it was never extinguished. Speaking of a journey she made in 1672, during which she regretted not having the company of her amiable cousin de Coulanges, she writes: "To feel joy we must be with joyous people. You know I am what people want me to be; I originate nothing." Which merely means that this charming spirit possesses all tones and could adjust itself to the notes of others. Certain it is that even amid sadness and vexations she continued the finest-tempered woman, with the most playful imagination ever seen. She had a way of her own, a gift of sudden and familiar imagery with which she could clothe her thought unexpectedly, as, indeed, none but she could do. Even when that thought was serious, even when sensibility was at the bottom of it, she used words that play upon it and give the effect of gaiety. Her spirit could never divest itself of that vivacious sparkle, that gaiety of colour. She was just the contrary of her good friends the Jansenists; theirs was the *sad* style.

And, now, if what I have here said should seem to some critical minds to have pushed admiration for Mme. de Sévigné too far, will they permit me to ask them a question? Have you read her? By reading,

I do not mean running hastily over her letters, nor singling out two or three which enjoy an almost classic reputation—such as those on the marriage of Mademoiselle, on the death of Vatel, on those of M. de Turenne and the young Duc de Longueville—but entering in and going with her, step by step, through the ten volumes of her letters, following all, *winding through all* (as she herself would say), doing for her as we do for "Clarissa Harlowe" when we have a fortnight's rain and leisure in the country. After that not very terrible trial let any one find fault with my admiration if he has the courage, and if, indeed, he remembers it.

VIII.

Bossuet.

VIII.

Bossuet.

THE fame of Bossuet has become one of the religions of France, it is recognised, it is proclaimed, and men honour themselves in bringing to it daily fresh tribute, in finding new reasons for its existence and its growth; they discuss it no longer. It is the privilege of true greatness to define itself more and more clearly as it recedes, and to command from a distance. What is singular, nevertheless, in this fate, this sort of apotheosis of Bossuet, is that he thus becomes greater and greater for us without, for all that, inducing us to think him necessarily right in certain of the most important controversies in which he was engaged. We love Fénelon, we cherish his graces, his noble and refined ingratiations, his chaste elegances; we forgive him readily for what are called his errors; but Bossuet combats them, not only forcibly, but to excess, with a species of hardness. No matter! the great voice of the contradictor carries you away in spite of yourself, and forces you to bow your head regardless of your inward attachment to him he is striking down. So with the long and obstinate pitched battles waged on the Gallican question. Whether you are Gallican or whether you are not, you applaud or you breathe a sigh over that spot of the career, but the illustrious course as a whole loses nothing of its grandeur and its majesty in your eyes.

I shall venture to say the same thing of the relentless war that Bossuet waged against Protestantism under all its forms. Every enlightened Protestant, making his reserves on points of history, will own, with respect, that he never encountered another such adversary. In politics also, however little of a partisan one may be of the consecration theory and the right divine such as Bossuet institutes and proclaims it, we should be almost sorry if that doctrine had not found so simple, so manly, so sincere an organ, and one so innately convinced. A God, a Christ, a bishop, a king—there, taken as a whole, is the luminous sphere in which Bossuet's thought evolves itself and reigns; there is his ideal for the world.

Just as in ancient times there was a people apart, who, under the inspiration and guidance of Moses, kept clear and distinct the idea of a God, an ever-present Creator, governing the world directly, while all the neighbouring peoples wandered from that idea, confused to them in clouds of fancy, or smothered under phantoms of the imagination, or submerged in the exuberant luxury of nature, so Bossuet among

JACQUES BÉNIGNE BOSSUET.
From a steel engraving.

moderns has grasped, more than any other, that simple idea of order, authority, unity, of continual government by Providence, and he applies it to all things without effort, and as if by undeniable deduction. Bossuet is the Hebrew genius extended and fertilised by Christianity, open to all the acquisitions of the intellect, but retaining something of sovereign prohibition and closing his vast horizon precisely where, for him, light ends. In tone and gesture he belongs to the race of Moses. He mingles the bearing of the Prophet-King with the emotions of an ardent and sublime pathos; he is the eloquent voice *par excellence,* the simplest, the strongest, the most abrupt, the most familiar, yet resounding with sudden thunder. Within the bounds of his rigid and imperious current flow treasures of eternal human ethics. It is through all these characteristics that he is still unique for us, and that, whatever use may be made of his words, he remains our model of the highest eloquence and the noblest language.

Jacques Bénigne Bossuet, born at Dijon, September 27, 1627, of a good and ancient *bourgeois* family of magistrates and members of parliaments, was brought up among books in the family library. His father, having entered, as dean of counsellors (a newly created office), the Parliament of Metz, left his children in care of his brother, who was counsellor to the Parliament of Dijon. Young Bossuet, who lived in his uncle's house, attended classes at the Jesuit college

of the town. He distinguished himself early by a
surprising capacity of memory and comprehension;
he knew Virgil by heart, and a little later he knew
Homer. His great pagan preference, if I may so express it, was instinctively first for Homer, then for
Virgil; Horace, to his taste and his judgment, came
later. But the book which, above all, determined the
genius and the vocation of Bossuet, and which became the regulator of all within him, was the Bible.
It is related that the first time he read it he was, as it
were, illumined and transported. He had found the
source whence his own genius was to flow, like one
of the four great rivers in Genesis.

Bossuet was destined in childhood for the Church:
tonsured when eight years of age, he was barely
thirteen when he was appointed to a canonry of the
cathedral at Metz. His boyhood and his adolescence
were therefore regular, pure, and wholly directed toward the Temple. He went to Paris for the first time in
September, 1642. It is said that on the very day of his
arrival he saw the entrance of Cardinal de Richelieu, in
a dying condition, on his return from his vengeance
on the south of France; the minister was borne in a
movable chamber covered with scarlet cloth. To have
seen, were it only once, Richelieu, all powerful in the
purple, and soon after to see the Fronde, civil war unchained, and anarchy, was for Bossuet a compendious
course in politics, from which he drew the sound lesson: better one master than a thousand masters, and,

better still, that the master be the king himself and not the minister.

Entering, for his course in philosophy, the college of Navarre, he distinguished himself in themes and addresses in public; he was a prodigy and a school angel before he became the eagle we admire. We all know that, being extolled at the hôtel de Rambouillet by the Marquis de Feuquières, who had known his father at Metz and extended his goodwill to the son, young Bossuet was taken there one evening to preach an impromptu sermon. In lending himself to such singular exercises, exhibitions at which his person and his talent were challenged, treated like a virtuoso of intellect in the salons of ·the hôtel de Rambouillet and that of de Nevers, it does not appear that Bossuet's vanity was touched in the slightest degree; there is no other example of a precocious genius thus lauded and caressed by society and remaining as truly exempt from all self-love and coquetry.

He often went to Metz to repose himself in study and a sterner life after his successes and triumphs in Paris. He was there ordained, successively, subdeacon, deacon, archdeacon, and priest (1652). He even settled himself in Metz for six years to fulfil assiduously his functions as archdeacon and canon. It was then that he preached the first sermons that we have of his, and his first panegyrics; also he took up arms for the first time as a controversialist against the Protestants, who abounded in that province. In a

word, Bossuet conducted himself like a militant young
Levite, who, instead of accepting at once an agreeable
post at the centre of all things in the capital, preferred
to inure himself and temper himself by bearing the
arms of the Word where duty and danger called him,
on the frontier.

Of Bossuet's earliest sermons, among those he
preached at Metz in his youth, one has been specially pointed out by the Abbé Vaillant; it is that for
the ninth Sunday after Whitsunday. Bossuet seeks
to show at one and the same time the kindness and
the rigour of God, the tenderness and severity of
Jesus. He begins by showing Jesus moved to pity
when he enters the city that is about to betray him,
and weeping over it; then he shows him irritated and
implacable, avenging himself, or letting his Father
avenge him on the walls and on the children of that
same Jerusalem. This sermon preached, as Bossuet
said in closing it, "as God has inspired it in me,"
has something youthful, eager, bold in places, rash,
and even strange. He tries to represent in the same
discourse the merciful Saviour and the inexorable
Saviour, the tender heart and the angry heart of Jesus:
"Listen first," he says, "to the sweet, benign voice
of this Lamb without spot, and then you shall hear
the roarings of the victorious Lion born of the tribe
of Judah: that is the subject of this discourse. . . ."

More might be said on this first period of Bossuet's
life, both at Metz and in Paris. We might inquire,

for instance, what his personal appearance was in his youth, at the age when he delivered these sermons, already so powerful, with a precocious authority through which shone a visible inspiration, embellished, so to speak, with a lingering *naïveté*. We are told that Nature had endowed him with a noble face; the fire of his mind shone in his glance; the characteristics of his genius permeated his speech. It is sufficient to consult his portrait in the Louvre, painted in old age by Rigaud, from which to form a true idea of what he must have been in his youth. The Abbé Le Dieu, in his "Memoirs, etc., on the Life and Work of Bossuet," says that "his eyes were gentle, yet piercing; his voice seemed always to come from a passionate soul; his gestures in oration were modest, tranquil, natural." But, better still, see his bust in the Louvre by Coysevox: noble head, splendid carriage, pride without assumption; forehead lofty and full, the seat of thought and majesty; the mouth singularly agreeable, sensitive, speaking even in repose; a straight and most distinguished profile: the whole with an expression of fire, intelligence, and kindness — a countenance most worthy of manhood, whether he is made to speak to his fellows or to gaze into heaven. Take from that face its wrinkles, shed over it the bloom of life and youth, dream of a young and adolescent Bossuet; but do not describe him too minutely to yourself, lest you miss the severity of the subject and the respect that is due to him.

When Bossuet quitted Metz to settle in Paris the effect was shown instantly in his eloquence; and to read his productions of that period is like passing from one climate to another. "In following Bossuet's discourses in their chronological order," says the Abbé Vaillant, "we see the old words fall successively like the leaves in autumn." Antiquated or trivial expressions,. repulsive images, lapses of good taste, which were less the fault of Bossuet's youth than of that whole epoch of transition which preceded the great reign, disappeared, leaving the new language free, unconstrained, sudden, unexpected, never to recoil, as he said of Saint Paul, "before the glorious degradations of Christianity," but ready to glorify magnificently its combats, its spiritual government, and its triumphs. Frequently called upon, after the year 1662, to preach before the Court, having also to speak in churches or before the great communities of Paris, Bossuet acquired immediately the language in use, all the while keeping and developing his own and stripping himself of that of the provinces. The provinces, however, through a discipline and practice of six years, had trained and inured him; the Court merely polished him as much and no more than he needed. He was a finished orator at thirty-four years of age. During eight or nine years, from 1660 to 1669, he was the great preacher in vogue, and in renown.

Bossuet's talent was anterior in origin and formation

to the period of Louis XIV, but he owed much of its completion and perfection to the young king. More than once attempts have been made to deprive Louis XIV of his species of useful influence and propitious ascendency over what is called his epoch; such attempts are unjust and exclusive. Bossuet in particular, as I think, shows us a great and striking example of the sort of benefits that the epoch of Louis XIV owed to the young star of the king from the day of its rising. Treated with distinction by Anne of Austria, and becoming, towards the end, her chosen preacher, Bossuet at first indulged in certain luxuries of intellect, certain diffuse and subtile discriminations that belonged to the taste of the day. Delivering before the queen-mother in 1658 (or 59) his "Panegyric of Saint Teresa," Bossuet, excited perhaps by the choice style of the Spanish saint, and carefully developing a passage in Tertullian which says that Jesus, before dying, desired to "sate himself with the delights of patience," does not shrink from adding : "Would you not say, Christians, according to the words of that father, the whole life of the Saviour was a *feast* at which the *meals were tortures?* strange feast! but one which Jesus deemed worthy of his taste. His death sufficed for our salvation, but his death did not suffice to quench that *marvellous appetite* that he had to suffer for us." There, assuredly, is the *bel esprit* in vogue during the Regency. But after he was summoned to preach before the young king he quickly learned to correct such sayings and repress them.

When Louis XIV heard Bossuet for the first time he liked him much and did a charming thing for him, very worthy of a youthful monarch who still had his mother: he sent a letter to Bossuet's father at Metz, "to congratulate him on having such a son." Whoso does not feel that delicacy is not fitted to feel the sort of influence that the young king had over the vast imagination and sound mind of Bossuet. Louis XIV had, at all times, the fit and proper word, just as he had, they say, correctness and a sense of symmetry in the glance of his eye. He had in him, and he had about him, something that warned others not to be excessive, and to force nothing. Bossuet, speaking in his presence, felt that in the matter of elevated taste he had before him a regulator. I wish to say nothing but what is incontestable: Louis XIV, very young, was useful to Bossuet in giving him proportion and all its *justesse,* accuracy. The great and consecrated orator continued to owe to himself alone and to the spirit that filled him his inspirations and his originality.

Here is a fact that can be verified: in the series of Bossuet's Sermons that have been classified, not in the chronological order in which he composed them, but according to the order of the Christian year, beginning with All Saint's day and the Advent and ending with Whitsunday, if you desire to put your hand with certainty on one of the finest and most irreproachable, take any one of those that are labelled : "Preached before the King."

It is true to say that in all the sermons or discourses delivered by Bossuet from 1661 to 1669 and later, there are wonderful passages, far more moving to readers of any class than the sermons of Bourdaloue so much read in these days. In the "Panegyric of Saint Paul," how he takes possession of the subject in its depths, by its most secret and supernatural side! Paul is "the more powerful because he feels himself weak"; it is his weakness that makes his strength. He is the Apostle, without art, of a hidden wisdom, an incomprehensible wisdom, that shocks and scandalises, but into which he will put no deceit or artifice :

"He goes into that polished Greece, mother of philosophers and orators; and, in spite of the resistance of that world, he there establishes more churches than Plato gained disciples by an eloquence that was called divine. He pushes still farther his conquests; he casts down at the feet of the Saviour the majesty of the Roman fasces in the person of a pro-consul ; he forces Rome herself to hear his voice, and the day is coming when that mistress-city will feel herself more honoured by an epistle from Paul's hand addressed to her citizens, than by all the famous harangues she has heard from her Cicero.

"Whence comes it, Christian? It is because Paul has means for persuasion that Greece could never teach and Rome has never learned. A supernatural power, taking pleasure in lifting up that which the proud despise, instils itself and mingles in the majestic simplicity of his words. Hence it is that we admire in his wonderful Epistles a certain virtue, more than human, which persuades against all rules—or rather which does not persuade so much as it takes captive the understanding: which flatters not the ear, but sends its blows straight to the heart. Just as we see a great river restraining, as it flows across a plain, the violent and impetuous force it has acquired in the mountains whence it draws its origin, so this celestial power, contained in the writings of Saint Paul, preserves, even in the simplicity of that style, all the vigour it brought with it from the Heaven whence it came."

Let us now take other sermons preached before the Court: that on Ambition (1666), on Honour (1666), on the Love of Pleasures (1662); beauties of the same order shine throughout them. On ambition and on honour, he says, facing Louis XIV, all that could warn him of the present and future idolatry of which he was the object, if any warning could avail. He seeks to show by the examples of Nero and Nebuchadnezzar, "what can be done in the human soul by the terrible thought of nothing being above his head. It is then," he says, "that immoderate desires grow daily more and more subtile, and double, if I may say so, their stake. Thence come unknown vices . . . ." And on the man, small in himself and ashamed of his smallness, struggling to increase himself, to magnify himself, who imagines that he can incorporate within him all that he amasses and acquires: "Be he count, be he seigneur," he says, "possessor of great wealth, master of many persons, minister of all the councils, and so on; let him magnify himself as much as he pleases, and yet it takes but one death to cast him down. . . . " The characteristic of Bossuet is to seize at a first glance the great ideas that are fixed bounds and necessary limits of things, suppressing the intervening spaces where the external childhood of man forgets and deludes itself.

Lest it be said that I seek in him only his lessons to the great and powerful, let me say that in that same sermon on Honour, where he enumerates and denounces the different sorts of worldly vanity, he does not forget the men of letters, the poets, those who, after their fashion, grasp at renown and empire:

> "They think themselves the wisest who are vain in their gifts of intellect—learned men, men of literature, the wits of the day. In truth, Christians, they are worthy to be distinguished from others, for they are the finest ornaments of the world. But who can endure them when, as soon as they are conscious of a little talent, they weary all ears with their deeds and their sayings, and because they know how to put words together, measure a verse, or round a period, think they have the right to make themselves listened to forever and sovereignly to decide all matters? O justness in life! O equality in manners and morals! O moderation in the passions! rich and true adornments of reasonable nature, when shall we learn to esteem you rightly?"

Eternal art of Poesy, principle, maintainer, and higher law of true talents, here we behold you, established, as it were by the way, in Bossuet's sermon at the very moment when Boileau in his "Satires" is striving to find you. But how much higher up springs the source, and from what surer regions in Bossuet than in the Horaces and Boileaus!

During the first years of his life in Paris he began his subsequently famous series of Funeral Orations. We have the one he pronounced over Père Bourgoing, the general of the Oratoire, and over Nicolas Cornet, grandmaster of Navarre, and the cherished master of Bossuet in particular. There are beauties in both these discourses; in that over Nicolas Cornet the question of Grace and Free Will, which were then agitating the Church under the names of Jansenist and Molinist, are admirably defined; and Bossuet, by the liberal manner in which he states them, shows to what point he is aloof from parties and soars above them. Bossuet needed ampler and loftier subjects; while awaiting them he magnifies and exalts those he treats, but we feel the disproportion. He thundered a little in the void on such occasions, or, rather, in two narrow a space: his voice was too strong for the building.

He must have been more at his ease and felt himself more at large in speaking of Anne of Austria, whose Funeral Oration he pronounced in 1667; and here is a singular thing: that discourse in which Bossuet must have given free course to the gratitude of his heart and to a display of historical magnificence, was never printed!

The death, in 1669, of the Queen of England [Henrietta Maria, daughter of Henri IV and wife of Charles I] gave him the most majestic and grandiose of subjects. He needed the fall and restoration of thrones, the revolutions of empires, all fates collected in a single life and weighing down a single head, as the eagle needs the vast profundity of the skies and

beneath him the abysses and the storms of ocean.
But let us here note another service done by Louis
XIV and his reign to Bossuet. He might have found
such great subjects during the disastrous epochs of
the Fronde and the civil wars, but they would have
come to him scattered and, in some sort, without
limits. Louis XIV and his reign gave him the frame
in which these great subjects were limited and fixed,
but not dwarfed. In the august, well-defined epoch
in the bosom of which he spoke, Bossuet, without
losing aught of his own expanse, or of the freedom
and boldness of his glance into the distance, found
around him on all sides this point of support, this
security, this encouragement, and also a subtile warning of which talent and genius itself have need.
No doubt Bossuet put his trust, first of all, in Heaven,
but as an orator his authority and calm force were
doubled by the sense that beneath him, and at the
moment that he pressed it with his foot, the soil
of France no longer trembled.

All those who have written on Bossuet have made
ample and continual use of the *Mémoires et Journal
sur la Vie et les Ouvrages de Bossuet,* by the Abbé Le
Dieu. A first and most natural inquiry is to know if
those Memoirs answer to the expectation formed of
them. I shall say at once that they do so only in
part; but, such as they are, they will fix with truth,
precision, and no exaggeration whatever, in the minds
of all readers who will allow them to do so, the

lineaments of that noble and upright figure of Bossuet. Its greatness, towards the end, may suffer a
little; I think it does, but its goodness gains.

Let us, however, distinguish a little: there are two
divisions in Abbé Le Dieu's work on Bossuet: the
Memoirs and the Journal. The Memoirs, written
shortly after Bossuet's death, on the spur of the
moment as it were, form a broad and animated
narrative, a picture of the life, the talents, the virtues
of the great bishop. In this work the Abbé Le Dieu
takes pains; he writes as if in view of the public;
his style is easy, it has development and happy turns
of phrase; we feel the man who lived with Bossuet
and who speaks of him worthily, with admiration,
with emotion. In the Journal, on the other hand,
written for himself alone and to serve merely as
matter for recollection, the abbé shows himself always filled with admiration and respect for the personage to whom he belongs, but his language does
not aid those ideas; his revelations are of all kinds
and not chosen; they are full of trivialities and plati-
tudes that we regret to see there. The Abbé Le Dieu
was a worthy ecclesiastic, hard working, author himself of several works on theological subjects; he was
attached to Bossuet in the year 1684, and remained
with him for twenty years (the last twenty years of
the great prelate's life) in the capacity of private secretary, and with the title of canon of his cathedral
church.

Le Dieu's Memoirs, very different from the Journal, are easy to read and copious; they show us Bossuet in his race and genealogy, his childhood and early education, his natural and continued growth. If any one ever seemed born to be a priest in the noblest and worthiest sense of the word, it was he. His pure childhood was followed by a pious adolescence and a youth already consecrated. Eliakim had but to grow, to continue himself in order to become a Jehoiada. The study of belles-lettres, which at first occupied him and in which he excelled, subordinated itself in his mind as soon as he had cast his eyes on the Bible, which happened to him in his rhetoric year. That moment, when he met with and read for the first time a Latin Bible, and the impression of joy and light that he received from it, remained always present with him through life; and he spoke of it in his last hours. He was, it may be said, revealed to himself; he became the child and soon the man of Scripture and the Sacred Word. The wonderful faculties he had received, and which early made themselves known, found their form and satisfaction, without effort, in the grave exercises that filled the life of a young priest and a young teacher — themes, controversies, sermons, conferences; he put all his senses and his beliefs into them, and in them he found his fruition.

What strikes me most in the traits that the Abbé Le Dieu has caught and collected of the early life and studies of Bossuet, is a first sign, a characteristic already manifest of the future great bishop — something facile and superior, which announces itself and takes position without struggle, without confusion, without interruption, yet without eagerness; it is the most straightforward vocation that can be conceived; his was the least struggling or thwarted soul that ever reached so high a region. He never ceased for a single day to be in his order and to walk his path.

Bossuet's success in the pulpits of Paris, when he went there periodically and rather frequently from Metz, are described by the Abbé Le Dieu with a vivacity and grace we should hardly expect to find in a mere record of sermons. These discourses, so praised by contemporaries that they came to be personified by the first words of their texts, always very happily chosen, the *Depositum custodi,* preached before the queen-mother, and the *Surrexit Paulus,* are made present and distinct to us, each with its particular physiognomy. The sermon called *La Vocation,* preached with the view of confirming the conversion of M. de Turenne (1668), was mentioned by the Carmelites, in whose chapel it was delivered, as a "sermon of exquisite beauty," and the explanations of the Epistles, made in their convent parlour about the same time, are said by them to have been of "enchanting beauty." It should be noticed that all such praises, which recur perpetually under the Abbé Le Dieu's pen, are to the effect that the man whom they called the "Angel of Meaux" was, as an orator, essentially remarkable for a character of sweetness and unction.

His Funeral Orations, now the most read of his works, have accustomed us to think chiefly of his splendid outbursts and his thunder, although many of those Orations (that on the Princess Palatine, for example) move us more gently and bring tears; but, in general, the first things we picture to ourselves when we think of Bossuet's eloquence are its thunderbolts. His theological duel with Fénelon, and the vigour he put into refuting him to the end and confounding him, have not lessened this idea of him, and have even made him pass for hard. He was not at all so in other matters. In the affair with Fénelon, Bossuet filled his office of teacher and incorruptible guardian of the truth; which, indeed, is a different, but not less essential aspect of the great mind, the wholly sacerdotal soul of Bossuet. I am speaking now of the orator only.

From the mass of testimony collected by Le Dieu, there is no means of doubting that the usual character of Bossuet's discourses, such as he made them with great outflow of heart and lively application of each word to his audience, was to be *touching,* to open the hearts of all as he opened his own, to bring tears ; in short, to persuade—the orator's great object. "How is it, monseigneur, that you make yourself so touching?" said the Mesdames de Luynes, those two noble and saintly nuns of Jouarre. "You turn us as it pleases you, and we cannot resist the charm of your words." Bossuet much preferred to preach the Word of God, in its simplicity and bareness, to the delivery of his celebrated Funeral Orations. "He did not like," says Le Dieu, "the latter work, which is very little useful, though it may shed edification." Feeling that this display and paraphernalia of solemn eloquence fatigued him to no purpose, except that of reputation and fame, he believed he did wrong to his own flock to continue it; therefore, after paying a debt of gratitude to the memory of the Prince de Condé, to which, indeed, friendship obliged him, he publicly announced that on that side his career was closed, reserving henceforth all his inward vigour for the service of his own people.

He was then at the age of which Cicero speaks, when the Roman orator says that his eloquence feels that it whitens: *quum ipsa oratio jam nostra canesceret;* he was in haste to employ all his maturity and sweetness for the Christian family entrusted to him. He bound himself to preach at Meaux whenever he officiated pontifically, "and never," says Le Dieu, "did any matter, however urgent it might be, prevent him from going to celebrate the great festivals with his people and proclaim to them the Sacred Word. At such times a father, not a prelate, spoke to his children, and the children made themselves docile and obedient to the voice of their common father."

Bossuet had all styles of eloquence; and this wonderful facility of speech, born of an inward source and fed by study and doctrine, together with the practice he had so early in the employments of the priesthood, explain to a certain point the tranquil composure, the precocious stability of a mind that felt it had only to continue its straight course, for that it was which would lead him to Jerusalem.

There are a dozen pages, among others in the Memmoirs of the Abbé Le Dieu, which I recommend to my readers; they are those in which he relates, from Bossuet's own lips, having frequently heard him speak on the subject, the manner in which the great orator conceived of eloquence in the pulpit and practised it. Here are the abbé's words, or rather those of Bossuet himself, for Le Dieu is obviously only his interpreter and secretary:

"Considerations of persons present, place, and time determined his choice of subject. Like the Fathers, he adapted his instructions or his reproofs to present needs; that is why, throughout Advent or Lent, he could not prepare himself in the interval between one sermon and the next. For that reason he never took upon himself those great Lents when a sermon must be preached daily. He would have succumbed and been exhausted by the labour, so great was his diligence and his utterance eager. When at work he threw upon paper his plan, his text, his proofs, in French or Latin indifferently, without restraining himself as to words, or turns of expression, or imagery: otherwise, as he was heard to say many times, the action would have languished, and his discourse would have become enervated.

"On this unformed matter he meditated deeply on the morning of the day when he had to speak; usually he wrote no more, in order not to distract his mind, because his imagination always went much faster than his hand could go.

" Master of all the thoughts that were present in his mind, he fixed
in his memory even the expressions that he meant to use; then, collecting himself in the afternoon, he went over his discourse in his
head, reading it with the eyes of his mind as though it had been upon
paper; changing, adding, cutting out, as if pen in hand. Finally,
when he was in the pulpit and pronouncing the words, he followed
the impression made upon his audience, and suddenly, effacing voluntarily from his mind what he had meditated, he fastened to the present
thought, and drove home the emotion through which he saw upon the
faces before him the touched or shaken hearts."

Such were the meditated improvisations from which
Bossuet drew his first great sermons, and to which
he continued faithful throughout the whole course of
his pastoral homilies. Bossuet, unlike Bourdaloue or
Massillon, never repeated his Lenten or Advent addresses; he renewed himself constantly; he was incapable of monotony, of uniformity, even in speaking
of that which did not vary; he wanted in his most
regular teachings a freshness of life, always present,
always to be felt; nothing of the craft, the profession;
he wanted action, emotion that was wholly sincere;
he needed that his whole soul, his imagination, wooed
by the Spirit from on high, should find their place and
spread themselves over all on each new occasion; he
could not endure in sacred oratory that words and
emotions should be arranged and regulated before-
hand; it was no longer, he thought, pouring from the
source of living waters.

Here is a remarkable fact: even when he composed
his Funeral Orations, " in which there was much narrative and little to change," or his discourses on doc-

trine, where the explanation of dogma should be clear and concise, "he wrote all," says Le Dieu, "on a paper with two columns, with several different expressions of the great emotions placed side by side, reserving to himself a choice in the heat of utterance, to keep, he said, liberty of action when following his effect upon his auditors; thus turning to their profit the very plaudits they bestowed." The abbé shows him to us at Meaux before he went up into the pulpit and after he came down:

"On his days for preaching, after composing his ideas in his study by reading Holy Scripture, or Saint Augustine, that grand and inexhaustible receptacle of Christian doctrine, he kept himself during divine service in quiet meditation and continual prayer; then, after a few minutes when he shut himself up alone before mounting the pulpit, he began to pour out his soul through his lips and the stream had only to flow. . . . When he had finished, and as if to shelter himself from plaudits, he returned at once to his house and remained there hidden, giving glory to God for his gifts and his mercies, without saying a single word either of his preaching or the success it had had. . . . And the remark to be made as to this," adds Le Dieu, "is on its true and sure character, for he did the same on all occasions. He considered himself as the organ, the channel of the Word, happy if he were the first to profit by it, and never, above all, being elated by his act."

It was in virtue of that same principle of modesty, and of just and rigorous distinction between the man and the deed, that on his death-bed, when the vicar of Vareddes expressed astonishment that he should wish to consult him, he to whom God had given such great and vivid light, he answered: "Undeceive yourself; God gives it to a man for others, often leaving him in darkness because of his own conduct."

His perpetual meditation on Holy Scripture, espe
cially after he felt that the end of his life was near, was
in keeping with his inward spirit:

"He had taken a great devotion to reciting frequently the 22nd
Psalm, ' My God, my God, why hast thou forsaken me? O thou
my succour, haste thee to help me.' He often went to sleep, and
woke up, still meditating on that Psalm, which he called ' The Psalm
of death, the Psalm of abandonment.'"

"Monsieur, I have always thought you an honest
man," said an unbeliever on his death-bed to Bossuet,
"I am now about to die; speak to me frankly, I have
confidence in you: What do you believe about religion?" "That it is a sure thing, and that I have
never had any doubt of it," replied Bossuet; and the
sincerity of those words strikes us in all that we read
of him to-day.

There was nothing of the man of letters in Bossuet,
using that term in its ordinary meaning; that is to
say, he never wrote merely to write, he had no crav-
ing to be printed; he generally wrote only when
forced to do so by some motive of public utility; to
instruct or to refute; and if the motive ceased, he
suppressed, or, at any rate, he put away what he had
written in a drawer. "Nothing was great in his
eyes but defence of the Church and religion." Such,
indeed, he appears to us, more and more, in the picture made of him by the Abbé Le Dieu, and such he
continued to his death.

The years when he was tutor to the Dauphin

[Monseigneur, son of Louis XIV], during which he
returned to mundane studies in order to teach them,
were those in which he occupied himself most with
belles-lettres, properly so-called. We find him re-
reading Virgil, and reading Homer with special enthusiasm. On these points the Abbé Le Dieu has not,
perhaps, all the exactness and knowledge of detail
that one desires; but one thing, at least, is very manifest, namely: that profane literature, in taking at that
time a large place in Bossuet's studies, hindered no
others and encroached on none; its limits were fixed
from the beginning; although we are told that he
sometimes recited Homer in his sleep, so much had
certain passages struck him the evening before; yet
he never felt in such reading that buoyant poetic
intoxication which in the soul and the charmed imagination of Fénelon produced *Télémaque.* Bossuet, in
short, remains for all time the man of the Word of
God; he loved that Word; essentially, he loved that
only. Isaiah, the Prophets, the Psalms, even the Song
of Songs — those were his chosen reading, for ever
dear; on them he was happy to grow old and die:
*Certe in his consenescere, his immori, summa votorum
est.* There was his *Hoc erat in votis,* and, as old age
came on, he permitted no diversion to this final occupation, the only one, to his eyes, worthy of the
sanctuary.

One never wearies of passing and repassing before
that grand figure, which presents the most exact con-

cordance and conformity with the epoch in which it appeared, and over which it may be said to have reigned. Bossuet throughout his whole life walked with his face uncovered; nothing in him, nothing in his actions nor in his thought is in shadow; he was the public man of great institutions and established order; sometimes their organ, sometimes their inspirer, sometimes the censor, accepted by every one, or the conciliator and the umpire. He was the most respected man of those times in the Catholic and Gallican order, and wherever speech could prevail. The words of that speech have come down to us in almost all their beauty—what more can we desire?

IX.

Boileau.

Boileau.

IX.

Boileau.

FOR more than a century since the death of Boileau, long and continual quarrels have been kept up over him. While posterity accepted with unanimous acclamation the fame of Corneille, Molière, Racine, and La Fontaine, it disputed constantly, or reviewed with singular rigour the claims of Boileau to poetic genius; and it was not the fault of Fontenelle, d'Alembert, Helvetius, Condillac, Marmontel, and, at moments, Voltaire himself, that this great classic renown was not impaired. We know the ground of nearly all the hostilities and antipathies that then assailed it: Boileau had no "sensibility"; and as in the eighteenth century *sentiment* mingled in everything, in a description by Saint-Lambert, in a tale by Crébillon, Jr., in a philosophical history of the two Indias, the fine ladies, the philosophers, and the geometricians took a great aversion to Boileau. Nevertheless, in spite of their epigrams and their scoffing smiles, his literary fame held good, and grew firmer day by day. "The poet of common-sense, the legislator of our Parnassus," kept his upper rank. Voltaire's *mot*, "Don't say harm of Nicolas, it brings ill-luck," made its fortune and passed into a proverb; the positive ideas of the eighteenth century and Condillac's philosophy, in triumphing, seemed to set a more durable seal on the fame of the most sensible, most logical, and most accurate of poets.

But it was, above all, when a new school of literature arose, when certain minds, few at first, began to put forward strange and unusual theories, and to apply them in their work, it was then that hatred of innovations brought men back from all sides to Boileau, as to an illustrious ancestor, to whose name they could rally in these encounters. Academicians rivalled one another in pronouncing his eulogy; editions of his works multiplied; distinguished commentators — MM. Viollet-le-Duc, Amar, Saint-Surin — environed him with assortments of their taste and erudition; M. Daunou in particular, that venerable representative of literature and philosophy in the eighteenth century, gathered around Boileau, with a sort of piety, all the facts, all the judgments, all the apologies, which were attached to so great a cause.

This time, however, the combination of worthy efforts did not sufficiently protect Boileau against the new ideas, at first obscure and decried, but growing and enlarging under the clamours. It was no longer a question, as in the eighteenth century, of

NICOLAS BOILEAU.
From a steel engraving.

piquant epigrams and satirical personalities; it was a strong and serious attack against the principles and the very foundations of Boileau's poetic art; it was a wholly literary examination of his devices and his style; a severe inquiry on the qualities of a poet, and whether they were or were not in him. Epigrams were no longer in season; so many had been made upon him formerly that it became bad taste to repeat them. I shall have no difficulty in avoiding them in the few pages I can here devote to him; pages in which I shall not seek to make a full examination, or to offer definitive conclusions. It is enough to talk freely of Boileau with my readers, to study him in his privacy, to look at him in detail, according to our point of view and the ideas of the present day, passing alternately from the man to the author, from the *bourgeois* of Auteuil to the poet of Louis the Great, not evading the great questions of art and style, elucidating them possibly, but without pretending ever to solve them. It is well, at each new literary epoch, to go over in our minds and revive the ideas that are represented by certain names that have become sacramental, even if we change nothing in them, very much as in each new reign new coins are struck on which the effigy is renewed without altering the weight.

In these days a lofty and philosophical method is introduced into all the branches of history. When it becomes a question of judging the life, actions, and writings of a celebrated man, we begin by examining and describing the epoch that preceded his coming, the society that received him into its midst, the general trend of minds; we observe and arrange, as a preliminary, the great stage on which the personage is to play his part; from the moment he appears, all the developments of the force within him, all the obstacles, all the repercussions are foreseen and explained; and from this harmonious spectacle there comes by degrees into the soul of the reader a peaceful satisfaction in which his intellect reposes. This method never triumphs with more complete and brilliant evidence than when it resuscitates statesmen, conquerors, theologians, philosophers; when applied to poets and artists, men of retirement and solitude, exceptions become frequent, and one has need to be cautious. For while, in the orders of other ideas — politics, religion, philosophy — each man, each work, takes its own rank, all make sound and number, the common beside the passable, and the passable beside the excellent, in art nothing counts but the excellent; and observe that the excellent in art may always be an exception, an accident of nature, a caprice of heaven, a gift of God. You may make fine and legitimate reasonings and deductions on prosaic races and epochs; and lo! it pleases God that Pindar should issue from Beotia and that André Chénier should be born and die in the eighteenth century. No doubt these peculiar aptitudes, these wonderful faculties,

received at birth, co-ordinate themselves sooner or later
with the epoch into which they are cast, and are subjected to certain lasting impressions. But even here,
the human initiative is in the first rank and is less subject to general causes; human energy modifies and, if
I may so express it, assimilates things; besides, does
it not suffice an artist, in order to accomplish his destiny, to create himself a haven, however obscure, in
the great movement around him, to find some forgotten corner where he can weave his web in peace, or
make his honey? It seems to me that when we
speak of an artist or a poet, especially a poet who
does not represent an entire epoch, it is better not to
complicate his history with too vast a philosophical
baggage, but to keep, in the beginning, to private
character, the domestic relations, and to follow the
individual closely through his inner self; sure that
later, when we know him well, we can bring him
into a strong light and confront him with his epoch.
This is what I wish to do very simply for Boileau.

Son of a father who was a clerk of court and of
lawyer ancestors (1636), as he says himself in his
tenth epistle, Boileau passed his childhood and his
early youth in the rue de Jérusalem, in a house built
in the days of Henri IV; having thus before his eyes
the *bourgeois* life and the life of the law courts. He
lost his mother when very young, the family was
numerous, and his father much occupied; the child
was left to himself and lodged in the corner of a

garret. His health was injured by it, but his talent for observation must have profited; sickly and taciturn, he noticed everything; and as he had not the dreamy turn of mind and his childhood and youth had never known tenderness, he early accustomed himself to look at life with common-sense, severity, and caustic bluntness. He was soon sent to school, where he was finishing his course in the fourth class when attacked by the stone; it was necessary to operate, and the operation left him with a very great infirmity that lasted all the rest of his life.

In school Boileau read, besides the classic authors, much modern poesy and many novels; and although he himself wrote, after the custom of rhetoricians, some rather bad tragedies, his taste and his talent for verses were already recognised by his masters. After graduating in philosophy, he was put to study law; on his father's death he continued to live with his brother Jérôme (who had inherited his father's office of clerk of the court), made himself a lawyer, but soon, weary of pettifogging, tried theology without more taste for it, or more success. He obtained a benefice of only 800 *livres,* which he resigned after a few years in favour, it is said, of the demoiselle Marie Poncher de Bretouville, with whom he had been in love, and who had made herself a nun. Apart from this attachment, which some have doubted, it does not appear that Boileau's youth was ardent, and he himself has stated that he was "very little voluptuous." These few known facts on the twenty-four first years of his life bring us to the year 1660, the period when he entered the literary world by the publication of his first Satires.

His exterior circumstances thus given, the political and social state of the country being known, it is easy to conceive what was the influence on a nature like that of Boileau of this early education, and of the domestic habits about him. Nothing tender, nothing maternal around the sickly and desolate child; nothing inspiring or sympathetic in the litigious conversations that went on around the armchair of his father, the old clerk, nor in the habits and ideas of a *bourgeois* family. No doubt the soul of a dreamy child might, in some period of analysis and inward examination, have gathered food and strength from this obstruction and repression; but the soul of Boileau was not fitted to do so. There was, it is true, the resource of mockery and burlesque. Villon and Regnier had already poured out abundant poetic ridicule on the manners and morals of the *bourgeoisie*, on that very life of citizens and pettifoggers; but Boileau had decorum in his mockery, sobriety in his smile, and they forbade him the witty debaucheries of his predecessors. Besides, manners and morals had lost their saliency since the regulating force of Henri IV had rolled over them, and Louis XIV was about to impose decorum.

As for any loftily poetic and religious effect of

splendid public buildings upon a young life begun between Notre-Dame and the Sainte-Chapelle, it is useless to think of it as possible in those days. The feeling of the middle-ages was completely lost; the soul of a Milton could alone have perceived something of it; Boileau saw nothing but a cathedral of fat canons and a choir-boy. Consequently, what was it that came suddenly, and for a first essay, of the glow, the fancy of his twenty-four years, of that poet's existence long so miserable, so repressed? Not the pious and sublime sadness of the Penseroso wandering by night, in tears, beneath the Gothic cloisters and the solitary arcades; nor the vigorous onslaught of a Regnier on nocturnal orgies in the dark alleys and the spiral stairways of the Cité; not the soft and unctuous poesy of the family hearth like that of La Fontaine at Ducis; no, it was "Damon, the great author," bidding farewell to the town, after Juvenal; it was satire on the intricacy of the streets of Paris; it was sharp and wholesome sarcasm on the wretched rhymers who swarmed in those days, having usurped a reputation in the town and at Court. Like his caustic elder brother, Gilles Boileau, he made war upon the Cotins and their like. He had, for his sole instigation, "the hatred of silly books."

I have just said that the feeling of the middle-ages was lost; it did not survive in France till the sixteenth century; the Greek and Roman invasion of the Renaissance smothered it. Nevertheless, while this great

and long neglect of the middle-ages was working to
an end (which did not happen till the close of the
eighteenth century), while the really modern era for society and for art in particular was still awaited, France,
scarcely recovered from the agitations of the League and
the Fronde, was slowly creating for herself a literature,
a poesy, tardy no doubt, and somewhat artificial, but a
mixture skilfully blended, original in its imitation, and
beautiful still in the decline of a society the ruins of
which it draped.   Drama apart, we may consider
Malherbe and Boileau as the authors, official and
authorised, of the poetic movement produced during
the last two centuries at the summit and on the surface of French society.   They are both distinguished
by a powerful infusion of critical wit, and by a pitiless
opposition to their immediate predecessors.   Malherbe
is inexorable for Ronsard, Des Portes, and their disciples, as Boileau was for Colletet, Ménage, Chapelain,
Benserade, and Scudéry.

This rigour, especially that of Boileau, may often
call itself by the name of justice: nevertheless, even
when they are right, Malherbe and Boileau are so in
the rather vulgar manner of common-sense; that is to
say, without the force of passion, without principles,
with incomplete and insufficient views.   They are
empirical; they attack real vices, but exterior ones,
the symptoms of a poesy that is rotten at the core; to
regenerate it they do not go to the heart of the evil.
Because Ronsard, Scudéry, and Chapelain seem to

them detestable, they conclude that there was no true taste, no real poesy among those ancients; they ignore and suppress out and out the great renovators of the art of poesy in the middle-ages; they judge blindly by a few passages in Petrarch, a few *concetti* of Tasso, to which the wits of the time of Henri III and Louis XIII were attached. And when, with their notions of reform, they decided to return to the antiquity of Greece and Rome, always faithful to that incomplete logic of common-sense, which never dares to drive things to a conclusion, they preferred the Romans to the Greeks; the age of Augustus presented to them at once the type of the absolutely beautiful.

However, these uncertainties and inconsistencies were inevitable in an episodical epoch, under a reign that was, in a way, accidental, and which never plunged deeply into either the past or the future. The arts, instead of living and cohabiting in the bosom of the same sphere, and being gathered back perpetually to the common centre of their rays, were isolated, each, on its own line and at its own extremity, acting solely on the surface. Perrault, Mansart, Lulli, Le Brun, Boileau, Vauban, though they had among them, in manner and method, general points of resemblance, had no understanding with one another, and did not sympathise, imprisoned as they were in the *technique* of their own work. In periods truly *palingenesic* it is quite the contrary; Phidias, whom Homer inspired, supplements Sophocles by his chisel;

Orcagna commentates Petrarch or Dante with his
brush; Chateaubriand understands Bonaparte. But
let us return to Boileau. It would be too harsh to
apply to him alone the observations that should fall
upon his century, but in which he has, necessarily, a
large share in his quality of critical poet and literary
legislator.

That is, in truth, the rôle and the position that
Boileau assumes in his first essays. From 1664, that is
to say from his twenty-eighth year, we find him intimately allied with all that the literature of that day
could show of best and most illustrious; with La Fontaine and Molière, already celebrated, with Racine,
whose guide and counsellor he became. The dinners
in the rue du Vieux-Colombier took place weekly, and
Boileau bore the palm for criticism. He frequented
the best company, that of M. de La Rochefoucauld,
of Mesdames de La Fayette and de Sévigné; knew
the Lamoignons, the Vivonnes, the Pomponnes, and
among them all his decisions in matters of taste were
law. Presented at Court in 1669, he was appointed
historiographer in 1677; at the latter period, through
the publication of nearly all his satires and his epistles,
of *l' Art poétique* and the first four cantos of the *Lutrin,*
he had attained the climax of his reputation.

Boileau was forty-one years old when he was made
historiographer; and it may be said that his literary
career ended at that age. During the fifteen years
that followed, down to 1693, he published nothing

but the last two cantos of the *Lutrin ;* and from that time to the end of his life (1711), that is, for eighteen years, he did no more than the satire *Sur les Femmes,* the epistles *à ses Vers, à Antoine,* and *Sur l' Amour de Dieu,* together with the satires *Sur l' Homme* and *Sur l'Équivoque.* We must look into his private life for the explanation of these irregularities; from it we may gather certain considerations on the nature and quality of his talent.

During the period of his growing fame, Boileau continued to lodge in the house of his brother, the clerk, Jérôme Boileau. This home must have been little agreeable for a poet, the wife of Jérôme being, it was said, crabbed and a scold. In 1679, on Jérôme's death, he went to live for a few years with his nephew, Dongois, also a clerk; but after making (in a carriage) the campaigns in Flanders and Alsace, he was enabled by the king's liberality to buy a little house at Auteuil, where we find him installed in 1687.[1] His health, always very delicate, became worse, and he suffered from an extinction of voice and deafness, which unfitted him for society and a Court life.

It is by following Boileau into his solitude at Auteuil that we learn to know him best; it is by observing what he did and did not do then, during more than twenty years, delivered over to himself, feeble in body but

---

[1] It was then that he took the name of his little property, Des Préaux, to distinguish him from his brothers. He is called, in all the memoirs of the time, M. Despréaux.

sound in mind, and in the centre of a smiling landscape, that we can judge with truth and certainty
of his earlier productions and assign the limits of his
faculties. Well! must we say it, strange, unheard-of
thing? — during this long sojourn in the country, a
prey to infirmities of the body which, leaving the soul
clear, disposed him to sadness and revery, not one
word of conversation, not one line of correspondence,
not one verse betrays in Boileau a tender emotion, a
true and simple feeling for the Nature around him.
No, it is not indispensable, in order to rouse us to a
deep and vivid sense of Nature's things, to go afar,
beyond the seas, through countries beloved of the
sun, the lands of the lemon and the orange, floating
all night in a gondola in Venice or at Baia, at the feet of
an Elvire or a Guiccioli—no, much less suffices. Look
at Horace, how he contents himself, for his reveries,
with a little field, a tiny spring of living water, a bit
of forest above, *et paulûm sylvæ super his foret:*
Look at La Fontaine, how he loves to sit down and
forget himself for long hours beneath an oak; how
marvellously he understands the woods, the waters,
the fields, the warrens, and the rabbits nibbling thyme
in the dew, the farms with the smoke rising from their
chimneys, the dove-cotes, and the poultry-yards. And
that good Ducis, who, himself, lived at Auteuil, how
he loves and how he paints the little smiling hollows
and the hillsides! "I walked a league this morning,"
he wrote to a friend, "over plains of heather and

sometimes among bushes covered with blossoms and singing." Nothing of all that in Boileau. What then does he do at Auteuil? He takes care of his health, he gives hospitality to his friends, he plays at skittles, he talks, after his wine, of Court news, the Academy, the Abbé Cotin, Charpentier, or Perrault, just as Nicole talked theology under the charming leafage of Port-Royal; he writes to Racine, asking him to kindly recall him to the memory of the king and Mme. de Maintenon; he tells him he is composing an ode in which he "risks things that are very novel, even to speaking of the white plume the king wears on his hat." The best thing he does is assuredly a clever epistle to Antoine; and even in that the good gardener is transformed into "the governor of the garden"; he does not plant, he "directs" the yew and the honeysuckle, he "exercises" on the wall-fruit the "art of la Quintinie"—there was Versailles even at Auteuil!

But Boileau grew old, his infirmities increased, his friends died; La Fontaine and Racine were taken from him. Let us say to his praise, at this moment when we are judging his talent with some severity, that he was more sensitive to friendship than to any other affection. In a letter, dated 1695, and addressed to M. de Mancroix on the subject of La Fontaine's death, we find this passage, almost the only touching words to be found in Boileau's whole correspondence:

"It seems to me, monsieur, that this is a very long letter. But the truth is, the leisure that I now have at Auteuil lets me, as it were,

transport myself to Reims, where I imagine that I am talking with
you in your garden, and see you again, as formerly, with all the dear
friends whom we have lost and who have disappeared *velut somnium
surgentis.*"

To the infirmities of age were added a lawsuit un-
pleasant to carry on, and a sense of the public misfortunes. After the death of Racine, Boileau never
set foot in Versailles; he judged sadly of men and
things; and .even in the matter of taste, decadence
seemed to him so rapid that he went as far as to regret
the days of Bonnecorse and Pradon. What one has
difficulty in understanding is the fact that in his last
days he sold his house at Auteuil, and went to die
(1711) in the cloister of Notre-Dame, in the quarters
of his confessor, the canon Lenoir. His principal motive, no doubt, was piety, as stated in the "Necrology
of Port-Royal"; but economy also had something to
do with it, for he was fond of money. The old age of
the poet-historiographer was not less sad and morose
than that of the monarch.

Boileau was not a poet, if we restrict that title to
beings strongly endowed with imagination and soul;
though his *Lutrin* reveals a talent capable of invention and, above all, of picturesque beauties of detail.
Boileau, as I see him, was a man of shrewd and sensible mind, polished and sarcastic; not fruitful; agreeably abrupt; a religious observer of good taste; a good
writer of verse; learnedly correct, wittily gay, the
oracle of the Court, and of Letters in those days;
just such as was needed to please on all sides—Patru

and Bussy, d'Aguesseau and Mme. de Sévigné, M. Arnauld and Mme. de Maintenon,— to impose on young courtiers, and make himself acceptable to old ones, and be esteemed by all as an honest man of merit. He is the "poet-author," knowing how to converse and to live, but truthful, irascible at the very idea of falsity; taking fire on behalf of the right, and attaining sometimes, through a sentiment of literary equity, to a species of moral sympathy and luminous resplendency, as in his Epistle to Racine. The latter represented well the tender and passionate side of Louis XIV and his Court; Boileau represents not less perfectly the sustained gravity, the upright good sense rising to nobleness, and the decent order of Court and monarch. Boileau's literature and poetic art are marvellously in accord with religion, philosophy, political economy, strategy, and all the arts of the day; it is the same mixture of sound sense and insufficiency, of views provisionally right, but seldom decidedly so.[1]

The point of view as to all that concerns Boileau has changed very much during the twenty-five years just passed. When, under the Restoration, at that brilliant moment of valorous attempts and hopes, younger generations came upon the scene, striving to inspire new life into style and form, and to extend the circle of literary ideas and comparisons, they met

---

[1] The foregoing was written in April, 1829. It did not wholly satisfy the writer, and in September, 1852, twenty-three years later, he returned to the subject in what here follows.—TR.

with resistance from their predecessors. Estimable, but hide-bound writers, with other writers less estimable, who would certainly have been in Boileau's day those he would have begun by castigating, put forward the name of that legislator of Parnassus, and without considering the differences of epochs and centuries, quoted his verses on all occasions as though they were the articles of a code. I did then what it was natural to do; I took the Works of Boileau by themselves; though not numerous, they are of unequal strength; some show the youth, others the old age of the writer. While doing justice to his fine and wholesome parts, I did not do it amply, nor did I associate myself heartily with the spirit of the man. Boileau as a personage and an authority is far more to be considered than his work; and it needs a certain effort to grasp him as a whole. In a word, I did not then do a full historical work upon him; I remained with one foot in polemics.

To-day, with the circle of experiences accomplished, and discussions exhausted, I return to him with pleasure. If it is permissible to speak of myself, I would say that Boileau is one of the men who have most occupied my mind since I have written criticism, and the one with whom I have most lived in idea. I have often thought of what he was, recalling what seemed lacking to me at an earlier time; and to-day I can speak of him, I venture to say, with a very keen and very present feeling.

Born November 1, 1636, in Paris, in the rue de Jérusalem, opposite to the house that was the cradle of
Voltaire, Nicolas Boileau was the fourteenth child of
his father, clerk of the Grand Chamber of the Parliament of Paris. Losing his mother at an early age, he
knew nothing of the tender care that usually brightens
childhood. His first studies were hindered by an
operation for the stone. His father destined him for
the Church, and he was tonsured. He did his theology
at the Sorbonne, disliked it, and after going through a
course of law, was called to the bar. In his twenty-
first year he lost his father, who left him some fortune, enough to make him independent of clients and
publishers, and, his genius goading him, he gave himself wholly to Letters, to poesy, and, among other
styles of poesy, to satire. In that family of clerks
and lawyers a satirical genius circulated. Two brothers of Boileau, Gilles and Jacques, were both stamped
with that same characteristic in different forms, which
it is piquant to notice here, because they serve better
to define the illustrious younger brother.

Gilles Boileau, lawyer and rhymester, who belonged
to the Academy twenty-five years before his brother
Nicolas, was one of those *bourgeois* and malicious wits
aiming for high society as a follower of Boisrobert, a
hornet race engendered by the Fronde, who sported
gaily during the ministry of Mazarin. Scarron, against
whom he had made a rather witty epigram, defined
him in a letter to Fouquet thus: "Boileau, well known

to-day for his backbiting, for his treachery to M.
Ménage, and for the civil war he caused in the Academy, is a young man who began early to damage
himself, and has since contrived to damage others."
Gilles Boileau, when travelling, carried the "Satires"
of Regnier in his carpetbag; usually he took up his
station before the third pillar in the great hall of the
Palais [law courts], setting the tone to the young wits
among the lawyers. He was called "Boileau, the
grammarian," and "Boileau, the critic." This is
enough to show that he lacked only more solidity
and more taste to have played the part of his brother
Nicolas; humour and satirical intention were not
wanting in him.

Jacques Boileau, otherwise called the Abbé Boileau,
doctor of the Sorbonne, long dean of the church at
Sens, subsequently canon of the Sainte-Chapelle, was
also of the same nature, but with traits that were
franker and more spontaneous. He had the gift of
repartee and witty sayings. It was he who, hearing
a Jesuit say that Pascal, then in retirement at Port-
Royal-des-Champs, was making shoes, like those
Messieurs, for penance, promptly said: "I don't know,
Reverend Father, whether he is making shoes, but
you must admit that he has delivered you a famous
botte" [thrust]. When he was performing the service
in the Sainte-Chapelle he sang with both sides of the
choir, and always out of time and tune. He was
fond of strange subjects and titles for his books, such

as: "History of the Flagellants," and "Short Coat of Ecclesiastics"; his Latin, for he usually wrote in that language, was harsh, fantastic, and anomalous. With his puns and his gaiety he makes me think of his brother Nicolas when the latter was facetious and in good humour. He resembled him in face, but with some exaggeration and caricature. Except for powers of reasoning, he was equal to him in mind. One day the great Condé, passing through the town of Sens, which was in his government of Bourgogne, was complimented by the Guilds and Companies of the town. Caustic as usual, he made game of those who were paying him compliments.

"His greatest pleasure," says a contemporary, "was to do some malicious thing to the complimenters on such occasions. The Abbé Boileau, who was dean of the cathedral church at Sens, was obliged to make a speech at the head of his Chapter. M. le Prince, wishing to disconcert the orator, whom he did not know, affected to advance his head and his big nose close to the dean, as if to hear him better, but really to make him blunder in his speech, if he could. But the abbé, who perceived his malice, pretended to be abashed and overcome, and began his speech thus, with affected terror: 'Monseigneur, your Highness must not be surprised to see me confused and trembling in appearing before you at the head of a company of ecclesiastics, for if I was at the head of an army of thirty thousand men I should tremble much more.' M. le Prince, charmed with that beginning, embraced the orator, would not let him finish, asked his name, and when told that he was the brother of M. Despréaux, he redoubled his caresses and kept him to dinner."

The Abbé Boileau seems to me to possess the brusquerie, the dart and thrust of his brother, without his refinement and his serious and judicial application of his wit. The originality of Nicolas Boileau, being of this mocking and satirical family, was that he joined to hereditary malice a portion of sound common-sense, so that those who had dealings with him, like Mathieu Marais, could say: "There is pleasure in listening to that man; he is reason incarnate."

In considering this line of brothers, alike, yet unequal, it seems to me that Nature, that great generator of talents, made a first sketch of Nicolas when she created Gilles; there she stopped, repentant; then she took up her crayon again and drew a bold stroke in making Jacques; but that time the stroke was too hard. The third time that she set to work the result was good: Gilles is the sketch, Jacques is the caricature, Nicolas is the portrait.

In his first Satires, composed and put in circulation in 1660, in those that followed almost immediately, and in the Satire dedicated to Molière in 1664, Boileau shows himself a skilful versifier, more exact and scrupulous than others of his day, much preoccupied in presenting elegantly certain special details relating to *bourgeois* citizens and poetasters; never approaching mankind or life on the side of feelings, like Racine and La Fontaine, nor on the side of moral and philosophical humorous observation, like La Fontaine again, and Molière; he does it from a point of view less extended, less fertile, but agreeable, nevertheless, and pungent. He was the author by profession, the poet of the Cité and the Place Dauphine, who placed himself in judgment over the illustrious writers spread out for sale at Barbin's, in the gallery of the Palais.

In his "Satires" and in his "Epistles," Boileau constantly lets us see the labour and the deliberations of his mind. In his youth it was always so ; there was something captious, capricious, vexed in young Boileau's muse; it never had the emotional ring of youth; it was grey-haired from the start; this became him as he matured, and in his second period he seems younger than at first, for all is then in keeping. This moment of maturity in Boileau is also the period when he affords the most pleasure. If he has any *charm,* properly so called, it is at this time only, the period of the first four cantos of the *Lutrin* and of the Epistle to Racine.

Boileau's muse, looked at rightly, had nothing of youth but courage and audacity. He needed both to attempt his enterprise, which was nothing less than to say to the literary men most in vogue, to the academicians who possessed the most influence: "You are bad authors, or, at any rate, very mixed authors. You write haphazard; out of ten verses, twenty verses, a hundred verses, you sometimes have only one or two that are good; and those are drowned in the bad taste, the loose style, the insipidity of the rest." Boileau's work was, not to return to Malherbe, already far behind, but to make French poesy submit to a reform of the same kind that Pascal had introduced into French prose. It is from Pascal, above

all and before all, that Boileau, it seems to me, derives; one might say that he is the child in literature
of the *Provinciales*. The poetical and critical purpose
of Boileau is very well defined in the following words:

"To guide and elevate French poesy which (excepting two or three
names), was going at random, and was decadent; to lead it up to the
level where the *Provinciales* had carried prose; but to maintain, nevertheless, the exact limits and distinctions of the two classes. Pascal
scoffed at our poesy and its conventional tinsel: ' golden age,'—' marvels of our time,'—' fateful laurels,'—' beauteous star.'—And they call
that jargon, he says, poetic beauty!"

The question for Boileau was to render poesy respectable to the Pascals, and to allow nothing that
sound judgment could reprove.

We must represent to ourselves the exact state of
French poesy when Boileau appeared, and take it
first among the best and greatest names: Molière,
with his genius, rhyming at full speed; La Fontaine,
with his carelessness, leaving the reins loose (especially in his first manner); the great Corneille, letting
his verses go as they would and never retouching
them. Thus Boileau was the first to apply to the
poetic style Pascal's method for the prose style: "If I
write four words, I efface three." He goes back to
Malherbe's law and gives it fresh vigour; he extends
it and adapts it to his epoch; he teaches it to his
young friend Racine, who without it might sometimes have gone amiss; he recalls it to La Fontaine,
already mature, and inculcates it on him; he even

brings Molière to think of it twice in his most perfected plays in verse. Boileau understood, and made his friends understand, that "a few admirable verses do not justify the neglect of others that surround them." Such is the true definition of his literary work.

But this one thought and purpose was fitted to kill that crowd of fashionable *beaux-esprits* and rhymesters, who owed a few happy lines to chance and to the multitude of their pen-strokes, and who were living on that credit and on tolerance. Also it struck no less directly the ceremonious and pompous oracles who had gained an imposing credit at Court by the help of an erudition without nicety of judgment and without taste. Chapelain was the leader of that old party still reigning. One of Boileau's first cares was to dislodge him in the estimation of Colbert, under whom Chapelain was a sort of head clerk of Letters, and to make him ridiculous in the eyes of all as a writer.

God knows what scandal was caused by this audacity of the young man! The Montausiers, the Huets, the Pellissons, the Scudérys shuddered; but Colbert comprehended, and that sufficed; it was enough that the minister understood the daring judge, that he laughed as he read and heard him, and that in the midst of his grave and heavy labours the mere sight of Boileau made him merry. Boileau was one of the rare and legitimate amusements of Colbert. Boileau has so long been presented to us in our youth as frowning and severe that we find it difficult to imagine him as he was in reality—the liveliest of serious minds, and the most agreeable of censors.

To put myself still more in his presence I went yesterday to see, in the Museum of Sculpture, the fine bust made of him by Girardon. He is there treated in a free, broad manner; the ample and indispensable wig is nobly placed on his forehead, and does not overweight it; his attitude is firm and even proud, the carriage of the head confident; a satirical half-smile flickers on his lips; the line of the nose, a little turned up, and that of the mouth indicate a jesting, laughing, satirical habit; the lips, however, are kind and frank, half-open and speaking, as if they could not withhold the jest. The bared neck gives to view a double chin, which is, nevertheless, more allied to thinness than to embonpoint; the neck, a little hollow, is in keeping with the weariness of voice which had troubled him from childhood. But seeing him as a whole, how thoroughly we feel that the living man must have been the contrary of sad or sombre, and not in the least wearisome!

Before taking to this rather solemn wig himself, young Boileau had pulled off more than one from other heads. I shall not repeat what is well known to all, but here is a little story which has never, as I believe, reached print. One day Racine, who was readily mischievous when the fancy took him, thought it would be an excellent trick to take Boileau to pay a

visit to Chapelain, who lived in the rue des Cinq-
Diamants in the Lombard quarter.   Racine had reason
to be grateful to Chapelain, having received encouragement from him on his earliest odes.   Using, therefore, the access he had to that learned personage, he
presented Boileau to him as M. *le bailli* de Chevreuse,
who, being in Paris, wished to become acquainted
with so important a personage.   Chapelain suspected
nothing; but, in the course of the visit, the *bailli,*
who was presented to him as an amateur of literature, having turned the conversation upon the drama,
Chapelain, learned man that he was, declared his
preference for Italian comedies, and extolled them to
the prejudice of Molière.   Boileau could not contain
himself; in vain did Racine make signs to him; the
pretended *bailli* took fire and was on the point of
betraying himself.   His introducer hastened to cut
short the interview.   On leaving, they encountered
the Abbé Cotin on the staircase, but luckily he did
not recognise the *bailli.*   Such were Boileau's early
pranks.   The point is: if such be played at all, to
place them judiciously.

Boileau's " Satires " are not, in these days, the most
pleasing of his works.   The subjects are rather petty,
but, when the author takes them on the moral side,
they turn to commonplace; such as the Satire addressed to the Abbé Le Vayer on human follies, and
that to Dangeau on nobility.   In the Satire and in
his "Epistles," the moment that works of the intellect

are not the special topic, Boileau is very inferior to
Horace and to Pope; and incomparably so to Molière
and La Fontaine; he becomes a mere ordinary moralist, an honest man of good sense, who is superior
only in details and in the portraits that he introduces.
His best Satire is the IXth. "It is perhaps the masterpiece of its class," says Fontanes. This masterpiece of satire is addressed to his *Esprit,* a favourite
topic, always the same, rhymes, method of writing,
portrait of his own imagination; he paints himself
more fully, with more development than ever, with a
fire that lights up his figure marvellously, and makes
him for all future time the living type of the critic.

Boileau's sensibility went, very early, into his reason
and remained one with it. His passion (for in this
direction he had passion) was wholly critical and
exhaled itself in his judgments. "The true in works
of the mind"—that idea was at all times his mistress,
his Bérénice. When his upright sense was shocked
he could not contain himself. Speaking in that Satire
of Truth he says:

> " 'T was she who in pointing the road I should follow
> Taught me hatred of books that are silly and hollow."

The "hatred of silly books," and also the love and
worship of good and beautiful works, was the lesson
he learned. When Boileau praises with full and
heartfelt meaning, how moved he is, and how he
moves us! how passionate and affectionate his lines:

" In vain 'gainst ' The Cid ' may the ministry league,
    All Paris for Chimène has the eyes of Rodrigue;
    In vain may the learned Academy censure it,
    The public, rebellious, resolves to admire it."

How generous the tone! how the eyebrows frown!
The grey eyes glitter with a tear; his verse is that
of wholesome satire, which "purifies itself in the
rays of good sense"—for good sense is there, with
warmth, and glow, and light. The Epistle to Racine after the production of *Phèdre* should be read;
it is a magnificent triumph of the sane sentiment of
justice, a masterpiece of critical poesy, alternately
sparkling, inflaming, harmonious, affecting, and fra-
ternal. But above all, his beautiful lines on the death
of Molière should be re-read—lines on which there
must have fallen an avenging tear, a tear of Boileau.

We reach, in the Epistle to Racine, the height of
Boileau's glory and of his vocation. He rises there
to his highest rank, the centre of a group of the illustrious of the epoch; calm, equitable, sure, powerfully
firm in his own style, which he has gradually
enlarged, envying no one, distributing soberly his
awards, classing even those who are above him—*his
dantem jura Catonem;* master of the choir, as Montaigne says; one of those men to whom authority is
delegated, and whose every word bears weight.

We can distinguish three periods in Boileau's career: the first, which extends to about the year 1667,
is that of the pure satirist, of the audacious, morose

young man, rather narrow in his views, just escaping
from a lawyer's office and still too close to the courts,
busy with rhyming and ridiculing silly rhymers, in
putting them in the pillory of his hemistichs, in
painting in relief, and with precision, the external
absurdities of his quarter, and in naming very loudly
the pretenders of his acquaintance: "I call a cat a cat,
and Rolet a swindler."

The second period, that from 1669 to 1677, includes
the satirist still, but a satirist who grows more and
more placable; showing circumspection and discretion
as he reaches fame; already on a good footing at
Court; becoming more wisely critical in every sense,
legislator of Parnassus in his *Art Poétique,* and more
philosophical in his broader view of man (Epistle to
Guilleragues), capable of delightful idleness and the
varied enjoyments of country life (Epistle to M. de La-
moignon), whose imagination, reposed but not cooled,
still combines and invents fearless pictures, profound
in their jocoseness, of a skill that rises to supreme perfection, to immortal art. The first four cantos of the
Lutrin express the spirit and mind of Boileau in his
honest leisure, in his serenity and his freest play, in
the pleasant calmness and the first glow of his after-
dinner leisure.

During the third period, coming after an inaction
of several years, under pretext of his office as historiographer and on account of illness, extinction of
voice, both physical and poetical, Boileau made a

moderately successful return to poesy (not so deplorable as persons have chosen to say) in the last two cantos of the *Lutrin,* in his final "Epistles" and "Satires," *L'Amour de Dieu,* and the melancholy *Équivoque* ending all.

There again, ideas and subjects fail him more, perhaps, than talent. Even in his disagreeable Satire against women, I have heard the most ardent admirers of the modern picturesque school commend the picture of sordid avarice so hideously shown in the persons of Tardieu and his wife. In that Satire there are some fifty lines *à la* Juvenal, which do not pale as we read them, even after we have read *Eugénie Grandet* or looked at some startling canvas of Eugène Delacroix.

But of this third and last period of Boileau, in which he allied himself more closely with Port-Royal and the Jansenist cause, I shall say but little here, the subject being too private and thankless. Moreover, it is one that I have long laid aside for the future.[1]

What was Boileau at Court and in society in his best days, before increasing infirmities and a gloomy old age overtook him? He was full of frank speech, witty sayings, and repartee; he spoke with ardour, but solely on subjects that he had at heart, that is to say, on literary matters. The talk once launched upon them, he put no restraint upon himself. Mme. de Sévigné tells us of a dinner at which Boileau,

[1] See "History of Port-Royal," vol. v., book vi., chap. 7.

arguing with a Jesuit on the subject of Pascal, gave a
scene of most excellent and naïve comedy at the
expense of the priest. Boileau carried his verses in
his mind, and recited them long before he put them
on paper; in fact, he did better than recite them, he
acted them, so to speak. One day, being in bed (for
he rose late), he repeated to Arnauld, who came to
see him, the whole of his third Epistle, in which
occurs the fine passage that ends with the words:

> "Hasten! time is flying and drags us with it:
> This moment when I speak is gone already."

He recited those last lines in so airy and rapid a tone
that Arnauld, naïf and ardent, easily moved, and a
good deal of a novice in the beauties of French poesy,
jumped from his chair and made two or three turns
about the room as if in pursuit of the flying moment.
In the same way, Boileau recited to Père La Chaise
his theological Epistle on the love of God in such
a way that he obtained (a more difficult matter) his
entire approbation.

"Doctors ought to order champagne," said Boileau,
"to those who have no intellect, just as they order
asses' milk to those who have no health; the first
remedy would be surer than the other." Boileau,
in his best days, did not hate champagne, good cheer,
and the bustle of social life; he spared himself less in
that respect than his friend Racine, who took care of
his health to excess, and was always in fear of falling

ill.   Boileau had more animation in society, more
social spirits than Racine; he let himself go to its
pleasures.   Until he was quite advanced in life he
received those who liked to listen to him and to make
a circle round him with pleasure.   "He is happy as
a king," said Racine, "in his solitude, or rather his
inn at Auteuil.   I call it so, because there is never a
day when there is not some new guest, often two or
three, who do not even know each other.   He is
happy in adapting himself thus to everybody.   As for
me, I should have sold that house a hundred times."
Boileau ended by selling it, but only after his infirmities had made life in it more difficult, and conversation
positively painful.   The extinction of voice, which
sent him to the Baths of Bourbon in the summer
of 1687, brought out the interest that the great people
of the kingdom took in him.   The king at table often
inquired about his health; the princes and princesses
also: "You were," writes Racine, "the topic of
conversation during half the dinner."

In 1677 Boileau was appointed, with Racine, to
write the History of the king's campaigns.   At first,
the courtiers made merry at the sight of the two
poets, on horseback, following the army, or in the
trenches, conscientiously studying the subject.   A
thousand tales, true or false, and doubtless much
embellished, were told about them.   Here is one
which is quite new; I take it from an unpublished
letter of Père Quesnel to Arnauld; this time the two

poets are not with the army, but simply at Versailles, where, nevertheless, the following misadventure overtook them:

" Mme. de Montespan," writes Père Quesnel in 1680, " has two bears, which come and go as they please. They passed one night in a magnificent apartment that was being prepared for Mlle. de Fontanges. The painters, on leaving their work at night, forgot to close the doors; those who have charge of the apartments were as careless as the painters; so the bears, finding the doors open, went in and ruined everything. The next day it was said that the bears had avenged their mistress, and other poetic nonsense. Those who ought to have closed the doors were well scolded, so they resolved to close them early in future. As much was said about the great damage done by the bears, great numbers of people went to see it, MM. Despréaux [Boileau] and Racine among them, towards evening. Going from room to room, absorbed in curiosity, or in pleasant conversation, they took no notice when the outer doors were locked, so that when they wanted to leave they could not do so. They shouted through the windows, but nobody heard them. Finally, the two poets *bivouacked* where the bears had the night before, and had leisure to think of their past poesy or their future History."

This tale shows that the subject of Boileau is not so uniformly grave and sad as one might think. Louis XIV, in protecting Boileau by his esteem, would not have allowed him to be seriously hurt by the Court jesters. The fine royal sense of the one appreciated the sound literary sense of the other. In 1683, Boileau, then forty-seven years old, did not belong to the Academy; he was paying the penalty of his early Satires. Louis XIV was out of patience with the delay. A vacancy occurred. La Fontaine, competing for it with Boileau, being accepted on the first ballot and proposed to the king as *subject,* or member (this

was then the custom), an adjournment was had to
receive the decision of the monarch, after which the
second balloting of the Academy would take place.
In the interval, another vacancy occurred; the Academy named Despréaux and presented his name to the
king, who said immediately that "the choice was
very agreeable to him and would be universally approved." "You can," he added, "receive La Fontaine
at once; he has promised to conduct himself properly."
But during the six months that had elapsed between
the two elections, the king (remarks d'Olivet) scarcely
allowed his own inclination to be seen, "because he
had made a rule to himself not to influence the suffrages of the Academy." We have since known
kings who were less delicate in that matter than
Louis XIV.

Let us recognise and hail in these days the strong
and noble harmony of the great century. Without
Boileau, and without Louis XIV, who regarded
Boileau as his Controller-General of Parnassus, what
would have happened? Would the great talents
themselves have fully rendered all that now forms
their most solid heritage of glory? Racine, I fear,
would have made another Bérénice; La Fontaine fewer
Fables and more *Contes;* Molière himself might have
stayed longer with his Scapins and might never have
risen to the stern heights of the *Misanthrope*. In a
word, each of those great geniuses would have yielded
more to his defects. Boileau, that is to say, the good

sense of the critic-poet, authorised and backed by
that of the great king, restrained them all, and compelled them, by his respected presence, to do their
best and gravest works. Know you what it is that,
in our day, is lacking to our poets, so full at their
start of natural faculties and happy inspirations and
promises? They lack a Boileau and an enlightened
monarch; the one supporting and sanctioning the
other. Thus our men of talent, feeling themselves in
a period of anarchy and want of discipline, quickly
follow suit; they behave, strictly speaking, not like
noble geniuses, or like men, but like schoolboys in
the holidays. We see the result.

Boileau, growing old and morose, believed that
sound taste was already compromised, and declared,
to whoso would hear him, that French poesy was
decadent. When he died, March 13, 1711, he had
long despaired of his contemporaries and of his successors. Was it a mere illusion of old age? Imagine Boileau returning to the world in the middle or
towards the end of the eighteenth century, and ask
yourself what he would have thought of the poesy of
that time. Place him, in idea, under the Empire, and ask
yourself the same question. It has always seemed to
me that those who were most ardent in invoking the
authority of Boileau were not those whom he would
most surely have recognised as his own. The man
who best felt and commented on Boileau, the poet, in
the eighteenth century, was Le Brun, the friend of

André Chénier, accused of too much audacity by prosaic rhymesters. Boileau was more daring and more
novel than most people, even Andrieux, thought.

Let us leave suppositions that have no precise end
and no solution possible. Let us take literary things,
such as they come to us to-day, in their confusion and
piecemeal condition; isolated and weakened as we
are, let us accept them with all their burdens, all
their faults, including our own faults also, and our
errors in the past. But, things being as they are, let
those who feel within them some share of the courage
and good sense of Boileau and the men of his race not
fail nor weaken. There is a race of men who, when
they discover beside them a vice, a folly, literary or
moral, keep it secret, and think only of making use of
it, and of quietly profiting through life by self-inter-
ested flattery or alliances; these are the greater number. But there is yet another race who, seeing the
false and accepted hypocrisy, have no peace until,
under one form or another, truth as they feel it is
brought out and proffered. Be it a question of rhymes
only, or of things more serious, let us belong to that
race.

X.

Racine.

X.

Racine.

THE great poets, the poets of genius, independently of their class, and without regard to their nature, lyric, epic, or dramatic, may be divided into two glorious families which, for many centuries, have alternately intermingled and dethroned one another, contending for pre-eminence in fame: between them, according to periods, the admiration of men has been unequally awarded. The primitive poets, the founders, the unmixed originals, born of themselves and sons of their own works,— Homer, Pindar, Æschylus, Dante, and Shakespeare,—are sometimes neglected, often preferred, but are always contrary to the studious, polished, docile geniuses of the middle epochs, essentially capable of being educated and perfected. Horace, Virgil, and Tasso are the most brilliant heads of this secondary family, reputed, and with reason, inferior to its elder, but, as a usual thing, better understood by all, more accessible, more cherished. In France, Corneille and Molière are detached from it on more sides than one; Boileau and Racine belong to it wholly and adorn it, especially Racine, the most accomplished of the class, the most venerated of our poets.

It is the peculiar property of writers of this secondary order to win for themselves almost a unanimity of suffrages, while their illustrious opponents, higher than they in merit, above them in fame and glory, are, nevertheless, brought into question in each new epoch by a certain class of critics. This difference in renown is a necessary consequence of the difference of talents. The ones truly predestined and divine are born with their lot; they are not concerned to enlarge it inch by inch in this life; they dispense profusely, and as if by both hands; for their inward treasury is inexhaustible. Without disquieting themselves, without rendering to their own minds a close account of their means of doing, they *do*. Their thoughts are not turned inward; their heads are not turned back to measure the way by which they came and calculate how much still lies before them; but they make long marches, never wearying, and never content with what they do. Secret things take place within them— in the breast of their genius — and sometimes transform it. They undergo these changes without taking part in them, without aiding them artificially, any more than man can hasten the time when his hair whitens, the birds the time when their plumage moults, or trees the change of colour in their leafage at the divers seasons. And, proceeding thus, by some great

RACINE.
From a steel engraving.

inward law, some premature, potent principle, they come at last to leave the traces of their force in sublime monumental works; works of a real and stable order beneath an apparent irregularity, as in Nature, intersected with gullies, bristling with crags, hollowed into depths — thus is it with those of one glorious family.

The others need to be born under propitious circumstances, to be cultivated by education, and to ripen in the sun. They develop slowly, knowingly, fertilising themselves by study, and give birth themselves to art. They rise by degrees; follow each step of the way, and never spring to their goal at a bound; their genius enlarges with time, and erects itself by degrees, like a palace to which each year a course is added; they have long hours of reflection and of silence, during which they pause to revise their plan and deliberate; so the edifice, if it is ever completed, is a noble, learned, lucid, admirable conception, of a harmony that charms the eye, and perfect in execution. To understand it, the mind of the spectator discovers without difficulty, and mounts with a sort of placid pride the ladder of ideas up which has gone the genius of the architect.

Now, according to a very shrewd and very just remark of Père Tournemine, we admire in an author only those qualities of which we have the root and the germ within us. Hence it follows that, in the works of the great, superior souls, there is a relative

level to which each inward spirit can rise, but cannot go beyond; a spot whence it must judge of the
great whole as it can. This is somewhat as it is with
the families of plants living at different elevations on
the Cordilleras; each unable to pass above a given
height; or rather as it is with families of birds whose
soaring in the air is fixed at a certain limit.

Now if, at the relative height to which each class of
minds can rise in understanding a poem, no corresponding quality is found to act as a stepping-stone,
a platform, from which to contemplate the country
round, if there are jagged peaks, a torrent, a gulf,
what happens? Minds that have found no rest for
their feet will return, like the dove to the ark, without
so much as an olive twig:—I am at Versailles, on the
garden side; I mount the grand stairway; breath fails
me half-way up, and I stop; but at last I see before
me the lines of the château, its wings; I appreciate their symmetry; whereas if I climb, from the
banks of the Rhine, some winding path that leads to
a Gothic dungeon, and stop short, breathless, half-
way up, it may be that a rise of ground, a tree, a
bush will hide the whole view from me. That is a
true image of the two poesies.

Racinian poesy is so constructed that at every height
are stepping-stones, and places of support for weak-
lings. Shakespeare's work is rougher of approach;
the eye cannot take it in on all sides; I know very
worthy persons who toil and sweat to climb it, and

after striking against crag or bush, come back swearing in good faith that there was nothing higher up; but, no sooner are they down upon the plain than that cursed enchantment tower appears to them once more in the distance, a thousand times more imperatively than those of Montlhéry to Boileau. But let us leave Shakespeare and such comparisons and try to mount, after many worshippers, a few of the steps, slippery from long usage, that lead to Racine's marble temple.

Born at La Ferté-Milon in 1639, Racine was orphaned at a very tender age. His mother, daughter of a king's attorney at Villers-Cotterets, and his father, controller of the salt stores at Ferté-Milon, died very nearly together. At four years of age he was confided to the care of his maternal grandfather, who put him, while still very young, to school in Beauvais. After the old man's death, he was taken to Port-Royal-des-Champs, where his grandmother and one of his aunts had retired. It is from there that the first interesting details of his childhood have been transmitted to us. The illustrious recluse, Antoine Le Maître, felt a special regard for him, as we see by a letter that he wrote him during one of the persecutions, in which letter he urged him to be docile, and to take good care, during his absence, of his eleven volumes of Saint Chrysostom.

The "little Racine" soon learned to read the Greek authors in the original; he made extracts and annotations in his own writing, and learned them by heart;

first, Plutarch, then the "Banquet" of Plato, with Saint Basil and Pindar in turn, and in his idle hours "Theagenes and Chariclea." Already he revealed his reserved, innocent, and dreamy nature by lonely walks, book in hand (which he did not always read), through those beautiful solitudes of which he felt the sweetness even to tears. His dawning talent was exercised at that time in translating the touching hymns of the Breviary into French verse, which he afterwards retouched; but above all, he delighted in celebrating in verse Port-Royal, the landscape, the ponds, the gardens, and the meadows. These youthful productions show true sentiment beneath extreme inexperience and weakness of expression and colour; with a little attention we can distinguish in certain places a far-off echo, a prelude, as it were, to the melodious choruses of *Esther.*

He left Port-Royal after three years' stay, and came to do his course in logic at the college of Harcourt in Paris. The pious and stern impressions he had received from his first masters weakened by degrees in the new world by which he was carried along. His intimacies with amiable and dissipated young men, with the Abbé Le Vasseur and La Fontaine, whom he knew from that time, gave him more and more a taste for poesy, romances, and the theatre. He wrote gallant sonnets, concealed from Port-Royal and the Jansenists, who were writing him, meanwhile, letters upon letters with threats of anathema. We find him,

in 1660, in communication with the actors of the
Marais about a play the name of which has not come
down to us. His ode on the *Nymphes de la Seine,*
written for the marriage of the king, was sent to
Chapelain, who "received it with all the kindness in
the world, and, ill as he was, kept it three days to
make remarks upon it in writing." The most important of these remarks related to the Tritons, who
never lived in rivers, only in the sea. This poem won
for Racine the protection of Chapelain, and a gift in
money from Colbert.

His cousin, Vitart, intendant of the Château of
Chevreuse, sent him to that castle on one occasion to
take his place in superintending masons, glaziers, and
other workmen. The poet was already so used to
the bustle of Paris that he considered Chevreuse a
place of exile, and dated his letters " from Babylon."
He relates that he goes to the wine-shop two or three
times a day, paying the score of every one, and that a
lady has taken him for a sergeant; then he adds: "I
read poesy, I try to make it; I read the adventures
of Ariosto, and I am not without adventures of my
own."

All his friends at Port-Royal, his aunt, his masters,
seeing him thus on the high-road to perdition, consulted together to get him out of it. They represented to him vehemently the necessity of a profession,
and they induced him to go to Uzès in Languedoc,
to stay with a maternal uncle, a canon of Saint-

Geneviève, with hope of a benefice.   We find him at
Uzès during the winter of 1661 and the spring and
summer of 1662, clothed in black from head to foot,
reading Saint Thomas Aquinas to please the good
canon, and Ariosto and Euripides to comfort himself ; much caressed by all the teachers and all the
priests of the neighbourhood on account of his uncle,
and consulted by all the poets and all the lovers of
the regions roundabout concerning their verses, on
account of his little Parisian reputation and his celebrated ode on "Peace": for the rest, going out but little,
wearying of a dull town, all the inhabitants of which
seemed to him hard and selfish; comparing himself
to Ovid on the shores of the Euxine, and fearing
nothing so much as to corrupt, through listening to
the *patois* of the South, the excellent, true French,
that pure flour of wheat on which men are nourished
around Château-Thierry, Ferté-Milon, and Reims.

Nature herself was only moderately attractive to
him.   "If the country had a little delicacy, if the rocks
were a little less frequent, I might take it for the
land of Cythera."   But the rocks oppress him, the
heat chokes him, the grasshoppers are louder than
the nightingales.   He thinks the passions of the South
violent and carried to excess; as for him, sensible and
moderate, he lives in silence and reflection; he keeps
his room and reads much, and does not even feel the
need of composing.   His letters to the Abbé Le Vasseur are cold, refined, correct, flowery, mythological,

and slightly satirical; the sentimental *bel esprit* that is to blossom out in *Bérénice* is perceptible throughout; there are numerous Italian quotations and gallant allusions; but no indecency such as young men allow to escape them, not a single ignoble detail; all is exquisitely elegant in its closest familiarity. The women of the region dazzled him at first, and a few days after his arrival he wrote to La Fontaine the following remarks, which give food for thought:

" All the women are brilliant, and they dress themselves in the most natural way in the world; as for their persons, *color verus, corpus solidem et succi plenum;* but as the first thing that was said to me was to be on my guard, I do not wish to say more about them. Besides, it would be profaning the house of a beneficed priest, in which I live, to make a long discourse on the matter: *Domus mea, domus orationis.* That is why you must expect I shall say no more to you on this subject. I was told: ' Be blind.' If I can't be that entirely, I can at least be mute; for, don't you see? one must be monk with monks, just as I was wolf with you and the other wolves of your pack."

But his naturally chaste and reserved habits prevailed when he was not led away by companions in pleasure. A few months later he answers very seriously a jesting insinuation of the Abbé Le Vasseur, that, God be thanked! his liberty was still safe, and that when he left that region he should bring back his heart as sound and whole as he brought it; and thereupon he relates a recent danger which his weakness. had happily escaped. The passage is little known, and it casts enough light into Racine's soul to make it worth quoting at length:

"There is a young lady here very well made, with a fine figure. I had never seen her nearer than five or six feet, and I thought her very handsome; her skin seemed to me bright and dazzling; her eyes large, of a fine black, her throat, and the rest that is uncovered rather freely in this region, very white. I had always had a somewhat tender idea of her, approaching to an inclination; but I saw her only in church, for, as I have told you, I am rather solitary, more so than my cousin advised. At last I wished to see whether or not I was mistaken in the idea I had of her, and I found a very civil occasion; I approached her and spoke to her.

"What I am telling you happened not quite a month ago, and I had no other intention than to see what sort of answer she would make to me. I spoke to her with indifference, but as soon as I opened my mouth and looked at her I became confused. I saw upon her face certain blotches, as if she was just getting well of an illness, and that made me change my ideas. Nevertheless, I remained there, and she answered me with a very gentle and very obliging air; and, to tell you the truth, I must have taken her on some bad day, for she is thought very handsome in the town; and I know several young men who sigh for her from the depths of their heart. She is even thought one of the most virtuous and gayest in the town. But I am very glad of this encounter, which has served to deliver me from a certain beginning of agitation; for I am studying now to live rather more reasonably, and not let myself be carried away by all sorts of objects. I begin my novitiate. . . ."

Racine was then twenty-three years old. The *naïveté* of his impressions and childlike heart that appears in the above narration marks a point of departure, whence he advanced gradually, by dint of experience and study, until he reached the utmost profundity of the same passion in *Phèdre*. His novitiate, however, was never completed. He grew weary of awaiting a benefice that was always promised but never came; so, leaving the canon and the promises, he returned to Paris, where his ode on *La Renommée aux Muses* won him another gift of money, an entrance at Court, and the acquaintance of Boileau and Molière. The *Thébaïde* followed rapidly.

Until then, Racine had found on his path none but protectors and friends. But his first dramatic success awakened envy, and from that moment his career was full of perplexities and vexations which his irritable susceptibility more than once embittered. The tragedy of *Alexandre* estranged him from Molière and Corneille ; from Molière, because he withdrew the play from him and gave it to the actors of the Hôtel de Bourgogne; with Corneille, because the illustrious old man declared to the young man, after listening to the reading of the piece, that it showed great talent for poesy in general, but not for the stage. When it was performed, the partisans of Corneille endeavoured to hinder its success. Some said that Taxile was not an honourable man; others that he did not deserve his fate; some that Alexandre was not lover-like enough; others that he never came upon the scene except to talk of love. When *Andromaque* appeared, Pyrrhus was reproached for a lingering of ferocity; they wanted him more polished, more gallant, more uniform in character. This was a consequence of Corneille's system, which made all his personages of one piece, wholly good or wholly bad from head to foot; to which Racine replied, with good judgment:

" Aristotle, far from asking us for perfect heroes, wishes, on the contrary, that the tragic personages, that is to say, those whose misfortune makes the catastrophe of the tragedy, shall be neither very good nor very bad. He does not wish them to be extremely good, because the punishment of a good man would excite more indignation than pity in the spectators; nor that they be bad to excess, because no one can feel pity for a scoundrel. They should therefore have a mediocre goodness, that is to say, a virtue capable of weakness, so that they fall into misfortune through some fault that causes them to be pitied and not detested."

I dwell on this point, because the great innovation of Racine, and his incontestable dramatic originality, consist precisely in this reduction of heroic personages to proportions more human, more natural, and in a delicate analysis of the secret shades of sentiment and passion. That which, above all, distinguishes Racine, in the composition of style as in that of the drama, is logical sequence, the uninterrupted connection of ideas and sentiments; in him all is filled up, leaving no void, argued without reply; never is there any chance to be surprised by those abrupt changes, those sudden *volte-faces* of which Corneille made frequent abuse in the play of his characters and the progression of his drama.

I am, nevertheless, far from asserting that, even in this, all the advantage of the stage was on the side of Racine; but when he appeared, novelty was in his favour, a novelty admirably adapted to the taste of a Court in which were many weaknesses, where nothing shone that had not its shadow, and the amorous chronicle of which, opened by a La Vallière, was to end in a Maintenon. It will always remain a question whether Racine's observing, inquiring method, employed to the exclusion of every other, is dramatic in the absolute sense of the word; for my part, I think it is not; but it satisfied, we must allow, the society of those days which, in its polished idleness, did not demand a drama more agitating, more tempestuous, more " transporting "—to use Mme. de Sévigné's language; a society which willingly accepted *Bérénice,* while awaiting *Phèdre,* the masterpiece of Racine's manner.

Bérénice was written by command of Madame [Henriette], Duchesse d'Orléans, who encouraged all the new poets, and who, on this occasion, did Corneille the ill-turn of bringing him into the lists in contest with his young rival. On the other hand, Boileau, a sincere and faithful friend, defended Racine against the clamouring mob of writers, upheld him in his momentary discouragements, and excited him by wise severity to a progress without intermission. This daily supervision of Boileau would assuredly have been fatal to an author of freer genius, of impetuous warmth or careless grace, like Molière, like La Fontaine, for instance; it could not be otherwise than profitable to Racine, who, before he knew Boileau, was already following (save for a few Italian whimsicalities) that path of correctness and sustained elegance in which the latter maintained and confirmed him. I think, therefore, that Boileau was right when he applauded himself for having taught Racine "to write with difficulty easy verses"; but he went too far if he gave him, as it was asserted that he did, "the precept of writing the second line before the first."

After *Andromaque,* which appeared in 1667, ten years elapsed before *Phèdre,* the triumph of which came in 1677. We know how Racine filied those years. Animated by youth and the love of glory, spurred by his admirers as well as by his rivals and detractors, he gave himself up wholly to the development of his genius. He broke completely with Port-Royal; and àpropos of an attack by Nicole on writers for the stage, he flung out a piquant letter, which caused scandal and drew down upon him reprisals. By dint of waiting and soliciting he had at last obtained a benefice, and the licence for the first edition of *Andromaque* was granted to the Sieur Racine, prior of Épinai. A monk disputed his right to that priory; a lawsuit followed, which no one understood; and Racine, weary of the whole business, desisted, avenging himself on the judges by *Les Plaideurs,* a comedy that might have been written by Molière; an admirable farce, the handling of which reveals a hitherto-unperceived side of the poet, and reminds us that he read Rabelais, Marot, even Scarron, and had his place in the wine-shop between Chapelle and La Fontaine.

This busy life, with its solid studies, to which were

added literary quarrels, visits to Court, the Academy after 1673, and perhaps, as some have suspected, certain tender weaknesses at the theatre—this confusion of vexations, pleasures, and fame, brought Racine to the year 1677, when he was thirty-eight years old, at which period he broke away from it to marry and be converted in a Christian manner.

His last two plays, *Iphigénie* and *Phèdre,* had roused a fresh storm against their author; all the hissed authors, the Jansenist pamphleteers, the superannuated great seigneurs, and the last remains of the *précieuses,* Boyer, Leclerc, Coras, Perrin, Pradon, I was about to say Fontenelle, Barbier-d'Aucour, and above all (in the present case), the Duc de Nevers, Mme. Des Houlières, and the hôtel de Bouillon, rose up in arms shamelessly, and the unworthy manœuvres of that cabal must have troubled the poet not a little; but, for all that, his plays had triumphed; the public went to them and applauded them in tears. Boileau, who never flattered, even in friendship, issued a magnificent letter to the conquering author, "blessing" him, and declaring the century that saw the "birth of his stately marvels fortunate." This was, therefore, less than ever the moment for Racine to quit the scene that resounded with his name; he had far more ground for intoxication than for literary disappointment; consequently, his resolution was absolutely free from the sulky ill-humour to which some have endeavoured to attribute it.

For some time past, since the first fire of youth, the first fervours of mind and senses were spent, the memory of his childhood, of his masters, of his aunt, the nun at Port-Royal, had again laid hold upon Racine's heart; and the involuntary comparison forced upon him between his peaceful satisfaction in other days, and his present fame, so troubled and embittered, brought him to regret a life that once was regular. This secret feeling, working within him, can be seen in the preface to *Phèdre,* and must have sustained him, more than we know, in the profound analysis he makes in that play of the "virtuous sorrow" of a soul that sees evil and yet pursues it. His own heart explained to him that of Phèdre; and if we suppose, what is very probable, that he was detained in spite of himself at the theatre by some amorous attachment he could not shake off, the resemblance becomes closer, and helps us to understand all that he has put into *Phèdre* of anguish actually felt, and more personal than usual in the struggles of passion.

However that may be, the moral aim of *Phèdre* is beyond a doubt; the great Arnauld himself could not refrain from recognising it, and thus almost verifying the words of the author, who "hoped, by means of this play to reconcile a quantity of celebrated persons to tragedy, through their pity and their doctrine." Nevertheless, going deeper still in his reflections on reform, Racine judged it more prudent and more consistent to quit the theatre, and he did so with courage, but without too much effort. He married, reconciled himself with Port-Royal, prepared himself in domestic life for the duties of a father, and when Louis XIV appointed him, at the same time as Boileau, historiographer, he neglected none of his new duties: with these in view, he began by making excerpts from the treatise of Lucian on "The Manner of Writing History," and he applied himself to the reading of Mézeray, Vittorio Siri, and others.

From the little that we have now read of the character, the morals, and the habits of mind of Racine, it is easy to foretell the essential fine qualities and defects of his work, to perceive to what he might have attained and, at the same time, in what he was likely to be lacking. Great art in constructing a plot; exact calculation in its arrangement; slow and successive development rather than force of conception, simple and fertile; which acts simultaneously as if by process of crystallisation around several centres in brains that are naturally dramatic; presence of mind in the smallest details; remarkable skill in winding only one thread at a time; skill also in pruning and cutting down rather than power to be concise; ingenious knowledge of how to introduce and how to dismiss his personages; sometimes a crucial situation eluded, either by a magniloquent speech or by the necessary absence of an embarrassing witness; in the characters nothing divergent or eccentric; all inconvenient accessory parts and antecedents suppressed; nothing,

however, too bare or too monotonous, but only two
or three harmonising tints on a simple background;
then, in the midst of all this, passion that we have
not seen born, the flood of which comes swelling on,
softly foaming, and bearing you away, as it were,
upon the whitened current of a beauteous river: that
is Racine's drama. And if we come down to his
style and to the harmony of his versification, we shall
follow beauties of the same order, restrained within
the same limits; variations of melodious tones, no
doubt, but all within the scale of a single octave.

A few remarks on *Britannicus* will state my thought
precisely, and justify it, if, given in such general
terms, it may seem bold. The topic of the drama is
Nero's crime, the one by which he first escapes the
authority of his mother and his governors. In Tacitus, Britannicus is shown to be a young lad fourteen
or fifteen years of age, gentle, intelligent, and sad.
One day, in the midst of a feast, Nero, who is drunk,
compels him to sing in order to make him ridiculous.
Britannicus sings a song in which he makes allusion
to his own precarious fate, and to the patrimony of
which he has been defrauded; instead of laughing
and ridiculing him, the guests, much affected and less
dissimulating than usual because they were drunk,
compassionated him loudly. As for Nero, though
still pure of shedding blood, his natural ferocity has
long been muttering in his soul and watching for an
occasion to break loose. He tries slow poison on

Britannicus. Debauchery gets the better of him; he neglects his wife Octavia for the courtesan Actea. Seneca lends his ministry to this shameful intrigue. Agrippina is at first shocked, but she ends by embracing her son and lending him her house for the rendezvous. Agrippina, mother, granddaughter, sister, niece, and widow of emperors, a murderess, incestuous, and a prostitute, has no other fear than to see her son escape her with the imperial power.

Such is the mental situation of the personages at the moment when Racine begins his play. What does he do? He quotes in his preface the savage words of Tacitus on Agrippina: *Quæ, cunctis malæ dominationis cupidinibus flagrans, habebat in partibus Pallantem,* and adds: "I merely quote this one sentence on Agrippina, for there are too many things to say of her. It is she whom I have taken the most pains to express properly, and my tragedy is not less the downfall of Agrippina than the death of Britannicus." But in spite of this stated intention of the author, the character of Agrippina is inadequately expressed; as an interest had to be created in her downfall, her most odious vices are thrown into the shade; she becomes a personage of little real presence, vague, unexplained, a sort of tender and jealous mother; there is no question of her adulteries and her murders beyond an allusion for the benefit of those who have read her history in Tacitus. In place of Actea we have the romantic Junia. Nero in love is nothing more than the impassioned rival of Britannicus, and the hideous aspects of the tiger disappear, or are delicately touched when they must be encountered. What shall be said of the *dénouement?* of Junia taking refuge with the Vestals, and placed under the protection of the people?—as if the people protected any one under Nero! But what, above all, we have a right to blame in Racine, is the suppression of the scene at the feast. Britannicus is seated at the table; wine is poured out for him; one of his servants tastes the beverage, according to the custom of the day, so necessary was it to guard against crime. But Nero has foreseen all; the wine is too hot, cold water must be added, and it is that cold water which must be poisoned. The effect is sudden; the poison kills at once; Locuste was charged to prepare it under pain of death. Whether it were disdain for these circumstances, or the difficulty of expressing them in verse, Racine evades them; he confines himself to presenting the moral effect of the poisoning on the spectators, and in that he succeeds. But it must be owned that even on that point he falls below the incisive brevity, the splendid conciseness of Tacitus. Too often, when he translates Tacitus, as he translated the Bible, Racine opens a path for himself between the extreme qualities of the originals and carefully keeps to the middle of the road, never approaching the sides where the precipice lies.

Britannicus, Phèdre, Athalie, Roman, Greek, and Biblical tragedy, those are the three great dramatic claims of Racine, below which all his other master-pieces range themselves. I have already expressed my admiration for *Phèdre,* and yet one cannot conceal from one's self that the play is even less Greek in manners and morals than *Britannicus* is Roman. Hippolytus, the lover, resembles Hippolytus, the hunter, the favourite of Diana, even less than Nero, the lover, resembles the Nero of Tacitus. Phèdre, queen-mother and regent for her son, on the supposed death of her husband amply counterbalances Junia, protected by the people and consigned to the Vestals. Euripides himself leaves much to be desired as to truth; he has lost the higher meaning of the mytho-logical traditions that Æschylus and Sophocles entered into so deeply; but in him we find, at any rate, a whole order of things — landscape, religion, rites, family recollections, all these constitute a depth of reality which fixes the mind and rests it. With Ra-cine all that is not Phèdre and her passion escapes and disappears. The sad Aricia, the Pallantides, the di-vers adventures of Theseus, leave scarcely a trace in our memory.

This might lead us to conclude with Corneille, if we dared, that Racine had a far greater talent for poesy in general than for the drama in particular. Racine was dramatic, no doubt, but he was so in a style that was little so. In other times, in times like ours, when the proportions of the drama are necessarily so different from what they were then, what would he have done? Would he have attempted it? His genius, naturally meditative and placid, would it have sufficed for that intensity of action that our *blasée* curiosity demands? for that absolute truth in ethics and characters that becomes indispensable after a period of mighty revolution? for that higher philosophy that gives to all things a meaning, that makes action something else than mere imbroglio, and historical colour something better than whitewash? Had he the force and the character to lead all these parts of the work abreast; to maintain them in presence and in harmony, to blend, to link them into an indissoluble and living form, to fuse them one into the other in the fire of passion? Would he not have found it more simple, more conformable to his nature, to withdraw passion from the midst of these intricacies in which it might be lost as if poured into sand? to keep it within his own channel and follow singly the harmonious course of grand and noble elegy, of which *Esther* and *Bérénice* are the limpid and transparent reservoirs? Those are delicate questions, to which we can only reply by conjectures. I have hazarded mine, in which there is nothing irreverent towards the genius of Racine. Is it irreverent to declare that we prefer in him pure poesy to drama, and that we are tempted to ally him to the race of lyric geniuses, of religious and elegiac singers, whose mission here below is to celebrate Love — love as Dante and Plato saw it?

The life of retirement, of household cares, and study, which Racine led during the twelve years of his fullest maturity, seem to confirm these conjectures. Corneille also tried for some years to renounce the theatre; but, though already in declining years, he could not continue the attempt and soon returned to the arena. Nothing of this impatience or this difficulty of controlling himself appears to have troubled the long silence of Racine. His affections went elsewhere; he thought of Port-Royal, then so persecuted, and took delightful pleasure in memories of his childhood:

"There was no religious house at that time," he says, "in better odour than Port-Royal. All that could be seen of it from without inspired piety; people admired the grave and touching manner in which the praises of God were sung there, the simplicity, and at the same time the propriety of their church, the modesty of the servants, the solitude of the parlour, the little eagerness shown by the nuns to enter into conversation, their lack of curiosity about the things of the world, and even about the affairs of their neighbours; in a word, an entire indifference to all that did not concern God. But how much more did persons who knew the interior of the monastery find subjects of edification! What peace! what silence! what charity! what love for poverty and for deprivation! Toil without intermission, continual prayer, no ambition except for the lowest and humblest employments; no impatience in the sisters; no whims in the mothers; obedience always prompt, and commands always reasonable."

Port-Royal had all of Racine's soul; thence he drew calmness; in behalf of it he offered prayers; he was filled with the moanings of that afflicted house when for the prosperous house of Saint-Cyr he wrote the touching melodies of the chorus of *Esther*. During these years of his retirement he wrote the History of Port-Royal, as well as that of the king's campaigns, delivered two or three discourses before the Academy, and translated certain hymns of the Church. Mme. de Maintenon drew him from his literary inaction, about the year 1688, by asking him for a play for Saint-Cyr. He woke with a start, at forty-eight years of age, to a new and wonderful career, taken in two steps: *Esther* for his first attempt, *Athalie* for his masterpiece. Those two works, so sudden, so unexpected, so different to the others, do they not confute our opinion of Racine, and escape all the general criticisms I have ventured to make upon his work?

Racine on Hebrew subjects is far otherwise at ease than on Greek and Roman subjects. Nurtured from childhood on sacred books, sharing the beliefs of the people of God, he keeps strictly to the Scripture narrative; he does not think himself obliged to mingle the authority of Aristotle in the action of the play, nor, above all, to place at the heart of his drama an amorous intrigue (and love is of all human things the one which, resting on an eternal basis, varies most in its forms according to the ages, and consequently leads the poet more surely into error). Nevertheless, in spite of the relationship of religions, and the communion of certain beliefs, there is in Judaism an element apart, inward, primitive, oriental, which it is important to grasp and put forward prominently, under pain of being tame and unfaithful; and this fundamental element, so well understood by Bossuet in his *Politique Sacrée,* by M. de Maistre in all his writings, and by the English painter, Martin, in his art, was not accessible to the sweet and tender poet who saw the Old Testament solely through the New, and had no other guide to Samuel than Saint Paul.

Let us begin with the architecture of *Athalie;* with the Hebrews all was figurative, symbolical; the importance of forms was part of the spirit of the law. Vainly do I look in Racine for that temple wondrously built by Solomon, in marble, in cedar, overlaid with pure gold, the walls gleaming with golden cherubim and palm-trees. I am in the vestibule, but I see not the two famous columns of bronze, eighteen cubits high, one named Jachin, the other Boaz; nor the sea of brass, nor the brazen oxen, nor the lions; neither can I imagine within the tabernacle the cherubim of olive-wood, ten cubits high, their wings stretched out and touching one another until they encircled the arch of the dome. The scene in Racine takes place under a Greek peristyle, rather bare, and I am much less disposed to accept the "sacrifice of blood" and "immolation by the sacred knife" than if the poet had taken me to the colossal temple, where King Solomon offered unto Jehovah, for a peace-offering, two-and-twenty thousand oxen and one hundred and twenty thousand sheep. Analogous criticism may be made upon the characters and speeches of the personages.

In short, *Athalie* is an imposing work as a whole, and in many parts magnificent, but not so complete nor so unapproachable as many have chosen to consider it. In it Racine does not penetrate into the very essence of Hebraic oriental poesy; he steps cautiously between its naïve sublimity on the one hand, and its naïve grace on the other, carefully denying himself both.

Shall I own it? *Esther,* with its charming gentleness and its lovely pictures, less dramatic than *Athalie,* and with lower aims, seems to me more complete in itself and leaving nothing to be desired. It is true that this graceful Bible episode is flanked by two strange events, about which Racine says not a single word: I mean the sumptuous feast of Ahasuerus, that lasted one hundred and eighty days, and the massacre of their enemies by the Jews, that lasted two whole days, at the formal request of the Jewess Esther. With that exception, and perhaps by reason of that omission, this delightful poem, so perfect as a whole, so filled with chastity, with sighs, with religious unction, seems to me the most natural fruit that Racine's genius has borne. It is the purest effusion, the most winning plaint of his tender soul, which could not be present where a nun took the veil without being melted to tears — an incident of which Mme. de Maintenon wrote: "Racine, who likes to weep, is coming to the profession of Sister Lalie."

About this time, he composed for Saint-Cyr four

spiritual canticles, which should be numbered among his finest works. Two are after Saint Paul, whom Racine treats as he has already treated Tacitus and the Bible; that is to say, by encircling him with suavity and harmony, but sometimes enfeebling him. It is to be regretted that he did not carry this species of religious composition farther, and that in the eight years that followed *Athalie* he did not cast forth with originality some of the personal, tender, passionate, fervent sentiments that lay hidden in his breast. Certain passages in his letters to his eldest son, then attached to the embassy in Holland, make us conscious of an inward and deep-lying poesy which he has nowhere communicated, which he restrained within himself for long years; inward delights incessantly ready to overflow, but which he never poured out except in prayer at the feet of God, and with tears that filled his eyes.

The poesy of those days, which formed a part of *literature,* was so distinct from *life,* that the idea of ever joining them came to no one; and once devoted to domestic cares, to fatherly affection, and the duties of a parishioner, a man had raised an insurmountable wall between the Muses and himself. Nevertheless, as no deep sentiment is ever sterile within us, this poesy, repressed and without issue, becomes a sweet savour, secret, yet mingling in every action, in the lightest words, exhaling itself by ways unknown, and communicating a good fragrance of worth and virtue.

This was the case with Racine; it is the effect made upon us to-day as we read his letters to his son, already a man launched upon the world; simple, paternal letters, written by the family hearth, beside the mother, and among the six other children; every line with the impress of grave tenderness, austere sweetness; letters in which reproofs as to style, advice to avoid the "repetition of words," and the "locutions of the 'Gazette of Holland,'" are naïvely mingled with precepts for conduct and Christian warnings:

"You have some reason to attribute the success of your voyage in such bad weather to the prayers that have been offered for you. I count mine as nothing; but your mother and your little sister prayed God every day to preserve you from accidents; and they did the same at Port-Royal. . . . M. de Torcy informs me that you are in the *Gazette de Hollande;* had I known it, I should have bought the paper to read it to your little sisters, who would think you had become a man of consequence."

He writes that Mme. Racine is always thinking of her eldest son, and that when they have anything "a little good for dinner" she cannot keep from saying: "Racine would have liked to eat that." A friend, returning from Holland, brought news to the family of the cherished son; they overwhelmed him with questions, and his answers were all satisfactory: "But I did not dare," writes the excellent father, "to ask him if you thought a little of the good God; I was so afraid the answer might not be such as I could wish."

The most important domestic event of Racine's last

years was the taking of the veil at Melun of his young-est daughter, then eighteen years of age. He tells his son of the ceremony and relates the details to his old aunt, still living at Port-Royal, of which she was abbess. He never ceased to sob during the service; from that breaking heart, treasures of love, inexpres-sible emotions flowed forth in those tears; it was like the oil poured out from Mary's vase. Fénelon wrote to him to console him. With this extreme giving way to emotion, this keen sensibility, growing more sensi-tive daily, we can understand the fatal effect on Racine of Louis XIV's speech, and of that last blow which killed him. But he was already, and had been for a long time ill—ill of the ill of poesy; towards the end, this inward and hidden predisposition degene-rated into a sort of dropsy, which delivered him over without strength or resource to the slightest shock.

He died in 1699 in his sixtieth year, reverenced and mourned by all, crowned by fame, but leaving, it must be said, a literary posterity that was not virile, well-intentioned rather than capable: such as Rollin and Olivet in criticism, Duché and Campistron in drama, Jean Baptiste and the Racine sons in ode and poem. From his own time until ours, and through all variations of taste, Racine's renown continues, with-out attack and constantly receiving universal homage, fundamentally just, and deserved as homage, though often unintelligent in its motives. Critics of little compass have abused the right of citing him as a model; they have too often proposed for imitation his most inferior qualities; but, for whoso comprehends him truly, there is enough, in his work and in his life, to make him for ever admired as a great poet and cherished as a heart-friend.

XI.

Madame de Caylus.

XI.

Madame de Caylus.

IT has often happened to me to speak of that happy
epoch of our language and taste that, in France,
corresponds with the end of the seventeenth century and the beginning of the eighteenth, when, after
the production of our greatest works, and in the close
neighbourhood of the best as well as the most charming minds, delicacy and refinement were extreme, and
corruption (meaning pretension, affectation) had not
yet come. To-day, I desire to show that perfect moment in a pleasing and somewhat distinct person,
who paints it for us with vivacity and grace, and who
paints nothing else. It would be easy to find greater
examples than Mme. de Caylus, who wrote with difficulty, and only accidentally, as it were; but such examples would prove other things, more things than I
have in view, and the delicacy of which I wish to give
an idea is in them complicated, in a measure, by the
talent of the writer. Here, on the contrary, in pausing
a moment with this woman of a pen so delicate and
light, we are not distracted from the point I am

especially anxious to indicate, a quality which those who knew her best designated, when speaking of her, as "pure urbanity."

Mme. de Caylus was the niece of Mme. de Maintenon, niece in the Bretagne way. The great d'Aubigné of the sixteenth century, the warrior-writer, the Calvinist-frondeur, the bold and caustic companion of Henri IV, had a son and two daughters; Mme. de Maintenon was the daughter of the son; Mme. de Caylus was the granddaughter of one of the daughters. The father of Mme. de Caylus, the Marquis de Villette, a distinguished naval officer who left Memoirs, seems to have had something of her grandfather about him in courage and intellect. Mme. de Caylus herself was not without likeness to her great forefather; beneath her womanly grace and her angelic air she has a sharp, keen, biting wit. She is a female Antoine Hamilton. At first she seems occupied solely with pleasures, amusements, and the trifles of society; but do not for a moment suppose that you are dealing with a weak or silly woman. Her mind is clear and firm, observing and sensible; it is, like that of Mme. de Maintenon, solid; but in Mme. de Caylus solidity lies hidden by a flower. Her depth, however, will be found by whoso seeks it; and, after living with her for a short time, we say to ourselves that there is nothing, after all, like a strong race when grace comes in to crown it.

Born in 1673, in Poitou, Mlle. Marguerite de Villette-

MARQUISE DE CAYLUS.
After the painting by G. Staal.

Murçay was carried off from her family, when seven years of age, by Mme. de Maintenon. The king was then converting, *nolentes volentes,* the Huguenots of his kingdom, and Mme. de Maintenon, following his example, made it her duty to convert her own family. So the young de Murçay was carried off while her father was at sea. An aunt, the father's sister, lent a helping hand to this abduction which had so good a purpose. We ought to hear Mme. de Caylus relate this early adventure:

" My mother had hardly started for Niort before my aunt, who was used to changing religion, and had just been converted for the second or third time, started too, and took me with her to Paris."

On the way they encounter other young girls, older in years, whom Mme. de Maintenon was claiming for conversion. These young people, determined to resist, were as much astonished as they were grieved to see the young de Murçay carried off without defence:

" As for me," she says, " content to go wherever they took me, I was neither " (grieved or astonished). . . . " We arrived together in Paris, where Mme. de Maintenon came at once to fetch me, and took me alone to Saint-Germain. At first I wept a great deal; but the next day I thought the King's mass so beautiful that I consented to become a Catholic, on condition that I should hear it every day, and that I should be guaranteed against whipping. That was all the discussion they employed, and the sole abjuration that I made."

From the tone in which Mme. de Caylus relates things held to be so important, we are led to ask what

she really thought of them.   Did she know, herself?
Like Mme. de Sévigné, her natural wit and liveliness
carries her away; the facts seem to her amusing, and
she relates them gaily.

Mme. de Maintenon brought her up, and did it as
she knew how to do it; that is to say, with taste, with
preciseness, and in perfection.   All her careless and
rather volatile graces, which might otherwise have
run the risk of emancipating themselves too early and
of playing at large, were regulated and brought to
good effect, appearing at the right time.   They married her at the age of thirteen, and rather badly.   It
was one of Mme. de Maintenon's assumed humilities
to marry this charming niece, whom the greatest
matches were seeking, in a mediocre way.   Mme. de
Maintenon was full of such refinements of modesty
and disinterestedness in view of distinction and glory;
in this case the child paid the cost of the aunt's virtue.
The husband given to her, M. de Caylus, very ordinary as to fortune, was in other respects most unworthy of her.   When he died in Flanders, in 1704,
"his death gave pleasure to all his family, he was
blasé, stupefied for many years with wine and
brandy," and they kept him on the frontier in winter as well as summer, expressly forbidding him to
approach either his wife or the Court.   It was to such
a man, with such warnings, that Mme. de Maintenon,
from principle, and in preference to all others, thought
it right to give a young girl whom she had brought

up with the utmost care, and of whom all eye-witnesses give us enchanting descriptions:

"Never," cries Saint-Simon, "was there a face so spiritual, so touching, so speaking; never a freshness like hers, never so many graces or more intelligence, never so much gaiety and liveliness, never a creature more bewitching."

And the Abbé de Choisy, who knew her at that time and later, and who enjoyed her at all ages, says:

"Laughter and playfulness shone in rivalry round her; her mind was still more lovable than her face; one had no time to breathe or be dull when she was near. All the Champmeslés in the world never had those ravishing tones of voice which she gave out in declaiming, and if her natural gaiety had allowed her to check certain little coquettish airs, that all her innocence could not justify, she would have been a perfect person."

Ápropos of this comparison with Mlle. Champmeslé, it must be remembered that Mme. de Caylus played Esther at Saint-Cyr, and played the part better, it was said, than the famous actress would have done. She was not educated at Saint-Cyr; she came too soon for that, but she witnessed its beginnings; and one day, when Racine recited to Mme. de Maintenon the scenes in *Esther,* which he was composing for that establishment, Mme. de Caylus began to declaim them so well, and in so touching a voice, that Racine entreated Mme. de Maintenon to let her niece act the part. It was for her that he composed the prologue of *La Piété,* in which she made her first appearance. But Mme. de Caylus, once launched, did not confine herself to the prologue, and she played successively all personages,

but especially Esther.   She had but one defect, and
that was to act too well and touch the heart too deeply
by certain accents.   "They continue to play *Esther,*"
writes Mme. de Sévigné to her daughter (1689).
"Mme. de Caylus, who was their Champmeslé, plays
no longer; she did too well, she was too touching;
they want only pure simplicity for those little innocent souls."   Mme. de Caylus is considered to have
been the last person, the last *actress,* who preserved
the pure declamation of Racine, the degree of cadence
and song that suited those melodious verses, written
expressly for the voices of a Caylus or a La Vallière.

My readers will now comprehend what I meant
when I spoke of the perfection of culture and taste in
a young woman who, at the age of fifteen, had seen
the birth of *Esther,* breathed its first fragrance, and
entered so fully into its spirit that she seemed, by the
emotion of her voice, to add something to it.

This emotion, with all that it promised of sentiments just ready to blossom forth, was not confined
to the voice of Mme. de Caylus.   I am not narrating
her life, and she herself in her *Souvenirs* scarcely
speaks of what relates to herself.   But Saint-Simon
informs us about her, as he does about so many
others, in a way that leaves nothing to be desired.
Through her satirical sallies, her vivacities of heart
and mind, and her *liaison* with the Duc de Villeroy,
Mme. de Caylus earned an exile from Court when
nineteen years of age.   She was exiled once, and pos-

sibly twice; at any rate, she was not less than thirteen or fourteen years away from Court, under a species of punishment. She consoled herself at first by living in Paris in the society of persons of intellect; it was there that she knew La Fare, who wrote for her some of his prettiest verses. She took a house and received her friends.

But after a while, whether for *ennui* or caprice, or in remembrance of *Esther,* she began to throw herself on the side of devotion, and a devotion that was not considered the proper thing. She took for her confessor Père de La Tour, a man of much intellect, without compliance, and best known as General of the Congregation of the Oratory. But this priest was suspected of Jansenism, and Mme. de Maintenon, with her strict, plain sense, always looking for whatever brought useful respect, would have preferred to see her niece without a confessor than with one who was looked upon with suspicion at Court. She did so much in the matter that, insensibly, the young widow abandoned her confessor and austerity, and resumed her worldly habits. She reappeared at Versailles, at the king's supper, in February, 1707, "beautiful as an angel." It was more than thirteen years since she had seen the king. But by her wit, her charm, and skill she repaired all, and her long eclipse was as if it had never been. She softened and reconquered her aunt, became once more necessary to her, was soon a part of all intimacies and of all private coteries, and her apparent favour was complete enough to obtain for her certain malignant satirical couplets, which curious persons may seek in the *Recueil* of Maurepas.

Mme. de Caylus remained at Versailles until the death of Louis XIV; put aside from that time as a person of the "old Court," she returned to live in Paris, in a little house within the gardens of the Luxembourg. There she lived, in semi-retirement from the world, among her friends and the Duc de Villeroy to the end, often having with her her son, the Comte de Caylus, an original and a philosopher, giving suppers to people in society and to learned men, mingling devotion, the ways of the world, liberty of mind, and the graces of society in the charming and rather confused measure of the preceding century. She died in April, 1729, aged fifty-six years.

The portraits that we have of her in her youth answer well to the idea given of her beauty by Saint-Simon, the Abbé de Choisy, and Mme. de Coulanges. Whether in morning robes, Court dress, or winter garments, she appears in each delicate, slender, tall, noble, elegant, and pretty; her tall figure gave her the grand air; her face was a little round, an angel face, in which sweetness was allied to mischief, with dainty lips on which raillery played easily, beautiful eyes whence sparkled charm and intelligence; grace and distinction over all. What more shall I say? Such a face had but to choose, it could be, at will, either Esther or Célimène.

As for direct testimony upon her intellect, we find
it in the volume of her Correspondence with Mme.
de Maintenon and in her *Souvenirs.* This little book
of *Souvenirs,* published in 1770 (forty years after her
death), with a preface by Voltaire, seems nothing to
us to-day, because all its anecdotes have long passed
into circulation, and we know them by heart without
remembering from whom we obtained them; but,
all the same, it was she who first told them delightfully. The book is in the style of the Memoirs
of Queen Marguerite, and of some of the historical
writings of Mme. de La Fayette: it is "an afternoon's
work." No effort is visible; "she never tries," they
said of her. Her pen runs negligently; but those
negligences are precisely that which makes the ease
and charm of her conversation. Do not ask her for
more than a rapid series of portraits and sketches;
in those she excels. Her light pen touches everything to the purpose; she takes from each person the
dominant feature and seizes all it is essential to show
in them. Mme. de Maintenon is there undisguised;
with her good qualities but without flattery; we can
even trace, here and there, beneath the praises, a tinge
of malice. Louis XIV is painted by just and neat
strokes which show him without exaggeration, and
with all his excellences in every-day life; we feel the
king, worthy of this great epoch in which men
thought and spoke so well. Mme. de Montespan,
who had so much piquancy and a unique turn of

humour and satire, imagined that she could govern
the king for ever, because she knew herself superior
to him in mind. Mme. de Caylus disposes in two
words of that pretended superiority, which only existed by chance, as it were:

" The king did not, perhaps, know how to talk as well as she, though
he spoke perfectly well. He thought justly, expressed himself nobly,
and his least prepared answers covered in few words all that there was
that was best to say according to times and seasons, things and persons.
He had, far more than his mistress, the sort of mind that gives advantage over others. Never in haste to speak, he examined, he penetrated
their characters and thoughts; but, as he was wise, and knew how
the words of kings are weighed, he often kept to himself that which
his penetration had discovered. If it was a question of discussing important affairs, the most enlightened and the ablest men were astonished at his knowledge, convinced that he knew more than they, and
charmed by the manner in which he expressed it. If he frolicked,
if he made jokes, if he deigned to tell a story, it was with infinite grace,
and a noble and elegant turn of manner and phrase that I have never
known in any one but him."

That is how Louis XIV spoke and kept his rank as
king through that epoch of intellect. Without flattery, and considering only the fulness and correctness
of his language in ordinary discourse, he might have
been one of the leading Academicians of his kingdom.

The observation of Mme. de Caylus is always direct
and prompt; she goes to the bottom of characters
without appearing to do so. When it is necessary to
picture Mlle. de Fontanges, with her beauty and her
peculiar style of romantic silliness, and to make it felt
how, even if she had lived, the king could not have
loved her long, she says it in two lines:

"We accustom ourselves to beauty, but we never accustom ourselves to silliness turning to affectation, especially when we are at the same time with persons of the mind and nature of Mme. de Montespan, whom no absurdity escaped, and who knew so well how to make it felt by others by means of that unique wit peculiar to the family of the Mortemarts."

Yet this same Mlle. de Fontanges, the vain and silly beauty, gave a lesson one day to Mme. de Maintenon, who exhorted her, with her stiff rectitude, to cure herself of a passion that could not make her happy: "You talk to me," replied the young woman, "of quitting a passion as one would take off a gown." The girl without mind was enlightened for a moment by her heart.

What distinguishes, at first sight, all these portraits of Mme. de Caylus is their delicacy; the vigour and firmness beneath them are often veiled. But there are moments when the true word comes to the surface, the keen expression breaks forth. The "impudence" of Mme. de Montespan, who grows bolder with her successive pregnancies; the "baseness" of the Condés, ambitious to ally themselves to the king by all his bastard branches; all such traits are boldly sketched, as became the granddaughter of old d'Aubigné. The king, having married the Duc du Maine, makes representations to his son about his wife, who is ruining him; "but," says Mme. de Caylus, "seeing at last that his remonstrances only served to make a son whom he loved suffer inwardly, he took to silence, and *let him wallow* in his blindness and weakness." There is nothing feeble in such tones. We feel, in reading these accomplished women, that Molière, not less than Racine, was present with his genius beside their cradle, and that Saint-Simon was not far off.

I could, if I chose, point out certain jollities in Mme. de Caylus which show her, in a softened style perhaps, a true daughter of Mme. de Sévigné. She knows how to change her tone when advisable and proportion her touch to her personages: "Mlle. de Rambures had the style of the Nogent family, to which her mother belonged: lively, daring, and all the mind that is needed to please even without being beautiful. She attacked the king and did not displease him. . . ." That is how she speaks when she could say all; and close beside it is a portrait drawn in two lines: "Mlle. de Jarnac, ugly and unhealthy; she has, so they say, a fine complexion which lights up her ugliness." None but Hamilton or a woman could find such shafts. "She had malice in her," says Saint-Simon.

Truthful and penetrating minds are often embarrassed by their rôle in this world: they tell what they see, the thing that is, and they run the risk of being thought malicious. Mme. de Caylus was only a truthful painter, who could not keep herself from catching objects to the life as she passed along, be those objects Mlle. de Jarnac, with her ugliness set in its finest light, or the bewitching Mlle. de Lowenstein, with her "nymph-like waist still further set off by a flame-coloured ribbon." The whole series of pictures in which she shows us the squadron of the dauphine's maids of honour, and, in general, the long file of Court ladies, resembles a gallery of Hamilton, same date, same cleverness of brush, same delicate causticity, at moments cruel. Mme. de Caylus is mistress, in her way, of the art of that continual irony in which she speaks, and which the wittiest of foreign women, even those who are naturalised among us, seldom catch. The Duchesse de Bourgogne, born in Savoie, though very French in many respects, never attained it; saying sometimes to Mme. de Maintenon: "Aunt, they turn everything into ridicule here!"

Of a truth, there were many things to ridicule. The anecdotes of Mme. de Caylus are little scenes which, lightly sketched in, leave an ineffaceable impression of the comic. Will you have a scene in which M. de Montausier, or Bossuet himself plays the comic rôle? It is on the eve of some Holy Week or jubilee; the king, who was now religious, wanted to sever himself from Mme. de Montespan, who, in her way, was becoming religious too. Whereupon the lovers part, and each goes his and her own way to mourn their sins. But here let Mme. de Caylus take up her inimitable tale:

"The jubilee over, gained or not gained, it was a question of knowing whether Mme. de Montespan should return to Court: 'Why not?' said her parents and friends, even the most virtuous, such as

M. de Montausier. ' Mme. de Montespan by birth and office ought
to be there, and she can live in as Christian a manner there as elsewhere.' The Bishop of Meaux [Bossuet] was of that opinion. There
remained, they added, one difficulty: Should Mme. de Montespan appear before the king without preparation? They ought surely to see
each other before meeting in public, to avoid the inconveniences of
surprise. On this ground, it was decided that the king should come
to Mme. de Montespan's apartments; but, in order not to give the
slightest subject for scandal to lay hold of, it was arranged that certain
respectable ladies, the gravest at Court, should be present at the interview, and that the king should see Mme. de Montespan in their
presence only. The king accordingly came to Mme. de Montespan's
apartments, as it had been arranged; but, little by little, he drew her
into the embrasure of a window; they talked in a low voice for some
time, weeping, and saying what is usually said in such cases; finally,
they made a profound bow to the venerable matrons and retired to
an inner apartment; the result was Mme. la Duchesse d'Orléans, and
later M. le Comte de Toulouse."

These were the last of the seven children that the
king had by Mme. de Montespan.

"I cannot," adds Mme. de Caylus, "keep myself
from saying a thought that is in my mind: it seems to
me that one can still see in the character, in the countenance, in the whole person of Mme. la Duchesse
d'Orléans traces of this struggle between love and the
jubilee." [1]

Was there ever a way of telling a story more
lively, gayer, bolder, more spontaneous, more natural!
Nothing half-told, or told too much; all is sketched
in, painted in, but nothing emphasised.

This leads us to the examination of another ques-

[1] A jubilee in the Roman Catholic Church is a solemn and general
plenary indulgence granted by the Pope on certain occasions and under certain conditions.—TR.

tion, which has already been touched upon, and with which the name of Mme. de Caylus has been mingled from the beginning. What is urbanity? in what does it properly consist? Is it wholly in the conciseness and appropriateness of a witty saying? is it in irony, in pleasantry, in gaiety, or must we seek it elsewhere? An abbé, a learned man, and a wit, the Abbé Gédoyn, the same who translated Quintilian, and translated him all the better because he had been a friend of Ninon (to be with Ninon was always useful),—the Abbé Gédoyn, I say, has written on this question of urbanity, and he ends his agreeable and learned treatise by adding a eulogy on Mme. de Caylus, remarking that of all the persons he had known there was none who showed in so living a manner what he meant by the word *urbanity*. Let us see what the amiable abbé understood by that word; we shall still be concerned with Mme. de Caylus.

According to the Abbé Gédoyn, *urbanity,* that wholly Roman word, which, in its origin, signified only softness and purity of the language of the city *(urbs)* in opposition to the language of the provinces, and which was for Rome what *atticism* was for Athens,— that word came after awhile to express the characteristic of politeness, not only of speech and accent, but of mind and manners, and the whole air of individuals. Then, with time and usage, it came to express still more, and to signify not only a quality of language and of mind, but also a sort of virtue and social and moral quality that made a man amiable to others, that embellished and made secure the social intercourse of life. In this complete and charming sense, urbanity requires a nature of kindness and gentleness, even in malice. Irony suits it, but irony that has nothing that is not amiable, irony which has been well defined as "the spice of urbanity." To have urbanity, as Gédoyn understands it, is to have *morals;* not morals in the austere sense, but in the antique sense: Horace and Cæsar had them. To have morals in this delicate sense, which is that of honourable persons, is: not to think more of one's self than of others, not to preach, not to insult any one in the name of morality. Harsh, rustic, savage, and fanatical minds are excluded from urbanity; the crabbed critic, accurate though he be, can make no pretension to it. Melancholy minds are not admitted; for a certain foundation of joy and gaiety is in all urbanity, there are smiles. If we consider the extreme pains taken by the ancients to give to their children, from the mother's breast, this delicate tact, this exquisite sensibility, we are struck with the difference in modern education:

"When one sees," remarks the great mind of Bolingbroke, "the care, the pains, the constant diligence that went to form the great men of antiquity, we wonder that there were not more of them; and when we reflect on the education of youth in our day, we are astonished that a single man arises who is capable of being useful to his country."

That remark, which seems very severe if extended over the whole of education, is evidently true if applied only to urbanity. Comparing on this point the education of our day with that of the ancients, we are surprised that anything remains to us of the word or of the thing. At the close of the seventeenth century, that is to say, the most glorious moment of our past, complaint of this decadence was already being made, and yet it was the golden age of urbanity. The women of that time, with the facility of nature which in all ages has distinguished them, succeeded better than men in presenting perfect models of that which we are seeking; they sowed the seeds of it, as it were, upon the air they breathed. It is in them, among those who wrote, that we shall more surely find proof of that becoming freedom and familiarity, that delicate satire, that ease in saying all things, which fulfilled the conditions of the ancients all the more because they themselves were unaware of it. "All that is excessive is necessarily unbecoming, and all that is *laboured* cannot have grace." So say Quintilian and Gédoyn, and we can verify the remark in reading the simple pages of Mme. de Caylus. The Abbé Gédoyn felt it so much (and it is to his honour) that, having ended his treatise with a sort of compliment to the Academicians before whom he read it, he hastens to add a postscript, indicating Mme. de Caylus as the most conclusive example, the supporting evidence of his words.

The *Eulogy* of Mme. de Caylus, printed at the end
of Gédoyn's treatise, which is from the pen of an M.
Rémond (one of those lazy dilettanti who have left but
a few lines behind them), shows her to us in a new
light even after the praises of Choisy and Saint-Simon.
We see her beautiful for many years, always agreeable, combining the flowers of mind of a Mme. de
La Sablière with the solid foundation of a Mme. de La
Fayette; with a gift of varied conversation and choice
of topics, sometimes serious, sometimes gay, by no
means hating the pleasures of the table, but redoubling
her sallies when there, and presiding as a goddess,
like the Helen of Homer:

"Mme. de Caylus," says M. Rémond, "led farther than Helen;
she shed a joy so sweet, so bright, a taste for pleasure so noble
and so elegant into the souls of her guests, that all ages and all
characters were made to seem amiable and happy. So surprising
is the power, or, rather, the magic of a woman who possesses a
veritable charm."

There may be, perhaps, in that word "charm," and
in the comparison with Helen of Troy, something
alarming and misleading, if we did not know that this
portrait of Mme. de Caylus was written in her last
years, after her youth; and the charms referred to are
those of her mind. It is thus that we must understand another passage in the same *Eulogy,* where it is
said: "As soon as men made her acquaintance they
were ready to quit their mistresses without a thought,
because they then began to please them less; it was

difficult to live in her society without becoming her
friend and her lover." These lively expressions of the
platonic writer only the better render that joy of the
spirit, that pure intoxication of grace unconsciously
shed around her.

For—to return once more to the conclusion of Quintilian, interpreted to modern minds by Gédoyn—ease,
discretion, delicacy, no emphasis, no driving to an
end, are, undoubtedly, conditions of urbanity; but all
would be as nothing without a certain spirit of joy
and kindliness that inspires the whole: "which is
properly *charm,*" said La Fontaine.

I shall not insist any longer on the lightsome graces
of the writer of the little book of *Souvenirs,* never
completed, but so agreeable, so prettily turned, that
we are glad to reread them and refresh our memories
with things well known, but especially to freshen our
taste for the swift and airy manner of telling them.
In the art of portraiture, without seeming to attempt
it, Mme. de Caylus is unrivalled. But where I especially ask my readers to follow me is into her Correspondence with Mme. de Maintenon. This goes
back to the time when Mme. de Caylus, a young and
pretty widow, was living in disgrace in Paris and
before her return to Versailles. Mme. de Maintenon
sends her good advice upon her conduct, so strict and
cold that it would have given any one who was its
object a desire to go against it. Mme. de Caylus
neither obeyed nor disobeyed it wholly. Once

returned to Versailles, we see her in her letters — or rather her short notes, written from one room to another — displaying all her grace and prettiness to soften her aunt, to amuse and brighten her. Mme. de Maintenon, so agreeable in mind, had a grave background, sad, and even austere; she had amassed a burden of *ennui* in amusing others; she had withered her own soul in striving to please, from her youth up, those who were greater than she. So, when she found herself alone, she enjoyed solitude as a relaxation and rest. Mme. de Caylus did all she could to obtain access to her aunt in those rare moments; she coaxed her, she teased her with all due respect to make her smile: "I don't know what the Academy would say of the word *acoquiner*," she writes, "but I feel all its energy in you." She calls herself the "superintendent of her pleasures," and complains that the office is dwindling in her hands.

Mme. de Maintenon had now become indispensable to the king and to the whole royal family, who never gave her a single instant's respite. Even when the king worked with his ministers she must be there. Oh! in those moments how Mme. de Caylus would have liked to sit smiling and silent beside her aunt! "Who does not see you, enjoys nothing," she cries ; "I have infinite regret in not sharing with you the back of M. Peletier"— doubtless M. Le Peletier de Souzy, a director-general and councillor of State, who worked every week with the king. Another day, she envies Fanchon, the chambermaid: "Why cannot I slip in under her form during the *absence* of M. de Pontchartrain's back ?"—M. de Pontchartrain being the least amusing of the ministers. Here is one of her prettiest letters, in which she speaks of herself as the "little niece," and claims from her aunt the favour of seeing her oftener.

"I reflect about your week; and I cannot think it well arranged that there should not be more in it of the little niece; why not have more of the little family? She will be just as stupid at cards as you could wish; she will work so sedately; she will listen, or read to you with so much pleasure. Finally, and this perhaps is the best way to make you receive her, she will go away at the slightest sign. If you choose to leave her with the company, she assures you, without hypocrisy, that she will find more time for it than is needed; she sees nothing in it, after all, but the coterie, and those marshals of France, who do not charm her to the point of not being able to do without them; she fears the ministers; she does not like the princesses; if it is repose you desire for her, she can only have it with you; if it is her health, she finds with you her regimen and remedy: in a word, she finds all with you, and without you nothing. After this sincere statement, order—but not as a *Néron*."

That term *Néron* often recurs under her pen to express gaily the negative habit of Mme. de Maintenon, inexorable in the privations she imposed on others as well as on herself. One day Mme. de Caylus sent her a little distaff; for Mme. de Maintenon liked to spin with her own hands; it served as an exhibition of modesty and simplicity added to all the rest. But listen to the pretty chatter with which Mme. de Caylus surrounds her distaff in sending it:

"Why have I not all the graces of a lively wit to introduce

into your solitude the liveliest of distaffs! It is pretty, if you will; but, besides that, it is given you by a person who, when she is beside you, would fain never lose it from sight. . . . Go, my distaff; there is no irony in saying that I envy you: nothing can be more true."

She is inexhaustible in her turns and returns of charming insistence on this perpetual theme; she tries to send to that old age, which seeks to mortify itself, a ray of her own brightness. "I am angry with the sun for shining so brilliantly into my room when you are not in it."

Towards the end, she enters so fully into her aunt's spirit that she is wholly one with it, and conspires with her in diverting the king: "It is certain that we are doing a great service to the State in keeping the king alive by amusing him."

Mme. de Maintenon, in spite of her airs of resistance, was not insensible to such winning grace. The Princesse des Ursins, in her letters to her, never ceased to praise her "friend" from the moment she returned to Court and to the favour of her aunt; she varies her praise in many keys: "There is nothing artificial about her; she is as lovable in mind as she is in face." "You will find infinite resources in her, no one having more intelligence, or being more amusing, without any malignity." Mme. de Maintenon in the end acknowledges in reply that she is almost conquered:

"It is true that I get on better with Mme. de Caylus than formerly, because she seems to me to have recovered from her ob-

stinacy about Jansenism, finding it difficult to be agreeably placed
among persons who think differently; her face is as charming as
ever, but she has a form that disfigures her much; for the rest, I
see no woman here so reasonable."

Whether this change was caused by some little
emotion entering Mme. de Maintenon's heart, or
merely by a liking for intelligence, it is certain that
she had a weakness for this niece that she felt for no
other person. She calls her her "true niece," and
after Louis XIV's death she turns to her with solid
friendship. It is true that Mme. de Caylus is perfect
in manner, respectful, and at the same time familiar;
she knows so well the proper distance to keep in
writing to her, the degree of information she must
give, the sad news of society and the vexatious truths
she must not conceal, and others on which it would
be useless to enlarge; she knows well how to be
serious as her pen runs on. "I say nothing to you
of the beauty of your letters," writes Mme. de Maintenon, "lest I should seem to flatter, and at my age
one must not change one's nature."

We might, however, take too serious an idea of
Mme. de Caylus if we confined ourselves to her letters. In writing to her aunt, she presents herself
without hypocrisy, but in her most matter-of-fact
and sober aspect; doubtless she allowed her to see
but one-half of her life. In her little house in the
Luxembourg gardens, which is isolated and quite
rural, and which was reached only by a long and

winding way, she appears to us like some country lady returning for a time from the grandeurs of Versailles:

> "It is a delight to rise early; I look out of my window over my whole empire; I take pride in seeing under my rule twelve hens, one cock, eight chicks; a cellar which I transform into a dairy; a cow pastured near the entrance to the great garden by a tolerance that may not be of long duration. I dare not ask Mme. de Berry to endure a cow. Alas! it is enough that she endures me."

The Duchesse de Berry, here mentioned, was that daughter of the Regent who filled the palace of the Luxembourg with her orgies. Mme. de Caylus, making allusion to them, says elsewhere, in a fancy full of thought: "I am very well pleased here; I lose not a ray of sun, nor a word of the vespers of a seminary (Saint-Sulpice) where women cannot enter; 't is thus that life is mingled—on one side, this palace; on the other, the praises of God."

Mme. de Maintenon, good churchwoman that she was, felt, surely enough, that this charming niece had not become a recluse, and that she was still receiving friends of all kinds. "You may know how to do without pleasures," she writes, "but pleasures cannot do without you."

Such was Mme. de Caylus, so far as we can resuscitate her from the few pages we possess, in which, after all, we have but the smallest part of herself. But, by the help of contemporary testimony, I feel sure that I have given her nought that does not

belong to her in seeking to defend her. This eldest
daughter of Saint-Cyr, this sister of Esther, who did
not confine herself wholly to that gentle part, is, as it
were, the last flower of the epoch, then closing, of
Louis XIV; in nothing did she breathe the spirit of
the coming age. Coming after the La Fayette, the
Sévigné, the Maintenon, cultivated by those women,
and admiring them, she resembled them only so far as
to detach herself from them; she shines as their follower, the youngest, the gayest, but with her own
distinct brilliancy, and her delicacy without pallor.

XII.

Fénelon.

XII.

Fénelon.[1]

THE volume which will here concern us—*Lettres et Opuscules de Fénelon*—is added as an indispensable complement to the twenty-two volumes of his *Œuvres* and to the eleven volumes of his *Correspondance,* that is to say, to the very fine and very good edition presided over by the Abbé Gosselin and the Abbé Caron. This new volume unites, with

[1] The following Essay is not a brief sketch of Fénelon's life, such as Sainte-Beuve gave of Molière, La Fontaine, and others; it is a review of his Letters, with incidental comments on his life and character. Some parts of it are here omitted. Fénelon was attached to the Seminary of Saint-Sulpice when the Duc de Beauvilliers, governor of the Duc de Bourgogne, son of Monseigneur, the only son of Louis XIV, selected him as tutor for the young prince. In that capacity he won the respect and affection of all until he came under the influence of Mme. Guyon and showed leanings toward mysticism. Mme. de Maintenon, the king, and the clergy influential at Court turned against him, and occasion was offered by his publication of a certain book, *Maximes des Saints,* to send him into exile in his archbishopric of Cambrai. With a beautiful nature, he was cautious, ambitious, and something of a time-server: had he possessed the courage of his opinions we might have known more of the mystical truth revealed by Mme. Guyon, who was then what we should now call a *seer,* or, perhaps, a medium. Had Fénelon been a stronger man the doctrine of Quietism, so called, might have done more work in the world.—Tr.

some writings not without interest and a few letters of business and administration, other letters of spiritual guidance, and especially certain charming letters of friendship and familiarity: in them we find the whole of Fénelon. Some of them are addressed to Mme. de Maintenon, by whom, as we know, Fénelon was greatly protected, consulted, and listened to until she had the weakness to abandon him.

Saint-Simon, in his Memoirs, has so vividly related the arrival of Fénelon at Court, his initiation into the little inmost circle of Mme. de Maintenon and the Ducs de Beauvilliers and de Chevreuse, the rapid rise of the fortunate prelate, so quickly followed by many vicissitudes, a great downfall, and that shipwreck of hopes which is to-day so touching a part of his fame, that one can only send the reader to such a painter, feeling it to be a profanation to rewrite the picture, even though we may think some points of it rash. Saint-Simon was gifted with a twofold genius seldom united to the degree we find in him: he received from nature the gift of penetration, almost of intuition, the gift of reading minds and hearts through the countenance, and of seizing thus upon the secret play of motives and intentions; he carried into this piercing observation of the masks and actors who swarmed around him in vast numbers a vigour, an ardour of curiosity that seems at times insatiable, and almost cruel: the eager anatomist is not more prompt to open the still palpitating breast, and to probe it in

every direction to find the hidden wound. To this
first gift of instinctive and irresistible penetration,
Saint-Simon added another, which also is seldom
found with the same degree of power, and the daring
use of which constitutes him unique in his own
special work: that which he had, as it were, wrenched
out with his relentless curiosity, he could write down
with the same fire, the same ardour, and almost with
the same fury of stroke. La Bruyère also had the
faculty of penetrating and sagacious observation; he
notices, he uncovers all things and all men around
him; he shrewdly reads the secrets on all the foreheads before him; then, alone in his study, at leisure,
he traces his portraits with delight, with skill, and
slowly; he begins them over and over, he retouches,
he caresses them, adding feature to feature, until he
finds them a perfect likeness. It is not so with Saint-
Simon, who, after his days at Versailles or Marly,
which I call his debauches of observation (so much
did he amass that was profuse, conflicting, and diverse), re-enters his own room at fever-heat, and
there, pen in hand, at full speed, without resting, without reading over his words, and far into the night, he
dashes down, all living, on his paper, in their amplitude and natural confusion, yet with an incomparable
clearness of relief, the crowd of personages he has
passed through, the originals he has caught on his
way and carried off, palpitating still, the majority of
whom have become, thanks to him, immortal victims.

A little more and he might have made Fénelon one of those victims; for, in the midst of the charming and delightful qualities he recognises in him, he harps perpetually on a secret vein of ambition which, in the degree which he supposes, would have made Fénelon quite another man to the one we like to see in reality. On this point, I think that this picture of the great painter ought to undergo, in order to be true, a slight reduction, and that his ardour of introspection has taken too much latitude. He did not penetrate and live at leisure in all parts of that amiable soul. Saint-Simon knew Fénelon through the Ducs de Beauvilliers and Chevreuse as well as a man can be known through his intimate friends. Personally, he knew him very little, and he tells us so: "I knew him only by sight, being too young when he was exiled." Nevertheless, to such a painter, that mere sight was enough to let him grasp and marvellously render Fénelon's charm:

" This prelate," he says, " was a tall, thin man, well made, with a large nose, eyes from which the fire and intellect gushed like a torrent, and a countenance the like of which I have never seen, and which, once seen, could never be forgotten. It united all things; yet the contradictions never clashed. It had gravity and gallantry, solemnity and gaiety; it equally expressed the learned man, the bishop, and the great seigneur; but what was manifest above all, and in his whole person as well as in his countenance, was elegance, refinement, intellect, grace, decorum, and, especially, nobleness. It required an effort to cease looking at him. . . ."

When a writer has once painted a man in that way, and shown him gifted with such powers of attraction, he can never be afterwards accused of calumniating him, even though he may be mistaken on some points. With Saint-Simon we can best confute and correct Saint-Simon himself. Read what he says so admirably about the Duc de Bourgogne, that cherished pupil of Fénelon, who never ceased to guide him from afar, even from his exile at Cambrai, through the channels of the Ducs de Beauvilliers and Chevreuse. The young prince, whom Saint-Simon shows to us first as haughty, impetuous, terribly passionate by nature, and contemptuous of all about him, of whom he could say: "From the height of his skies he looked on men as atoms with whom he had nothing in common, whatever they might be "—this same young prince, at a certain moment, transformed himself, and became a wholly different man, pious, humane, charitable, as well as enlightened, attentive to his duties, wholly absorbed in his responsibility as future king, and daring to utter, he the heir of Louis XIV and in the salons of Marly, a saying fitted to make the very arches crumble: " A king is made for his subjects and not the subjects for him." Well, that young prince thus presented by Saint-Simon, whose death tore from him—from him, the inexorable observer—words of emotional eloquence and tears, who was it who thus transformed him? Allowing for the part due to that which is mysterious and invisible in changes of heart, even that which is called grace; allowing for the share of the venerable Duc de Beauvilliers, the excellent governor, who, I ask, among human instruments, played so large a part as Fénelon? Near or far, he never ceased to guide his pupil, to inculcate upon him, and to insinuate into him that maxim of *father of the nation:* "that a king is made for the people," and all that hangs upon it.

We now know, in some respects, more than Saint-Simon knew: we have the confidential letters of Fénelon, addressed at all periods to the young prince; the notes that he wrote down for him, the plans of reform, all the papers then kept secret but now divulged, and which, allowing to human ambition the place it must always hold in every man even in his virtues, show the latter as belonging to the highest rank, and place for evermore in its full light the generous and patriotic soul of Fénelon.

Bossuet also, in concert with the Duc de Montausier, trained a pupil, the first dauphin, Monseigneur, father of the Duc de Bourgogne; it was for that royal and little worthy pupil that he composed many admirable works, beginning with the *Discours sur l'Histoire Universelle,* of which posterity will for ever reap the benefit. But looking at the matter closely, what difference of care and solicitude! Monseigneur, no doubt, was less amenable to instruction, possessed as he was by a gentleness that amounted to apathy. The Duc de Bourgogne, with passions and even vices, had at least an inward impulse revealing the

sacred fire. "Eager and excitable natures," says
Fénelon, "are capable of terrible errors; passions and
presumption lead them astray; but also they have
great inward resources, and often they return from
very great distances . . . whereas, one has little
or no hold on sluggish natures." Yet we see that
Bossuet did very nearly, in order to conquer the
laziness of his pupil and spur his sensibility, what
Fénelon did in the second case to subdue and har-
monise the violence of his. The first great man did
his duty with amplitude and majesty, as he was wont
to do it, and then passed on. The second continued
his attentions and fears, his ingenious and vigilant
cares, his insinuating and persuasive appeals, as if he
were held to them by some bond of nature itself; he
had the tenderness of a mother.

To return to the present volume; I have said that
we there find some letters which Fénelon, lately arrived at Court, addressed to Mme. de Maintenon, still
under the spell of his charm. The tone of his *Lettres
Spirituelles* is, in general, delicate, refined, easy, and
very agreeable to gentle and feminine minds, but a
little soft and tainted with the jargon of Quietist
spirituality; we feel the near neighbourhood of Mme.
Guyon. Fénelon is also too much given to infantile and
mincing expressions, such as Saint-François de Sales
addressed to his ideal, his Philothea. Speaking of the
familiarities and the caresses which, according to him,
the Heavenly Father bestows on souls that become

once more childlike and simple, Fénelon, for example,
says: "One must be a child, O my God! and play at
thy knee to deserve them." Theologians have quarrelled with these expressions, and others like them,
from the point of view of doctrine; severe good taste
would suffice to proscribe them. And it is here that
the manly and wholesome manner of Bossuet, brought
to bear upon all subjects, asserts its superiority.

I know, in speaking thus of Fénelon's letters, the
exceptions that ought to be made; some are very fine
on all points and very solid; such, for instance, as the
one to a lady of quality on the education of her daughter; such also as the *Lettres sur la Réligion,* supposed
to have been addressed to the Duc d'Orléans (the
future regent), and which are usually placed at the
end of the treatise on *L'Existence de Dieu.* But I am
here speaking only of the *Lettres Spirituelles,* properly
so called, and I do not fear that those who have read
a goodly number of them will contradict me.

Mme. de Maintenon, while receiving Fénelon's letters, and enjoying their infinite delicacy, judged them,
nevertheless, with the excellent mind and the good
common sense which she applied to all that did not
exceed her mental range and the horizon of her daily
life. She had doubts about certain expressions a little
too vivid and somewhat rash, the details of which I
need not give here. To clear her mind, she consulted another confessor, Godet, Bishop of Chartres,
and Fénelon was called upon to explain and justify

himself. In his explanation (which we find in this volume), by which he endeavours to reduce his mystical and rather strange expressions to their proper value, I am struck with an habitual skill in turning a subject, which is one of his characteristics. While maintaining his expressions, or, at any rate, justifying them by means of respectable authorities, he ends every paragraph by saying, and repeating, under various forms: "A prophet (or a saint) has already said before me something equivalent, or even stronger; nevertheless, *I submit.*" That constant affirming of submission, reiterated at the end of every justification that he offers as convincing, produces in the long run a singular effect, and actually ends by annoying those who are least theological. I call it an irritating gentleness, and the impression given supports the remark of M. Joubert: "The mind of Fénelon had something softer than gentleness, more patient than patience"; which also is a fault.

What, of a certainty, is not faulty, is the general character of his piety; that which he feels and that which he inspires. He desires in it joy, lightheartedness, sweetness; he would banish harshness and sadness: "Piety," he said, "has nothing weak, nor sad, nor constrained; it widens the heart, it is simple and pleasant, it makes itself all things to all men to win all." He reduces nearly all piety to love, that is, to charity. But this gentleness in him is not weakness or fawning compliance. In the few letters of

advice to Mme. de Maintenon that are given in this
volume, he lays his finger on essential things; on that
"self-love that seeks to take all upon itself"; on that
slavery to consideration by others; that ambition to
appear perfect in the eyes of persons of note,—in
short, all that constituted the foundation of her prudent and self-glorifying nature. There is in the *Lettres
Spirituelles* a certain variation by which we see
Fénelon adapting and proportioning himself to individuals, and he must have had this same variety in his
conversation. The *Entretiens,* transmitted to us by
Ramsay, in which Fénelon developed to him the
reasons that ought to lead every one, as he thought,
from deism to Catholicism, are of a breadth, a simple beauty, a full and luminous eloquence, that leave
nothing to be desired. Just as *L'Entretien* of Pascal
and M. de Saci is one of the finest testimonies to
Pascal's mind, so these *Entretiens* with Ramsay give
the highest idea of Fénelon's manner, and surpass in
breadth of tone most of his letters.

The most interesting part of the volume just pub-
lished is a series of familiar letters addressed by
Fénelon to one of his friends, a soldier of merit, the
Chevalier Destouches. During the last wars of Louis
XIV, all who were most distinguished in the army
(the army itself passing at each campaign through
Cambrai) visited Fénelon and received his hospitality.
With the attraction that was natural to him, he re-
tained from these passing acquaintances more than

one lasting friend. His friendship with the Chevalier
Destouches was one of the closest and tenderest.
Destouches, then about forty-three years of age,
served with distinction in the artillery; he was a man
of intelligence, cultivated, taking special delight in
Virgil. Dissipated withal, given to pleasures, to
those of the table, which, for him, were not the
only ones; and we are forced to admit that his intimacy with Fénelon never entirely cured him, inasmuch as he is supposed to have been the father of
d'Alembert, by Mme. de Tencin, in 1717. However
that may be, Fénelon loved him, and that word redeems all. The kindly prelate says it to him in many
tones, scolding him, schooling him, and seeing plainly
that he succeeded very little in reforming him.

" If you were to show my letter," he writes to him one April day,
" to some grave and stern censor, he would not fail to remark: ' How
can that old bishop (Fénelon was then sixty-three) love a man so
irreligious!' It is a great scandal, I acknowledge; but how can I correct it ? The truth is, I find two men in you; you are as dual as Sosie,
without any duplicity; on the one side you are bad for yourself; on
the other you are true, upright, noble to your friends. I end by
words of protestation, taken from your friend, Pliny the Younger:
neque enim amore decipior. . . ."

That is to say: " Affection does not blind me; it is
true I love with enthusiasm, but I judge, and with all
the more penetration because I love."

This correspondence with the Chevalier Destouches shows Fénelon to us in the sad years of his
exile (1711–1714), amusing himself. sometimes with

innocent playfulness, sporting, like Lelius and Scipio, after loosening his belt. He seems to have proposed to himself a wager in this correspondence, as if he had said to his rather libertine friend: "You love Virgil, you like to quote him; well, I'll send you Horace; I don't require, in order to beat you, any other auxiliary than he, for I can manage to insinuate into you nearly all the Christian advice that you need, or, at any rate, all that would be useful to your life, by disguising it under the verses of Horace." Horace, in fact, appears on every page of the letters; he speaks as often as Fénelon. These letters give an idea of what the latter's conversation must have been: most charming and distinguished in his hours of gaiety and sportiveness; they are the table-talk, the "after-dinner" talk of Fénelon, all that we can fancy most playful and smiling in the moral key. We catch, as though we were present, the habits of feeling and thinking, the exact tone of this fine nature. Destouches had sent the bishop a few Latin epitaphs: "Those epitaphs," replies Fénelon, "have great force, each line is an epigram; they are historic and learned. Those who made them have much wit, but they meant to have it; whereas wit ought to come by chance and without reflection. They are made in the spirit of Tacitus, who *digs into evil.*" Farther on, after quoting Homer on Peace, Fénelon recalls a stanza by Malherbe: "There we see the ancient who is simple, graceful, exquisite, and here is the modern who has his own

beauty." How well said that is! how well observed
the proportion, the shades, between the ancient and
the modern writer, and how we are made to feel that
he prefers the ancient!

That year, 1711, was an important one for Fénelon.
The first dauphin died in April, and the Duc de Bourgogne became the heir, and to all appearance the immediate heir to the throne. In his distant exile at
Cambrai Fénelon was felt by all to receive the rays of
that coming grandeur, and to reign already by the side
of his royal pupil. Consulted in writing on all matters political and ecclesiastical, umpire much listened
to secretly in the quarrels of Jansenism, once more a
teacher and oracle, already the great rôle was his.
But, all of a sudden, misfortunes fell. The Duchesse
de Bourgogne died on the 12th of February, 1712;
the Duc de Bourgogne followed her on the 18th, at
twenty-nine years of age, and all the hopes, all the
prospects—shall I dare to say all the secret ambitions?
—of the prelate vanished. We find traces of his profound grief in his correspondence, but his words are
simple, true, and cast far from him all censorious
thought. Learning of the death of the princess he
writes to Destouches (February 18th):

"The sad news that has come to us, Monsieur, from where you
are, takes from me the joy that was the soul of our intercourse: *Quis
desiderio sit pudor.* . . . Truly the loss is very great for the
Court and for the kingdom. They say a thousand good things of
the princess and increase them daily. One must be deeply pained for
those who regret her with such just sorrow. You see how frail life is!

Four days, and those not sure! Each man thinks he is secure, as if he were immortal; the world is but a mob of living, feeble, phantom beings, about to rot; the most dazzling fortune is but a flattering dream."

Those are not the grand tones, the strong beating wings of Bossuet in his pulpit, crying out: "Madame is dying! Madame is dead!" But with less lightning, less thunder, Fénelon's words are not less eloquent, and quite as piercing.

On learning of the death of the Duc de Bourgogne, Fénelon writes but one sentence; it is brief, deep-felt, and all it should be: "I suffer, God knows; but I have not fallen ill, and that is much for me. Your heart, which feels for mine, comforts me. I should be distressed to see you here; take care of your own bad health; it seems to me that all I love is about to die." To write thus to the Chevalier Destouches in such a sorrow was to place him very high.

The rebound of the world's favours after this cruel death was quickly felt by Fénelon. The night before, he was the man of the coming reign, the centre of all future hopes; on the morrow he was nothing, his dream had crumbled away, and if he could forget it for a moment, the world was ever there to remind him. A man of importance, a friend of Destouches, had offered his daughter to Fénelon's nephew; the day after the death of the Duc de Bourgogne this man withdrew his promise. Fénelon was not surprised; nor did he blame the father's attention to the solid

establishment of his daughter; he even praises and
thanks him for the promptitude of his action:

"As for your friend," he writes to Destouches, "I entreat you not
to be angry with him for this change; at most his blame is to have
hoped too much from a frail and uncertain support; it is on such frail
hopes that the worldly wise are too accustomed to fasten certain
projects. Whose will not forgive others for such things would become
a misanthrope: we should avoid such perils in our own lives, and forgive them in our neighbours."

Admirable and serene, or, at least, tranquil in mind,
Fénelon knows the world and mankind to their
depths; he has no illusions about them. But he
is not a misanthrope, and had he ever become one,
it would have been in a manner that resembled no
other:

"I am very glad, my dear, good man," he writes to Destouches, "that
you are pleased with one of my letters that they have read to you.
You are right in saying and thinking that I ask little of nearly all men;
I try to give them much, and to expect nothing. I find I am the better for this bargain; with this condition, I defy them to deceive me.
There is a very small number of true friends on whom I rely, not from
self-interest, but from pure esteem; not wishing to obtain something
from them, but to do them justice in not distrusting their hearts. I
should like to serve the whole human race, and, above all, good men;
but there is scarcely any one to whom I am willing to be under obli-
gation. Is it from haughtiness and pride that I say this? Nothing
could be sillier or more out of place. But I have learned, in growing
old, to know men, and I believe that it is best to do without them,
without letting it be known." "I pity men," he says elsewhere,
"though they are seldom good."

This rarity of good men, which seems to him "the
shame of the human race," brought him to stronger
love for his chosen friends: "Comparison only makes

us feel the more the value of true, sweet, safe, reasonable persons, open to friendship and above self-interests." Once only do we find him showing any inquiring interest in others, and then it is for Prince Eugène, in whom he thinks he perceives a truly great man. He owns that he would like to know him and observe him:

"His actions in war are grand, but what I esteem most in him are qualities in which what is called fortune has no part. They tell me he is true, without ostentation, without haughtiness, ready to listen without prejudice, and to answer in precise terms. He goes apart by himself at times to read; he values merit; he adapts himself to all nations; he inspires confidence. That is the man you are about to see. I wish I could see him, too, in our Low Countries; I own I have a curiosity about him, though I have little left for the human race."

The death of the Duc de Beauvilliers, in 1714, broke the last tie that bound Fénelon to the future: "True friends," he wrote to Destouches on this occasion, "make all the sweetness and all the bitterness of life." In these new Letters we find a few other details on the last year of Fénelon's life (1714). The peace just signed imposed fresh duties upon him.

"That which ends your work," he writes to Destouches, "begins mine; peace gives you the freedom it takes from me; I have seven hundred and sixty-four villages to visit. You will not be surprised that I wish to do my duty—you whom I have seen so scrupulous in doing yours, in spite of your wound and your infirmities."

Six weeks before his death, during one of his pastoral visitations, his carriage was overturned and he came near being killed; he relates the incident very pleasantly:

" A rather long absence has delayed the answers I owe you. It is true, dear man, that I was in great danger of losing my life, and I do not now see how I escaped; never was any one so willing to lose three horses. My servants called out: ' All is lost! save yourself! ' I did not hear them, for the windows were up. I was reading a book, with my spectacles on my nose and a pencil in my hand; my legs were in a bearskin bag, about as Archimedes was when he perished at the siege of Syracuse. The comparison is conceited, but the accident was frightful."

He gives the details. A mill-wheel started to turn as the carriage was on a bridge without parapets; one of the horses was frightened and sprang off, and the rest followed.

Until the last, in spite of his inward sadness, and though his heart was ever sick after the death of his cherished pupil, Fénelon could smile, and without too much effort. He had by nature that light-hearted gaiety, which is not either volatile or false; in him it was the natural impulse of a chaste, equable, and temperate mind; he had that joy of which (as he says so well) "frugality, health, and innocence are the source." In his last letter he jokes Destouches on the "pretty repasts" to which the chevalier was given, at the risk of being forced to repent. "It is at Cambrai," he says, "that people are sober, healthy, light-hearted, content, and gay under rules." In reading this familiar correspondence, I am made to find once more in the whole of Fénelon something gay, quick, lively, slow, easy, insinuating, and magnetic [*enchanteur*].

Among the pleasantries to be found there, are some that relate to the quarrel between the Ancients and

the Moderns, which was then at its height in the
bosom of the Academy, growing more and more
vehement when peace was signed in Europe. La
Motte, a friend of Destouches, had translated and
travestied the Iliad of Homer, and he sent it to
Fénelon, asking his opinion. Fénelon was here rather
weak. Invoked as judge and arbiter by both sides,
he evaded the subject. He thought that in matters
that did not concern the safety of the State people
might, perhaps, be more accommodating than in
others, and more inclined to politeness. He answered La Motte with compliments and praises, but
did not commit himself on the real point; he got out
of it by quoting a line of Virgil, which leaves the victory undecided between two shepherds: *Et vitula tu
dignas, et hic.* . . . It was Fénelon, the translator, the continuator of the Odyssey, the father of
Télémaque, who could talk thus. How is it possible
to push tolerance to such a point! Evidently, Fénelon had not that irritability of good sense and reason
that forces a man to say " No!" with vehemence; that
prompt and honest faculty, a little brusque it may
be, that Boileau brought to literature, and Bossuet to
theology. In this we again find a feeble side.

Each man has his glory and his shadows. We
may find Fénelon in fault on certain points. Bossuet,
in theology, pushed him hard. I find him equally refuted and forcibly reprimanded in connection with his
Dialogues sur l'Éloquence and certain of his assertions

about ancient authors, by Gibert, a well-informed man, with a vigorous and in no way despicable mind. But of what importance to-day are such mistakes and inaccuracies? Fénelon had the spirit of piety, and also the spirit of antiquity. In himself he unites the two spirits; or, rather, he possesses and contains them, each in its own sphere, without contention, without struggle, without discordance of any kind; and that is a great charm. For him, the battle between Christianity and Greece did not exist, and *Télémaque* is the unique monument to this fortunate and well-nigh impossible harmony.

Télémaque is not the pure antique. The pure antique to-day would be more or less imitation and *pastiche*. We have had striking instances of the antique studied and made over with passion and knowledge. *Télémaque* is another thing; something far more naïf and original even in its imitation. It is the antique laid hold of naturally and without effort by a modern genius, a Christian heart, which, fed on the speech of Homer, recalls it freely and draws from it as from a spring, but remakes and transforms it unconsciously while in the act of remembering it. This beauty thus turned aside, softened, not impaired, glides a full stream in Fénelon's channel, overflowing into a fountain always playing, always sacred, which adapts itself easily to its new slopes and its new shores. To appreciate *Télémaque* as it should be, there is but one thing to do: forget, if you can, that

you read it in childhood. I had that happiness a year
ago; I had, as it were, forgotten *Télémaque,* and I
was able to read it again with the freshness of
novelty.

From the literary point of view, many have greatly
praised and striven to define Fénelon, but nowhere
has it been done, as I think, with a happier expression
of feeling and a more touching resemblance than in
the following passage, which relates to his eloquence
as much as to his person: " What he made people
feel were not transports, but a succession of peaceable
and ineffable feelings: there was in his discourse I
know not what tranquil harmony, I know not what
sweet slowness, I know not what long, lingering
graces that no expression can render." It is a Choc-
taw who says that in " The Natchez." It is strange
to meet with such a speech in the mouth of an Ameri-
can savage, but it is not less beautiful and perfect and
worthy to be inscribed at the close of Fénelon's own
pages.

Fénelon was, above all else, a perfect and supreme
director of consciences. I go at once to the objection
that can be made to this statement. As such, as ar-
bitrator of souls, he had his errors, he went astray, he
yielded too completely to his tastes and predilections.
There was in his life a critical moment, when the inclination and the particular vocation that he felt for inward direction and for the delicate mysteries of piety
misled and slightly intoxicated him. Meeting in Mme.

Guyon a tender and subtile soul, who apparently revived all the traditions of the most saintly and the
most admitted fervours, he forgot himself too much
in speculating with her and in vying with her in
research and relinquishment. Let us pass a sponge
over that moment of illusion and forgetfulness, in
which, moreover, we cannot take a single step without obscurity and bewilderment. It is not for us, and
this is not the place, to enter into elucidations of what
they called "the different degrees of Prayer" [*les
divers degrès d'Oraison*]; we can only remain upon
the threshold, and with difficulty there. I shall therefore take Fénelon wholly outside of that affair of
Quietism, and simply as a most delicate, most perceptive, most adaptable and acceptable guide that
many anxious souls consulted and some devoted
friends.

The *Lettres Spirituelles* bear specially on these points
of the inward life, and by them he teaches how to
make true progress in the "art of loving God." This
volume, well known and valued as it is, is not the
one that I chiefly recommend to people of the world,
nor is it the one that I prefer. It is too exclusively a
collection of inward matters, leaving out all that relates to events, persons, and society; all, in short,
that would give it reality. The best way, as I think,
to read the *Lettres Spirituelles* of Fénelon, when it
is desired to make a slow and just use of them, is
to read them in connection with the edition of the

Correspondance in eleven volumes. There we find
the names, dates, events, and all the circumstances
that make the matter living.

For example, we know the Comtesse de Gram-
mont; she was a Hamilton, sister of the spicy and satirical writer, Antoine Hamilton, and wife of the Comte
de Grammont, so well known for his Memoirs, written down for him by his brother-in-law. Brought
very young to France by her parents during the civil
wars in England, she was educated at Port-Royal; for
which she always preserved an attachment. Returning later to France as Comtesse de Grammont, the
most noted woman at Court, haughty, brilliant, of
easy virtue, but respected and esteemed through all
her dissipations, she retained, when growing old, the
remains of beauty, and made herself acceptable at all
times to Louis XIV, to the point of giving umbrage
now and then to Mme. de Maintenon. Saint-Simon
and Mme. de Caylus tell us all this, and do not leave
us ignorant of the vagaries of temper and character
that made her a person even more interesting than
amiable. Well, the Comtesse de Grammont is one of
the spiritual correspondents of Fénelon; not precisely
one of his penitents, although he seems to have been
the person who contributed most to bring her back
and fix her to ideas of religion; and it was not until
Fénelon was in exile at Cambrai that the countess returned to her former ways at Port-Royal and declared
herself openly on that side. Until then, and so long

as Fénelon was within reach, she kept a middle course.

It was towards the age of forty-five that the Comtesse de Grammont began to change her ways, and to think of regulating her life. She had much to do:

"You have a great deal to fear both within and without," wrote Fénelon. "Without, the world smiles upon you; and the part of the world that is most capable of feeding pride gives yours all that can gratify it in the marks of consideration you receive at Court. Within, you have to surmount a taste for a refined and dainty life, a spirit haughty and disdainful, and a long habit of dissipation. All that, taken together, is a torrent that will sweep away even the best resolutions."

He advises her, as a true remedy, to save, each day, some hours for prayer and reading; but were it only half an hour, he says, in the morning; and half a quarter of an hour taken from excitements and well managed would still be good. "It is in such moment's that we renew ourselves before God, and repair in haste the breaches the world has made."

Silence, above all, seems to him a great remedy, and the only one in the moments thus snatched from the world. Imagine the sister of Hamilton, like him in mind, in satirical charms, in subtile, imperceptible, elegant, pitiless, and vengeful irony —imagine her cutting off all that and leaving to others the honours of conversation! "You cannot conquer your disdainful, mocking, haughty spirit except in holding it chained by silence. . . . You cannot fast too rigidly from the pleasures of worldly conversation. You must humble yourself incessantly; you will rise again only too soon." He knows the spot he touches, and he returns to it repeatedly: "Preserve inward meditation even in conversation; you have more need than others of this antidote." But this silence to which she is required to condemn herself must not be a "cold and disdainful silence"; for self-love driven back has many byways of return; "it must, on the contrary, be a silence of deference to others." Thus does Fénelon, on every tone and with infinite skill, endeavour to instil charity for one's neighbour into the sister of Hamilton.

But he sees another rock, another peril within her: "You have more need to be humiliated," he tells her, "than to receive more light." These lights of religion, as he very well knows, the countess received from childhood at Port-Royal; she has greater need, in turning from the world to religion, to learn not to pass from one self-love to another, not to seek to excel or to be a marvel in a new sense:

"What I desire for you is smallness and simplicity of mind. I fear for you a *luminous* and lofty devotion, which, under pretext of seeking the real and lasting thing in reading and in practice, nourishes in secret I know not what of grandeur that is contrary to the child Christ Jesus, simple and despised of the sages of the century. We must be a child with him. I pray him with all my heart, madame, to take from you not only your defects, but also your taste for grandeur in virtue, and to humble you by grace."

There is nothing in these letters of Fénelon to Mme. de Grammont, that exceeds what the delicate good sense of the most enlightened director of consciences should counsel and prescribe.

Some of the letters addressed to her do, however, go much farther and develop the important and always intelligible points of Fénelon's doctrine of piety. The Stoics, Epictetus, for instance, lay it down as a principle that to be happy and virtuous we must withdraw ourselves within ourselves and within the bounds of all external things that depend upon us; cutting off whatever is without, raising the drawbridge, as it were, so that all communication be merely formal, and not affect uses sentially. Fénelon, like all true Christians, found that way of attaining to virtue and happiness very gloomy and insufficient; it is not in seeking solitude, in withdrawing within self, that he thinks it possible to find peace; for in us, in our nature, is the root of all our ills; so long as we remain selfishly shut up within ourselves we are exposed to all painful and sorrowful impressions:

" Our temper exposes us to that of others; our passions clash with those of our neighbours; our desires are just so many points at which we lay ourselves open to the darts of other men; our pride, which is incompatible with the pride of our neighbour, rises like the waves of an angry sea; all fight us, all attack us, we are exposed on all sides by the sensitiveness of our passions and the jealousy of our pride."

The remedy, to his mind, is to find peace by coming out of self; to rise by prayer, and lose that self as much as possible in thoughts of the infinite Being, the fatherly Being, loving and good, and always present;

to obtain, if possible, that his will be substituted for ours: "Then shall we know the true peace reserved for men of right will . . . ; then can men do naught against us, for they cannot touch us through our desires nor through our fears; then shall we will all and will nothing. This is to be inaccessible to enemies, to become invulnerable." That in the doctrines of the later Stoics, and even in Epictetus and Marcus Aurelius, there was a beginning of this method of conceiving the enfranchisement of the spirit, I do not deny; but such thoughts did not have their full illumination and accomplishment until Christ brought into the world the idea of God that he came to reveal. The doctrine of Fénelon, freed from certain refinements of expression and over-niceties peculiar to his manner of feeling and writing, is no other than the Christian doctrine in its most spiritual vigour.

In his correspondence with Mme. de Montbéron he thinks he is, or says he is, sometimes cold and uncertain: on the contrary, he enters, in a keen and rapid manner, into all the delicacies of Divine love; he explains in clear, prompt terms its theory, as we should say, its precepts; he makes it simple, but a simplicity we do not perceive at a glance. As he has to do with a soul more scrupulous, more subtile than that of Mme. de Grammont, he goes farther and deeper than with the latter. He insists upon the rather subtile point that, in prayer, we must try to hush ourselves to let the spirit of God speak in us:

"There is no longer real silence," he says, "when we listen to ourselves. After having listened, we answer, and in that dialogue a secret self-love silences God. Peace for you is in a very delicate simplicity."

It is in this doctrine of silence and quietude in prayer that we find the germ of what is called Quietism, which may become illusion. I say no more, and pass on hastily. In general, Fénelon's "delicate simplicity" is not that from which we start, but that to which we return by force of mind, of art, and of taste. I will not try now to investigate and define it, having still to show its more serious aspects. . . . To-day I have only skimmed my subject; but, in truth, these matters of spirituality cannot be given in great quantities at a time. It remains to show Fénelon on his firmer and stronger sides, in his correspondence, half spiritual, half political, with the Duc de Chevreuse and the Duc de Bourgogne — the close of the reign of Louis XIV as seen from Cambrai.

Among Fénelon's letters there are none more interesting and more instructive than those he wrote to the Duc de Chevreuse. It was through him, principally, that Fénelon, during the seventeen years of his exile at Cambrai, continued to correspond with his pupil, the Duc de Bourgogne.

The Duc de Chevreuse, like the Comtesse de Grammont, was a former pupil of Port-Royal; but, unlike the countess, he did not preserve an affection for it. He always, however, retained some effect of it in his

mind, his method of reasoning, close and logical, and
in his erudite, polished, and pure language. It was
for the Duc de Chevreuse, when a child, that Arnauld
composed the *Logique,* called that of Port-Royal. The
duke did not profit by it in the sense and spirit that
Arnauld expected. One of the remarks of that judicious "Logic" is, that the greater part of men's errors
come less because they reason ill on true principles
than because they reason well on false ones. The
Duc de Chevreuse, such as we see him in Saint-Simon
and in his correspondence with Fénelon, appears to
us precisely a type of the men who reason wonder-
fully, reason too well, reason on everything, and *ad
infinitum,* only the principle from which they start is
false and contestable.

"One was lost," says Saint-Simon, "if one did not stop him
in the beginning; because as soon as he had been allowed to pass
two or three propositions which seemed simple, and which he made to
result from one another, he led his man by beat of drum and colours
flying to his end. People felt he was wrong, but he reasoned so
closely that there was no finding a joint at which to break the
chain "

The Duc de Chevreuse, honest, sedulous, laborious,
treating all questions methodically, exhausting himself in combining facts and drawing inductions and
conclusions for ever, had something in him of the doc-
trinaire and the statistician combined (we still have
some of the kind): with much intellect, worth, capacity, and knowledge, he never came to be more
than a good, wrong mind [*bon esprit faux*]. It was

certainly not worth while to write the most simple
and sensible of *Logiques* expressly for him, and attain,
in his person, such results.

Fénelon did his best to correct the Duc de Chevreuse in his intellectual excesses and to cure him of
them:

"I always fear," he writes to him in 1695, "your excessive tendency to reason; it is an obstacle to the silence and inward composure
in which God communicates himself. Let us be simple, humble, sincerely detached from men; let us be calm, meditative, not arguers
with God. The men you used formerly to listen to are dry, cold,
critical reasoners, opposed to the true inward life. However little you
listen to them, you will always hear endless arguments and dangerous
inquiries which will put you insensibly away from grace, and cast you
back into your natural self."

It was, in truth, the whole nature of the Duc de Chevreuse that he was trying to remake from head to foot;
Fénelon's counsels are given in lively and personal
terms, which now serve as features for a faithful portrait of the good duke. "I have often remarked that
you are always in a hurry to go from one occupation
to another, but that, nevertheless, each of them leads
you too far. You follow your spirit of anatomy into
everything. You are not slow, but you are long."
And again: "You are too accustomed to let your mind
plod." To the Comtesse de Grammont, satirical and
pungent, he counsels "fasting from worldly conversation"; to the Duc de Chevreuse, absorbed in his
speculations, he counsels "fasting from ratiocination":
"When you cease to reason you will die to self, for

reasoning is the whole of your life. . . . The more you reason the more you give food to your philosophic life. Yield yourself up to simplicity and to the mania of the Cross."

The Duc de Bourgogne holds naturally a large place, the largest place, in Fénelon's Correspondence during these years, and it is to us the most interesting part of it; it is like a semi-poetic and romantic light suddenly thrown for our benefit upon history. Young princes, the objects of so many prayers and hopes, who never lived to fulfil them, those to whom the voice of peoples, like the voice of the poet, has said: "If 't is given thee to vanquish the inimical Fates, thou shalt be Marcellus"—these incompleted figures that imagination often crowns, present, as they flit by, a problem that the most serious and least visionary minds may well meditate upon, at least for a moment. It is thus with the Duc de Bourgogne; we cannot, as we cross these last years of Louis XIV, meet the original, singular, and puzzling figure of Fénelon's pupil without asking ourselves: "What wholly different results would have come in history, what turn would things have taken for France, had he lived?"

I shall say at once that the idea of the Duc de Bourgogne which we obtain in reading Fénelon is not exactly the same as that which is given by Saint-Simon. And here is a singular thing: we get from Saint-Simon a stronger and more favourable impression of the Duc de Bourgogne than we do from Fénelon.

Whether it was that the latter, in his distant exile, did not fully know the good qualities tardily developed in the young prince, the superior merits praised so highly in the last year of his life, or whether Fénelon was too disposed to judge him always as a child, towards whom, as former master and tutor, he was bound to be more severe and exacting than he would be to others, it is certain that Fénelon's letters are continually filled with censure, most distinctly pronounced, except in those of the last eight months of the prince's life.

What Fénelon wrote to the Duc de Bourgogne he never ceased to repeat to him through the channel of the Duc de Chevreuse; he is hurt in his religion as an enlightened Christian, in his tenderness as foster-father, in his patriotism as a citizen, to see a prince who ought to be so dear to all good Frenchmen becoming, as he thinks, an object of contempt and general exasperation. Fénelon's letters of this date throw a melancholy light on the decadence of public spirit, and the deterioration of characters and social morality. The young and rising generation, full of new desires, enduring impatiently the long reign and the mute subjection imposed by Louis XIV, ought, it seemed, to turn with favour to an heir more or less like themselves, who already announced such contrary maxims. Far from it: in place of that favour they showed only dislike against the future king, because they knew him to be virtuous and religious.

Vice and debauchery, muzzled at the close of Louis XIV's reign, feared to be still more so, and in another manner, under his grandson. Nevertheless, as much heedless want of reflection, much mere vogue and fashion, were, after our French custom, mingled with all this, it came to pass that during the last year, when the Duc de Bourgogne, then become dauphin by the death of his father, put himself, with little effort, into an attitude of pleasing and of winning good will, public opinion suddenly veered round to honour him and extol his transformation, so that when he died, a few months later, the loss was mourned as irreparable, as that of a blessing torn from the human race.

Saint-Simon shows us, visibly, the whole of this movement, the flux and reflux, in which he swims himself, and which is much less felt in the calmer and by no means enthusiastic Correspondence of Fénelon. During the whole year of 1710, and in the beginning of 1711, he never ceases, when touching that delicate chord, to make it ring the one sound: sustain, correct, enlarge the heart of the young prince; he desires, and demands of Heaven for him, "a heart as wide as Ocean." It is necessary that from that moment he should practise his royal rôle "by correcting himself, by taking much upon him, by adapting himself to men in order to know them, to manage them, and learn how to put them to work." In vain is he told good things of the prince, he will not be satisfied "until he knows him free, firm, in possession of the power of speaking (even to the king) with gentle and respectful force. . . . If he does not feel the need of becoming firm and vigorous, he will never make any true progress; it is time now to be a man."

Fénelon, who has been accused, and with reason, of being sometimes visionary, and who had a corner of poesy and idealism in his nature which, in his youth at least, he liked to transport into human things, guards himself from this tendency when he judges and exhorts the Duc de Bourgogne. He feels, with all his mind and all his nobility of nature, what are the qualities necessary for a king, for the head of a nation, for one of the masters of the world. He desires, therefore, to inspire his pupil with boldness of action, nobleness in his behaviour and bearing; the art of conversation, of all that adorns, imposes, and gives to power its gentleness and majesty. "Let him be small and ever smaller under the hand of God, but great and grand to the eyes of men. It is for him to make virtue joined to authority loved, feared, and respected. It is said of Solomon that men feared him, seeing the wisdom that was in him." To the very end he distrusts and combats in his pupil what was in the latter an inveterate habit until he was twenty-eight years of age, namely, too much reasoning, too much speculation as opposed to action, and a certain petty and trivial compliance, both in serious matters and in his recreations: "Puerile amusements lower the mind, weaken the heart, degrade the man, and are contrary to God's order." Fénelon, in the whole of this moral appeal, is not chary of his expressions.

In all that I have said, I have had no other intention than to recall certain traits of the noble, lofty, courageous piety, both social and royal, of Fénelon, without presuming to draw (which would be cruel and almost impious in regard to him) any inference, any consequence, against the future of his cherished pupil, against that future which it was not given to men to know or to see develop. The Duc de Bourgogne, disappearing in his first bloom, remains one of those confused and flattering hopes that all may construe and interpret as they choose. Have we not seen Saint-Simon admire him all the more because he had, as it were, grafted upon him and upon his future reign his own whole system of quasi-feudality?

Fénelon himself, like his pupil, was a hope; he appeared in politics as one of those floating lights that the breeze of public opinion sends vacillating from one side to the other, according as men take them and welcome them. His ideas and his various plans demand a long explanation, the last word and conclusion of which would be, as I think, doubt. That which is certain is that the true Fénelon, such as he shows himself in this correspondence, and in his last years, is not precisely the Fénelon whom the men of the eighteenth century — Ramsay, d'Alembert, and others — have successively presented to the public

and extolled. The Fénelon who, in 1711, seems to
desire and pray for an Assembly of Notables, but who,
at the same time, is wholly occupied in opposing
Jansenism, even mitigated Jansenism, in refuting M.
Habert, in making an excerpt of the true doctrine of
St. Augustine: the Fénelon who declares that "the
liberties of the Gallican Church are actual slavery,"
who fears laic power far more than spiritual and ultra-
montane power, and who dreads the danger of schism
as much as the invasion of France—that Fénelon is
certainly not the one whom the philosophers of the
following century have fashioned and remodelled to
suit them.

The long reign of Louis XIV had strained all ener-
gies and wearied, in the long run, all conditions of
men and their souls. Towards its close, and in spite
of conventional laudations, the faults of that régime
were felt by all reflecting minds, and struck the eyes
of all who knew how to see. And who would see
and feel them more keenly than Fénelon? His policy
was, above all, moral. It was what it must have
been in a man of sensitive feeling, piety, and delicacy,
who had seen the Court very closely, and had suffered
from it, and now, at the end of a long reign, watched
its disadvantages and ill results, its last abuses and its
disasters. In his exile, and notwithstanding his remaining confidential intercourse with the Court, he
was not fully informed of the state of things; he says
himself, constantly, that the general state of affairs

has not been explained to him, and he is right; he judges only as the public judged, or, as he says, "by the scraps of government he sees on his frontier." But even so, and without needing further information, all men of sense, honest men, the Fénelons, the Vaubans, the Catinats, saw the defects, and sought, each on his own line, remedies in counteraction and in the reversal of that which was. All such projects of dismissed and exiled men, malcontents, or patriotic dreamers, are necessarily vague and somewhat chimerical when it comes to applying them. But there was then a general inspiration, a natural breath, as it were, diffusing itself through all classes of lofty minds or simply human minds, sensible and gentle. Each had his plan of correction for that government of Louis XIV, now nearing its end. Fénelon was merely the man most in sight; the most popular among the many makers and inventors of plans and programmes.

He never gave to his plans and programmes a final touch; he never proposed them as other than first ideas, to be sifted and moulded into practice. His great innovation was to think and to say, in face of the monarchical idolatry of Louis XIV, that "kings are made for subjects, not subjects for kings." By inculcating that maxim in the Duc de Bourgogne, engraving it, as it were, upon his heart, he did not think of any act of positive reform, still less of philosophy and democracy, as we should now say: he was merely going back to the religion of

Saint-Louis. However laudable such maxims may be, they leave out, almost entirely, the question of public policy, properly so-called. A policy truly novel, but so necessary after Louis XIV, required, in order to succeed in its application, all the correctives and all the precautions which, later, were lacking— for Louis XVI failed solely from having practised faithfully, but without art, this very maxim of the virtuous dauphin, his father, and of the Duc de Bourgogne, his grandfather.

Fénelon knew men, and appears not to have relied much upon either their goodness or their gratitude; he says so in more than one place to the Duc de Bourgogne, and with a singularly intense accent, showing that he had no illusions on that point: "When a man is destined to govern men, he must love them for the love of God, and not expect to be loved by them. . . ." I refer my readers to that whole passage, which it is painful to transcribe in its ugly truths. There are moments when Fénelon's experience brings him very near to bitterness; but in him bitterness stops short and soon softens; it never resembles the misanthropy of others. I find in one of his letters to Mme. de Montbéron, when he was nearing his fiftieth year, a very keen and circumstantial painting of the insipid, arid, disillusioned life he was leading: "As for me, I live in cold peace, obscure and languishing, without ennui, without pleasure, without thought of ever having any; without prospect of any future in this world;

amid an insipid and often thorny present. . . ."
Such moments of aridity and disgust in Fénelon are
described in terms which show that his weariness of
soul did not resemble a vulgar ennui.

As he grew older, causes for sadness increased; he
lost all his friends. The short year during which the
Duc de Bourgogne shone, only to be extinguished,
passed like a flash. Fénelon, courted once more for
several months, then dropped again on the death of
the duke, had full opportunity to revive his ideas of
the vanity and baseness of the world. Yet, in the
midst of it, his delicate, pure nature, blessed with
unction, and adorned with grace divine, recovers itself and resumes the upper hand. I find a letter from
him on the death of his best friend, the Abbé de
Langeron: it is sad, it is charming, it is light-hearted.
Fénelon believed without effort in all that is spiritual
within us; his piety had wings.

As we advance in the Correspondence, in the letters
near its end we perceive a gleam, as it were; we feel
a something that resembles mirth. There is the same
disgust of life, but with it I know not what of fellow-
feeling that corrects it. He loses the Duc de Chevreuse; and he delights in keeping about him at
Cambrai the grandchildren of his friends, the sons
of the Duc de Chaulnes, and in surrounding himself
with all that happy youth. He loses the Duc de Beauvilliers: "As for me, who have been deprived of seeing him for so many years," he writes to the widowed

duchess, "I still talk to him, I still open my heart to him, I believe I meet him before God; and though I do mourn him bitterly, I cannot think that I have lost him. O what reality there is in that close intercourse! . . . A little while, and we shall mourn no longer. We die ourselves, and what we love is living, and dies not again." This presentiment, this involuntary sensation of a soul that approaches the end of its earthly way and is about to reach its goal, shows through all of Fénelon's last letters, and communicates itself by many a little sign of joy to the reader. These last letters have the effect upon me of the last days of a mild winter, beyond which I feel the springtime.

XIII.

Comte Antoine Hamilton.

XIII.

Comte Antoine Hamilton.

THE modern vice that has done, perhaps, the most harm in these latter days is the pompous "phrase," the declamatory grand words that some writers play with, others take seriously, and which all the first who used them, even those who played with them, took seriously also. I do not mean that we are ill of that malady only, nor that it is not allied to many others; but I think that disease is one of the most contagious, the one more directly injurious of late years, and that it is doing a good work to endeavour to cure it. Whatever could contribute to bring back to us our first clearness of expression, to rid the French language and the French mind of pathos and emphasis, of the false colour and the false lyricism which mingles in everything, would be a true service rendered not only to taste but also to the public mind. To accustom ourselves to write as we speak and as we think, is not that to put ourselves in the way of thinking rightly? After all, great efforts are not needed in France to return to that clearness, for it is not only good form among us, it constitutes the basis of our language and of the spirit of our nation: it was its tendency and evident quality for centuries, and in the midst of all that has since been done to change it we still find numerous and excellent specimens of it to-day.

I shall go farther and say that, whatever may be done, clearness is and always will be a prime necessity in a nation eager and hurried like ours; which needs to hear quickly, and has no patience to listen long; we are brought back to our original quality by our very defects.

Nevertheless, among the celebrated writers of our language, all are not equally fitted to give us the impression or show us the image of this perfect clearness. No doubt some examples of it are found in all ages, even among our classics; witness Philippe de Commines and Montaigne. In spite of the pedantry of false knowledge and the remains of barbarism, this tendency and particular turn of the French mind did not fail to come to the light, and original natures took the lead in it. But it was not until a certain period more equally enlightened, that this clearness became habitual and, we may say, universal among good writers, passing into common usage. That period is quite recent; I date it towards the close of the seventeenth century. It was not until the middle of that century that French prose, which had done its grammar with Vaugelas and its rhetoric under

COMTE ANTOINE HAMILTON.
From an old print.

Balzac, emancipated itself all of a sudden, and became the language of a perfectly polished man in Pascal. But what one man of genius then did, and what other superior minds trained to the world, such as La Rochefoucauld and Retz, practised also, it needed an interval of time to bring others to profit by, and for the coin with the new effigy to circulate.

La Bruyère marks distinctly the new era; he inaugurates a species of régime wholly modern, in which clearness of expression seeks to combine itself with the action of the mind. Besides La Bruyère, we find other examples less striking but, perhaps, more facile, more natural. Fénelon, in his non-theological writings, is the lightest and most graceful model of the kind. Certain distinguished women, with the tact they receive from nature, did not wait for La Bruyère's example to show their vivid and inimitable sense of the fit and the appropriate in language.

At the close of the seventeenth century, and during the first half of the eighteenth, there came a period by itself for purity and the easy flow of French prose. When the second half of the latter century came, when Jean-Jacques Rousseau appeared, it was enriched with loftier, more brilliant, and wholly novel features; our prose gained in the shading of impressions and descriptions, but declamation was then introduced; false enthusiasm, false sensibility, had their course. This "declamation," from which we suffer still [1850], has taken many forms for nearly a cent ury; it has had its renewals and changes of colour with each generation, but it dates in the first instance from Rousseau.

But however that may be, between La Bruyère or Fénelon and before the advent of Jean-Jacques, there came a calm, enlightened period of moderation, in which we find the language such as we speak it, or might speak it, and such as nothing has yet made ancient. "Our prose," says Lemontey, "stopped at the point where, being neither too curt nor too formal [*hachée ni périodique*] it became the most supple and elegant instrument of thought." We may certainly, as amateurs, prefer other epochs of prose than that; it would not be difficult to show moments when our prose took on more fulness and grandeur; but for habitual and general use I know none more perfect, more convenient, or better suited for intercourse, than the language of that date. For principal examples I take, at a first glance; Le Sage, the Abbé Prévost, Mme. de Staal (de Launay), Mme. du Deffand, Fontenelle, Vauvenargues, Montesquieu finally, and Voltaire, already in his variety and richness. I find also, at the very beginning, the incomparable writer of Memoirs, Saint-Simon, and a unique narrator, on whom I pause for a few words to-day— the very agreeable Hamilton.

Antoine Hamilton, one of the most Attic writers of our literature, was neither more nor less than an

Englishman of Scotch descent.   We have seen other
foreigners—Horace Walpole, the Abbé Galiani, Baron
de Béseuval, the Prince de Ligne—possess, or assume,
the French spirit marvellously well; but Hamilton
does so to a degree that allows no other element to
be seen; he is that spirit, that wit itself.   Educated
from childhood in France, living afterwards at the
semi-French Court of Charles II, at all times a pupil
of Saint-Évremond and the Chevalier de Grammont,
with a vein in him of the Cowleys, the Wallers, and
the Rochesters, he was a cross between all that was
most acute, refined, and witty in the two races.   England, which had taken Saint-Évremond from France,
restored him in the person of Hamilton, and it was
full consolation.   Louis XIV gave subsidies to Charles
II, he gave him also a mistress: the emigration of
James II returned both to Louis XIV, in the persons
of a great warrior, Berwick, and (what is more rare)
a charming writer, a light and airy chronicler of
elegancies.

What is known of the life of Hamilton?   Very little.
He was born, they say, in 1646, in which case he
would be a little younger than La Bruyère and a little
older than Fénelon.   In the flower of his age he was
at that Court of Charles II which he describes to us so
vividly; but the Hamiltons of whom he speaks were
his brothers; personally, he gives himself no rôle.
Whatever rôle he may have played, he was, first and
last, an observer.   Endowed with a keen sense of the

ridiculous, and a most penetrating social perception, he could distinguish the faintest shades and fix them with a light, ineffaceable stroke.   He makes no difficulty in admitting that he gladly amused himself at the expense of those who deserved it.   Returning to France on the Revolution of 1688, in the suite of his legitimate king, he lived there in the best society, compensating himself for the ennui of the pious little Court at Saint-Germain by visits to the Berwicks and the Grammonts.   He made couplets in the style of Coulanges, and wrote letters to friends, mingling prose with verse, in the style of Chaulieu.   He was intimate with the latter, and frequented the Vendômes and the society of the Temple.   We find him in demand at Sceaux, where the Duchesse du Maine held Court of *bel esprit*.   Dangeau wrote to him àpropos of a letter of his to Berwick, which was thought to be full of delicate praises: " It is wholly in the style of the best-bred persons at Marly."

But this kind of vogue would only have led him to be appreciated by his friends and the societies he enlivened: it would not have procured him a distinct place and physiognomy among the chroniclers of that day.   Speaking of the expedition of the Pretender in 1708, and of the seigneurs who took part in it, Saint-Simon mentions Hamilton confusedly: " The Hamiltons," he says, " were brothers of the Comtesse de Grammont; they were the leading lords of Scotland, brave, full of intelligence, and faithful.   Through their sister, they mingled much with the best company of our Court; they were poor, and had each their own little corner of singularity." Here then is our Hamilton confounded with the others of his family, and, for all distinctive mark, we are told that they had each "their own little corner of singularity!" And there he would still remain for us if, when already old, in his sixtieth year, he had not taken it into his head, in order to amuse his brother-in-law, the Comte de Grammont, then over eighty years old and still charming, to write down the latter's youthful adventures when Chevalier de Grammont; to make himself, in short, his Quintius Curtius and his Plutarch, in merriment.

This is the only work of Hamilton that is worth re-reading to-day; as for his verses and even his *Contes,* they need not be mentioned. His verses, praised, however, by Voltaire, praised even by Boileau (who must have grumbled as he wrote that polite letter), are entirely out of date for us, and almost unreadable; they are nothing but a string of rhymes in which, here and there, a happy thought flashes out. How is it that in witty works that have pleased good judges when born, there should be so much that decays with time and dies out? There is a Voiture in every man of wit who is nothing but that; I call by Voiture's name the wit of fashion that has but one season and which a breath wilts; there is much of Voiture in Hamilton's verses. Pure poesy is not to be looked for in him.

He has that of his day in sportiveness; he knows the right quantity for the French mind at that period: "Whatever its ornaments," he says, "in a lengthy narrative poesy is always wearisome." He likes Horace, but he seems not to know what Milton was. Shakespeare is to him as if he were not; though it seems as if the roguish Ariel disguised itself and, all unknown, glided into his prose.

His *Contes* might have something more, perhaps, of this Ariel fancy if they were less confused. He wrote them on a wager to amuse his sister, the Comtesse de Grammont, and in imitation of the "Arabian Nights"; they are full of allusions, the meaning of which escapes us. Still, through them all, something natural and piquant is felt. The Duc de Lévis, who believed he continued them, was merely insipid. If I wished to give an idea of them by some modern production I should name the pretty fantasy of Alfred de Musset's *Merle blanc*.

But the *Mémoires de Grammont,* they last; it is to them that the fairy has given all her grace. The manner seems made expressly to illustrate Voltaire's words: "Grace in expressing itself is worth more than what is said." The foundation is slender; not precisely frivolous, as persons have called it; it is not more frivolous (light and airy as it is) than all human comedy. There are many heavy treatises that are more frivolous, though without the appearance of it. The hero of the Memoirs is the Chevalier, afterwards the Comte de Grammont, the man most in fashion in his day, the ideal of a French courtier at a period when the Court was all in all, the type of that airy, brilliant, supple, alert, indefatigable personage, repairing all faults and follies with a sword-thrust or a witty saying. Our century has seen some fine remains of the race in the Vicomte Alexandre de Ségur and Comte Louis de Narbonne. The characteristic of that light race was in never being false to themselves. Grammont, dangerously ill and urged to religion by Dangeau, sent for that purpose by the king, turned to his wife, who was very devout herself: "Countess," he said, "if you do not take care, Dangeau will filch my conversion from you." Which did not, however, prevent the conversion, in the end, from being sufficiently sincere.

But Grammont himself does not matter very much to us. Though the hero of Hamilton's narrative, he is often only its pretext. It is the manner of showing him that makes the charm. Envious folk (and Bussy was one of them), while granting to the Comte de Grammont a gallant and exquisite wit, added that the expressions of his face and his tones often "gave value to things he said that were nothing at all on the lips of others." Hamilton made good use of Bussy's remark by giving to Grammont his every accent, and perhaps by lending him some. Nothing can equal his manner of telling and narrating, easy, happy, uniting the trivial to the choice, with a perpetual yet almost unconscious satire, an irony that glides and does not force itself, and a perfected art of disparaging. He says, somewhere, of the Duke of Buckingham, who was paying court to a beauty:

"She did not dislike backbiting; he was father and mother of it; he wrote ballads and invented old women's tales, over which she went crazy. But his particular talent lay in catching the absurdities in people's talk, and mimicking them in their presence without their perceiving it. In short, he could flay all kinds of personages with so much grace and charm that it was difficult to do without him when he chose to take the trouble to please."

I think I catch in that portrait a reflection of Hamilton himself; but it is more especially when he paints his sister, the beautiful Miss Hamilton, who married Grammont; it is on that charming page, among so many others, that indications escape him which I trace back to himself, applying them not to his muse (solemn term that does not suit him), but to his grace as a writer:

"She had," he says, "an open forehead, white and smooth, hair well-plaited and docile to the natural arrangement it costs such trouble to produce. A certain freshness that borrowed colours cannot imitate, formed her complexion. Her eyes were not large, but they were lively, and her glances signified all that she wished them to say; her mouth was full of charm, and the outline of her face was perfect. A delicate little turned-up nose was not the least ornament of a face that was very agreeable. . . . Her mind was a good deal like her face. It was not by aggressive vivacity, the sallies of which only stun and bewilder, that she sought to shine in conversation. She avoided still more that affected slowness of speech, the weight of which sends us to sleep; but, without being in haste to speak, *she said what it was necessary to say and no more.*"

That is how, in his perfect diction, he appears to me himself. Shall I add that in this very portrait of his sister his malicious [1] pen does not refrain from an insinuation on hidden beauties, which proves that, if need be, his indiscretion respects nothing. We have since had other Memoirs of courtiers and celebrated dandies. The Maréchal de Richelieu, that spoilt child of the eighteenth century and of Voltaire, that last type of the consummate courtier who took the place of the Comte de Grammont, also desired his historian. Soulavie edited from his notes volumes full of scandal and diverting adventures, more or less vulgar. The flower of the genus was not in them, it had been plucked already: I do not know if there was no other Comte de Grammont, but it is certain that there has been but one Hamilton.

Also there is but one age for certain fortunate works. That a gentle, polished mind, penetrating, shrewd, and refined, shedding upon surrounding things and on its neighbour a universal airy satire— that such a mind should be born into the world does

---

[1] It may be well to say here that *malicieux* is one of the many words identical in French and English which have not the same meaning in both languages. "Malicious" in English means harbouring enmity without cause; proceeding from extreme hatred or ill-will (Stormonth). *Malicieux* in French means inclination to do little mischievous things (*méchancetés*); little mischievous things done for pastime (Littré). We have no word or expression in English that translates, or can represent *malicieux;* "mischievous" is the nearest ; but it is quite inadequate, and conveys neither the delicate humour nor the roguishness.—Tr.

not suffice.   All things about that mind must be ar--
ranged to favour its possessor; the climate, as it were,
must be prepared; in the midst of fools and vulgari-
ans who, in all ages, swarm in the world and in the
best society, a well-assorted company of choice minds
must assemble apart, and be able to listen and reply
to him, losing nothing if he speaks low, and asking
from him no more and nothing else than he can say.
In the second half of the eighteenth century the world,
in this respect, changed; declamation obtained the
upper hand, and a certain false keying-up became
necessary.   Minds like those of Hamilton would have
been much less enjoyed; in fact, they must have
forced the tone to be felt at all.   At the pace the world
is now going, will this species of rare minds be lost
entirely?   Not entirely, I think; but it will be less
and less in view, and seen in a less good light.

Meantime, it is profitable to put ourselves back,
now and then, into a liking for these facile writers, in
whom there is nothing old or worn.   "This work,"
says Voisenon, speaking of the *Mémoires de Grammont,* "is at the head of those we ought to re-read
regularly every year."   That is better advice than one
might expect from Voisenon.   Grace, I know, cannot be taught and is never learned; in fact, it would
be knowing it to attempt to copy it.   It is good,
however, to talk of it sometimes, and circle round it;
something of it always remains.

To analyse these Memoirs of Grammont would be

a thankless and stupid task, for it is manner and the method of expression that give them value; as for the narrative, after a certain moment, it goes pretty much as God pleases. The opening adventures are the most interesting and the most consecutive. The first loss at cards in Lyons with the horse-dealer, the revenge of the chevalier at the siege of Turin, the game with the Comte de Caméran at which, foreseeing he meant to cheat, de Grammont has himself secretly supported by a detachment of infantry—all these are scenes of pure comedy. We feel at once how ideas of morality have changed since then, when the historian, even in jest, could do honour to a hero so lacking in honesty. It is true that when Hamilton, at the close of Louis XIV's period, related the first exploits of his hero under Richelieu, he was speaking of another century and of things that were nearly fabulous. At any rate, the Abbé Prévost did not think he ruined his Chevalier Des Grieux in the mind of the reader, by attributing the like peccadillos to him. We must conclude, therefore, that on this point of morality we have improved upon those times. The personages that Hamilton meets by the way and shows to us become instantly living. Who does not remember, if once he has seen them, the grotesque Cerise, the worthy governor Brinon, and, above all, Malta, the chevalier's second, Malta so natural, so heedless, so full of wit! He had no brains, says Retz, but Hamilton puts in action his naïve giddiness

and makes us love him. At Turin, gallantry begins;
the beautiful ladies are mentioned by name; it is still
another trait of manners and morals that these Memoirs could have appeared in the lifetime of Hamilton,
with all these names and revelations, without causing
an uproar. People were more easy-going in certain
ways than they are now.

When his hero goes to the English Court the style
of the historian changes a little; we enter a gallery
of portraits and find a complication of adventures
which, at first, we have some difficulty in disentan-
gling. Unity ceases; we have alternately the recollections of Grammont and the recollections of
Hamilton, which combine or cross each other. Still,
with a little attention, we end by recognising where
we are, at a Court ball, as it were, amid that bevy of
English beauties, the most refined and the most aristocratic in the world, whose every charm the painter
has rendered with discrimination. I have before my
eyes the magnificent edition of the Memoirs published in London in 1792, with numerous engraved
portraits; those beauties defile before me, the squadron of maids of honour to the queen and the Duchess of York; I read the opposite page, and I find that
the writer with his pen is the greater painter.

"This lady," he says of a Mrs. Wettenhall, "was what is properly
called a wholly English beauty, kneaded of lilies and roses; snow
and milk as to colours, made of wax in regard to hands and arms,
throat and feet, but all without soul or air. Her face was of the
prettiest, but it was always the same face: you might say she took

it from a case in the morning and put it back at night, without using it during the day.. But how could she help it? Nature had made her a doll from childhood and doll to her death remained the white Wettenhall."

So of one, so of others, but among them no resemblance. Hamilton is not the Van Dyck of that Court; he has not the gravity of a great royal painter; but he is a painter apart, of his own kind, with his soft, shrewd, malicious brush. The roguish Ariel frolics through all this part of the Memoirs, and often takes delight in tangling the web. What mystifications, what madcap tales, what pretty episodes throughout this incessant imbroglio! What an ironical contrast between this life of youth and jollity and the final expiation at Saint Germain! The last page, which sums up in marriages these various whimsicalities of love and fortune, ends delightfully the charming tale, which was beginning to drag slightly.

The style, generally happy, natural, negligent, fastidious without being *précieux,* is not free, in two or three places, from an appearance of studied nicety and fine writing, which betokens the approach of the eighteenth century. In fact, Hamilton, may be said to begin the eighteenth century. Already he has the curt phrase of Voltaire. Bossuet has made a timely exit from the world just as Hamilton begins to write. He is one with La Fare, Sainte-Aulaire, Chaulieu, with that little group of choice voluptuaries who mark the transition between the two ages. He lays a finger, as it were, on the *Lettres Persanes,* published one year after his death. But, in the *Lettres Persanes,* jesting begins to attack grave things, and to take on a bitterness that Montesquieu afterwards regretted. Hamilton never jests, at any rate never with pen in hand, except on light matters: he scoffs in low tones only. He is one of the happy, lively spirits who brighten the opening of the new century before declamation began with Rousseau, and before the propaganda to which Voltaire set fire. Epicurean, perhaps, on many points, he at least had the prudence to feel that, to be at his ease, it was not desirable that all the world should be so too.

Hamilton died at Saint-Germain, April 21, 1720, in the seventy-fourth year of his age, with feelings of great piety, it was said, and after receiving the sacraments; in the matter of death he became once more the man of the seventeenth century. A few "Reflections" in verse show that he did really, like La Fontaine, have his day of sincere repentance. I find, among the *Anecdotes Littéraires* of the Abbé de Voisenon an incident relating to Hamilton which needs clearing up: " The Comte de Caylus," says the abbé, "who saw him often at his mother's house, assured me more than once that he was not amiable." Can it be that Hamilton was not amiable in society? in spite of all such assurances, could we ever believe it?

Hamilton, when the Comte de Caylus saw him at his mother's house, was an old man, wearied perhaps; moreover, we think of him as being, at all times, capricious, and rather unequal in moods, like his sister; he had that " corner of singularity " of which Saint-Simon tells us. He himself says, somewhere, that he knows when to hold his tongue, and that he did not much like talking. With his malicious causticity and the sly lip for which he was so well known, he needed silence around him; and, perhaps, when Caylus met him at his mother's house there may have been too much youth and tumult to suit him.

XIV.

The Princesse des Ursins.

XIV.

The Princesse des Ursins.

DURING the negotiations for the Peace of the Pyrenees, Mazarin, talking one day with the prime minister of Spain, Don Luis de Haro, spoke of the political women of the Fronde, the Duchesse de Longueville, the Duchesse de Chevreuse, and the Princess Palatine, as being each of them capable of overthrowing ten kingdoms:

"You are very lucky in Spain," he added; "you have, as everywhere else, two sorts of women, coquettes in abundance, and very few good women; the former think only of pleasing their lovers, the latter their husbands; neither have any ambition but for luxury and vanity; they know only how to write, the one set their love-letters, the other their confessions: neither know what flour is made of, and their head swims if you talk to them on business. Our women, on the contrary, be they prudes or coquettes, old, young, silly or clever, want to meddle in everything. A well-behaved woman" (I allow the cardinal to use his own language) "would not sleep with her husband, nor a coquette with her lover, unless they talked to her during the day of State affairs; they want to see all, hear all, know all, and, what is worse, do all and tangle all. We have three among others, Mmes. de Longueville, de Chevreuse, and the Princess Palatine, who put us every day into more confusion than there ever was in Babylon."

"Thanks be to God," replied Don Luis, with little gallantry, "our women are what you say; provided they handle the money, whether of their husbands or lovers, they are satisfied, and I am very glad they do not meddle in affairs of State; for if they did, they would assuredly spoil things in Spain as they do in France."

Those are harsh words on both sides, which would raise a terrible quarrel if fully discussed. It seems that the philosopher Condorcet did formally take upon himself to reply in a dissertation (inserted in the Journal of the Society of '89), in which he pleaded for the "admission of women to civic rights," adducing in support of their claims the great historical examples of Queen Elizabeth of England, the Empress Maria Theresa, and the two Empresses Catherine of Russia; and he adds, speaking of French women:

"Was not the Princesse des Ursins worth a little more than Chamillart? Is it thought that the Marquise du Châtelet could not write a better despatch than M. Rouillé? Would Mme. de Lambert have made such absurd and barbarous laws as those of Keeper of the Seals d'Armenonville against the Protestants, domestic thieves, smugglers, and negroes?"

The Princesse des Ursins herself treated the same question less solemnly and more agreeably in one of her letters to Mme. de Maintenon. The latter had written to her, complaining of the frivolity of the talk that reigned more than ever at the Court of Versailles: "Yes, madame," she writes, "the greatest difficulty lies in the little resources to be found in the men; they are nearly all selfish, envious, insincere, insensible to the public good; they consider all sentiments contrary to their own as romantic and impracticable." To which Mme. des Ursins replies:

PRINCESSE DES URSINS.
From an old print.

" You make me a portrait of most men, which is not much to their advantage; and what I think the worst of it is, that it seems to me rather natural. They return us the same; for if one is to believe them, we have most of their imperfections and few of their good qualities. Yet it is certain that they have contemptible pettinesses, and they tear each other to pieces even more than women do. . . . The knowledge that I have of the world attaches me still more to you; I find there all the virtues and the goodness that are lacking in others."

This is how, while complimenting each other, two political women talked of men in their tête-à-tête, and took their revenge on Don Luis de Haro and Mazarin.

But, in a letter dated soon after, the truth is perceptible; I catch a confession there which proves that revenge is never quite complete, even to the eyes of the heroines who indulge in it. The Queen of Spain, forced to quit Madrid at the approach of the enemy, was obliged to part with most of the ladies of her suite. Three hundred remained in Madrid, not caring to accompany her, though many, with a little good will, could have done so; and these ladies soon after left the palace to go, some to their homes, others to convents, in short, wherever inclination or interests took them. On the queen's return to the capital, finding them absent or dispersed, it was thought a good time to practise economy; soldiers were just then more needed than female attendants of doubtful fidelity. Mme. des Ursins proceeded to cut off at one stroke the three hundred ladies of the queen. We can imagine the outcry. Mme. de Maintenon, however, writes to congratulate her: "As I never lose my interest in you, I am delighted that you have three hundred less women to govern." So she herself and Mme. de Maintenon thought three hundred women more difficult to rule than three hundred men—what more could we ask?

The Princesse des Ursins, who has led me to touch this delicate chord, was a woman in politics not, I think, of the first order, but very superior as such to Mme. de Maintenon. Having played in Spain an important rôle for thirteen years, interrupted only by a short dismissal, then abruptly thrown down, as if uprooted in the twinkling of an eye, without leaving behind her either partisans or minions, she has excited contradictory judgments, most of them severe. Short of being historians, we should have little chance of forming a close appreciation of her fame were it not that we possess nearly the whole of her correspondence with Mme. de Maintenon. It is through those letters that we are able to approach her closely, to enter her mind, and pronounce an opinion upon her with more esteem than has usually been given to her.

In spite of her name [Orsini] and her foreign rôle, Mme. des Ursins was wholly French, of the blood of the Trimouilles, and the daughter of M. de Noirmoutier, who was so mixed up in the intrigues of the Fronde, and so closely allied with Cardinal de Retz, whose Memoirs end with a complaint of his unfaithfulness. At the same time, Mlle. Anne-Marie

de La Trimouille, through her mother, was almost
a *bourgeoise* — a *bourgeoise* of Paris. Her mother,
Aubry by name, belonged to an old family of the
robe and the finances.   The exact date of the
daughter's birth is not given, but it must have been
about the year 1642.   She married in 1659 her first
husband, the Prince de Chalais, of the Talleyrand
family.   A duel having forced him to quit the kingdom, she followed him to Spain, then to Rome,
where she became a widow.   She was young,
beautiful, with much intelligence, much worldly
knowledge, grace, and the gift of language.   She
sought the protection of the French cardinals, more
than one of whom was not insensible to her charms.
Saint-Simon, who paints her to perfection in her
first form, shows her to us again in the fulness of
her beauty and the grandeur of her bearing, which
she well knew how to maintain through all her
vicissitudes:

"She was tall rather than short, with blue eyes that invariably
said what it pleased her that they should say; with a perfect figure,
a beautiful bust, and a face which, without beauty, was charming.
Her air was extremely noble, with something majestic in her whole
bearing, and graces so natural and so continual in all things, even the
most insignificant, that I have never seen any one to compare with
her in body or mind, of which latter she had a great deal and of all
sorts: a flatterer, caressing, insinuating, cautious, wishing to please for
the sake of pleasing, and gifted with charms from which it was impossible to defend oneself when she chose to reign and fascinate.
And with it all, an air that, in spite of its grandeur, attracted rather
than alarmed; a delightful gift of conversation, inexhaustible, and
withal, very amusing from all she had seen and known of countries

and people; a voice and manner of speaking very agreeable, with a gentle air; she had read much, and she was a person of much reflection. A great choice of the best company, much practice in keeping it and even in holding a Court; great politeness, yet with great distinction, and, above all, much care not to put herself forward except with dignity and discretion. She was, moreover, the person in the world best fitted for intrigue; who had passed her life in it in Rome by her own choice; much ambition, but a vast ambition far above that of her sex and of the ordinary ambition of men, and an equal desire to be and to govern. . . ."

I pause in the quotation of this portrait which the inexhaustible painter does not end so soon. Such was the Princesse des Ursins in Rome at the time she made her second marriage with Prince Orsini [called Ursins in French], Duc de Bracciano. Mme. des Ursins was at that time called Mme. de Bracciano when in Paris, where she sometimes went for long visits, giving little balls for marriageable heiresses, which always ended at ten o'clock in the evening. But her usual residence was Italy and chiefly in Rome. Becoming a widow for the second time, and without children, it seemed that her remarkable qualities, much appreciated by friends, were not likely to be exercised on a wider field than that of a brilliant society, when an unforeseen necessity occurred to bring her forward.

Louis XIV, in accepting the crown of Spain for his grandson, the Duc d'Anjou, married him to a princess of Savoie, sister to the Duchesse de Bourgogne, the wife of his brother. It was necessary to find a guide for the young queen (a child only thirteen years of age), an experienced adviser to form her, to train her

not to shock expectations around her, but to play her
part with dignity.   It was found that Mme. des Ursins
alone united the difficult conditions of this post: she
had lived in Spain, knew the language and the customs, and held the rank of grandee through her husband.   The Cardinal of Porto-Carrero, who was the
influencing personage in Spain, had formerly, when in
Rome, been very much in love with her in common
with many others.   She knew intimately all the southern Courts and those who figured at them.   It was
therefore decided that no one was so fitted as Mme. des
Ursins to fill the place of *Camerara mayor,* or Superintendent of the Household of the queen.   Until then, her
ambitions and her intrigues had been spent on accessory
and secondary affairs.   She now felt that the game was
about to come into her own hands, but she carefully
avoided seizing it too eagerly; in fact, she made herself entreated for what was really the object of her
secret desire.   She was not less than fifty-nine years
old when this career opened to her (1701).   Mme. de
Coulanges, on hearing the news, while considering
Mme. des Ursins very worthy of the office, thought
that at her age nothing agreeable in life could be expected; this came of her being a woman only, incapable of conceiving in her sex other passions than those
that were loving and tender.   Mme. des Ursins, who
added to those passions the ambitions of men, entered
upon her new rôle with a zeal, an ardour, an activity
that were more than virile.

Two distinct epochs are to be noted in her thirteen years of influence in Spain. From the first she
charmed the young queen, a gracious and really intelligent pupil, became necessary to her, and, through
her, became equally so to the young king, Philippe V,
a prince of upright mind, brave in war, but timid
in character, with an imperious temperament, which
made him blindly dependent on his wife (*uxorius*);
in a word, chaste, devout, and amorous. During the
three first years Mme. des Ursins worked to establish
herself firmly in the minds of these two royal personages; she put aside all rival influences, foiled them by
every means in her power, excited endless clamour,
and for want of enough discretion and prudence deserved to receive her recall by order of Louis XIV.
In this first downfall she displayed qualities far more
rare and more dextrous than any she would have
shown under permanent good fortune. Like a good
general who proves his skill in a retreat, she managed
her own so well that she induced Louis XIV, instead
of obliging her to go at once into exile in Italy, to see
her and hear her at Marly and Versailles. There, on
the ground, in person, she reconquered her influence, and at the same time she learned to understand
better the line of policy she ought henceforth to
follow.

Returning to Madrid all-powerful and upheld by
authority, she reigned there, absolutely, in the interior
of the palace, resolved in future to remain in perfect

accord with the Court and Cabinet of Versailles, at any rate until the day when that Cabinet should put itself in disaccord with the interests of Spain. It is from the date of her return that we have the series of her letters to Mme. de Maintenon, in which it is such pleasure to hear her and study her. It happens to us almost as it happened to Louis XIV; the moment that Mme. des Ursins succeeds in being heard, she recovers her place in our minds.

I must nevertheless say one thing on this first period (1701–1704) on which so many narratives have been written. Louville, one of the principal agents of French influence on Philippe V before the arrival of Mme. des Ursins, shows himself unjust and insulting towards her; he speaks of her, like an evicted rival, with all sorts of abuse, in Memoirs that were taken from his papers and published under his name. The Memoirs of Noailles, edited by the Abbé Millot, are more equitable. Without entering into the detail of intrigues, it is evident that Mme. des Ursins contributed, from the first, to guide the queen wisely and to lead her into a path where she made herself welcome to her new subjects and cherished by the Spanish people. The graces and the intelligence of that child-queen would not have sufficed without the direction of this constant guide, who became that of the young king also, in many ways. With the delightfully jesting tone peculiar to her, Mme. des Ursins is very amusing to listen to on this topic:

" In what an office, good God! have you put me!" she writes to the Maréchale de Noailles. " I have not a moment to rest, not even time to speak to my secretary. It is no longer a matter of reposing after dinner, or of eating when I am hungry; I am only too happy if I can snatch a bad meal at odd moments, and then it is very rare that I am not called off the moment that I sit down to table. Mme. de Maintenon would laugh if she knew all the details of my office. Tell her, I entreat you, that it is I who have the honour to take the dressing-gown of the King of Spain when he gets into bed, and give him his slippers when he gets up. To that point I have patience; but every evening when the king enters the queen's chamber to go to bed, the Comte de Benevento (grand chamberlain) puts into my arms his Majesty's sword, a chamber-pot, and a lamp, which I usually spill upon my clothes—it is too grotesque. Never would the king get up if I did not open his curtains, and it would be sacrilege if any one but I entered the queen's room when they are in bed. Lately the lamp went out, because I had spilt half of it; I did not know where the windows were, because we had arrived at that place in the night; I came near breaking my nose against the wall, and we were nearly a quarter of an hour, the King of Spain and I, stumbling against each other, trying to find them. Her Majesty is so pleased with me that she sometimes has the goodness to send for me two hours before I want to get up. The queen enters into all these jokes; but I have not yet secured the confidence she gave to the Piedmontese waiting-women. I am astonished at that, for I am much better than they; I am sure they never washed her feet or took off her shoes and stockings as neatly as I do."

She had to pass through these domestic cares in order to reach affairs of State and bring the young couple to do so likewise. During the campaign in Italy, which Philippe V insisted on making in person, Mme. des Ursins, according to the duties and prerogatives of her office, never left the young queen for a single instant. She was with her at the sessions of the Junta, and, under pretext of initiating her in public affairs, she herself obtained their secrets. She knew

how to make use of etiquette, to put it forward, or
modify it, or loosen it altogether, according to her interests.   She comprehended the sort of concessions
demanded by the spirit of the Spanish people and
what reforms it would permit.   She judged the minds
of the grandees at first sight, and was under no illusions as to the degree of support she might expect
from them.   "With those people," she writes to M.
de Torcy, "the safest way is to show firmness.   The
more I see them closely, the less I find that they deserve the esteem I once thought no one could refuse
them."   According to her, the Spanish nation, in the
person of its grandees, had given itself to a son of
France solely from the belief that France alone could
protect and defend it.   France remaining victorious
and powerful, Spain was safe; but after each defeat
in Germany or Flanders, the eyes of the grandees
turned back to the archduke, and their fidelity did not
hold good.

The merit and the art of Mme. des Ursins were to
know, in so short a time, how to turn to good account the favours and affability of the queen, and thus
render her truly popular among the real Spanish people in the centre of the kingdom; it was a miracle to
see how the roots of this new royalty struck into the
hearts of the old Castilians so that it resisted the
storms of many tumultuous years.   The exact situation was this: the queen ruled the king; for in spite
of the counsels that surrounded him, in spite of the

admirable instructions of Louis XIV, "the force, the impulse that decides men were not in him; he had received from heaven a subaltern and even subjugated spirit." Now the queen who, in 1704, had just completed her fourteenth year, needed a person to rule and govern her, "and give her good advice and courage." Mme. des Ursins was essentially that person. Did she always use this private and uncontrolled influence in a purely devoted and disinterested way? It would be rash to affirm that she did. Louville, her rival and enemy, a man of talent and ardour, but full of passion, presents her to us as the wickedest woman on earth, who ought to be driven out instantly: "so sordid and thieving that it is a marvel." He brings the same accusation against Orry, an able man whom Louis XIV had sent into Spain to put some order into the finances. These accusations do not seem to me warranted. Maréchal de Berwick, who held himself above all such odious bickerings, does more justice to Orry, and gives the impartial reader reason to think that Mme. des Ursins was still cleaner in this respect, and that she felt, as she herself said, "very easy and free in carriage." "I am a beggar, it is true," she writes to Mme. de Noailles after her arrival in Spain, "but still more am I proud." Recounting later to Mme. de Maintenon the indignities of that kind charged against both of them, she speaks in a tone of lofty irony and sovereign contempt which seems to exclude all pretence.

But what seems certain, though rather strange at first sight, is that Mme. des Ursins at over sixty years of age still had lovers. "She has morals on a see-saw," wrote Louville to the Duc and Duchesse de Beauvilliers. The Sieur d'Aubigny, a sort of steward of whom she made an equerry, occupied in the *Retiro* an apartment adjoining that of the princess, at the window of which he was seen one day to brush his teeth. "He was a tall, handsome fellow, very well made and free and agile in body and mind," not at all the "brute beast" that Louville describes him. But he was bold and rather insolent, as one who felt his rights. One day when Louville entered, with the Duc de Medina-Cœli, Mme. des Ursins's apartment, where she took them to converse more freely, d'Aubigny, who was installed at one end, seeing only the princess, and thinking her alone, apostrophised her in terms of brusque familiarity of the crudest kind, which put them all into confusion. Mme. des Ursins's feminine defect was on this side: "gallantry and devotion to her person was her ruling weakness, surviving everything else to final old age." It is Saint-Simon who says it, and he does her ample justice for her lively and lofty qualities.

This d'Aubigny has been mentioned as the principal cause of Mme. des Ursins's first downfall. After having caused the dismissal of Cardinal d'Estrées, whose place was filled by his nephew, the Abbé d'Estrées, Mme. des Ursins discovered that the latter, contrary to agreement, was writing despatches to the Court of France without her knowledge. She intercepted one of these despatches and there read the particulars of her relations to d'Aubigny; but what piqued her most was a final remark of the ambassador that many per-- sons thought them married. The great lady rose to her full height, and in her wrathful indignation wrote on the margin of the despatch: "As for marriage, no!" This, at least, is the story that circulated. The despatch thus commented upon went to the courier, and must have reached Louis XIV.

But the letters that we have of the king show that this extreme piece of folly was not needed to turn him against Mme. des Ursins. The complaints against her were at that time universal, certainly at Versailles, and at a distance it was difficult to distinguish those which had foundation from those which had none. Judging from what we know of Louis XIV's mind, he must have thought it an amazing thing that such im- portance should be given at the Spanish Court to a woman whom he had placed there to serve him. Finding resistance in his grandson and the young queen to Mme. des Ursins's recall, he wrote to them in the tone of a father and a king:

"You ask my counsel," he says to Philippe V, "and I write you what I think; but the best counsels become useless when persons wait to ask them and follow them until after the harm has happened. . . . Up to this time you have given your confidence to incapable or self- interested persons. . . ." (Speaking of the recall of Orry and another agent.) "It seems that the interest of those particular men fills your mind altogether, and while it ought to be occupied only with great views, you lower it to the cabals of the Princesse des Ursins, with which I am incessantly wearied."

And to the queen Louis XIV writes more explicitly still:

" You know how I have desired that you should give your confidence to the Princesse des Ursins, and that I neglected nothing to induce you to do so. And yet, forgetting our common interests, she has given herself up wholly to an enmity of which I was ignorant, and has thought only of thwarting those who have been charged to conduct our affairs. If she had had a faithful attachment to you she would have sacrificed her resentment, well or ill-founded, against Cardinal d'Estrées, instead of making you take part in it. Persons like ourselves ought to hold themselves above the quarrels of private persons, and conduct themselves in accordance with their own interests and those of their subjects, which are one and the same. It was necessary, therefore, to either recall my ambassador and abandon you to the Princesse des Ursins, leaving her to govern your kingdom, or to recal lher, herself. The last is what I have thought it my duty to do."

In these words so firm and so royal, we see plainly the true cause of Louis XIV's displeasure; and Mme. des Ursins's marginal note, true or false, is only a secondary matter.

The great king thought he ought to take extreme precautions to strike a blow at the right time. He chose a moment when the King of Spain was with the army and separated from the queen, fearing that the latter in her despair would throw obstacles in the way of its execution.

I send to the fourth volume of Saint-Simon all those who would admire the presence of mind with which

Mme. des Ursins, thus suddenly recalled as if by a thunder-bolt, did not allow herself to be disconcerted, the tranquillity of her demeanour, the art with which she managed her retreat slowly, in good order, yield-ing the ground foot by foot, without affecting to disobey, but taking measures to provide for her re-turn. After a first stoppage at Toulouse, from which place she continued to correspond with her royal pupil, and where she succeeded in warding off the exile to Italy, she received the much-desired order to go to Versailles, and from that moment she no longer doubted her final success and triumph.

Arriving in Paris January 4, 1705, visited imme-diately by all persons of consequence, she went, eight days later, to Versailles, and after her first interview with Louis XIV, it was evident from the way he treated her that she was no longer an accused person, coming to render account of her conduct, but a con-queror who had got the better of her enemies. We see her loaded with favours and marks of distinction, "such as no subject ever had before"; and on one of the trips to Marly, Louis XIV did her the honours as if she were "a lesser foreign queen." At the Marly balls she was easy, dignified, unconstrained, turning her eyeglass on every one; at one of the balls she carried a little spaniel in her arms as if she were in her own house, and (what was still more remarked upon) Louis XIV caressed the dog several times, when he returned to converse with her, which he did nearly all the evening. "Never was any one seen to soar so high."

Mme. des Ursins, who had imagination and was a little subject, we are told, to being dazzled, may have been, during these months of favour, slightly intoxicated; but it is certain that while she displayed all the charms of her continual and inexhaustible conversation, she keenly appreciated the mind of the king. She returns, in her subsequent letters, too frequently to the subject, and enters too particularly into what she discovered in him, not to make us feel on her part a sincerity deeper than flattery. She never speaks of the king except as "the most amiable man in the world," the "best friend," the "most courteous of men." Some have even gone so far as to suppose that Mme. des Ursins's views went farther, and that "the age and health of Mme. de Maintenon tempted her." She may have asked herself whether the prospect of taking her place in France were not better than what she would find in Spain. But these are conjectures too easy to make about the heart of a woman and quite impossible to verify.

What seems to me certain is that, independently of public affairs, she obtained a personal triumph of mind. Mme. de Maintenon, Mme. des Ursins, and Louis XIV were for some time under one and the same charm: "I often recall the idea of you and of your amiable presence that charmed me so at Marly," writes Mme. de Maintenon a year later; "do you still retain the tranquillity that enabled you to go from most important conversations with the king to the foolery of Mme. d'Heudicourt in my cabinet?" Mme. des Ursins, who was there as a bird of passage, delighted in pleasing, and the sense of success redoubled her charm. Louis XIV was fascinated both by her grace and her capacity. He had expected to find her a belated woman of the Fronde; instead of which, he found one who by nature was fitted to be a person of authority and government, but who, for all that, did not cease to be a woman of delightful social art and with the grandest air. With her as a third, intercourse with Mme. de Maintenon became rejuvenated. Of the three personages, if I may venture to say it, Mme. des Ursins was the one who was most in command of her situation, who had considered all points of it intelligently; she was the one of the trio most aloof from her rôle, and, consequently, she played it best.

Once re-established in Spain, Mme. des Ursins, now in unison with Louis XIV, followed a more cautious, regular, and really irreproachable course towards those who had sent her there. The letters that she writes to Mme. de Maintenon, which began immediately after her departure from Paris, if they do not show us to the full her vigour and brilliancy, at least allow us to divine them; and they give us, unmistakably, the principal lines of her character. The mind of Mme. des Ursins was a serious mind, practi-

cal, a little cold and dry at bottom, but frank, reso-
lute, and bold.   Unlike Mme. de Maintenon, she had
political ideas; she dared to avow them and push
them to execution.   She commits herself, before all
else, to the complete re-establishment of the authority of the King of Spain.   Àpropos of a claim set up
by the grandees against the captains of the guard,
she wishes to see the whole cabal of the nobles (who
are profiting by the weakness of the new régime to
create titles and prerogatives for themselves) broken
up; otherwise Spain was likely to fall into the same
difficulties France was in before the Fronde, "in the
days when Frenchmen did nothing but thwart one
another."   She is of opinion that the leaders of that
party ought to be made to feel the displeasure of the
king before any word can be received from France; so
that it may appear to be a resolution taken by the
King of Spain, and not suggested from abroad.

"Do not feel alarmed, I entreat you, madame, at these resolutions,"
she writes to Mme. de Maintenon; "it is fortunate that the grandees
have given us so good an occasion to humiliate them.   They are proud
men without force or courage; they are working to annihilate the
authority of their king; I am furiously angry with them for all they
have done since they entered the Council."

This virile tone carries us far away from Mme. de
Maintenon.   A thing more important, in Mme. des
Ursins's opinion, than satisfying the grandees is to
have troops and find means to pay them, after which
"we can laugh at the rest."   "Would to God," she

exclaims, "that it was as easy to get the upper hand of the priests and the monks, who are the cause of all the revolts that you hear of!"

She has ideas on war (I do not say they are the best, but she has them), on plans of defence, and on the choice of generals; she states them all, excusing herself from arguing upon them, but she argues all the same. She sees dangers in advance, lays them bare, and spreads them out, without allowing herself to be discouraged. She shows the Spanish troops such as they are, the important fortresses destitute of everything, "according to the custom of Spain"; she demands energetically from France succour, men, and, after vehemently asking in the body of the letter for big battalions, she adds in a postscript that she has advised the King of Spain to order prayers. She has little flatteries of this kind suited to Mme. de Maintenon.

A few days after the arrival of Maréchal de Berwick, in writing to thank Mme. de Maintenon for that succour, she speaks of Saint-Cyr, knowing that nothing would please her so much, and well aware of the "weakness of mothers":

" The queen likes your ' Rules ' for Saint-Cyr very much; our ladies wish to have them, and I am having them translated into Spanish to give them that satisfaction. If her Majesty were not bound by very different engagements than those of your young ladies of Saint-Cyr, I really believe she would wish to be one of your pupils."

The flattering creature knows how to say just the

proper thing, but there are days when, displeased to feel that Spain is being neglected and abandoned by Versailles, she is frank to rudeness.

One of her finest letters is addressed to M. de Torcy, the minister. Going back to the principle of the Spanish Succession, Mme. des Ursins shows what basis should be made of the fidelity, so recent in date, of the Spanish nation to the House of Bourbon, and what was the true political lesson of it; towards the grandees, to prevent the division of the monarchy; towards the people of the provinces, to sell their wool. Those who desire these advantages from France will, she thinks, decide to get them with the archduke, if France does not provide them. She ends by submitting her views as to the means of defending Spain as soon as possible from an impending invasion from Portugal, and also from Catalonia. Then, after having said all that she had in her heart, and saying it boldly, she effaces herself in a skilful postscript and re-enters her feminine rôle of lofty propriety.

The dangers that she foresaw were realised in the campaign of 1706; the Court was reduced to leave Madrid, which the Portuguese threatened and Berwick was unable to protect. The miseries and incidents of the journey across the still faithful provinces are related by Mme. des Ursins in a playful tone. She contents herself with cheering those about her, consoling them, inspiring firmness and a sort of joy; not

seeing things "in black," but obeying her easy humour and a certain inclination to hope that came to her
by nature:

"It often happens, madame," she writes to Mme. de Maintenon,
"that when we think all is lost, some fortunate event occurs to change
the whole face of things. . . . I turn the medal, and expect
consolations that will soften our troubles. I would, madame, that
you could do the same, and that your temperament were your best
friend, as mine is the one on which I can best rely. . . ."

Mme. de Maintenon, who, in spite of her excellent
mind, was for ever tormenting herself and lamenting,
was constantly praising her for a natural tranquillity
that she envied, for her courage mingled with good
humour, and for "the fine blood that left nothing sour
or gloomy in her." It was, in truth, an original and
most distinctive trait in Mme. des Ursins's character
that she was a person so tranquil fundamentally beneath a form so active, and through a life so agitated.
It was to this that she owed, after her great fall at
seventy-two years of age, the ability to rise again and
die in peace at the age of eighty. But there are still
other traits in her nature that put her in perfect contrast to her friend, Mme. de Maintenon.

When we read the letters of Mme. des Ursins with
those of Mme. de Maintenon that reply to them, the
natures of the two women come out in a contrast that
they themselves are the first to feel and to indicate.
Mme. de Maintenon affects to appear less than she is;
she likes to let more be divined than she shows; she
slips aside, seems to shun notice, makes herself small

and modest, going so far as to say that she does not know how to deal with great people. Mme. des Ursins, on the contrary, very willingly puts herself forward, and brings all her person into play. We feel at times that she exceeds her limits as superintendent of the royal interior, for she does not fear to seem to step beyond them, and let something be seen of the political authority, the mainspring of which she holds in her hand. She likes both to be, and to appear to be. Their ideal of the future is different and marks the opposition of their natures, although ambition may not be less in the one than in the other. Mme. de Maintenon, sated and weary, aspires only to shut herself up at Saint-Cyr, as an impenetrable refuge; communicating only with timid and submissive young girls, resting the greater part of the day, wrapped in veils and hidden behind curtains. The greatest act of her queenship that she clings to performing is to seem to abdicate. Mme. des Ursins, always in the spirit and the enjoyment of public appearance and power, dreams, for her last retreat, of a tiny State of which she should be the independent sovereign; where she could, in her leisure hours, govern at last in her own name, and display herself in the sunlight — that was her *pot-au-lait,* her true castle in Spain. Of the two ambitions, the one that played the modest was really the wiser ; the other seems more sincere: but, after all, these were only two different manners of playing queen when they were not queens.

The most agreeable part of this Correspondence is that which precedes and follows the victory of Almanza. That victory, gained almost in spite of himself, by Maréchal de Berwick, April 17, 1707, restored for a long time the affairs of Philippe V, who thus reconquered his capital and a good part of his kingdom. The letters of Mme. des Ursins, even during the flight and the disasters, breathe courage and hope; but from that moment of victory they take a marked tone of gaiety and brilliant raillery, which shows her to us at her best.

The account of the joy caused at Marly by the news of the victory of Almanza is in itself a living picture. France was beginning to feel unused to victories. The preceding year had seen the deplorable and disastrous day of Ramillies; reverses alone seemed to be expected. Suddenly, on the side where it was least expected, the news of victory arrives. Mme. de Maintenon relates to Mme. des Ursins the first effect produced:

"You know Marly and my apartment; the king was alone in my chamber, and I had just sat down to table in my salon, through which every one passes; an officer of the guards cried out at the door of the room where the king was: 'Here is M. de Chamillart!' [Minister of war.] The king answered, 'What! himself?' because, naturally, he was not expected. I threw down my napkin, quite agitated; M. de Chamillart said to me, 'It is good!' and entered where the king was, followed by M. de Silly, whom I did not know; you can believe, Madame, that I entered, too; I then heard of the defeat of the enemy's army, and returned to my supper in high good humour."

This little scene, very well related by Mme. de

Maintenon (I have slightly abridged it), struck the excited imagination of Mme. des Ursins, and brought back an echo that makes it more vivid still:

"All that you represent to me, madame, from the officers of the guards entering to announce the coming of M. de Chamillart, while you were supping in your salon, till the king went to the door himself with this great news, seems to me so natural that I think I see you flinging down your napkin and running to hear what was told; Mme. Dangeau flying to write to her husband; Mme. d'Heudicourt walking about as if she had good legs but not knowing where she was going; M. de Marsan jumping on a chair, in spite of his gout, with as much ease as if he had been a rope-dancer. As for Monseigneur the Duc de Bourgogne who is, I think, a little subject to absent-mindedness, I am surprised that in the first moments of his joy he did not take some lady for a billiard-ball and give her a stroke with the cue that he held in his hand."

All this part of the Correspondence shows these two celebrated women much to their advantage, in all the vivacity of their mutual interests and in full accord. Mme. de Maintenon, with her usual preciseness, adds to this impression when she replies:

"I have just reread your letters to see if I have replied to everything. *Mon Dieu!* Madame, how content you are, and how playfully you jest! There is never any blackness in what you say, but now there is a joy that gives me all the joy of which I am capable. To render it complete we must have peace, but on conditions that will satisfy us."

I remark, in passing, the little sentence: "There is never any blackness in what you say"—meaning sadness for blackness.

This peace, of which the timid and sensible Mme. de Maintenon writes incessantly, became in the

following years a stumbling-block in her intercourse
with Mme. des Ursins, who is much less eager for it,
and does not wish it at all except on the best conditions for Spain. Here again we see the differences in
the natures of the two women defining themselves
clearly. Mme. des Ursins hopes, even in extremity;
she is not of those who abdicate easily. The King
and Queen of Spain, to whom she had devoted herself, have lofty sentiments, "as lofty as the rank in
which God has placed them; they are incapable of
base acts. They have resolved to lose life itself rather
than do aught that is unworthy of what they are " —
that is to say, they will defend their crown, fighting
until death, and she is incapable of giving them any
other advice. But the moment comes when France
despairs; when the ministry, especially, inclines to
peace at any price; when Mme. de Maintenon, overwhelmed with anxiety, preaches or insinuates the
same. The consequence of this discouragement would
be the abandonment of the crown of Spain, and almost the dethronement of Philippe V by his grandfather, if Louis XIV consented to it. At that idea
Mme. des Ursins rebels, her courage rises, all her
blood boils; she writes letters of "fire and blood" to
Mme. de Maintenon, turns for support to the Spanish
nation, and, aided by the noble queen, flings the king
resolutely into the arms of his subjects. This is her
finest moment—the moment when her generosity,
her proud soul, her courage, and the resources of her

mind display themselves to great advantage, and turn to the public good as much as to her honour. The correspondence with Mme. de Maintenon changes from this moment; sharp and bitter irony comes to the surface.

The war of the Spanish Succession, which ambition on the part of France began, and which ambition on the other side continued, was of a nature which, up to that time and for many previous centuries, was considered extraordinary and stupendous, whether from the military or the historic point of view. A great contemporaneous mind and actor in those memorable scenes, Bolingbroke, said of it: "The battles, the sieges, the surprising revolutions that took place in the course of this war, were of a kind the like of which cannot be found in any period of the same length." However that may be, it was certainly permissible in those days of disaster to differ in opinion as to the remedy and the means of coming out of such overwhelming evils. Mme. de Maintenon longed for escape like a woman, and like too many of the men of that day; like a woman of feeling, who sees the evil very closely, who suffers from it in herself and for others to whom she is attached, who has nothing of the heroine in her, who is wholly resigned and Christian, seeing the hand of God not only in repeated defeats and reverses, but even more directly in the natural scourges that fell upon France, such as the winter of 1709 (the severity of which had not been

known for more than a century), and in the famine
that followed it, Mme. de Maintenon, in view of
such evils, bows her head, kneels down, and — provided repose and relief from this excessive suffering
come—does not recoil before any necessity:

"We can no longer make war," she writes to Mme. des Ursins:
"we must bow our heads beneath the hand of God when he wills to
overthrow kings and kingdoms. That, Madame, is what I have
always feared. . . . We have experienced a succession of misfortunes such as France cannot recover from except by a long peace;
and famine, the worst evil of all, has driven us to our last straits. I
own that all my fears never went so far as to foresee that we should
be reduced to desire to see the King and Queen of Spain dethroned;
there are no words, Madame, in which to express such sorrow; the
King is filled with it."

The word "dethroned" is uttered! She may
afterwards have wished to retract it, but Mme. des
Ursins refers to it perpetually, and never forgave it.

Mme. des Ursins, who is of a wholly different race,
nurses and expresses very contrary opinions. She
has always believed that the resources were greater
than people said, if only the men were not so discouraged; she cannot understand those generals
(Tessé, for example) who distrusted themselves, and
who always had an air of expecting to advance to
defeat. She is of opinion that "nothing can be done
unless it is undertaken." She fastens to Villars and
seems to divine that the man whom everybody called
mad was destined to be their saviour: "For," she says,
"there are too many wise men, or at least too many

who think they are when they risk nothing. I am persuaded that one must sometimes let risks be run, provided they are not pushed to temerity; that belongs only to heroes of romance." This last defect, she feels, is that of Villars, but she pardons it in him, even in the midst of the national humiliation: "Maréchal de Villars talks and acts," she says, "like those heroes of romance who think they carry victory wherever they go; I would like to have such airs here now, so opposed to those who are dashing us over the precipice."

The whole Correspondence of Mme. des Ursins during that fatal year of 1709 redounds to the honour of her generosity and the loftiness of her soul, as well as to her perspicacity of judgment; for, at the last, events proved her right; the throne of the Bourbons in Spain remained erect without causing that of Louis XIV of France to be much lowered.

A gap occurs in the correspondence of the two women at the moment when it cools and grows bitter. Mme. des Ursins requested one day that her letters be burned, and Mme. de Maintenon, to obey her, seems to have burned a part of them. Those lost letters, very curious for history, must have been less regrettable for charm and interest. Mme. des Ursins makes us share her feelings and carries us with her without difficulty, so much does her resistance to the peace seem a direct inspiration, a cry of patriotism and honour; we not only pardon her obstinacy, we admire it. But, so soon as we suspect a personal ambition and cupidity, the impression becomes quite the contrary, and her noble part is injured in our eyes. It is certain that towards the end of this bloody period, and during the slow negotiations that closed it, she did all she could to obtain from the contracting powers a sovereignty of her own in the Low Countries. The King of Spain held firmly to that condition, so indecorous and so disproportioned to the great interests involved; he refused to sign the peace with Holland unless the Dutch not only placed Mme. des Ursins in possession of that sovereignty, but agreed to guarantee it to her against the Emperor. This is the most serious blame that can be laid upon the memory of Mme. des Ursins; a fault of conduct through vanity. She deserved that Bolingbroke, who knew her weakness and what could be obtained from her by giving her the title of Highness, should remark, during the negotiations of that period: " There is a real advantage for us in flattering the pride of that old woman, inasmuch as we have not the means of gratifying her avarice." This affair of the sovereignty completed the rupture between herself and Mme. de Maintenon. The sound and judicious mind of the latter recovers all its advantages here; her modesty would never have conceived an ambition so out of all proportion, her sense of fitness would never have allowed her to commit such a blunder.

The catastrophe that hurled Mme. des Ursins from

her high position remains one of the most singular, most dramatic, and most unexplained events in history. We know that the charming queen to whom she belonged, having died at the age of twenty-six, Philippe V instantly desired to remarry. Mme. des Ursins took possession of him, kept him under a species of humilating subjection, and chose for him, intentionally, the least important of the princesses of Europe, with the express intention of creating her as if by her own hands, and forming her to her own interests.

Elisabeth Farnese, Princess of Parma, the object of this choice, and chosen only because Mme. des Ursins little knew her, arrived in Spain. The king advanced to meet her on the road to Burgos, and Mme. des Ursins herself went on from there to the little town of Xadraque. When the new queen arrived there, Mme. des Ursins received her with the customary formalities. Then, having followed her into her apartment, she became aware that the queen's tone instantly changed. Some say that Mme. des Ursins, having taken exception to a part of the queen's dress or coiffure, the latter treated her as an impertinent servant and became very angry. Others relate (and these different accounts supplement one another without actually conflicting) that Mme. des Ursins, having protested her devotion to the new queen, and assured her Majesty "that she might count on finding her always on her side with the king, to maintain things as they should be in regard to her and to procure for her all the satisfactions that her Majesty had a right to expect, the queen, having listened quietly until then, took fire at these last words, and replied that she needed no one between herself and the king, that it was impertinent to make her such offers and to dare to speak to her in that manner." What is certain is that the queen, dismissing Mme. des Ursins with contumely out of her apartment, sent for M. Amezaga, lieutenant of the body-guard, who commanded her escort of honour, and ordered him to arrest Mme. des Ursins, put her instantly into a carriage, and take her to the frontier of France by the shortest route and without making any stop by the way. As M. Amezaga hesitated, the queen asked him if he did not have a special order from the King of Spain to obey her in everything without reservation; and it was true that he had it.

Mme. des Ursins was therefore arrested, and taken off instantly by six horses across Spain, still in her Court dress. It was then midwinter and she was over seventy-two years of age. A waiting-woman, and two officers of the guard were put in the carriage with her.

"I know not how I have borne up under the fatigues of this journey," she writes to Mme. de Maintenon eighteen days after the scene at Xadraque. "I was made to sleep on straw, and to fast in a way very different from the meals I am accustomed to. I did not forget to mention in the details I took the liberty of writing to the King (Louis XIV) that all I ate was two stale eggs a day; I thought that circumstance would excite him to have pity on a faithful subject who has in no way deserved, it seems to me, such contempt. I am going to Saint-Jean-de-Luz to rest awhile and hear what it pleases the king shall become of me."

From the latter town she writes again, still to Mme. de Maintenon:

"I shall await the orders of the king here at Saint-Jean-de-Luz, where I am living in a little house near the sea. I see it often agitated, sometimes calm: such is the life of Courts; that is what I have known; that is what has happened to me; that is what excites your generous compassion. I readily agree with you that we can find no stability except in God. Certainly none can be found in the human heart, for who was more sure than I of the heart of the King of Spain?"

Everything combines to show that it was the King of Spain himself who, forgetting the long services of Mme. des Ursins and weary of her rule, from which he dared not free himself, gave the order to his new wife to take the dismissal on herself; and she, who, as well as Alberoni, her adviser, was of the race of intrepid gamblers in politics, did not hesitate a moment in making for her first essay this masterful stroke. Elisabeth Farnese felt herself too strong a personage to exist beside Mme. des Ursins on the same stage.

This was the same Elisabeth, born to reign, of whom the great Frederick said: "The pride of a Spartan, English obstinacy, Italian shyness, and French vivacity made up the character of that singular woman; she marched audaciously to the accomplishment of her designs; nothing took her unawares, nothing stopped her." Being of that character, it is not surprising that she took advantage of the opportunity offered her to make a clean sweep on her first arrival.

Under this terrible fall, Mme. des Ursins, the first shock over, recovered all her force, all her self-possession, and her apparent composure; not a complaint, not a reproach came from her lips, nor a word of weakness. She had long rendered account to her own mind of the nothingness of human life; she told herself, seeing her enemies triumphant and her friends in consternation, that there was nothing to be surprised at; that the world was but a comedy in which the actors were often very bad; that she had played her part better, perhaps, than others, and that her enemies ought not to expect her to be humiliated because she could play it no longer: "It is before God that I ought to feel humiliated," she said, "and I do."

After quitting France, where Louis XIV was then dying, and where the Duc d'Orléans, her declared enemy, was about to be master and Regent, she went to live in Rome, her old residence, the city of fallen grandeur and decent disgrace. From long habit, she set herself to govern the household of the King and Queen of England, in order to govern something. There she witnessed the arrival, overthrown in their turn, of more than one of those who had caused her downfall. She died in December, 1722, at more than eighty years of age.

The publication of official papers and the despatches of French ambassadors during the period of Mme. des

Ursins in Madrid (if that publication is ever made) can
alone determine with precision the full importance
and quality of her political action.   As for her literary
merit, I presume to say that Mme. des Ursins only
needs less negligent editors to become one of our epistolary classics.   Her letters are full of living pages,
which give us not only the manners and morals of
the Court of Spain, but those of French society towards the close of the reign of Louis XIV.   No one
really knows the Duchesse de Bourgogne, Mme. de
Caylus, and many other persons of agreeable renown,
until they see them daily passing in and out through
this Correspondence.   In spite of fortunate and choice
exceptions, it is plain that the great century is becoming corrupt; the young women of that day are growing strange in manners and in morals; they are about
to be the women of the Regency.   They do not
yet smoke, as they do to-day, but they take snuff.
The pretty nose of Mme. de Caylus is daubed wtih
tobacco.   The Duchesse de Bourgogne sits up all night,
sups, and, from the advice perpetually given to her,
appears to have done all she could to kill herself.
Mme. des Ursins, who thinks Mme. de Maintenon too
severe on her young and charming relations, especially
on Mme. de Noailles and Mme. de Caylus, exhorts
her to surround herself with her nieces, who would
brighten and rejuvenate her life.   Whereupon Mme.
de Maintenon, with her most piquant rigidity and
rectitude replies — and it is clearly understood that

what follows is not intended to apply to Mme. de
Caylus, nor to Mme. de Noailles:

"You lecture me on strangers and on my relations: I own to you,
madame, that the women of these days are intolerable to me; their
senseless and immodest clothing, their tobacco, their wine, their glut-
tony, their coarseness, their laziness—all that is so opposed to my taste
that it seems to me, and with reason, that I cannot endure it.   I like
modest women, sober, gay, capable of serious things and playfulness;
polite, jesting with jests that cover praise, whose hearts are kind, and
their conversation lively and awake;   yet simple-hearted enough to
own to me that they recognise themselves in this portrait, which I have
made without design, but which I think very just."

It is indeed Mme. des Ursins whom the portrait resembles in her best moments; certainly in its principal
features, and especially in that of "jests that cover
praise."   That is the method of charming most habitual to this choice spirit, just as her defect was a turn
for too frequent irony and a satire that was carried too
far.

I had the intention, in writing of Mme. des Ursins,
to show some of the objections to political women,
of whom she is a type, for all that such women can be
that is distinguished, and at the same time incomplete, excitable, ostentatious, and vain.   The subject
studied, I have not the courage: she rendered real services and; we are glad to take her as we find her, able
and skilful in difficult conjunctures.   Still, in uniting
these two personages of notable appearance before
the world, Mme. des Ursins and Mme. de Maintenon,
these two able women of the first order, may I be

permitted to recall, upon the background of an earlier
period, behind and below them, the figure of a simple
spectatress of the comedy of a Court; a person who
had no genius of intrigue or of action, but a sound,
equable good sense, gentle and delicate, a calm, safe
judgment, the wise, sincere, and virtuous woman of
those Court regions — Mme. de Motteville.